THE ENLARGEMENT OF THE PRESIDENCY

THE
ENLARGEMENT
OF THE
PRESIDENCY

REXFORD G. TUGWELL

OCTAGON BOOKS

A DIVISION OF FARRAR, STRAUS AND GIROUX

New York   1977

Reprinted 1977
by special arrangement with Doubleday & Co., Inc.

OCTAGON BOOKS
A DIVISION OF FARRAR, STRAUS & GIROUX, INC.
19 Union Square West
New York, N.Y. 10003

Library of Congress Cataloging in Publication Data

Tugwell, Rexford Guy, 1891-
    The enlargement of the Presidency.

    Reprint of the ed. published by Doubleday, Garden City, N.Y.
    1. Presidents—United States. 2. Executive power—United
    States. I. Title.
[JK516.T8   1977]   353.03'13   77-10935
ISBN 0-374-98031-4

Manufactured by Braun-Brumfield, Inc.
Ann Arbor, Michigan
Printed in the United States of America

DEDICATION

THIS BOOK IS FONDLY GIVEN TO MY MOTHER IN HER NINETIETH YEAR. It is about Presidents; and all her life she has been intensely concerned with them. Some she has disliked to the point of inventing irregularities, repeating disparagements, and darkly suspecting scandals. For one of them she had an affection which went beyond all restraint and precluded any questioning whatever. But usually she has been informed, shrewdly appraising, understanding, but never willing just to live and let live; they must answer to her for everything.

Her recollections go back to Garfield, Cleveland, Harrison, and McKinley; but she has never valued recollection, except to prove a point. She has had the future in mind, and her criterion has been adequacy in meeting the problems she could see coming up.

She lived to see Eisenhower defeat Stevenson; and this blow, coming upon her in her later life, almost destroyed an already shaky faith in democracy. Her faith was thus feeble because, having lived all her life in safe Republican country, she doubted the competence of the majority to make wise choices. This gave her an added interest in affairs because in her view the Republican Presidents were so vulnerable that defense of them reduced her neighbors to nonsense. This delighted her, but it did not enlarge her faith in the intelligence of the electorate. When one of her favorite Democrats was in the White House, her encomiums could be hard to endure; but not even all the Democrats won her approval. One recent one, she felt, might almost as well have been a Republican. He did not, she said, "measure up."

This seems to me a sound way of appraising statesmen. If there were enough Americans with my mother's sense of what constitutes fitness for the Presidency, the Republic would be much safer. As long as she lives I, at least, shall consult her judgments.

Meanwhile I do hope she will like this book in spite of her disrespect for the past.

FOREWORD

WHEN, DURING THE LATE 1950S, THE ANNUAL EXPENSE OF THE PRESI-
dent's office began to exceed five million dollars, there was a spate of critical comment. It may have been justifiable to deplore the budget for household and staff of a President whose comments on the cost of other
agencies had been so free, who had characterized the Democratic Congress as "spendthrift," and who had referred repeatedly to the extrava-
gances of his predecessors. And in the same frame of reference it was
relevant to note that the Eisenhower remuneration was twice that of
Franklin D. Roosevelt, that there were 615 persons on the payroll of the
Executive Mansion as against 502 when he had taken office, and against
162 in 1938 when the outrageous New Deal had been in full operation.

Actually the style for the Presidency set by Washington, who appeared
in the streets of New York and Philadelphia in a chariot drawn by four
white horses, accompanied by suitable outriders, footmen, and other servants, was no more than matched by the splendor of this latest of his
successors. But Washington had not deplored the excesses of others; he
had not, in fact, allowed himself the least partisan expression. He probably
felt that the Republicans of his day (soon to become Democrats, to many
a schoolboy's confusion) were not to be trusted in positions of confidence;
but he was rigidly unwilling to admit such forebodings while President,
as he considered, of *all* the people; and he cannot be imagined ever to
have allowed himself the faintest censorship of his colleagues' style of life.

Other Federalists—Washington was a Federalist, beyond question, even
though he admitted to no factional preference—were no more reluctant
than the Republicans of our generation to criticize the democratic tendencies of their opponents. Jefferson's adherents constituted a "mob," they
were led by "demagogues," and their irresponsible policies would ruin
the nation. After Washington retired he could admit such sentiments, but
not while he was President.

The lesson to be learned from Eisenhower's comments on the conduct
of his predecessors is that Presidents who live in White Houses should
not cast aspersions—not, at least, until they have taken a careful look
around and read a history book. If the *Washington Post*, on May 14, 1959,
the day after one of his more disparaging press conferences, had been
on his reading list, he would have seen upward of a column devoted to a
report on his own expenditures and emoluments which should have embarrassed him considerably. In addition to some comparison with previous Administrations, this account went on to say, after telling what it
had cost to recondition two cabin cruisers which had replaced the traditional yacht—and there had been a good deal of complacency about dispensing with the yacht—that they had been used for a total of nine days
and ten hours. It also said:

. . . The President has at his disposal a fleet of limousines, planes, helicopters, and a motorized golf cart. . . . The only aircraft assigned directly to the White House is the Columbine, a Super Constellation, which cost $81,576 to operate last year, not including the pay of 8 guards and 11 maintenance men.

The two engine Aero-Commander used for short flights is supplied from the Special Air Missions Group of the Air Force. The Missions Group is also paying for three Boeing 707 jets now on order at a cost of 14 millions. . . . The helicopters used by the President are provided by the army and marine units in the area. . . . At least 20 cars are rented on a regular basis for the use of the President and his staff, and more are made available when the need arises.

The President himself is reported to use three cars: a recent model Cadillac, a bubble-top Lincoln costing about $30,000 and a Chrysler Imperial equipped with a sliding roof. Two heavily constructed Cadillacs costing about $65,000 each are occupied by Secret Service men who accompany the President. Chauffeurs for the fleet are provided by the army.

Washington is said not to have been much disturbed by the snorts of disapproval over his regal trappings emitted by Senator Maclay and others; and indeed there have always been reasons for Presidents to shelter themselves in the convenient cocoon of praise from those around them and to summon up a sense of mission when enemies' appraisals became unpleasant. Unfortunately, to be President is to be Chief of State, and the Chief of State of a great power cannot be and live as other men. Even Jefferson found literal equality impractical. And Eisenhower's equipment for travel, communication, and even the pleasures of life were not excessive for one in his position. He stood, as Washington did, in the place of father to the nation; and a father has to fill the role for which he has been chosen. If he has been unfairly spoken of, those who have done it may have been more concerned with his hypocrisy than with his extravagance. Such criticisms would be amply justified.

Behind the expansion of the White House budget there is something of vastly more importance than can be gathered from accounts of the show put on by the occupant of the Mansion. What happens there has at least some relation to the amazing expansion of the nation. Since Washington, it has grown from one of thirteen to one of fifty states, in population from a few million to nearly two hundred million, from a poor backwoods kind of country to one of urban sophistication, from one of self-sufficient localities to one whose position in the world is among the first in possessions and in power, and whose technical achievements have reduced time and space to a fraction of their significance no more than a generation ago. Like the American worker, who has attained his unmatched productivity by using the energies of nature rather than his own muscles, the President must increase his competence for expanding duties by calling into his service every possible human and mechanical aid and every device it is possible to conceive. None of these will make him either a better or a more intelligent individual, but they will furnish him with more accurate information, surround him with massed judgments, and keep him from being harassed by duties others could perform as well.

The President has, indeed, become so important not only to Americans but to all the people of the world that any possibility of improving his performance must be explored and experimented with. If a country estate for relaxation, a yacht for pleasure, more planes for getting about will add the least bit to his competence, they will be worth many times their cost. We have been disgracefully stingy with our Presidents in the past. Only recently was the Congress persuaded to provide them with a pension for retirement, and then it was one they should have been ashamed to see published to the world. So presidential staffs are caviled about; vacations, entertainments, favors to their families are criticized. We Americans would be better occupied in studying such an enlargement or reorganization of the office as might make it more efficient for its mission than in the trivia of such appurtenances. And it is in the hope of contributing to a discussion of more depth that this book has been written.

As the study progressed it seemed more and more obvious that some drastic change was becoming necessary. The concern felt by Woodrow Wilson has not died out. And his suggestion that we adapt to our uses the British Cabinet (or parliamentary) system is periodically rediscovered. He was first alarmed by the feeble condition into which the Executive had fallen when he began to study it in the 1870s. More vigorous Presidents succeeding those of his youth—Cleveland and Theodore Roosevelt —caused him to modify his belief that constitutional change must be contemplated; and as President himself he found that he could operate successfully in the existing system. But Harding followed Wilson, and Coolidge followed Harding. The doubts of students again became active. But the second Roosevelt met the depression of the thirties and faced another world war in inspiring fashion. His early success was magnificent. But as his years passed, the overwhelming burden that fell on him caused another sort of doubt to be felt. The risk run by the democracy was not only that of electing weak Executives; it was a much more frightening thought that even the most competent ones, equipped with all the devices of modern administration and with all the staff members they could manage, could not meet the demands of the office. Between the two likely failures—that of having a President intellectually unequal to the recurrent emergencies of contemporary life, and having one capable of meeting any human challenge but unable, for all that, to stretch his strength and will to compass the responsibilities of his office—there is not much to choose.

However it is looked at and, I believe, the harder it is studied, the more the conviction will grow that we have reached an impasse. I had no intention of trying to establish this as a fact, but the reader will see that I could not escape the conclusion.

Since reaching it, I seem always to be discovering others who are similarly concerned. I should like to quote one of them: Marquis Childs, the experienced political analyst. He was commenting on the refusal of the Senate to confirm the appointment of Lewis Strauss to the Cabinet and saying that refusal was very unusual but something, also, which underlined the not at all unusual conflict between the Executive and Legislative Branches, made more trying by the tendency lately shown by the electorate to choose a President whose party cannot win a legislative majority. Taking the Strauss incident as a text, Mr. Childs asked what will become a familiar question to readers here:

> Can this country afford in an era of global responsibility a government that periodically breaks down as the power is divided between the two separate branches of government . . . ?
>
> This might, if there were leadership from the White House, be the moment for a great constructive debate on the American system versus the Parliamentary system. A debate would air the advantages and the limitations of dividing the powers of government as we do under the Constitution. (*The Washington Post*, June 24, 1959)

What Mr. Childs specifically suggests would be a continuation of the debate begun by Wilson in 1884 in his *Congressional Government*. Like Wilson, most contemporary commentators seem to confine themselves to the alternatives offered by the British and American systems. But there is at least one other possibility; that, I have ventured to suggest, is such an overhauling and enlargement of the Presidency as would make it adequate for the demands upon it, at the same time creating a device—such, for instance, as electing Representatives at large instead of in districts— to make it more probable that President and Congress would generally agree on policy. It might be a grave mistake to modify too greatly the tension between the Branches concerning their respective powers; but more general agreement on policies would be a happy change. And, if I may repeat what I have often said before, an adaptation of planning devices, now well known and long-tested, to our governmental situation would remove from the area of controversy a considerable percentage of the matters over which disagreements have been most common in recent years.

But I have not meant here to suggest remedial devices—merely to bring the reader, if I could, to the point of seeing that they are pressingly necessary.

For careful processing of the manuscript for this book—as for two preceding it—I am indebted to Mrs. Jeanne Hansen. I shudder to think what it would have been like without her shepherding care.

R.G.T.

THE ENLARGEMENT OF THE PRESIDENCY

THE PRESIDENTS

1. GEORGE WASHINGTON	two terms	1789–1797
2. JOHN ADAMS	one term	1797–1801
3. THOMAS JEFFERSON	two terms	1801–1809
4. JAMES MADISON	two terms	1809–1817
5. JAMES MONROE	two terms	1817–1825
6. JOHN QUINCY ADAMS	one term	1825–1829
7. ANDREW JACKSON	two terms	1829–1837
8. MARTIN VAN BUREN	one term	1837–1841
9. WILLIAM HENRY HARRISON	one month	1841
10. JOHN TYLER	three years, 11 months	1841–1845
11. JAMES KNOX POLK	one term	1845–1849
12. ZACHARY TAYLOR	one year, four months	1849–1850
13. MILLARD FILLMORE	two years, eight months	1850–1853
14. FRANKLIN PIERCE	one term	1853–1857
15. JAMES BUCHANAN	one term	1857–1861
16. ABRAHAM LINCOLN	four years, one month	1861–1865
17. ANDREW JOHNSON	three years, 11 months	1865–1869
18. ULYSSES S. GRANT	two terms	1869–1877
19. RUTHERFORD BIRCHARD HAYES	one term	1877–1881
20. JAMES ABRAM GARFIELD	six months	1881
21. CHESTER ALAN ARTHUR	three years, six months	1881–1885
22. & 24. GROVER CLEVELAND	two terms	1885–1889 & 1893–1897
23. BENJAMIN HARRISON	one term	1889–1893
25. WILLIAM MCKINLEY	four years, six months	1897–1901
26. THEODORE ROOSEVELT	seven years, six months	1901–1909
27. WILLIAM HOWARD TAFT	one term	1909–1913
28. WOODROW WILSON	two terms	1913–1921
29. WARREN GAMALIEL HARDING	two years, six months	1921–1923
30. CALVIN COOLIDGE	five years, six months	1923–1929
31. HERBERT HOOVER	one term	1929–1933
32. FRANKLIN DELANO ROOSEVELT	twelve years, one month	1933–1945
33. HARRY S. TRUMAN	seven years, 11 months	1945–1953
34. DWIGHT D. EISENHOWER	two terms	1953–1961

★ I ★

IT WOULD HARDLY BE EXPECTED THAT LATE IN THE SECOND CENTURY
of its existence any written document would still effectively dominate
a government established under it; yet the Constitution adopted in Philadelphia late in the summer of 1787 does still furnish the structure and
control the working of the Federal Union. And any inquiry concerning
the government's powers or the relations of its Branches to each other—as
well as its relations with the states—has to start with that original and
(almost) unamended charter.

Actually, there have been twenty-two formal changes in the Constitution, but it can still be said that none of them goes to the form or substance
of the Republic. Most have to do with directives for, or limitations on,
governmental action. The first ten are customarily called the Bill of Rights
and were adopted so soon after the Convention (they were ratified in
1791) as usually to be thought of as part of the original. They are limitations on the power of government to abridge the liberties of citizens.
Others, such as thirteen, fourteen, and fifteen, adopted just after the
Civil War were the result of that conflict. One abolished slavery; the
others provided for the protection of Negroes as citizens.[1]

One amendment repealed another—the prohibition of commerce in al-
coholic beverages; another provided for the legitimizing of the income
tax, another for the direct election of Senators, and still another for allowing women to vote.

Only three in any way affected the Presidency—the subject of this book
—and only one of these was important to its operations. The Twelfth
changed the procedure of the President's election, separating the voting
in the Electoral College for the President from that for the Vice-President
(1803); another, the Twentieth, shortened the interval between election

---

[1] Although fourteen has been used to protect corporate rights rather
more than those of individuals, a result of corporate development and
sympathetic interpretation by the Courts.

and inauguration (1933); and a third, the Twenty-second (1951), prohibited a third term.

It was important to enlarge the suffrage by abolishing racial and sexual discrimination, to revise election procedures, and to shorten the long interval between the choice of the President and his investment; but none of these changes altered the primary structure. The Twenty-second Amendment did alter it drastically.

Interpretations of the Constitution, it should be said, differ; they differ because of its sometimes ambiguous language and also because certain of its provisions have become irrelevant or insufficient. But these qualities have had their own usefulness; they have allowed escape from strict constructions which might have bound too tightly an expanding society. The outstanding characteristic, and the one responsible for the remarkable endurance of the Constitution, is related to these faults (or ambiguities); it is that interpretations may and do differ and change and that none is universally and permanently accepted. They are made; they fade into mere expressions of opinion; they continue to exist as part of an accumulating gloss; and they are considered respectfully. But, however pretentious or authoritative they may seem, they may not stand. No one has a final say.

It is largely because of this that it has not become much clearer with the passage of time what the President may or may not do, or even ought to do, to comply with the Constitution he has sworn to uphold. It has allowed his office to be enlarged with the demands made upon it and to meet the exigencies of a more and more complex civilization. The directions he finds in the Constitution are bafflingly general, and he must make his own interpretation of their meaning. There is no one to whom he may apply for a higher reading than he himself may make.

The Supreme Court, on occasion, has ventured to give the President advice amounting to orders; so, even more often, has the Congress. But there is always the indisputable fact that the Executive is an independent —if co-ordinate—Branch; and that, because of this, the other Branches— Legislative and Judicial—cannot define his powers and duties any more than he can define theirs. When they have tried to do so, the President of the moment may have resisted or may have acquiesced; but, whatever his attitude, his successors in their time have refused to be bound by his example. Not infrequently Presidents have felt compelled to remind Court and Congress that they might not limit, circumscribe, or in any way define the presidential powers and duties; and they have proceeded on their way regardless of attempted interference. Who could prevent?

Formal approaches—study of the Constitution itself and of the intentions of its framers—have their own interest; so have the elaborate commentaries accumulated during its history; but the Presidency in being is best understood by studying the conduct of its occupants, its gains and losses and its gradual accommodation to the other institutions it affects and is affected by. And this is especially true of its relations with the other Branches. With them it is intimately entangled.

We can read the words of the document, and we can study the discussions preceding its adoption in 1787; but as things stand in our later day, both duties and powers, although not changed in nature, are obviously wider and deeper than could possibly be deduced from these exercises. It is proposed here to study the Presidency in a behavioral way, for the most part, with due attention to the influence on it of opinion and interest. What it is today, the Presidents have made it; but they have not acted in a vacuum. They have been men of views, with affiliations, with ambitions, and with visions. And these have not been left behind when they have taken office. But on the whole the institution has been enlarged, and our study will be concerned mostly with the incidents of its enlargement.

It may be useful to summarize the more important and obvious of the constitutional specifications.

The President's *duties*, then, are:

To take care that the laws are faithfully executed.
To act as Commander in Chief of the military forces.
To appoint and commission all officers of the government.
To recommend to the Congress "such measures as he shall judge necessary and expedient."
To report on the state of the nation.

But let us see. This bare statement says nothing of his duty to be the Chief of State and the leader and mentor of the nation; to be the head of a political organization with responsibility for the formulation of a program; to devise domestic policies calculated to ensure well-being; to control foreign relations so that the national security is assured; to see to it that the legislation necessary to desirable objectives is written and passed; and to make sure that the administrative services are competent for the faithful execution of the laws with which he is charged.

It says nothing, either, about the unremitting and infinitely wearing effort a President must sustain to conciliate and persuade an often recalcitrant Congress or a hostile Court; the delicate and urgent task of choosing the close assistants who will carry out—or obstruct—the policies he stands for, including the Cabinet, whose members, if properly chosen, may be useful as advisers as well as administrative aides; the constant concern he must maintain with patronage and other political claims, such as the giving of favors and the recruiting of support all necessary to the continued vigor of his party; the mobilizing and using of public opinion through many media to maintain his touch with the electorate; the acting as seer and prophet, visualizing the nation's possible future in the world and in time; and the directing of a whole people toward the enhancement of their welfare and their honor.

His *powers*, now to be enumerated, will be seen mostly to turn upon duties to which they are indispensable and from which they are often indistinguishable. Neglect of the one can be fatal to the other. To be President is to be a servant of the people, but at the same time to be their conscience and their guide. His powers, then:

> To appoint (with Senate approval) Ambassadors, Justices of the Supreme Court, "and all other officers of the United States."
> To make treaties (subject to Senate approval).
> To call the Congress into extraordinary session.
> To veto legislation (but with the possibility that the veto may be overridden by a two-thirds vote of both Houses), or to approve it.
> To command the military forces.
> To pardon offenders against Federal laws.

This says nothing of the positive and massive compulsion that looms behind the threat to call a special session for the passage of particular legislation. There is implied in this the tremendous appeal of the President as a popular leader having for support the mandate of a majority vote. The millions who have voted for him will be predisposed to think him justified in his estimate of a crisis. They will tend also to believe an attempt to coerce an obstructionist Congress justified; no member of that body has behind him, ever, more than a fraction of the votes a President has attracted; and legislators always come from far smaller districts than the nation as a whole—which is the presidential constituency. He will, besides, have the frightening means to reach, with one or another appeal, almost every one of those who made him their choice; and nothing is more respected by the professional politicians than the expressed sentiments that may be induced to overwhelm them by any skillful and determined President. This power would make him, if he had no other, national and party leader.

The enumeration says nothing, again, of the President's power to commit the Congress and the nation to courses he has, in his own way, determined to be the wise and expedient ones. By the time these have reached the Congress for consideration they may have been so far forwarded as to be very nearly irreversible. They may have become the nation's well-identified policies. This power has been growing both in domestic and in foreign matters. The domestic economy is no longer made up of separate and inconsiderable units, no one of which is of much importance to the whole. The President may, by conferring or by using pressures of various sorts, affect the policies of the vast aggregations, under one management, that make up the modern complex. He may even threaten government compulsion, something the most recalcitrant industrialist shudders to contemplate. Whether the Congress approves or not, he may influence industrial policies.

This is even more true of foreign policy. It is he—or his subordinates—who represents the nation in all its dealings with other governments, including the negotiating of treaties. These, of course, must be approved by the Senate, but as the situation of the United States in the world becomes a more and more responsible one, and as the dangers of irresponsibility become more and more obvious, the reluctance of the Senators to reject an agreement reached by long negotiation as a result of a well-understood policy is more marked. Besides, by a kind of tour de force—an extension of presidential prerogative—matters which once would have been the subject of treaties have become ones to be settled in Executive agreements not subject to ratification.

There is also the President's superior facilities for marshaling weapons in the recurrent contest he must carry on with the other Branches. He may or may not appoint; and the longing of congressional politicians for patronage is one of supernal strength. He may hold them in line with amazing facility so long as he has appointments to distribute—and he usually has, although they are much more numerous at the beginning of new Administrations—which accounts, in some part, for the well-known sweetness of the "honeymoon." Also, he may or may not dismiss; and while this is not a weapon of comparable value, it still has its uses. Since Washington's Administration it has been settled that the President may discharge those whom he appoints.[2] The Constitution does not say that he may; but in the laws establishing the first three Departments—State, Treasury, and War—it was explicitly stated. Hamilton and others of his sort believed that no such authorization was necessary. It was an "implied power." To which the Jeffersonians made the reply that the Constitution was an enumerating document. All powers intended to be granted were so designated. But they had to deal with a distinctive "vesting clause," presently to be discussed, which gives the President a peculiar advantage

[2] Two exceptions must be noted. First the challenge may possibly recur which was made by the Congress when the Tenure of Office Act was passed. It was repealed, as we shall see; but another might be tried. Then there are the conditions sometimes attached to dismissals. When the Congress authorizes appointments, it likes to say that they may be terminated only for certain causes. The Courts have seemed to approve; but the Presidents have not agreed. It is a matter on which the Constitution is completely silent, as it is on so many others, and this leaves all Branches free to make their own interpretations respecting their powers and duties. There are famous incidents to be examined. But the rule is that the President may dismiss those whom he appoints, except those in the independent agencies and in the Courts; about this we shall have more to say.

—makes him, in fact, the possessor of "residual powers," especially if we are to believe the strong Presidents who have had recourse to them and have so vigorously defended their use.

Nor does the enumeration say anything of the "pre-natal" effect of the veto power. The anticipation that the President may disapprove not only prevents many legislative projects from becoming law but strongly influences their nature as they are discussed and take form in the legislative process. Actual veto was very seldom resorted to, in fact, during the early years of the Republic. Cleveland was the first President to use it freely. But it was always there, a big stick behind the door, regarded with infinite respect by the legislators. Its possession, as will be noted, has made the President's influence on legislation very important. A number of students have spoken of him as the "First Legislator," an idea we shall want to examine; but what there is of truth in it is at least partly derived from his possession of the veto.

So vast an influence could not be inferred by examining the sparse words of the Constitution.

And nothing has been said yet of perhaps the most potent of all the powers possessed by this novel creation of the framers, one that has expanded and grown more pervasive with the recurrent crises of the twentieth century—this, of course, is his mandate to command the military forces. How far beyond the actual disposal of these forces in the field, on the sea, and in the air this power may be extended was somewhat explored by Polk, further pushed by Lincoln, and widened to encompass the whole economy during the world wars by Wilson and Roosevelt. We shall need to pay close attention to this development.

But perhaps we ought to observe at the outset, of this and other extensions of presidential powers, that they have only sometimes—not nearly always—been made at the expense of, or despite opposition from, the Legislative Branch. Most of the accruals, taking them in bulk, have been delegated or authorized, whether or not the Constitution required it, which was often not a settled matter, by the Congress. That body has had many seizures of panic during which the President has been turned to for rescue. Recovery from panic, with the passing of the crisis, has usually been rapid; but something of a precedent usually has been established, even though it may not have been a firm one, and some residue has remained of powers never fully returned to their original claimants.

But these matters we shall be examining at length and in detail as we go along. It has been meant to insist here only that the constitutional enumerations are extremely curtailed, that time has piled on the Presidency a vast accumulation of duties and the powers to carry them out, not at all to be understood by examination of the original document. Who would guess from it that much of the law of the land, in our time, was never passed by the legislators at all, but emanated from administrative agencies? That law is a kind of extrapolation of broad directives contained in authorizing Acts. So with the presidential powers: the Constitution is a narrow authorizing charter, broadened by experience and filled out by presidential initiative.

★ 2 ★

WHEN THE INTENTION OF THE FRAMERS IS COMPARED WITH PRESENT
reality there is one especially conspicuous departure: it was expected
that the President would be selected by a class of experienced and responsible citizens from among themselves. Election by universal adult
suffrage was not even suggested. And when James Wilson put forward
the proposal that the President should be directly elected by those possessing the suffrage, then severely restricted by property qualifications, it
was not approved, and the indirect Electoral College method was substituted. This was only after protracted discussion of legislative selection,
a method many delegates found it hard to dismiss, it being so familiar
from British and American practice. But Wilson and Gouverneur Morris,
reinforced finally by Madison, carried the day for separate election, even
if by few people and indirectly. The importance of this was that the
President consequently owed his grant of power to the same source as
the legislature and was therefore equal and independent.

It was, however, several decades—and several Presidencies—after ratification before the President made himself clearly and indisputably
separate and beyond legislative control. Candidates were for some time
chosen by congressional caucus, and this created a debt and established
affiliations. It was not until the party convention replaced the caucus that
all lingering similarities with the parliamentary system were erased. Van
Buren, in 1832, was the first President nominated in this way. This
development—and, indeed, the whole party system—was not anticipated
by the framers. Yet it *was* intended that the separate-but-equal principle
should create a system of checks and balances. And that system began
to operate from the very first when Washington found that the Senate
would not consent to become an advisory body but was determined to
review his suggestions with complete detachment. This was his first lesson
in the nature of the new government. When the Senators refused to consult with him orally and privately, he retired in profane disillusionment
and never offered another opportunity for such an affront.

Washington had been present at the Convention discussions; and his understanding of the Presidency might, it seems, have been more realistic than it was. He was led into the humiliating experience with the Senate, probably, because of his hope that the new government would be a co-operative one with the single purpose of seeking the general good. He found that political realities were more complex than that. The public interest was frequently confused with that of individuals and localities, and politicians would not, or could not, follow him in his high-minded purpose.

The idea of separated powers had behind it the theory of laissez faire and pas trop gouverneur. The pursuit of individual and local gains, it was believed, would somehow produce a common good; and if government did not interfere, the country would flourish. The almost immediate formation of turbulent political parties, the rise of demagoguery, and skepticism concerning even his good intentions disconcerted Washington; he opposed parties; "factions," he called them. He believed they might pull down the new government as they had ruined the old.

He set himself, as Chief Executive, to be also guide and mentor to a people confused and disturbed by political adventurers. He was certain that he was right in this, and he thought his prestige would prevail. He never acknowledged himself to be a party man even when attacked by one and supported by the other of the newly constituted groups. He said that the first wish of his heart was, if parties did exist, to reconcile them.[1] In this he began what most Presidents have had the impulse to continue, the detached and disinterested representation of all the people, not just his partisan supporters. His successors would be unable to sustain the role. The dilemma of one who must lead his party, yet guide and represent the whole nation, would be a recurring torment and would never really find resolution. Many would attempt a compromise, and some would find one temporarily; but each would discover that the impossibility of really succeeding was inherent in the chosen instruments of democracy.

There must be free choice, and when there is, men are likely to differ. Their differences must be settled by majority rule: each gives consent to that just by being a citizen. When differences become organized into a program of proposed public actions and support for them hardens, parties are born. A President owes his position to affiliation with those who have one or another view; he is chosen because the view of his party commands a majority. His subsequent effort to command the support of *all* the people cannot transcend the disappointment of the minority in his election. The most they will grant is limited approval for his behavior in strictly national matters. This, to most Presidents, is a cause of frustration.

It was a disappointment to Washington, who was not chosen because

[1] John Marshall, *Life of Washington* (Philadelphia, 1805–7, 5 vols.), V, 675.

he represented certain views but because he was a towering symbol of national unity. But even he could not for long disguise his preference for certain policies—those of Hamilton, Adams, Jay, and the other nationalists which differed from those of Jefferson and his Republicans. As time passed it became clear that the Federalists were a restricted group of the well-born and the propertied; they were not even a majority of those limited few who could vote; and as the limited few became more numerous, the dissident majority became larger. The Federalists were under the fatal handicap of being by definition a minority.

The contest between those who would later be Federalists and those who would be Republican-Democrats was the principal source of contention in the Convention itself. There were those who wanted a strong and those who wanted a weak national government. And there were those who wanted a strong and those who wanted a weak Executive. They were roughly the same people. James Wilson, who, with Gouverneur Morris, must be given the most credit for having invented and unremittingly pushed the idea of the Presidency as it emerged finally, would have made it stronger. He would also have made the central government more powerful.

Madison, to whom the Constitution owes so much, had given more thought to the Federal principle itself than he had to its various parts. When he came to the Convention, he was still hazy as to the Executive; and the Virginia Plan, introduced by Randolph, his colleague, would have made the Executive subordinate to the legislature by allowing that Branch to choose the other. This would have resulted in a parliamentary system similar to that of Britain; but of course it did not prevail.[2]

It may have been unfortunate, for reasons we shall better understand later, that plurality for the Executive came to be identified during the Convention with governmental weakness. Because this was so, however, all those rated as nationalists, as opposed to the supporters of states' rights, centered on the single individual as possessing a desirable "unity" which would be lacking in a group. How such a group might be constituted to achieve unity and yet give added wisdom and security was not explored because the nationalist group prevailed in the processes of compromise.

Wilson intended that the single Executive, elected by the people, should obviate not only any influence on him by intervening states but also any influence by the Legislative Branch. The government, if it was to

[2] The very brief account here of the attitudes and discussions at the Convention may be supplemented by reference to Farrand's *Records of the Federal Convention*, (New Haven, 1934–37, 4 vols.), to Charles C. Thach's *Creation of the Presidency* (Baltimore, 1922), to N. J. Small's *Some Presidential Interpretations of the Presidency* (Baltimore, 1932), and to various constitutional histories.

be national, must flow from all the people; and if it was to have strength, must have an Executive who would resist popular whims or legislative interferences. He must be single. He would thus have more "energy, dispatch, and responsibility." He must have no council, which would, in a sense, destroy his "unity." So it was decided, finally. Various modifications of this idea were proposed, but none was accepted. He was named "President," he had no advisory council, and he was to be independently elected.

Various other characteristics went with this conception. The independence of the President was made more real by giving him the legislative veto, although it finally became a modified one. Similarly, it was determined that he should be elected for a limited period but that he should be re-eligible without limit. Also, he was given the original responsibility for making appointments, even of judges; and he was made Commander in Chief.

The previous acceptance of the tripartite form furnished a framework within which the arguments about relationships could take place. All were independent, but they were also interdependent. None had clear unchecked powers. Each must share power with the others. The Congress must anticipate veto if the Executive was displeased. The Executive must ask the Congress for funds and the Senate for confirmation of appointments and approval of treaties. The Court was to interpret the Constitution, but its members were appointed by the President and its jurisdiction was subject to determination by law.

It was agreed that powers were to be limited in order to prevent oppressions; but whether it was realized what tense situations were being provided for future negotiation, what opportunities for raiding and counterraiding, cannot be known. The President had one considerable advantage to be used in these future battles and one corresponding disadvantage. The advantage was that only he represented the whole nation as against legislators' representation of states or districts. It was he, therefore, who naturally became the leader in crisis, and, as it would turn out, even in ordinary times, if he was capable of leadership. The disadvantage was that he could not make moves of any but the most limited sort without congressional approval. That Branch disposed of the necessary funds.

But the extent of the powers and the effectiveness of the checks were subject to interpretation. And since each of the three Branches was independent, each might look at the Constitution in a different way—and none could claim a final authority. But also, since the powers of each impinged on those of the others, each in defining its own defined in some degree those of the others. This was the inner conflict of the system which was permanent. It could never be resolved. It would never come to more than uneasy compromises resting on temporary tolerances.

Compromises between conflicting theories and between opposing interests account for many of the features of the Constitution. The Senate would not have been established with equal representation from the states if the smaller ones had not feared the larger ones. And the President would not have been elected independently of the legislature if the device of the Electoral College had not seemed to remove his choice some way from direct election. There were other compromises; in fact, Wilson, sponsor of the strong Executive, was disappointed that the adherents of legislative supremacy should have got so much. Especially he deplored the origination of money bills in the House and the assignment to the Senate of the power to confirm. He thought the whole scheme, as it emerged from the discussions, had "a dangerous tendency to aristocracy."[3] The President would not be, as he should, a man of the people, but "the Minion of the Senate." But what Wilson really was against was divided powers; he wanted a responsible President, and he regretted his checking by a Senate.

Morris, however, felt that those who had wanted a strong President had generally prevailed. The Senate had lost the exclusive power to appoint the judges which it had had in earlier drafts and had lost also its right to participate in the election of the President. The sentiment against presidential appointment of officers of the government without any check had been a general one. On the whole, the compromise was as good a one as could have been reached.

Once all the decisions had been made and the structure was complete, there remained to the Convention the delicate task of writing an acceptable draft. To do this a committee was appointed consisting of Johnson, Hamilton, Gouverneur Morris, Madison, and King. The committee entrusted the writing to Morris. It is to him, therefore, that the Presidency owes the tremendous advantage given to it by the style of the "vesting clause." It might not be thought that such a rewriting task could, if it were approved, have any considerable influence on substance. That there were possibilities of furthering his own preference, Morris knew; and he took full advantage of them.[4] He was later accused of making a positive change in the welfare clause; but what he did for the Presidency was nothing of this sort; he merely left it as it was. The legislative grant of powers in the finished draft read: "All legislative powers herein granted shall be vested in a Congress." The judicial power was indicated to be completely described by saying: "the judicial power shall extend to . . ." and then enumerating. But the Executive power was described thus:

[3] Farrand, Records, II, 522–23. Cf. also Thach, op. cit., 136.

[4] That he knew is shown by letters to Livingston and Pickering quoted in Farrand, op. cit., III, 404, 419.

"the executive power shall be vested in a President of the United States of America."

Concerning this, Thach has remarked:

> In modern parlance, this phrase was to prove a "joker." That it was retained by Morris with full realization of its possibilities the writer does not doubt. At any rate, whether intentional or not, it admitted an interpretation of executive power which would give to the President a field of action much wider than that outlined by the enumerated powers.[5]

It is, in fact, the constitutional foundation for that Rule of Necessity which we shall see bulking larger and larger as we recount certain incidents in the history of Presidential enlargement.[6]

[5] Op. cit., 138–39.

[6] Concerning the "unity" of the Executive, which so much concerned Wilson and Morris, and the suggestion of plurality, which was lost because it was identified with weakness, Lord Bryce, many years later, would have something to say in his *American Commonwealth*, I, 35: "That a single head is not necessary to a republic might have been suggested to the Americans by those ancient examples to which they loved to recur. The experience of modern Switzerland has made it still more obvious to us now. Yet it was settled very early in the debates of 1787 that the central executive authority must be vested in one person . . . The explanation is to be found in the familiarity of the Americans, as citizens of the several states with the office of State Governor (in some states then called President) . . ."

Wilson seems to have taken his example from the state of New York, where his "unity" was most nearly approached.

★ 3 ★

IT HAS TO BE RECALLED TO WHAT EXTENT THE DELEGATES TO THE Convention were working without precedent to guide them. There were semi-democratic governments in the world, and there had been well-known republics; but none assumed that the people were sovereign, none was suited to the circumstances of a nation being established on the shores of a vast continent most of which was still a wilderness, and, especially, none suited the aspirations of those vigorous individualists whom the delegates represented.

For these reasons the framers had no guide to the extent they might go in providing new devices. Their instructions were vague. They were to strengthen the Union; they had not been told to create the framework for a new government; and doubts about this tormented the meeting from the very first. These doubts prepared the way for the Paterson (New Jersey) plan. The question whether a new Constitution might be written was one that each delegate had to settle in his own mind before he could consent to the radical changes being proposed. Some did it forthrightly, knowing that their departure from instructions was a gross one; some were more ambiguous and gave consent because they could see no way to avoid it if any real strengthening was to be done. Some, of course, did not agree at all; but these were not many, although they were influential in certain states, such as Virginia.

The finished document certainly exceeded instructions. The government it provided for was so different in conception from the Continental Congress as to bear very little resemblance to it. Yet the departures were in the direction of the strengthening of the Union which had been set as almost the only instruction. And it was on this basis that the Executive provided for could be justified. His choice separately from the legislature was a novel idea; but there was no doubt that it did lend power to the center. Yet its creators were quite right in anticipating that it would be attacked in the coming discussions about ratification.

What saved the Executive in the Convention was what in the end saved the new government as a whole. This was the desperate condition of the country and general recognition that the weakness of the Union was responsible. The backwoods democrats disliked the prospect of a stronger government; in fact, the less government there was, the better they were suited. Yet they did not like the results of weakness when these results were brought home to them. Their frontiers were not safe, for instance, and those frontiers were so deep as to make up most of the country. They wanted improvements even if they did not want to pay for them. And the state politicians were unremitting in their hostility. So it went. They hated being faced with the dilemma that had gradually become insistent; but they finally, if reluctantly, ratified.

Even so, ratification might not have taken place, or might have been indefinitely delayed, if the Convention had not exceeded its instructions in another instance. It was provided that ratification should be by state conventions, not by the state legislatures which had sent the delegates to the meeting; and it was provided that the Constitution should become operative when nine, not thirteen, states had acted. There was no warrant for these arrangements, and there were loud outcries from the state politicians who were obviously being circumvented; but both novelties were accepted. They were not easy ones to argue against, and again there was the urgency of escaping from decay.

It cannot be too much emphasized that the really unique innovation of the new Constitution was the President it established. Nor can it be too much insisted on that he was made independent of, in many ways opposed to, and yet inescapably co-ordinate with, the other Branches; and that, in creating him, the framers established a state of tension and uncertainty which would be unremitting. It was this sharing of powers and unwilling co-operation in duties that would, they thought, protect the individuals of the nation from too considerable a concentration of power in any Branch and yet would provide a government able to command respect at home and abroad and so be able to protect the national interest.

Other chiefs of state in national governments had not usually been thus responsible to the people except through another elected body which could also make laws. What was better known was the British King, whose authority derived from divine appointment or who was, at any rate, independent of, and above, his subjects. This might be mostly theoretical, and he might actually be controlled by nobles or, more recently, the Commons, but to go all the way in establishing an Executive broadly based on the whole people, as sovereign, was a tour de force of such magnitude as to command respect and wonder. The colonials, after their experience with an absolute monarch in the person of the Royal Governors, came with the utmost reluctance and after sad experience to the admission that a strong Executive was necessary, and when their representatives in the Convention created one he had to be hedged about with countervailing powers. Also, he had to be subject to impeachment for cause. But that he had stature and that he lent strength to the Federal government could not be denied. The underlying logic of those who, after the Convention, took up the task of arguing for ratification was good enough. But it was probably not the logic of those who wrote *The Federalist* papers, or of the other politicians who became advocates, that carried the cause to completion. It was the disillusion of the whole country with simple confederation. Its opposite was, by contrast, acceptable.

This disillusion had, in fact, been very much present in the minds of the delegates. They had seen the old government practically expire while still nominally in existence, its organs incapable of carrying on the most elementary functions.[1] And it was not because able officials were not to be had; it was because the government's structure was defective and its powers insufficient. This explains the receptiveness of the delegates to a Federal scheme with specific powers delegated to the central organs, and among these the President in a prominent situation. Consent to the change even in the Convention being far from unanimous, it could be anticipated that there would be contention about ratification. But what Washington and perhaps others did not foresee was that the contention would go on into the post-ratification period and grow worse rather than better. And certainly the first President did not regard it as possible that Jefferson might lead an opposition which would overthrow the nationalists and reinstitute many of the ideas and devices rejected by the Convention.

The argument was made at once that the President provided by the Constitution was almost indistinguishable from a king, and this theme was pursued throughout the ratification debates. Washington, searching his soul, would have found no kingly ambitions, even if he did desire great dignity and prestige for the President, representing the people. In *The*

---

[1] John Jay, who had served the Confederation long and faithfully, and would also serve the Federal Union, had attended the dying as a frustrated official. He had written to Washington in 1786: "When government, either from defects in its construction, or administration, ceases to assert its rights, or is too feeble to afford security, inspire confidence, and overawe the ambitious and licentious, the best citizens naturally grow uneasy and look to other systems." It is interesting, too, that Jay had a clear idea of what the best other system would be: "I promise myself nothing very desirable from any change which does not divide sovereignty into its proper departments. Let Congress legislate—let others execute— let others judge." (*Correspondence and Papers of John Jay*, 4 vols., edited by H. P. Johnson [New York, 1891]. The quotations are from III, 126.) Even if Jay did fail of election as a delegate, he was, as John Adams remarked, "nevertheless very much present." So, it might be said, was Adams, whose views were similar.

Federalist, Hamilton undertook to demonstrate how little the President resembled the British King or even the colonial Governors. He was, said Hamilton, much more like the Governors of the states under the Confederation.[2] And there is ample reason for believing that the strong executive of the New York constitution did actually serve as a model for Wilson and Morris, who were so persistent in the constitutional debates. This is a point of some importance for those interested in understanding the inner nature, the spirit, of the government. Its genesis was in American experience tempering a theoretical construct and modifying a British institution.

It is undoubtedly true that something like half the delegates were inclined, especially at first, toward a parliamentary government, including a limited monarchy. Hamilton said in his formal speech that he favored this solution but that he did not expect to see it adopted. As it was finally shaped, the Executive was very little like the British monarch; nevertheless, he was given potential powers of considerable magnitude. They exceeded in many ways those remaining to the Crown after the British revolution, and they would in time make him the most potent Chief of State in the world. Presently the kind of persons—the Federalists—who fought so hard for his acceptance would be having second thoughts. And for their successors—Whigs and Republicans—it would become necessary, so they would think, to whittle down his powers considerably. He would become, in their eyes, even more than the Congress of whom they would have expected it, the *vox populi.* Whenever they would capture the Presidency in later years, they would weaken it by intention. It threatened their privileges.

---

[2] This was in No. 69 of *The Federalist.* Commenting on this, Professor R. L. Schuyler has said: "If a provision of the Constitution is similar to one found in the Articles of Confederation or in a state constitution, and also resembles some law or custom of the English Constitution, it is surely farfetched to infer that the borrowing was from what was remote, rather than what was at hand and known through intimate experience." *The Constitution of the United States* (New York, 1923), 155–56.

★ 4 ★

WASHINGTON, SOON AFTER HIS DEATH, WOULD BE SO HIDDEN IN MISTS
of adulation as to be more legendary than real; but in the years after the
war he was the best known of living men. He was aging and somewhat
withdrawn, but he could be seen in the streets of the towns, visited at
his estate, and consulted by those who had need of his advice. The regard
of most Americans rose to an intense emotion in the veterans who had
served in the armies he had commanded. When the Convention was over
and the Constitution submitted to the people in their state conventions,
they knew that the General was committed to the new scheme. He let it
be known that he considered it a satisfactory framework for a national
government and that a national government was necessary to cure the
feebleness of the Confederation. Even if *The Federalist* had never been
issued or the many other polemics undertaken, his judgment would have
been enough to ensure ultimate acceptance. The state politicians would
have done their best to prevent it, appealing to the "love of liberty" under
which localism was hidden. But Washington's solid judgment would certainly have outweighed all other considerations.

It had been with deepening concern that he watched the government
in New York fall to pieces after the military victory had been won. It
could be said of him that he was American before he was Virginian at a
time when numerous others of his prominence refused to put the nation
before the states. They were as influential in Virginia as in other places.
Watching the effect of their activities, he came to see that his retirement
had been premature. There was still work to be done that only he could do.
He must offer himself as a nucleus about whom the nationalist sentiment
could gather and to whom sensible patriots, able to see further than the
borders of their states, might look for leadership. It could begin with consideration of the absurd restrictions the states were imposing on each
other's commerce; and this was the reason for the Annapolis meeting in
1786. This effort came to nothing because of localism, the evil he had identified as responsible for the country's decline; but the failure was softened
by one success: another meeting was appointed to take place in Phila-

delphia in 1787 with widened terms of reference. They included, at Hamilton's suggestion, the strengthened Union that rather surprisingly became part of the delegates' instructions from most of the states.

Hardly anyone in the thirteen states could have been unaware of Washington's concern. His expression of it must have strengthened those with nationalist leanings and must have alarmed those who feared that the nationalists would prevail. The support coming to him was in encouraging volume. But he was much opposed in his own state. The Governor, Edmund Randolph, was hesitant; Patrick Henry, the formidable demagogue, was furiously opposed; and George Mason was determined to prevent centralization. To all of these the idea of a strengthened center represented a setback in the long struggle for individual liberty, the essence of the Revolution. It was only by the smallest of margins that Madison was chosen as one of the Virginia delegates—which is appalling, considering the contributions he was to make.

But if the situation in Virginia seemed unfavorable to strengthened Union, that in New York appeared to be even worse. Clinton, the state's most potent political figure, preferred to keep entirely apart. Hamilton was becoming more and more discouraged, and John Jay was losing favor because of his nationalist expressions. Yet the tide was running toward unionism. And the moderate group assembled at Philadelphia met the problem they had to solve without evasion. There were dissenters, some even who would not join in the conclusion. But when it was finally done, it was a national government, not an assemblage of state representatives. And at the very heart of it was the President. He, more than any other of its inventions and compromises, represented the hopes of those who, like Washington, had wanted unity and discipline.

The President's duties and powers had been made less specific than they might have been if there had been any experience with such an office; and they were limited, in accord with the theory of checks and balances, by grants to the other Branches, of powers interpenetrating it. When they adjourned, having approved Article II, none of the delegates could have had any very definite picture of the official they had created— except that he would be very much like Washington. How long he might serve, what his relations with the other Branches might turn out to be in practice, whether he would be more Executive or Chief of State—these and other developments were left to the future. He was definitely independent because he owed his office to the sovereign people; and if he shared his powers with others, they also shared theirs with him.

That the Washington figure was in the delegates' minds as they shaped the office and as they consented to the silences his voice might fill, we know from more than inference. It was suggested more than once that he ought to be the first incumbent, and it was with this in view that the heavy duties and the significant symbolism were agreed to. The silences, it was expected, would be filled reasonably as was his habit. That this was so, emboldened the Convention to mold the central figure to heroic size.

The expectation was met. Washington, who had thought himself retired from public life, proved to be a powerful and creative President. He still remains among those who have contributed most to the shaping of the office. Even after the leveling efforts of Jefferson and Jackson, it retained much the style he gave it; it still does as succeeding individuals occupy it. He was not always certain how he should act. He often consulted those he could look to for advice; but this did not mean that he was unwilling to take responsibility or to make decisions; it meant rather that he took his responsibilities seriously and wanted to make his decisions with all the judgments before him that could be assembled. He did not lean on others, but he respected their opinions.

It was required that he should be bold as well as cautious; but he did not hesitate to experiment, as he was used to doing at Mount Vernon in his agricultural operations, choosing what seemed best among the possibilities. Perhaps no other President except Eisenhower has known so well how to use a staff, something both seem to have owed to military experience. This is a technique that politicians do not acquire, that they naturally find unacceptable. It does not comport with the intrigue and amicism of politics; and most Presidents are raised to office from that life.

We have inherited an image of Washington, coming down to us from bowlderized accounts of his life and from the official portraits, which is that of a man who is elderly, cold, and aloof. And it is true that from 1777, when he took command of the army, to 1783, when he resigned his commission, he had of necessity been withdrawn and reserved, one who took advice very formally and worked out his decisions in solitude. Commanders carry their responsibilities in this way because they must; and in his case it has to be recalled that he was always harassed by shortages of materials as well as of men and that he was so poorly supported by the Congress as to be left sometimes without the most elementary necessities for campaigning. If he was morose, it is no wonder. And if he hid the real situation from his soldiers, it was in the country's cause.

But it is also true that in this hardest of schools he acquired patience; and that, better than any of the others, he learned to look beyond discouragement to the objectives of independence and Union. In his camps, when it was possible, his official family saw a kinder side of his nature, and many of them had cause to be grateful for his support and sympathy. He was not always cold and dignified. And there were occasions when his wrath was something to see. He was not a man who would suffer stupidity and disloyalty without taking the measures these military sins required. When the victory had been won, all his countrymen knew his virtues, but they also knew of his conduct under provocation, of his kindness and his generosity. He was no monolith to them.

An early determination on Washington's part when he took command of the armies that he would accept no pay for his services had a certain importance. It allowed him to feel that his own patriotism was untainted, and naturally it became generally known. Even after the war a suggestion that he accept a gift of money from the Congress (made by the Pennsylvania Executive Council) was rejected—this in spite of the notorious expensiveness of Mount Vernon. The estate had become a kind of resort for passing visitors of all sorts, and even the most casual of these were entertained in the General's ceremonious way. Their stays were often prolonged, and altogether it was known to be difficult for him to meet the outlay involved. This may have been largely because he was land-poor—basically he was a wealthy man—but at any rate he was usually short of cash. He had come home from the war, as he had foreseen, with reduced resources and increased obligations. During the years between 1783 and 1789 the humiliations he underwent in this way were galling to so proud a country gentleman. But again, when Virginia voted him a gift, he refused it. And in his first inaugural he said that he would take no pay as President. He allowed the government to bear the expense of his establishment and the ceremonial it required, but he always remained an unsalaried servant of his nation.

In this self-denial his only imitator would be Herbert Hoover, the reason being in most cases that none of the other Presidents could afford it. No President has left office with a fortune; many of them, on the contrary, left office so impoverished as to have been embarrassed.[1]

Luckily it was otherwise with Washington. At any rate, this, and his determined non-partisanship, created in the first years a model President that all the earnest efforts of Jefferson's Democratic-Republicans failed to obliterate. The President would somehow emerge, even from the murkiest equalitarian periods, with much the same nobility that Washington intended to give him. Even the meanest of the Presidents have seemed to be transformed by the office, and the most mediocre have risen some distance toward the expectations of a people needing at their head a symbolic figure of virtue.

Washington's successes as a military commander were not often of the spectacular kind. He had not the wherewithal to win many battles, being more usually required to steady his men in retreat and to mitigate the

---

[1] That other Virginia gentleman, James Monroe, was an example. He was forced to dispose of his home at Oak Hill and spend his last days in his son-in-law's home in New York City. And Jefferson, for all the appearance of Monticello, was practically bankrupt in age—he had to sell his library to the Congress—and latter-day Presidents who survived long had to find means to support themselves; not easy for an ex-President anxious not to demean the office he has held.

hardships of their life in the field than to raise their spirits for fighting. But he learned to value a thorough knowledge of the enemy's dispositions and a studied estimate of his intentions. He grew very clever in outwitting forces much stronger than his own. He was helped in this by having been a British officer. He knew the regulars. And when he was President he put to good use what he had learned of the nature of legislatures when as Commander in Chief he petitioned for supplies and fended off conspiracies against his leadership. What he did not already know, he quickly learned.

When on April 14, 1789—a time when Mount Vernon was in its most attractive dress for spring—Charles Thomson, Secretary of the Congress, appeared to notify the General of his unanimous election, he was ready with an equally formal reply. He had known for some time what he must do. He had, as was his habit when preparing to be away, written out in meticulous detail instructions to George Augustine Washington, his nephew and manager, for the conduct of the estate during his absence. And he was already engaged in the painful answering of applications from those who would like to share in the patronage they anticipated he would have at his disposal.[2]

It is impossible not to feel a certain sympathy for the retired General with the devotion to country life and the means to enjoy it fully—and who, moreover, had given years to the task of making a new nation in which gentlemen could be safe on their estates and with clear consciences —who was now being forced by his sense of duty to accept a position he regarded as an onerous obligation. He had become, in Americans' regard, the representation of their hopes, once so full and now so tenuous. Through him they might still advance into that nationhood they had intended to establish yet had drawn back from as its disciplines had been revealed in practice.

[2] Cf. the letter to Samuel Vaughan, to whom he was indebted for a handsome Mount Vernon chimneypiece and whose son wanted a job: ". . . from the moment when the necessity [of accepting the Presidency] had become more apparent, and, as it were, inevitable, I anticipated in a heart filled with distress, the ten thousand embarrassments, perplexities, and troubles to which I must again be exposed in the evening of a life already nearly consumed in public cares. Among all these anxieties . . . I anticipated none greater than those that were likely to be produced by applications for appointments. . . . My apprehensions have already been but too well justified." Quoted in D. S. Freeman, *George Washington* (New York, 1954), VI, 160.

★ 5 ★

THE ESTABLISHMENT OF THE FEDERAL GOVERNMENT UNDER THE NEW
Constitution offered another chance after the wasted one succeeding
independence; but the redemption of the promises so often reiterated
in the arguments for ratification, depended now on a vigorous government
embodying them. And the center of that government must be the President
provided for with such pains by the framers. Only one man fitted
the conception; its grandeur would not survive the tenure of a lesser man
than their greatest. This was Washington, and wearily he acknowledged
his duty. He must accept the consequences of what he had caused to
be begun.

Since he was experienced in public life he was only too well aware
that people hoped for too much. He, if not they, knew that he was human
—in some ways so insufficient that he would have to labor for adequacy.
But he must try. He saw the role he had to play in general outline but
not in detail, and there were important matters about which he knew
his ignorance to be complete. The proprietor of an estate on the Potomac,
even the commander of an army, had cause to learn little about commerce
or finance, especially in its public aspects. He had helped to make an issue
of the tariffs among the states; it had been the issue leading to the
Annapolis meeting; but his knowledge was more practical than general.
Also, he was neither a lawyer nor a student of government as so many of
his colleagues at the Convention had been. He was only an earnest, devoted patriot, somewhat slow, but of impeccable integrity. He had risked
hanging for treason; he would not excuse himself from risking less for the
nation he had helped to make.

In the company he was about to enter he would be uneasy. Others
would be agile where he would be stolid; they would be devious; they
would very likely check him on occasion. His reserve would be invaded;
his dignity would suffer. But, on the other hand, he was regarded with
such popular respect that no politician would risk attacking him openly,
and his prestige might enable him to stifle the inevitable squabbling in
and about the capital. The same prestige might overcome the reluctance

of state officials to allow the Federal government the authority intended by the Constitution. Furthermore, he did at least have a definite view of the foreign policies needed to re-establish the nation's position among the powers. There was trouble all around the borders. Three rapacious empires gazed inward at the feeble new nation, and they were continually inciting their Indian allies to aggression. In such matters he would be competent because of long experience and that slow cogitation by which he finally arrived at sound conclusions.

So in April of 1789 the first President reluctantly prepared to leave the greening fields of Mount Vernon for the journey to New York. That he did not realize the true nature of that taut and always-quivering structure created by the framers, we can infer from certain of his early concessions of advantage to the Congress. But there were some important gifts of power that came to him unsolicited. In the matter of dismissing as well as appointing his subordinates, about which the Constitution had been silent, the Congress yielded without argument. The statutes setting up the first three of his Departments were specific on the point. There was thus established a custom of first importance. If the Congress had insisted that this vacant line in the instrument be written in their favor, he might have acquiesced in innocence, and this would have been a disaster for the Presidency. And if he had fought for the privilege, there would have been precipitated a most unedifying struggle for the first years of the new Republic.

But, important as structure and functioning were, Washington's first concern was merely for appearance. Fortunately what came easiest to him was also what he believed to be appropriate. He exercised his normal dignity, somewhat exaggeratedly, in the new environment, setting thus the presidential style. Some years previously, at the end of the war, he had moved from city to city, a hero, endlessly entertained and eulogized, escorted through the countryside by local guardsmen, honored as the local resources allowed. He had eaten innumerable meals, drunk hogsheads of wine in response to toasts, and reviewed hundreds of troops of militia. He had only to heighten his performance as the first citizen of the land, set apart by his office, and responsible to all but not to any. He could succeed in this because he was already the first citizen. And it was his conception of the presidential role.

We have a kind of self-portrait of this mature and splendid public figure accepting responsibility for the creation of his new office; even so great a man could be humble:

> In our progress toward political happiness my station is new, and, if I may use the expression, I walk on untrodden ground. There is scarcely an action, the motive of which may not be subject to a double interpretation. There is scarcely any part of my conduct

which may not hereafter be drawn into precedent. Under such a view of the duties inherent in my arduous office, I could not but feel a diffidence in myself . . . and an anxiety for the community . . .

It was to be a government of accommodation as well as a government of laws. Much was to be done by prudence, much by conciliation, much by firmness.[1]

But in office he gained certainty, and later he said with firm confidence:

The powers of the Executive of this country are more definite, and better understood, perhaps, than those of any other country; and my aim has been, and will continue to be, neither to stretch nor relax them in any instance whatever, unless compelled to it by imperious circumstances.[2]

This is the first statement by a President of the interlocked Rules of Necessity and Restraint. We shall find Washington's successors repeating them occasionally, but, much more important, we shall see them operating in accord with their precepts. Restraint when possible, action dictated by necessity when circumstances compel! Such is the presidential rule. It was impressed on the first President; it would be a guide for the others. It accords with the spirit of the Constitution—or, it might be better to say, the Constitution as Presidents see it.

But the crises in which resort must be had to extraordinary powers are not common, and for Presidents the dictates of restraint are more usually heeded. There are many operations of a running government in which conciliation of the legislature is worth attending to. Washington was aware of this. He tried to defer and to consult so far as his sense of deportment allowed. He was among the most circumspect of men, and there was seldom complaint that he lacked consideration for those about him.

The sober and dignified Washingtonian President would not hold to the original style quite without modification. When political parties formed about the Presidency as they had already formed about the Governorships of the states, men of lesser stature, and sometimes of lesser integrity, would be elected to the office. The role of party leader would, however, even if reluctantly, be played by every one. Washington's impulse to repudiate politics could often be seen operating; but one who had accepted party support, and perhaps even been a party leader, could not suddenly drop his affiliations. Still, even such partisans as Jefferson and

---

[1] *Life and Writings of Washington,* Jared Sparks, (Boston, 1839), X, 69. For comment on this statement, cf. *Some Presidential Interpretations of the Presidency* by N. J. Small (Baltimore, 1932), 14 ff.

[2] Ibid., 422.

Jackson would have moments when the nation became everything and the party nothing.

The personality Washington found it appropriate to emphasize by his ceremoniousness on all occasions, set the Presidency apart. Especially when he went abroad in the streets, it was in such splendor as could be managed in New York and Philadelphia—cities of no more than twelve thousand, but the largest in the nation. At his inauguration, to which he proceeded through cheering crowds and in the company of attending notables, his ornate coach was drawn by four matched horses, and he himself sat alone, wigged and powdered, as he rode through the streets, attended by outriders. On that day, as on others, he saluted the multitude from the portico of Federal Hall, bowing graciously but with reserve, then allowing himself to be seated. He was approached by Chancellor Livingston and after a time rose to take the oath and kiss the Bible, with Vice-President Adams, Governor Clinton, and officers of the Congress looking on. He again saluted the crowd, re-entered the Senate Chamber, took his place on the dais, and read his first inaugural.

This address is of interest, in its relation to the Presidency, because of its insistence at the outset of this first of all Administrations on the basic significance of the Union. But Washington, as most of his successors would also do at first, assumed that the Congress meant to be equally a Federal organ. He was soon to find that its members yielded to national needs only at his insistence—unless there might be a frightening crisis, when his urging was less necessary. But at the beginning he was inclined to defer. He felt sure, he said, "that no local pledges or attachments, no separate views or party animosities," would "misdirect the comprehensive and equal eye which ought to watch over this great assemblage of communities and interests . . ." It was a mistaken assumption. During his later years in office factions would become obstreperous and offensive, and the struggle to maintain the integrity of the central government would become more and more fierce, to end in the Jeffersonian revolution, at the heart of which was distrust of the Federal power and a reversion to the easy anarchy of localism.

By that time Washington the President would not be so universally treated with respect. Gradually the Republican partisans would gather courage to deprecate what he stood for and finally would actually attack him individually as an aristocrat, a friend of the wealthy, a believer in government by the elite. But there were victories at first. It was important that Hamilton's financial schemes were adopted. They were calculated, it will be recalled, to identify the interests of the creditor classes with the Federal government and so to buy their support. It may have been a costly purchase, but it was a successful one. As to the Presidency itself, the three Departments Washington wanted were established—State, Treasury, and War—also, provision was made for a government attorney and for a postal system. As to appointments, Washington did what he must. Like his successors, he struggled to save the highest offices for quali-fied candidates regardless of affiliation—the Supreme Court, for instance, to which he named John Jay as the first Chief Justice, and as Associates, James Wilson, John Rutledge, William Cushing, John Blair, and Robert H. Harrison (who declined). These were distinguished lawyers, but a geographic distribution had been made. Represented were New York, Pennsylvania, South Carolina, Massachusetts, Virginia, and Maryland—a precedent which would always be respected.

As in the beginning, so throughout his two terms he deliberately sought to establish a line of conduct for Presidents which would emphasize their national standing. He meant to be so firm a model for those who came after that his example would reach far beyond his own years. When he took pains that he should always appear in public in elaborate state, when he opened his residence to selected citizens with suitable formality, when he made journeys to various parts of the country, and when he made careful addresses to the Congress, he was making sure that as President he appeared as one apart, above controversy, the embodiment of national conscience and principle.

Also in other ways, less general and more practical, he affected the office permanently. It must always be recalled that he was breaking ground, finding his way. He had to determine, for instance, how he should treat the heads of Departments once they were appointed, and whether he should look to them for advice; also, he had to relate his own functions to those of the Congress and the judiciary. The Congress was at first in-clined to concur because it could not deny; his prestige was too over-whelming. But even when opposition arose his attitude toward it con-tinued to be courteous. The outward deference of his first inaugural was maintained. Nevertheless, he gradually found that he must become, if not a leader in legislation, at least an influence on it, and he began to let it be known how he regarded important issues, even controversial ones. As to the Department heads, he firmly made them his subordinates and sepa-rated them from the Congress. And this would remain the rule until the attempted tour de force of the Republican Radicals in Andrew Johnson's Presidency, when the Congress would assert its superiority by seizing the removal power it had allowed Washington to exercise without protest.[3]

[3] The Tenure of Office Act would not be agreed to by President John-son, of course; it would be passed over his veto. And eventually it would be repealed. As we proceed there will be other, more lasting, modifications of the presidential control over the Executive establishment. Perhaps the most important of them will be represented by the series of semi-inde-pendent agencies, of which the first will be the Interstate Commerce Com-mission. These will result from the growth of the business system and

Other contributions made by Washington, besides those having to do with presidential deportment and the business of the Executive, were equally important. For instance, his overwhelming prestige was largely responsible for a new respect accorded the nation by other governments. One important incident in his conduct of foreign affairs went a long way toward gaining this regard. This was really more than an incident, since it involved the complications precipitated by the revolution in France and the relations to it of the United States, as well as the quarrel then going on between the French and the British. During its course Washington set several precedents, one being that it was the President who was to determine on and proclaim neutrality between belligerents; also, that it was he who was to receive (or not to receive) foreign envoys and to dismiss them if they became persona non grata; that it was he, in fact, who was to transact all business of whatever kind with other nations.

About these matters the Constitution had been as calculatedly silent as about so many others. In Article II it was said that the President, "by and with the advice of the Senate," should have power to "make treaties, provided two-thirds of the Senators present" concurred; also, that he should "appoint Ambassadors, other public Ministers and Consuls . . ."; and that he should "receive Ambassadors and other public Ministers." But that was all. It was not said that he should decide great matters and commit his country to courses which might have the most serious consequences. And the situation with which he was confronted made it necessary for him to proceed, on this rather thin instruction, to the determination of his own powers. The Constitution did award to the Congress the declaring of war, and it also mentioned the raising and support of armies,

---

the necessity of finding some way to direct and control it. They are often spoken of as "semi-judicial," but they are semi-legislative and semi-executive as well; and their place in a tripartite government would from the first be anomalous. The industrial revolution was something that the framers did not anticipate. They could conceive, in their time, of no other possible system than the laissez faire which had so recently replaced the restrictive mercantilism. This had, in fact, been one of the annoyances leading to the revolution. Justice Holmes would have occasion to remark that the Constitution did not enact Spencer's *Social Statics*—meaning laissez faire. But if the framers had thought it necessary to mention economic affairs, it would have been laissez faire that would have governed their thinking. As it turned out, a policy for business regulation would have to be found without constitutional guidance. It would be a very difficult matter, involving divisiveness and acrimony. These problems were far ahead in Washington's time, but his firm establishment of the Executive would have an important part in their solution when leadership would be most urgently needed.

the provisioning and maintenance of a navy, and the calling out of the militia to repel invasions. These specifications would seem to limit the role of the Executive in such matters to the direction of the armed forces as Commander in Chief after wars had begun. Still the commitment involved in receiving Ambassadors and that of deciding on neutrality were clearly decisive. Ought he to consult even in these preliminary matters which might make a declaration of war almost inevitable?

He thought not. And the precedent has stood.

★ **6** ★

SO WASHINGTON HAD TO FEEL HIS WAY. AND ON OCCASION HE ASKED his principal advisers to give him their opinions. When the war on the continent made it necessary to decide whether the United States should remain neutral, he submitted a list of questions to Hamilton, Jefferson, and Randolph.[1]

1. Shall a proclamation issue for the purpose of preventing interferences of the citizens of the United States in the war between France and Britain? Shall it contain a declaration of neutrality? What shall it contain?
2. Shall a minister from the Republic of France be received?
3. Would a reasonable interpretation of their obligations to France under the existing treaty of alliance permit the United States to remain neutral under the present circumstances?
4. Is it necessary or advisable to call together the two Houses of Congress, with a view to the present posture of European affairs? If it is, what should be the particular object of such a call?[2]

This was one of those occasions when the puzzled President found it convenient to "require the opinion in writing of the principal officer in each of the Executive Departments."[3] He uncovered violent disagree-

[1] Legal representative whose office would later become the Attorney-Generalship.

[2] Sparks, op. cit., X, 533.

[3] Not much used thereafter; it was made unnecessary by the custom of holding Cabinet meetings, although sometimes Presidents liked to have memoranda as background for discussion. Monroe did this in preparation for the Doctrine, for instance. But advisory opinions from Attorneys General were common—*vide* the second Roosevelt's memorandum from Jackson on his Court reorganization plan in 1937. But later Presidents, many of them, disliked discussion in Cabinet of important issues, which may

ments and cannot have been much helped. But it was his way to make a deliberate approach; and perhaps the differences sharpened his own perceptions. Jefferson, the Secretary of State, opposed the issuance of any proclamation at all; he thought it more expedient to have the Congress decide. But Jefferson was already beginning to act more like a rival politician than an adviser.[4] On the other hand, Hamilton thought the case for presidential prerogative quite clear. He argued that the general doctrine of the Constitution vested the Executive power in the President, and this was subject only to the exceptions and qualifications expressed in the instrument. Foreign relations were assigned to the Executive; neutrality had to do with foreign relations and so was within Executive competence. Since the Constitution did not forbid the issuance of a proclamation, the authority to issue one must be presumed.[5]

Washington finally concluded that his powers ran to the warning he had in mind, and he caused a proclamation to be framed by John Randolph. Having made this decision, it was logical that he should follow it

---

have been because the group had grown so large. Among ten or twelve confidences could hardly be exchanged without risking leaks.

[4] That this was a political attitude adopted for effect is suggested by its inconsistency with his later refusal, when President, to be bound by a Court decision with which he did not agree: the President then became an independent agent. Besides, he later came around to saying that the transaction of business with foreign nations must be exclusively Executive. *Works*, Ford ed., (New York, 1905, 12 vols.) VI, 261; VII, 250. Cf. also Small, op. cit., 57. Jefferson, of course, was a partisan of France, as was Hamilton of Britain; and Washington's sympathies ran against the disorder of revolution. He dreaded the implications of French influence in the United States, and this made him lean toward the British point of view.

[5] There was beginning the controversy, so long to be continued and so deeply involved with other issues—slavery, for instance, in another generation, and the disciplining of business in still a later one—between the "strict constructionists" and those who held to the doctrine, stated here by Hamilton, of "implied powers." We shall see a reversal of attitudes, so that so strong a conservative as Taft will argue vehemently against "residual powers" for the President.

It should be noted that in this case Hamilton was also arguing for strictly separated powers. He declared that the President might decide for himself what the Constitution required of him, but so also might the Congress. This important implication of the principle of tripartite government would often be ignored when convenient but would always be come back to because it must. So long as the Constitution stood unamended, each Branch was its own mentor.

by enforcing its requirements; and he proceeded to prosecute infractions of neutrality on the sole authority of his proclamation. He seems to have thought, however, as enforcement proceeded, that consultation with the Congress would be expedient; and he requested that a supporting law be passed. This request doubtless affected the views of future Presidents. It was readily complied with. But Lincoln in the Civil War crisis, and other Presidents in lesser ones, would keep foreign policy well within the Executive realm of decision. It was a delicate matter and one likely to precipitate angry reactions, especially after the building up of immigrant minorities who would have remaining affiliations with their former countrymen. Both Wilson and Roosevelt, in the world wars, would have such difficulties. And Roosevelt's struggles to obtain from the Congress the neutrality legislation he wanted would have a satisfactory outcome only when it was almost too late. But he would wait for the Congress to act.[6]

Another cluster of happenings, centering in the *affaire Genêt*, helped fix presidential control over foreign policy. In this instance, also, Washington was required to establish precedent in an important constitutional area. He had again to expand the meaning of the duty imposed upon him to "receive" Ambassadors. If he could receive them, could he also *refuse* to receive them? And, once they were received, was their status permanent? Could he revoke their credentials if he thought it expedient? He saw at once, when he considered these questions, that there might be involved such provocation of another government as would result in war or the threat of it. He again asked the advice of his counselors.

It was not so complicated a matter to receive Genêt as Minister; but when the Frenchman undertook to argue for American military support in his country's conflict with Britain, and when he continued to propagandize and to agitate, the question of his continued acceptability was raised. The nation was being seriously divided at a time when it could not afford the hostility of either empire. Washington decided that it was within the presidential power to require the Minister's recall. The French government acquiesced, and, as it turned out, the peace was not breached; it had been a wise decision and in the national interest; but more important even than the immediate issue was the acceptance from then on of the rule that Presidents might recognize and might at least rebuke, by demanding the withdrawal of envoys, other governments whose actions became provocative.

This decision of Washington's was not challenged, and the precedent

---

[6] On the other hand, Roosevelt's own views would be made manifest throughout the years of hesitation before the nation made up its mind; he would be neutral only in a legal sense. And, as we shall see, aids to the Allies would not be delayed for congressional approval.

was long assumed to govern. Jefferson thus recognized the Napoleonic regime in 1804, and Wilson directed the Ambassador in St. Petersburg to establish relations with the revolutionary government of Russia in 1917.[7] But it would have been strange if there had not been a challenge by the aggressive Congresses of the Civil War years; and there was. The House at that time voted resolutions, passed on to it by its Committee on Foreign Affairs, declaring that the Congress had a right to "an authoritative voice" in such matters. To this Seward, Lincoln's Secretary of State, replied that this was a "purely executive question" and that decisions about it belonged constitutionally "not to the House . . . nor even to the Congress, but to the President."[8]

It is interesting that even so firm a tradition, accepted as ruling for more than half a century, should not have been respected when another Branch felt able to attempt its reversal. We shall see that this is true of all precedents, well established or not. They are never fixed for good and all. After the attempt by the Civil War Congress to seize control of foreign relations, as it was reaching for so much else, there were no other such important incidents until Wilson's Administration; but then the Senate ventured to dictate what must be done in crises involving Mexico and Russia. Wilson was indignant and said so, even though it might by then have been argued that Executive action had been stretched beyond toleration by Theodore Roosevelt in the Panama incident and that some check might be advisable.[9] However weak his constitutional case, Wilson succeeded in avoiding the potential interference. He had to do it, however, by political maneuver, and his experience made later Executives more cautious. F. D. Roosevelt, who had momentous foreign problems, usually took the greatest pains to conciliate Republican partisans and to admit appropriate legislators, especially the Senators, to the preliminaries of negotiation whenever there was any likelihood of irritation.

The discretion of later Presidents, after the willfulness of Wilson, has not affected—indeed, it has strengthened—the rule that foreign business is the President's to deal with. In negotiation, if the Senators are consulted, it is purely a consultation; and if resolutions are passed, they are usually of Executive origin and designed to show the unity of national opinion. So far has this gone that foreign affairs can be said to be an area

[7] Wilson also recognized Poland, Finland, Armenia, etc., the succession states of World War I, by formal notification through the Department of State.

[8] This matter has been examined by various students, for instance by Small, op. cit., by J. G. Randall, and by others.

[9] Panama's alienation from Colombia will be further discussed as one of Roosevelt's contributions.

within which the President is representative not of his party but of the whole country. He is to be supported even when not wholly approved. There are limits to this, and not infrequently there are Senators or others who will not conform, but the success of the Executive in monopolizing the lead and the quick return to bipartisanship after every spate of dissent show where the stabilized norm will lie. Washington's practical sense and cool wisdom are largely responsible. A wrong turn at the beginning could have made the Senate the master of this field, with results too horrible to contemplate equably.

At least one other debt owed to Washington by his successors ought to be noted. It was incurred during the course of the Whiskey Rebellion. As a result of Washington's conduct when confronted with the problems of civil disobedience, there would never again be any doubt of the President's power to intervene when events made it desirable. In fact, by then the Congress would have delegated it to him,[10] but this too would have been because Washington demonstrated the wisdom of firm action under one direction. When he first was confronted by virtual rebellion in western Pennsylvania against the revenue laws, there was no guide to the view he ought to take. Since the Constitution said that the Congress must "provide for calling forth the militia to execute the laws of the Union, suppress insurrections and repel invasions," it was not apparent that the President might take the initiative.[11] Part of the difficulty was removed when in 1792 the Congress passed an Act providing that when an Associate Justice or a District Judge should certify that the execution of the laws was being opposed by "combinations too powerful to be suppressed" by ordinary means, the President might call out the militia of the state beset by disorder. Also, if that state should not furnish force enough, he might, if the Congress was not in session, call out the militia of other states. But he might employ these troops only for thirty days after the beginning of the ensuing session.

The passage of this Act doubtless relieved Washington's mind, but there is reason to believe that he would have acted anyway. The refusal of the considerable number of citizens in western Pennsylvania to comply with Federal law was a serious challenge to the government. No move was made to meet it fully until 1794, almost three years after defiance had become notorious, and when enforcement was undertaken there was congressional authorization. But the delay was not because determination was lacking; it was because Washington wanted to make certain that in this first use of force he had ample justification.

Unless the government did act, it would be called impotent; but if it

[10] Rev. Stat., secs. 5298–5299.

[11] Art. I, sec. 8, par. 15.

acted precipitously it would be accused of oppression, thus confirming what had so often been said by dissenters to be the consequence of setting up a strong Executive. The President, it had been prophesied, would use the standing army for compelling obedience to his will. These allegations were still being made—they were part of the opposition propaganda—and they were the reason for Washington's caution. He tried other means, hoping to avoid the use of force. He urged the United States marshals to intensify their efforts and in 1792 issued a proclamation calling on the offenders to desist. Even about this he requested the opinions of his advisers. They were unanimous; but that Jefferson was reluctant is known.[12] He must have been even more reluctant to see Washington set out on an enforcement campaign, even though two years more of defiance had passed; and he did in fact express himself as fearful that either other states might refuse their militia or that if Pennsylvania should be "invaded" the discontent would be still more aggravated. But the others approved without reservation.

Washington by then had argued with himself until he was quite clear as to what he must do:

> If after these regulations are in operation opposition to the due exercise of the collection is still experienced, and peaceable procedure is no longer effectual, the public interest and my duty will make it necessary to enforce the laws respecting this matter; and, however disagreeable this would be to me, it must nevertheless take place.[13]

When the insurrectionists refused to comply and the proclamation (of August 1794) was flagrantly disobeyed, Governor Lee of Virginia was appointed to command the militia and instructed to proceed to the area of revolt. Washington himself prepared to take the field as well, thus demonstrating the determination of the government to enforce the law.[14]

The demonstration sufficed. Moonshiners, recently so defiant, vanished into the hills and were not heard of again as a threat to government. The militia had no call to use force. But the demonstration was complete that the Federal government was supreme, that it would not suffer de-

---

[12] He wrote to a friend that it was "another instance of my being forced to approve what I condemned uniformly from its first conception." *Works*, Ford ed., VI, 261.

[13] Sparks, op. cit., X, 259.

[14] There were altogether four proclamations, only one of which was required by the Act. This extreme caution, backed by unmistakable firmness, was characteristic of Washington as President and one of the important legacies to his successors.

fiance by any interest, and that its Executive could and would act when the laws must be enforced by other than ordinary means.

We shall see, a century later, how another President confronted a similar crisis. This was Cleveland, and the circumstances were furnished by the Pullman strike in Chicago. In 1893 none of the caution used by Washington was thought necessary. The President did not even confer with the Governor of the state as to the necessity for Federal interference, but sent in the army without hesitation. The Governor (Altgeld) protested, but the President relied on an Attorney General who considered that interference with the mails imposed a duty to see that the laws were faithfully executed. And there was no recourse.

The general opinion, after consideration, was that Cleveland had been precipitate and poorly advised and that Washington's had been a more reasonable solution; but the matter was confused because Cleveland was intervening in an industrial dispute, and it was later said by critics that interference with the mails was cited merely as an excuse for disciplining the strikers. But it cannot be denied that the President prevailed. The rule is clear that the President may do what is necessary to see that faithful execution is carried out. Different Presidents have had different ideas about delay and consultation and about the means to be used. But they have seen their duty in the clause of the Constitution that requires of them the guardianship of peace, order, and welfare. And there is always before them the warning of Buchanan; if he had been another Washington—or a Jackson—in his reading of these directives, events in the nation's ordeal of dissension might have been different, and, who knows, the Civil War might possibly have been averted. When the nation needs a President, the need is not a limited one.

As Washington's second term ran on, the factionalism his prestige and cautious firmness had stifled gradually rose again to the surface, and even he could not prevent ambitious politicians from arousing the emotions of susceptible dissidents. He ended with his dignity impaired, suffering the slanders of those he more and more despised, again fearful for his country's future. He was especially sad that the office he had sought to set in a new pattern should have become involved in the factionalism. He knew that if things had been bad for him they would be worse for John Adams; and they were, indeed, much worse. Adams, after four years, and after defeat by Jefferson in a mean campaign, would retreat to Braintree to the tune of derisive songs shouted in the streets and taverns, in fear of violence from mobs in the cities he must pass through on his journey. He would not wait to receive his successor with due courtesy.

Jefferson had deliberately instigated much of the derogation in which Washington was involved, it is sad to say, and had defeated Adams by methods unbecoming in so voluble a popular mentor. It was a much-impaired Presidency that he inherited, but it was he who had impaired it in deliberate pursuit of a theory. He distrusted Federal authority and presidential power, and he meant to reduce them to what seemed to him consonance with true democratic principles.[15]

[15] David Cushman Coyle's *Ordeal of the Presidency* (Washington, D.C., 1960), may be consulted for an extensive study of the calumnies visited on Chief Executives beginning with Washington. It is a strange and sinister phase of democracy in operation.

★ 7 ★

IT MAY BE THAT LATER GENERATIONS OUGHT NOT TO QUESTION THE sources of the rich inheritance they possess but ought merely to be grateful. Curiosity, however, will not be denied; and it is impossible not to marvel at the conversion of Jefferson, who discovered so late that there is more to being President than appears to an ambitious candidate. His acquisition of the Louisiana Territory—much more than what we now call Louisiana; an indefinite area, in fact, stretching out into the unknown Northwest—was an imperial addition to the nation. It is, however, not its size but the manner of its taking that interests us here. It was done through one of the most momentous of all the enlargements of the presidential power, and by a President who had believed it ought not to be done in the way he settled on. National necessity overcame his principles.

It has to be said of Jefferson generally that his scruples in public life were not too unruly. But in this instance the departure from his professed beliefs was drastic. It was by presidential arrangement, and without other authorization, that the vast areas involved were acquired. He agreed to pay sixteen million dollars—an immense sum then—on his own responsibility. Presidential prerogative could hardly be stretched farther.

Jefferson had built his public career on opposition to the theory of Federal supremacy held by Washington, Adams, Hamilton, Jay, and the other nationalists. So far as the Constitution was concerned, he preferred to read the Tenth Amendment literally: powers not specifically granted might not be assumed by the Federal government; they belonged to the states. He was not the first advocate of states rights—there had been others at the Convention—but he was the first to occupy the Presidency.

It was because Washington and Adams had been advocates of Federal supremacy that they were the targets of Jefferson's long and devious campaign to undermine their influence and eventually to supplant them. Even though he was Washington's Secretary of State (he resigned during the second term) and Adams's Vice-President, he had worked industriously to discredit them and to build up an opposing Democratic-Republican faction whose central tenet was decentralization. If there was one commitment more emphatic than any other in his party's creed, it was strict constructionism. Indeed, as is now known, he was the real author of the Kentucky Resolutions, which would have allowed the states to hold Acts of the Congress unconstitutional and of no effect.[1]

This curious effort to undermine the Federal power did not succeed. Chief Justice Marshall executed a tour de force which seized for the judiciary the privilege of interpretation.[2] Although Marshall prevailed over Jefferson in this matter, the attempt underlines the extreme position from which Jefferson had to move when he was required to decide whether the western lands were to be acquired at once or whether he was to jeopardize the acquisition by waiting for a constitutional amendment authorizing it. He decided that there does, in fact, exist an overriding public interest which must govern a President's conduct regardless of all else.

Concerning this, we may note here in a preliminary way—it will come up again and again—that Presidents usually act thus only when they are substantially certain that they have rightly read the public mind and that approval will flow to them in the necessary volume if questions should be raised. Of course a President acting on this imputed authority knows that no consent after the fact—even ratification by a Congress under the pressure of popular approval—can make what he does more legal. Nor can it make what he does more consistent with his former views. He simply relies on popular support to obscure these departures, usually avoiding argument. But this usually suffices to protect him from serious criticism and has always prevented his successful impeachment. Emergency assumptions of power have been questioned and opposed. The opposition has always originated in a minority, usually a small one, and often partisan. More importantly, it has come after the fact, and so has not prevented the taking of the action. Once done, and successfully done, the event has proved to be its own advocate.

Other Presidents, as we shall see, followed Jefferson in this. Jackson, Polk, Lincoln, Cleveland, the two Roosevelts, and Truman reached out beyond the ordinary scope of their power. And in only one instance did they fail. The President who failed was Truman. The incident of his defeat bulks very large in the later history of the Presidency, perhaps the most serious setback it has ever suffered.[3]

[1] The complicated intrigue involving these "resolutions" was carried on while he was Vice-President.

[2] Marshall was Adams's last-hour appointment made with a view to perpetuating Federalist principles. The case referred to here was *Marbury* vs. *Madison,* later to be discussed.

[3] This was the seizure of the steel mills during the Korean war, which the Supreme Court declared to be unlawful.

But Jefferson was the first to exceed his writ—which is ironic. He had been so determined a detractor of the Federalists and so long an advocate of decentralization that his violent reversal was extremely hard to justify. He was the representative in America of those principles of revolution that had swept France while British and American conservatives watched in horror. His long campaign to raise the French and lower the British in the regard of his countrymen had been a successful struggle to possess men's minds. He and his followers held that the Hamiltonian policy was calculated to attract the wealthy by making them wealthier. By using their enhanced power, they would accomplish, Jefferson said, what Hamilton had always wanted—and had failed to get at the Constitutional Convention—a monarchy, supported by an aristocracy able to keep the rabble in its place.

It was the rabble Jefferson had depended on for his support. The incidents of his rise have been awkward for his many apologists to explain. There was about them a characteristic lack of openness that frequently had the appearance of conspiracy. His intrigues did not stop short of personal attacks if they were necessary to discredit his opponents. He was, however, the first real professional in politics to have a national success, even if at some cost to his reputation as a man. His biographers naturally argue that the means he used were necessary to the ends he won. This is a hard admission to make, but it has to be said that if Jefferson had not been at the head of a ruthless and corrupt machine which outdid his opponents in political scandalmongering he would not have possessed the personal power necessary to acquire Louisiana as he did, confident that his action would have congressional and popular approval.

At any rate, however it was done, we must say of Jefferson's action that it furnished an invaluable example for successors who felt that the public interest required them to assume powers they formally did not possess. Also, it must be added, it was done in such a way, or with such concurrence, that it was not seriously challenged. And this too was an example it was well for others to learn.

The departure from reiterated conviction was in response to a real enough emergency. The small nation along the seaboard was not very respectfully regarded by the more powerful states of Europe, and especially during Jefferson's Presidency, when Napoleon was extending himself so mightily. Spain, among other nations, lay helpless in the Emperor's grasp; and Louisiana, at the outlet of the Mississippi, and the Floridas, farther east, were Spanish possessions. What with Britain on the north and west, and Spain, a French puppet, on the south and west, there was in the United States a feeling of constriction which was intolerable to an aggressive pioneering people whose ambitions for westward expansion were rapidly rising. West of the Appalachians the route of commerce ran to the Gulf; to have it threatened was more than irritating, it was intolerable. The control of New Orleans was the key; whoever held it might blockade one of the nation's most useful ports. This was the basis for a persistent separatist sentiment which lasted until the outlet to the Gulf was secure.

In 1802 the Spanish did close the port of New Orleans. It was done, as was learned later, on Napoleon's orders. He was preparing to take over Louisiana and he preferred to take it with commerce already stopped. In the background was his tremendous victory over the Austrians at Marengo. After it he felt able to look to the conquest of another continent. Sometime before, as a kind of consolation gift, he had presented the vast trans-Mississippi West to Spain. This recompense for her losses elsewhere, he now felt, had been an unnecessary gesture to the senile empire and he regretted it. He would take it back, develop its riches, which must be immense, and at the same time contain the aggressive Americans within their present boundaries. The Spanish, confronted with Napoleon's demand, temporized, as was their habit; and the Emperor, furious at the delay, began a series of forcing moves. He first made peace with the British. He then sent an expedition to suppress a revolt against France being led by Toussaint L'Ouverture in Santo Domingo. It was his intention, as soon as the revolt was put down, to use that island as a base for the seizing of New Orleans and the occupation of Louisiana. Talleyrand, his Foreign Minister, however, persuaded the Spanish to give in by pledging that Louisiana, under French control, would not be sold or otherwise alienated. The Spanish fear was, of course, that if the Americans should get possession of New Orleans they would push on out toward California, down into Mexico, and perhaps even farther. They were few, but they were showing an alarming propensity for expansion.

It seems that for two years negotiations about this complex affair went on without Jefferson's knowing anything about them. It was not until 1802 that American Ministers Rufus King in London and Robert R. Livingston, newly arrived in France, warned him of Napoleon's probable intentions. In April of that year DuPont de Nemours, a businessman of Delaware, happened to tell the President that he was going to France on business of his own. He would, he said, be glad to do anything he could to improve relations between his old country and his new one. Jefferson regarded this as a timely opportunity and at once asked him to come to Washington for a conference. De Nemours wrote that he could not come, but in the communication he indicated his approval of the suggestion he had heard that Louisiana might be acquired. It was true that Jefferson had already drafted a letter to Livingston about the matter, but how De Nemours could have known that he was about to ask for the cession of New Orleans to the United States was a mystery. The possibility that the proposal might be widely known frightened him. There was evidently need for haste. He entrusted the Livingston letter to De Nemours, gave him permission to read it, and asked him to impress on the Emperor the certain consequences of a seizure of New Orleans. What he had to say to Napoleon was that such an action would force a union of Britain and the United States, something he knew would be an unpleasant prospect. He put it plainly: "The day that France takes possession of New Orleans fixes the sentence which is to restrain her forever within her low water mark. It seals the union of the two nations who in conjunction can maintain exclusive possession of the ocean. From that moment we must marry ourselves to the British fleet and nation."[4]

Before De Nemours arrived in France with this letter (containing, he felt, too emphatic a threat) Livingston had already begun negotiations. He was handicapped by lack of instructions and inability to communicate with the President at home. He was also frustrated by the bland French denial that there was any intention of taking New Orleans. By the time De Nemours arrived, however, he had learned that Talleyrand intended to negotiate only after the transfer to France had been made. Matters stood thus when in 1803 James Monroe was sent to Paris to see what he could do toward hastening a settlement. There was by now furor everywhere along the Mississippi and its tributaries, and the Federalists were making an issue of the Administration's inaction when confronted with French aggression.

Jefferson was by now deep in a dilemma of his own making. His theory had called for emasculating the Federal government and transferring most of its functions to the states. This process had led to enfeeblement not only as against the states but also as against other nations. His drastic economies had nearly extinguished the navy, and there was no army to speak of. It is true that the Congress had given him authority to raise and pay a militia if necessary; but, as is now known, he had no intention of doing so. He meant to make armed forces unnecessary by avoiding conflict. He accepted the congressional permission largely to keep his trans-mountain partisans quiet. That was his reason, also, for sending Monroe abroad, rather than a belief that anything would be accomplished by it. His whole position was threatened and he must have time and a certain freedom. If war should come, the government's weakness would expose the nation to humiliation and his policy would be completely discredited. He must find another way.

In explaining his actions a year later, he maintained that he had been temporizing, actually, because he had foreseen that trouble would develop between France and Britain. This, if it proved serious, would give him an opportunity to sell American favor to the highest bidder. Since it

[4] Letter to Livingston, April 18, 1802, *Works*, Ford, IX, 363–68.

did come and since the politician's solution did succeed, he must be given credit for a marvelously daring and delicate maneuver.

One of his difficulties was that he began by being quite convinced that constitutional authority for acquiring territory to be added to the national area was lacking. An amendment was needed, and especially if it was the President who was to negotiate. Gallatin, Secretary of the Treasury, did not agree. He thought the authority existed. But Levi Lincoln, the Attorney General, had doubts. After listening and thinking it over, Jefferson still felt, as he said, that it would "be safer not to permit the enlargement of the Union but by amendment of the Constitution."[5]

Monroe was not happy to be chosen for so uncertain a mission as a negotiation for which his principal had little enthusiasm, but he felt that he must go. He, De Nemours, and Livingston were all "to work together." As it turned out, although the inevitable jealousies among the negotiators developed, these were unimportant. Events elsewhere—the ones Jefferson had gambled on—brought the affair to a conclusion. Napoleon's expedition to Santo Domingo was all but destroyed, which disrupted his scheme for a Caribbean base from which to move into Louisiana. And anyway, he was by now turning toward the subjection of Britain, and a Louisiana involvement would be something more than a nuisance; as Jefferson had said, it would bring in the United States—for what that was worth—as a British ally. So before Monroe even arrived in France, Napoleon had given in. On April 11 he had instructed Talleyrand to ask Livingston *if the United States would like to have the whole of Louisiana.*

There followed some involved exchanges. When Monroe arrived shortly, he and Livingston, consulting, appear not to have risen very quickly to the opportunity—the implications of Talleyrand's proposal escaped them. They had been concerned—as had Jefferson—with New Orleans and with the Floridas. These were the subjects of the political agitation to which Jefferson was reacting. They were embarrassed by the offer of the vast unknown Northwest; they even told Talleyrand that they were interested only in the lesser objectives. Then too, the price seemed very high and they were afraid to promise it. Bargaining of this sort went on for nearly a month, but they finally agreed. The size of the nation was to be at least doubled—and they had been hesitating!

Jefferson, fairly netted in his own machinations, had gone through three stages. At first he was certain that there must be amendment, so much so that he had prepared two drafts; then he thought it would be sufficient if, after he acted, the Senate ratified at once and proceeded to an amendment legalizing the transaction ex post facto; but finally he came all the way around to the position that the urgency of the opportunity justified

---

[5] Letter to Madison, August 30, 1802, *Jefferson Papers*, L.C.V. 126, 21692.

him in proceeding on his own. He had meanwhile made sure, of course, that ratification in the Senate would be forthcoming. The cause of this rapid conversion was a practical one. He became aware that Napoleon might change his mind. That dictator, having sold something he did not own, was soon deluged by bitter protests. He was inclined to seize any excuse for canceling the whole transaction. It was no time to quibble, and Jefferson acted with commendable speed. His turnabout was not a graceful one; anyone could see that it was altogether determined by expediency. He allowed himself to be pushed (or arranged for it) into the new position, but it was somewhat embarrassing to avow what had always heretofore been Federalist doctrine. He told supporters that he would rather "ask an enlargement of power from the nation" than "assume it by a construction which would make our powers boundless." He admitted that "our peculiar security is in possession of a written Constitution. Let us not make it a blank paper by construction." But he went on at once to add, "If . . . our friends shall think differently, certainly I shall acquiesce with satisfaction, confiding that the good sense of our country will correct the evil of construction when it shall produce bad effects."[6]

Thus having accepted direction as he had never done before, he proceeded to slip the ratification through the Senate, as he said, *sub silentio.* The Federalists objected loudly, but Jefferson had a firm ascendancy, and on October 20 the Senate approved the treaty by a vote of 24 to 7. On the twenty-second, the President was authorized to take possession of all the lands involved and to administer them until provision could be made for their permanent organization. There was somewhat more of a row in the House, which, if it did not ratify treaties, still had to be asked for funds and for the authority to set up a government in the new territory. There were still Democratic-Republicans who thought Jefferson's way of proceeding a dangerously arbitrary one. But he went ahead, and almost at once he sent the few available troops to New Orleans, characteristically arranging simultaneously for a local insurrection, and called for volunteers, anticipating resistance from the badly treated and highly indignant Spanish. But by December all was finished. The Spanish had handed over to the French, and the French to the United States.

Jefferson, as Presidents seized of office do, had conveniently forgotten his scruples. He pointed proudly to the achievement: "Tho' we shall be only the 2nd. of the civilized nations in *extent* of territory, we shall be the first in what is cultivable," he said.[7] And, since this was undoubtedly true and immensely important, it served as statesman's justification.

[6] Letter to Nicholas, September 7, 1803, *Works,* Ford, X, 10, 11, 21.

[7] Letter to Page, November 25, 1803, *Papers,* 136, 2357, quoted in Schachner, *Jefferson,* (New York, 1951, 2 vols.), 754.

An account of the momentous purchase has to be set against Jefferson's conduct in office otherwise. Only when this is done does its significance as an advance in the evolution of the Presidency become apparent. He had from the first made an unmistakable show of reversing Washington's symbolism. He had walked alone in the streets to official occasions, worn shabby clothes, and generally paraded a commonness not natural to a Virginia gentleman. Going farther, he had drastically contracted government activities, abolished many taxes, and weakened regulations wherever they were in effect.

He had thus made himself, as President, a conspicuous symbol of pluralistic organization in contrast with the Federal unity of the twelve preceding years. It was a deliberate and unmistakable derogation. When Washington had retired, Benjamin Franklin Bache, writing in *Aurora*, a Democratic-Republican paper, had expressed the view that the hearts of the people ought to beat with exultation that the name of Washington had ceased giving currency to political iniquity and legalized corruption. This was the Jeffersonian line; and the Presidency, in his possession, had to be the opposite of everything Washington and Adams had stood for.

The disparagement had drastic implications for the balance of governmental powers. If the Federal government was to be severely limited in scope, so was the Presidency within that government. Weakening the Executive was easier for the Democratic-Republicans, because the Congress was so completely under the control not of Jefferson as President but Jefferson as political boss. The talent for, and the habit of, intrigue had gone with him into the Mansion. The Presidency and party leadership were not yet permanently identified, but their union in Jefferson's Administration was for the moment complete.

When it came to deciding on the Louisiana Purchase, the commitment to strict construction might have proved fatal; Jefferson might have insisted on being guided by his principles, either because of stubborn faith in their validity or because he feared their too conspicuous abandonment. But he must be supposed to have been aware, as all good politicians are, that inconsistency is an unimportant sin. It is soon forgotten, and the sooner if the action involved is concluded rapidly and successfully. As to the struggle he may have had with his conscience, obviously the prospective gain to the nation must have overwhelmed his concept of the Executive. Then too, there was a potent interest to be thought of across the Appalachians. Anyway, he acted, and the euphoria aroused by the acquisition of so vast a domain completely cloaked the doubts of the orthodox.

The resulting sense of expansion and largeness did more. It reversed what had been a noticeable decline into something like national neurosis. The cult, so persistently pursued, of central torpor and extreme parsimony had made the nation so weak as to induce a kind of shame. There was a visible lethargy. But the conclusion of the purchase set flowing new rivers of energy and ambition. Because it was again growing, the nation felt itself once more virile. Ambition returned. There were new lands to conquer and settle, and this might not be the end; already there were intimations of further conquest. The logical boundary of so intrepid a nation was surely the Pacific Ocean.

Jefferson's preference for a curtailed government and a restrained Presidency was not shared by his immediate successors, but this was not so much because they did not in principle agree with him—they did; it was the politically popular attitude to assume—but rather because recurrent crises clearly called for the maintenance of an alert and competent government in Washington and a President who could and would act when necessary. It was not long before the Presidency was accepted, even by those reluctant to admit their own conversion, as a bulwark of democracy rather than a threat to it. Jefferson's practice was more important than his preaching. And there would soon come that curious reversal in which it would be discovered that the President and not the Congress was the palladium of libertarian values.[8]

[8] Jefferson later said, in defense of his departure from what he had defined for himself as allowable, that "those who accept great charges have a duty to risk themselves on great occasions, when the safety of the nation, or some of its very high interests, are at stake." This is the second statement of that Rule of Necessity that Washington first formulated. Coming from one who had so often denied the presidential power to invoke it, there is a double significance in the admission.

★ 8 ★

JEFFERSON HAD UNWILLINGLY USED THE FEDERAL GOVERNMENT AND the Presidency in such ways as to enhance both. But during the incumbency of his successor, Madison, there was on the whole a retrogression. Attention was wrested away from the West and the problems of expansion and was turned to the humiliations of a war the country was not prepared to carry on, and whose incidents were the cause of shame. Especially the capture of the city of Washington and the burning of the Capitol and the Executive Mansion had about them a sinister suggestion of incapacity. It was not easy to accept a weakness so serious that enemies could land from the Patuxent, march practically unopposed into the city, and have their way with it while the President fled one way and his wife the other.[1] A rising nation was entitled to more security than this and more vigor in its leaders.

The malaise in Washington was to an extent relieved by Jackson's victory at New Orleans over the same forces that had put General Winder's men to flight. And more was made of it, by a people grasping for even slight reassurance, than was warranted by the event itself. But the full recovery of confidence came gradually; and it was not until Monroe, following Madison, with a brilliant Secretary of State to aid him, asserted a grand continental hegemony that the national pride was rehabilitated. The claim may have gone beyond the nation's then ability to sustain it in a test, but the test was not called for. The pride may presently have risen beyond the tolerance, almost, of the rest of the world; but it assisted in the subsequent conquest of a continent as westward

---

[1] The fleeing President was trying to overtake the fleeing army. He crossed the Potomac into Virginia and then recrossed into Maryland at Great Falls. When he got as far as Brookeville he learned that the British were re-embarking. Next day he returned to find the Mansion destroyed. The "Madison House" still stands in Brookeville. It was the home of Postmaster Caleb Bentley, who had been appointed by Jefferson. Dolly, with a few possessions fled further into Virginia but came to no harm.

movement again became uppermost in men's minds. And the incident was an important demonstration of the position now occupied by the President, at least with respect to foreign affairs.

It has to be said that even before the enunciation of the aggressive Doctrine—in Monroe's second term—there had been a gradual enhancement of the office. Jefferson's systematic undervaluation of his powers had not survived as a policy into the Administrations of his younger colleagues. Madison, as President, had lost none of the clarity of mind that he had so often shown in the past, but as he grew older his inconspicuous person seemed to wither. He had none of the graceful presence so notable in the other Virginians. He was a small man with a weak voice who spoke hesitantly. He was called "Little Jemmy," rather in derision than with affection. He commanded none of the respect as Chief of State that he had so quickly won and so easily kept as second to his more impressive principals in the affairs of former years.

But the Madison regime was enlivened and the Presidency was given a saving tone by the legendary Dolly, possibly the most brilliant of all presidential wives. Even after the Executive Mansion was burned by the British and the Madisons had taken up residence in temporary houses while repairs were made, Dolly managed to maintain her position with irrepressible vitality. She seems to have charmed everyone but her social rivals.[2] She had been Jefferson's hostess when her husband was Secretary of State—Jefferson being a widower—and she had only to enlarge and glorify an already familiar role. Washington society, with her to set its standard, became almost unbecomingly gaudy for a democracy. Equality might be a political profession with the Democratic-Republicans, but its practice stopped short of the Mansion. The contrast of the modest and unassuming Madison with his blooming, exuberant wife was remarked by all contemporaries who left any record. But it was a useful partnership—she to maintain social prestige, he to work faithfully if unimaginatively at his presidential tasks.

One remarkable development during the post-Jefferson regimes down to Jackson's Administration was the growth of a small but capable civil service to carry on the limited functions of the Departments. The efficiency of these career officials resulted from the monopolization of government positions by a social elite. There was a closed circle of "better people" to whom the opportunities for office were confined. This, again, seems somewhat inconsistent with Jeffersonian theory; but, after all, Madison and Monroe were gentlemen. White House society (the Mansion began to be called the White House after its partial rebuilding and its

2 The "house of a thousand candles," razed in 1958, was used as a Mansion from 1815 to 1817. For a time, also, the Madisons used Octagon House, which has been preserved.

painting to efface the scars and stains left by the burning) sometimes seemed, after Dolly's time, so punctilious and stiff as to be oppressive. Dolly was able to make her entertaining bright and interesting without sacrificing the dignity appropriate to the President's position.

Meade Minnigerode once commented on this:

> Except as surviving individuals, the Federalists had practically ceased to exist . . . Mr. Jefferson's Republicans were firmly in power—one faction or another seeking the advantage, the Livingstons, the Clintons, the followers of John Randolph, the new men in Congress, John Calhoun, Henry Clay—but now they were calling themselves Democrats, and it was a curious thing how Republican, how Federalist, almost, they had become with the years. They talked quite freely of a loose construction of the Constitution. Mr. Jefferson's purchase of Louisiana had taught them that—and they supported the right of the Federal government to effect internal improvements; they had incorporated a Bank of the United States, without falling into a fit at the recollection of Alexander Hamilton; they were advocating high tariffs and protection, and Mr. Calhoun and the South approved them for a while.
>
> In other respects too they had travelled a long way from Mr. Jefferson's Republicanism. The election of 1800 had been a victory of "the people," a triumph over "despotism" and "aristocracy"—but Mr. Jefferson's own Administrations had been as despotic as one could wish, and the term Dominion of Virginia had two meanings in many minds; Mr. Jefferson's successors, in their mode of life, their social habits, and their intellectual attitude, had shown no lack of aristocratic instinct. The Madisons had restored the Presidential levees and pomps; the Monroe's had brought fastidious elegance to their regime; the business of government remained primarily an occupation for gentlemen; the people at large had no more to do with it than the man in the moon.[3]

And John Quincy Adams, for all that he was a member of a strict and frugal New England family and was no gentleman in the Virginia sense, nevertheless conducted himself in office as a conscientious member of the ruling class. But it was before he became President that the notable Doctrine was promulgated and made good. That it could issue from the White House, requiring no legislative backing, and reverberate in all the chancelleries of the world was of immense importance to the Executive. The Doctrine established itself at once as the most unarguable of all American foreign policies. This was remarkable, but it was more remarkable that it should have happened at a time when there was intense rivalry for

[3] *Presidential Years 1787–1860* (New York, 1927), 126.

the presidential succession and when many thunderers in the Congress would gladly have seized any available opportunity for political advantage.

The explanation of this is that the Doctrine was one of those simplifications of a people's determination which gain immediate and massive response. It was bold. In the countries of the Holy Alliance, whose statesmen provoked its formulation, it was denounced as effrontery and condemned as inadmissible; but actually it was never challenged except in words. Its warning to the old empires to keep out of the Americas was recognized as literally meant and quite possibly enforceable. From that time on, the President of the United States was a world figure to be treated with cautious respect; also, he was regarded with new pride among Americans themselves. The Jeffersonian belittlement of the office thus came to an end during the succession of his disciples and before the old Democrat himself had quite passed from the scene.

Monroe seldom neglected to consult his predecessors when important decisions were to be made, and Jefferson had already expressed himself as being in favor of leaving Europe to Europeans and establishing barriers between them and the Americas. Madison, too, was of the same opinion. But when the advice of these two was actually requested, it was in connection with a preliminary suggestion made by Canning, the British Minister, that his government and that of the United States should join in a statement declaring a common intention not to acquire further territories in Latin America, the idea being that this would, by implication, constitute a warning to all others not to acquire any either.

Both Madison and Jefferson would have accepted the British suggestion. But Adams objected. He thought it a trap. As worded, it would prevent any further annexations by the United States as well as Britain—and expansion to the south was still, to his mind, a desirable possibility. Because of his opposition the Doctrine became an independent declaration of policy rather than a joint manifesto, and it was confined to plainly warning others that they must keep out. If he had not insisted, it is entirely possible that Texas might still be a republic and California one of the states of Mexico.

Adams had from the beginning dealt with the complex issues created by the rebellions in the Spanish territories. Monroe, much disturbed by an agitation carried on by Henry Clay, would have recognized the new republics prematurely if he had not been restrained by Adams. That experienced diplomat was anxious to see them separated from Spain but was not convinced that they were in the least democratic. Clay and Monroe seemed to regard Bolivar and San Martín as liberators of the Washington sort, struggling for liberty as well as independence. Adams was skeptical. He had been disillusioned by such offers as that of the Argentine to make the infant Don Carlos an absolute monarch if independence should be conceded. And Bolivar showed no liking, so far as he could discover, for representative institutions of any sort. The revolutionary envoys who implored the Secretary of State for recognition were given a very chilly reception. He preferred to wait until he could see what kinds of governments were planned and until it was clear that there was no chance of reconquest by Spain. But from the first he had been emphatic in opposition to any and all European activities in the Western Hemisphere. As early as 1818 he had instructed Ministers Gallatin in Paris and Rush in London to make plain the American position.

There was real danger that intervention might be undertaken. The Holy Alliance—Russia, Austria-Hungary, and Prussia—had declared itself ready to promote "piety and peace" throughout the world. With Napoleon out of the way, the pretensions of the Alliance ran to world hegemony. But the Czar seemed to have some unexplained kindly feeling toward the United States, in spite of her revolutionary origins, and would have had her join the closed circle of powers. Adams told him in abrupt terms that such a relationship would be incompatible with American institutions; it was not to be thought of.

Russia was, at the same time, throwing out tentacles of empire reaching well down the coast of California. In that area there were almost as many complications to deal with as in South and Central America. In addition to the Russian worry, there was potential trouble with the British. The Northwest was a vast unoccupied area, not yet controlled by any power, but both empires were claiming it. The Russians had given a government-backed trading company "rights of settlement," and one of this company's posts was only fifty miles north of San Francisco. Further to confuse matters, the British and Americans were supposed to be occupying "jointly" this and other areas under an agreement made in 1818.

The Czar, in 1821, in a new ukase, granted "exclusive" development privileges to the Russian company, and "foreign" ships were forbidden the waters north to the Bering Sea. No attention was paid to this prohibition by either Britain or the United States until a Russian ship appeared in Pacific coastal waters and began enforcement operations. This drew the two nations together for defense; they notified the Russians that they would resist. It was in this exchange that Adams formulated what afterward became one part of the Doctrine. Russia had no right, he said, to any territorial establishment on the continent; the United States regarded the Americas as improper places for any new colonial establishments.

This was an intimation of the Adams vision. He had on other occasions said, in Cabinet meetings, that the Spanish possessions on the southern border and the British ones on the northern must be annexed. The world must get used to regarding the proper dominion of the United States as the North American continent. Exchanges during these years with the

British also, through Canning, then Minister in Washington, showed how strongly he felt about this and how far he would go to convert the President to his view. He was insisting in all his talks with the Minister that the Northwest, up to what is now the Canadian city of Vancouver, belonged of right to the United States. He was plain-spoken; in fact, there can hardly ever have been such blunt—and often angry—exchanges between professional diplomats as occurred in these negotiations.

The significance of this was not only that an American claim to exclusive ownership was being made, but that an American spokesman had demanded and received British respect for his candor. Adams, conscious of speaking for the nation, would neither be bullied nor cajoled. And when a little later Canning succeeded Castlereagh as Foreign Minister and Britain was isolated in opposition to the Holy Alliance on the Continent, he knew how to win co-operation from the Americans. He had only to treat the President and his Secretary of State with the consideration due them as representatives of a newly powerful nation—something British diplomats had been slow to learn.

When presently Canning proposed that the United States join with Britain in a declaration concerning the southern republics, it was a proposal for a "promulgation of views," and it was made to statesmen disposed to receive his communications with respect. Specifically, he would have had the policy statement say that neither nation would view the transfer of any portion of the republics' areas "to any other power with indifference," but also he would have added that neither intended to occupy any such territory for itself.

This was the statement that Monroe was inclined to accept but that Adams, knowing Canning and being suspicious of the British, saw as dangerous. He was not impressed by the advice of Jefferson and Madison that the offer ought to be accepted; rather, he was roused to more active opposition, and it was in the next meeting of the Cabinet that what is now called the Monroe Doctrine was formulated. Adams felt not only that the possibility of annexing Cuba should be kept open and that Texas ought to be annexed, but that any declaration about such matters ought to be purely American. It ought not to be admitted that the British had any legitimate interest.

The Secretary had some difficulty in getting his way, but he had a sharp, realistic, close-reasoning mind that was hard to evade and he overbore his opposition. Throughout the month of November in 1823 the matter was repeatedly reverted to in the Cabinet. In the midst of these discussions Baron Tuyll, the Russian Minister, delivered a note which, when Adams absorbed its meaning, he found intolerably offensive. It was an announcement that the Czar's government, faithful to the political principles of the Alliance, could not receive agents of any of the new revolutionary governments; it went on to say that it approved the neutral attitude of the United States and hoped that it would be continued. What this meant, Adams saw, was that the United States was not to receive any such envoys either and was not otherwise to assist the revolutionary regimes—on penalty of Russian displeasure.

In subsequent talks with the President, Adams pointed out that no one had asked the Russians about their willingness to receive South American emissaries and noted, further, that the new republics had already been recognized—but only by the United States. The British, for instance, had avoided it. The Russian note seemed to him intended as a rebuke; it was more—a threat. The Holy Alliance meant to put down revolutions wherever they occurred in the world. Its members would support the sacred principle of legitimacy denied by the revolutionists of the Americas. It could even be suspected that the eventual intention was to restore to Spain all her former possessions.

As though this note had not been provocative enough, the Russians presented another. This was a sort of wandering and exultant account of the success of the induced counterrevolutions in Spain and Portugal. It included a lecture on the superiority of autocratic over republican government, well calculated to enrage so thorny a democrat as Adams. It disturbed even the more equable Monroe, and Adams was allowed to frame a reply which was a lively exposition of republican theory. He could lecture too. But his note disclaimed any intention on the part of the United States of imposing republicanism by force or even of interfering in European affairs, and it concluded with the hope that the Europeans would "equally abstain from the attempt to spread their principles in the American hemisphere, or to subjugate by force any part of these continents to their will."

This was, as afterward could be seen, preliminary to the more formal declaration which was still being discussed. Monroe, at almost the same time, however, submitted to his advisers the first draft of the message to the Congress which was to contain the full statement of the Doctrine to be known thenceforward by his name. More argument followed. It had now become a general one involving apprehension lest the Holy Alliance should attempt to extirpate the republicanism its members regarded as so dangerous to the absolute monarchies. Nevertheless, Monroe, in the draft submitted for Cabinet discussion, took very high ground. He rebuked the European powers for intervention in Spain and Portugal, to which Adams had no objection; but he also went far afield, as Adams felt, in making an emphatic declaration favoring Greek independence. What Adams preferred, he said, was that the message should deal only with the Americas. To bring in the Greek issue was to spread the American protest too widely. If kept to this hemisphere, it had a defensible geographical logic. Also, he preferred to stress self-determination rather than republicanism. He pressed Monroe in Cabinet and in private, and finally the

President gave way and the message was written as Adams wanted it to be.

So the declaration was issued as a proclamation of supremacy for the United States in the Western Hemisphere. It warned against European interference of any sort. The Holy Alliance powers were offended. Metternich voiced the reaction. It was, he said "a new act of revolt, more unprovoked, fully as audacious, and no less dangerous than revolution itself." The Americans "had" cast blame and scorn on the institutions of Europe most worthy of respect, on the principles of the greatest sovereigns, on the whole of those measures which a sacred duty, no less than an evident necessity, has forced our governments to adopt to frustrate plans most criminal.

In spite of the hostility in Europe, this presidential warning was respected. From its first announcement it formed, along with Washington's admonition against entanglement in European affairs, the most enduring guide to the foreign policy of the nation. That the President had himself taken the initiative served to define further the meaning of the constitutional duty "to make treaties." He would make treaties in a fashion determined by his own judgment.

WHEN ADAMS'S LONG SERVICE AS DIPLOMAT AND CABINET MEMBER WAS followed by succession to the Presidency, it was quite in accord with his behavior theretofore that he should be a vigorous occupant of the office and an ardent conservator of presidential prestige. He was, however, caught in circumstances for which he was poorly suited and was defeated in most of his endeavors.

The struggle to succeed Monroe among Jackson, Calhoun, Crawford, Clay, and Adams had been a nasty one, and the bitterness carried over into the new Administration. The election had been thrown into the House. Crawford, although stricken by paralysis, had forty-one electoral votes. This was enough to make Clay's election, with thirty-seven votes, impossible. Together they had only seventy-eight. The choice had to fall between Jackson, who had ninety-nine, and Adams, who had eighty-four. For a time none of the candidates would withdraw, but it was obvious that whichever one of the two leaders got Clay's votes would win. In the end, Clay's enmity for Jackson led him to give Adams his support, thus making him President.

When, following the maneuvering involved in this struggle, Adams made Clay his Secretary of State, Jackson, who had felt himself cheated anyway, was more than ever infuriated. He at once accused Adams of corruption and double dealing. The Presidency, he claimed, had been bought, and the price had been the Secretaryship for Clay. The whole country reverberated with outcries from Tennessee, and Jackson's vow of vengeance echoed loudly in his supporters' propaganda.

Their resolve to oust Adams was proclaimed at once, and they began one of the most prolonged and unrestrained attacks any President would ever be called on to sustain. It was, moreover, so successful that Adams's re-election soon became very unlikely. Defense against the attacks of those who have no scruples is difficult in any circumstances; for a minority President, with no considerable popular appeal, it was impossible.

The unremitting hostility of the Jacksonians was not the only reason for Adams's political failure. He refused to make any of the concessions obviously called for by the changing character of American politics resulting from wider suffrage and the admission of new states. He was a man of the most upright character, but he had also the stiffness that goes with such virtue. Not only was he opinionated, he had excellent reasons for his opinions, got from arduous courses of study. In latter-day terms he would be called an "egghead," and there never was a time when intellectuals were less valued. He refused to use his office to feed patronage-hungry politicians at first and, when he did give way, used it clumsily. He rebuffed those who had been his most useful supporters and rewarded his detractors (in New York, for instance, he capitulated to the Clintonians, who had been his enemies, and refused favors to Thurlow Weed and his friends, who had been on his side). He sponsored policies, also, which were laudable but had no wide appeal. He could be seen afterward to have been remarkably right and very far-seeing in the nation's interest; but the democracy was bent on immediate exploitation of its apparently endless resources, and there was no time for conservation and no patience with long-range plans for development.

But such partisans as Adams did have—mostly in New England—were about as unscrupulous as their enemies. They accused Jackson and his followers of all varieties of chicanery, some of it credible and some not; and this extremism, of course, made it easier for Jackson and his people to justify their own drumfire of abuse. The slanderous methods used in this campaign were a discredit to Jackson, but it must be said that they were a beginning consistent with the most whimsical, arbitrary, and unprincipled of all presidential regimes. Whatever his objectives—and they were often worthy ones, sometimes indispensable to the nation's future—they were usually demeaned by the methods used to promote them. The General belonged to the new frontier beyond the mountains. Its people were crude, uneducated, obstinate in their ignorance, and determined to capture the government as they had conquered the wilderness—by treachery and violence if boldness and resolution proved not to be enough —and to use it for their own profit.

So Adams had only one term, and an unhappy one at that. But his contributions were more considerable than those of some two-term Presidents. They began, as we have seen, even before he succeeded Monroe, in the development of the declaration which established once for all the leadership of the Executive in foreign affairs. But he must also be credited with an equally important custom of taking the lead in domestic planning. He gave the nation the benefit of his restless initiative and his broad intelligence. It was not made use of—the Jacksonians saw to that— but it set a mark for presidential responsibility beyond any reached by his predecessors; it stood as an example for the strong Presidents to come.

Strict-constructionist views had prevented the Jeffersonians from accepting the President as planner; the Federal government could not engage in internal improvements; such activities belonged to the states and to local governments. Madison and Monroe had modified the strictness of this party prohibition. But Adams, in his first message, ignored it altogether and went even farther than the Federalists had gone, years before, in outlining a comprehensive scheme of national development. He wanted the government to survey and build highways and canals, to maintain aids to navigation, to establish observatories, to improve rivers and harbors, to send exploring expeditions into the West, and to create a national university. All this would be come back to in the future, and Adams would be understood to have shown the way to indispensable presidential initiative in national works the Federal government must undertake. But at the time his spirit and knowledge were wasted. The frontiersmen had their way.

The significance of such documents as Adams's inaugural and several other of his state papers outlining policies consistent with the nation's certain expansion is that he accepted the role of leader. It had been, as we have seen, the Jeffersonian view that the President had mostly the duty of preventing the government from encroaching on the rights or stifling the initiative of the citizens. Strictly construing the Tenth Amendment yielded this conviction.[1] There was, of course, a considerable enumeration of powers (in Section 8 of Article I); and there was the wide permissive declaration of the Preamble,[2] whose apparent intentions could not always be met within the equally apparent restrictions of the Tenth Amendment. So that even Jefferson was compelled to resort to sophistical arguments to support actions essential if the obligations of the Preamble were to be met. Jackson would be even more tortured by the dilemma of the general welfare threatened by the very liberties so valued by the strict constructionists. Adams had none of these difficulties. His intelligence and shrewd sense told him that there must be a national program and a national leader if there was to be a genuine Union, and that the President must show the way. He set the Preamble above the amendment. But the times were leveling ones; and the majority, the new voters, were intent on destroying all symbols of class and all evidences of superiority. They meant to reduce the strongholds of privilege, they said; but what

[1] "The powers not delegated to the United States by the Constitution, nor prohibited by it to the States, are reserved to the States respectively, or to the people."

[2] "We the people of the United States, in order to form a more perfect Union, establish justice, insure domestic tranquility, provide for the common defence, promote the general welfare, and secure the blessings of liberty to ourselves and our posterity, do ordain and establish this Constitution for the United States of America."

they really meant was that they wanted privileges of their own without earning or deserving them.

The justification among the Jacksonians was the same as that used by the Jeffersonians—the principle of equality. They sought to extend it in a fantastic way: not only opportunities should be equal, but places and rewards also. They could, because abilities, again, were equal. Anyone could do anything. The rapacity thinly concealed by this philosophical justification nearly destroyed the government altogether. It actually so demeaned its offices and procedures that the effect would be felt throughout the rest of the century.[3]

> [3] And even longer. Far into the twentieth century political scientists could trace the effects of this first overwhelming anti-intellectual success. We are dealing here with something as real and sinister as it is imponderable. It might be said that integrity in the public service is like virtue in general—always being undermined, always needing defense, never securely established. When the "evils of politics" are spoken of, this must be the worst of them. The substitution of personal and private gratification or rewards for concern that the public interest should be served is easily erected, in a democracy, into a virtue whose falseness is not easily exposed.
>
> Mr. Gerald Johnson, as late as 1959 (in the *New Republic* for May 18), wrote of the Twenty-second Amendment as owing its adoption to this weakness. As late as that, he thought, Americans could allow the very structure of their government to be undercut on the principle that he called "pass the biscuits":
>
> . . . *No doubt the amendment was in part spite-work, a studied insult to the memory of Franklin D. Roosevelt; but beyond that it had a strong appeal to politicians of mediocre or less ability. It is an expression of the old "rotation in office" idea, one of the pernicious encrustations on democratic theory.*
>
> *The idea was perfectly expressed by one of those curiosities constantly being thrown to the surface of the seething pot of Texas politics. Some years ago he ran for office on the injunction, "Pass the biscuits, Pappy." The basis of this plea is the theory that public office is not a public trust, but a public handout, earned by work, not for the public, but for the party.*
>
> *It is a theory cherished by inferior men, constantly annoyed by the success of their betters. This annoyance is fearfully exacerbated when a really adroit politician wins victory after victory. It was lifted to the level of madness when Roosevelt four times won the gaudiest office of all and it became evident that there wasn't a politician smart enough to lick him in a fair fight . . .*
>
> *So they determined to make it impossible for any man, no matter how superior, to exasperate them in that fashion . . . the Twenty-second Amendment was adopted by some 5,000 men, all of them politicians—a majority of the 531 members of the House and Senate, and majorities in the Legislatures of 63 states. This amendment was not, like the Twenty-first, ratified in the several states*

The Adams relation to the Constitution was a special one. It had been his father who, through letters and other writings, had spread the tripartite theory among the intelligensia; any government, he had contended, must inevitably be arbitrary if a single Branch should both make and execute the laws. Charles Warren, when speaking of this once, went on to say[4] that this principle seemed to be understood but that old habit was very strong, and the state legislatures, as their constitutions were written, invariably were given authority outweighing that given to other Branches. There had been some years of state experience by the time the Federal Constitution came to be written, and the tripartite principle was somewhat better understood. There was a deliberate purpose, at that time, to restrict the legislature and increase the powers of the Executive:

Accordingly, in the Federal Constitution, the Executive Branch of the new government was vested with new and enlarged powers of veto, of pardon, and of appointment (from which has been implied a power of removal) as well as powers to receive foreign ambassadors and Ministers (from which has been implied a power to conduct all foreign affairs), power to make treaties, and extensive powers over the army and navy militia. (It may particularly be noted that it was the Massachusetts Constitution of 1780, drafted by John Adams, which formed the basis for the Executive article in the Federal Constitution.[5]

---

by conventions elected for the purpose; so no one except politicians had a chance to vote on it. . . .

We must pass the biscuits in order that as many as possible of the hungry may be fed. Skill, sharpened by experience in the office, counts for nothing. The trust and confidence of the people count for nothing. The possible lack of any man of equal competence counts for nothing. All that counts is that sustenance shall be evenly distributed to the ravenous, whether they are competent or not . . .

[4] In an illuminating lecture in the Boston University series of Bacon Lectures on the Constitution, called "Presidential Declaration of Independence," 1939.

[5] Op. cit., 78. Cf. also, by the same author, *The Making of the Constitution* (New York, 1928).

Adams's contribution was indeed a decisive one. His was the clearest conception of the tripartite form, expressed over and over to those who afterward were influential in the making of the Constitution. In answer to Richard Henry Lee in 1775, for example, who had written to him asking for his views, Adams wrote:

A legislative, an executive, and a judicial power comprehend the whole of what is understood by government. It is by balancing each of these powers

What was written and what was practiced, however, had a tendency to diverge. Legislators did not lose the lingering conviction that there was something special, something closer to the core of popular sovereignty, in being elected by a small constituency. Executives had theretofore been the agents of an alien and inimical power, and the President was still felt to be something resembling a king or one of his Governors. He must be held within strict limits by a somewhat superior opposing force—a coalition of local representatives.

Whatever the framers intended, and however much those in the Convention who feared legislative oppression argued, there remained a lingering suspicion. This was the ground line of the Jeffersonians, and they were to find as time passed that the checks and balances of the Constitution were actually so weighted that the legislature could assert itself successfully in contests with cautious or weak Executives.

The process known to political theorists as "congressional trespass" did begin at once when the government was organized—in spite of Washington's prestige. The first President, careful of the new Constitution's fabric, was reluctant to insist on having his way in matters beyond his clear competence. In spite of the several accretions to the Executive which have been noted, he was very delicate in his trading with the Congress. Even the painful experiences with the Jeffersonians late in his Presidency failed to shake his conviction that the seemly course was to keep himself free of "faction." His method lasted out his time; at least he clung to it, even if at the last with a good deal of pretense.

But when Jefferson succeeded, having humiliated Washington, defeated John Adams, and demonstrated what intrigue could accomplish within the new government, he deliberately moved away from the equal-powers theory. It was, with him, as though no Constitution had been written. He had not been present, and he had not approved. The Executive, to his mind, was a dangerous agency, to be subordinated and to follow rather than to lead. He himself pretended elaborately not to be a leader. He managed to be one, and to maintain his principles, by a sub rosa manipulation of the disciplined congressional majority he so closely

---

against the other two, that the efforts in human nature toward tyranny can alone be checked and restrained and any degree of freedom preserved in the constitution.

Even though Adams was abroad when the Constitution was actually being written in Philadelphia, the members of the Convention were all made aware of his views, if they had not been before, by his then current pamphlet, *Defense of the Constitutions of the United States of America,* written as an answer to attacks on the principle of separation by the Frenchman Turgot, who, like many others before and since, would concentrate them in one whole.

controlled. But he diminished the presidential office at the same time that he gained in personal power. This he did in the interest of a theory that agrarian smallness was a positive good, that largeness and regulation were inherently bad, and that the President was the agent of the centralizers.

It is one of the monumental ironies of American history that one of the first—and one of the most important—uses of vast putative presidential powers in response to national necessity should have been undertaken by Jefferson himself. But if the Louisiana Purchase was carried out by the eloquent defender of strict construction, it is thus that the Presidency has often been enlarged—against the intention of those who meant to weaken it but who found their attitudes impractical.

It has often been enlarged in another way, of course: by the deliberate interposition of strong Presidents who were sure they knew what was best for the national interest and were determined to accomplish it. Adams might have been one of these. He was, however, never in a position to make good his resolution. He was almost the antithesis of Jefferson in offering leadership and defining inspired objectives. Yet his Administration was one during which there was a steady reversion to Jefferson's principles, not, this time, because of the principles themselves, but because they lent themselves to the intentions of the new majority issuing from the frontier.

This, we must understand, was a significant turning point in American history—and in the history of the Presidency. With Adams, the nation had the chance to shape constitutional practice in the way it must be shaped for a burgeoning society with the need to establish organs of Union. It chose the easier way of evading the difficult disciplines. After Adams it would enter on a detour lasting many decades, to be recovered from only gradually and reluctantly against the resistance of many divisive interests and over the objection of determined individualists. Perhaps at this point we ought to anticipate in a summary way this theoretical disagreement which was to prolong itself through so many coming decades.

Those who held the Jeffersonian view that the Legislative Branch ought to be paramount were soon taking a peculiar view of the Presidency, obviously derived from Jefferson's success. The President's powers, they said, came to him because he was, by the Constitution, made Chief Legislator. He had grown with legislative growth. He had his importance by sharing in legislative supremacy.

This argument would have it that the framers established an independent Executive only in a limited sense, for administration, not for leadership and national planning. As President, he was meant to be a shadowy figure who took on substance because of his relation to the legislative process. The framers' reluctance to confer ample powers had overcome their desire for more effective government. So thoughtful a student as H. L. McBain interpreted the Constitution in this way; and others have agreed, or agreed in substance.[6] McBain argued that the policies of government in which people found themselves most interested were legislative ones:

> Executive policies are of small moment. Even the fact of administrative scandals is fleeting. Our Presidential campaigns, to the extent that they are conducted upon any clear-cut issues of policy, are fought out normally upon the record of legislative achievements . . . and proposals for constructive legislation ahead. We elect the President as a leader of legislation. We hold him accountable for what he succeeds in getting Congress to do and in preventing Congress from doing . . .[7]

The legislative role of the President is certainly important, but it is perhaps not so exclusively important as McBain would have us believe. Since his essay was written (in 1937) there has been an even more notable development of a trend evident even then—the delegation of powers to the Executive Branch. This has led, because the delegations are general, to the making of an enormous body of administrative law. This, it might be said, makes the President more, rather than less, a legislator; but this is not the sense in which McBain meant the term.

There has, of course, been a countervailing tendency to extend legislative jurisdiction into the field of the Executive, and also to set up hybrid agencies (later to be discussed) not really controlled by either Branch but having an existence of their own under the minatory supervision of the Court. The Executive is thus diminished; officials not responsible to the President are designated for administrative duties, and agencies outside the Executive are given responsibilities belonging properly to him.

These opposite tendencies, confusing to the strict separationist, have been put in motion by a kind of pragmatic response to troublesome problems. What has happened has often depended on whether at the moment the President was Republican or Democrat, whether he was vigilant or lax in protecting his prerogatives, whether he was an efficient administrator or more gifted in the arts of the politician running for office. It appears paradoxical to say that the President has become stronger as the result of this practical approach and at the same time has lost immense areas of the territory within which, constitutionally, he should be supreme.

[6] *The Living Constitution* (New York, 1937); for another example of the use of the term "Chief Legislator," cf. Louis Brownlow, *The President and the Presidency*, Public Administration Service (Chicago, 1949).

[7] Op. cit., 116. We shall see that Woodrow Wilson, in his early phase, thought the President ought to be even more firmly attached to the legislature. He favored going all the way over to the parliamentary system, thus reversing the most important of the Constitutional Convention's decisions. Of this, more later.

It is nevertheless exact. What the President has lost is what most of those who approach the Presidency as professional politicians are glad not to have as responsibilities—the control and management of the administrative and regulatory machine. What he has gained is the leadership in ideas and policies which result from his separate election and his constant communication with his national constituency. This is apart from what he may do in crisis when broad powers devolve upon him either by congressional delegation or by simple appropriation. In ordinary times he has both more and less than early Presidents had, and the reasons for both losses and gains are to be found in the developments we see beginning especially with Jackson.

During the Administration of Adams these tendencies were forming themselves. He foreshadowed the leaders among his successors, but he was unable to force the action that would make good his leadership. The legislature was aggressively resistant to his urgings, but the resistance was negative. It was not intent on diminishing the President so much as on replacing him. The movements we recognize as the major ones affecting governmental structure would begin with his successor.

But Adams does furnish one generalization of some significance. It is that a President must have more than a formal designation for his office if he is to be marked as a success. He must have a hold on people's minds and hearts which may be exploited in the interest of leadership. Adams, it may be said at this distance, ought to have given way to Jackson when he realized that he would be a minority President with an opposition certain to increase. Jackson, whatever his other faults, was a genuine political captain, capable of bringing to bear the force of his popularity in the interest of the causes he felt to be important. The unhappiness of Adams's experience would be repeated by very few of his successors, but when it did happen it would be for the same reason—lack of support throughout the national constituency.

★ IO ★

BECAUSE HE HAS TOLD US SO MUCH ABOUT IT IN HIS REVEALING
Diary, the Adams tenancy is convenient for visualizing the President in
his Mansion with its traditions maturing and himself endeavoring to enlarge his services to the nation. It was now generally called the "White
House," a fond and possessive colloquialism. It was his place of being,
his seat. It was, along with him, the symbol of nationhood, the center of
the power and influence conferred on him by his electorate. It was also
the frame, the enclosure where he spent his working days and nights,
the office for those who must consult him, and for directing the administrative personnel of government. It was by now a known geographic
reality, just as the edifice being built on Capitol Hill was the seat and
center of the Congress. It could be said that the White House and its
occupant were the physical embodiments of Article II of the Constitution.

The President was usually at home, but all Presidents are travelers, more
or less, for reasons of health or for relief from exhausting routine labors.[1]
Then too, they must show themselves, must inspect, must be heard, and
above all must keep in touch and estimate public opinion. But, for all
of them, their journeyings and their sojourns elsewhere have been no more
than interludes in a long fixed residence. Some, wearied by the continual
pressures coming in upon them and by the unending procession of favor
seekers, as well as by the ever-renewed piles of papers to be dealt with,
have spoken of the House as a prison and of prospective retirement as a

[1] The malarial swamps to the south were a menace for many years
until the Tiber was covered and drainage begun, but this would not be
until the post-Civil War period. Meanwhile it was a matter of necessity
to escape during the hot months. Even when malaria was less a risk, the
heat of Washington's torrid summers, especially along the Potomac bot-
toms, was almost unbearable. Air-conditioning began to be used, room by
room, in the early thirties, but it was never very satisfactory until the
rebuilding of the House in the Truman Administration; and summer White
Houses, established at a beach or in the mountains (at the President's
own expense), became the rule.

release. Yet, as Professor McBain once shrewdly remarked, "History does not record many instances of available candidates who shun or shy this high office because of the injustice of its exactitudes—or for any other reason."[2] None, at any rate, has ever resigned or even, so far as we know, seriously considered the possibility.[3]

It is hardly necessary to say that the complexities of social change, coming so rapidly by this time, were being felt in the White House as elsewhere. One effect of the restriction on Federal activities insisted on by Jefferson, and less consistently but still to an extent by Madison and Monroe, was to keep the Presidency relatively simple as an institution. This was the effect, too, of congressional jealousy. The power of the purse was used with niggardly rigor. And the President never had adequate assistance. The allowances for housekeeping and for entertainment were frequently the subject of rural legislators' heavy humor, an acute embarrassment to one who must maintain a certain dignity and support what must at the minimum be an elaborate establishment.

Furthermore, Presidents, as party violence grew, had often to withstand attacks of a sort which undermined the authority of their office and their prestige with other nations. The party leadership they were called on to assume was wholly inconsistent with being Chief of State. This was becoming more apparent during Adams's time and would become an acute embarrassment, from which escape would futilely be sought, for many of his successors. The framers not having envisaged parties, the President they had planned would not have been subject to this sort of ordeal. But no return was made to the original conception. The embarrassment would go on and on, one of the anomalies contributing to the final impossibility, for any man, of discharging all the duties of the office. Adams would not, then, be the last to find the office a kind of torture; he was called by conscience for great things and found himself dealing with small, even ignoble, ones, through long and tedious days.

This seemed hard to him. But what he—or his predecessors—would have said if they could have been translated forward to the White House of Wilson, say, or that of any of Wilson's successors, it is difficult to imagine. If we accept Adams's estimate, as well as that of other early Presidents, they did in every day all that one individual could do and bore all that could be borne. If, then, we visualize the responsibilities of the twentieth-century Presidents, it must follow that duties and requirements have

[2] Op. cit., 117.

[3] Except Lincoln, for a different reason. When he thought his opponent might be elected during the Civil War, he concluded that he ought to shorten the interval between election and inauguration by turning the office over to him at once—which could then have been done by appointing him Secretary of State and himself resigning.

changed or that Presidents have in some way found relief—or both. And, actually, that has been so. As duties have grown heavier and become more consequential, the office has been expanded and the whole Executive establishment repeatedly reorganized. The President himself has been given assistants and relieved of many former tasks so that he may concentrate on fewer and more important ones. A modern President may well be less harassed, because he is so much better protected and equipped than the early ones, especially those who were compelled to adopt the extreme equalitarian posture made fashionable by Jefferson and firmly fixed by Jackson. But it still remains too great an undertaking for any individual.

Chief Executives following Jefferson were under some compulsion to behave as he had. They must walk in the streets unattended, callers might come in upon them unannounced, they could have few assistants, and they could have only meager allowances for entertainment. There was a gradual recovery from this extremism until Jackson arrived with his horde of frontiersmen; after him, no President for fifty years would really try to establish such conditions that he could carry on his work effectively; it would have run against an impervious presidential stereotype. Before Jackson, such an office was not so inadequate as it afterward became. The nation was still comparatively small, even if rapidly growing, and so was the untidy small town of Washington. The government was small, too, and relations could be intimate even among the potentially hostile Branches.

When Adams was inaugurated and the Presidency was thirty-five years old, the personnel of government had been stable through several terms, some individuals having served for the better part of their lives. There had been respect for the service and protected tenure for its officials. The Departments were rather tradition-bound, and the Cabinet members had the established routines of limited responsibility. Franklin, Washington, and most of the other framers were long gone, but John Adams and Jefferson still lingered on, in retirement, watching their successors from a distance. They were as far apart as Virginia and Massachusetts, a wide separation in other than the geographical sense, but they were in touch with each other again after many differences, finding that after all they had many agreements. They were soon to die on the same day, a strangely appropriate one, the fiftieth anniversary of the Declaration of Independence. Both, as they approached the end of life, had much in mind the glorious incidents of the past; they were more proud than regretful, Jefferson of the Declaration, Adams of the Constitution.

Adams the younger, hearing that his father approached death, and departing on the difficult journey to New England—even with the utmost crowding it took more than four days—was a man feeling very sorry for himself. He did not start back for Washington from Quincy until October.

He left, he said, with the "anxious and consoling hope" that his stay in Washington would not last too long. After three years he would settle in the old home for life. All his schemes for reuniting the factions of the party were failing. He had conciliated Clay, but there were the intransigent Jacksonians with whom he could do nothing. None of his program of national improvements, he could see, was likely to be enacted. He had been mistaken to become a minority President.

His life in the White House, under continuous political attack, was almost impossible to sustain. His long diplomatic training—as well as his character—imposed on him a routine of administration and of protocol. The chores of office were his to do, and he did them thoroughly. He was required, among other matters, to decide on new army regulations, to pass on the findings of courts-martial, to approve pay scales, promotions, and even the course of study at the Military Academy. He had also to spend much time poring over plans and inspecting progress on the Capitol, then under construction. But especially he had, day after day, to see and listen to a clamorous horde of visitors pushing in to ask for jobs or favors—the familiar complaint of Presidents.

As a result, the night hours, when rest should have been possible, had to be given to correspondence, to the composition of state papers (no Adams would have used a ghost writer), and to the keeping of the *Diary*. This running account of his activities was written in Adams's own hand. He had only his son John as secretary; he had no stenographer and no copyist. But the *Diary* was not one of the more resented chores. He poured into it, with Adams talent and with Yankee bitterness, all his frustrations and disappointed hopes. By mid-term he was finding it hard to keep up his account, much as it meant to him. On December 7, 1826, there was an entry showing this:

> I wrote very little this evening, and my *Diary* now runs in arrears day after day . . . The succession of visitors from my breakfasting to my dining hours is inexpressibly distressing, and now that members of the Congress come and absorb my evening hours, it induces a physical impossibility that I should keep up with the stream of time in my record. An hour's walk before daylight is my only exercise for the day. Then to dress and breakfast I have scarce an hour. Then five-and-twenty visitors, or more, from ten of the morning till five in the afternoon, leave me not a moment of leisure for reflection or for writing. By the time evening approaches, my strength and spirit are both exhausted . . .

Other passages reflect the same dispirited fatigue, the Adams conscience contending with the demeaning claims of politics and the wearing compulsions of duty. But there are others, for Adams was also a man of many interests. He noted a lively pleasure in the gardens, for instance. He was writing about such matters during the next spring and seemed somewhat happier with the turn of the season. The Washington burgeoning is spectacular; he went abroad when he could to enjoy it:

I rise generally before five . . . write for one or two hours in this *Diary*. Ride about twelve miles on horseback. Return home about nine; breakfast; and from that time till dinner between five and six, am occupied incessantly with visitors, business, and reading letters, dispatches, and newspapers. I spend an hour in the garden and nursery; and an hour of drowsiness on a sofa and two hours of writing in the evening.

Not many Presidents have been capable of so sharing with posterity the troubles and satisfactions of the life they led in the White House, but some others have given us sufficiently factual accounts. All of them were, before long, unhappy and harassed. Only a few found themselves possessed of the talents for so complex and demanding a job, and as a consequence a feeling of inadequacy soon succeeded the euphoria of victory; and the Mansion, for this reason as well as others, became rather a place of strain and sadness than of confidence and accomplishment.

It has been at best the scene of hard labor and, for its occupants generally, unhappy incident. This makes it all the more remarkable that Presidents have been—generally again—devoted and persistent in their work, jealous of their position, and alert to enlarge its powers. The very centrality of the Presidency made the burdens what they were; but it also increased, by a kind of compensating action, the willingness to be dominated by its duties. There have been exceptions, but the procession of the Presidents must be said to be a sequence of aging and weighed-down men struggling against disrupting influences, conscious of carrying almost alone national responsibilities, and constantly discouraged that so much that ought to be done could not be accomplished.

Few of the Presidents' familiars—Cabinet members, party chieftains, congressional leaders—seem ever to have had any consideration for them. The Presidents, although there has been an endless curiosity about them, their families, and their friends, have been mostly regarded as exploitable sources of influence, favors, or jobs. They could assist or obstruct the ambitious; their word, or the withholding of it, could affect events. They have been looked at in this way, appraised coldly, used for personal or political purposes without mercy—and allowed to go into retirement worn out, but with no provision for their remaining years. They have often been regarded by the public as benefactors; they have even, some of them, been regarded with veneration; but none has had any general sympathy for his limited human capacity, for his exhaustion after prolonged strain, for his need to rest, to relax, and finally to retire.

Adams suffered in these ways as his predecessors had done and as his successors would do; in 1824–26 Jefferson was near bankruptcy at Monticello, Madison, at Montpelier, was somewhat better off but only because his private means had not been exhausted, and Monroe was losing Oak Hill to his creditors. The elder Adams was a poor man too, comparatively speaking; and the younger one had no very cheerful prospects on retiring. What he could look forward to was the resumption of a profession he had not practiced since his youth and then not for long. It was a typical outlook.[4]

One of Adams's difficulties—one that was becoming more and more serious for all Presidents—was the inextricable mixture of his domestic with his official life. The White House as a home is expected to be a model for all homes in the nation, and at the same time it is expected to be used for official purposes of all sorts. Even its domestic quarters are something less than private. Visiting statesmen in variety are expected to be entertained, and with appropriate attention.[5] Then too, the social season involves the use of the House for immense receptions, for official dinners, and for the entertainment of important persons of all sorts. The organization for this sort of thing would become very elaborate in the twentieth century. In Adams's time it had all to be managed by the President and his wife. This intermingling interferes with the private life of weary men and women, reducing the opportunity for repose and relaxation besides imposing an additional trying duty.

Also, it has to be noted that Presidents' wives have been, more often than not, quite incapable of meeting the demands of their position as chatelaine and as the organizer of official society. The menopause is usually upon them and the infirmities of age are making inroads; and, besides, they have often been by nature and habit suited to a very different regime, more humble and less demanding. Their husbands did not choose them as young women to be mistresses of a White House in age. Many have either broken down under the strain, have retreated into invalidism, or have simply not attempted to become real partners in the Presidency. Adams's wife was one of these. During his term she was, in spite of her long conditioning in diplomatic posts, unhappy and insufficient.

Before Adams, wives had been more helpful, usually for special reasons.

[4] In Adams's *Diary* on July 4, 1826, when Jefferson lay dying at Monticello, he spoke of attending a commemorative service at the Capitol. He noted the speeches and the reading of the Declaration, then added: *Governor Barbour delivered an address . . . soliciting subscriptions for the relief of Mr. Jefferson. Mr. Rush, also, on the floor of the House, made a short address to the same purpose. Not more than four or five subscribers were obtained . . .*

[5] A situation considerably relieved in later years by the use of Blair House, across Pennsylvania Avenue, and its next-door neighbor.

Martha Washington had presided quietly but with dignity in her several official homes; it had been no considerable change from the regime at Mount Vernon, where she entertained important persons and managed a large establishment. Abigail Adams had been more effective as a presidential wife than her husband had been as President. Jefferson had been a widower but had had the help of his daughters and then of Dolly Madison. Eliza Monroe had been the first of the White House invalids. But she would be followed by a dozen others, so that the average of capability would be very low. Some Presidents have used their wives' invalidism to escape social duties. McKinley, for instance, did this. But Adams had a literal conscience, and to a former diplomat protocol was important; also, White House entertaining had become a tradition; it was one of the important supports of presidential prestige. What his wife could not do, Adams tried to do himself.

Nevertheless, the regime of the Adamses had a comparative simplicity that later Presidents must have envied. From the *Diary* we learn that the Mansion's grounds, in later years so meticulously parked and tended, then ran in rough pasture down to Goose Creek and the Potomac, so that a President, if he could find an hour of leisure, might walk there. And Adams, alone or with his son, often went to the river to swim in the early morning. Then there was a garden of flowers and vegetables where the experimental fancy of an amateur could be indulged.

The close relation of home and working quarters would not be changed until separate offices were established, first as a wing of the mansion and then in nearby locations. For Adams, in spite of his wife's invalidism, there could be hardly any separation. But no occupant of the White House has better represented the democratic spirit. Jefferson had rather paraded his commonness but was incurably interested in his kitchen and wine cellar; the Monroe regime, after the Madison brilliance, had been dull but had given the House an outfit of lovely French furnishings which Adams inherited. He used his inheritance with thrift and appreciation. Plain living and high thinking might well have been the family motto. This Adams liked to walk in the streets, work in the garden, and cultivate his mind. He also liked a home, but the White House was not that.

The House itself was, however, a more agreeable environment for Adams than for his successor. Jackson's careless flamboyance clashed with the quiet dignity about him. The Adams manner fitted the reserved classicism almost perfectly. The building, which even in later years, when flanked by office wings and surrounded by adjunct buildings, would still keep its pleasantly antique air, was still a monumental center in a rural scene. It would still glow serenely on its green lawns after the rebuilding in the 1950s; but in Adams's day its effect was imposing, standing alone as it did in its rough environment. It seemed conspicuous then, as though waiting for suitable neighbors so that it might relax; and it never seemed to tolerate happily the invasions of its precincts by office seekers.

It had been meant to look southward toward the marshes bordering the Potomac, across fields which pastured a cow or two and a few sheep. But its northern front always seemed the main one and was recognized as such, of course, by the construction of Latrobe's portico. Across the way, to the north, was the President's square, later to be called Lafayette Park and, somewhat incongruously, to have as its centerpiece a huge rearing horse with General Jackson in the saddle. Beyond was St. John's Episcopal Church, built in 1817. The houses, later to be so famous, around the square were mostly not yet built; but the Dolly Madison house stood on one corner, its tenant gone, its use for the Cosmos Club not yet to begin for some time. There were, in fact, only three residences on the square, and since they were so widely spaced, the scene was almost as rural as the outlook to the south.

The House had no plumbing. Its sanitary arrangements were those of most estate mansions; water came from wells and was not piped inside. For living, as for working, the modern student is apt to think it had few amenities. These would be added in time, but meanwhile it was possible to resent the almost constant critical barrage of the politicians who represented it as a place of luxury in which presidential families reveled.

There have been few Presidents who have not at some time been criticized for their behavior as tenants of the Mansion. Usually the complaint is about extravagance, but occasionally they are accused of making off with publicly owned furniture or silverware. Adams was once denounced for having acquired a billiard table. It turned out to have been bought with his own funds, whereupon his determined critics maintained that it was a gambling device. Monroe had suffered in the same way. In retirement, poor as he was, he was accused of having taken away furniture bought with public funds. For this kind of attack the widest publicity is always available, which may be embarrassing in the midst of important business to which the President ought to be giving his attention.

Many Presidents have wished to escape from living in a nationally owned House. Having a private establishment would at least make them invulnerable to the attacks of congressional demagogues. But no serious move of this sort has ever been made. If most Americans seem not to approve very much of their Presidents' living at public expense, they insist on their continuing the ordeal. Perhaps this is one of their more subtle implied duties—to be a kind of readily available foil for those politicians who, by attacking them, call attention to their own contrasting virtues.

One of the improvements of the Presidency in more recent years is the partial separation of the public activities from the domestic and social ones. This became imperative with the increase in the size of the Executive bureaucracy. But the President and his family would still not escape

the close scrutiny of eager busybodies. And the latest President would
still be embarrassed by familiar charges of carelessness with appropriated
funds. It was incident to the jealousy among the Branches. Presidents
would come to consider it one of the penalties of office; and future ones,
as they made their way upward in the political hierarchy, would always
be conscious that such possible attacks must be minimized. It would affect
their domestic arrangements and their professional or business affairs. But
their precautions would never be adequate. Cracks in their façades would
be found and enthusiastically exploited. They seldom seemed to marry
women of discretion, and even more seldom to pick subordinates of impeccable honesty.

The old House, often rehabilitated and several times entirely rebuilt,
would still stand, more than a century after the Adams occupancy, on its
common, giving an impression of serenity often at variance with the anxieties within. It could not be guessed from its appearance what harassments
and unhappinesses it often harbored. A very few times it has been the
scene of unworthy events; more often it has heard the preliminaries of
high decision concerning the national security and been the center of
planning to ensure domestic tranquility.

No other Chief of State is thus confined to a single official home in the
center of a capital city. All have been furnished with residences elsewhere
for relaxation, for withdrawn conference, and for family living. If American Presidents have gone elsewhere for such purposes it has had to be
to places they themselves provided or that were loaned to them by
friends.[6] For some, identification with an estate has been an asset. Wash-

[6] Except that some have made use of official quarters on army or navy
posts. Lincoln went in summer to the Soldiers' Home on a hill a few miles
away, Roosevelt to Catoctin Mountain, Hoover to a camp under the
Blue Ridge, Eisenhower to Augusta, the Colorado mountains, or Newport, etc. I am indebted to Horace Sutton, the travel writer, and to *The
Saturday Review* (September 20, 1958, 35–36), for the following lively
compendium of presidential vacationings:

*Newport has been visited by no less than seventeen Presidents while in office.
Monroe arrived in a sailing vessel; John Quincy Adams was the first to use
the Redwood library, the oldest in continuous use in the country; Arthur went
year after year; FDR was the first to view the American yacht races from
there. Grant was the first to fish, the first to enjoy a clam bake, and the first
to attend a GAR reunion. He also was the first to have a bit of trouble fitting
into the social patterns. The other Newporters were Washington, Jackson, Tyler,
Polk, Fillmore, Hayes, Cleveland, Harrison, T. Roosevelt, Taft, and Truman. Eisenhower was the first to golf there.*

*For nearly a century White Sulphur Springs was the summer capital. Being
in the lower Alleghenies, in West Virginia, it was cooler than Washington and
a President could make it there in three days by steamboat and stagecoach.*

ington and Mount Vernon, Jefferson and Monticello, Franklin D. Roosevelt and Springwood at Hyde Park (Warm Springs, also, in his case) have been part of each man's picture in the public mind.

There was, however, a long equalitarian period, beginning when the frontiersmen captured the capital and Jackson moved in, and running on through the "log-cabin" Presidents to Fillmore, when *not* to have been a country gentleman was a prerequisite. William Henry Harrison, who was born a Virginia blue blood, as much as was Washington or Madison, and who certainly did not live in rural poverty even in Indiana, had to be pictured in the "Tippecanoe and Tyler too" campaign of 1840 as a "log-cabin and hard cider" candidate. There was a kind of popular conspiracy about this. No one could have believed that a man fit to be President was as "common" as many of them were pictured as being. Yet there was a demand that such a standard should be set and that conformity with it should appear to be maintained. The pretense was so general as to seem incredible to later generations, yet it was very characteristic of a long period of American politics which yielded Presidents from Jackson to McKinley.

It was part of this same demand for common men in office that led several Presidents to renounce ambitions for a second term. This was considered a very creditable sacrifice, since it would give others a chance at the office. And the others, in a land of equality, would be just as competent. The most notorious of the "log-cabin" Presidents was the first—Harrison. How he might have gone about living in accordance with expectation is not known. He was the oldest of all (sixty-eight when he was inaugurated) and was worn out by the fantastic proceedings of the campaign. He lived only a month in office. He happened to be succeeded

---

The first President on the property was Jackson, followed by Van Buren, John Tyler, and Millard Fillmore . . . President Wilson's visit in 1916 was the last by a President until President Eisenhower came in 1956 for talks with President Ruiz Cortines of Mexico and Prime Minister Louis St. Laurent of Canada.

As for Coolidge, he returned to the Vermont Hills where he had been born, delighted in donning a farmer's smock, the blue jeans of that day . . . Hoover had a fishing lodge on the Rapidan river in Virginia. Garfield's choice was Elberon, N.J. and he died there after having been shot in the railroad station in Washington. Grant liked Elberon too, and stayed a half a mile from Garfield's home. Cleveland supposedly went fishing in Buzzard's Bay in 1893, but the real reason was to recuperate from an operation on the roof of his mouth which had been performed aboard a friend's boat. Washington pined for Mount Vernon but he apparently found New York a summer festival and lived in the city in two or three houses which were set aside as Executive Mansions. Truman seemed to prefer winter vacations and pictures of him in a loud sport shirt under the Key West sun must be an indelible memory to all readers over six.

by Tyler, who was an authentic landed planter and who refused to behave as was expected of him—he was chosen, it will be recalled, to placate the Clay faction and turned out to be not only not common but also not Whiggish—and was as unpopular with the party he had been chosen by as any President in the whole succession. He did not have to renounce a second term. None was offered.

It is apparent that the silences of the Constitution have allowed the Presidency to be remade a little by each of the Presidents—and by the strong ones, more than a little—as well as by the forces playing upon it in a changing society. And one of the more important materials for manipulation has been the style each adopted as he came to live in the Mansion. Traditions gradually gather about the residence and limit the changes available to new occupants; but in a way the House itself is a kind of gently neutral, if firmly classic and all-containing, frame for what is inclusively called an "Administration." And Presidents, within elastic limits of taste and tolerance, can do much as they wish. Yet there is certainly a recognizable and unchanging style. It was created in the early Presidencies—those of the Jeffersonians and the Adamses, with the first General-President overshadowing all. What the White House was by 1828, it would, in a very real sense, remain for good and all.

★ II ★

ADAMS, LATE IN LIFE, USED SOME PICTURESQUE LANGUAGE TO CHARAC-
terize his successor. One of the words he used was "ruffian," and this was
perhaps not an exaggeration if the Adams point of view was accepted.[1]
Jackson was indeed a kind of manic Jefferson. As a youth and as a
young man he was wild and reckless. In a later time he would have been
called a delinquent. His roistering was notorious. But when later he became an official, and especially when he was an officer of volunteers, he
was a severe upholder of regulations and a harsh disciplinarian. That was
the pattern of his life. He had, of course, studied law in the casual fashion
of the frontier, but without notable results. William Graham Sumner once
commented on this:

> In the generation before the Revolution the intellectual activity
> of the young men, which had previously been expended in theology,
> began to be directed to the law. As capital increased and property
> rights became more complicated there was more need for legal train-
> ing. In an agricultural community there was a great deal of leisure
> at certain seasons of the year, and the actual outlay required for
> an education was small. The standard of attainments was low, and
> it was easy for a farmer's boy of any diligence to acquire, in his
> winter's leisure, as much book learning as the best colleges gave. In

[1] When Jackson was re-elected to his second term, Adams, then sixty-
five and a member of the Congress, confided to his *Diary* that he considered the President to be intoxicated "with powers and flattery." He
went on to say that all the circumstances were "calculated to make him
entertain an exalted opinion of himself, and a contemptuous one of others."
Also, that "his own natural passions contributed to this result."
There were other remarks of a similar sort both before and after. But the
climax of his indignation was reached when Harvard University conferred
a honorary degree on Jackson. He refused to be present and wrote that he
could not bear to witness the disgrace of his Alma Mater in awarding her
highest honor to a barbarian who could not spell his own name.

truth, the range of ideas, among the best classes, about law, history, political science, and political economy, was narrow in the extreme. What the aspiring class of young men who were self-educated lacked, as compared with the technically "educated," was bits of classical and theological dogmatism which the colleges taught by tradition, and the culture which is obtained by frequenting academical society . . . What the same aspiring youths had in excess of the regularly educated was self-confidence, bred by ignorance of their own short-comings. They were therefore considered pushing and offensive by the colonial aristocracy of place-holders and established families . . . The restiveness of the aspiring class was one of the great causes of the Revolution. The lawyers became the leaders in the revolt everywhere . . . The men whose biographies we read because they rose to eminence present us over and over again with the same picture of a youth with only a common school education, who spends his leisure in reading law . . . but only the select few succeed . . . most fall back into the ranks of farmers and store keepers. Andrew Jackson so fell back.[2]

Jackson fell back; but he rose again in a different way, not as a frontier intellectual, but as a man of action. As President he would disclose possibilities that no one until then had imagined the office to possess. But it would be done in the midst of such confusion that its significance would be largely overlooked. Also, the most important disclosures would be made in his effort to escape from a dilemma into which his own emotionalism had led him. His threat of disciplining South Carolina would be as inconsistent with his professed beliefs as the Louisiana Purchase had been with those of Jefferson. But Jackson was not one to weigh ideas about government in general, about government in the United States in particular, or about the place in it of the Chief Executive. He was not, in fact, one to be troubled about conformity with principle or tradition. Really, after the younger Adams, there would not be another President who would be much bothered by such considerations until the accession of Wilson in 1913. In this, many of them would resemble the aspiring but uneducated individuals described by Sumner. Even Lincoln had beginnings of the same sort as Jackson. Hayes did have a year at the Harvard Law School, but he was the only lawyer-President—and there were a dozen of them—between Adams and Taft who did not acquire his legal training by "reading" in the office of some older practitioner after having had little or no schooling.

It ought to be said that a President—and Jackson is an illustration—need not be a thinking man, in the sense of having a *conscious* orientation

[2] *Andrew Jackson* (New York, 1898), Chap. I.

within his culture and his government, to have an important effect on the office. Even if he acts from pure instinct and is notoriously irregular, he may, in crisis, show that something may be done which had theretofore been considered to be prohibited. It may not be as wise as a philosopher's behavior, but it can be quite as consequential.

The politician has a kind of rationalizing mechanism others find it difficult to understand. It has no necessary relation to reason; it need not be consistent with any pattern; it need only be approved by a majority of the voters—this is regarded as complete vindication. If the historian finds a man of Jackson's sort incomprehensible, that is because he *is* incomprehensible. Jackson, as one of the political breed, did one thing after another in response to impulse. Where the successive impulses originated could sometimes, but not always, be guessed. They often seemed to have different origins because they expressed such inconsistent convictions. But when the strictly political test was applied, these inconsistencies tended to disappear or to become unimportant. Large majorities emphatically approved whatever he decided to do. They even seemed to approve his mistakes and to follow him through his reversals.

In trying to find clues to his success, it can never be forgotten that he was the apotheosis of his constituency and that this identity of purpose and of habit enabled him to divine what they would almost certainly approve. So he would have no doubt that they would follow him—or a majority would—in standing firmly for Union however much they distrusted government. In order to understand the importance of this it is necessary to recall that the Democratic-Republicans who had been following Jackson's leadership *did* really resent any interferences in their affairs, even the collection of taxes; and they disapproved of "internal improvements" carried out by the Federal government.

It was in what amounted to frenzy, with all the destructive impulses of revolution, that they seated Jackson in the White House and swarmed over Washington, dirtying the Mansion and trampling through the Departments. Their muddy boots and coonskin caps were symbols of liberty, including the liberty to do as they liked with what they had conquered by their votes.

While the new Democrats were rising to power, disaffection was spreading through the South and along the border. At its heart was the same idea that had been embodied in Jefferson's Kentucky Resolutions: a state might accept or reject a Federal enactment at its own option; it might refuse to obey a Supreme Court order; it might resist attempts at enforcement. The South's special grievances required that kind of justification. It was, it is true, inconsistent with everything else its influential elite believed. They regarded authority as naturally moving downward from a narrow aristocracy. But they allowed their need for economic resistance to supplant their general theory of sovereignty for the occasion. They specifically feared that the North was moving toward the abolition of slavery; and it was more than feared—it was known—that measures being pressed by the North would cripple the southern economy. Already there was a "tariff of abominations," signed by Adams, to point to. Matters were rapidly coming to a crisis.

There is an almost exquisite irony in the situation of Jackson, the frontiersman, the champion of the small farmers, and the hero of the shopkeepers and artisans, when the consequences of his contradictory professions came home to him. He had followed his unthinking impulse to support a horde of Georgia settlers seeking to dispossess the Cherokee Indians who held lands in the western part of the state. He had to support this indiscipline—if he was to support it—against a Federal treaty and against a Supreme Court decree upholding it. Before he knew what he was doing, he was committed to nullification in an important instance; and nullification was only a short remove from secession.

When he did see what he had got into he reacted with characteristic directness, aggravated, no doubt, by irritation at his own carelessness. It might easily by then have been too late, but his aggressiveness prevailed. And it has to be said that his firm stand settled for years to come the supremacy of Federal power and the paramountcy of the President within the Federal government.

The Cherokee troubles—to pursue the incident somewhat further—had begun long ago. Washington had made a treaty with all the Gulf Indians in 1791 by which they were given territorial and other guarantees in exchange for their title to large original holdings. But the white population grew, the tidewater plantations became exhausted, and there was a persistent movement into new areas to the westward. The Indians were directly in the path of this migration, holding lands the whites were determined to possess. The treatment of the Indians by these migrant settlers is one of the more shameful passages in American history. The coveted lands were taken by force or trickery, but anyway were taken. When treaties interfered they were ignored or deliberately violated. Worst of all, the justification offered for these outrages was one of convenience only; no pretense of right was made. The Indians, it was said, were an inferior people; therefore any kind of treatment, however rascally, was allowable. And it was condoned by the state authorities.

Presidents before Jackson had done what they could to check the rapacity of the settlers. New treaties had repeatedly been made guaranteeing the Indians possession of land farther toward the West, but they had always been broken by individuals or by local and state governments. There had on occasion been Federal interferences, but the enforcement efforts had been feeble in comparison with the massive determination of the offenders. The consciences of Monroe and Adams had been troubled, and Adams had once ordered the army to intervene. But when Jackson had to deal with the matter, sentiment overcame him. He had no troubled conscience. He was himself an old Indian fighter, and he shared the prejudices of the most ruthless settlers. No actions on their part were too extreme to be forgiven; he would keep no one from exploiting Indians.

The specific trouble, of interest to us here, was the more difficult because the Cherokees were so advanced and settled a people. They were a good deal more civilized, than many of those who were demanding that they be ejected from their territories. For their displacement by the Georgians there was no possible excuse except the ugly one of covetousness; their advanced arts were, to the Georgians, an added source of irritation. As their treaties with the Federal government were violated again and again, each violation was accompanied by loud trumpetings from the demagogue who happened to be Governor of the state. Adams's attempt to oppose the aggressions had been feeble, but Jackson actually encouraged the aggressors.

He finally found himself supporting an invasion of lands supposed to be specifically protected by treaties he was, as President, sworn to uphold—they were laws. He either did not, or would not, recognize the implications until he was very deep in the consequent dilemma. Meanwhile, however, he had done something very important for the Presidency —he had defied the Court. And no matter what the occasion, and regardless of the correctness or mistakenness of the interpretation, any instance of presidential assertion of the right to interpret is bound to be important. This is especially true if the correction succeeds; and this one did. It seemed more important at the moment, of course, that a powerful Chief Executive had supported a state in ignoring Federal law; but the two end consequences were utterly at variance with each other—an aggressive Executive in a feeble government was an anomaly. And this raised an issue that could not finally be dodged. The President would sooner or later have to say whether he chose the Federal supremacy that went with a strong Executive or states' rights that went with a weak one. Just then the South was in a mood to seize on the implications of his support for states' rights. There was acute irritation anyway, not only about Federal interferences in favor of the Indians, but about the growing abolitionist movement in the North. Any suggestion that slavery might be brought to an end by Federal action was furiously resented.

Then too, there was the matter of the hated tariff favoring manufacturers in the North but bearing heavily on the agricultural South. There were enraged outcries, and southern politicians, shown the way by Calhoun, were preaching nullification and interposition more and more openly. It seemed to the southerners that Jackson's outspoken attitude in the matter of the Cherokees gave consent to their contention that a state might not be coerced. They presumed on it. But their very extremism brought Jackson to seeing, finally, what he ought to have understood from the first: he was being supposed to favor, as Jefferson undoubtedly had, the right of the states to accept or not to accept Federal sovereignty at their own option.

It was therefore with surprise and consternation that southerners at a dinner in Washington, held to advance the political fortunes of Calhoun, heard Jackson, when called on to rise, glare about him belligerently and offer the toast: "Our Federal Union—it must be preserved!"

This dinner was held on Jefferson's birthday (April 13) in 1830. Calhoun was then Vice-President, and since he had just made a speech extolling liberty above Union, the President's toast was taken as a direct and calculated rebuke. There followed during the next few months several threats of nullification, and defiant resolutions were passed by the legislature of South Carolina. But Jackson made it unmistakably clear that he would if necessary use force to uphold Federal law, and South Carolina failed to enlist other states in displays of defiance. So the movement subsided.

A President had again proclaimed a national policy and had caused it to be respected. That it was inconsistent with his former views and actions was less important than his obvious present determination. In a crisis he had declared himself to be the primary formulator of the people's will and shown himself to be capable of taking any necessary measure to see that it prevailed. And there had been no effective opposition.

Jackson thus helped to prepare the way for Lincoln and others. Without saying so directly, he had reaffirmed the Rule of Necessity. That this was a real contribution as the country moved into the new era of libertarian democracy, we can see at this distance, knowing what other presidential declarations it resembles.

Another of his contributions was the securing of authority over such industrial and social organizations as performed public functions. In what is usually spoken of as "the battle of the Bank," his power was established in an important area not theretofore pre-empted by the President. In a fierce campaign he destroyed the controls being exercised by a private concern and asserted the authority of the government over the financial system—and made good the assertion. He was thus successful in driving out of government a baneful influence. He considered this fight, when he retired, to have been his most useful one, and perhaps he was right.

The chief of the private fiscal monopolists challenged by him was Nicholas Biddle of Philadelphia, who had become the president of the Bank in 1823. But the institution itself went farther back—to 1816, when its charter had been granted. It was a fairly close replica of Hamilton's original invention, which had gone out of existence with the expiration of its charter in 1812. When renewal had been refused, a large number of local banks were organized, and these, completely out of control, produced a chaotic situation. The system was extremely insecure—if it could be called a system

—and it produced before long an intolerable inflation. Much against their wishes, the Democratic-Republicans had been forced to come to Hamilton's solution of a private bank with government participation, and Madison had signed the measure establishing one.[3]

It is not possible to describe here the operations of this institution or to follow the methods by which it managed to get control of government rather than acting as the agent by which the government controlled the fiscal system of the country. The Bank had been declared to be constitutional in a famous Supreme Court decision—*McCulloch* vs. *Maryland*—but this did not deter Jackson, who was quite clear that a President had his own duty to make his own interpretation. In his first message to the Congress he said that both the constitutionality and the expediency of the law creating the Bank were questionable. He said further that it must be admitted to have failed in establishing a uniform and sound currency. He suggested that something better could be devised, "founded on the credit of the government and its revenues." In his messages of 1830 and 1831 he again referred to the matter.

But it was in the campaign of 1832 that the issue became a heated one. Jackson's Whig opponent supported the Bank, and the campaign became an out-and-out struggle between its supporters and its opponents. For Jackson, as a practicing politician, the Whig commitment to the Bank was fortunate. He loudly and bitterly denounced "the money power" and by doing so consolidated his own support. He was always at his best, as most professionals are, when he had a visible and vulnerable enemy. The result in this instance could be seen in the election returns. Jackson's popular majority was 123,936 in a total vote of 1,290,493.[4] The electoral vote was 219 to 49, with a few votes going to the nullification ticket and a few to Wirt of Vermont.

The main phases of the struggle occurred after the election, during Jackson's second term. The old General was by now convinced that he had an appointment to destroy the Bank; and although he was chronically ill and often hardly able to be about, he summoned strength enough on various occasions to denounce his opponents and expose their maneuvering for recharter. In the course of the various engagements Biddle suborned Congressmen, bought up newspapers, precipitated a panic by re-

---

[3] Its capital was fifty-five million, seven million subscribed by the government in 5 per cent stock, seven million by the public in specie, and twenty-one by the public in U.S. bonds. Twenty directors were elected annually by the stockholders and five were appointed by the President. The government undertook to charter no other institution, thus establishing a monopoly.

[4] Excluding South Carolina, whose electors were still chosen by the legislature.

stricting credit, and generally proved by his behavior that all Jackson was claiming about his nefarious machinations was true. Jackson was bound to win, and did. The Bank was liquidated.

The difficulty with all this from the point of view of public policy was that what he fell back on was the use of state banks as government depositories. And he did, at a certain stage, remove deposits from the Bank and entrust them to a number of such institutions. There was no adequate suggestion of a substitute for the other fiscal functions of the Bank. There was a boom in state-bank stocks, a flood of inflated currency, and then general fiscal chaos. This was added to by the curious circumstance—curious, that is, to later generations—that there was a Treasury surplus. Since there was no debt to use as a Treasury balancing mechanism and only deposits of surplus to be made, the government lost control of fiscal policy almost completely. Commercial credit was subject to indefinite inflation along with the currency. But Jackson accepted no responsibility for the results of his policy. And, as a matter of fact, he was not held responsible by the public. He finished his second term on a high tide of popularity and left the problem to his successor.

He may have been mistaken to disestablish the Bank without providing more adequately for the carrying on of its fiscal functions. But that the Bank served him well in its travail cannot be denied. Also, it has to be noted that he did vindicate the power of the government in economic affairs; and, in the government, the authority of the President. If he did it in a destructive way, which may be admitted, it must also be admitted that it was thereafter understood by everyone that the government's finances were not to be managed by private interests for their own profit.

★ 12 ★

SOMETHING MUST BE SAID ABOUT STILL OTHER ENLARGEMENTS OF THE
Presidency that are due to Jackson, and especially the Doctrine of Direct
Representation. It was this which aroused Webster to his most spectacular
forensic furies and caused violent mental turmoil among the Whigs generally. From this time on, a strong Presidency was to be supported by the
Democrats, with the Whigs and Republicans permanently opposed. It
was Jackson who asserted that Presidents must be powerful because they
were "the people's men" in a sense more real than could be said of legislators. This was soon expanded to justify claims to presidential powers
far beyond those enumerated in the Constitution. The President must be
able to meet the responsibilities flowing from his direct representation of
the ultimate sovereignty in a democracy—the whole people.

It is no doubt anomalous that so much of the prestige of the later Presidency should have been gained for the office by so determined an individualist as Jackson. He professed to be a strict constructionist, and this
would certainly not allow for implied powers. But the contradiction is more
seeming than actual. The advances he fought for were personal. If they
limited the liberties of others, those others were not entitled to any; they
were the exploiters of his constituents. Contradictory as it seems, the fixing in the American tradition of the Doctrine of Direct Representation is
closely related to the caprices and irregular methods of Jackson and to
his ruthless destruction of the old civil service. The people's man had a
kind of mandate to represent them independently and without being influenced by those who might have been contaminated by special interests.
This, it will be seen, made a kind of virtue of the spoils system. The spoilsmen were loyal President's men; through them he could make sure that
the policies he formulated in the people's interest would be put into execution.

As an extension of this theory the Jacksonians spoke of the "rotation"
involved as highly desirable. It recognized the equalitarianism of the middle border. Any man could do any job; government positions were privileges and ought to be shared out so that as many as possible could gain

something from victory. This was the rationale. Because it fitted perfectly the desires of politicians both high and low, it was seized on and argued for as though an important truth had been discovered and must be propagated. And if the politicians found it convenient, it was actually widely believed among the voters. But their belief in it was greatly encouraged by the living illustration of Jackson himself.

The pioneer life in which a man depended upon himself alone with his family, and in which, with an ax and a squirrel rifle, he was as good as any other man, was the source of equalitarian individualism. It had always been prevalent on the fringes of settlement and in small towns; but these were vastly extended as migration flowed across the mountains into the West and homes and villages were set up in the wilderness. These communities, small and sometimes lost in the vast forests stretching to the plains across the Mississippi, were nevertheless aggressively certain that the future was theirs. The writers of the Constitution had been aware of these sentiments and beliefs, and most of them had feared the effect on government. They had tried to take precautions against the very developments now taking place.

The provisions of the Constitution concerning the Presidency, except for modifications of electoral methods, was unchanged. But the rise of parties and the subjection to them of the electors had made the President a people's man in spite of the precautions of the framers. Jackson was merely the first politician to take full advantage of the new developments and to exploit the silences of the Constitution.

But he was a new breed of leader, shrewd, wary, and determined to have the position he felt himself entitled to as the chosen champion from the border lands. He was only the first of such heroes, and his election only the first assertion of trans-Appalachian power. There now began the dignification of ignorance which was to last the rest of the century. The educational level of the unschooled farmer was to be the standard for their representatives in government. And the new class was not content with getting the persons it approved into office; it insisted that they behave in ways approved in their primitive communities. Good manners were ridiculed as effete; knowledge and expertness were held to be affectations; and such tests were applied all the way to the top of officialdom.[1]

The rise to power of the new class was consolidated by the spread of adult male suffrage. Once they had the vote, the men of small or no property easily overwhelmed those of wealth and influence who had thereto-

---

[1] The first reversal of this attitude would be delayed until Hayes, who had had a college education, became President (in 1877) and began to insist on the reconstitution of the civil service; but progress would be slow even after that.

fore managed governmental affairs. And it was natural that they should choose public officials of their own sort. Why not? They believed themselves capable of filling any position. Unfortunately most of them had no tradition of service, no talent for administration, and only an elementary sense of duty. They were politicians, intriguers, opportunists. Their capture of the upper echelons of government, presided over by Jackson, was a disaster to the public service. The disaster would be unrelieved until even they had attained a certain maturity, perhaps we should say until mass education began to have its effect. Yet it has to be said that it democratized the government, which for some time had been monopolized by an upper class.

Cabinet members, under Jackson's capricious management, were not much better off than the lowliest clerk so far as security went. They were liable to instant replacement and, in fact, none lasted through Jackson's eight years. This may have seemed unbearable to the Secretaries involved, but it had an effect of another sort on the presidential office. It enhanced the central figure immensely. There had grown up a custom of regarding Cabinet members as "constitutional advisers." There was no warrant for this in the Constitution, of course, but there was an explanation for it in the natural desire of important men, often political rivals of the President, who sometimes regarded themselves as more worthy than he, to enhance their own prestige. Also, it had fitted the habit of mind of former Presidents who had come to their policy-making and their administration of the public's business with due care and consideration. When they required from their Secretaries written memoranda, or when they asked for consultation on important issues, they were behaving in a manner consonant with their training as statesmen rather than as politicians. Without substantial agreement, reached by thorough discussion, they were reluctant to make commitments. This kind of consideration had preceded the formulation of such policies as expansionism to the South and West, trade and fiscal policies, relations with France and Britain, and the treatment to be accorded the Indian nations. Also, the Monroe Doctrine, as we have seen, had been thus prayerfully approached.

Jackson disestablished this custom of consultation among a governing group, and he had as little compunction about it as about his other departures from Washington tradition—his contemptuous treatment of the Supreme Court, for instance. It was this careless individualism that resulted in such inconsistencies as his reversal of himself on the issue of nullification. The threat of Federal force to be used against the South Carolinians if they should persist in their defiance—which his former attitude in the Cherokee matter had seemed to condone—was the second thought of a man who had not really had a first thought and had not consulted others who might have guided him.

This contempt of Jackson's for the precedures of consultation had one result that must be noted: it resolved the long-disputed status of the Secretary of the Treasury, who might have seemed, from the duties prescribed for him in the Act establishing the Department, to have a duty to report to the Congress rather than to the President.[2] What President Jackson and Secretary Duane said to each other, after several previous exchanges concerning the removal of government deposits from the Bank, is retold in L. D. White's *The Jacksonians:*

[2] This has to do with the contradiction between the "take care" clause of the Constitution, which gives a duty to the President, and the "necessary and proper" clause, which gives an apparently overriding authority to the Congress. An extensive and illuminating discussion of this matter may be found in Corwin's *President: Office and Powers,* 1948 ed., III. There is there brought into focus the inherent opposition for which there is no possible resolution except mutual restraint and tacit agreement. The general rule, Professor Corwin says, has been stated by the Court to be that when any duty is cast by law upon the President it may be exercised by him "through the head of the appropriate department," whose acts become, in effect, the President's acts. In fact, most orders emanating from heads of departments, even under powers conferred by statute on the President, do not mention him. The discussion goes on:

Suppose, on the other hand, that the law casts a duty upon the subordinate executive agency eo nomine, does the President thereupon become entitled, by virtue of his "executive power" or of his "duty to take care that the laws be faithfully executed," to substitute his own judgment for that of the agency regarding the discharge of such duty? An unqualified answer to this question would invite startling results. An affirmative answer would make all questions of law enforcement questions of discretion, the discretion moreover of an independent and legally uncontrollable branch of the government. By the same token it would render it impossible for Congress, notwithstanding its broad powers under the "necessary and proper" clause, to leave anything to the specially trained judgment of a subordinate executive official with any assurance that his discretion would not be perverted to political ends for the advantage of the administration in power. At the same time, a flatly negative answer would hold out consequences equally unwelcome. It would, as Attorney General Cushing quaintly phrased it, leave it open to Congress so to divide and transfer "the executive power" by statute as to change the government "into a parliamentary despotism like that of Venezuela or Great Britain, with a nominal executive chief or president, who, however, would remain without a shred of actual power." Or, in other words, it would leave it open to Congress to destroy unity of administration in the national government, as it has long since been destroyed in the state governments. There are some critics, indeed, who profess to believe that this has already happened.

This comment of Professor Corwin's opens the whole subject of constitutional vagueness and the possibilities that lie in the aggressive action on the part of any of the balanced and checked Branches.

"A secretary, sir," said Jackson, "is merely an executive agent, a subordinate, and you may say so in self-defence." To which Duane replied, "In this particular case, congress confers a discretionary power, and requires reasons if I exercise it. Surely this contemplates responsibility on my part." Here was the heart of the matter. On September 23, 1833, Jackson solved the problem by summarily removing Duane. To Van Buren he wrote, "In his appointment I surely caught a tarter in disguise, but I have got rid of him."[3]

When Jackson defended his position, in a message to the Senate, he put the presidential view about as clearly as it would ever be stated:

. . . It was settled by the Constitution, the laws, and the whole practice of the government that the entire executive power is vested in the President of the United States; that as an incident to that power the right of appointing and removing those officers who are to aid him in the execution of the laws, with such restrictions only as the Constitution prescribes, is vested in the President; that the Secretary of the Treasury is one of those officers; that the custody of the public property and money is an Executive function which, in relation to the money, has always been exercised through the Secretary of the Treasury and his subordinates; that in the performance of these duties he is subject to the supervision and control of the President, and in all important measures having relation to them consults the Chief Magistrate and obtains his approval and sanction; that the law establishing the bank did not, as it could not, change the relation between the President and the Secretary—did not release the former from his obligation to see the law faithfully executed nor the latter from the President's supervision and control.[4]

But, like other constitutional issues, this matter is never finally settled; however quiet the issue may remain for a while after such a victory, it may—almost certainly will—arise again, perhaps with the same exhibition of ill temper on either side. As to the President's control of his subordinates, the bloodiest engagement was yet to take place between another President and another Congress. But Andrew Johnson would be fortified in his battle with the Congress over Stanton, his Secretary of War, by Jackson's previous victory. And in the long run, Jackson's view would seem

[3] One in his series of studies in administrative history (New York, 1954), 37.

[4] J. D. Richardson, *A Compilation of the Messages and Papers of the Presidents, 1789–1910*, 11 vols. (New York, 1911), III, 85 (1834). White, above, was also following Richardson's account.

to have been accepted—although no one could say that the whole question would not again be revived in some future crisis.

If Jackson had trouble with his formal Cabinet, there was, it should be noted, the famous Kitchen Cabinet to be relied on. Those usually listed as among these confidants are Andrew J. Donelson, Amos Kendall, Duff Green, Francis P. Blair, Major W. B. Lewis, Isaac Hill, and Roger B. Taney. Donelson was a Jackson protégé and acted as his secretary, Lewis lived at the White House and ran political errands, Taney gave the kind of legal advice Jackson wanted, especially in the Treasury struggle, and later, of course, was rewarded by appointment to the Chief Justiceship. None of these was prominent enough to have been included in a Cabinet list. They were of a peculiar sort, to become better known in public life from this time on. Their attachment was personal—their loyalty too—and their duties had to do either with party intrigue or with the carrying out of confidential missions. Some of them were clever and helpful, and as a coterie they were more than a match for the conservatives of Jackson's opposition, and some were later made members of the regular Cabinet.

There had been something of the sort before. Washington had consulted Jay;[5] Jefferson had depended a good deal on his political henchmen; but as an informal institution the kitchen assistants so overshadowed the regular Cabinet that it amounted to a new invention. There can be no doubt that it had the effect of enlarging the President's person indefinitely by repairing his lacks of various sorts, and it undertook duties that would otherwise have been beyond his strength and range—and perhaps beneath his dignity. They saw people he could not see, gathered information he could not otherwise have known, wrote speeches and messages, devised legislation, formed a liaison with the congressional leaders and with influential politicians elsewhere, saw that political debts were paid and the right people rewarded. That their services broadened his influence could be inferred, if there were no other way, by the cries of rage from members of the Congress who resented increased presidential effectiveness, and from outsiders who had reason to fear his displeasure. And this is to say nothing of political opponents who were infuriated by this "unconstitutional" resort.[6]

[5] And been refused a consultative opinion he should have known better than to ask for. Our knowledge of presidential advisers of this sort has been enriched by Professor L. W. Koenig's *The Invisible Presidency*, (New York, 1960.)

[6] It should be noted that Tyler would resort to the same device when his policies came into conflict with those of the Whigs, who inadvertently had opened the way to the White House by making him a Vice-President of convenience. There would be an exodus from the Cabinet and unusual need for unorthodox consultations. In general, Whigs and Republicans

Somewhat related to this, because it had also to do with practical politics, was the sudden change in the procedure of nomination for the Presidency, which until then had been by congressional caucus. These meetings of Representatives and Senators had been effective in keeping for them a certain control of the Executive Branch; whoever was nominated owed his selection to the legislators. Now a convention, made up of delegates who might very well be politically unfriendly with members of the Congress, would make the selection. It greatly increased the party influence of state politicians.

The change was due to Jackson's quarrels with the Senate and the unlikelihood that a caucus would accept his choice of Van Buren to succeed him.[7]

Van Buren was the product of one of the most corrupt, but also one of the best-disciplined, machines in the country—that of New York State— and he was thoroughly familiar with all the techniques of selecting candidates and managing party business. The two old professionals moved to create the machinery which would not only nominate Van Buren and punish the recalcitrant legislators but would provide a nominating system the state machines could control. It was, they said, more democratic.

The convention as a nominating device had been suggesting itself, anyway. It was generally used in the states. But also it had become quite

---

would frown on the practice; its future extension would be mostly in Democratic regimes—that of F. D. Roosevelt being a conspicuous example. But the Republicans would always seem to have a larger number of prominent citizens on call, who, when consulted, were not resented as "upstarts" and did not even need to be attached to government. They would never be called a "Kitchen Cabinet"; they were approved as "advisers."

[7] Van Buren's unpopularity could be gauged by the Senate's refusal to confirm him as Minister to Britain. But he had ingratiated himself with Jackson in many ways—particularly in the affair of Mrs. Eaton, wife of the Secretary of War. Senator Eaton had married Peggy O'Neill, before becoming Secretary under circumstances regarded by Washington socialites—including Cabinet wives—as suspicious. They refused to receive her, and this infuriated Jackson, who had had his own troubles with gossips and social censors in earlier years. He undertook to force the issue. The affair became a notorious one. The more the women resisted, the more Jackson insisted that they be disciplined by their husbands. Almost alone among the upper echelon of officials, Van Buren paid conspicuous attention to the lady. The irritated husbands pointed out that he was free to do so because he had no wife or daughters to deal with; but his conformance endeared him to the willful old General as almost nothing else could have done.

customary for groups of various sorts, meeting unofficially, to make nominations they hoped would be accepted. So it was not entirely novel for the Democrats of New Hampshire to send out a call for a meeting. What was novel about it was that the call was a national one for a major party meeting in Baltimore. Its validity as a political and party arrangement would obviously depend on its general acceptance; but with Jackson and Van Buren sponsoring it, the chances for its success were good.

By 1832 the party system had taken fairly definite form. Curiously enough, it had progressed most rapidly during the Administration of the younger Adams, who was the least political of Presidents. This was because of the feud carried on by Jackson and his followers after the loss of the Presidency in 1824, and because they were so determined to win in 1828. Jackson had been "nominated" to succeed Adams many times before 1828. The numerous meetings to support his candidacy and the numerous resolvings of state legislatures controlled by his machine had begun almost before Adams's inauguration. They were given a formidable boost by the campaign to impugn Adams's motives in appointing Clay to be his Secretary of State. That Clay had furnished the electoral votes necessary and that as President Adams had immediately reciprocated with appointment to the premier Cabinet post made it easy for the opposition to claim that there had been a "deal." The "corruption" claimed to be involved was distorted and inflated to an extent credible only in the strange realm of politics. No one could reasonably suppose that Adams would thus "buy" votes; and if his appointment of Clay was partly out of gratitude, this was not an unusual reason for the selection of Cabinet members. It was certainly not "corrupt." But it served, nevertheless, to float many indignation meetings, even of state legislatures, which passed resolutions "nominating" Jackson; and these—not a congressional caucus—put Jackson into the running again and at once.

When Jackson's first term was coming to an end, he determined to ditch Calhoun, who had been his Vice-President, and to substitute for him Van Buren, who was much more tractable. Van Buren had been Secretary of State, but his feud with influential Senators was compromising. It seemed to him that if he escaped temporarily from the party struggles by becoming Minister to Britain the enmity might subside. It was a good enough scheme, except that the Senators saw through it and refused to confirm him for the mission. He had no alternative but to fight, and it would be pleasant to be able to preside over the Senate after having been refused preferment by its members. Jackson was even more annoyed than Van Buren himself. It was at least partly this annoyance that made him decide on a second term, with Van Buren as Vice-President, when he was already aging and worn and would rather have retired.

The old General in the White House, with his overwhelming popularity, and Van Buren with his shrewd management were an unbeatable combination. It was especially effective because by now the presidential electors in all the states but two were elected directly and not by the state legislatures. A convention to set up the nominees, and a rousing campaign to select pledged electors, resulted in the tremendous victory of 1832— and fixed the convention procedure firmly in the political system.

There had already been two conventions of lesser parties when the New Hampshire Democrats were persuaded to issue their call for a national meeting to be held in May. The Anti-Masons and the National Republicans had nominated Jackson's rival, Clay. They had also adopted resolutions denouncing Jackson and all his followers; these were the progenitors of the party platforms that were to become so traditional a part of political life from that time forward. Thus in the heat and controversy of active politics are its customs created.

★ 13 ★

HOW CONSIDERABLY JACKSON'S INNOVATIONS EXTENDED THE PRESIDEN-
tial influence has been increasingly appreciated with the passage of time.
However weak some of his successors, or however much they professed
devotion to congressional supremacy, the customs established while the
electorate was growing and grouping itself behind the irascible Tennes-
sean would never be completely abandoned even in the worst days for
the Presidency. For considerable periods there would be a return to the
rule that Presidents must confine themselves to the execution of laws made
by an omniscient Congress. This view would have its longest run in the
peculiar circumstances following the Civil War. But the first really strong
President following the Republican succession from Grant to Arthur would
again assert the prerogatives of his office and find them not much impaired
by two decades of intervening subservience. The Constitution had, after
all, not been altered.[1]

That such vital changes as came about through the adoption and spread
of the Jacksonian political devices could take place without any change
in the Constitution itself emphasizes the breadth and depth of the silences
in that instrument. By exploiting them Presidents have found indefinite
resources to hand in carrying out the increasing responsibilities of the office. Much has depended, of course, on persuasiveness in mustering general consent among the governed. As we have seen, the sparse specifications of the Constitution did not include directions for the organization
or operations of the Executive. It might almost be supposed from reading
it that he was expected to carry on all its functions personally, except

[1] We shall see how a famous political theorist—Woodrow Wilson, later
to become President himself—would first conclude, from observing the
Republican succession, that there was no hope in the Presidency and that
congressional supremacy would have to be recognized and that body
required to accept the responsibilities of leadership, and then, observing
a strong President in action—Cleveland—would conclude that he had been
too hasty in generalizing.

that in separate passages "officers" are mentioned who must also be involved in administration. That there were to be Departments with heads subordinate to the President was made apparent only in that vestigial sentence—a survival from an earlier draft—saying that he might "require the opinion, in writing, of the principal officer in each of the Executive Departments, upon any subject relating to the duties of their respective offices."

A close reading of this sentence would seem to indicate that he might not ask of them any opinion *not* in writing and *not* having to do with their respective duties. It not only does not suggest the existence of an advisory council but seems to assume that there will be none. And of course we know that the Senate was expected to advise, something it promptly refused to do, at least in the way, and on the scale, that the framers anticipated. Also, in connection with the mention of Departments, there has to be read the "necessary and proper" clause of the Congress's enumerated powers; this says that the Congress shall "make all laws which shall be necessary and proper for carrying into execution" the other enumerated powers and "all other powers vested by this Constitution in the government of the United States, or in any Department or Officer thereof."

The Constitution does not say that the Congress may or shall set up Departments as it does say, in the judiciary article, that it shall provide the courts inferior to the Supreme Court. But there is no doubt whatever that funds for any such establishment must be provided by the House, because all money bills must originate there. And this has always been taken to mean that there must be legislation authorizing their initiation. The Congress may have gone very far in specifying what Departments may or may not do and how they may be organized, but Presidents have not cared to challenge the right of the legislators to do this. They have, however, become aroused when congressional interference with operations was threatened. It is at the beginning of administration that they have judged their responsibility for faithful execution to begin.

There is another clause that refers to "other officers of the United States" than the Ambassadors and judges spoken of specifically; in this there is more than a suggestion that the Congress shall have a part in the setting up of their offices and in their selection. It is said that their appointments shall be "established by law" and that the Congress *may* delegate the selections.[2]

[2] The relevant passage reads: ". . . and he shall nominate, and by and with the advice and consent of the Senate, shall appoint Ambassadors, other public Ministers and Consuls, Judges of the supreme Court, and all other officers of the United States, whose appointments are not herein provided for, and which shall be established by law: but the Congress

There had been one view of the meaning of this before Jackson; there was quite a different one, as we have seen, among his partisans. But it has to be noted that there were distinctions made between the powers given to the President and those given to the Congress. As a result, when the Departments of State, of War, and of the Treasury were authorized by law, State and War were recognized as coming within the President's responsibility, but the Treasury, as an extension of the Congress's primary fiscal responsibility, was treated differently. So when the Post Office was authorized in 1792 it was not assigned to the President.[3] Jackson, however, when he undertook to instruct the Secretary of the Treasury, ignored these distinctions. In his view, *all* the Executive Departments were his to direct, and his exclusively.

In other matters as well as this he had no compunction at all about reversing the views of his more staid and intellectual predecessors. It was in the same style that he dislodged career officials. He more than tolerated the spoils system; he directed its operations from the White House.

It should perhaps be noted that although political preferment had not previously become a rule in the Federal service it had been raised to a system in several of the larger states, such as New York, Pennsylvania, and Jackson's own Tennessee. It was now merely transferred to Washington by professional state practitioners. A long time and many reformist campaigns would be required to eliminate it.[4] And even then the reforms would have very mild beginnings. The moving of the spoils system from Tennessee to Washington was quite consonant with the convulsive political changes during the twenties and thirties of the nineteenth century. The nation had until then been a republic, but it had been something less than a democracy. Universal suffrage for an unready electorate was bound to result in abuses. It resulted also in what Professor Corwin has spoken of as the "occultation" of Jackson, even though he exhibited so many of the typical faults and shortcomings of those who had elected him. One historian has said about him:

There had been no reason for the rejection of Mr. Adams and the election of General Jackson save a personal preference for Jack-

---

may by law vest the appointment of such inferior officers, as they think proper, in the President alone, in the courts of law, or in the heads of Departments." (Art. II, sec. 2.)

[3] Nor was Interior when it was organized in 1849. But Navy, in 1798, was. This seems to follow the same theory of constitutional attributions.

[4] Jackson first brought the Postmaster General into the Cabinet. It was done because he had so many jobs to distribute. It was an easy transition to customarily appointing party chairmen to the Postmaster-Generalship.

son. If that was a good reason for substituting one President for another, it was surely sufficient to justify "rotation" in the minor offices, rotating out those who did not, and rotating in those who did, approve and assist in making the greater substitution. No President before Jackson had so good a reason as he to regard his elevation as a personal triumph, or to assume that the whole responsibility of government was entrusted to him. That fact may explain why he felt justified in displaying anger when the Senate . . . rejected his nominations; why he discarded the old custom of consulting the members on momentous public questions, and sought the advice of a coterie of politicians, his devoted slaves, who were derisively styled the "Kitchen Cabinet".[5]

But there is no doubt that, even if for reasons no respecter of orderly government could approve, the Jacksonian changes had a profound effect on the presidential office itself and that these effects were lasting ones. They were thus lasting because they broke up old patterns and interpretations. They showed as nothing had done before how enormous were the areas of the Constitution remaining to be given content by determined Presidents. Those coming after Jackson would find that the national needs could be met within the original compact as thus interpreted. This was not true of some weaker ones, of whom the most conspicuous was Buchanan; but all the strong ones would find their latitude sufficient. The interpretation necessary to action might be novel but the President would have the right to make it, and its acceptance would depend on his ability to persuade the electorate of its reasonableness.

To hold their gains in the no man's land of tripartite government, Presidents have relied on other means than public persuasion, of course; and one other developed to its very limit by Jackson and believed to be most effective by Professor White as by others, was the seizure and expansion of the removal power. The permanent effect on the Presidency of this successful foray was immense:

> . . . the power of the Presidential office was expanded to proportions hitherto unknown or unthought of . . . it was directly felt in every part of the country . . . it increased year by year as the country grew and officeholding multiplied.[6]

It was logical enough for Jackson to have advocated a single term for Presidents, thus applying the rotation principle to Presidents as well as

[5] Edward Stanwood, *A History of the Presidency* (Boston, 1898), 151–52.

[6] *The Jacksonians*, op. cit., 33.

others, but he was doubtless glad to have this remain a theoretical matter. It was pointed out to him that there was a fallacy involved—only a party chief who could win could seize jobs for the faithful—but after the commitment in his first inaugural it was difficult for him to retreat. In five annual messages he repeated his first statement that "it would seem advisable to limit the service of the Chief Magistrate to a single term of four or six years"; but whatever he said, he was, very soon after his first inauguration, planning for a longer stay in office. Major Lewis (of the Kitchen Cabinet) was, within a few months, writing to a Pennsylvania legislator, enclosing the draft of a letter urging the General, in the warmest terms, to run again. It was to be signed by as many of the lawmakers as were willing and then to be sent to Jackson. It was actually signed by sixty-eight members. To assume that Jackson could have been ignorant of Lewis's solicitation is to strain credulity. At any rate, in response to this and a tide of similar resolutions and communications, he did consent; and, as the election of 1832 approached, the Kitchen Cabinet really applied itself to the preliminaries. There was no trouble about the nomination, but there was some opposition in the election. The two-party system was taking shape.

The platform of the National Republicans demanded that every citizen who had regard for the honor and welfare of the nation, and for the preservation of the Union, vote for Henry Clay. Clay had been thought to be a likely victor, but Jackson won decisively with 219 electoral votes to 67 for his opponents; and this, in his opinion, was the essential confirmation that his policies were approved.[7]

---

[7] Forty-nine of the 67 votes in opposition went to Clay; the others went to Floyd and Wirt. Floyd's support was from South Carolina and Wirt's from Vermont. There were special reasons for each, interesting ones in American political history. Wirt was the Anti-Mason candidate, this movement being then at its height—one of those protesting ones so characteristic in the United States. They never have succeeded, but they have often had a considerable effect on the major parties. This would be true of the Wallace Progressive candidacy in 1948; it lost, but it substantially altered Democratic policy.

Floyd represented that nullification sentiment in South Carolina which had been manifest for some time and would grow into the rabid dissent of the next decade, ending in the Civil War.

It was in this year that Delaware abandoned the choosing of electors by the legislature; this left only South Carolina still using the old method. Twenty-four states took part in this election, the same as in 1824, but the number of electors was enlarged by the reapportionment resulting from the census of 1830.

It ought also to be noted that the "two-thirds rule," which would be adopted by successive Democratic conventions until 1936, originated in

In the end, after his eight years of power, Jackson retired to his home in Tennessee, leaving Van Buren to succeed him. Even in the succession he had his way, although the enthusiasm for Van Buren was limited to a few officeholders.[8]

As he made his way toward Tennessee and the Hermitage, the retiring President was almost mobbed again and again by hero worshipers. The electorate was still his. They had wanted a leader of their own sort who would show the way to genuine popular rule. Jackson, in their name, had broken the power of the financial monopolists who were so hated by the farmers and small businessmen. One of the worst depressions-*cum*-panic in all American history would result almost at once, directly traceable, as many believe, to Jackson's hopelessly muddled policies. Van Buren had to meet this crisis as best he could. It was a very poor best, and the government would pass out of Democratic control as a result. The Jacksonians would have a shorter run than the Jeffersonians. But the mobs who cheered the old man in 1837 would probably not have supported a wiser and more disciplined policy; both he and they had to learn the hard way that economic facts are stubborn and that economic policies, to be successful, must recognize them.

For our purpose here we are interested less in the particular policies Jackson developed, or even in their success or failure, than in his use of his office to promulgate and support them. He had a program, and he used his popularity to force its acceptance. He subdued strong opposition both in and out of the Congress; he filled the government establishment with followers who would carry out his orders; he treated his Cabinet members not as counselors but as subordinates to carry out plans they were not asked to consider; he fostered and mercilessly pilloried useful enemies for the delight of the electorate; he invented political devices to extend and consolidate his power and to perpetuate his policies (such

---

this year. It came about in conjunction with a resolution regulating the number of delegates. Theretofore the states had sent an indeterminate number. It was now said that they might have the same number of votes in the convention as they had presidential electors but that nominations would be by a two-thirds majority.

[8] Every President, and particularly every strong one, who has lived to retire has considered the succession to be one of his responsibilities. In most cases he has been able to impose his choice on the party convention; and in most cases, too, he has seen his candidate elected. But experience would not seem to indicate that these choices are likely to be good ones. In no instance has an "heir" also proved to be a strong President. The cases of Van Buren, Taft, Hoover, and Truman may be cited in point. But also the successors of Jefferson can hardly be said to have been among the more successful of Presidents.

as the party convention); and he found and inspired devoted followers who would work for him, in and out of office, with the faithfulness a politician must command who is to rise to the top. His influence on the office was greater, possibly, than that of any other of its occupants, and all that influence was used for enlargement.

For whatever reason—perhaps from ignorance, perhaps from arrogant indifference—he outraged many traditions and violated many precedents; but he established the President as an open and responsible leader, not afraid to command a party, not afraid, either, of appealing directly to the electorate in order to coerce the other Branches. He was always conscious of embodying the sovereignty of the people who elected him, in a way and to a degree that no other official did. He was immune to any other influence than his perception of the people's interests; and he considered that his judgment in this matter should be supreme. To him as to no predecessor President would future strong leaders in his office look for precedent, encouragement, and guidance. The man who accepted no tradition and no precedent established ones of vital importance for those who followed him, the most important of them being that none need be accepted.

★ 14 ★

JACKSON, THE SEVENTH PRESIDENT, WAS NOT THE FIRST TO FIND HIM-
self in active conflict with the Congress. It had happened to both Washington and John Adams, somewhat to their surprise. The thornier legislators had proved able to irritate Presidents almost beyond toleration, and
it would always be more or less so. But naturally the more imperious and
intractable Executives met the most resistance—or thought they did; and
it sometimes seems almost as though the enlargement of the office is mostly
due to such conflicts. This is only seeming. Such incidents are spectacular,
but actually there has been more advancement from delegation than from
conflict, as will become apparent as we proceed. Nevertheless, the exchanges between the White House and Capitol Hill have often filled the
areas between the two with sounds of battle, and sometimes the battles
have had results of some consequence to our institutions.

Presidents have had to learn sooner or later that no one will protect
their prerogatives for them. Some have taken this discovery in one way,
some in another. Some proceed from an initial understanding of the presidential position; many more have to be taught by experience that they
face several hundred potential, sometimes active, detractors. It is an
interesting exercise to run through the list of Chief Executives and classify
them in this respect. The range is wide, from those who did not understand at first and who never really found out, to those who from the first
took the initiative without illusion and met congressional aggression head
on. Grant was the most extreme case of one who allowed himself to be
anesthetized and bound; F. D. Roosevelt, at the other extreme, had a
completely sophisticated understanding of the inherent conflict and took
immediate measures to meet it. Others range from the stubborn resistance
of Tyler to the fatal supineness of Buchanan. Truman required about a
year to awaken, but he had begun with the betraying weakness of having
been a Senator. Eisenhower dreamed away six years before he awoke to
his situation and began a lethargic defense of his budget which gradually
turned into something like leadership.

But if the conflict is to make any sense, it has to be understood how widely the theory is held that the legislature is supreme in a democracy. This is a view that comes natural to members of the Congress, especially; and when it does not, their indoctrination occurs very quickly and thoroughly. This is expected. But when the same theory is accepted and defended by Presidents—as it often has been—it seems a kind of treachery. This was Jefferson's view, and we begin to encounter it again in the post-Jackson period. One explanation for the boldness with which this doctrine was proclaimed then is that it was a reaction to the methods of the old General. His establishment of himself as a dictatorial power was violently resented.

The Whigs, who opposed Jackson and, after he was gone, succeeded in electing two Presidents—Harrison and Taylor—had been exasperated by repeated defeats. Jackson had achieved the acceptance of his theory that Presidents were the direct and special representatives of the people and had prevailed in the contest to determine whether he could appoint and control his subordinates. On every front of the contest he had won. The Whigs were the more exasperated because these ought theoretically to have been their own positions as they had been generally the Federalist ones. The traditional conservative view was that legislators, as representatives of the people, directly elected, were less to be trusted than a single Executive chosen by a college of electors. One man ought to be easier to reach and influence than many Congressmen, and especially one chosen by the elite. It was a disappointment that radical democracy should have seated itself in the White House and undertaken to enhance the Presidency for its own purposes. The resentment was chewed over and over. It was especially exasperating to have to find justifications for such a reversal as the Whigs must now undertake.

A satisfactory theoretical solution to the Whig dilemma was never found. They would go on believing one thing and practicing another; but politics is a supremely practical art, and the contradiction was usually ignored. Their Presidents were not very satisfactory. Both were elected in degrading campaigns; both died in office and were succeeded by Vice-Presidents who could not be depended on (Tyler refused to be guided and Fillmore was so weak as to be a discredit). But the debates of the period involving the presidential powers tended to center on specific issues and to avoid the general question of constitutional meanings. Webster was the outstanding orator who undertook to attack the presidential citadel. He argued against Tyler's view of the veto power, and it was he, also, who attacked the doctrine of direct representation with a show of indignant resentment at so base a perversion of the framers' intentions. Clay and John Quincy Adams (now a Representative) joined in these debates. But the result was inconclusive. The President held his ground whenever he exerted himself to do so. The resort of the Whig captains would have to be the capture and holding of the Presidency. They must find men they could trust not to push its prerogatives and who would accept counsel from the elite.

In the period from Jackson to Lincoln—from the thirties to the early sixties—there were repeated controversies about presidential powers. Sometimes they seemed to be decided one way, sometimes another. Jackson's views were more or less wholly accepted by Polk[1] and more or less by Tyler. But both Harrison and Taylor repudiated them as good Whigs should and affirmed a belief in legislative supremacy. They did bridle a bit and show some annoyance when the more aggressive Congressmen presumed to give them directions, but on the whole they behaved decorously. There were some others during this period who were weak and confused about most things, including their own responsibilities. Fillmore, who filled out Taylor's term, Pierce, and Buchanan belonged among these. But there were occasions when even they asserted themselves, and the office came to Lincoln not disastrously impaired, although it had been badly used. There were even two advances: the use of the veto for reasons of policy as well as because of doubts about constitutionality, and the development of the role of Commander in Chief during the Mexican War. Each deserves attention.

As to the veto, until Jackson's time it had, as Adams critically observed, been "exercised with great reserve".[2] He was right. In all the preceding Administrations there had been only nine vetoes. Six of these had been on constitutional grounds, and only three had been because of disagreement over the issue involved.[3] But Jackson had vetoed twelve measures, one of these being his spectacular rejection of the rechartering of the Bank. And it was he who brought to the support of the policy veto the Doctrine of Direct Representation. It was in his second inaugural that the matter was stated as he saw it; he would, he said, be reluctant to oppose his judgment to that of the Congress; but he also contended that he had an "undoubted" right to withhold his consent when measures seemed to him undesirable; it was he who represented all the people and he must protect their interests. No President after that felt that he must confine himself to constitutional objections; on the contrary, they were apt to leave these to the Court and use the veto only when they objected on policy grounds. But it was Tyler who precipitated the argument with Adams and Clay; and, curiously enough, it was James Buchanan, later to be the weakest of

[1] Who was even known as "Young Hickory."

[2] *Memoirs,* ed. by C. F. Adams, (Phila., 1874–77), VIII, 230. Entry of June 6, 1830.

[3] White, op. cit., 28–29; and E. C. Mason, *The Veto Power; Its Origin, Development and Function in the Government of the United States* (Boston, 1890), *passim.*

Presidents, who put into words for the Democrats what was to be their general position for the future.

It was Clay's contention that, since a two-thirds majority of both Houses was required to pass a law over the veto, the President's legislative power was equal to that of nine Senators and forty Representatives. This, he said, represented an actual negative control over legislation.[4] It went even further; it acted as a preventive; even the threat of veto was effective, almost as much so as its actual exercise. This was intolerable; and he proposed that the Constitution should be amended to provide that a simple majority should overcome presidential intervention. Buchanan's reply was an appeal to the Doctrine of Direct Representation. Clay's contention, he said, rested on the assumption that the Congress represented in some special way the people's will. This was simply not true. On the contrary, the President, who was directly responsible to the people, more nearly represented them than any other Branch. Besides making the point that the President was elected by all the people and not just part of them, he also contended that this was the least to be dreaded of the Executive powers: it could not result in any new law; it could actually bring about no change of any kind; it could only arrest and hinder hasty actions, and that only until the people could finally decide by voting.

The matter rested there; it still does. No one suggests any more that this presidential prerogative ought to be curtailed. The Whigs were sullen about it. They said that when they came into control the Executive would be restrained. And actually Harrison, their first President, in his turgid inaugural, did maintain that it was "preposterous to suppose that the President . . . could better understand the wants and wishes of the people than their own immediate representatives." Tyler, who succeeded to office on Harrison's death, was, however, heretical in this as in most of the Whig doctrine;[5] he vetoed two Bank measures and two tariff bills which were especially wanted by the conservatives. This made them so furious that they seriously proposed impeachment; they also proposed a constitutional amendment to restrict the veto; but nothing came of either threat.

On the other hand, although the Whigs at this time, and the Republicans later, forwent their intention of modifying the veto, they only reluctantly,

[4] He argued from the indisputable fact that when he spoke no law had ever been passed over presidential objection. Cf. White, op. cit., 31-32.

[5] Clay considered that he had earned the nomination, but the professionals decided that he could not win. From their point of view they were right to nominate Harrison and Tyler; that is to say, it was a winning ticket. But Harrison, who was "safe," did not live to embody their ideal President. Tyler, so hastily selected, disappointed them.

and never quite wholly, withdrew from their position that the Congress was the premier power. President Hoover would still be saying so in the 1920s, and so would Eisenhower in the 1950s. It was the Doctrine of Direct Representation that galled the Whigs intolerably. They were more and more certain that since this considered the President to be the people's man and thus a demagogue responsive to the ill-considered temporary demands of the irresponsible and ill-informed voting majority, it was dangerous to property and generally to traditional institutions. Later students of government might find it difficult to understand why a device so necessary to the balance of power should have been in question half a century after the beginning of operations under the Constitution, but actually it was the center of a considerable and long-continued controversy. The veto itself was not so important; it was whether it might be used against the interests of the elite that was in question. It was only now that the President was becoming the people's man, and it was therefore now that his powers were suspect for the first time. The deeper conflict will doubtless continue as long as tripartite government continues. And efforts to alter the balance of power will persist. The Twenty-second Amendment was an incident in this struggle—the first notable victory, as a matter of fact, in the long Whig-Republican campaign begun by Webster and Clay in the aftermath of the Jacksonian revolution.[6]

The other notable expansion of the presidential power in the post-Jackson period was contributed by Polk. This was the filling out of the brief phrase in the Constitution which designated the President as Commander in Chief.[7] And it was a real filling out. There had not been any considerable contribution made by Madison during the War of 1812; nearly all crucial questions remained unanswered as Polk undertook to discipline Mexico and expand the national territory. He did not solve all of them, but he did establish precedents of value to Lincoln, to McKinley, to Wilson, and to F. D. Roosevelt in the later wars they would be called on to direct.

In many ways the Mexican War was the most complicated and difficult of all American conflicts. In the first place, it was a war of convenience for a President who had in mind to use it for results far beyond the immediate

---

[6] The effect of this amendment was, by prohibiting a third term, to transfer the party chieftainship from the President to the more permanent legislative leaders, and through them to the financial and business elite who have always been the strategists, controllers, and beneficiaries of Republican policy.

[7] What the Constitution says about this (in Art. II.) is only that "The President shall be Commander in Chief of the army and navy of the United States, and of the militia of the several States, when called into the actual service of the United States . . ."

one of defeating the Mexican army. This made its preliminaries extraordinarily complex for the President, since he had to conceal his real purpose and bring about hostilities for invented reasons. Such a tour de force was not one Polk would have been thought capable of by any student of his former career, but it was brought off brilliantly. This done, organization for the conflict had to be undertaken from a beginning as unready as can possibly be imagined. There were few men, few materials, and little knowledge; Polk had to conjure them up out of a miscellany of Indian fighters, obsolete munitions, ignorant physicians, and antique transport. Before it was over many reputations would be ruined, some few enhanced, and Polk's own brilliance in strategy and management amply demonstrated. He showed, in the midst of the most distracting difficulties, what a President could do when he knew precisely what he wanted and was endlessly industrious in achieving it. He was, of course, not too scrupulous, but his maneuvering had the same justification as Jackson's —it was in the national interest, which it was for him, as President, to interpret. The ethics of this may be questionable; but the results, it must be admitted, have been uniformly successful throughout American history for all the Presidents who have been comparably single-minded. Polk was another President who showed the way for his successors.

The Whigs, the abolitionists (a growing group) and many of the northerners in his own party opposed the war and looked with the gravest suspicion on all his moves calculated to precipitate it. They were not in the least fooled by his dissembling, yet the sentiment he was able to arouse was so powerful that the opposition quickly lost its strength and dwindled to hidden hampering. In addition, the generals he had to depend on were Whigs and turned out to have ambitions of their own.[8] The scale of operations was, for the time, and with the available means for transportation and communications, immense. And, added to all the other difficulties, the field of deployment and fighting was in a treacherous climate where disease was a much more formidable opponent than the enemy. Nevertheless, in spite of everything, Polk contrived a victory and, beyond the enemy's surrender, the objectives he had set himself to gain— the acquisition of immense western territories, including California.[9]

[8] This would happen as well in some subsequent wars, although Presidents must have been warned by Polk's troubles: Lincoln with McClellan; Johnson with Grant; Wilson with Theodore Roosevelt and Wood; Truman with MacArthur—these are conspicuous later instances. Roosevelt largely escaped, although he handled MacArthur and some others with notable delicacy. He knew well enough that practically all of his top-echelon commanders were conservative Republicans.

[9] Incidentally, but almost as part of the same operation, he settled the old Oregon boundary dispute with Britain. This perennially irritating

The scope and range of Polk's activities as a President exploiting the constitutional position of Commander in Chief can be comprehended best by making a partial list of them. He determined strategy; he made up his mind what men and what supplies were required; he supervised the estimates of funds needed and saw that the Congress was pressed to supply them; he appointed all the generals and many of the other officers; he chose the method of raising the army and supplying it; and he generally directed the campaigning. Also, while the war was coming on and while it was being fought, he conducted the affairs of government with close attention to every detail, treating his Cabinet as strictly subordinate, just as Jackson had done. More than any other President except Cleveland, he insisted that he should be the managing director of all the government's business. His worst fault in administration was the insistence on following every detail of administration. Even in his time it was more than any one individual could do. In the end it so exhausted him that he died within a few months of his retirement—at the end of only one term. But his performance was a superb demonstration that the whole of government was presidential business. Later Presidents would learn, because they must, the techniques of delegation. The utmost development of these, carried even beyond democratic tolerance, would not in the end suffice. In future, however, because of Polk, there would be less doubt about the presidential scope. No matter how he contrived it, the Executive must furnish leadership and management; must invent and must somehow get done all necessary to the national destiny.

Historians of the future were apt to register surprise, much as his contemporaries had done, that Polk should so suddenly have displayed the qualities of greatness. It is evident that he was underestimated throughout his pre-presidential career. He is often spoken of as the first dark-horse presidential candidate—meaning that he was nominated by the Democrats because they could not choose between more likely but competing contenders. In this case these were Van Buren and Cass, both old political veterans, lifelong officeholders, and party managers. In this they were much like Polk, who had spent many years in the Congress as Jackson's most faithful retainer and had gone back to Tennessee to run for Governor when it was required of him. But Van Buren had been President and by all the rules entitled to a second chance, which he very much desired. And Cass was a better-known public man who had a military as well as a civilian record and had been Governor of Michigan. Polk had never in his life said or done anything spectacular. No one considered that he had a politi-

---

question might well have resulted in another British-American war. The settlement was a genuine compromise. Not the least of Polk's presidential accomplishments was the outwitting of the American fire eaters who wanted to press the national claims to a conclusion without concession.

cal existence at all apart from Jackson's. He was pale and lank; he had none of the outgoing ebullience usually possessed by successful politicians. He was, however, from the border state of Tennessee and he had the blessing of the old General, who was tired of Van Buren's pretensions.

The convention that nominated Polk started off by giving Van Buren the majority he expected; but it did not reach two thirds, and on subsequent ballots it dwindled. As Van Buren's strength faded, Cass's vote increased, until it seemed that he might accumulate the required two thirds. But by the seventh ballot it was apparent that the professionals would have to look elsewhere if they wanted to win. On the ninth ballot they contrived the nomination of Polk. The news was sent from Baltimore to Washington by the brand-new telegraph, and the story goes that Washingtonians looked at one another and asked: "Who the hell's Polk?"

★ 15 ★

IF THE CITIZENS OF WASHINGTON ASKED ABOUT THE OBSCURE DEMO-
cratic nominee of 1844 in puzzlement, they soon found out who and what
he was. In the election he defeated the experienced Whig politician,
Henry Clay—"Prince Henry"—who was at last having his chance after
many disappointments. When the victor left Tennessee to be inaugurated
he said that he intended *to be President* and, if there was a war, that he
intended *to be Commander in Chief*. He made good his intentions.

Polk, like the younger Adams, kept a diary. It lacks the Adams literary
quality, but it does enable us to follow him as he acted. There are at least
some of his decisions whose preliminaries can be seen as he saw them.
This is a boon to historians, who mostly find that Presidents are enigmas,
and especially the ones they consider to be among the most consequential.
Lincoln, Wilson, and Roosevelt, for instance, presiding over the nation's
worst ordeals, left no such record. In Polk's case they are the more wel-
come because his emergence was so surprising and his performance so
amazing. He had worked hard and made himself useful to his seniors in
the party, accepting his political duties humbly and carrying them out
faithfully. But so had others of his contemporaries. His preferment had
a large element of the accidental, but it is also true that he was ready
when the time came. While he waited and served he had prepared
himself. He was ready not only for the nomination but also for the
Presidency; he knew precisely what he wanted for the nation, and he
knew how he intended to accomplish his objectives.

As he assumed office Polk had to deal with one of those monstrous,
inevitable-seeming crises that sometimes confront nations. It was the
same one that would run on into the Civil War fifteen years later when
less decisive Presidents allowed it to get out of control. The slavery issue
was not yet so acute as it later became; there was still time for compromise. Polk's conception was that the acquisition of the vast areas
between Texas and the Pacific would provide ample room for the extension of slave territory; it was also necessary to complete the Union.

He felt that the divisive forces, rapidly becoming dangerous, would be moderated, possibly dissipated, in the grand adventure of conquering and settling a new empire. The South was growing more and more irritated as new lands in the North and West opened up and were organized. Extensions in the South would serve to placate the dissidents.[1]

For the time being Polk's vision and his success in carrying the national boundaries to the Pacific gave everyone enough to think about and do. It was a magnificent conception. But the war with Mexico was not necessary to its consummation, as could be seen afterward, and Polk's reputation as a statesman suffers as a result. To him it seemed a necessary preliminary, and a good deal of ingenuity went into bringing it about in such a way that the Mexicans would appear to be the aggressors. Only such an appearance would support the scheme for the enormous acquisitions he had in mind. Texas, of course, was the key. Whether or not annexation should be carried out had been a disputed matter for years, and Tyler, at the last moment of his Administration, had finally made up his mind. He had sent off a messenger accepting; and Polk might have recalled him, as he was urged to do. He refused, thinking the Mexicans would be stirred to conflict by the affront. When they were not, he ordered an army detachment under Taylor down to the Rio Grande, far into territory to which the nation could have only the flimsiest claim. Then he said that if the Mexicans should cross the river it would constitute an act of war. This was one of those assumptions statesmen sometimes find convenient. And the best of them succeed in convincing others that their fictions are realities. Polk's undertaking was difficult, but earnestly, and with a show of complete conviction, he worked to prepare first his Cabinet, then the Congress, and finally public opinion for the inevitable questioning of his aggression.

The Mexicans did finally react. They had been tormented by incompetent dictatorial regimes which were as unstable as they were corrupt; they were poor and oppressed as a people; but the dictators did maintain armies. There were more trained troops at the disposal of their generals than were available to Polk; and General Zachary Taylor, on the border, with an ill-supplied and disease-riddled army, might be supposed to have been in some danger of defeat. Polk was taking long chances; but only military victory could put him in position to claim California as he meant

[1] Both Florida and Texas became states in 1845. They were presently matched by Iowa and Wisconsin, the one admitted in 1846 and the other in 1848. But this uneasy parity would again become unbalanced by the admission of California in 1850, Minnesota in 1858, Oregon in 1859, and Kansas in 1861. And the South would become more and more bitter and intractable.

to do. He looked to Taylor with hope, but a hope that was half apprehension.

The Whigs did not approve. They regarded the whole scheme as an attempt to establish slavery permanently in the Southwest. Also, they were more interested in financial matters and in high tariffs than they were in expansion.[2] But, even if they objected, they were afraid to refuse funds for the army in the field. What they did do was to leave most of the fighting to those who were interested. When Polk asked for volunteers, most of them came from the South and West; the Northeast lagged.[3]

Once at war, Polk was strict in allowing his general strategy to dominate his dispositions; he sent expeditions not only into northern Mexico but into California as well. There was resistance in the South and a famous victory for General Taylor (which made him President), but in the West there was very little fighting. Seldom has so rich a conquest been made so cheaply and by so few. The luster acquired by the soldiers in the field tended to obscure the leadership furnished by Polk and the magnificence of his strategic conception. He himself was inclined to work hard, say little, and allow events to occur as he wanted them to occur. He had an obstreperous opposition to placate, and dissembling was indicated. But one result of this was that the Whigs made the most of his mistakes and belittled his accomplishments. When there were victories, they were won by Whig generals; when there were deficiencies, it was Polk who was blamed. His task was harder because of his chosen method, but also because he suffered from a tormenting suspicion of those around him which seemed to become progressively worse. He worked unremittingly; he took all the responsibility; he was a hard, lonely, and humorless Commander in Chief. But he clung to his central position and would allow none to share it.

In some of these matters his *Diary* is amazingly revealing.[4] Consider, for instance, the entry of May 11, 1846. This passage succeeds others telling how he maneuvered to provoke the Mexicans, how he seemed to have failed and had prepared a message to the Congress making a wholly

[2] Not by any means the loudest among them, but as forthright as any in opposition to war and annexation, was Representative Abraham Lincoln of Illinois. Not even he, however, dared to vote against appropriations asked by Polk for the war.

[3] Asking for short-term volunteers was one of Polk's few mistakes. There was a delay of months, while an attack on Mexico City impended, because enlistments ran out and soldiers simply went home.

[4] The quoted passages are from the Nevins edition (New York, 1929), 86 ff.

specious claim of wrongs, ones so imaginary that he was fairly certain they could not carry conviction. Then the Mexicans had been suddenly accommodating. They had crossed the Rio Grande, and he could claim with a better show of conviction that there had been an invasion. Even this was thin, and he could not be sure of its acceptance. He was in torment for fear all his plans would fail because of congressional skepticism.

> I refused to see company generally this morning. I carefully revised my message on the Mexican question . . . I addressed notes to Senators Cass and Benton requesting them to call. General Cass called first . . . he highly approved. Col. Benton called before Cass left . . . I found he did not approve . . . He was willing to vote men and money for defense of our territory, but was not prepared to wage aggressive war on Mexico. He disapproved the marching of the army from Corpus Christi to the left bank of the Del Norte, but said he had never said so in public. I had a full conversation with him, and he left without satisfying me that I could rely upon his support. . . . I inferred that he did not think the territory of the United States extended west of the Nueces river.

There is no doubt that everyone saw through Polk's subterfuges. Benton was a leading Democrat, and if he did not accept the President's explanation, others certainly would not. A few Democrats joining the skeptical Whigs would ruin everything. He went on:

> At twelve o'clock I sent my message to Congress. It was a day of great anxiety with me. Between five and six P.M. Mr. Slidell, United States Minister to Mexico, called and informed me that the House had passed a bill carrying out all the recommendations of the message by a vote of 173 to 14, and that the Senate had adjourned after a debate without coming to any decision . . .

The compliance of the House did little to relieve his fears. It was the Senators who were likely to prove recalcitrant. Calhoun was objecting violently to the preamble of the proposed declaration fastening blame on Mexico. And Calhoun in the end could only be persuaded to abstain; he would not approve, fearing, apparently, that war would strengthen the President and weaken the Senate and the states. Then too, he had all and more of the usual senatorial jealousy. Benton came again to the White House, and Polk called in Marcy and Buchanan, Secretaries of War and State, and there was further argument. Benton demanded to know the extent of the commitment. Polk could not tell him, but said that

> if the war was recognized by Congress . . . with a large force on land and sea I thought it could be speedily terminated. Col. Benton

said that the House had passed a bill declaring war in two hours, and that one and a half hours of that time had been occupied in reading the documents which accompanied my message, and that in his opinion in the nineteenth century war should not be declared without full discussion and much more consideration than had been given to it in the House. . . .

Benton stayed and worried the subject for hours. He was not impressed by Buchanan's reiteration of the thesis that a state of war existed because the national territory had been invaded and that the Congress could not very well refuse to recognize the fact. The three—the President and his Secretaries—agreed after the Senator left that he would be in opposition. The President noted:

> The part taken by Mr. Calhoun in the Senate today satisfies me that he too will oppose the bill passed by the House today if he thinks he can do so safely with reference to public opinion. The Whigs in the Senate will oppose it on party grounds probably, if they can get Mr. Calhoun, Mr. Benton, and two or three other Senators professing to belong to the Democratic party to join them, so as to make a majority against the bill. . . . I am fully satisfied that all that can save the bill in the Senate is the fear of the people by the few Democratic Senators who wish it defeated.

But the President was too apprehensive—or else the Democratic Senators were very much afraid of public opinion—because on the next day the *Diary* noted the passage of the bill by 42 votes to 2. It was, he said, a great triumph for the Administration. On the next day after that he began to carry out his plans. General Scott was called in to present his ideas about the army. Polk found them incomplete and told him to come back later in the day with a more formal report. At the same time he felt that he must appoint the General to the command of the army to be raised, although he did not consider him "in all respects suitable"—which was a remarkable understatement.

The *Diary* entry for that day, which must have been written late at night after everyone had left, the proclamation made, the preliminaries over, and all set in motion, tells of a conversation with Buchanan. It reveals how little, until then, the Secretary of State had understood what vast affairs were in motion. In it the reader now can see much of what Polk had had in mind all along:

> Mr. Buchanan read the draft of a despatch which he had prepared to our Ministers at London, Paris and other foreign courts, announcing the declaration of war against Mexico, with a statement of the causes and objects of the war, with a view that they should com-

municate its subśtance to the respective governments to which they
are accredited. Among other things Mr. Buchanan had stated that
our objective was not to dismember Mexico or to make conquests,
and that the Del Norte was the boundary to which we claimed; or
rather that in going to war we did not do so with a view to acquire
either California or New Mexico or any other portion of the Mexican
territory. I told Mr. Buchanan that I thought such a declaration to
foreign governments unnecessary and improper; that the causes of
the war as set forth in my message to Congress and the accompanying documents were altogether satisfactory. I told him that though
we had not gone to war for conquest, yet it was clear that in making
peace we would if practicable obtain California and such other
portions of the Mexican territory as would be sufficient to indemnify
our claims on Mexico and to defray the expense of the war which
that power by her long continued wrongs and injuries had forced
us to wage. . . .

Buchanan was inclined to argue. If it was not said to the other powers
that we did not intend to acquire California, it was likely that both France
and England would join with Mexico. It would be impossible to settle
the Oregon question, which was still a cause of irritation, and war with
England, at least, would be likely. Others of the Cabinet joined the argument, mostly against Buchanan. Polk became as heated as his Secretary
of State. He told him that

> before I would make the pledge which he proposed, I would meet
> the war which either England or France or all the Powers of
> Christendom might wage, and that I would stand and fight until
> the last man among us fell in the conflict. . . .

There was a good deal more of this. Polk's harangue went on for some
time; Buchanan in return "was very earnest in expressing his views and
enforcing them." But Polk's vehemence was proportional to the doubtful-
ness of his case; and he was, after all, the President. The difference ended,
according to Polk, when he stepped to his table and

> wrote a paragraph to be substituted for all that part of Mr. Bu-
> chanan's proposed despatch which spoke of dismembering Mexico,
> of acquiring California, or of the Del Norte as the ultimate boundary
> beyond which we would not claim or desire to go. I strongly
> expressed to Mr. Buchanan that these paragraphs in his despatch
> must be struck out. Mr. Buchanan made no reply, but before he
> left took up his own draft and the paragraphs which I had written
> and took them away with him. . . .

The President had come to believe, as perhaps statesmen must, that his inventions were facts and that his cause was just. The last entry in the *Diary* for that day said that he was

much astonished at the views expressed by Mr. Buchanan on the subject . . . The Cabinet adjourned about eleven o'clock P.M. and I retired to rest much exhausted after a day of incessant application, anxiety, and labour.

This last cannot have been an exaggeration. The President was not only formulating the strategy of conquest but was accepting the duty of convincing everyone that his specious arguments were sterling truth. Also, he was setting the machinery in operation which would bring Mexico to the conference table willing to cede the territories he wanted. As Mexico was being defeated, he would also, by making a reasonable concession to the British, set the nation's northern boundaries. With all this done, he would leave office—he had made a one-term pledge as was becoming fashionable —having presented the nation with a gift of inestimable value in the broad lands and the rich resources of the Southwest.

It was an imperial conception, and Polk was the man to transform it into reality. As the *Diary* goes on in the same meticulous and humorless way through the years, the picture unfolds as seen by a President's eyes, and it continues until the story is told of his return to Tennessee, ill and worn, by way of the sea, the Gulf, and the Mississippi. He must have remembered Old Hickory coming home to the same state twelve years earlier. The reception he got was cordial enough, but it had none of the enthusiasm which had marked Jackson's progress to the Hermitage. Polk was genuinely sick and would live only a few weeks. That he was near his end no one realized, however, and he himself was more worried about his successor than about his health. He wrote, after accompanying General Taylor, the new President, to the Capitol and returning to his hotel:

On going up to the Capitol California was alluded to . . . Something was said which drew from General Taylor the expression of views and opinions which greatly surprised me. They were to the effect that California and Oregon were too distant to become members of the Union, and that it would be better for them to become an independent government . . . These are alarming opinions to be entertained by the President of the United States . . . General Taylor is, I have no doubt, a well-meaning old man. He is, however, uneducated, exceedingly ignorant of public affairs, and, I should judge, of very ordinary capacity. He will be in the hands of others. . . .

Polk did not say that he ought not to have renounced a second term or ought to have given more thought and effort to the election of a suitable successor. But it was with no easy mind that he said good-by to Marcy and Buchanan on the pier at Baltimore as he embarked for the long journey home. In this, he was like most Presidents who live to retire or be replaced.

★ 16 ★

REFERENCES HAVE BEEN MADE, AND OTHERS WILL BE MADE, TO THE
Doctrines or Rules of Restraint and of Necessity. The relation between
the tripartite Branches somewhat resembles the strained tension of
individuals held in check and prevented from acting as urgent impulses
command. It must be supposed, however, that, as in individuals again,
there are other and countering impulses. These will counsel caution, warn
that giving way to immediate urges may bring danger. It is the nature of
the Branches to press against restraints; but this expansionism is controlled by a discretion which perhaps corresponds with an individual's
instinct of self-preservation. The cold war in government is not always
active, but it often is, and it is always potential.

And it is never settled. The most that can be said is that repeated engagements have established fairly firm ground for each Branch on its
constitutional base. It is in these citadels that aggressions are planned
and it is from them that forays are made. The occupants are always
changing; and so, somewhat less often, are their captains. Some of these
are more belligerent than others, and some have more discretion than
others. So first one, then another, Branch gains some territory, old and
long in dispute or new and just opened to occupation. But the fortunes
of the conflict are not exclusively determined by the readiness and
competence of the participants. The climate of the day and the terrain of
the field may favor one or the other. Gains sometimes come with surprising ease, some are even conceded without struggle, but others come hard
and may be fought for throughout years without appreciable result.

In the years before the Civil War the Presidency fared sometimes well
and sometimes ill—well in the Administrations of Washington, Jackson,
and Polk; and ill, for the most part, in those of others. This was, in the cases
of the Adamses, because of frustrations—the situation was unfavorable. In
the case of Jefferson it was because of commitment to congressional
supremacy and deliberate withdrawal.

The Rule of Necessity is seldom invoked except in grave emergency
when the state of tension between the Branches is momentarily in abey-

ance. National danger has that effect. The Rule applies only to one Branch —the Executive—and is, to the extent that it has formal recognition, supposed to be strictly temporary in its operation. This has been generally true. Powers conferred or appropriated in crisis have been given up when the crisis has eased. But it is incontestable that the scope of the Rule has widened with time and with the increasing urgency of the crises the democracy has met. It is difficult to say that it has limits at all, or, if it has, what they are.

Frequently what has been done by invoking the Rule has been ratified by at least one other Branch, thus re-establishing for the system of government its former character—its state of tension, its perennial suspicion, its unwilling co-operativeness. But because it is so generally recognized that the Rule does lie latent in American institutions and is, indeed, necessary to supplement the inherently illogical character of their arrangement, it is necessary to recognize that it has its justifying reference in the nature of the Presidency as the premier people's office. If the President were not the surrogate of the electorate, one exercise of such powers as have repeatedly been used in emergency would shatter the whole structure. As it is, this presidential Rule no more interferes with the normal functioning of the system than does the relief valve of a steam boiler. It provides for an emergency and ceases to function when the emergency passes.

Only the Presidents who have been most deeply aware of the inner nature of the institution they embodied have understood what was required of them and have acted in accordance, thus preventing disaster. Buchanan did not thus understand, and the resulting explosion nearly ended the life of the Republic. This one failure—the most notable, but not the only one in presidential history—points to a question we shall have to examine again and again as we proceed. What can be done to make it more certain that when the nation requires of the Presidency that it act in accordance with the latent Rule there shall be some assurance of adequate response? There will be other times—as in the past—when weakness and hesitation may be fatal to the nation.

It may seem, as we go on, because the states of emergency in which the Rule of Necessity has been governing are so dramatic and have given such scope for leadership, that these are the periods when the Presidency has been most likely to be enlarged. But that, of course, is not so. The general expansion of the President's management over the varied functions assigned more and more to government by a developing society is the field of enlargement which is more permanent and more basic. We have to begin to note here, with Polk, how definite the expansion has become and how it has changed the Presidency. It will be a change which will go on, not steadily, but inexorably.

And this is not all. The leadership function of the Presidency will, as we shall see, have a remarkable enlargement. We shall come finally, in

Wilson's time, to recognize a Rule of Responsibility. And this will be because, beginning about then, the President will have to assume the direction of economic and social affairs, grown complex and dangerous, lest they threaten the welfare of the electorate. No more will be said about this now, but it ought to be kept in mind. It is not only in emergencies of war that the office we are studying has been required to assume untraditional powers. They have come to it also in the less spectacular exigencies of peaceable progress. And these have usually become permanent.

So far in this study we have not said very much about administration; we must now begin to give it attention. It is not at all exaggerated to award Polk credit for being the first of the Presidents to understand the principles of public business. And it is therefore an appropriate place to begin speaking seriously of the government's household.[1]

We noted that when Polk was leaving Tennessee to become President he said that he would be a real Chief Executive. The *Diary* shows what this meant in daily practice. To select one day among many others, and to read his notes, is to be given a view of a competent nineteenth-century President at work, one who was complete master of his situation, however worn and driven he might be. The month of September is as appropriate as any, because he was so alone at his job in Washington; most of the Cabinet were summering in more agreeable climates. And 1848 is an appropriate year, because, since it was late in his term,[2] his habits of work had settled. On this particular day he made some remarks about his method; it was Saturday, the twenty-third:

---

[1] Until the time of Polk, as White's administrative history has shown (*The Federalists* and *The Jacksonians*), the bureaucracy was not conspicuous, and the ordinary citizen was hardly conscious that there was a Federal government. It had a very restricted range except in war. Even taxation was not direct, so that Tocqueville, for instance, writing in the thirties, could say that "the administrative power in the United States presents nothing either central or hierarchical in its Constitution," and again that "nothing is more striking to a European traveller . . . than the absence of what we term the Government, or the Administration." The United States was still a loose democracy, its individuals going their own way, independent and willful. Only very gradually would the demands of a more integrated society make themselves felt so that there must be more discipline and order. The Executive establishment would grow in response to this need; and the need for the President to assume Executive responsibilities would grow accordingly. (The quotations from Tocqueville will be found on pp. 70 and 88 of Vol. II, *Democracy in America*, 2 vols. Reeve translation, Cambridge, Mass., 1863.)

[2] He was to have only one. He had renounced a second before the beginning of his first.

The Hon. James Buchanan, Secretary of State, who has been absent from Washington on an excursion to the North for the last three weeks, returned this afternoon, and about nine o'clock P.M. called to see me. Mr. Walker and Mr. Marcy are still absent, but I hope will return next week. I have not had my full Cabinet together in Council since the adjournment of Congress on the 14th of August last. I have conducted the government without their aid. Indeed, I have become so familiar with the duties and workings of the government, not only upon general principles, but in most of its minute details, that I find but little difficulty in doing this. I have made myself acquainted with the duties of the subordinate officers, and have probably given more attention to details than any of my predecessors. It is only occasionally that a great measure or a new question arises, upon which I desire the aid and advice of my Cabinet. At each meeting of the Cabinet I learn from each member what is being done in his particular Department, and especially if any question of doubt or difficulty has arisen. I have never called for any written opinions . . . preferring to take their opinions, after discussion, in Cabinet and in the presence of each other. In this way harmony of opinion is more likely to exist.

If this day resembled others, as probably it did, stacks of commissions had been signed, many letters had been written, dozens of people who crowded the corridor outside his second-floor room had been seen, and directions for operations in several different departments had been given. There was one secretary for all the multifarious duties of making appointments, arranging interviews, and communicating with subordinates. There were from time to time several clerks borrowed from the departments for copying letters, inscribing commissions, and making records; but an immense amount of detail had to be carried in the President's own mind, and he had to make decisions about unimportant matters of which he might easily have been relieved. It happened that Polk had an avidity for detail that gave him no rest. It had been that way during the war, and it was still that way in 1848, although the nominations for his successor had been made and he knew that he would be retiring from office next March. Either Taylor, Cass, or Van Buren would succeed him; and none of these was likely to follow his pattern of work. Still he kept at it.

It would be 1857, in Buchanan's term, before Presidents had the assistance of a staff. Until then they would be dependent on members of their family or assigned clerks from the Departments; and borrowing was a matter that members of the Congress were apt to view with suspicion as circumventing their power of the purse. In spite of his handicaps, and in spite, too, of having crises to surmount which might well have taken all his attention, Polk undertook to make a reality of the principle sought to be established by Washington, that the Executive Branch of the government was one whole to be managed by the President alone. Until this time—and there were reversions afterward—there had been much ambiguity about this. When Departments were established, the Congress was apt to go into detail about organization; and when appropriations were made, the disbursing officers were apt to be named. It was doubtful what control the President could actually exercise, and there was a good deal of variation in practice.

Even Washington, with his immense prestige, had not settled these matters; and the Adamses, who were intelligent administrators if they had been free, were so engaged with survival that they made only contributions of intention. The Jeffersonians were indifferent, being violently opposed to centralized direction and to Washington's unity. Jackson would have been able to make some gains if he had not been indifferent as well as temperamentally unfitted for administration. It was Polk who inherited the hitherto anomalous working procedure and brought it into order.

For the first time Cabinet members were not allowed to communicate with the Congress officially without the President's visa; and for the first time the Department estimates went through the President's hands on their way to the Appropriations Committees. We have a picture of Cabinet members being made to sit before the presidential desk and read aloud their proposed reports. Similarly, they were required to gather together the estimated expenditures of their bureaus and submit them for the President's approval. It was this—and the control of communications and of the budget, even in crude and poorly co-ordinated form—that showed the way to later planned programs for the future and gave reality to Washington's principles.

Washington himself had been an excellent administrator. In the army he had learned the value of staff work, something few other Presidents have ever done or have been temperamentally inclined to do. He was methodical about gathering information, taking counsel, and making firm decisions. And he then followed through carefully. He had a sense of possession concerning the nation which can be guessed to have been the same as that he felt for his estates at Mount Vernon. This care for the country reached out to every sort of improvement and was invulnerable to compromise in favor of predatory interests. No other President down to Polk shared these abilities and interests. Jefferson was a builder; he created at Monticello and at the University of Virginia unique institutions showing a high order of ingenuity, but they were single and limited; he seems to have felt that the nation was made up of men like himself, each of whom would, if he were able, make similar improvements. This was a very different matter from being personally responsible for the condition of all the broad land as later Presidents would have to be. Polk might well have been one of the later ones. He had the ability to bring a vision into focus and to invent the means for its realization. And he could follow through, day by day, as he maneuvered into being the necessary laws, agencies, and regulations, as he appointed and supervised the personnel, and as he generally watched over the progress of operations. But it was not yet time for the Rule of Responsibility to become effective. The role of government was still limited, and the role of the President in that government still restricted. Also, until Cleveland, no President would be nearly so capable an administrator as Polk; none could have assumed the duties of a later time. And the Presidency, as a result of this and of other handicaps, was lagging in its development.

There were several reasons for this, quite apart from the unwillingness of the Congress to implement any expansion of the Executive. But it must be said that Presidents did not press very hard for administrative aids and would hardly have known what to do with larger appropriations if the Congress had been willing to grant them. This was not so likely to be the case if they came to the higher office from state Governorships—as Polk did—where they had had to direct varied operations; but they were usually much more gifted in the political than the administrative arts. These talents are very far apart, and it is unusual to find both possessed by one individual. We are here touching one of the problems of democracy which was not overwhelmingly important to the shapers of early American institutions but which, as the country developed, began to show itself as a grave defect, without any attractive suggestion being made for its correction. To state it baldly, the talents necessary for acquiring the Presidency have seldom been associated with those necessary to perform its duties successfully; or, to put it more precisely, the talents necessary to perform *all* its duties successfully. The logical escape from this democratic dilemma is such a contrivance as will multiply presidential talents. But in Polk's time political observers had not yet been made aware of the nature of the developing problem. Polk's experience offered his successors some lessons they may well have studied with profit. These would begin with his perception from the very start that he might take counsel but that he would never be excused from making up his own mind and that he must direct and supervise administrative operations industriously. Successors could have learned some negative lessons, too, one being that, unless administrative skills are studied and the techniques of delegation used, the job will be a killing one; it was for Polk, and it would be for others.

Polk was tormented with suspicions, but there were reasons. If any employees—or any officials—were capable and conscientious, it was not because these had been requisites for their appointment. What counted was influence; and the rapacity of job seekers was scandalous. They had no mercy on the President, who did most of the actual appointing, and he had only the feeblest defenses against their importunities. They swarmed into his unprotected office—which was also his house—just as they had when Adams had complained of their greediness, and made their demands in person, frequently accompanied by a political sponsor to whom the President must at least be polite. Repeatedly he confided his disgust to his *Diary*—and it must be recalled that Polk was a professional politician who would have a certain tolerance. On October 19, 1848, he wrote:

> I transacted the business on my table and at two o'clock opened my office . . . Quite a number of persons came in, several of whom were begging for money and others, who from their appearance were too lazy to work, were asking for office. The office of the President is generally esteemed a very high and dignified position, but I really think the public would not so regard it if they could look in occasionally and observe the kind of people by whom I am annoyed. I cannot seclude myself but must be accessible to my fellow citizens, and this gives an opportunity to all classes and descriptions of people who obtrude themselves upon me about matters in which the public has not the slightest interest. There is no class of the population by whom I am annoyed so much, or for whom I entertain a more sovereign contempt, than for the professed office-seekers who have besieged me ever since I have been in the Presidential office.[3]

But these "loafers" were the ones who, in one way or another, got the jobs; and they conducted the affairs of government. The President cannot have had any more respect for them in office than he had had when they were importuning him for appointment. This is certainly one reason why the more conscientious Presidents have brought themselves to the edge of exhaustion day after day. They have had confidence only in what they themselves have done or what they have carefully overseen. Polk mentioned his concern (on January 7, 1847). The officeholders, he said, held the balance of power between the two parties. They could destroy the popularity of any President, no matter how good he was. And this, of course, accounts for the continuing ordeal, through so many Administrations, of Presidents who must suffer the indignities they all resented.

And very often they could have little more confidence in the abilities, the industry, or the disinterestedness of the heads of their Departments.

---

[3] Earlier in the same year he had noted that he no longer had offices to give away and that this added to his harassment. And in an entry for June 21, 1847, he had said: "When I opened my office at one o'clock it was filled with them . . . The herd of loafers who thus annoyed me seemed to act as though they had concluded that the government was about to come to an end . . ."

Polk did not trust Walker (Treasury), Mason (Navy), Marcy (War), or Buchanan (State). Very often he concealed his plans from all or some of them, and although, as we have seen, he spoke sometimes of his Cabinet as a "council," his consultations with them were used mostly as part of an apparatus for getting done what he had already determined on—as we have seen him instructing Buchanan. It was not an accident that his Secretary of State was a prominent Pennsylvania politician in charge of a powerful machine, or that Marcy had a similar standing in New York. Neither was a competent administrator, and both were inordinately ambitious. They could not be trusted, but they could be used if a President took the trouble.

During the whole of the Jacksonian period there was a lack of rapport between Presidents and Cabinets which was totally at variance with the theoretical relationship. It made administration difficult and the President's life much more arduous than it might have been. But this lack of harmony was the direct result of the party system, and no President found any way to establish himself as Chief Legislator and further his policies except to load his Cabinet with approved party men from various regions and from various factions. Very few owed any loyalty to the President. The most that could be said was that they belonged to the same party and therefore had the same general aims. But often this was a superficial similarity apt to vanish under strain.

This problem would remain an unsettled one, varying in its seriousness. Tyler's whole Whig Cabinet resigned at once (except Webster, who stayed awhile to finish a negotiation); in all, Tyler had three Secretaries of State, three Secretaries of the Treasury, four Secretaries of War, four Secretaries of the Navy, and two Attorneys General. Polk held his Cabinet nearly intact for his four years, largely because of his combined firmness and leadership; but in the four Taylor-Fillmore years there were three Secretaries of State, two of the Treasury, three of War, three of the Navy, four of the Interior, and so on. Such dissension and temporary occupancy of Secretaryships was bound to affect administration, especially as the Secretaries were never chosen for this sort of competence. Since the Departments tended to be filled with office seekers of doubtful ability, and since they were headed by indifferent Secretaries, it is remarkable that any public business was satisfactorily carried on. The burden on the man who occupied the White House was enormously heavier because he could not count on competent assistance; it is no wonder that a conscientious individual should have tried to do everything himself and become exhausted in consequence.

It was obvious for many years before any reforms were undertaken that the position of the President as Chief Executive was an impossible one. Eventually the office-seeker problem would move toward solution, although in a democracy liable to fairly drastic policy changes from one term to another, it remained inevitable, even desirable, that replacements should take place in the upper echelons of the service. These would be very extensive as the expansion of governmental services took place. But it remained true that Cabinet members were very largely chosen for party reasons. These might be complex because parties were coalitions and had very different ideas in different regions and among different classes. Even if they had been so disposed, Presidents were not able to think first of their responsibilities as Chief Executive in naming their Secretaries. Their other responsibilities—Party Leader, Chief Legislator, Policy Maker, Constitutional Representative of the people—came first. Other Presidents after Polk would have to go through times of trial with incompetents in the most sensitive Cabinet posts, and sometimes these appointees would exhibit the disloyalty natural to a rival, and this would make matters worse.

If the Presidency had not been enlarged by certain of its incumbents, this would not have been true. They might have sunk back to ministerial functions, as Whig theory would have had them do, and given way to congressional supremacy. They might have taken a restrictive view of the veto and not have used it except for reasons of constitutionality; they might not have developed that response to national necessity which actuated even Jefferson; and they might have handed the conduct of war over to the military and not have taken so seriously their duties as Commander in Chief. But no President after successive enlargements of the office had taken place could ever quite go back to older conceptions. Even if he had made commitments to the Federalist-Whig-Republican theory, he soon found in office that compliance, at least literal compliance, was impractical. And those who came nearest to honoring it in practice turned out to be the least respected Presidents—Grant, Taft, Harding, Coolidge, and Hoover, for instance.

Just to name those who have come closest to following the "least government" rule shows how it can affect the reputations even of otherwise competent Presidents. Hoover was a distinguished administrator; but he did not believe in doing enough, and disaster and discredit overtook him. The laissez faire of Harding and Coolidge prepared the way for the debacle which overtook Hoover. Similarly, Grant was a notable general but a miserable President because he accepted direction from businessmen and legislators who had elevated him for their own purposes; and those who discuss him now hardly know whether to venerate him for his military victories or to castigate him for the weakness and corruption of his Presidency. Eisenhower was almost as bad, except that, in his case, his constitutional duty to take the lead in foreign policy was accepted, and foreign policy was the most serious issue of his administration. This tended to cover the deficiencies of his domestic performance.

★ 17 ★

WHEN THE FRAMERS OF THE CONSTITUTION, DRAWING AUTHORITY
from Locke and Montesquieu,[1] decided on a modified counterchecking
scheme of separated powers, the Branch least favored by their attention
was the Judicial. In view of this, it is amazing to see what has been attempted and accomplished by the generations of Justices. In spite of scant
justification in the document itself, the Supreme Court has set itself up
as the arbiter of government, discriminating between what is and what
is not allowable to the other independent Branches; it has seen its assumptions of authority grow more respected with the passage of time,
and it has come finally to rebuking both President and Congress and sometimes being allowed the privilege. This, of course, is because—and purely
because—of its monumental prestige with the public, fostered by the legal
profession and honored by a Congress made up largely of lawyers.

Judicial supremacy is not a principle that can be found in the Constitution; but so clever have the Justices been in fostering a reputation for
detachment and wisdom that they have been able to create a mythical
Constitution which they customarily use as a standard of reference.

The course of events leading to this position of oversight is not obscure.
The phases of intense conflict among the Branches can be distinguished

[1] Locke was an important intellectual influence in eighteenth-century
America; but Montesquieu's Esprit des Lois is very generally credited
with the central structural idea of the Constitution. For instance, Woodrow
Wilson, in his Constitutional Government (New York, 1911), 55–56, said:
"The makers of our Federal Constitution followed the scheme as they
found it expounded in Montesquieu, followed it with genuine scientific
enthusiasm. The admirable expositions of The Federalist read like thoughtful applications of Montesquieu to the political needs and circumstances
of America. They are full of the theory of checks and balances . . ." Cf.
also Montesquieu in America, 1760–1801, by P. M. Spurlin (Baton
Rouge, 1940). But see also the convenient Political Ideas of the American
Revolution by R. G. Adams, 3rd, ed., (New York, 1958).

in retrospect, and the emergence of the Court as arbiter has occurred in well-known incidents; it has retreated on occasion from its advanced forward positions with undignified precipitation—as in 1937 when it reversed itself on social legislation to avoid drastic reorganization; on other occasions, especially when Justices with strong convictions—such as Marshall, Taney, and Brandeis—have prevailed, it has boldly seized the initiative and invaded the field of social policy. But its posture of dignity and its air of aloofness have so impressed the public generally that it can call on immense reserves of prestige in its worst crises. It even vies with the President for support when the ground of its appeal seems secure. True, it has several times been mutilated and has oftener been threatened; but it has recovered from each attack and has attained a position as participant in the making of laws and their administration that would not have been imagined to be possible by anyone in the beginning.

The Court's expansion has to an extent been at the expense of both other Branches; but mostly, as is true of the Presidency, it has been due to the sheer growth of society and to the more important place in society of government. Both the Executive and the Congress have at times, as we shall see, felt themselves reduced to impotence when they confronted certain momentous issues of modern life and were unable even to understand the problems involved. When this has happened the Court has had no difficulty in establishing itself as the determiner of standards and so, although usually by indirection, the maker of policy.

In his preface to *The Struggle for Judicial Supremacy*[2] Robert H. Jackson, later to be a Justice himself, marveled at what had happened:

> As created the Supreme Court seemed too anaemic to endure a long contest for power. It has no function except to decide "cases" and "controversies," and its very jurisdiction to do that was left largely to the control of Congress. It has no force to execute its own commands, its judgments being handed over to the Executive for enforcement. Its Justices derive their offices from the favor of the other two Branches by appointment and confirmation, and hold them subject to an undefined, unlimited, and unreviewable Congressional power of impeachment. They depend annually for the payment of their salaries and the housing and staffing of their Court upon appropriations by Congress. Certainly so dependent an institution would excite no fears.

Nevertheless, as he went on to say, in spite of an apparently hopeless vulnerability, the Justices have repeatedly overruled and checked both of the other Branches. The Court

---

[2] (New York, 1941.) The quotations are from pp. vii–x.

has been in angry collision with the most dynamic and popular Presidents in our history. Jefferson retaliated with impeachment; Jackson denied its authority; Lincoln disobeyed a writ of the Chief Justice; Theodore Roosevelt proposed recall of judicial decisions; Wilson tried to liberalize its membership; and Franklin D. Roosevelt proposed to "reorganize" it.

Yet it not only survived, but, armed only with "the moral force of its judgments," attained a virtual monopoly as the source of Constitutional dogma. This is surprising enough, but surprise turns to amazement when

> we reflect that time has proved that its judgment was wrong on the most outstanding issues upon which it has chosen to challenge the popular Branches. Its judgment in the Dred Scott case was overruled by war. Its judgment that the currency that preserved the Union could not be made legal tender was overruled by Grant's selection of an additional Justice. Its judgment invalidating the income tax was overruled by the sixteenth amendment. Its judgments repressing labor and social legislation are now abandoned. Many of its judgments against New Deal legislation are rectified by confession of error. In no major conflict with the representative Branches on any question of social or economic policy has time vindicated the Court.
>
> Yet, by 1933, *by the efficacy of its words,* the Court had not only established its ascendancy over the entire government as a source of constitutional doctrine, but it had also taken control of a large and rapidly expanding sphere of policy. It sat as an almost continuous constitutional convention which, without submitting its proposals to any ratification or rejection, could amend the basic law. And it had used that supremacy to cripple other departments of government and to disable the nation from adopting social or economic policies which were deemed inconsistent with the Justices' philosophy of rights[3]

The singularly spare phrases of the Constitution referred to by Jackson were those in Article III: "The judicial power shall extend to all Cases . . . arising under this Constitution," and those in Article VI: "This Constitution, and the laws of the United States which shall be made in pursuance thereof . . . shall be the supreme law of the land . . ."

---

[3] The italics were not in the original text. It may be recalled that Jackson, as an experienced government attorney as well as a Justice, was writing from a background of frustration. He had been Solicitor General and Attorney General during the preparation and trial of cases the Court had used to defeat New Deal intentions.

Lawyers who write about the Constitution are apt to be disappointed with this skimpiness and for what seems to them the incredible neglect of the subject during the Convention. They are inclined to feel that the omission was because of a general contemporary understanding that the judiciary was to interpret the law. The Constitution was law; there was no need to be explicit. For this they have some references to adduce. One is that laws were "revised" in colonial practice by the Privy Council in London; another is that there were a few cases in the states during the decade before the Convention in which laws had been invalidated by the courts for being unconstitutional. This practice, it is said, was well known to the lawyer delegates. But there is also the considerable discussion of a Council of Revision which bears on this issue. This idea was finally abandoned in favor of Executive veto; and one reason for its abandonment, it is argued, may have been that the courts were understood to have the power of review.

But however they arrive at it, the consensus seems to be that review was intended to be part of the governmental apparatus. This rather forced conclusion is defended both by those who regard the framers as practical men setting up a system favorable to their interests and by those who regard the Constitution as deriving from a set of fundamental principles. One scholar usually identified with the theory of economic determination is C. A. Beard,[4] who, from his study of background and debates, reached the conclusion that of the twenty-five delegates who could be said to be dominant in the Convention, seventeen were known to have declared, directly or indirectly, for judicial control. There were only five who were opposed. This accorded with the Beard thesis that the men of property who made up the meeting saw in the courts a most necessary further check to the democratic vagaries of the Legislative Branch. It will be recalled that the more convinced liberals—and the radicals—of the time did not participate in the discussions. Patrick Henry "smelled a rat," Samuel Adams was not chosen to represent Massachusetts, and even Jefferson was not present. The conservatives had things pretty much their own way. For such a group, the argument runs, it was not necessary to spell out the utility of Court interpretation; it would be understood.

Beard has had a lasting influence; even those who do not agree admit that economic influences were present. They point out, however, that the Constitution was not shaped in disregard of theory and experience. A framework had to be found; principles and precedents had to be considered. It was, they say, out of the experiences of the Revolution that the document really emerged; it was, indeed, the very embodiment of the revolutionary idea that there is law higher than any made by a legislature.

[4] *The Supreme Court and the Constitution* (New York, 1912), and *Economic Interpretation of the Constitution* (New York, 1913).

It is to be found in nature and in the inalienable rights of man. These, no legislature may violate, and when it attempts to do so it must be reversed. One historian of the Constitution was particularly eloquent about this:

> The doctrine of . . . "judicial review" is the last word, logically and historically speaking, in the attempt of a free people to establish and maintain a non-autocratic government. It is the culmination of the essentials of Revolutionary thinking.
>
> Over and over again in the Revolutionary argument we find assertion that the Parliament was bound and limited by the constitution; the colonists attributed to Britain a principle which they were to make actual in their own constitutions; and the courts, when opportunity arose, assumed the right, in their independence, to act upon that principle and make the Revolutionary doctrine as real as their own position permitted.[5]

There are others, of whom Professor Corwin is one, who feel that something is to be allowed for both these arguments but that, at any rate, the power of judicial review, so soon seized by the Justices (in 1803), was not one that was usurped; it belonged to them by usage and common sense. The layman, considering this subject, is perhaps likely to be attracted by the confession of William Draper Lewis:

> There is one explanation of this failure by the Convention to act that I submit with diffidence. It is that there existed among the leaders a fear that, should the matter be seriously argued in the Convention with insistence on a definitive decision, the Constitution's adoption by the Convention, or by the people of the several states, would be jeopardized because it would create a long wrangle over who should be the final interpreter, the Congress, the Supreme Court, or some body especially created for that purpose. Perhaps also there was a belief that if nothing were said the Supreme Court or the Congress would become the ultimate arbitrator, either of these solutions being satisfactory to the more federally-minded members.[6]

It might be recalled also that Hamilton in *The Federalist* mentioned judicial review as something hardly necessary to argue for:

> The interpretation of the laws is the proper and peculiar province of the courts. A Constitution is, in fact, and must be regarded by the

[5] *A Constitutional History of the United States,* by A. C. McLaughlin (New York, 1935), 310–17.

[6] *Interpreting the Constitution* (Charlottesville, 1937), 12. Lewis was for many years dean of the University of Pennsylvania Law School.

judges, as a fundamental law. It therefore belongs to them to ascertain its meaning, as well as the meaning of any particular act proceeding from the legislative body. If there should happen to be an irreconcilable variance between the two, that which has the superior obligation and validity, ought, of course, to be preferred; or, in other words, the Constitution ought to be preferred to the statute, the intention of the people to the intention of their agents.[7]

Whether it is to be concluded that the elaborate justifications of the lawyers and historians, from whatever point of view, do make a case for holding judicial determination to be a doctrine intended by the Constitution, there is no doubt that it was presently made to seem so by Chief Justice Marshall. But it can be understood why there has been a rather hectic effort to find some better foundation than the logic which maintains such intervention between legislation and people *to be needed and therefore to be justified*. Ours is supposed to be a government of laws, not of men. Review is a very important tenet. If it was merely manufactured by men, the fact that the men have been Justices hardly makes the case better. There is, in truth, no very secure defense. Interpretation is an invention convenient to the courts—but not always to others.

Our interest here, of course, is in only one phase of the judicial power—that especially affecting the Executive, though restraints on him have often come as restraints on the Congress, both Branches being intimately linked in policy-making and in legislation. This, in fact, is quite well illustrated by the leading case in the matter, always cited as the fundament of review—*Marbury* vs. *Madison*.[8] This and a succeeding case, *McCulloch* vs. *Maryland*,[9] which declared that the Constitution conferred implied as well as explicit powers, are both important in the history of the Presidency. Marbury, it should be noted, was asking for a writ of mandamus against the President, under the provisions of the Judiciary Act of 1789. He had been appointed to a minor position by Adams, retiring as President, but his commission had not been delivered when the change of Administration took place. The Court held that Marbury was entitled to his appointment; that Madison (incoming Secretary of State, acting for President Jefferson) had wrongly withheld his commission. But it also held that the provision of the Judiciary Act under which the case had been brought was unconstitutional; it wrongfully gave the Court jurisdiction. Since it had no jurisdiction, the Court held itself powerless to grant the petition.

[7] No. 78.

[8] 1 Cranch, 137, 175 (1803).

[9] 4 Wheat 316 (1819).

The circumstances were complicated and the atmosphere was charged with political electricity. But in reading the Chief Justice's words, the student is struck with their seeming remoteness from the controversy that gave rise to the case. Marshall's opinions were notable for their apparent judicial detachment. It contributed enormously to the immediate acceptance of what seemed to many, on consideration, to be outrageous presumptions. Jefferson, who raged inwardly at the Marbury decision, was stopped from protesting because nothing was required of him. The Court had committed an effrontery, but only in words that needed no enforcement. There was, in fact, no effective rebuke. The Democratic-Republicans were furious at the survival into their regime of Federalist ideas, but nothing was done. And successor Courts blandly assumed, as though they had received a valid directive, that they might continue to sit as "continuous constitutional conventions." Another Chief Justice, in much later times, would remark with an air of announcing familiar doctrine that the laws were what the judges said they might be.[10]

It is, of course, one thing to examine an Act of the Congress for its accord with the Constitution, and quite another to say to the President that he may not behave in ways he is convinced are required by his sworn constitutional obligations. There is even less warrant for this sort of prohibition than there is for declaring a law to be unconstitutional. But Marshall had said in effect that it could be done—even if he did not do it. What this might come to when a weak President confronted a strong Court would not fully appear until President Truman bowed to the judges' definition of the Rule of Necessity in the steel-seizure case.

The difference mentioned here is not one of principle—the principle is the same; if the judges can "interpret" the Constitution, they can do it for Presidents as well as for Congresses. It is rather one of politics and power. For it is the President who, in the archaic symbolism of legal scholarship, controls the sword. The Congress has the lesser power of the purse, and the judges have only the position of arbiter. They rest, really, on the practical need for an agency which can resolve differences, interpret ambiguities, and extend meanings—which can, in other words, fill the silences of the Constitution with the voice of authority. This is all very well, it is sometimes acknowledged, so long as the other affected powers—of the purse and of the sword—agree to submit. But suppose they do not agree. It is the basic fact of this matter that in such a case the ultimate decision

[10] This was Chief Justice Hughes in a Columbia University lecture. What he said was: "The Court is the final interpreter of the Acts of Congress. Statutes come to the judicial test . . . with respect to their true import, and a federal statute finally means what the Court says it means." *The Supreme Court of the United States* (New York, 1928), 229–32.

would not be made by the judges but by public opinion. How this might be done is not shown in that Constitution because, although it made differences inevitable, it left their resolution to the arbitrament of conflict. But Americans can always take issues to the polls if they are sufficiently important and can get some sort of ruling. It may be one which the losing Branch may not give in to gracefully—this was true of the Court when it opposed F. D. Roosevelt—but it cannot in the long run resist. Nothing can be clearer than that the last word is not that of the Court but of the people. But this is not a conclusion that the judges are anxious to have emphasized.

The Courts have been discreet in their sizing up of opportunities to advance the judicial power. They have guarded themselves with procedural fences shutting out of their jurisdiction any issues they prefer not to consider. A refusal of jurisdiction is final. And they have allowed it to be known that they will refuse all "political" cases. This in practice means any matter of policy they feel it is better for them to avoid and to allow to be settled by legislation or Executive action. Actually there have been many "political" opinions, some of them very controversial. But the Court has somehow always managed to maintain the reputation of being "above politics," a very useful defense. This policy of discretion—with occasional shrewdly chosen departures—has allowed the Justices, as Jackson noted, to emerge from their retreat on selected issues and establish themselves in advanced positions. They have executed some very successful forays in this way. On the whole, judicial review has established the Court, *in practice,* as the arbiter it has from the first sought to become. This has affected the Presidency adversely, of course, but there has always remained the President's right of refusal to accede. It has been open to him to say that, with respect to his powers, only he can decide.

It has been suggested that another dictum of Marshall's, quite as unjustified by a literal reading of the Constitution, is responsible for legalizing the implied powers so necessary for the support of the explicit ones of the Constitution. It is not necessary to conclude, as is often done, that the government and the President would never have come into possession of those powers if Chief Justice Marshall had not recognized and established them; but the fact is that he did and that it was an important contribution. The case involved was *McCulloch* vs. *Maryland,*[11] in which the state of Maryland was told that it might not interfere with the Federal government's operations even if those operations were not mentioned in

[11] The words of Marshall, it should be recalled, were no more than an application of Federalist theory. Hamilton had argued for implied powers and so had Washington. But Marshall fixed the principle as precedent.

the Constitution, only provided that what was being done was necessary to an activity authorized in the document.

This would seem at first to contradict the conclusion of the Court in *Marbury* vs. *Madison*. In that case it was said that there were limits not to be transcended; in *McCulloch* vs. *Maryland* it was said that they might be transcended. But the reasoning of the Court was that, although the limits certainly did exist,

> the sound construction of the Constitution must allow to the national legislature that discretion, with respect to the means by which the powers it confers are to be carried into execution, which will enable that body to perform the high duties assigned to it . . . Let the end be legitimate, let it be within the scope of the Constitution, and all means which are appropriate, which are plainly adapted to that end, which are not prohibited, but which consist with the letter and spirit of the Constitution, are constitutional.

But the Court, in *McCulloch* vs. *Maryland,* had a second issue to meet. A state had undertaken to impede a Federal function by taxation. This, said the Court, it might not do, because the power to tax involved the power to destroy. It was because Federal law was supreme in its own field that the states had "no power, by taxation or otherwise, to retard, impede, burden, or in any manner control, the operation of the constitutional laws enacted by Congress to carry into execution the powers vested in the general government . . ."

Thus the principle was established that there were implied powers, that they might not be limited by action of the states, and that there were limits to them, but that the limits were known only to the Court. In any needful instance litigants would be told what they were. This added to the scope of Federal power and gave notice that the Court would defend and sustain its operations, but at the same time it opened the way to enlarged powers for the Executive.

The Jeffersonians were no more pleased by the second decision than they had been by the first. The case had arisen out of differences concerning political theory; the controversy surrounding it was exacerbated by the depression following the War of 1812. There was angry resentment among the debtor classes, and there was widespread suffering from unemployment and ruined markets. The disaffection was worst in the border country, but farmers and small businessmen everywhere were hard hit by the deflationary fiscal policies of the Bank. The Democratic-Republican party was always made up mostly of such people. Against them the Federalists could never bring to bear a majority. They might be rich and well-born, but there were never enough of them. When Jefferson, after years of mostly subterranean campaigning succeeded to the Presidency, there began a long period—which really ran on into the even more radical Jackson era—when decentralized government, loose administration, easy money, slack controls, and a de-emphasized Executive would be the policy marks of the dominant politicians. Standing against this trend—and represented by the opinions just cited—there was only the Supreme Court, with Chief Justice Marshall as its spokesman. There was a long duel between Court and Executive which seemed to be partly resolved with the passing of Marshall and the advent of Taney. How that resulted we shall see.

★ 18 ★

LINCOLN, TOO, WAS CONFRONTED WITH A NATIONAL CRISIS. LIKE POLK, even more boldly than Polk, he moved to meet it without allowing legal niceties to stand in his way. His earliest actual mention of necessity as his compelling reason for acting was in a message to the Congress on the fourth of July, 1861, when he asked for ratification of the measures he had taken during the previous three months. He had moved to meet the challenge of rebellion, using means, he said, which, "whether strictly legal or not, were ventured upon, under what appeared to be public demand, and a public necessity; trusting then, as now, that Congress would readily ratify them."[1] He justified his most flagrant action in this way:

> Soon after the first call for militia, it was considered a duty to authorize the Commanding General in proper cases . . . to suspend the writ of habeas corpus . . . I have been reminded from a high quarter that one who is sworn to "take care that the laws be faithfully executed" should not himself be one to violate them. Of course some consideration was given to the questions of power and propriety before this matter was acted upon. The whole of the laws which were required to be executed were being resisted . . . in nearly one third of the states. Must they be allowed to finally fail of execution . . . ? To state the question more directly, are all the laws, *but one,* to go unexecuted, and the government itself to go to pieces, lest that one be violated?[2]

Many public officials, not only Presidents, have found themselves in this dilemma and have had to choose which of two contradictory directives they would honor. For Presidents the choice is peculiarly an ordeal; they have, in the first place, a duty to the whole nation; and, in the second place, means at their disposal which, used with energy, are adequate to

[1] S. Ex. Doc. 1, 37th Cong., 1st sess., 9.

[2] This was also an answer to Chief Justice Taney, who had rebuked him for suspending the writ of habeas corpus.

any emergency. Not many others besides Presidents have had to act in comparable crises or to violate, in their acting, personal rights of comparable value.[3] Lincoln, who was the truest, most instinctive, of democrats, was determined; but he was also uneasy. He finally brought to his support the war powers of a Commander in Chief. He believed, he said, that no law had been violated. He thought the Constitution allowed habeas corpus to be suspended "when, in cases of rebellion, or invasion, the public safety" required it. He had decided, he said, that there was "a case of rebellion . . ."

There is no passage in the Constitution conferring such a power on the President. This was something he knew perfectly well; and so he argued in his message that the relevant constitutional provision was "equivalent to a provision . . . that the privilege may be suspended . . ." He was clearly making his own interpretation and asking that it be accepted.[4] But it is certain that he would not have retreated in any case.

[3] Lincoln probably felt about this as he once told John Hay he felt about war itself—that the central idea pervading it was the "necessity . . . of proving that popular government is not an absurdity." (*Diaries* of Hay, Dennett ed., 19.) On the matter of Lincoln's appeal to necessity, it is relevant also to quote Professor Clinton Rossiter, who, speaking of the passage just repeated, said:

In other words, in an instance of urgent necessity, an official of a constitutional state may act more faithfully to his oath of office if he breaks one law in order that the rest may endure. This was a powerful and unique plea for the doctrine of paramount necessity. It established no definite rule for the use of emergency power in this country, but it does stand as a fateful example of how a true democrat in power is likely to act if there is no other way for him to preserve the constitutional system he has sworn to defend. ("Our Two Greatest Presidents," Heritage, February 1959, 100.)

[4] On the contrary, there is language giving the Congress explicit power in such matters. The President is Commander in Chief; but it is said that the Congress shall have power to declare war (Art. I, sec. 8, par. 11). Also that it shall have the power "to provide for calling forth the militia to execute the laws of the Union, suppress insurrections and repel invasions" (par. 15). But Lincoln could point to the deliberate substitution of "declare" for "making" on August 17, 1787, on motion of Madison and Gerry. This would, they argued, "leave to the Executive the power to repel sudden attacks." Jefferson was doubtful, but Presidents have since exercised the prerogative repeatedly. Cf. J. R. Rogers, *World Policing and the Constitution*, who lists 149 episodes between the undeclared war with France in 1798 and Pearl Harbor, a catalogue which Corwin and Koenig (*The Presidency Today* [New York, 1956], 47) cite as sufficient evidence that the President may "judge whether a situation requires the use of available forces to protect American rights . . . outside the

In considering the series of presidential actions taken during the spring months of 1861 it is desirable to understand the actuality of the necessity.[5] In the first place, the Confederate States of America had been formally established. The seceding "nearly one-third" was made up when South Carolina was joined by Mississippi, Alabama, Louisiana, Georgia, Florida, and Texas. In the second place, a loyal majority in the Congress did not exist until the southerners in it had actually departed. Furthermore, questions remained about the border states—Virginia was in process of seceding and Maryland might well follow. It can be understood that Lincoln was compelled to act and that he avoided calling the Congress with good reason.

Contemporary accounts describe the feverish atmosphere of the capital. A considerable number of residents were violent southern partisans, and an even larger number were active sympathizers. W. O. Stoddard, who was a minor secretary in the White House, writing some years afterward, spoke of the city as a "hot-house of secession." He told of walking in the evening through streets ringing with southern songs issuing from deliberately opened windows. All the better people, it seemed, were openly and provocatively hostile to the government.[6]

In this environment of almost open enmity Lincoln had to devise new policies and find new ways to implement them. It was not at all clear who among the civil and military staffs would remain loyal. Defections were occurring in thousands. Southern officers were joining the rebellious forces, and many civil servants were staying on only to do as much damage as they could before being discovered and replaced. To make matters worse, Lincoln had to contend with more than the usual swarm of demanding job seekers. The Republicans were taking over after years of Democratic control, and the spoils were rich. The second-floor offices of

---

United States . . ." But this does not go to the case of insurrection. For that Lincoln had to break ground. He had no justification. All his measures except suspension of the writ were based on the theory that the rebellion from the outset "possessed the dimensions of a public war" (op. cit., 32).

[5] Besides suspending the writ of habeas corpus, Lincoln proclaimed rebellion ("of combinations too powerful to be suppressed by the ordinary course of judicial proceedings") asked for 75,000 volunteers, proclaimed a blockade of southern ports, increased the size of the regular army and navy, asked (in May) for 300,000 additional volunteers, authorized expenditures without congressional approval, and took over rail and communication lines between Washington and Baltimore. Some of these we shall discuss further.

[6] *Inside the White House in War Times* (New York, 1890).

the White House were besieged; long lines of applicants stretched down the stairs and out of doors. They were increased as many would-be officers turned up looking for commissions in the new armies.[7]

To handle his work Lincoln had the same meager staff as his predecessors—with the addition of one secretary, authorized in Buchanan's time:

> There never has been and there is not now any excessive liberality in the appropriations made by Congress for paying Presidents and conducting the business of the National Executive. The President's salary, in 1861, is just what it was when such a dollar as is paid to him, or even a silver dollar, would go twice as far in defraying household expenses. The salary of his private secretary is only $2,500, with no provision for an assistant. When the work to be done imperatively demanded a second, it was necessary to appoint him, at first, as a clerk in one of the Departments, and then an army officer with special detail . . . Since Mr. Lincoln's term began, something has been done towards refitting the "reception" part of the interior, but the remainder of that, and of the outside, are untouched, and the basement continues to carry somewhat the air of an old and unsuccessful hotel . . .[8]

The beginnings of war for the United States have always been chaotic; the beginnings of the Civil War were fantastically so. It was in the midst of utter confusion that Lincoln had to come to his conclusions and make his dispositions. He waited—as Presidents have usually done—for an overt act of the enemy, in this case the firing on Fort Sumter, and then made his moves. Out of them there came two precedents in presidential relations with the Judicial Branch. One was the suspension of the writ; the other had to do with the proclamation of blockade and what are known as the Prize Cases.[9]

The matter of the writ arose in Maryland. It was not a Supreme Court case; Chief Justice Taney was on circuit duty and so acted alone when he ordered General Cadwalader, the military commander, to appear before him bringing "the body" of John Merryman. It was, however, a repre-

---

[7] Cf. the account in Nicolay and Hay's *Lincoln,* 10 vols. (New York, 1890), III, 443.

[8] Ibid., 49. Lincoln suffered peculiarly from congressional niggardliness and from the penchant of bucolic Congressmen for exploiting extravagance or misbehavior in the occupants of the White House. Mrs. Lincoln was neither a saving nor a tactful person, and he himself was nothing of a manager.

[9] 67 U.S. 635. The matter of the writ is cited as *Ex Parte Merryman,* 17 Fed. Cas. 144.

sentative issue. Merryman was one of many; a whole system of arrests for subversion or suspected treason was at stake. And the location was one in which conspiracy might have especially dangerous results. But what was involved was one of democracy's most precious guarantees, and Taney was in a strong moral position. He took advantage of it. This was the same Chief Justice, of course, who had committed the Court to the Dred Scott decision.[10] And it may be best to consider the effect of that earlier opinion before going on to the conflicts of the war it helped to bring on. Its importance, for our purpose here, is that it had provoked Lincoln, even before he became President, into making a distinction of some importance. It was one that other Presidents would find useful when confronted by a Court bulwarked by dignity but determined to have its own way on a public issue. Taney's attempt to force the acceptance of his view amounted to a reinforcement of Calhoun's doctrine that there was a compact among the states that the Federal government must honor. That compact made the territories the joint possession of the states; this being so, any citizen of any state could take his property with him into the territories without interference, because such interference would be a taking of property without due process.

Calhoun had spent the last years of his life formulating this principle and agitating for its acceptance, and of course it was accepted by at least the southern wing of the Democratic party. It denied the validity of the Missouri Compromise,[11] and it inflated the issue on which the Republican party was founded. It was because of this that Lincoln had become a Republican after having been all his life a Whig. He knew how delicate an issue it was. He had debated it with Douglas in 1858 up and down the Illinois counties. He had reluctantly come to a conclusion and, conservative though he was, felt compelled to argue for it. The next step, he said, would be for the Court to say that slavery could not be made illegal in any state, since that too would involve the taking of property without due process. The nation could not endure half slave and half free; the advocates of slavery would not have it so; they were determined to have all or nothing. Therefore, they must have nothing.

There was, said Lincoln, a conspiracy to bring about the legitimizing of slavery. He spoke of a suspicious concurrence between Justices and Presidents, and in one sentence linked "Stephen and Franklin and Roger and James": a Senator, a Chief Justice, and two Presidents.[12] Among

[10] 68 U.S. 254, 19 Howard 393 (1857).

[11] Which would have limited the expansion of slavery; it was repealed in 1854.

[12] Stephen A. Douglas, Roger B. Taney, Franklin Pierce, and James Buchanan.

them they intended to fasten the institution of slavery on the nation forever. He resorted, as he so often did, to parable:

> We cannot absolutely know that all these exact adaptations are
> the result of preconcert. But when we see a lot of framed timbers,
> different portions of which we know have been gotten out at differ-
> ent times and places by different workmen—Stephen, Franklin,
> Roger, and James, for instance—and we see these timbers joined
> together, and see they exactly make the frame of a house or a mill,
> and all the tenons and mortises exactly fitting and all the lengths
> and proportions of the different pieces exactly adapted to their re-
> spective places and not a piece too many or too few, not omitting
> even scaffolding—or, if a single piece be lacking, we see the place
> in the frame exactly fitted and prepared yet to bring such a piece
> in—in such a case we find it impossible not to believe that Stephen
> and Franklin and Roger and James all understood one another from
> the beginning and all worked upon a common plan or draft drawn
> up before the first blow was struck.

The historic point about Lincoln's position in this debate and in his
"house divided" speech[13] was that henceforth he would be what he had
not at all intended to be—the champion of the abolitionists. This
made him unacceptable to the South, so unacceptable that they would
not tolerate him in the White House. For years now "northern men with
southern principles" had been elected. Especially Pierce and Buchanan
had been this kind of "doughface." They may have believed, and certainly
acted as if they believed, that the way to a peaceful solution of the most
dangerous difference of their generation was to give in to the southerners.
They had a kind of missionary zeal in this cause. Buchanan felt that his
contribution to the nation must be peace; and peace would be assured if
the slave interests were placated.

It was with this end in view that Buchanan played the part that later
became known in bringing about the Dred Scott decision and consequently in precipitating Lincoln's determination to be heard. Buchanan
had said in his inaugural in 1857 that the Supreme Court was about to
rule on the legality of the Missouri Compromise, that it was to the Court
that the determination of the issue belonged, and that he himself would
submit cheerfully to the verdict, whatever it might be. What was not
known was that he already had been informed, from exchanges with the
Justices, what it would be. The passage about it in his speech had, in
fact, been suggested by one of them—Catron.

It was an instance in which the Court might easily have declined juris-

---

[13] This was his acceptance when nominated by the Republicans of
Illinois to run against Douglas for the Senate in 1858.

diction; indeed this would have been the normal thing to do. Justice Catron was a Jacksonian and a strong unionist, but he felt that the excitement then building up might be stifled by a decision even though the Missouri Compromise, under which the case was brought, was no longer law. Buchanan, as President-elect, nudged him as well as other Justices, and they finally agreed to do what a majority had been inclined not to do —decide an issue they knew to be thoroughly "political."

Taney, Chief Justice, was only too willing. And his opinion, when prepared, read like a speech in a hot political campaign. He spoke of Negroes as "degraded," he described the Constitution as the "compact" Calhoun had been saying it was, and he said that slaves were property. The Missouri Compromise, reserving the territory beyond the Mississippi as a free area, was unconstitutional. So Taney defined the issue on which the campaign of 1860 was fought.

Lincoln can hardly have thought of himself, before that time, as being unacceptable to anyone, so conservative and understanding had he been. Of course he had been a Whig—had remained one until there were hardly any left. And he had opposed the Mexican War and Democratic expansionism; if it had been up to him Texas and California would never have been added to the Union at the cost they involved. But all this was lowkeyed and reasonable; he made no cause of his opposition to southern desires.

Even after he was elected his character was not sized up accurately. There were very few who considered that he might react uncompromisingly to southern provocation; there were many influential northerners who would have had him accept, without objection, the departure of the seceding states from the Union, and he might have agreed to this solution. It had, however, been made difficult by the course of the campaign so recently past; he had had to go farther toward a commitment than he had ever gone before; and besides, the southerners were pushing bitterly, in defeat, toward extreme rebellion. He had really only the choices of allowing the Union to be broken up—and possibly, in time, reunited on the terms of the secessionists—or of enforcing the view of the unionists that the nation was indivisible, that secession was impossible, and that attempts to alienate citizens or territories were treason.

But Lincoln, the new President, had to consider not only what he ought to do but also what he could do. Was it possible to enforce the concept of the indivisible Union? The man who had seemed so ill prepared for the ordeal he faced, who was so much less imposing than many of those about him, had seemed to move during the interval between election and inauguration in a kind of waking dream. While the South was seceding or preparing to secede, and while the abolitionists and others in the North were clamoring for some kind of punishment, the lawyer from Illinois considered, in what interludes he could steal, the policies he must adopt.

And when he had reached the Presidency, when Virginia was about to join the Confederacy and Maryland seethed with sedition, he still seemed uncertain of his course.

It was truly a dilemma. If he moved vigorously and quickly, he must move without congressional consent, and he must expect any measures he took to be called unconstitutional by the existing Court. He must have searched carefully through the precedents established by his predecessors even after he had made up his mind what he must do. What *was* a President? It was Whig-Republican doctrine that he was one who executed the will of the Congress. And the Chief Justice of the United States had declared a few years before, after one of Seward's pronouncements, that if Seward should be elected President—as then seemed likely—he would refuse to administer the oath. He had consented to administer it to Lincoln, but he was still an adherent of southern views. Moreover, a majority of the Court were from the South, and two others from the North were known to be "doughfaces." There was hostility in both the other Branches which would bristle at the least provocation.

At this distance we can see how right, and even inevitable, were the conclusions to which Lincoln found his way in the lurid surroundings of that spring. A President was a leader; he was answerable to the people, and beyond them to something else—call it their better nature, their destiny as a democracy. He must choose the hard duty, so foreign to his peaceable disposition, of preserving the Union, even if it meant the violation of every other precept of the Constitution. Those precepts were not, he made up his mind, written into the document to enable those who, invoking their literal meaning, would destroy the whole of which they were part. Because he had been elected by all the people he must, even without the consent of Congress or Court, do what was necessary.

★ 19 ★

ONCE A REPUBLICAN MAJORITY WAS ESTABLISHED IN THE CONGRESS, Lincoln hoped his talents as a politician would enable him to manage it. There was no difficulty about the first authorizations; the heat of rebellion melted all objection. It was different when the old hands in the Congress began to interfere with the running of the war. But he took infinite pains to maintain decent relations with the "radical" group even after the Committee on the Conduct of the War began its investigations and its members began to act as military experts.

It was the Court that he had no way to influence—except as it was amenable to public opinion. And the Chief Justice was joined by several others in regarding southern opinion as the true guide. What could Lincoln do? There was in the background his stated opposition to the Dred Scott decision, but as President could he openly disregard the Judicial Branch? There was a nice point here. In one of the debates with Douglas —at Galesburg in 1858—he had said that he believed the decision "was improperly made." And he had added, "I go for reversing it." It was in this connection that he insisted on the distinction, afterward so useful, between "resistance" and "opposition." He accepted the Court's finding, he said, so far as Dred Scott was concerned and so far as others in Scott's position were concerned; he would not resist. He did not suggest that the Court be defied. But he felt free to criticize the ruling; he thought it was wrong; and he thought the Court ought to reverse it because it was neither in accord with the Constitution nor with sound public policy. Now that he was President, it was undoubtedly one of his aims to create a Court that would reverse the decision. When Taney died—in 1864—he appointed Salmon P. Chase to the Chief Justiceship with something like that in view, although by then other issues were more important. At the time of the Merryman incident, he had had no vacancies to fill. And it was urgent, as hostilities broke out, that he should do something to secure the situation in eastern Maryland. At one time Washington was cut off almost completely and rioting secessionists were barring the passage of

Federal troops from the North. Bridges were being blown up, railroad tracks ripped away, and roads blocked. Just then, too, a special session of the Maryland legislature in Annapolis seemed on the verge of taking the state out of the Union. It was not impossible that Washington itself might become the capital of the Confederacy.

Lincoln ordered the commanding general in Baltimore to imprison those suspected of conspiracy to secede and hold them without trial. One of these was Merryman. When the Chief Justice demanded that he be brought into court, the general refused, saying simply that he took his orders from his Commander in Chief. Taney thereupon declared him in contempt of court. Lincoln, he said, had violated the Constitution in suspending the writ and holding the prisoner without trial. It was an able opinion, and Taney was undoubtedly correct in his contention. The Constitution authorizes suspension if there is "rebellion," but it does not authorize the President to do it.

It was not long before the secessionists in Maryland were subdued and order restored, and it was not much longer until the Congress ratified what Lincoln had done. He had saved the Union, he believed, by ignoring temporarily a prohibition which, if obeyed, might have destroyed it. The Rule of Necessity was justified by the result. It is, however, nearly as interesting to follow the Merryman incident to its indeterminate conclusion as it is to notice Lincoln's behavior at its beginning. For Merryman was held in detention for forty-nine days, after which he was released to the district court in Baltimore. This was what Taney had said should have happened in the beginning. He was still under indictment for treason but was not held in prison, and his "recognizement" in the sum of $20,000 was "respited." His case was continued, he was not prosecuted, and the issue faded from public notice. Was Taney right or was the President justified?

It is a characteristic of expeditions by the various Branches into the silent places of the Constitution that there is no decisive and satisfactory ending. Discretion, withdrawal, indeterminateness, and subsequent claims of having prevailed cover the whole with confusion; and it is only after a long time that it can be seen whether or not the incident counted for permanent advance on the part of the aggressor. In this case there is the fact that Lincoln did cause Merryman to be detained for the critical period and that his action was ratified by the Congress. Also, it was admitted by Taney that the Court could do nothing about it. But any future President with an impulse to do the same thing would have to reckon with some moving passages from Taney's opinion.

The Constitution actually says that "the privilege of the writ of *habeas corpus* shall not be suspended, unless when in cases of rebellion or invasion the public safety may require it." But who was to say when this exceptional condition existed? Lincoln considered, at least with the Congress not in session, that he had the responsibility. But the limitation on arbitrary arrest is a privilege embedded not only in the Constitution but in people's minds. No President can take it lightly, whatever the provocation. Lincoln was probably very relieved when the Congress consented to what he had done, and in general he very probably agreed that Taney was right, not in saying that the suspension was a power that only the Congress possessed, but in objecting to military intervention in civil processes.

Lincoln, the Illinois lawyer, must have winced as he read Taney's sentences:

> . . . even if the privilege . . . was suspended by act of Congress and a party not subject to the rules and articles of war was afterwards arrested and imprisoned by regular judicial process he could not be detained in prison or brought to trial before a military tribunal . . .

> And the only power therefore which the President possesses where the "life, liberty, or property" of a private citizen is concerned is the power and duty . . . which requires "that he shall take care that the laws be faithfully executed."

From this point on, however, Taney was in disputed territory, so far into it that no Chief Executive could afford to admit the correctness of his reasoning. Speaking of the faithful execution of the laws, he went on to say:

> He is not authorized to execute them himself or through agents or officers civil or military appointed by himself, but he is to take care that they be faithfully carried into execution as they are expounded and adjudged by the coordinate branch of the government to which the duty is assigned by the Constitution. It is thus made his duty to come in aid of the judicial authority if it shall be resisted by a force too strong to be overcome without the assistance of the executive arm. But in exercising this power he acts in subordination to the judicial authority. . . .

To suppose that the President could act on his own judgment, said Taney, was to suppose that he had had

> conferred upon him more regal and absolute power over the liberty of the citizen than the people of England have thought it safe to intrust to the Crown—a power which the Queen of England cannot exercise at this day and which could not have been lawfully exercised by the sovereign even in the reign of Charles the First.

He drove it home. If the President had any such power,

the people of the United States are no longer living under a government of laws, but every citizen holds life liberty and property at the will and pleasure of the army officer in whose military district he may happen to be found.

His conclusion must have been harder to take for a man of the Lincoln sort than the rest of the reasoning. For Taney asked himself what was the duty of the nation's highest judicial officer who had done all he could but "had been resisted by a force too strong" for him to overcome. What he did do was to cause the record to be filed in the Federal circuit court and a copy transmitted under seal to the President. "It will then," he said, "remain for that high officer, in fulfillment of his constitutional obligation . . . to determine what measures he will take to cause the civil process of the United States to be respected and enforced."[1]

Lincoln, the President, affected not to be moved; and he prevailed, even though nothing he could find to say had the eloquence or the authentic reference to tradition of Taney's sentences. He must have thought them the more dangerous for being so true, and he must have considered his own fate a hard one: to have violated a liberty so that in future there could be any liberty at all.[2]

[1] Official Records, 2 ser. I, 576–85; 17 Fed. Cas., 153. Cf. *Constitutional problems under Lincoln* by J. G. Randall, rev. ed. (Urbana, 1951), and, by the same author, *Lincoln, the President; Midstream* (New York, 1952). Cf. also *The Supreme Court and Judicial Review* by R. K. Carr (New York, 1942).

[2] It can be imagined what a furor there was about the Merryman case and the issues involved. Newspapers, some of them, denounced Taney, described him as senile or traitorous, and advised him not to interfere in military matters; but there were also sober reflections that Merryman might have been punished by civil processes. And there was a center of discontent in the Congress. These matters are summarized in Warren's *The Supreme Court in United States History*, (Boston, 1932), II, 368 ff.

It cannot be said that anything was settled, and Lincoln went on for the next several years behaving as he had been. In direct violation of Taney's prohibition he set up a censorship and persisted in authorizing the arrest and trial of civilians by the military.

In a letter in 1863 to Erastus Corning (*Complete Works*, VIII) he explained what he considered to be his justification:

Thoroughly imbued with a reverence for the guaranteed rights of individuals, I was slow to adopt the strong measures which by degrees I have been forced to regard as indispensable to the public safety . . . I concede that the class of arrests complained of can be constitutional only when in cases of rebellion or invasion the public safety may require them; and I insist that in such cases they

In December 1862, and in time to have some effect on the war, the Prize Cases were decided in a group.[3]

They are of greatest interest to us now as showing the typical behavior of the Court in genuine emergency. There is an almost irresistible impulse to acquiesce when strong leadership is offered, even if—as was true in the Prize Cases—the reasoning has to be tortured to reach the favorable conclusion.

It had been the deliberate policy of Lincoln to treat the conflict as a rebellion; to maintain that the southern states had not left the Union—because they could not; that there was, therefore, no "war." If there was no war, there could be no belligerents. This had been the basis of Secretary of State Seward's case for preventing the recognition of the Confederate states by foreign governments. In the Prize Cases there was the added complication that Lincoln's proclamations blockading the Confederate ports had been issued without any other authority than his own judgment that they were necessary. This had been done in April, some weeks before the Congress had ratified his various emergency Acts. There was a kind of dilemma. If there was no war, there could be no war powers. Anyway, only the Congress can declare war. So, even if it had not been the Administration's fiction that there was no war, one could not be said to exist; and if it did not, there could be no legal blockade and no prizes could be validated in the Federal courts.

There was a certain rough common sense about the Court's brushing aside of this restricting argument. There was also a certain sophistical justification that courts ordinarily do not use. It is true that four Justices out of nine dissented and that these included the Chief Justice. But the

---

are constitutional whenever the public safety does require them, as well in places in which they may prevent the rebellion extending as in those where it may already be prevailing.

Taney might be said to have been vindicated, when the war was over, by the decision in *Ex Parte Milligan.* The Court, in this opinion, restated a principle. "The Constitution," it said, "is a law for rulers and people, equally in war and in peace . . ." Lincoln had found this too simple. He had asked, "Which law?" for he found two. But the Court had no sympathy with Executive dilemmas. It went on to say: "No doctrine involving more pernicious consequences was ever invented by the wit of man than that any of its provisions can be suspended during any of the great exigencies of government."

The Court that issued this opinion had a majority of Republicans; nevertheless, it unanimously denounced the establishment of military tribunals in states where the civil courts were open.

[3] 2 Black, 635.

majority said there was a war; it had not begun, however, until July 13, 1861, when the Congress had recognized its existence, and captures of prizes before that date were invalid. But Justice Grier, speaking for the majority, said that even if a President may not initiate a war, he must resist rebellion. This rebellion may be war; war may be unilateral; and it may exist without a declaration by either party. The President was bound to meet it in the shape it presented "without waiting for Congress to baptize it with a name." It was unreasonable, when foreign governments had recognized it, to ask the Court to "affect a technical ignorance" of a civil war "which all the world acknowledges to be the greatest . . . known in all the history of the human race."

But this was not all. Counsel for the claimants argued against the retroactive authorization of presidential acts. And they had this to go on: Lincoln had said in asking for congressional approval that he had done nothing which was beyond the competence *of the Congress*. This was usurpation, counsel said; it would make the President the "impersonation of the country." Constitutional government would come to a stop whenever a President thought the nation in danger. Lincoln had acknowledged the necessity for ratification; this was an admission that his actions had been illegal.

The majority of the Court met this by refusing to admit that ratification had been necessary. The ratifying measure was upheld, but if it had not been passed there was still no defect in the President's acts. Even if there had been, moreover, the ratification had cured it. This seems to say that a President may in emergency do things beyond his ordinary powers and that they may be made legal afterward by congressional approval. There is some reason to think that Lincoln felt himself to be in this position. But the Court avoided this by saying that the President had not exceeded his own powers; he had merely taken measures to resist rebellion, and when he did so war existed.

Here we are certainly on the far frontier of the Rule of Necessity. The exercise by the Executive of a power allocated specifically to the legislature stretches the theory of our government intolerably. Lincoln simply did not want a Congress, known to be hostile, in session during the dangerous spring weeks of 1861. It might endanger the Union. But this approaches the justifications we have more recently heard for dictatorship; and it was undoubtedly a certain squeamishness that caused him to ask for ratification in terms of *congressional* rather than *Executive* powers. That this would put the Court in an extremely embarrassing position he had not foreseen.

Considered as an incident in the development of the Executive in our history, Lincoln's behavior between March and July of 1861 shows that the limits of necessity are not to be defined except by the nature of a national danger; it also shows the President, in relation to the Congress and the Court, in a position of at least temporary supremacy which both were willing to recognize and legalize. The Presidency was immensely larger because Lincoln acted to preserve the Union—how much larger, however, no one could say.

We have seen that the Court by a bare majority sustained him. How that majority was constituted and maintained is a valuable lesson in presidential behavior.

As it existed in 1861 there were nine members. This was the Court of the Dred Scott decision, and it would certainly not have decided the Prize Cases as was done in 1863. But by this time Lincoln had been able to make three appointments—Swayne, Freeman, and Davis—and all of them were of the majority in the decision. They had been selected because their views accorded with presidential policy. The fourth and fifth of Lincoln's appointments were made for the same reason. These were Field and Chase (for Chief Justice). Aside from appointments in place of other Justices, also, the Court was enlarged by one in 1863. This was the position to which Field was appointed.

Once the Prize Cases were behind him, Lincoln had other concerns in which the Court was likely to be involved, notably the legal-tender controversy and the issue of slavery. He did not live to learn of the Court's disposition of these. The slavery issue was taken away from the Court by the Thirteenth Amendment; after Taney's replacement the Proclamation would have been upheld anyway. But in certain postwar cases acts of the Administration were invalidated, although the theory of the war was sustained in *Texas vs. White*.[4]

There are always those who regard the Court as untouchable, and usually those who thus venerate it are also those who would have appointments made because of strictly legal eminence. Those who have such qualifications are often lawyers who have prominent clients and have risen to the highest places at the Bar, or they may be judges in the lower courts who have commended themselves to their legal colleagues. The profession always has a panel of sorts for every vacancy. But Presidents do possess the appointive power; and when they face emergencies or when they have policies likely to be examined in Court, they are less interested in the purity of the bench than in agreement with what they desire to do. We have seen that Buchanan was circumspect to the point of slyness in influencing the Dred Scott decision. The same characteristics marked all his relations with the Court. Lincoln was a different sort. He meant to proceed with his affairs and to use his constitutional position to make his proceeding as smooth as possible. He was not so foolish as to rasp the sensibilities of the high-minded, but he was not in the least

---

[4] 7 Wallace 700 (1869).

affected by their advice. He knew only too well that it would result in trouble for himself.

Lincoln's successor had as troubled relations with the Court as with the Congress. President and Congress could not agree on the judiciary. The Court was reduced to eight. The number, however, was again raised to nine in Grant's time. This was less because Grant wanted it than because the Congress, to which he was thoroughly subservient, demanded it. But it was done, and for a specific political purpose. It was necessary to have two votes for the constitutionality of the legal tenders. When Justice Grier resigned, there was one vacancy; the Congress created another by enlarging the number, and Strong and Bradley were appointed. The Republicans thus gained their majority.

Grant was always naïve in such matters, and when he was accused of packing the Court he was at a loss how to reply. The issue had been too direct and specific for him to evade. He suffered in silence, undefended by the congressional clique by whom he had been pushed into his embarrassment. Nevertheless, the effect was the same. The press and the profession might be horrified, but the Constitution was interpreted as the congressional majority wanted it to be.

★ 20 ★

LINCOLN MAY HAVE BEEN CONCERNED ABOUT JUDICIAL ATTITUDES, BUT
he did not allow the Court to influence his policy. He need not. He occupied in the public mind the usual position of the Executive in emergency; he practically constituted the government. Even the Congress, furnished with colorful characters both voluble and aggressive, was not
allowed to deflect him from the course of action he had chosen. No President, and especially a man of Lincoln's sort, could have ignored the Congress altogether; but the impression gained from a study of his relations
with it—when it was somewhat belatedly summoned—is that he carefully
and with patience managed matters so that legislative interference was
kept at a minimum. Professor Randall, careful student of the President,
put it this way—that Lincoln went his way and the Congress theirs. But
this was no happy arrangement, and often patience and tolerance were
tried to the limit, for in the whole history of the Republic there never
has been so bitterly vindictive and so headstrong a group as the "radicals"
of the Civil War years.

The Republican majority was adventitious. If the seceded states had
been represented the Democrats would have had control. This was a point
made by co-operationists in the South, the moderates who were against
secession: Lincoln, they said, was not an abolitionist; he was, in fact, suspect by the radicals among the Republicans. If this was so and the South
had a congressional majority, why leave the Union? Why not manipulate
it?[1]

But the immoderates among them had lost all sense of reality. They
had for many years insisted that their view of the Constitution be completely accepted and had demanded approval of their "peculiar institution" as not only necessary but moral. Once the South Carolinians—always
the most intransigent—gave way to xenophobia, the less moderate politicians in the other states began an appeal to belligerence that presently

[1] *The Secession Movement, 1860–61*, by D. L. Dumond (New York,
1931), 130–31.

could not be stopped. Still, neither Lincoln nor most of the southern leaders regarded war as inevitable or, until the last moment, even as likely.
The southerners misjudged the distance they could go without being
checked; they also thought they could go on gaining their ends by threat
and blackmail as they had been used to doing since Jackson had for once
called their bluff. They cannot have suspected that the inexperienced
and ungainly man from Illinois would resort so quickly to force when
challenged.

When the breach widened beyond repair Lincoln was alone in the
White House trying to dispose of the claims pressed on him by the avid
office seekers and to find his feet in the unaccustomed world of administration. Not least among his troubles was the attitude of his Cabinet,
several members of which felt themselves more qualified to manage the
nation's affairs than he. Among them, however, were politicians of such
influence that he must dissemble in their company, appearing to learn as
he listened. In the midst of all the turmoil he somehow came to his resolutions and quietly took action—shocking action to those still of a mind for
compromise. But about the process by which he arrived at the conclusion
that temporizing would only tempt the South to further outrages and that
there must now come an end to conciliation, we are quite in the dark.
Even more than most Presidents, he made his decisions without explaining how or why. Of him Herbert Agar, for instance, trying to penetrate
the workings of his mind, has said, in words only slightly different from
those used by other thoughtful students, that he was always learning
and always increasing, somehow, in wisdom:

> He was the most sincerely thoughtful man America has produced
> —probably the widest in sympathy and understanding—and he died
> before he had expressed his wisdom. All he accomplished was to
> save the American Union; he never explained why he thought it
> worth saving . . . he would not have fought the Civil War for the
> sordid end that resulted. But for what end did he fight it? What was
> this Union of his dreams?[2]

Behind the Gettysburg Address and the second inaugural, as Mr. Agar
noted, the latter-day American feels some formed and well-understood
plan for the future. It was never brought to materialization; but if Lincoln
never really told the people of the North what they were fighting for,
as he saw it, that does not seem so strange if the circumstances are kept
in mind. He was only the recent and quite nominal head of a relatively
new but already deeply divided party. The faction opposed to his long-
range hopes, so far as they were disclosed, was the most voluble in the
Congress and the most unscrupulous; it had constantly to be conciliated—

2 *The American Presidents* by Herbert Agar (London, 1936), 177.

the more so as its demands were so often disregarded. How could he have been candid unless he had been willing to appeal for public support; and was the beginning of civil strife an auspicious setting for a battle with the legislative leaders?

He was thus handicapped in fulfilling the presidential mission of education and persuasion and could come at it only by indirection. He must hope—as Wilson and F. D. Roosevelt would hope—that public sentiment would move in the direction he felt he must go. This suggests itself as a reason for his circumspection. There is also to be considered the viciousness of his opponents without, as well as within, the Congress. There is a temptation to use the most extravagant adjectives in the attempt to describe the cruelties visited on him. But of course it has happened to others. Incredible things were said about Washington, and if they could be said about him they could be said about anyone. The Presidency ought perhaps to be a place of dignity, protected by democracy's regard for itself, if by no other restraint; but it has never been so, and Lincoln suffered more than most. He did have the advantage, in dealing with the hostile Congress, of representing to Americans what they most wanted from the costly struggle with the rebels. This may have been only vaguely defined, and there may have been more savagery and less kindness in the public mind than in Lincoln's. But in this he was known to represent a higher mindedness than most individuals could sustain but which the collective conscience demanded.

There is a passage in Professor Randall's account of this time which at once outlines the differences between President and Congress and goes some way toward supplying the explanation wanted by the puzzled student. He was discussing the Crittenden Resolution—passed in 1861 but never reaffirmed—declaring that the restoration of the Union was the sole purpose of the war. Such a declaration would serve Lincoln's purpose very well, and there were those from the border states, in addition to loyal Democrats and less aggressive Republicans, who felt that the radical policy, in addition to being unchristian, was tending to solidify the South instead of weakening it. Professor Randall went on to say:

> What were called "war aims" were, of course, in reality peace aims. The purpose of war itself is to kill, maim, destroy, break down morale, annihilate enemy fighting power, and produce victory by force. What that victory shall signify, and what a nation is "fighting for," can never be achieved except by peace, and by conditions and attitudes as they persist during years of peace. There were honest souls who felt, as did Lincoln, that it would be most unfortunate for the country to continue to be divided by sectionalism and partisanship after the conclusion of a war whose avowed purpose was the reuniting of the Union.

This matter of purpose that looked beyond war to long eras of peace was properly a function of both Congress and the President. If there could be harmony between executive and legislative minds, and if that harmony could be kept on a high level, something constructive might be accomplished. If not there would be a sorry sequel to Lincoln's high resolve that the nation's dead should not have died in vain.[3]

The sorry sequel eventuated, and it ran on into years and decades of bitterness and division that Lincoln would have prevented if he could. Perhaps he might if he had lived; he was a politician of talent, and he was on the side of conscience. He might well have succeeded in "binding up the wounds" that, as things were, stayed open; but that he would have had a mighty struggle is plain. The winning of the war would have been nothing compared to it—that is, to him personally. The war finally, at its climax, brought him much praise and silenced even his detractors; but the peace would have occasioned a tussle with those who, now that they had a victory, wanted to exploit it.

We may not pursue Lincoln's relations with the Congress into this phase; death intervened. But it would certainly have been instructive for our purpose here. As things are, we have for inspection only the situation of a President being circumspect and conciliatory. He did present the Congress *faits accomplis* in the eighty-day actions and in the Emancipation Proclamation; but these were not, as it turned out, provocative. They were within the limited areas of agreement.

But as the war drew out its bloody and destructive later phases it was evident that presidential and congressional ideas were less and less compatible. Lincoln's hope of keeping the border states loyal was constantly menaced by Radical belligerence, and there was a sinister tendency to castigate the South as a whole, moderates along with extremists. Lincoln was less interested in slavery than in Union; but to hear the loud voices from the Hill, it would be thought that slavery was the single cause that obscured all others. He would have reformed the institution; he would not have punished the individuals involved in it. As early as the first year of war he was apprehensive about this. It is true that he signed the Trumbull bill providing for confiscation of Confederate property, but he did it with the explanation that he felt it unwise; and it was obviously unenforceable. Emancipation did not arrive by that route, and the confiscation of property achieved under it was negligible.[4]

---

[3] *Lincoln the President: Midstream* (New York, 1952), 114.

[4] This whole matter became extremely complicated, so much so that legislators changed sides in the debates and a modifying resolution was passed which involved the substance of the Act. Argument was drawn

The source of congressional aggression most of the time was the Joint Committee on the Conduct of the War, which ever since has served as a model of irresponsible legislative mischief-making. It was meddlesome, obstructive, and imbued with a carping determination to interfere; it had no positive virtue, and it was an added harassment for an already terribly harassed Commander in Chief. Such a committee might conceivably have served a good purpose, as was shown during a later war when Senator Truman was chairman of a similar group; but to Lincoln it was an unrelieved nuisance, serving mostly as a convenient vehicle for the expression of all the irritations and grievances inevitable in the organization of a vast national effort requiring some discipline on the part of citizens and some recognition of duty to country.

The committee made no effort to get any complete account of the controversies it looked into. It was determined to discredit humane generals. To them a man, however brave and able, who did not accept radical doctrine was a "traitor," and they did not hesitate to use any method to blacken his reputation. I quote from Professor Randall:

The harrying of victims was not confined to actual Committee proceedings which were relentless enough; there was also an accompaniment of wild rumor and irresponsible publicity . . .

If one asks how the officious maneuvers of this committee affected the President, the first observation is that the prominently active members were anti-Lincoln men such as Wade, Chandler, and Julian . . . In a conversation with Ward Hill Lamon the President is reported to have said: "I have never faltered in my faith of being ultimately able to suppress this rebellion and of reuniting this divided country; but this improvised vigilant committee to watch my movements and keep me straight, appointed by Congress and called the 'committee on the conduct of the war,' is a marplot, and its greatest purpose seems to be to hamper my action and obstruct the military operations."[5]

---

out through two sessions. Lincoln's point of view was paid little attention, and in the end the muddle was so difficult to untangle that proceedings were undertaken with little success in the courts. Cf. Randall, *Constitutional Problems under Lincoln*, 276–80.

[5] *Lincoln the President: Midstream*, 132–34. In illustration Professor Randall cited the case of General Stone, who was blamed for the defeat at Ball's Bluff in October 1861. The committee listened to the most irresponsible stories of the General's "disloyalty," caused him to be arrested through the Secretary of War, Stanton, who was always very close to them, denied him a hearing, and subjected him for a year to a barrage of defamation. Not until a year after his arrest was he informed of the charges.

But Lincoln had been a member of the Congress during an earlier war which had had political overtones. Polk had managed it with Democratic advantage in view and had thoroughly disliked having to use Whig generals—a suspicion he must have felt thoroughly justified when one of them became a candidate for the Presidency. Lincoln, recalling Polk, cannot have been surprised if his own partisans reacted similarly about Democratic generals—and they too were justified when McClellan became the opposition candidate in 1864. But as Commander in Chief, Lincoln was responsible in a way no Congressman was, and he seems to have paid little attention to the affiliations of the men he needed as officers. That this annoyed his fellow Republicans, there was ample evidence. There were times when the more radical leaders gave way to rages as unrestrained as those of the avowed Copperheads. And this tendency grew worse as difficulties deepened. For the war went badly for the North until Grant's conception of its conduct was accepted. When operations were directed toward the destruction of the southern forces rather than the capture of strategic places, the weight of the North began to prevail. Until it did, Lincoln was on the defensive, and the criticism was often unrestrained. Fortunately the change came before the election of 1864.

To carry the weight of a wearing and prolonged war, whose incidents were largely defeats, for purposes disagreed with by the most voluble Congressmen of his party—this was Lincoln's ordeal. If he persisted in holding to the reuniting of a nation in spite of a congressional majority who wanted to ravage and despoil the conquered states, it was because of a deep integrity which he was incapable of compromising. It is impossible to think of many of his predecessors in office who would have so persisted, and certainly none of his immediate ones—Buchanan, Pierce, or Taylor. Lincoln was a professional politician, as were Buchanan and Pierce; but he was also a statesman in a sense that they were not.

It is true that in considering Lincoln's relations with the Congress we have something of a special case. It can almost be said that the United States has a different kind of government for times of crisis, one in which the usual limitations on the Executive are ignored and in which the Congress very nearly abdicates. But such times have been few and of short duration. There has almost always been a reaction from them, also, in which the Congress had been more than usually aggressive—as though to recover lost prestige.

It is preferable to say about this that at one time the Executive advances into the indeterminate ground of the Constitution, and at another the Congress forces back the presumptuous President. Both are influenced, as cir-

---

He answered so completely that he had to be restored to command, but his career was ruined. He presently resigned.

cumstances dictate, by a restraint with the familiar overtones of self-preservation. Each must grope for the support of the public, and success is governed by its volume. The caliber of a politician is measured, in one of its dimensions, by the ability to sense the strength likely to be commanded in popular entreaty. Often Presidents, even the cleverest of them, have misjudged probable response to appeals and have gone too far or not so far as they might. This is obviously a delicate business, apt to be confused by the conviction of need for emergency action or even by simple annoyance at opposition, both likely to be exaggerated by strain and by an overgrown sense of importance. And Congresses have misjudged, too, the distance they could go in opposing a President. Many Houses, facing the fatal biennial judgment of the electorate, have found themselves largely replaced; and even Senators whose elections happen to occur at a time of presidential wrath have suffered political disaster.

After Lincoln's eighty days, accordingly, there followed a period of congressional aggressiveness, and there was ample material for criticism in the awkward business of getting the war under way and in the early defeats of the Federal armies. So Lincoln's handling of his congressional relations, if not exactly usual, were carried on in an atmosphere mostly unfavorable to the forwarding of his plans. The risk of opposing the war was never accepted by the legislators. Funds were voted and authority delegated. But there were constant investigations, not of what ought to have been investigated, but of matters beyond Congressmen's competence; and there was almost constant criticism whenever it could be calculated to reflect on the President himself or would discredit appointees for whom he had a responsibility. Partisans of the Radicals were immune from this, and Lincoln had opportunity to learn all about the dangers that exist in alliances between members of the Cabinet and legislative cliques.

★ 2 I ★

WHAT IT MUST HAVE BEEN LIKE TO BE FACED WITH THE MOST TERRIBLE need in the nation's history and try to move the machinery of government, as it existed in the 1860s, into speedy action can be realized in later circumstances only by a flight of the imagination. It was through Department heads that the services must be activated and controlled; Lincoln's worst problem, therefore, was his Cabinet. He could ignore them in his decision-making, but their role in administration could not be diminished.[1] Consider, for instance, the case of Cameron, Secretary of War. This Pennsylvania boss was appointed because he was in a position to demand recognition. He was the political dictator of his state, and his lust for the perquisites of office was so voracious that it overcame all opposition. At the nominating convention in Chicago, Lincoln's managers had very simply traded a promise of office for his support. They thought they had to have it; and they expected Lincoln, although he had not been consulted, to pay the debt.

There was a good deal of indignant protest—Cameron's reputation was well enough known—and Lincoln was embarrassed. He asked Cameron to relieve him of the obligation undertaken in his name, but the request was refused, and he felt forced to honor the bargain. In about a year Cameron would be replaced, but the incident of his appointment reveals the pattern a President must follow in forming his Administration.

A new President sits down at the head of a table facing a Cabinet, not of friends or even of prospective loyal associates, but of representatives he has felt compelled to accept by political arrangement. They have in com-

---

[1] Later Presidents would learn to do so by creating new agencies; but with these many of the same problems arise, perhaps not at once, because they are usually created in emergencies, and the Executive has considerable leeway in such circumstances. But if they survive, their heads present the same difficulties of choice as those for heads of full Departments, and their bureaucracies will establish the same inertia.

mon only membership in a party recently victorious in an election.[2] Individuals among them may not agree with the plans made by the
President, and they may regard themselves as his political rivals—an impulse likely to grow stronger as they are encouraged by the interests that
gather behind them.

The principle of disarming enemies by inviting them to join you is well
illustrated by Lincoln's search for a southerner. The evidence that he made
some effort of this sort is clear. Moreover, he wanted a real one; indeed,
if one was from farther south than another it would make him preferable.
He would have taken a slave holder if one had been available who was
otherwise acceptable. His criterion seemed to be "good standing"; he
wanted a man "with a living position in the South."[3] But he recognized
that he could not go farther to capture enemies than his party associates
would approve. He was as acutely conscious as any ordinarily chosen
President must be that, if he had a part in the legislative process, the
legislators had a part in Executive operations. It was very unusual for
such an appointment to be rejected; still it was possible, and the possibility operated as a reminder that counseling was called for.[4] This was
one of the reasons why Lincoln's Cabinet was so far from being an intimate
entourage and could be more realistically described as a collection of
powerful party figures. They were gathered physically about the President
for Cabinet meetings, but they had no intention of really working under
his direction. Presumably they represented, taken all together, the aims
and views of the party; but in a two-party system the spectrum of attitudes could be—and in this case was—so wide that disagreement was more
likely than harmony.

In the end Lincoln did not find the southerner he wanted. He would
have three Secretaries from below the Mason-Dixon line, but none with

[2] To this rule there may be exceptions, of course, and there usually
are. That is to say, the President may be allowed a choice or two of his
own. Also, he may insist on representation of allied political forces—as when
F. D. Roosevelt appointed western progressives or when he formed a
coalition Cabinet at the beginning of World War II.

[3] Cf. Randall, *Lincoln the President: Springfield to Gettysburg*, (New
York, 1945), 267–68.

[4] The only rejections up to that time had been one of Jackson's nominees
(Taney as Secretary of the Treasury) and four of Tyler's after his quarrel
with the Whigs and his replacement of the Cabinet members who resigned
in consequence. Subsequently, Johnson, Coolidge, and Eisenhower would
have confirmations refused. But it was unusual. The disposition to allow
the President his own choice of Department heads was a strong one.

that "living position" he had mentioned.[5] Besides Cameron, his other selections were Seward for State, Chase for the Treasury, Welles for the
Navy, Bates for Attorney General, Blair for Postmaster General, and Caleb B. Smith for Interior.[6] All were the results of prolonged consultation
and urgings among the politicians, of careful consideration and maneuvering on his part, and of eventual party agreement—by compromise—on
assignments. None was a choice made by Lincoln out of friendship or
trust or for any other personal reason. The most magnificent figure among
them was fittingly, it seemed, Seward, who was made Secretary of State.
He was a party grandee of long standing and vast self-esteem who considered, as many others had done, that he should have been the presidential nominee. He was not very gracious to the interloper. The tolerance
and grace shown by Lincoln in response to Seward's condescension shows
his indifference to personal slight when the public interest was involved.

Chase had been another rival for the nomination, with rank in the
party second only to that of Seward, and almost as much convinced
that he should have been the candidate. Lincoln was attracted to him by
the peculiar circumstance that he had once been a Democrat. This fitted
the new President's intention of appealing for support among a wider
following than merely the "Old Whigs." Welles was the inevitable New
Englander. He too was a former Democrat, and some of the party elders
would have preferred Charles Francis Adams or one of the other old-
timers. But Hamlin of Maine, the Vice-President elected with Lincoln,
preferred Welles and was allowed his choice.

Bates of Missouri was an anti-slavery man but, like Lincoln, a moderate;
he was opposed to secession and had advocated the suppression of rebellion. He seems, on the whole, to have been more Lincoln's sort than any
of the others; also, he was more nearly an individual choice. Blair saw to it
that his availability was well advertised. He was not actually selected
until the last moment, but it was natural that a Marylander who had
kept his balance should be brought into the Cabinet. He had been counsel
for the plaintiff in the Dred Scott case and so was known to be on the right
side of the slavery issue. The remaining Secretaryship, Interior, which
went to Caleb Smith of Indiana, was incident to another Chicago bargain.

[5] They were Bates of Missouri, Blair of Maryland, and (although not
at first) Speed of Kentucky.

[6] Of these, only Seward and Welles would remain until Lincoln was
assassinated. Stanton would succeed Cameron in January 1862; Fessenden, Chase in 1864; and McCulloch, Fessenden in 1865. Speed would
replace Bates in 1864; Dennison, Blair in the same year; and Smith would
be replaced by Usher in 1863, to give way to Harlan in 1865. Altogether,
he would have thirteen Cabinet members.

He was a pressing applicant, not a choice Lincoln would have made if he could have helped it.

It was a Cabinet meant to pacify the demanding politicians, not please the President; but neither the radicals nor the moderates of the party were very happy, and even before inauguration there was a first-rate row to be settled. Egged on by Thurlow Weed, his New York colleague, Seward informed Lincoln that he positively would not serve in the same Cabinet with Chase, and not until the day after the ceremony did he relent. Even when he began his duties it was known that he had not brought his family to the capital; he was prepared to leave at any moment.

What began thus inauspiciously went on in much the same way. Professor Randall, contemplating the opening of Lincoln's ordeal, remarked with compassion:

> The Cabinet should have been an instrument to assist and sustain the President, but under Lincoln it was never that. It has been seen that his Administration began with a crisis before the official council was installed, and, had Lincoln known it, this might have been taken as a warning that his period of rule would be a series of minor crises, with now and then a major one.[7]

It is with such materials and in such circumstances that Presidents must make up their minds as they take office what their relations with their associates shall be. It is expected that there will be "an Administration," and this means that the government as a whole will be a kind of entity, having direction and pattern, and that its chief members will have participated in policy-making and will be in charge of its execution. A competent President will manage something of the sort no matter what the difficulties. He may have to mediate, to persuade, to soothe; he may have to ignore minor indisciplines and manifestations of ego; he may have to counsel with some at exhausting length; he may at worst have to enforce his decisions by threats. But somehow he ought to present an impression of a united group which can attract confidence. In the realm of actual execution he must act mostly through the heads of his Departments. Kitchen Cabinets cannot have more than a half life. They may be useful, even indispensable, but they cannot be administrators. Heads of Departments and agencies have vast bureaucracies under their management with work to be done, and they must be given direction if not instructions. They must therefore see and talk with the President. Relations may be strained; the President may lack confidence in them; but, even if he does, he must dissemble; they cannot be altogether ignored.

In this instance, because the country hung breathlessly on the words of its leaders, and especially Lincoln, as the Union fell apart and civil war

[7] Op. cit., 312.

came on, all the small differences were exaggerated and all the large ones were seized on by the partisan politicians. But still Lincoln's problem was not in essence different from that of other Presidents.

Some begin by miscalculating their coming conflicts with the Congress and their certain difficulties with Cabinet members. This costly ignorance and unrealism seem the stranger when the new President has come from service in the Congress and is presumably a professional who should have no illusions; but Presidents of this sort are apt to have the notion that because they belong to the congressional "club" they will be treated with a certain consideration and that their Cabinet will refrain from intriguing with the legislators. Besides, they carry over into the Presidency the idea, so persistently promulgated in the Legislative Branch, that the Chief Executive is exclusively an administrative officer and that only the Congress establishes policy and makes laws. This should make his job a simple one.

It is one of the paradoxes of American political life that the public generally tends to accept the congressional view of this matter at the same time that it condemns a President who does not give a clear lead and exert a firm discipline. Among the many perplexities Presidents discover, if they do not already know of them, and must finally confront, this is one of the worst, especially when they are reluctant to be convinced. Lincoln ignored the problem; but if he had remained in office beyond the war he would have had to face it—as his successor had to, in a form made worse by Lincoln's avoidance.[8]

When a President first has a meeting of his Cabinet—as is expected of him—each Secretary is still wondering what his relations will be and is cautiously feeling out his colleagues. He is even more interestedly exploring the expectations of the President. Lincoln's first meeting was more than usually thorny. As Bates recorded in his *Diary*, it was "formal and introductory only—in fact uninteresting."[9]

The men in the Cabinet group, having been chosen for no consistently similar reason, had not been enthusiastically received even in Republican territory. There were several who were presumably representative of the most populous states—New York, Pennsylvania, and Ohio—and although there was no real southerner, there were two who were from border states. There were those who held a variety of views on slavery, on the tariff, and on lesser matters; and even about secession there were degrees of intensity. The party's factions were well enough represented; but not even this appeared to have been a guide to selection. The members

[8] A detailed account of Lincoln's Cabinet may be found in Burton J. Hendrick's *Lincoln's War Cabinet* (Boston, 1946).

[9] The Bates *Diary* in the Library of Congress was published in 1933 as Vol. II of the *Annual Report* of the American Historical Association. The reference here is to p. 72.

did not agree with Lincoln nor among themselves; they did not pull the same way. Only a study of the conflicting influences bearing upon Lincoln can explain how each appointment came about.[10]

In other words, in the pull and haul of political and personal jealousies, and in payment of promises made in his name to secure the nomination, Lincoln had made the most expedient choices. No principle was involved.

Presidents do not escape the penalties of any mistakes they may make in Cabinet selections; troubles incident to the incompetence or insubordination of such close associates are certain to become embarrassing. Some of the most involved and exhausting passages in many Presidents' lives have arisen from intolerable situations of this sort which they have had to find some way to compose. Lincoln's need to get rid of Cameron was fairly typical, although it was unusually pressing because of the war. Inattention to duty made his separation imperative; but he had a political machine whose good will could not be dispensed with. He was appointed to an important Ambassadorship—a device used in many such cases—and his incompetence was more or less minimized by Lincoln's assumption of blame.[11]

Lincoln was also embarrassed similarly by Blair and by Smith. But his troubles of this sort were fewer than those of some other Presidents—beginning with Washington, who failed to reconcile the views of Jefferson and Hamilton. The President must always be aware that no matter how unsuitable an appointment may prove to be, there is nearly always a political faction which may be incited to protest removal. There must therefore be a weighing of two possible embarrassments against each other, and if action must be taken there must also be an earnest attempt to reduce resentment and salve injured feelings.

That there is no constitutional status for the Cabinet and that an incompatible group is likely to result from the processes of selection has not prevented the myth of Cabinet as Council from persisting. And the myth

[10] Randall, op. cit., 270.

[11] This episode was complicated by certain of the emergency actions taken at the start of the war. Lincoln transferred governmental powers to three private individuals and advanced them two million dollars. This they spent without bond in forwarding troops and supplies during the early interruption of traffic by revolutionaries between New York and Washington. In the sequel to this, he was, in 1862, condemned by the House, chided by several Senators, and rebuked by the Supreme Court. It was indeed an extreme invocation of the Rule of Necessity. But as is usual in such instances, the rebukes came after the crisis had been overcome. As is usual, also, he was supported in his illegalities by public opinion.

has sometimes, as myths do, been able to embody itself in reality. There have been instances of Presidents announcing as they took office that *they* would depend on Cabinet advice; some have; and actually, but infrequently, voting has been allowed. There have been a few occasions when a majority vote has been respected.

Because of the persistent public assumption that there exists something like a corporate Cabinet, elaborate pretenses have been resorted to by some Presidents. Cabinet members have been inclined to co-operate in this fiction since their reputations were involved. But the publication periodically of members' notes or diaries has invariably revealed the nonexistence of any secure relationship beyond that guaranteed by the presidential interest in the Secretary's assistance or support; and this is complicated by the constitutional provision that appointments to the Executive establishment may by law be vested in inferior officers. A Cabinet member appointed because of his relationship with a congressional group, possibly part of a majority, may in some such way populate his Department with employees who owe more loyalty to him or to his congressional friends than they do to the Chief Executive or even to the party; and the President may find that he can do very little about it. Then too, he may, as Lincoln did, inherit a bureaucracy which is hostile and cannot be trusted to execute faithfully policies they happen not to approve. This, Lincoln said, accounted for his having entrusted two million dollars to a private committee for expenditure.[12] In cases of this sort the Cabinet member may be as helpless as the President; but if his Department is organized in this way and he can find no way to change it, the information he may contribute and the validity of his judgments cannot be valued very highly by the President.

There is an infinitude of reasons why a President must be grateful to the framers for not dignifying further than they did the heads of Departments. One is that they may already be rivals for his power. This is naturally truer of the more prominent or the "stronger" among them, but it may in lesser degree be true of others as well. The situation has grown worse as new Departments have been added. They are created, it will be recalled, under the "shall be established by law" phrase in Section II of Article 2 of the Constitution. This does not prevent the Executive from setting up new agencies, and he has often done so under some general authorization without asking the Congress; but they must have funds if they are to operate, and unless he has been given, as infrequently happens

---

[12] Randall, op. cit., says: "Lincoln himself stated that the civil service contained so many disloyal persons that he had to go outside the field of officialdom and confide governmental duties to chosen citizens who were 'known for . . . ability, loyalty, and patriotism.'" This referred to *Works*, VII, 192.

in emergencies, certain general funds, he must request an appropriation. The Congress then takes the opportunity to ask itself whether it approves the agency or the President's initiative in establishing it. If it does not, and withholds funds, the situation is no better than it would have been if authorization had been asked in the first place.

Since the Congress usually authorizes the agencies of the Executive establishment, it is apt to set them up on its own terms and in the way it approves. This has led to the organization of a Department of Agriculture, a Department of Commerce, and a Department of Health, Education and Welfare, not to mention numerous administrations, corporations, etc. The heads of these agencies are first and most importantly concerned in forwarding the interests of those who are their sponsors. They do not usually regard themselves as representatives of the public; and whatever counsel they may give the President is accordingly more advocacy than helpful advice.[13] Very often the group behind them builds them up until they have—if they did not have it before—an exaggerated view of their own importance. This runs to ambition for the Presidency itself in not a few instances. They actually succeed to the office only rarely, but the unlikelihood of promotion seems not to cause discouragement. Those so taken with presidential fever are difficult members of the official family, and some have had to be disciplined. The President is lucky indeed who has a few loyal, wise, industrious, and able Secretaries; but his chance of getting them is not very good.

It is at least partly because of this that Presidents have so often resorted to Kitchen Cabinets—following Jackson's example. They must have some dependable and confidential assistants; and if they cannot get them officially, they must get them in another way. It always annoys the members of the Cabinet when others work intimately with the President, and especially if the others are made intermediaries between themselves and their Chief. It annoys members of the Congress almost as much when their favorites are neglected. They regard such interlopers with suspicion and scrutinize their activities minutely in the hope of finding material for denunciation. Harassment is usually the lot of the unofficial helper, but Presidents seldom have much difficulty in finding those who will take the risk. The attractions of influence at the center of power outweigh the penalties of its possession.

Generally a President has three possibilities in managing his counselors when he does gather them together and seeks advice. He may make a proposal of his own and ask that it be studied and then discussed; he may authorize others to make suggestions, then listen and decide; or he

---

[13] A more and more important part in this selection process is played by economic pressure groups—business, finance, labor, agriculture, education, etc., working through professional politicians.

may pose his problem and require that he be presented with an agreed solution, thus reducing his function to one of ratification. There is still the other alternative sometimes resorted to: he may ignore his associates; but this has become less likely as problems have multiplied and the Presidency has become more highly institutionalized.

Each President has a different way of getting advice and of using those about him to get things done. Lincoln was not a man who found consultation easy, and he seems to have developed no customary way of getting advice. His responsibility was very personal, and its fatigues etched themselves on his face. They deepened his natural melancholy, and the months and years in the White House aged him far more than their number ought to have done. He did not delegate easily; he was not skillful in finding or using assistance. He had no very useful unofficial helpers, although no President ever needed the services of a Kitchen Cabinet more. He found an energetic Secretary of War as a second choice, but it was one whose judgment was always doubtful and whose political alliances were ruinous to his loyalty. And there was even more difficulty in finding a successful general; five were tried before Grant showed the way to success.

There is no hiding the truth that Lincoln was a clumsy President who succeeded only through the costliest experimentation. He had the indispensable virtues of integrity and steadfastness. They were undoubtedly worth more to the Union than all the efficiency conceivable, but the nation could have used both. And the need for reshaping the Presidency in such a way that in time of crisis administrative competence may be joined with statesmanship is one sharp lesson to be learned from the Lincoln experience.

★ 22 ★

LINCOLN IS ESPECIALLY INTERESTING IN THE CONTEXT OF THIS BOOK because he accomplished so much with so little. Bringing the nation successfully through the Civil War with the means he had at his disposal was a remarkable achievement, but to have done it in spite of his casual ineptitude for administration was an even more remarkable one. He was, in a way, the apotheosis of the old-fashioned President. He thought things out by and for himself, he had the acute sensitivity to people's thinking which is so indispensable to the democratic politician, and he had a divine flair for turning it to the uses of goodness. He stood off, in doing this, the Congress and the Court. When necessary, he asked for and got sacrifice and discipline; he got them more and more grudgingly from officials and the military as the war went on, but more and more willingly from the people. He began as an inexperienced country lawyer unused to large affairs, and his education was costly, but he somehow kept the confidence of his constituency and in the end succeeded.

On the other hand, he overcame none of the weaknesses inherent in the contemporary administrative situation and in his own lack of competence. Every operation of the government, including military affairs, was hopelessly muddled. Whenever any decision was made beyond his own personal reach it was as likely as not to be inconsistent with his policy. He seems in retrospect to have been incredibly unaware of the dangers in the rapidly growing capitalism of his time and he certainly took no measures to meet them; he was a backwoodsman in his conception of the economy. And in view of his special crisis, it has to be said that his primitive abilities were utterly inadequate for meeting the complex demands of war on a national scale. The thin resources of the South ought to have caused collapse and defeat within a year. That they did not was due as much to Executive blundering as to courageous resistance.

So, on the whole, Lincoln's success is a remarkable example of the tolerance and resiliency of democracy, of its ability to throw up leaders and support them while, wastefully and dangerously, they lead the way to appointed destinies. He is also an example of the futility of Whig-

Republican theory. The party politicians thought they had in him the type of candidate their interests required and which they have often uncovered. When they found themselves mistaken they were half glad and half sorry. They were glad to have Lincoln take all the responsibility for war, but they dissented from most of the policies responsible for ultimate success and deprecated their dissemination from the White House. In this they were in no novel position for them. They would always look for weakness—that is, subservience—and always hope that strength, for their purposes, would result from their choice.

It was the Republican—as it had been the Whig—thesis that Presidents should occupy themselves mainly in protecting the interests and forwarding the activities of the elite. Their slogan might have been "Weak to regulate but strong to protect"—that is, weak to regulate business but strong to protect property. Then there was the supplementary contradiction that, although the Presidency was to be kept small and restrained, it was still to be conducted with "businesslike efficiency." To find men who would run a tight presidential office and who would yet defer to financiers and industrialists, eschewing any tendency to become leaders of popular causes—this was the difficult task of party leaders. But they were to have a not inconsiderable success. The Republicans' era would last, with only the Cleveland interlude, until 1912. During that time they would select some poor Presidents but only one that threatened their interests.

Lincoln, before he was nominated, was scrutinized very carefully for unorthodox economic views. He was found to have none. And in this matter he gave little cause for dissatisfaction. It may be that the war kept him from the discovery of his own and the party's deficiencies. He was busy enough raising armies and trying to find military leadership. And of course the customary inflations of war settled for the moment the problems of economic and social adjustment which otherwise would have clamored for solution. If to the tasks imposed on him by the conflict there had been added those of undertaking industrial regulation, social reform, and organization for welfare, the Presidency would have become more of a nightmare than it was. It did begin to escape from his control when he suggested the kind of peace the businessmen and their political allies disliked. Compassion and the healing of wounds were no part of their intention. The prospect of money-making in occupied territory very easily linked itself with a hypocritical moralism. They would exploit the South while they reformed it.

When Lincoln set himself against this determination, the great struggle of his life was entered on; but he was spared this additional ordeal. He died as it was beginning. The auguries concerning it were good in one way but not in others. He had grown wiser and more sophisticated, and he had an immense prestige now as the organizer of victory. But there were many of the victorious who had grown savage with fighting, and there were many more who had lost members of their families and were in no forgiving mood. To have controlled these impulses would have been a heroic task.

And then the system of which the Presidency was the center had not been changed in the least, and the institution itself was the same inadequate one it had been when Buchanan left it. Let us see what that meant. There was almost no equipment for the work of administration. The office was not much more complex than would have been required for a township, say nothing of a county or a state. The devoted team of Nicolay and Hay was there for secretarial duties, but borrowing from the army was the only way clerkly tasks got done—and then there were sharp reprimands from the critics. Lincoln had to write many of his letters in longhand, and he drafted his speeches and messages at odd times and on odd bits of paper. He had only the two rooms on the second floor of the mansion for his business, and because the rest of that floor was occupied by the family, he really had no proper working quarters. He habitually wandered across the way to the telegraph room in the War Department but on critical occasions was actually unable to get the intelligence needed to reach decisions. He sometimes used the offices of Department heads for conferences because they were more convenient than his own.

Associated with the administrative handicaps he never found ways to overcome was the difficulty that he had no organized means of communicating either with the Congress or with the public and so was unable to meet very effectively a responsibility that he yet recognized as inescapable. Because of the lack of organization and the inadequacy of his office he could seldom find time or the necessary seclusion for calculation and planning. Sometimes he simply shut his doors; but walks in the grounds or the three-mile journey to the Soldiers' Home, used as a summer retreat, were almost the only solitude he could count on, aside from other infrequent trips away from Washington. He was, of course, not protected by a regular secret service, although he had an unreliable protection from bodyguards or military escorts which did not prevent a bullet from piercing his stovepipe hat when he was riding toward the Soldiers' Home one evening or, of course, his tragic assassination in Ford's Theatre in 1865. It is generally true to say that he had to formulate his policies and make his decisions in most unfavorable circumstances. He carried memoranda about with him in his pockets or in the band of his hat, however, and continued the habit, perhaps learned when circuit riding in Illinois, of thinking things out while in motion with reference only to his own brief reminders. He had no confidant, and he could never count on having research or investigation done by others.

All this was not so awkward for him as it might have been for another individual or even for a modern President with a more complicated domestic situation to manage. Also, as an old politician Lincoln was not averse to proceeding by indirection and on instinct or hunch. And his expectation of results was gauged to a realistic appraisal of the support and assistance he could expect.[1]

There was something similar, in a bizarre way, between the disorganization of the White House and the state of the Capitol, where the legislators did business. That edifice, supposedly completed in Monroe's Administration after having been gutted by the British in 1814, but long outgrown, was now a shambles of excavation, temporary barriers, scaffoldings, and mammoth piles of material; it was also hidden by summer dust or soiled by winter mud. It was as yet uncrowned by its dome. But at least it was being expanded to an architectural plan.[2] The Presidency was expected to be carried on, with its enormous war burdens, on the same scale as heretofore even though its offices were not enlarged. Perhaps it would be honest to say that Lincoln concurred. His small office on the second floor was somehow consonant with his nature.

Lincoln's behavior and that of those who were involved in the events of his Administration have been examined with great care by devoted scholars. The curiosity about him and about his associates has been insatiable. But the limitations of his office, the lack of recording, and the secrecy with which he came to his conclusions have made it impossible for

[1] A good illustration of this indirection is furnished by his insinuation into several minds of the idea that the Republican party ought to become a Union party for the purposes of the 1864 election and that Andrew Johnson might profitably be substituted for Hamlin as the vice-presidential candidate. But no one could quote anything definite he had said. Nicolay was allowed to go to the Baltimore convention without answers to questions Lincoln must have known he would be asked, and even came back to Washington because of the harassment he was subjected to. But still he was given no satisfactory directions. The Pennsylvania boss, Cameron, being a politician, knew better how to act on sketchy information and was the agent of most use. This incident was fantastic, but it was not more so than many others. Lincoln was often slow to make up his mind and was even slower to act, and when he did decide or act the results were frequently not those that might have been predicted. He was bland, uncommunicative, evasive, and unsatisfactory. It was a country-lawyer performance. Even Hay's urbanity was often tried, and the unhumorous Nicolay found himself in acute discomfort. As for the Cabinet, its members made their own various accommodations to a man who grew in stature, obviously, but as he grew became more of an enigma.

[2] The dome was supposed to be a symbol of the Union. Responsible for it was Thomas Walter, official Capitol architect, 1861–65. Senate and House wings were added to the central building in the same reconstruction.

historians to be what they regard as "definitive" about much of it. To an extent, of course, this is true of all Presidents. They alone are so situated in their place of lonely power that they can move the pieces on the chessboard of national action without confiding to anyone what they have ultimately in view, and they often feel compelled to maintain an even deeper secrecy because of their distrust of those about them. They are aware that many of their associates are under almost irresistible pressure and they know fairly well where it comes from, so they take their own precautions. Lincoln was peculiarly vulnerable because of the terrible strain everyone was under and the divided loyalties by which so many were tormented. Existing as he did at the center of the storm, he had always to be calm himself and somehow to reach decisions involving the continued existence of the Union. There are still passages in his life that are being argued over, all these years later, and perhaps there always will be.

Professor Eisenschiml, examining closely the events between the inauguration and the beginning of hostilities, has concluded that the war was plotted and was deliberately induced—by Lincoln.[3] The point about such differences, for our present purpose, is that he was not a natural organization man and that, even if he had been, the conflicts centering in his person would have forced him to be extraordinarily secretive. Also, it has to be added, as we have seen, that his equipment made it utterly impossible to do a satisfactory job of administration. Commenting on the Eisenschiml thesis and speaking of the first days of the Lincoln regime, Bruce Catton has observed with more moderation:

> Some very odd things did happen here, in all truth. It took Lincoln a long time to make up his mind about things; Secretary Seward was assiduously following a policy of his own; contradictory orders were being issued; sheer inexperience with the intricacies of government led to a succession of blunders—and, all in all, the record contains a good many unanswered questions, most of which can be summed up in the blanket question: What on earth was going on here anyway?[4]

Later wars, and especially those we call "world wars," would have a radical effect on the presidential establishment, but the Civil War did not. This was partly because of Lincoln and the Cabinet, but it was also

[3] In *Why the Civil War* (New York, 1958). But there was nothing very novel about this conclusion. Other historians—Ramsdell of Texas, in 1937, and even later, Coulter of Georgia—preceded him. This school is inclined to contend that Lincoln was either a schemer with a villainous intention or a blunderer whose stupidity passes comprehension.

[4] *The Saturday Review*, May 24, 1958, 18.

because of the special jealousy with which the Congress soon began to regard him and his conduct. The Radicals understood almost at once that they had a man in the White House they could not trust—a wily one— and they determined to circumvent him wherever they could. They could not openly oppose him as Commander in Chief, although they became more and more bold in checking him in this role; but they were vigilant against what they regarded as his weakness for compromising with the southerners. They did not mean to stop with victory, either; the enemy must be destroyed as well as defeated.

As we study Lincoln we are confirmed in the belief that there are numerous ways of enlarging the Presidency. Presidents of his sort make no contribution to the effectiveness of the machinery through which they must operate but nevertheless they magnify, sometimes even glorify, the potential of leadership inherent in the office. They become the custodian, as he did, of the nation's conscience. They represent its better self.

Such a President—and there had already been several when Lincoln arrived—sees into the future in one or another respect so clearly that people's intentions are defined by him in ways they recognize when he speaks but would not have arrived at for themselves. Lincoln on slavery, when he got around to it, and on Union, from the first, defined the patriotism and aspirations that men recognized as their own. It might have been so with his view of Reconstruction. It was made explicit in the Gettysburg Address and in the second inaugural. But it is easy, for men who are not pressed, to fall into the betraying emotions of revenge. Only inspired leadership can keep them true to a better plan.

This role of the exemplar with national vision was played by Washington and Jackson; and Lincoln, too, was a people's prophet. In view of this, it is instructive to consider what his domestic policies might have been if he had not had to deal with the war. Perhaps he might not have been so blind to the developing problems of industrialism as it now seems. So shrewd a commentator as Professor Binkley thinks so. Lincoln, he feels, was a tribune of the people, and that sort is bound to keep faith with them when the issues are drawn:

> This doctrine [of presidential duty] was the beginning of his dif-
> ficulty with the directorate of the Republican party. It was a Demo-
> cratic dogma repulsive to the former Whigs, from whose ranks many
> of the Republican party had come . . . These politicians welcomed
> no popular leader of the sort Lincoln was assuming to be in the
> Presidential office. The real Lincoln could never be a satisfactory
> type of President to the great industrial and financial leaders that
> came in time to constitute such an influential element in the party.
> Only a mythical Lincoln could make that group happy at any
> time before or since his death. While never actually a rabble-

rouser, he could not play the role of tribune of the people without seeming to be a potential one . . .[5]

Whatever conclusion is preferred concerning Lincoln's possible policies in the new kind of struggle, it is an argument that is bound to be unsatisfactory. To later generations he has become the savior of the Union and the emancipator of the slaves. They honor him for that contribution and are grateful. His successors in the Presidency must always be humble as they see the multitudes streaming to the shrines set apart to commemorate his deeds and his words and the man himself. There is an almost insatiable curiosity about the unhappy and unprepared country lawyer who rose so magnificently to the challenge of a moral duty and who was so obviously transformed and given strength by his reliance on the truth that was in him. All Presidents must hope to succeed him worthily; most of them, in their own ways and in the degree possible to them, have. And at least some of them must have repeated to themselves his definition of the Rule of Necessity:

I felt that measures, otherwise unconstitutional, might become lawful by becoming indispensable to the preservation of the Constitution through the preservation of the nation.

[5] *President and Congress* (New York, 1947), 292.

★ 23 ★

WHEN THOMAS A. R. NELSON ROSE IN THE SENATE CHAMBER ON AN April day in 1868 to defend President Andrew Johnson, the first impeachment trial under the Constitution was well along.[1] That it had begun at all in the spring of 1868 was a circumstance explicable only by political reference.[2]

It was a presidential election year, and Andrew Johnson was not a Republican. Lincoln's choosing him as a running mate had been motivated by his conspicuous Unionist beliefs. That he had succeeded to the Presidency was proving to be nearly as tragic for the nation as Lincoln's death—it had ended the hope of moderate men that the extremists could be circumvented and the nation's disunion healed. Impeachment was the final stage of the Radicals' scheme to fix themselves in power.

The besetting fear of Stevens, Butler, Wade, and the rest was that they might become a minority in a reconstituted Union; and it was to keep the position they had had since the elections in 1866, won on the tide of victory, that they were pursuing their present course. They had passed a series of Reconstruction Acts and the Tenure of Office Act over Johnson's

[1] Nelson was one of three defense counsel; he was not the first to speak, but he followed immediately George S. Boutwell's intemperate denunciation of Johnson. This tirade had gone far beyond the requirements of Boutwell's responsibility. Nelson had been born and brought up in the same section of Tennessee as Johnson. As a Congressman, immediately preceding the war, he had been opposed to southern extremism. He had indeed stood with Johnson for Union, although he had not usually agreed with him in politics. He was now retired but had been willing to act for the President in the impeachment. He spoke out of an indignation that was deeply felt.

[2] Impeachment was voted in the House in February 1868; the Senate proceedings began on March 5; the actual trial began on March 30; and the first vote was taken on May 16. The Republican convention was held while the trial was in progress.

veto. They were now determined to oust him and install President *pro tem* Wade of the Senate in the White House for the remaining months of the term. By preventing the South from participating in the election they would perpetuate their control.

Out of his violated sense of justice, Nelson, for the defense, appealed for a fairness he cannot really have expected to be shown:

> Who is Andrew Johnson? When treason was rife in the Capitol . . . where was Andrew Johnson then? Standing here, within ten feet of the place in which I stand now, solitary and alone in this magnificent chamber, when "bloody treason flourished over us," his voice was heard arousing the nation. Some of you heard it . . . He who has periled his life in a thousand forms to put down treason—he is now stigmatized as a traitor himself . . .[3]

What Nelson said in his address to the Senate sitting as a court was perfectly true. There were certainly no reasons of disloyalty, neglect of duty, or refusal to perform the duties of his office which could be adduced for impeachment. The congressional Radicals had begun by interfering with Lincoln's management through the Committee on the Conduct of the War and had progressed to the advanced position established in the Tenure of Office Act. If the Congress could take from the President the power to manage and, if necessary, remove his subordinates, it could go on to further victories. The President would be taught to fear impeachment if he did not accept the guidance of the legislative strong men. They would reduce him to ministerial status.

That this was what was in the prosecutors' minds was evident. They sought to becloud the issue when directly challenged, but the truth was that none of the causes for impeachment mentioned in the Constitution was really applicable.[4]

---

[3] A report of the trial was published as a Senate Document in 1868, Fortieth Congress, second session, 3 vols. The references here are to these volumes. The full index may be consulted for pages. The reader is also referred to George Fort Milton's *Age of Hate* (New York, 1930), and to D. M. Dewitt's *Impeachment and Trial of Andrew Johnson* (New York, 1903), as well as to many shorter accounts in general historical works.

[4] Art. II, sec. 4, reads as follows: "The President, Vice President and all civil officers of the United States, shall be removed from office on impeachment for, and conviction of, treason, bribery, or other high crimes and misdemeanors." The procedure for impeachment is specified in Art. I, sec. 3: "The Senate shall have the sole power to try all impeachments. When sitting for that purpose, they shall be on oath or affirmation. When the President of the United States is tried, the Chief Justice shall preside:

Failure of the President to agree with their views might seem to them treasonable, and apparently it did; but such an allegation was absurd and they were furiously aware that it was generally so regarded. Even before the trial got under way they were searching desperately for more secure ground. In spite of entertaining the most implausible witnesses and reaching for the most unlikely charges, they never found the slightest foundation for their attempt.

There could be, and there was, difference of opinion about the constitutionality of the Tenure of Office Act, since the Constitution had been as silent about the removal of officials as about so much else; but what the congressional "managers" of the impeachment denounced the President for was for having an opinion of his own even about this. He must, they said, give up his doubts and conform without protest to the congressional view.[5] Concerning this, George S. Boutwell, one of the House managers in charge of the prosecution said:

> To the President in the performance of his executive duties all laws are alike. He can enter into no inquiry as to their expediency or constitutionality. All laws are presumed to be constitutional, and whether constitutional or not, it is the duty of the Executive so to regard them when they have the form of law . . .
> Hence it follows that the crime of the President is not, either in fact or as set forth in the articles of impeachment, that he has violated a constitutional law; but his crime is that he has violated a law, and in his defense no inquiry can be made whether the law is constitutional.

This was extreme, but not more so than many other Radical diatribes. Nevertheless, the managers, in drawing up the indictment on which the President was to be tried, had wrangled endlessly about what should or

---

And no person shall be convicted without the concurrence of two thirds of the members present."
A following paragraph sets limits to the punishment that may be imposed.

[5] The Tenure of Office Act was one of a series of measures, including, at that moment, the first of the Reconstruction Acts, which were corollary to the impeachment. The Radicals were exasperated by Johnson's removal of their partisans from office—perhaps more so than about any of his other actions, although he had delayed unconscionably in beginning the discharge of officials disloyal to him. But it was not their exasperation or their reaction to it which was so important in itself; it was their willingness to effect a far-reaching constitutional revolution because of such an impulse, which was a frightening omen for the future of representative democracy.

should not be included. They settled finally on ten articles which included almost every possible allegation; but then, on further contemplation of the scarcity of fact, added another which was a kind of recapitulation of all the others—as though restatement could make the compendium of opinion, gossip, rumor, and vague hostility somehow more plausible.[6] They evidently had some hope that their complaints would carry conviction even beyond the Senate chamber, where they believed they had a majority anyway. At least Boutwell, speaking to the tenth article, made the claim that

> the common law of crimes, as understood and enforced by Parliament in cases of impeachment, is in substance this: . . . that, when any officer is guilty of an act contrary to the good morals of the office which he holds that act is a misdemeanor for the purpose of impeachment and removal from office.

A "high crime" had no other definition than the political judgment of the Senate: this in effect was what was being said. But it was the all-inclusive eleventh article that gave the prosecutor his widest scope and aroused him to the most unrestrained invective. The recapitulation made it quite plain that the President's really heinous crime was his objection to the congressional plan for reconstruction. Proceeding to a review of Johnson's policy from the very first, Boutwell worked himself up to denouncing the President as a traitor, a tyrant, a usurper, and an apostate. The scheme of this miscreant, he shouted, was no less than to obtain

> command of the War Department and of the army, and by their combined power to control the elections of 1868 in the ten states not yet restored to the Union . . . to inaugurate a policy throughout the ten states by which the former rebels, strengthened by the support of the Executive here, and by the military forces distributed over the South, would exclude from the polls every colored man, and to permit the exercise of the electoral franchise by every white rebel . . . to control the rebel states . . . to secure the election of delegates to the Democratic national convention favorable to his own nomination to the Presidency . . . This being done he had only to obtain enough votes from the states now represented in Congress to make a majority of electoral votes; and he would defy the House and the Senate should they attempt to reject the votes of the ten states, and this whether these states had been previously restored to the Union or not . . . and he would have been inaugurated on the fourth of March next President of the United States for four years . . .

[6] These Articles of Impeachment may be found at the beginning (pp. 6–9) of the proceedings referred to above.

Concerning this fanciful forecast, it has to be said that there have been Presidents of the United States both before and since Johnson who might conceivably have evolved such a strategy for maintaining themselves in power and might have carried it through. But that Johnson had, no one for an instant believed. Possibly it would have been better for the nation if he had.

Appealing to the Rule of Necessity and asserting his equal right to interpret the Constitution, he might have maintained that the conquered states, never having left the Union, because that was a constitutional impossibility, had, in the ways he and Lincoln had prescribed, fully reconstituted their governments and were therefore functioning entities. He might also have maintained that the Tenure of Office Act was not, in his view, constitutional. He might have refused to accept or be controlled by it. And he might have used force to establish his authority—he was, after all, Commander in Chief of a still vast army. He did none of this. He accommodated himself to laws passed over his veto which he said were unconstitutional and unwise and which were directed solely to emasculating the presidential office and enhancing the powers of a congressional clique. He had been as little provocative as a President could very well be and had submitted to humiliations that several of his predecessors would have rebelled against. Nevertheless, Boutwell, in a wild flight, ended his oration thus:

> Never in the history of free government has there been so base, so gross, so unjustifiable an attempt upon the part of the Executive, whether Emperor, King, or President, to destroy the just authority of another Department of the government.

This was indeed the gravamen of the Radical complaint. Johnson had attempted to "destroy the just authority of another Department"—the Congress.

It is impossible not to feel that the fevered vindictiveness with which the managers for the House conducted themselves, in spite of Chief Justice Chase, who attempted from time to time to return the affair to the level of a judicial proceeding, had its origin in a sense of guilt, an unconscious recognition of unseemliness, and perhaps some understanding that for a temporary passion they were upsetting the intended balance of the government. At any rate, the later student feels himself once again observing the most extreme result of that irresistible conflict among the Branches which was written so carefully into the Constitution. This particular crisis, with its resort to intransigent hostility, gave all the Branches, for the future, a valuable lesson concerning respective situations under the Constitution and what they must remain—indeterminate, dependent on the restraint of each to create and maintain a successfully working government. But it was not a lesson that was learned easily or all at once, and it was never openly admitted by anyone, much less any of those involved in the impeachment. The Rule of Restraint operates best when aggression obviously will not succeed.

It should be noted that the Supreme Court had an opportunity to become party to this quarrel but refrained at some cost to its dignity. It suffered almost the same humiliation as the President from the Radicals in the third Branch. While the impeachment trial was in progress the case of one McCardle was before them.[7] The Radicals feared that the decision might be unfavorable to their view. To prevent this, they passed, again over the President's veto, the Act of March 27, 1868, which severely restricted the Court's jurisdiction, even in pending cases. The effect of this was to substitute the majority in the Congress for the Court. It opened the prospect of congressional trials in all cases likely to be decided by the Court in ways not approved by the legislators.

But the majority need not have troubled itself; the Court's circumspection approached what seemed to its critics at the time to be judicial cowardice. There was an interval after the closing of argument before the restraining act was passed when a decision might have been issued. The Justices postponed action, obviously waiting for the Congress to act. This, at least one of them felt, was cause for shame. Justice Grier, when the case was called, read a statement expressing his own chagrin:

> By postponement of this case, we shall subject ourselves . . . to the imputation that we have evaded the performance of a duty imposed on us by the Constitution, and waited for a legislative interposition to supersede our action . . .

Since this was precisely what the Court had done, the Justice was right in supposing that postponement out of fear would have an adverse effect on the Court's reputation.[8] Indeed, Gideon Welles, one of the few loyal members of Johnson's Cabinet, wrote concerning it in his *Diary:*

> The Judges of the Supreme Court have caved in, fallen through, failed in the McCardle case. Only Grier and Field have held out like men, patriots, Judges of nerve and honest independence. These things look ominous and sadden me. I fear for my country when I

---

[7] *Ex Parte McCardle,* 6 Wall., 318. McCardle was a Mississippi editor who had been arrested and held for trial by a military commission under the authority of one of the Reconstruction Acts. He had petitioned for a writ of habeas corpus in the Federal Circuit Court, had lost, and had taken an appeal to the Supreme Court. The constitutionality of the Reconstruction legislation was at issue.

[8] Cf. *The Supreme Court in American History* by Charles Warren (Boston, 1932), II, 482.

see such abasement. Fear of the usurping Radicals in Congress has intimidated some of these Judges, or like reckless Democratic leaders, they are willing their party should triumph through Radical folly and wickedness . . . The action of Congress, and particularly the Senate in taking from the Supreme Court certain powers to prevent a decision in the McCardle case, is shameful and forebodes an unhappy future to the country . . .[9]

Welles was not a disinterested observer, and Justice Grier may not have been as wise as the majority of the Court. At any rate, the postponement raises the question whether in the heated atmosphere of that spring the Court was not the sole Branch which allowed itself to be guided by the Rule of Restraint. The temptation is to speak of caution, in any of these governmental conflicts, as cowardice; and this performance of the Court was very generally so regarded. But when discretion, which is the better part of wisdom, runs over into cravenness is at least difficult to determine. The judges thought that giving way before the aggressive drive of the ignorant and reckless men who were leading the Legislative Branch was best. As it turned out, it was the outrage of moderate men which in the end defeated the Radical purpose. It was not any opposition the President —who finally chose to fight—could muster. Perhaps the Court was right.

This inevitably leads to wonder whether Johnson might have gone farther in appeasement and avoided a direct clash with the aggressors. It is true that he finally became belligerent, especially in several of his speeches; but it is also true that he tried to be conciliatory in his first months in office and found that his enemies fed on compromise. The affronts were more than he could continue to endure, and later judgment tends to criticize him more for postponement and conciliation than for opposition. If there is a lesson of this sort to be learned from the contrast here, it is that there is no definition of scale to which a beleaguered statesman can appeal for guidance. The Rules of Necessity and Restraint are shaped by repeated experiences—like the common law—and limits are occasionally marked out in one or another way. But they are only there as cushion-like borders, and the warning markers are not at all clear.

Johnson certainly tried his best to find the limits beyond which even the most reckless legislators would not go. There were none for men who had no respect for the structure of their government and who were driven by passions of which they had lost control. The result was one of the few instances in the history of this relationship when an issue was allowed to come to a defining climax. For all those caught in the tide rips of fear and hate swirling through the nation as the war ended and Lincoln was

[9] This entry was made on March 20, 1868.

assassinated, we can find a certain sympathy. For none is that sympathy more stirred than for the unfortunate man who happened to be President.

It must be recalled that Johnson, like Lincoln, had had a reasonable plan for post-war pacification and that it had been in practical effect for a year when it was reversed by the Radical attack. Lincoln had been killed in April 1865. In December, Johnson told the assembling Congress what the policy—his and Lincoln's—had accomplished. It had been, he said, a "healing" period. A decision had had to be made about the territory lately in rebellion. It could have been held as a conquered area and kept in subjection by force, but this would have been an impossibly expensive and provocative way to proceed. The "true theory" was that all the pretended Acts of Secession had been from the beginning without force or effect. The states could not commit treason, and those whose citizens sought to do so had had "their vitality impaired but not extinguished, their functions suspended but not destroyed." The suspension could be ended. Whenever a state did not perform its offices, there was all the more need that the Federal government should maintain the state's authority and cause it to resume the exercise of its functions. On this principle, the President said, he had "by almost imperceptible steps," endeavored to restore the rightful energy of the governments.

This will be recognized as deriving from a firm belief in states' rights such as would be expected from Johnson. His Unionism was a Federal principle which he regarded as the original meaning of the Constitution. States must not secede; but, also, their powers must not be invaded. There was nothing in this for which he might be criticized; it was the generally professed conception even of the Republicans—except that the Radicals preferred to ignore it, along with other professions, when it appeared to hinder their immediate intentions.

Johnson went on to note that provisional Governors had been appointed, conventions called, Governors subsequently elected, legislatures assembled, and Representatives and Senators chosen; also that the United States courts had been reopened. This was a picture of a nearly completed reconstitution of civil government in the American pattern. And if the Civil War had been fought to re-establish the Union and purge the South of the secessionist threats which had been endemic for decades, then it could be said to have come to a victorious conclusion which the Presidency had brought to the stage of reassumed functioning. Also, slavery had gone forever, even if civil rights for Negroes were still not agreed on—these were still traditionally matters for state determination.

That there were risks in this procedure, Johnson admitted. But they were fewer than the risks in any other course. The full acquiescence of the states must be gained, and to gain it he had freely exercised his constitutional pardoning power (as had Lincoln). And he had invited the southern states to ratify the Thirteenth Amendment. Until that was done, the past could not be forgotten; when it had been done, the nation would be reunited "beyond all power of disruption."[10]

[10] This was an exceptionally able state paper and as a message unusually eloquent as well as clear in exposition, all of which is better understood by knowing that it was ghost-written by the historian George Bancroft. It was not the first presidential paper to be prepared in this way; many even of Washington's had been prepared by others. But it was certainly one of the most successful. This was perhaps because Bancroft was a sincere admirer of Johnson. From the time both had been together in Washington during the Polk Administration, Bancroft had followed the courageous career of the Tennessee politician with growing respect and had offered his services at a time when he considered that Johnson's need for them was considerable. The encomiums were general, and even the Republican press was for the moment won over.

★ 24 ★

THE FESTERING DIFFERENCE ABOUT THIS MATTER OF RECONSTRUCTION
went back to Lincoln's "ten per cent plan." This had given a general
amnesty and had restored property to all former rebels who would take
an oath of loyalty to the Union; it had also provided that whenever ten
per cent of the electorate of a state had taken the prescribed oath they
might set up a government which Lincoln had promised to recognize.
But the Congress had refused to seat Senators and Representatives from
states which had complied, and in the election of 1864 had refused to
count their electoral votes.

The congressional alternative to Lincoln's scheme had been embodied
in the Wade-Davis Bill.[1] This provided that the Congress, not the President, should preside over the Reconstruction; also that a majority, rather
than ten per cent, would be required for the reconstitution of a government. Lincoln stifled this flare-up with a pocket veto, but not until he
had brought upon himself the denunciation of the so-called Wade-Davis
Manifesto, which sought to put him in his place:

> The President must understand that the authority of Congress is
> paramount and must be respected . . . and if he wishes our support
> he must confine himself to his executive duties—to obey and execute,
> not to make the laws—to suppress arms by armed rebellion, and
> leave political reorganization to Congress.

The arrogance of this was about as extreme as any later shown to Johnson
and makes it doubly plain that the issue which came to its crisis in his
impeachment was not one made by him. Of course in one sense it was not
even made by Lincoln. It was as old as the government of independent
powers separated by the vast gulfs of silence which exploration never
seemed satisfactorily to chart or expeditions in force to conquer. It happened that the Civil War aroused sufficient passion and populated the
Congress with enough headstrong legislators, pushed by hatred and
tempted by power, so that the usual restraints failed. There may never

[1] Of July 8, 1864.

have been a Congress from the very first which did not have its Wade or Davis or Stevens or Butler, but never before had there been so many of them, and never before had they commanded a majority.

It must be recalled, also, in assessing the forces so fiercely loosed during the postwar years, that for once the most powerful interests in the nation had for allies the greatest number—the northern electorate fell in behind the plutocracy. Even then this was not so powerful an alliance as the congressional strength it mustered would seem to indicate. Grant's majority in 1868 would be only some three hundred thousand in a total of nearly eight million votes.[2] This narrow victory, even with patriotic claims and with the South excluded, is sufficiently indicative of the distrust aroused by the extremism of the Radicals, but it was also a lesson to the Republicans.

There was a burning hatred still of a just-defeated enemy which barely served to rally the greatest number. And the most powerful had grown afraid of Lincoln and were even more afraid of Johnson. If the southern states were readmitted and a democratic majority again re-established, it would in all likelihood repeal much of the legislation the Radicals had been able to pass—high tariffs, favorable to the manufacturers in the North and unfavorable to the South's agriculture, and benefits for the railroad and financial interests. These had to be defended at all costs, even the sacrifice of the most precious political principles—or what had hitherto been regarded as the most precious.

Thad Stevens was at least honest when he said that the southern states ought never to be recognized as "capable of acting in the Union, or of being counted as valid states, until the Constitution was amended so as to secure perpetual ascendancy to the party of the Union." It was not intended that what had been won by war should be lost by votes. That others might not agree on exactly what had been won by that war was merely a temporary confusion, and the Radicals did not much care how it was cleared up. It seemed to them that for what they had in mind a simple amendment would do—one providing for Negro suffrage. This would cause new rebellion in the South which would need to be repressed, and it would tie to the Republicans those humanitarians who were so determined to enforce Negro rights. Of these there were many, and they were as fanatical in their cause as the Radicals were in theirs—perhaps more so, since they were upholding rather than undermining a principle. At any rate, it made an effective partnership, one that was almost too much for Lincoln. And Johnson was not of Lincoln's size.[3]

[2] The totals were Grant 3,012,833 and Seymour 2,703,249. The electoral vote was, of course, more one-sided, 214 to 80.

[3] The partnership mentioned here would be sufficiently adhesive to keep the party in power through four presidential elections.

Speculation as to whether Lincoln would have succeeded better than
Johnson may be fruitless; it is impossible to be certain; but Lincoln's
prestige as a finally successful war President, and the impact of his personality—he was generally spoken of toward the last as Father Abraham
—would have been valuable aids. As it was, the Radicals made an impressive record. Still, when it is looked at closely, it can be understood
that their victories were rigged and that they were forced to make many
compromises. They failed to oust Johnson and so did not seat Wade in
the White House. Their reconstruction aims were largely achieved, however, and Lincoln might possibly have prevented this; but he would have
had difficulty in preventing the selection of Grant as candidate in
1868, and the Unionist coalition would have disappeared. The post-war
malaise—the corruption, the general moral slackness—that permeated the
government might have taken place with Lincoln in retirement almost as
easily as with Lincoln dead. These periods are never admirable in democracies.

It also has to be said that Johnson, in spite of being a lifelong professional and having had an extraordinary number of successes in electoral
contests, was nothing like so able a political strategist as Lincoln. He
allowed the election of 1866 to become an outright struggle between himself and the Radicals, although it was not a presidential election year, and
he was outmaneuvered. He was a Democrat among Republicans, and his
enemies had captured the Republican organization. Anyone who supported Johnsonian policies or candidates was likely to be called a Copper-
head, and this was too much for most of the moderates. A National Union
convention was held in 1868, but it did not result in any effective election machinery; Lincoln's party had obviously served its purpose and was
being abandoned. The business interests and practically the whole of the
northern press were Radical supporters. The result in 1866 was the election of a Congress whose majority was hostile to the Administration; and
in these circumstances Johnson seems to have lost his head—as indeed he
had begun doing in the campaign when he undertook the famous "swing
around the circle"—and began to trade insults with the opposition. This
was just what the Radicals needed, and they at once set their objectives
higher than they had dared to theretofore. They could now, they thought,
put Johnson out and install their own man in the White House, even if it
was Ben Wade, whose record in many respects was so hard to defend.

They almost did. The one-vote margin against impeachment was a
terribly thin victory for the Presidency.[4] For all that, it was as momentous

___

[4] The one vote was furnished by Edmund G. Ross of Kansas, who had
been an abolitionist and had led a colony to Kansas in 1856, but whose
make-up was such that he resented Radical pressure and was at the same
time offended by the injustice of the proceedings. He had seemed to be of

a one for the office as any in all its history. And it was the more so because the charges were political rather than ones involving any sort of criminality or misfeasance. But it owed very little to Johnson and a great deal to his blustering enemies. It seems curious to us now that for so long a time the general estimate of Johnson should have been pretty much that established by the oratory of his detractors. The extremism they exhibited was well enough recognized and was even repudiated politically, but their picture tended to perpetuate itself. Actually it was just about the reverse of the truth. Johnson was nothing like the sinister, devious man of intrigue with treasonable intentions conjured up by the speechmakers in the Congress. Actually he was a man of rigid principle—including integrity in office and personal rectitude. But he let himself go in campaigns. He was, in fact, called "the best stump speaker in the nation."[5]

That he was extreme, and even rabid and irresponsible, on the platform is true; and when he gave way to his impulse to sway the crowd before him, he often made more enemies than friends. The campaigning allowable to a President, in the voters' minds, is not at all the same as that allowable to local politicians or even to candidates in their first campaign, something Lincoln had known but that Johnson never learned. But Johnson's worst weakness was none of those attributed to him by his detractors. Instead of being sinister and aggressive, he was overcautious, indecisive, and inclined to delay even when acting had become imperative. His intelligence must have warned him within two months of his well-received address to the Congress in December 1865 that he must make some drastic changes in his Administration if he was to carry through the reconstruction on which he had embarked. There were unmistakable signs. In February 1866 he had to veto the Freedmen's Bureau bill, passed in spite of his arguments and in spite of the relative smoothness with which the pacification of the South was being completed. But in this, as in so much else, he stopped at argument and did nothing effective to carry his policy into effect. He allowed Stevens and others to make inroads everywhere, and he suffered their affronts with what came to seem fear. Worst of all, he kept in his Cabinet several members—Stanton being the most notorious—who were actively associated with his congressional enemies. He refused to take the initiative, and his procrastination in making de-

---

Radical persuasion but turned the other way while the trial was on. Toward the last, when it became apparent that his was a needed vote, his determination hardened as the threats against him multiplied, and he quite calmly voted against impeachment.

[5] A reputation that Seward said was deserved; but he also said that a President ought not to be a stump speaker—a shrewd canon for Presidents to keep in mind.

cisions allowed the subversion of his Administration to go on almost unhindered.

The veto of the Freedmen's Bureau bill was not overridden, but it was Johnson's last success of that sort. What he could expect must have been apparent enough when the polished Sumner spoke of him in a Senate speech as "an insolent drunken brute in comparison with which Caligula's horse was respectable."[6]

When they failed to succeed with the Freedmen's Bureau bill over Johnson's veto, Stevens in the House and Sumner in the Senate sponsored a civil rights measure which Johnson also vetoed. But this time the veto did not stand. The long roll of defeats had begun. The bill provided that the states might not discriminate among citizens because of color or race. Even though they had prevailed, the Radicals were doubtful about constitutionality and they proceeded at once to prepare a Fourteenth Amendment which would have the same effect.[7] They were taking no chances.

Johnson might have done better in the campaign of 1866 if he had accepted this amendment with approval and made it the basis for the return of the southern states to the Union. Instead he campaigned vigorously for states' rights and seemed to be contending that the southerners should be allowed to treat the Negroes among them in any manner they chose. This infuriated the former abolitionists and even many of the moderates. During his final two years, after his failure to persuade the electorate to return a moderate Congress, he was to have very few supporters.

Then, also, there were those disloyal members of his Cabinet, and

[6] The reference here was a typically unfair one. There had been an embarrassing incident at Lincoln's second inauguration when Johnson seemed to be drunk. He was a man of moderation in this respect, unlike many of those who criticized him; he had been ill and was unable, evidently, to carry successfully a stimulant given him by a friend.

[7] This very important amendment actually went much farther. It reduced congressional representation when Negro suffrage was limited; it disqualified many former officials and officers of the Confederate states; and it had one provision which was afterward to be of immense use to corporate interests. This article said: "No State shall make or enforce any law which shall abridge the privileges or immunities of citizens of the United States; nor shall any State deprive any person of life, liberty, or property, without due process of law . . ."

This was intended to protect Negroes; but it was interpreted to be applicable to corporate persons as well as individuals, and in this way the courts for many years found that business regulations of any sort were takings of property without due process.

especially Stanton, who as Secretary of War was in a strategic position. The Reconstruction Acts had in effect replaced civilian with military government in the states, and the military commanders had enormous powers. Worse even than this, the Congress had finally made these generals responsible to Grant as General of the Army rather than to the President, the constitutional Commander in Chief. This, together with the Tenure of Office Act, had left the President helpless.

Instead of rebelling and refusing to allow his powers to be thus taken away, Johnson had in effect acquiesced by doing his part in enforcing the Reconstruction Acts. He had argued that they were unconstitutional, but he had not refused to comply with their requirements. When the Act which took from him the control of the military was passed over his veto, however, he seems to have made up his mind that he must act. But as before, he argued the case in his veto message and then delayed. If words could have accomplished anything, his message was clear and compelling enough:

> Within a period of less than a year . . . Congress has attempted to strip the Executive Department of . . . essential powers. The Constitution, and the oath provided in it devolve upon the President the power and duty to see that the laws are faithfully executed. The Constitution, in order to carry out that power, gives him the choice of agents, and makes them subject to his control and supervision. But in the execution of these laws the constitutional obligation upon the President remains, but the power to exercise . . . is effectually taken away. The military commander is, as to the power of appointment, made to take the place of the President, and the General of the Army the place of the Senate; and any attempt on the part of the President to assert his own constitutional powers may, under pretense of law, be met by official insubordination. . . .

But presidential words were wasted; the congressional clique had the votes to override. They were wasted also on such power-worshipers as Stanton. The Secretary of War, as he had done all his life, gave his allegiance, for what it was worth, to those into whose control the powers of government were being gathered: not for him the fruitless loyalty of a subordinate. His intrigues with the Committee of Fifteen, which had now replaced the Committee on the Conduct of the War, were not exactly open, but they were well known in Washington. Johnson as well as others knew of them.

That the President's veto message stated exactly his situation is shown well enough by Grant's instructions to one of the commanders (Sheridan) who was asking whether he should conform to the Attorney General's opinion about the time of registration for voting in his district. He was told that such an opinion would not control him (Grant), if he were in Sheridan's place, "further than he might be convinced by the argument." This has its own interest, in fact, as coming from a future President who was, even so early, beginning to assist in undermining an incumbent one.[8]

During a considerable period of delay and confusion, with the military commanders taking charge in the South, Johnson continued to meet with his Cabinet. He was one of the Presidents—and this was characteristic— who accepted the Cabinet as an advisory council, and he took its advice on all matters of significance. This naturally made it a more serious matter that some of them should virtually be acting as spies for his political enemies. Stanton occupied an anomalous position. He was in constant touch with the Radicals in the Congress and still occupied himself with presidential advice—some of it very good, for Stanton, for all his lack of character, was an able man. It was because Johnson could not quite be sure of his disloyalty and because he was sure that dismissal would cause a first-rate row that he hesitated to discipline his Secretary of War. Then too, it is quite possible that he felt somewhat inferior. After all, Stanton's role during the war years and afterward, when Lincoln's assassins were being sought, had been a prominent one, and he had disposed of enormous power when Johnson had still been relatively obscure.

But when he was informed that the Supplementary Reconstruction Act, which had so embarrassed him, had virtually been drafted by Stanton, Johnson determined that something must be done. Even then he waited, and the matter did not come to an issue between them until he discovered that he had been hoaxed into confirming the military commission's sentence of Mrs. Surratt to death for having taken part in the conspiracy to assassinate Lincoln. There had been a recommendation for clemency which he had not been allowed to know about, and the concealment could only have occurred at Stanton's orders. This embarrassment was so annoying that he finally sent a note asking Stanton to resign. Stanton refused to leave "before the next meeting of Congress." Then Johnson suspended him and directed Grant, after some humiliating negotiations, to act as Secretary ad interim. Stanton, after having made a show to impress the clique to whom the future belonged, vacated his office, as he said, because force was being used to compel his action.[9]

---

[8] An even less lovely exhibit of this peculiar approach of Grant to the responsibilities of public life was his behavior while the impeachment trial was taking place. He turned lobbyist for the House managers and actively solicited votes against the President.

[9] One of the impeachment charges would be that this dismissal violated the Tenure of Office Act, a charge that Johnson, instead of meeting directly, avoided by claiming that Stanton was not covered, since he was a Lincoln appointee and had never been reappointed by himself. There

It was the furor over Stanton's dismissal that made it certain that impeachment actually would be tried. Until then it had been more threat than reality. Now the Congressmen persuaded themselves that they might act. Still it was delayed for some months because the Committee of Managers for the House had so much difficulty in formulating a set of charges with any semblance of justification. There was plenty of rage but no high misdemeanor to point to. The difficulty grew worse rather than better as the arguments went on. Their safest resort was the assertion that the framers had intended to embody in the Constitution a doctrine of congressional supremacy. This was something that, once claimed, could not be argued about with any finality. It had merely to be accepted; and once it was, much else followed. It was presently made to seem that it was traitorous to question so obvious a dogma.

Much time was consumed and streams of oratory were emitted in the preliminaries to impeachment, but the activists were certain that they possessed the votes, whether or not they had a case. The contempt for orderly procedure, the carelessness with facts, and the partiality of the judges made the impeachment trial itself one of the passages in American political life which require the most apology. It was rough, vulgar, disgraceful. But it had the effect of being so repulsive and at the same time so subversive of precious principles that all the issues involved in it were in the end settled as they ought to have been, and the institutions that had been in jeopardy were saved. The tribunal itself decided the issue of Johnson's removal. Time and the imperatives of government under the Constitution settled the others.

The Tenure of Office Act was repealed in Cleveland's Administration; the reconstruction went its way in strife and corruption until Hayes, to get the Presidency, made a deal for the southern electoral votes which involved the withdrawal of the last troops. Out of apparent defeat and betrayal in Johnson's and Grant's Administrations the Presidency actually emerged as strong as before. A succession of Republican incumbents did not insist on their prerogatives, and the Senate continued to think itself supreme, but in the end the impairment faded away, the balance was restored, and the powers necessary to the office were found when the next crisis arose.

Andrew Johnson was a tragic figure because he was caught in a situation he was powerless to control. It was the same one which had tormented Tyler before him. Both were Presidents without parties and therefore without the bulwarks needed to resist inroads upon their prerogatives.

---

were endless arguments about this. But Johnson was correct, and the Radicals had obviously made a mistake in making an issue of so doubtful a case. Like so much else in the impeachment, this was a weak support for the real political aggression.

Both were picked—and elected—not as Presidents but as vice-presidential conveniences for Presidents. Neither could have achieved the White House on his own; neither was able to go on to a second term.

The use of abuse and excess to which there must be reaction is certainly an awkward and costly way for a people to learn the meaning and value of their institutions; but there is one virtue in such lessons—they do not have to be repeated. There have been no more impeachment trials and no more attempts to pass Tenure of Office Acts. Also, the President's position as Commander in Chief is immensely stronger than it would have been if Congressmen had not undertaken to direct the military occupation of the conquered South with such horrifying results.

One lesson was not learned. There have been other vice-presidential choices of convenience, and some of them have turned out badly for the Republic. It must be concluded that the lessons have not been sufficiently disastrous. But what a people could learn, it would have been thought, must have been learned from Johnson, so excellent a man and so hopeless in the Presidency.

THE PRINCIPLE OF SEPARATION DOES OFTEN LEAD TO CONFLICT; AND conflict does interrupt the public business. It is certainly true that when one Branch asserts a prerogative and the claim is contested by another Branch nothing much can be accomplished until a truce is arrived at. And if a settlement is reached which seems in one or another way extreme, there is an uneasy feeling that the end has not been reached and that the question will soon be reopened. There seems almost to be a force in the equilibrium fixed by the Constitution which tends toward re-establishment. No discernible rule governs this tendency, and the time required for returning to the norm varies with the circumstances. What must always be recalled is that the conflict involved in separation is the active agent in restoring balance. To delete it from the Constitution would be to destroy a vital element.

This tendency to equilibrate is well illustrated by the events of the years just following the Civil War, when congressional aggression caught Johnson in an exceptionally weak position. He never recaptured the initiative, and not until Cleveland's Administration would the situation really be restored. But even in the weak regime of Grant there was a certain stirring of presidential assertion. And in the Administrations of Hayes and Garfield, committed though they were to the theory of congressional supremacy, there was a certain movement back into territory lost by Johnson. At the end of the first Republican succession, when Cleveland became President (in 1885) he very quickly found whatever power he needed. And when after another interval Wilson succeeded (in 1913), the same was true. The Constitution had its own way.

There were several separate and easily distinguishable incidents in the return to normal relations after the postwar raids of the Radicals. The first was Grant's rather feeble demand for repeal of the Tenure of Office Act. This resulted in some modification; but the changes, when Grant had finished compromising with the Senate oligarchs, were unimportant. The Senators were left, as they had been, with a strangle hold on the Executive. The second incident was the struggle of Hayes with the Senate over appointments to his Cabinet. The third was the Garfield-Arthur row with Senator Conkling. And the fourth was Cleveland's calm reassertion of his prerogatives and his complete refusal to relinquish them.[1]

In the first of these incidents, Grant might have won the repeal of the Tenure of Office Act if he had been at all resolute. But he wavered and gave in as he did in every instance when the Stalwarts (as the hard core of professionals were called) brought pressure to bear. His awe of them was pathetic. In his first message to the Congress he attacked the Act as "inconsistent with a faithful and efficient administration of the Government." To follow up, he refused to make any nominations as long as the Act was in effect. This left Johnson's appointees in office, and there they would remain until the Senate gave in. The House, led by Butler, who as much as anyone had been responsible for the measure in the first place, voted for repeal. But the Senate had gained a position it had no intention of relinquishing, and in conference with the House a new law was framed which would require the President to continue to submit nominations until the Senate approved of one, the old officeholder meanwhile keeping his job. The President was persuaded to sign, and the Senate kept its superior position vis-à-vis the Executive.

For a moment it had looked as though one presidential prerogative might be recovered from the debacle of the Johnson Administration. But Grant was not the man to recover anything, and if he had been he would not have known what to do with it. The erosion of the Presidency was more serious because of his complaisant inferiority than because of Johnson's defeats. Johnson never lost a battle without so carefully defining its significance that in time the correctness of his position would persuade reasonable men. Indeed, while he was in process of losing, many of those who defeated him came to see that he was right. The trouble with Grant was that he had no conception of the Presidency which at all corresponded with the realities of the office.

There is reason to believe that in electing Grant the people had thought they were restoring the Presidency to the position it had traditionally occupied. It is true that they had not supported Johnson, but at that time (in 1866) Reconstruction had been uppermost in their minds; they were

---

[1] President Hayes, in retirement after his single term, watched his successors, Garfield and Arthur, challenge and defeat the Senate. He was inclined to take credit for having made the presidential victories possible. In his *Diary* (for May 17, 1871) he wrote: "If the boss system is to go down, as now seems probable, I can say I struck the first and most difficult blows . . . The principal steps have been (1) the appointment of the Cabinet in 1877, (2) the defeat of Conkling in the Custom House conflict which made a business house institution of the New York Custom House, (3) the defeat of Conkling and Platt and their dismissal from public life in 1881." Cleveland's contribution was still to be made.

choosing between a hard and a soft policy toward the defeated enemy. They might have preferred to do this without downgrading the President; and Grant seemed to offer the same policy with restored leadership in the Presidency. But the Senators knew him better than the electorate. He had already been their tool too long for them to have any fear of his independence. They put him in his place at once, and he struggled only feebly.

This feebleness certainly did not come from a lack of courage or even from a deficient understanding of organization—he had shown both qualities as a general—it came rather from a kind of innocence, an ignorance of political affairs which would seem incredible if it were less well documented. He would execute the laws as he had done when he was a general. Even then he had thought the President less entitled to obedience than the lawmakers; and now that he was President he intended to stay in the subservient position he believed the President ought to occupy. This allowed him to regard the Executive establishment as not very different from the army. His Cabinet was a staff and not an advisory body to be concerned with national policy. He looked to the legislative leaders for orders. But as to this he was inconsistent. He did not pick a group of able associates, as he had done for the army. He surrounded himself with incompetents, and when a few of them showed signs of independence he dismissed them on the advice of the Senators he so much feared and appointed others who were approved because of their willingness to accept orders from the Hill.

What legislative supremacy of this sort really implies was described quite vividly by George F. Hoar, later a Senator but at that time a member of the House of Representatives and a Republican:

> The most eminent Senators, Sumner, Conkling, Sherman, Edmunds, Carpenter, Frelinghuysen, Cameron, Anthony, Logan— would have received as a personal affront a private message from the White House expressing a desire that they should adopt any course in the discharge of their legislative duties that they did not approve. If they visited the White House, it was to give, not to receive advice. Any little company or coterie who had undertaken to arrange public policies with the President and to report to their associates what the President thought would have rapidly come to grief.[2]

This situation existed throughout Grant's Administration; and the division of responsibility, together with the infusion into the government service of incompetents, created a situation that gradually worsened into widespread malfeasance. It was easy for the expanding business interests to

---

[2] In his *Autobiography of Seventy Years*, (New York, 1903), 2 vols., II, 46.

take advantage of the prevailing irresponsibility, and the resulting bribery and subversion reached into the White House itself. This was one of the few instances in all its history in which the presidential office was touched by scandal. This in itself was humiliating enough, but it was far worse that the structure of the government should have been distorted. Concerning this, Professor Burgess once thought that the Senate was succeeding in "the overturning of the check and balance system and the substitution of the parliamentary system for it." And it really did seem to contemporaries that the Senators had moved into the first and controlling place.

However final this arrangement may have seemed at the time, it became apparent as soon as Grant left the White House that presidential incompetence rather than senatorial strength was responsible. There was a very marked reaction throughout the country to Grant's failure; and when the Presidency itself was involved in the prevailing immorality, the Republicans realized that their candidate for 1876 must present a complete contrast in this respect. It was no easy matter to find an incorruptible candidate who would still hold the view of the Presidency insisted on by the Senate. One who would promise to prevent such occurrences in the Executive establishment as had discredited the outgoing Administration would hardly accede to senatorial control.

Difficult as this may have seemed, the Republicans thought they had succeeded when they nominated Rutherford B. Hayes. He had been one of the best of the political generals in the Civil War—had, indeed, been a dashing commander, much liked and admired by his Ohio volunteers. This had resulted in his becoming Governor, and even against stiff opposition he had been re-elected twice. This war service combined with a demonstrated political attractiveness ought to give him electoral strength. But he had two other attractions. He had been noted for the austerity and incorruptibility of his gubernatorial regime, but also he had resisted innovation and expansion and was as conservative in financial matters as the most particular taxpayer could desire. There were those who knew that the brilliant soldier had become an excessively cautious and stodgy civilian and that as Governor he had been more dull than creative, but they mostly kept quiet. And even the liberals among the Republicans, who had been in active revolt against Grant, found him acceptable.

Hayes had a popular opponent; and from the first, with the deplorable Republican record as a handicap, it looked as though the Democrats would win. It was by one of the most questionable maneuvers in American political history that the Republicans did finally seat their candidate in the White House. It was done by being more dishonest than the Democrats in buying the electoral votes of several of the southern states still under carpetbag rule. In effect Hayes promised—or the promise was made for him—that the military occupation would be ended if he became President. The contest was thrown into the House, which could not agree, and finally a bipartisan commission was set up with a Supreme Court Justice (Bradley) as an added member. Bradley was a Republican, and the matter was decided by his unhesitating party vote. This was obviously against the country's wishes; Tilden, the Democratic candidate, had had a clear popular majority,[3] but he refused to contest what was a very doubtful decision. The discussions and deals had gone on almost to the day of inauguration. The excitement was intense and all the materials were prepared for a continuing conflict. But a strain of decency and of concern for the nation shown by Tilden allowed Hayes to enter on his term without the disturbances which might well have resulted from the steal.

It must be said that Hayes justified Tilden's moderation in one respect— he refused to allow the Senators who had intimidated Grant to dictate in the same way to him. He may have been party to the deal for the southern electors, but that was the last chance anyone ever had to accuse him of questionable conduct. He proved to be one of the stiffest and most austere of all Presidents. He even carried the temperance cause into the White House, or allowed his wife to do so, and entertainment during his regime had the quality of a midwestern Protestant parlor society. The country welcomed it after the murky moral atmosphere of the former Presidency.

But Hayes's conscience extended, as well, to his administrative responsibilities. He had no intention of letting loose on the Federal establishment a new crowd of spoilsmen designated by the senatorial clique. He was well aware that he would have to deal with the vicious defense of their power by Conkling and Platt of New York, Simon Cameron of Pennsylvania, and James G. Blaine of Maine. Each of these—and others of their group—were expecting to place nominees in the Cabinet where they would be most effective. Unknown to them, the new President had taken a resolution not to appoint any holdover from Grant's Cabinet and, in fact, not to appoint anyone "to take care of anybody"—and he had written it down in his *Diary*.[4] In accordance with this determination he sent a list of nominees to the Senate for confirmation without consulting any of the Stalwarts. This was a shock to men so used to subservience in the White House, but they suffered a worse one when they heard about the new Cabinet, for Hayes had chosen a list of unexceptionable and independent citizens. Among them was one of Conkling's bitterest enemies, William M. Evarts, who was to be Secretary of State; and Carl Schurz, who was a liberal and a reformer and had led a long fight in the party against Grant

[3] Of about 250,000 in a total vote of some 8,000,000.

[4] On February 19, 1877, when the excitement about the electoral deal was at its height.

and the spoilsmen. Of the Republican regulars, only John Sherman of Ohio was appointed, but he was recognized as well qualified for the Treasury, where Hayes proposed to put him. He was, moreover, entitled to that traditional courtesy of the Senate—confirmation without inquiry.

The challenge to their power was met by the Senators with what they obviously believed would be a flattening blow to the upstart President. They referred the nominations to committees and let it be known that they would not emerge. But they immediately suffered the severe shock of discovering that the President had an irresistible force of public opinion on his side. Editorialists fumed against the Senate dictatorship and exhorted the President to stand firm, and an unprecedented correspondence deluged the offending legislators. In many cities mass meetings and demonstrations were organized which adopted strong resolutions. This outpouring surprised and gratified Hayes and dismayed his opponents. Almost at once confirmations were forthcoming; the Senate was completely defeated.

This event deserves a place among the historic victories in the long struggle of the Executive to maintain his place in the American system, and the more so, perhaps, because it was the result of spontaneous indignation. Hayes had not appealed for public support; he had merely acted in accordance with his view of the presidential position. The public had seen enough of legislative interference and irresponsibility and was disgusted with Grant's subservience. Hayes was not prepared to do more than behave in an upright and forthright way; he was no leader, but his conscience was strict, and against it the queasy political intentions of the legislators had no chance.

One unfortunate circumstance in Hayes's battle for his prerogatives was that he was committed to a single term. If he had fought the professionals all the way through to a second nomination the gains he made would have been more secure. He was succeeded by a fellow Ohioan who also had been a general of volunteers and a machine politician. This was James A. Garfield. Assassination cut short his service, but he had a chance to—and did—carry on another movement begun by Hayes. This was the civil service reform that would not end until the Federal service was purged of political favoritism in all its reaches up to the policy level. Such a consummation would be a long time on the way, but from this time on it would always be visible as an inevitable end.

In his inaugural, Hayes had mentioned this matter, and of course it was another count against him in the reckoning of the Senate Stalwarts. A year later, when military withdrawal from the South was substantially completed, he said to his *Diary* that the civil service ought to be next. He chose what was regarded as an impregnable Stalwart citadel for a beginning. This was the New York Custom House. From top to bottom it was a grazing ground for Senator Conkling's unofficial deputies. They paid little attention to their duties and much attention to keeping the political machine in order. It might have been thought that Hayes would consider such a stronghold a risky place to begin his attempt at reform. But in this his disinterest in the future gave him a certain boldness, and after an appropriate report made by an investigating committee of prominent citizens[5] he issued an Executive order prohibiting Federal employees from taking part in political activities.

What followed has a special interest for us because it involved a future President—Chester A. Arthur—who was Collector of the Port. It was not Arthur but a second-in-command, Alonzo B. Cornell, who became the first person to be disciplined and so to precipitate the more general conflict over the issue of senatorial interference; but Arthur could hardly be exonerated, and when Cornell openly defied the President by acting as chairman of a Republican convention Hayes demanded the resignation of all three of the top officers. When these were refused, Hayes sent to the Senate the names of three successors. They were referred to a committee presided over by Conkling himself, which was an indication of the Senate's attitude. In that special session, and in the regular session following, confirmation was refused; but during the following interval Hayes discharged the three and appointed three substitutes. When senatorial approval again appeared doubtful at the next session, the power of public opinion was again manifest. In his quiet and determined way the President had made such an impression that the Stalwarts saw their privileges threatened. And when Secretary John Sherman, within whose Department the custom houses were included, told his former colleagues that he would resign if his administration was hampered by employees not selected by himself, uneasiness rose to panic. In his rage Conkling made one of the most intemperate speeches the Senate had ever heard. This caused such a reaction that confirmation of the appointees followed and Conkling had to accept what to him was an almost unbearable humiliation.

These oratories over the Legislative Branch had results of importance for the Presidency. So, also, did certain others. Hayes defeated the Democrats' attempts, after they gained majorities in both Houses in 1878, to use appropriation bills for the repeal of authority for using Federal troops to "keep the peace at the polls." This would have returned to the states complete control of congressional elections. True, the law authorizing this protection had been a war measure, but the purpose of the Democrats was admittedly to nullify the principle of the Fifteenth Amendment, that it was a Federal responsibility to protect national elections and to see to it that no citizen was deprived of his right to vote. Five times during the Democratic Forty-sixth Congress attempts to take from the Executive his power to manage the military in the national in-

[5] One of whom was a Roosevelt.

terest were vetoed. In his messages returning the bills Hayes put the matter quite clearly. He could not and would not surrender his constitutional responsibilities or see them modified in any way. He believed and said that public opinion was opposed to such a compromise on his part. It demanded "greater vigor," rather than less, in the enactment and in the execution of laws framed to prevent violence and corruption; and, he said, this kind of control was as badly needed in New York City as in the South. The fifth of these vetoes left certain operations to be carried on without authorization, since an appropriation bill had to be disapproved to get at the rider. But Hayes emerged from the contest with all the honors.[6]

Hayes is generally thought of as one of the least interesting of all the Presidents, the epitome of conservatism and negative rectitude; but, regarded as a defender of his office, he must be thought of among its firmer occupants. His contests with the Stalwarts ended in complete victory which would lead on to the repeal, somewhat later, of the Tenure of Office Act; his advocacy of civil service reform began a significant administrative change; and his refusal to allow congressional politicians the inroads they sought to make on his prerogatives added another to a long list of presidential rejections of the persistent theory of congressional supremacy. His successors would have reason to regard him with unusual gratitude.

[6] It is true that the laws sought to be repealed by these Democratic riders were even then obsolete, something Hayes acknowledged in his veto arguments. He had no intention of using the force they authorized, but he felt the reserve power to be necessary. During Cleveland's time the Democrats did wipe the measures off the books, but not in circumstances inimical to the Presidency. Whatever the President's constitutional powers, they remained unimpaired.

★ 26 ★

NEITHER GARFIELD, WHO SUCCEEDED HAYES, NOR ARTHUR, WHO FIN-
ished out Garfield's term after his assassination, is usually rated among the
more effective Presidents. On the contrary, their mediocrity is thought of
as consonant with the times. It was business leaders who were moving
into the places of highest regard in the American culture; and politicians,
even in office, were looked at with a kind of tolerant suspicion. All were
lumped together as doubtful characters.

Some of the central figures in the public affairs of the postwar years
were indeed touched by corruption. As we have noted, Chester A. Arthur
was dismissed from his post as Collector of the Port of New York by President Hayes. James G. Blaine, a perennial presidential candidate, was
deep in the business of dispensing influence for a price. And Garfield, the
lay preacher, had profited, if only to a token extent, from the distribution
of Crédit Mobilier benefits.

It would doubtless be taken as exaggeration to say that Garfield and
Arthur were ennobled by accession to the Presidency, but it is a fact that
both disappointed those who had fully expected to use them for doubtful
purposes. Garfield engaged the Blaine faction in a contest as sharp as that
Hayes had had with the same Senate group; and Arthur notably advanced
the cause of the merit system, something hardly to be expected from a
former spoilsman. How else explain the reversal of expectations created
by their previous behavior than by attributing it to the assuming of presidential duties?

It was not an appropriate time for the appearance of giants in public
life, and there were none. The alternatives to the chosen Presidents in
the contemporary political society were not better and may well have
been worse. The alternatives to Hayes—Blaine or Morton—would have
been no improvement.[1] And if Grant or Blaine had been chosen instead
of Garfield it cannot be imagined that things would have gone better for

---

[1] Bristow might; he was one Grant associate whose reputation survived
the association, but he was not really a likely nominee.

the nation. Even if the Democrats had won with any of their candidates after Seymour in 1868—Greeley, Tilden, or Hancock—the resultant regime could hardly have been an improvement. None of these gave any sign of being potential statesmen of the more forceful presidential tradition.

Garfield, when he became President in 1881, had behind him a long legislative experience. He had been elected to the Congress while he was in the army and had chosen to resign his commission—unlike Hayes, who stayed with his regiment until the war was over—and go on with his political career. For him, as for many another politician part way to success, the Civil War had offered a difficult problem. To volunteer would be to interrupt progress toward chosen objectives and to enter a profession calling for abilities of a specific kind and with harsh tests for success; an officer in the Civil War was quickly tested. But to stay at home would be to risk a future in which any candidate for office would need a service record. Many of the ambitious chose to volunteer, and of these there were some who were discarded because they failed in the field; but there were many, and among them Hayes, who found an exhilaration in army life which they had never thought possible. For the first time they were free of conventions and released into a rough man's world. They exhibited courage, intelligence, and adaptability. They were a main reliance of the Union Army.

It was not a very professional war. There was a good deal of movement, personal courage was important, and technology played a small part. A volunteer, even one who had nothing to offer but willingness and ambition, who was innocent of mathematics and every other demanding discipline, could still be promoted on merit. Of course many entered as higher officers, even as generals. Many were elected by volunteers to lead them or were appointed by Governors. This was often a mistake; lost battles were hard to explain. And the whole process of trial and error in the discovery of military competence was horribly costly in men and money. Hayes was one of the best of these volunteers. Garfield did not find life in camp and field so agreeable; his health was intermittently bad, and his service had none of the brilliance Hayes's often had. He was glad, in the middle of the war, to retreat to Washington. The Congress was for him a natural venue. It required the talents he possessed, and he had little difficulty in being re-elected.

He was in process of advancing to Senator, after being Floor Leader for the Hayes Administration, when he was nominated for the Presidency. His nomination came as the result of a long rivalry between Conkling and Blaine to control the White House. They were not satisfied to share the Senate leadership. Blaine wanted the presidential nomination for himself; Conkling, to oppose Blaine, conceived the plan of putting Grant back in office for a third term. Grant had been sent on a well-publicized world tour as a kind of American exhibit, and his deficiencies as President had been to an extent forgotten in the flood of publicity from abroad about his reception by kings and emperors and his regal progress through Europe and Asia. Conkling thought that with the aid of the veterans he could put him back in office. He nearly succeeded, but Blaine proved too strong. When neither would give way at the convention of 1880, and when Sherman failed to attract support in spite of an eloquent nominating speech by Garfield, the orator himself was recalled to the minds of the delegates as a regular of the right breed who had a gifted tongue—as they had just seen—and whose origin and history fitted the tradition.

During the campaign Garfield was becomingly silent, as was the fashion for candidates then. But the campaign was a characteristically violent one. There were charges that Garfield had been much more intimately involved in the Crédit Mobilier affair of 1872 and 1873 than he had. No one actually believed that he was corrupt in any direct sense, but if he had not to a certain extent shared the Grant looseness it would have been a miracle. And toward the end there was a furor about a forged letter, picturing him as favoring Chinese immigration, in an attempt to influence the western vote. What enabled him to win was a deal he made with the Conkling-Grant group which turned their apathy into activity. He defeated Hancock by a very small margin.

The Republicans were holding onto the Presidency by very small margins in all these post-war elections. But their men in the White House were establishing a presidential pattern which was at once an advance and a retreat. That is to say, the role of the President was narrowed; he was not to be a people's advocate, a policy-maker. He was to accept his lead from elsewhere in society—from the Senate and from the industrialists and financiers. Yet Hayes had recovered much of the ground lost by Grant. He asserted his control over the Executive establishment, and his constitutional powers were mostly regained. He did not advance into the area marked out by Lincoln for all his successors when he became Father Abraham. He was something less than the symbol for the nation which was the presidential destiny. Yet there was a rectitude about him which at least restored respect.

Hayes had given the Stalwarts a rude shock by appointing his own Cabinet without consulting them; now Garfield offended Conkling by appointing one Robertson to the Collectorship of the Port of New York. Whether this was a double cross or not after a deal made during the campaign—as Conkling contended—it was regarded as a deadly offense. Robertson, in defiance of Conkling, had been an anti-Grant delegate at the convention. Garfield had been implored by most of those who were his political advisers not to offend the Senator, but he had persisted. In a letter concerning the quarrel he said that it would "settle the question whether the President is registering clerk of the Senate or the Executive of the United States." This was the proper high ground for him to take. He did not arrive at it in the way he implied, but he did arrive at it.

If Garfield's engagement did not settle the whole question of whether Senators should be deferred to in appointments they were interested in, which it distinctly did not, since this would continue to be fought over in succeeding Administrations, it went some way toward demonstrating that if the President chose to make an issue of the matter he would very likely win the resulting struggle. Conkling was in about as strong a position as any Senator could be, and he was decisively defeated. Conkling's plan for having his way was to see that all the new Administration's appointments except Robertson were confirmed, and then to adjourn. Garfield heard about this from Blaine, who, playing a curious role, which shows something of the qualities of professionals when they come into conflict, showed him how to counter the senatorial scheme. The President, he said, could simply withdraw all nominations except that of Robertson, leaving that the sole issue before the Senate. Then he could let it be known that no other appointments would be made until Robertson was confirmed. As Blaine had foreseen, the opposition collapsed. And Conkling, losing his head as rage overcame him, resigned from the Senate. He had decided to appeal for vindication at home in New York. If he should be re-elected by the legislature, as he fully expected, his position would be a happy one and the President would have been notified, in effect, that he must allow appointments to be determined by the Senators from the states where the appointees were to serve. But, to Conkling's obvious amazement, the legislature repudiated him and stood by the President. It was a notable victory for the office in a most unlikely place.

In the course of the imbroglio among the Republicans, extending back into the maneuvers before the convention of 1880, Garfield played no very glorious part. If his conduct led to some enhancement of the Presidency, it was more because that conduct was politically convenient, or because he was led into it by a kind of weak consent to what was convenient for others, than because he acted from principle. He was undoubtedly a man who knew what behavior was proper under the circumstances, but no one can believe that he was guided by this knowledge. He was torn between two warring factions and allowed himself eventually to be captured by one of them after dallying with each until he was so confused and exhausted that he hardly had any power of choice. If he afterward gave his motives a higher value than they deserved, it was an understandable attempt at justification. But the student of the Presidency cannot give him credit for a resolution which he lacked.

After making his mid-campaign deal with the Conkling forces in New York, he owed them a certain patronage. In the post-election trading among the professionals he tried weakly to placate them by favors so obviously less valuable than those awarded to Blaine and his people that they were as furious with him as they would have been had they been entirely left out. He had, of course, been so humiliated by the nomination of Chester A. Arthur as his running mate that a person of more firmness would have revolted then and there. Arthur was Conkling's chief man in New York; he had been dismissed by Hayes for unbecoming conduct; he represented everything dishonest and subterranean about machine politics. But Garfield had not only accepted Arthur, he had consented to the gathering about him of all the evil elements of the party as the campaign progressed. He had even recanted a known leaning toward tariff reform since it did not suit the business interests to whom the party looked for funds.

During the campaign Garfield had gone to New York to meet Blaine and seek his support. Blaine had refused to attend the meeting and had sent several lieutenants instead, led by Arthur, who was presumably now Garfield's rather than Conkling's second. Blaine was a much easier ally. He was active in support, free with advice, and even inclined to take over political direction, although Garfield was experienced enough. It was not too strange that Blaine should be made Secretary of State when the new Administration was formed. He had no competence for the first place in the Cabinet; nevertheless, after the fashion of politics, it was looked on as a just reward. It did, however, make a serious problem of somehow rewarding the Conklingites for their rather reluctant co-operation. Levi P. Morton claimed that in the New York conference he had been promised the Treasury. It was now refused him on the advice of Blaine, who had come into the open as the mentor, politically speaking, of the President-elect; and the Conkling people were furious. Garfield, in desperation, and for one moment disregarding Blaine, invited Conkling to his home for discussions. He offered the Senator a Cabinet position, only to have it refused. From then until inauguration—some six weeks—there were complex and hurried offers made to Conkling's supporters; there were refusals; then there were acceptances. By March, Garfield was so mired in a slough of shady deals and promises that it seemed unlikely he would ever be able to emerge into Executive authority.

Garfield's unhappy situation as he began his Presidency was later commented on by the historian E. P. Oberholtzer:

> The new President was overwhelmed by men who seemed to be involved in some conspiracy to usurp his functions, and direct him in the performance of his duties. In his zeal to restore "harmony," respect "claims," recognize "wings" and "sections" he multiplied his difficulties manyfold.
>
> The mischief maker at his council table was Blaine, who desired to use the administration . . . for the advancement of his own po-

litical fortunes. It was his policy to berate other men, if they were his enemies, for their insincere purposes, their incompetency to hold government office and their corruption . . . But he would promote the advancement of men of as bad or of worse instincts, if they would forward his personal plans . . . In choosing Blaine . . . Garfield had awakened the suspicions of the Independents and forfeited the right to their confidence. He, at the same time, by this token, had completed the affront of Conkling. Hayes, Sherman and others warned Garfield as the scene unfolded. They urged him to be President—he should not surrender the authority of his office to the prime minister.[2]

This is not the picture of a hero who, in appointing a Blaine supporter to the Collectorship of the Port of New York, was acting out of regard for high principle. He was not even seeking to establish the principle that a President may make appointments regardless of the preferences of local politicians. He was merely favoring Blaine rather than Conkling; he was a tool in one of the savage engagements between these stronger and more ruthless men. What the Presidency gained as a result was marginal.

It was the worse, perhaps, because in affronting Conkling he removed

the efficient public officer whom Hayes had established in the place, not for the improvement of the service, but to make a position, controlling valuable patronage, for an adherent of a faction which was notoriously hostile to Conkling, and for no better reason whatever. In attacking Conkling he was satisfying Blaine . . . who now made no secret of his pleasure. That Robertson was an "independent," which Garfield averred, was a wholly specious claim. Robertson was "independent" of Conkling, but in no fine or honest sense, and the new President, by this act, at once made a complete disclosure of the infirm character which he had brought into the campaign, and which was to mark his conduct now that he was President.[3]

If there is a lesson in all this it must be that later generations of Americans have some curious persons and some even more curious courses of conduct to thank for the shaping of their government. There can be no doubt that the victory of Garfield in the ensuing contest over the confirmation of Robertson is an important precedent in the general progress toward the President's independence and especially his control over the Executive Departments and agencies. That it began in intrigue and was

[2] *A History of the United States since the Civil War* (New York, 1931), IV, 108.

[3] Ibid., 113.

carried out by a politician's cleverness which owed nothing to any appeal for higher motives, we must set down as a vagary of the processes which have created our institutions. All evidently cannot be done in the odor of virtue.

★ 27 ★

THE ENTIRELY UNEXPECTED STRENGTH OF CHARACTER DISPLAYED BY Chester A. Arthur on becoming President deserves to rate as another of the significant incidents in the gradual return of the Presidency to a state of strength after the strains and distortions of the post-war period. No accession could have been less auspicious. Arthur's known record of subservience to the Conkling machine, his compliant and casual behavior as a local officeholder, his dandyism and love of luxury—all led to the supposition that he would be a negligent Executive and the tool of the same machine in Washington that he had been in New York. There came about, however, a kind of transformation. The politicos were disappointed, the moderates and liberals were agreeably surprised, and the office of the President was the better for his having occupied it.

Garfield and his group, after the nominating convention, had been in such a state of euphoria and so anxious to conciliate the Conkling-Grant faction that they had offered their beaten opponents the vice-presidential nomination without making any conditions or asking for any guarantees. It was a mark of the cynical annoyance of the New Yorkers that they named Arthur instead of any one of a number of other individuals who might have been considered suitable. The Garfield group had gagged a little before accepting as they had promised to do. When they did, it was with the specious explanation that the Vice-Presidency was an innocuous office and that no one could seem to have a better life expectancy than the robust Garfield.

It is not too much to say that the whole nation—even those who had participated in foisting Arthur on the Garfield ticket—were aghast at the thought of Arthur as President. Until the moment of his accession he had still, while Vice-President, been acting as Conkling's second, trying to counter the Blaine influence in the Administration. It was not until he appeared in a different guise entirely in the White House that some other things about him were recalled: he had had a New England origin, his father had been a preacher, he had gone to Union College and earned a Phi Beta Kappa key, he had been a lawyer who was reputed to be smart, and he had used his practice to forward the anti-slavery movement.

It was in his favor politically that he was a large, beautifully tailored and affable gentleman. In this he was a worthy successor of Hayes and Garfield. And, as the country soon discovered, he was considerably better equipped with brains than either. But there was character, too, evidently; he now gave up his association with Conkling, he caused the vigorous prosecution of certain frauds in the Post Office Department which could have been stifled, and he showed a lively interest in the civil service reform Hayes had spoken for but which Garfield had seemed to fear. These were indeed strange vagaries for a person of the sort everyone supposed him to be when he was sworn in to fill out Garfield's term.

Arthur would have had to be more stupid than the average not to understand that Guiteau's bullet, which had been fired in the name of Stalwartism, had put an end to an attitude toward public affairs which had existed since Jackson's time. Guiteau felt so outraged at not being given a job that he felt justified in assassinating the man who could have given it. He had no qualification for it, but neither did others who were more successful. He merely felt that all the plums should go to the Stalwarts. With Garfield out of the way and Arthur in the Presidency, the right people would be rewarded. The whole country understood that Guiteau was a logical result of the factional squabbling that was now perennial. The conspiring and name-calling were finally pointed up with a bullet. For Arthur to have accepted Guiteau's mandate and become the Stalwart man in the White House would have marked him as no better than the assassin himself. The nation was horrified by Garfield's martyrdom, and it went as far as any democracy is likely to go in acknowledging public responsibility for the political atmosphere which had generated assassination.

The becoming conduct of the new President went a long way toward redeeming the promise Garfield had failed to fulfill. Change, of course, had been made far easier by the tragedy; but Arthur must be given credit for having allowed the forces of reform to have their way. There was very general recognition of democratic failure. An editorial in *Harper's Weekly* was one among many comments which helped to establish a new spirit. It insisted that "the ferocity and insanity of party spirit, bred by the spoils system," had been the moving cause of the assassination. It went on to say that the throwing into every election of a hundred thousand places as the prize of success was directly to foster such crimes. The conclusion was that "the abolition of the spoils system is now the most essential and important public duty."[1]

[1] In the issue of July 23, 1881.

Of the atmosphere as Arthur began, Oberholtzer says:

Throughout the country men, without regard to party, were impressed by the need for a new system of distributing the offices
so that seekers after them might no longer plague the President,
and the administration of government could be made more honest
and efficient. Even those who were so dense of intellect as scarcely
to know what was meant by the words "civil service," and those
who were so heedless of the public weal as to attach no importance
to the demand for reform in this field had now had an object lesson
that they could understand, and politicians, whose very existence
depended upon patronage which they could distribute to the "workers," were for once on the point of being overborne.[2]

The Pendleton bill was not passed until 1883, and Arthur's advocacy
of it was something less than fanatic. But then Pendleton, whose name
was given to it, was no reformer either. Both the Senator and the President—as well as those who merely voted for the Act—responded rather
to one of those irresistible waves which carry democracies from one era
to another. The country was sick and tired of political jobbery, although
it seemed to have refused its opportunities to say so. It had awarded
Grant a second term and very nearly a third. After Hayes it had voted
for Garfield and Arthur, who were certainly not advertised as reformers.
But there was violent revulsion after the assassination, and the system began to seem wicked as it never had before. It must be said also that,
beginning about this time, there was a more alert and less partisan press
than there had ever been in the past, and this made the President's position much more secure. He could appeal more readily, and with quicker
response, to public opinion. From now on this would be a developing
resource of the Presidency. The more effective Presidents would again
and again win their way by such appeals. There was nothing really new
about this, of course; Jackson had been thus supported, and others had
depended on opinion to gain their ends. Johnson had lost out, but he would
be almost the last President who would lose an outright contest of this
sort. The pervasive press was a presidential tool of immense value.

At any rate, public opinion was now ready to resist the further development of political chicanery. The arguments for a merit system had
by now been made over and over by a small group of reformers—led by
the Civil Service Reform League—and examples of its opposite had been
exposed with considerable thoroughness. Hayes had made something of
the issue, and, although he had not awakened much support the Garfield
assassination had caused a searching of civic consciences and had suggested
other possibilities. Arthur, in his first message to the Congress, had said

[2] Op. cit., 130.

that he would approve an Act to establish a Civil Service, although he disliked the particular proposal being advocated by the reformers. In his later message (in December 1882) he recognized, he said, that "the people of the country, without distinction of party," had an earnest wish for action: "such action should no longer be postponed." So immediate was the response, and such was its volume, that an obviously reluctant Congress passed the pending bill with as little discussion as possible. So Chester A. Arthur, the Conkling spoilsman from New York, signed the first Civil Service Law and appointed the first Commission under it. Nothing that ever happened to the Presidency gave more relief to the occupants of the office. It began a transformation of the whole Executive Branch which would enable the President, for the first time since the Jackson debacle, to command an effective working force. It also led to relief from the distasteful and exhausting melee of office seekers into which every new President was plunged and from which he extricated himself with embarrassment, if at all. These changes did not come about quickly. The Pendleton bill did not go very far in the desired direction, but it was one step which implied others, and they followed as they were bound to do.

Arthur and the Congress were more willing to undertake this reform because the Republicans were under pressure. They were close to being regarded as the party of corruption after the exposure of vast Post Office frauds; and the fact that Arthur behaved in exemplary fashion in prosecuting those responsible gave him rather than the party a certain credit. When his Administration was no more than halfway through it began to be apparent that the party's long run of luck was about over. What the Democrats had barely missed in two previous elections, they seemed almost certain to gain in 1884. There had been a spectacular campaign in New York State in 1882 in which Grover Cleveland had been elected to the Governorship. Better government and civil service reform had been the pleas which had elected him.[3] The year 1883 saw some other changes of which the Pendleton Act was a kind of corollary. Seth Low was re-elected Mayor of Brooklyn, and Tammany was on the defensive. In Pennsylvania, Ohio, and Massachusetts there were occurrences which the Republicans could only read with foreboding. But if the Civil Service began on a wave of reform not likely to continue and was only a grudging sop thrown to the reformers by the professionals, it was the beginning of something which in a distant future would be the end of them, at least in their old free-swinging and open incarnation.

Arthur's assertion of an independence and courage no one had believed him to possess so endangered his position with the professionals that he was not renominated. He was forced to give way to Blaine, who now

[3] They had also re-elected Theodore Roosevelt to the New York Assembly, something significant for the future.

emerged from his place as President-maker and dictator of Republican policies to become a candidate. He was an inner-circle party man and was, moreover, immensely popular. He seemed an ideal candidate. As it turned out, the Republicans had presumed too much on the credulity and patience of the public. Their long occupancy of the White House—since the retirement of Buchanan in 1861—was ended in 1885 by the accession of Grover Cleveland, who had had an amazing rise from the mayoralty in Buffalo to the Presidency after only two years in the Governorship. His election re-established the rhythm of party alternation. Throughout the Republican supremacy there had been about as many Democratic as Republican voters—sometimes more—but something had always seemed to prevent their capture of the White House. Campaigns and elections were not scrupulously conducted in those years, but the Republicans were perhaps even less scrupulous than the Democrats. Grant, Hayes, and Garfield were all elected in doubtful circumstances or for reasons extraneous to the office they were to occupy. In the Blaine-Cleveland race, Cleveland had the better of an exchange of villifications, and anyway, the electorate was tired of humbuggery and boss rule. Cleveland was at least a sturdy and independent citizen.

With the resumption of alternation between the parties, expansion of the civil service began to have an interesting effect on the Presidency. As the merit system grew in popularity under the steady encouragement of reformers' propaganda, it occurred to outgoing politicians that they could prevent at least some of the losses they were about to suffer by adding to the number of protected job holders. By the end of their time in office, the Departments were filled with their partisans; they then "covered them in"—that is, gave them civil service status. And this gradually became a regular matter as party control alternated. There was resistance and there was sabotage, there were also setbacks and a great deal of congressional resistance, but the list of permanent jobs grew with each party change. The enormous relief this gave to the President can hardly be measured, but some estimate of its effect can be had by recalling the ordeal of Lincoln in the tragic circumstances of an oncoming civil war and comparing it with the relatively decent change at the beginning of more recent Administrations.

What later became a regular feature of expiring Administrations was begun when it was clear that Cleveland had been elected. Throughout the government there was a reduction (as far as that was possible within the rules) of the number of patronage positions. Examinations were required for many more. The Democrats would thus have fewer jobs at their disposal. But by that time the Pendleton Act had been passed and was in process of establishing its machinery, and this was an even greater contribution to the merit system; it, too, would not have been favorably considered if the Republicans had not been pretty certain that they would lose the next election. When the Congress met in December 1882, they had already lost the House. Arthur's message told them that the country demanded reform and promised to support it himself. It was in this atmosphere of party desperation that the first Civil Service Law was passed. It won in spite of sneers and ridicule from the professionals (Conkling spoke of it as "snivel service reform"). In nearly every similar situation thereafter more or less the same antipathy would be registered. Nevertheless, the movement would go on.

In the period before the Spanish-American War, however, the most notable gain for the Presidency came not from this long-needed reform, important as it was, but from the reversal of Republican theory and practice as soon as Cleveland succeeded. He was a vigorous and stubborn man, conservative and careful, but jealous of his prerogatives and alert to the public interest. His conservatism hampered his approach to the problems of depression during his second term and was responsible for his interference in the Pullman strike. But that incident is of special interest in the presidential history.

This interest lies in the recurrence of a President to the Rule of Necessity, in abeyance (and in disfavor) since its invocation by Lincoln in the emergency of war.

★ 28 ★

IN SEVERAL STRIKING INSTANCES WE HAVE SEEN AN ENLARGEMENT OF
the Presidency come about through actions taken with the utmost reluctance by Presidents of the moment. So both Jefferson and Jackson had to
reverse professed positions, and Lincoln, although he admitted nothing,
knew well enough, as lawyer and politician, that he had exceeded the
limits of what had theretofore been thought allowable to the Executive
even in the gravest circumstances. It may now also be recorded that Cleveland exceeded these limits. To suppress disorders incident to the Pullman
strike of 1894 in South Chicago he called in the army with no sort of
consultation with the state authorities. Since he was a lawyer, it may be
presumed that he was fully aware of his offense. He was a matter-of-fact
person, not given to theoretical examination, and he was therefore not
tormented by doubt; but the only possible excuse he could have adduced
for the employment of armed force was the Rule of Necessity referred
to here a number of times previously.

Concerning the particular situation in which Cleveland, by implication,
invoked the Rule, the Constitution is perfectly clear; the relevant passage reads as follows:

> The United States shall guarantee to every State in this Union a re-
> publican form of government, and shall protect each of them against
> invasion; and *on application of the legislature, or of the Executive*
> (*when the Legislature cannot be convened*) *against domestic vio-
> lence.* (Art. IV, sec. 4.)

The italicized words indicate the circumstances in which the President
may intervene in domestic crises; these did not exist when Cleveland
moved troops into the riotous area. He did not wait for a request, because
he thought the disorders had reached a dangerous intensity and because
Federal interests were involved. The evidence seems to indicate that there
would have been no serious consequences if he had not intervened. For
our purpose here, however, this is less important than that he exceeded the
constitutional limits for presidential action and that he not only succeeded
but was widely praised. There was no effective dissent, except from the

strikers and the Governor. The strikers happened to be led by Eugene V. Debs, who was in disfavor as an incendiary radical, so there was active minority protest. But there was also massive majority support. And the complaints of the Governor were ignored.

The impulse to this drastic presidential behavior came from the widespread fears among the well-to-do that revolutionary movements were under development and becoming dangerous to their interests. There was some reason for this apprehension. There were deplorable conditions. Booming industry oppressed its employees; there was no security for a worker or for his family beyond his pay check, and this might be cut off without reason or notice. Places of work were dangerous, hours were cruelly long, and living conditions were intolerable. The struggle for collective bargaining was just beginning on a large scale, and the suggestion that it ought regularly to be resorted to seemed subversive not only to employers but to most of the public as well. Cleveland was not an unsympathetic man—he had grown up in the knowledge of these conditions —but he was in authority, and authority is supposed to preserve order.

It is at least interesting to note that this was Cleveland's second term and that during his occupancy of the Presidency he had felt no responsibility for avoiding or in any way ameliorating the conditions which precipitated this—and other—disturbances. His meeting the worst of many such crises with stern violence instead of an attempt at probing or mitigating the causes is directly traceable to the view he held of his presidential duty. This is to say that, although he was a Democrat, he fully shared the Whig-Republican view of the scope of Federal power and the role of the Chief Executive in domestic matters. These did not extend to the maintenance of prosperity and certainly not to the increase of well-being. Even when the maintenance of tranquil conditions was necessary, it was expected that it would be done by local or state authorities. Cleveland's expectations were equally orthodox until he was forced to consider his obligation in particular circumstances.

He would have been amazed and indignant if he had been accused of contributing to the depression of 1893. Yet even then political parties and their leaders were certainly beginning to be held accountable for hard times and were claiming credit for prosperity when it existed. This was the period of the money-madness, too, when the free coinage of silver was being advocated as a relief from the restrictions of the gold standard. This was a political cause; it had fanatical propagandists and many supporters, and it was directly concerned with economic conditions. The agitation got its drive from the distress of debtors—notably the farmers who had borrowed to purchase land and now had to pay up in hard money. But they had little to pay with. There had been destructive droughts; also, the prices of their products were ruinously low. It was the resulting distressful conditions which were causing them to protest. And as for workers, unemployment, starvation wages, and high living costs furnished them with legitimate grievances. It was beginning to be fanciful to say, as conservatives did continue to repeat, however, that government must leave business alone, that freedom of enterprise was necessary to prosperity.

This was Cleveland's position too. He was a rock in the path of monetary reformers, a gold Democrat. He was not so naïve as to believe that tariffs, for instance, had no effect on business. He was in favor of lowering them, although he was unable to prevail on the Congress to accept his advice. But on the whole he was a conservative whose views differed very little from the prevalent ones of businessmen and bankers. The well-being of farmers and workers on which tranquillity might rest was none of his affair. But the tranquillity was. He did not hesitate to take direct and unprecedented action to preserve it.

Those who have felt that Cleveland acted intemperately and unjustly in the Pullman strike have still had a certain sympathy, usually, for the solid, temperate man who happened to be President when the tides of change were mounting and the old conceptions were proving to be so hopelessly incapable of containing them. The rigid notion of freedom for businessmen regardless of the effect on the economy; the "liberty" of the workman to starve when unemployed and of the farmer to suffer when his crops failed or could not be sold; the right of creditors to collect debts regardless of disaster to debtors—all these were maxims of a system believed in by Americans generally, even by those who lost their jobs or their farms or were ruined in depressions.

There were not many who accepted an outright alternative to the system which included these characteristics and produced these results. It was still one which seemed to produce progress. If some suffered, others gained; if there were hard times, prosperity soon returned. It was only necessary to hang on, to tolerate deflation, and wait for the upturn. Debs was a socialist who believed in meliorative reform, even in the common ownership of productive facilities. But he had more followers as a labor leader than as a philosopher. There was much more political strength in the "western revolt" whose prophets were Sockless Jerry Simpson, Ignatius Donnelly, Mary Elizabeth Lease, and, most refulgent of all, the Boy Orator of the Platte, William Jennings Bryan, who was just beginning to make himself heard.

The strike of the railway workers in Chicago occurred in midsummer of 1894, when one of the most serious depressions in American history was at its worst. It happened to come at a time when the President was particularly exasperated by the long-continued agitation of the cheap-money advocates and worried by the unrest of a people enduring the miseries of hard times. He was also perplexed by the perennial tariff controversy which had got itself mixed with the money question. He had just been defeated—had felt forced to allow a measure he thought unwise to become law without his signature. It had been dictated by "the trusts" and represented a further affront to the agrarians. He had hoped for a different result but had felt compelled to allow the congressional majority its way.

He was in the midst of troubles, then, when he had to meet the emergency situation in Chicago. This helps to explain his actions even if it does not excuse them. Our interest in his exceeding of the formerly established limits of Executive action requires no judgment concerning its actual necessity. Both he and—as it turned out—the country believed the necessity to be overwhelming. It was upon this belief, however unjustified, that he acted and, in doing so, demonstrated that any President might so act.

We must believe, relying on his biographers,[1] that his current preoccupations caused him to accept the advice of Richard Olney, his Attorney General, as to both the seriousness of the situation and the action he must take. Olney was prejudiced in favor of one side of the suddenly acute controversy; he was also an intemperate reactionary. He planned—"artfully," Professor Nevins says—a course of action calculated to carry out the intentions of employers who had long looked for a suitable opportunity to crush the growing labor movement. Olney was so intimate with the employers as almost to be one of them. When a railway strike was called, it seemed to him the occasion he had been looking for to show labor its place. If it was necessary to provoke more violence than would otherwise have developed and to exaggerate that which did occur, it would be in a good cause.

The Chicago workers had particular grievances. The Pullman Palace Car Company had reduced wages, in a series of cuts, by about one fourth, pleading poor business. At the same time it had held undivided surpluses of many millions and continued to distribute them as dividends. The whole weight of the economizing because of slackened activity was expected to be borne by the wage earners. There were other reasons for disaffection, one of them being the rapacious management of the Pullman company town in which many of the employees lived. The line-up was precipitated by the existence on either side of a militant group looking for trouble. If the General Managers Association was out to teach workers a lesson, the American Railway Union was intent on capturing railway labor by showing that it could do more for its members than the more conservative brotherhoods. The ARU had been organized only the previous year but, with Eugene V. Debs leading it, had quickly acquired a large membership. While the union was meeting in Chicago in June the Pullman Company was asked to accept arbitration in the dispute it was then having with its employees. The company refused, and the ARU de-

[1] Particularly Allan Nevins, whose *Grover Cleveland: A Study in Courage* (New York, 1934), is sympathetic but realistic.

clared a boycott and called a strike. This brought the union into conflict with the organized officials of the twenty-four railroads making up the General Managers Association.

Within a few days there were reports in Washington of the interruption of mail services and of the blocking of freight traffic in the Chicago interchanges. But also there were reports of incipient violence. The city was crowded with derelicts and casuals deposited there by the depression. Besides, there were more than a hundred thousand legitimate workers who were without jobs and were desperate for income. There had been demonstrations, and the streets were never free of milling crowds. The permanent residents were already uneasy; and the strike, with potential outbreaks of violence, induced a public panic. The newspapers were exhibiting a kind of frenzy, led, naturally, by the *Tribune*, which said in a headline on June 28, "Debs Is a Dictator," and on the thirtieth, "Mob in Control." Two days later its headline screamed, "Mobs Bent on Ruin."[2] This hysteria was baseless. It was intended to precipitate action on the part of the government which would suppress all protests against the current conditions. It was a businessmen's demand for protection from the results of policies they had insisted on. The newspapers were their organs; the propagandists displayed even more enthusiasm for the reactionary cause than was warranted by the attitudes of their clients.

So the stage was set, but the actual presidential intervention seems to have been undertaken almost entirely because of Olney's initiative in finding reasons for acting and in showing the way to act. The procedure was to procure an injunction against the strikers and then to enforce it against violators. Olney himself saw no particular need to be so meticulously legal. He said later that in his opinion the President might have used the army to prevent interference with the mails or with interstate commerce "without waiting for action by the courts and without justifying the proceeding as taken to enforce judicial decrees."[3] But if it was preferred that there be legal grounds, they would be found, first in the Anti-Trust Act, which made any combination in restraint of trade illegal and which applied to labor as well as to business, and second in the right of any court of equity to enjoin a threatened public nuisance.

Olney had been a railroad lawyer and even a director, and he had been a member of the General Managers Association; this was sufficient indication of his interest. But, beyond this:

> His natural bent had always been towards the defense of property rights, and particularly corporation rights. Moreover all Spring he had been struggling with disturbances caused on the western rail-

[2] Ibid., 614.

[3] This was in a letter to Henry James, ibid., 616.

roads by the Coxeyites or commonwealers. He had been aroused to a high pitch of indignation by their tactics, and had perfected a technique for dealing with them . . . Most of the roads were in the hands of Federal receivers, and the courts could not look on without an effort to save their property. They had therefore issued orders to Federal marshals to protect the railroads—orders which Olney had found were seldom effective because marshals could not find enough deputies to enforce them. In these circumstances, Olney had instructed the judges and marshals to join in applications to the Department of Justice for help from the Federal army . . .[4]

This was also the technique used in the Chicago situation. Olney dictated the procedure of provocation and directed the courts and marshals with aggressive confidence. He presently had a real emergency in being and could proceed to suppression. Cleveland, if without much consideration because of his preoccupation with other pressing matters, gave consent and was soon drawn into active participation. At the beginning of July he took command, and for a week or more it is said that he hardly slept. He held long conversations with General Miles and with others who were on the scene and acted on the information thus obtained. There was by then something like a reign of terror on Chicago's south side, whether induced by "anarchists," as Olney said and as the newspapers repeated, or provoked by the violence of the "suppressors," as the labor leaders contended. On the seventh of July there was a pitched battle between the troops and the mob of strikers. Seven were killed and many were wounded. On the tenth Debs and other labor leaders were indicted and arrested for obstructing the mails. Order was gradually restored.

There was a long aftermath. Governor Altgeld protested bitterly that he had not asked for assistance as the Constitution clearly required, and there were many others who believed the violence to be the result of provocation. Hardly any student since has found it possible to excuse Olney's partiality and savagery, although they give him credit for resourcefulness. Cleveland never apologized; indeed, his view of the matter was summed up in his remark that if it took the entire army and navy of the United States to deliver a post card in Chicago that card would be delivered.

This remark would seem to indicate that he rested on his constitutional duty to see that the laws were faithfully executed. He, like Lincoln, had found two conflicting directives and had chosen to obey one. What Olney had been interested in and what he had involved the President in was intervention in a labor dispute on the side of the employers. No other conclusion can be reached, and that was the real reason for the wave of

[4] Ibid., 615.

approval that swept the country. Labor had got out of hand and was threatening property. This must be stopped, and Cleveland stopped it. As one correspondent wrote, "The nation does not exist if anarchy and destructive despotism take the place of law."[5] He was speaking for a good many frightened citizens. Cleveland may well not have considered that he had done more than protect the Federal interests. But the whole nation seemed to feel that it had been rescued from threatened revolution; it was grateful to have so stern a disciplinarian in the White House. Clearly the Rule of Necessity was overwhelmingly approved; and if there were later reservations and protesting criticisms, it was then, as usual, too late. The incident was closed and the record written. A President, in emergency, is expected to act.

[5] Ibid., 625.

★ 29 ★

CLEVELAND WOULD SEEM TO HAVE BEEN POTENTIALLY THE ABLEST AD-
ministrator in the line of the Presidents. He had a complete grasp of the
government's activities—or as good a one as it was possible to have without
budget or personnel offices and with only the customary personal staff
of a few people; he was capable, too, of furious concentration; the piles
of work on his desk occupied him through long hours of the day and
night. Consequently he developed that bad habit of frustrated managers
—the compulsion to do everything himself so that it would be done in a
way he considered to be proper. This made it impossible for him to devote
the attention he should have given to some of the larger issues. They had
a way of coming upon him unexpectedly. This was what happened in
the incidents considered here. But he radiated power and confidence,
and if he had not been in public life he would probably have gone on
from his practice of corporate law to become one of those captains of industry who were then so prominent. His solid body conveyed the impression that there was on the job a man who made up his own mind and
would tolerate no nonsense. His leadership was quickly accepted by the
electorate and never was questioned.

It is true that he was defeated for re-election in 1888, but this was not
because of a national decision against him; he had a majority of the popular vote, but it happened not to be reflected in the Electoral College.
In 1892, after four years of Benjamin Harrison, who met so perfectly the
standard of respectable nonenity, Cleveland was re-elected. This is the
only instance of re-election after defeat and is to be thought of as a kind of
payment for courage and integrity. It did not mean that there was as yet
an acceptance of the necessity for a transformed Presidency. There was a
mounting crisis of sorts, but it was not yet one which would force governmental changes corresponding with those in the economic world. So we
have the picture again of a man, terribly overworked, struggling to meet
his obligations without the equipment for his task, even, perhaps, the
ideological equipment which would release him from the limitations of
custom. He did nothing to enlarge his office, but he insisted that the Presi-

dent should be strong in the matters to which his obligation extended. He regarded it as his duty to ensure tranquillity, and we have seen how far he would go to carry out that duty. He was equally firm and decisive in the conduct of foreign affairs, as we shall see. And of course his was the final battle of the several needed to dispose of the Tenure of Office Act, thus pushing the Legislative Branch back out of disputed ground within the Executive enclave.

In the controversy with Britain over Venezuela something was added to tradition; and it may be noted that it was done for the specific purpose of gathering into the presidential ambient all the negotiations with another nation and of keeping there the initiative in their conduct:

> . . . his aim was at one sharp stroke to bring the whole matter into his own hands, compel England to yield to arbitration, and put Congress in a position where it could not interfere . . .[1]

As in other instances, this presidential initiative evoked an instant and enthusiastic response. Even in the Congress there were speeches offering support, and some came from the opposition. The response, indeed, went beyond anything Cleveland desired. It uncovered a sinister strain of belligerence which had had no stimulus during the years of peace while the nation was growing so powerful. This same xenophobia would issue during the McKinley Administration in the attack on Spain, the most senseless of all American wars, and in the lingering imperialism of Theodore Roosevelt, one of the heroes of that war. Some contemporary commentators deplored the risks taken by Cleveland for the slight gain of an expanded and confirmed Monroe Doctrine, but more were delighted that the nation was at last asserting itself. Senator Lodge, who would be one of the Roosevelt circle and would still be waving the flag when Wilson's League of Nations reached the Senate, made one of the most bellicose speeches. But if the President's firmness called out a dangerous response, it was quickly calmed by his success.

The controversy into which Cleveland and Olney[2] injected themselves concerned one of the then least valuable areas of the earth's surface—the borderland jungle between Venezuela and British Guiana. Ever since Britain had taken the territory from the Dutch, and especially since Venezuela had become independent, there had been argument about the boundary. Several attempts at settlement had failed, and the tempers of the British had gradually risen. The Venezuelans were difficult. It looked finally as though there might be an attempt to conclude the matter uni-

[1] Nevins, op. cit., 640.

[2] The same Olney who as Attorney General had maneuvered his Chief into the interference in Chicago was now Secretary of State and exhibiting the same qualities.

laterally by force. It was felt by watching Americans, who were inclined to be critical of Britain anyway, that this involved the Monroe Doctrine. They managed in a short time to work up a minor frenzy. Several attempts to reason with the British were either ignored or evaded, with the inference, it seemed to the irascible Olney, that it was no business of the United States.

At length a note was "fired" at Britain which was described as "a twenty-inch gun." It called attention to frequent suggestions of good offices, but it also said that the "United States has made it clear to Great Britain and the world that the controversy is one in which both its honor and its interests are involved." There was also added a sentence destined to become as famous as that about the delivery of the post card in Chicago. It said that "today the United States is practically sovereign on this continent, and its fiat is law upon the subjects to which it confines its interposition." It took the British some time to react to this declaration; not until months later was a reply delivered in Washington. This long delay irritated Olney and gave Cleveland, as well, time to become wrought up at what he regarded as arrogant inattention. When the reply did come it was based on a construction of the Monroe Doctrine narrow enough to allow Lord Salisbury the contention that the United States was not called on to interfere. In a boundary dispute involving European nations, he said, the interests of the United States were not involved; and this one had been prolonged by a most unreasonable attitude on the part of the Venezuelans. The matter would not be submitted to arbitration.

This communication called out Cleveland's special message to the Congress of December 17, 1895. He asked for an appropriation to be used by a commission to be appointed by himself which would determine the boundary in dispute. Once it was drawn, he said, he would see that it was respected. The words he used were these:

> When such a report is made and accepted, it will, in my opinion, be the duty of the United States to resist, by every means in its power, as a wilful aggression upon its rights and interests, the appropriation by Great Britain of any lands . . . which we have determined of right belong to Venezuela.

But it was even more important that he drafted a last paragraph saying that he was fully alive to the responsibility he incurred and keenly realized the consequences that might follow. He was, nevertheless, firm in the conviction that

> there is no calamity which a great nation can invite which equals that which follows from a supine submission to wrong and injustice, and the consequent loss of national self-respect and honor, beneath which are shielded a people's safety and greatness.

The British decided on discretion, the dispute was settled, and the incident passed into the nation's records. One of its results was the awakening of the British—and other European nations then actively extending their territories—to the opposition in the United States that could instantaneously be aroused by any such ventures in the Western Hemisphere. The Monroe Doctrine was still very much alive. At home the effect was to demonstrate the popular conviction that the President had seized a proper occasion to assert his prerogatives. He had grasped and expressed the latent feeling of the electorate. He was the leader, they the led; and this was as it should be.

Years afterward, commenting on the incident in *Presidential Problems*,[3] he was inclined to accept the whole responsibility for himself and to slight the part Olney had played in setting up the controversy, much as he had set up the Chicago situation, so that intervention would be called for. He was even inclined to be eloquent about the worthiness of a people who had come to his support so powerfully. But he had never been a perceptive man, only an industrious and determined one. He spoke, in the later disquisition, of the "sublime patriotism and devotion to their nation's honor exhibited by . . . the plain people of the land . . ." He also went on to say that there could be few of our fellow citizens who, in retrospect, did not acknowledge the good that had come to our nation through this episode:

> It has established the Monroe Doctrine on a lasting foundation before the eyes of the world; it has given us a better place in the respect and consideration of the peoples of all nations, and especially of Great Britain; it has again confirmed our confidence in the overwhelming prevalence among our citizens of disinterested devotion to American honor; and last, but by no means least, it has taught us where to look in the ranks of our countrymen for the best patriotism.

What he did not say, but what is now apparent, is that he advanced the Presidency immensely by foreclosing the leadership in foreign affairs which might have escaped him if he had temporized. It can also be seen at a distance that he acted in one of those moments of intense understanding, a presidential moment, when he was at one with the people whose representative he was. He understood what was required of him and proceeded with appropriate energy to do it. That the sentiment he personified was belligerent and meretricious and that the risk he incurred was not worth any possible gains from it are historical conclusions. His resolution, however unjustified by the circumstances, was of immense use to the office he held.

[3] (New York, 1904.)

But there is still another credit to be recorded for Cleveland in the history of the Presidency. He brought to an end the protracted aggression upon it represented by the Tenure of Office Act, which was still in effect, even if modified, as he began his first term. It had been passed, it will be recalled, in Johnson's Administration and amended in that of Grant. It had caused trouble for Hayes, Garfield, and Arthur. It remained for Cleveland to liquidate it. This would not end the impulse of the Legislative Branch to assert itself in the Executive field, but it would bring one phase of the struggle to a definite end.

It will be recalled that by the terms of the original Act no official requiring confirmation by the Senate could be removed without the approval of that body. When the Senate was in recess there might be a suspension for cause, but within twenty days of the Senate's meeting again the reasons for suspension must be reported; if concurrence was not forthcoming the official would be reinstated. In 1869 the act had been modified to provide that a President might suspend without reporting his reasons; and reinstatement, if the Senate failed to approve, was dropped in favor of a provision allowing the President to make repeated nominations until one was approved. It will also be recalled that Grant might have secured a repeal but that his deference to the Senators had prevented. One of these Senators had been George F. Edmunds, who had also been one of the authors of the act. This same Edmunds was still a Senator as Cleveland began his Presidency and was now, through seniority as well as ability, very influential. He also commanded—or thought he did —the Republican majority which still held over in the Senate in spite of the Democratic victory in 1884.

There were several reasons why an early clash between the Republican Senate and the Democratic President was certain to happen. This was the first victory for the Democrats since the election (in 1856) of Buchanan, and the demand for offices was tremendous; but the Senators, some of long standing, had whole regiments of protégés nicely placed in the Departments, and they were bound to protect them if they could. If the Tenure of Office Act could be invoked they might at least bargain with the President. Edmunds, with Senator Sherman and other elders supporting him, immediately asserted that both dismissals and nominations were within senatorial discretion. It was proposed to use the same means of coercing the President that had. been used before. It had not succeeded then, but Edmunds felt that his position in this instance was impregnable. He commanded a majority, and Senate concurrence was necessary to appointment; unless satisfactory nominees were offered, and unless Republicans were protected in their jobs, confirmation would simply be withheld. For support he relied on appeal to the public against Democratic spoilsmen.

There was another issue involved in this, as Cleveland saw at once.

The Senate demanded information from Department heads about both dismissals and appointments. The strategy was to make public such of this information as would show that injustices were being done and that dismissals were purely political. They reckoned without Cleveland. It might be that he had risen to the Presidency very quickly from the Mayoralty of Buffalo and might not at first be competent to deal with national and international issues, but he was experienced in politics and he understood the relationship in the American system between the Branches. He had had hard lessons in Albany, where he had dealt with a hostile legislature. He knew better than to compromise.

He instructed his Department heads, when they were asked by Senate committees for information concerning nominees, to send only information about nominations. About these the Senate did have a duty to concur, but it had no right to interfere with dismissals and had none to confidential information on which appointments were based. This last was an important distinction now made clearly for the first time. A President, Cleveland reasoned, could actually be acquainted with only a few of the appointees he must approve; he must rely on information from sources he trusted. These must be protected or they would be closed. The Senators might have such information as was open to everyone; they might even inspect endorsements; they would not be given anything more.

At the beginning of 1886 the President and the senatorial majority stood publicly opposed on this issue. There were evidences of a lively public interest. The Senate opened the battle in February by resolving in Republican caucus that confirmation would be refused for appointees who were to succeed suspended officials unless the reasons for the action were submitted. The resolution was supported by a report from the Judiciary Committee—written by Edmunds himself—making the appeal most likely to be persuasive: that the Congress ought to have access to all documents in public offices created by themselves. It was evident that the Senators expected wide support for this position. The President would obviously be thought to have something to conceal if he should refuse such information.

But Cleveland was a stubborn man and, in such matters, resourceful. He knew that he could win such a contest in the long run because it was he who must nominate in the first instance; and he might simply refuse, leaving the onus of neglected offices on the Senators. But also, as other Presidents had done, he might proceed to make recess appointments. If confirmation was refused, he might regard the office as vacant and reappoint the same individual. This was unsatisfactory, but it could be done.

But the battle was really won by his message of March 1, 1886. In this he said flatly that he believed the Tenure of Office Act to be unconstitutional (an opinion afterward concurred in by the Supreme Court); but even if it were not, the directions concerning the submission of information had been repealed in 1869. Even further than that, the demands were unreasonable. He had confidential information that no one else had any right to inspect. He might or might not have relied on it. It might be injurious, because irresponsible or prejudiced, to the candidate he had finally chosen. His main reliance, however, was on what the Senators ought to have anticipated, the same one Jackson had appealed to—he had a duty to the people flowing from his election by them to the Presidency, and neither party pleas nor threats such as were made in the resolution of the caucus would discourage or deter him from following in the way he was convinced led to better government. In the heat of controversy, this large man, who was ordinarily a stolid, even lethargic, individual, could find a vein of righteous eloquence worthy of his preacher father. It accomplished his purpose.

Not only did his nominations begin to be confirmed and requests for information concerning dismissals cease, but in the course of the next year a bill was introduced, favorably reported by Senator Edmund's own Judiciary Committee, and passed, repealing the Tenure of Office Act altogether. It was a really notable victory for the Presidency.

IT IS NOT UNUSUAL TO HEAR CLEVELAND REFERRED TO AS "A THIRD KIND of President"—the other kinds being represented usually by Buchanan at one extreme and Jackson, Lincoln, or Theodore Roosevelt at the other.[1] Cleveland is placed in the center of a scale running from "strong" to "weak." Accepted as this moderate type, he has a certain interest for students of the Presidency.[2]

If we look carefully at Cleveland's life we can see some of the reasons why he became this kind of Executive. The man from western New York conformed, not literally, but in a symbolic way, to the log-cabin tradition so long dominant in American politics; that is to say, he had been a poor boy who had made his own way in the world. In fact, he was a minister's son whose father had died while he was still a boy and had left him without resources and with pressing family obligations.[3] So he was self-made

[1] The first Roosevelt, on occasion, praised Washington and Lincoln as the predecessors he admired most. Cf. letter to Sir George Trevelyan, cited in Rhodes, *The McKinley and Roosevelt Administrations* (New York, 1927). Rhodes was sent a copy of this interesting letter, which will be referred to again.

[2] Sydney Hyman, for instance, has spoken of Cleveland in this way. Cf. his article, "What Is the President's True Role?", the *New York Times Magazine*, September 7, 1958, 17 ff.

[3] Photographs of the various houses occupied by the family of Richard Cleveland in Caldwell, N.J., where Grover was born, and in Fayetteville and Holland Patent, N.Y., where they spent some years, show them to have been commodious frame structures conforming to the village type of the forties and fifties. The minister was respectably housed. He was, however, paid a very meager salary, not enough to command educational and other advantages as his children grew up. But in this a minister's family was not much worse off than most others. And the education of those years was gauged to the needs of boys who must also work for a living and perhaps contribute as well to the family exchequer. Cleveland's

and self-educated, as Americans preferred their Presidents to be. But that kind of criterion was at the latter end of its predominance. The frontiersman was losing out to the settled farmer and the businessman. Presidential candidates were likely to come from the populous industrialized states— Cleveland from New York, Harrison from Indiana, McKinley from Ohio, Roosevelt from New York, and Taft again from Ohio. And not for a very long time would there be another serious aspirant from the South. The gentlemen were through, the businessmen were coming up, and they were likely to be much less interested in a log-cabin origin for their candidates than in safe opinions. Before very long they would be speaking of "practical" men and looking with suspicion at anyone who "had not met a payroll."

Lacking a man who had met a payroll, the next best thing was a lawyer with business clients. Cleveland qualified in this. When as a young man he found himself in Buffalo he was forced to do all sorts of odd jobs while he studied law at night. He was practical, all right, even to an extreme. He seems never to have raised his eyes beyond the immediate task he had to get through. And of course he was rewarded after a hard struggle. He had an uncle in Buffalo who might have done a good deal more for him than he did—Lewis F. Allen, a substantial man of many interests. The Allens lived in a large house just outside the city. It stood in fine grounds and overlooked the wide, racing Niagara River as it funneled out of Lake Erie on its way to Lake Ontario by way of the upper rapids and the Falls.

It was to this house that Cleveland went when he first thought of making a career in Buffalo. The living there was ample in the fashion of the fifties. Among other properties, his uncle also had a place on Grand Island farther down the river, where he maintained a pioneering herd of shorthorn cattle. He had started a herd book and was keeping it up to advance the breed, something of importance to Grover, because although his uncle offered him no allowance he did give him the job of attending to these records for a time until he could find permanent employment.

Grover seems not to have expected more consideration than he got, and this too was characteristic; he was independent by nature. At any rate, he profited very little from connection with his prominent uncle beyond temporary shelter and an introduction to a reputable law firm in whose offices he was allowed to "read." He was not paid, but this too was customary and he never thought himself ill used. For a few years he was a casual visitor in the Allen home, but gradually he developed other friend-

---

boyhood almost duplicated that of Garfield and Arthur and, farther back, of Andrew Johnson, Lincoln, and Grant. Of all the Republican succession, only Hayes was more fortunate. He lost his father but was sponsored by a well-to-do uncle. The Democrats on the whole were from a more prosperous parentage—Buchanan, Pierce, and Polk, for instance.

ships and connections and presently dropped completely out of the family circle. Meanwhile he went back for short spells to bring the herd book up to date or to enjoy one of his aunt's Sunday dinners. And occasionally he stole a day to hunt or fish on Grand Island.

To understand why Cleveland became the kind of President who would leave an unusual impress on the office, it is necessary not only to know the kind of heritage he had but also to see him growing up in the western New York environment and preparing himself to take advantage of the opportunity which would hurry him to the White House from the mayoralty of Buffalo. It was a strange, almost bizarre, career, if the usual political chronicle is kept in mind. In the first place, Mayors seldom rise to other offices. In fact, only Andrew Johnson, before Cleveland, ever held such an office. It is Governors or the occupants of other prominent offices who are more usually considered to be eligible. And although Cleveland became a Governor—which was strange in itself—he came from the wrong end of the state to have any appeal as a presidential candidate. In the second place, he seemed entirely the wrong sort of person: a Democrat, a bachelor, with a corpulent body and a rather repellent personality. It was all wrong, and yet it happened.

Buffalo gradually accepted Cleveland as one of its own. The city was growing fantastically and boisterously as the young man was becoming a lawyer, establishing his practice, serving a term as Erie County sheriff, and retiring comfortably to practice again. From a city of some forty thousand in 1850 it grew to eighty-one thousand in 1860 and went on expanding at a booming rate thereafter. Part of the swelling population was transposed from New England, but there was a swelling increase of German and Irish immigrants before the Civil War. It was a crude, undisciplined, unplanned, ugly, and unsanitary town. Along the lake front there were grain elevators, docks, and processing plants. These were intermingled with saloons, dance halls, seamen's flophouses, and an occasional rescue mission. And the city itself was not much more sightly, although Delaware Avenue and Niagara Square were becoming pretentiously residential, with heavy stone-and-plate-glass houses approaching the mansion class. It was here that Millard Fillmore, a stout, pompous old gentleman when Cleveland was rising at the Buffalo Bar, had his home and drove out in his well-sprung coach. But there were still no pavements, no water or sewer systems, and few of the other appurtenances of civilized urban life.

Cleveland's law offices, when he was a reader and afterward when he was a member of various partnerships, were all in the central business district. For years he lived in rooms close to his office, rejecting all suggestions that he remove to a more suitable residential neighborhood. He resisted with equal determination the lures of marriage and family life. He valued his freedom, he enjoyed the atmosphere of the saloons, and he devoured his work. The fact was that he lived mostly for his practice, not because of any concern to advance the profession or to do good in its work, but because of a compelling instinct for laborious tasks of the sort he was always being presented with. He found that in them his rather narrow but formidable energies were engaged to the full.

He accepted all kinds of cases, but he always avoided representing clients who seemed to him not justified in doing whatever they were up to. Naturally he more and more engaged in civil practice, and more and more his clients were corporations of larger and larger size. When, however, he might have become counsel for the New York Central Railroad in Buffalo, the goal, it might have been thought, of any lawyer's ambition, he refused. This was shortly before he ran for Mayor, and the reason for his refusal is an interesting one. He simply did not care to be disturbed in a way of life and work where he was so comfortably grooved. What he was doing was well within his competence, he was becoming moderately wealthy, and he did not care to become part of so demanding an organization as the rapidly growing railroad was certain to be. The interest in this rejection of an opportunity of much promise to a lawyer is that in so short a time his placid life of office lawyering would be exchanged for the fevers of a public career. He did not want the city for a client any more than he wanted the New York Central, but somehow he could not see his way to a refusal.

He led a most peculiar personal life during the years of his rise to local prominence, not at all like that of most successful political leaders. As a young man he had made acquaintances of his own sort. In his thirties and forties he still kept his bachelor's flat near his office. His rooms were well, even richly, furnished, for he could well afford some luxury. But the part of town where he lived tended toward blight as the better businesses moved uptown. He ate in restaurants, mostly of the sort more properly called saloons. He often spent evenings playing cards and drinking beer, of which he was fond but which was grossly enlarging his paunch. Many of his cronies were political hangers-on and many were even disreputable, but he found them amusing.

This kind of life seemed not to interfere with his work, and certainly, although he enjoyed the company of free-and-easy companions, he was not touched with the corruption of their lives. For him this was relaxation, as other men took theirs at home with their families. And at the same time he was acquiring a reputation for competence. No one in court or in lawyers' discussions of pending cases was ever so well prepared as he; to the last detail he was master of the facts and of the relevant law. This made him known as completely dependable. If there was any one characteristic by which everyone recognized him, it was this; and it was, of course, the core of his public character as well; it was the reason he was turned to when Buffalo's better citizens despaired of breaking the defenses

of the corrupt ring which controlled the vices of the waterfront and pro-
cured the protection of the city's officials.

A succession of businessmen, elected as reformers, had failed to bring
about much change, for reasons of the same sort that would intrigue Lincoln Steffens fifty years later. *The Shame of the Cities* was not the text of
new sins; they were part of the very life of such blowzy agglomerations as
Buffalo. And a ponderous and incorruptible man such as Cleveland was
could do little more than check the plague for his term in office. But this
he could do and did.

Even before this, however, he had had a term of office, so that he knew
quite thoroughly what he was up against. For some strange reason, years
before, he had served as sheriff, probably because the fees were high and
because it was a natural part of the political ward work he had been doing.
For he had served a complete apprenticeship as a heeler and doorbell
ringer while he was also learning to be a lawyer; and the politicians had
found him as hard-working and dependable as had the fraternity of the
Bar. But he was also honest. He said nothing about it, but he never participated in any of the numerous grafting schemes he must have seen going on, and never asked anything for himself in all the hard work he did
in the political slums.

They had known the kind of sheriff he would be, but it had been convenient to have that kind just then. And he had given the office the kind
of administration, almost exactly, that he would afterward give his higher
ones. He had seen that all its duties were done faithfully and honestly;
he had mastered the minutiae of his work; he had governed his subordinates closely—and he had not been re-elected. But when a man was
needed for the Mayoralty under peculiarly trying conditions, he was exactly right. And so it turned out. He made no spectacle of ending graft
and corruption, but he ended it. He knew all about what had been going
on, and he stopped it.

Somewhat the same kind of man was needed for the Governorship in
1882—one who stood apart from the factionalism which had split the
Democrats. Tammany and anti-Tammany were in their traditional positions of antagonism. This made a New York City candidate difficult to
find. When the Republicans nominated Charles J. Folger, who was subservient to the Arthur-Conkling-Gould faction, the Democrats had only
to offer a solid and honest man. The reform group in New York, led by
Abram Hewitt, united with Cleveland's upstate friends to nominate him.
He was elected by a plurality of nearly two hundred thousand, a remarkable total. He made no speeches; his campaign was well run but unexciting.
It was of a piece with the whole Cleveland story.

His Governorship was marked by the same sort of hard, detailed study
at first while he learned his job, and then by straightforward attendance
to state business with such assiduity that he soon seemed to be the very

personification of the Executive. It was always known where he could be found—that was in his office or in the mansion. It was always known where he stood—that was in the position that had about it the aura of common sense. He could not be fooled, and he would not be influenced. He soon had the inevitable Governor's quarrel with Tammany which all his friends said was fatal if he wanted the presidential nomination, but he was not in the least swayed. And in the end, as it usually has, Tammany's enmity proved to be an asset. For in 1884 the Democrats needed a Cleveland and the country demanded a Democrat.

When Cleveland went to Albany from Buffalo it would have been difficult to find a prominent citizen in western New York who had thought so little about the state and its peculiar problems. And this was true again when he went to Washington from Albany. He was as innocent as a child of the large thoughts a statesman must have about his nation's position in the world, about its responsibilities, and about its security. He probably had never considered, either, the role of government in an industrialized society, knit together by networks of transportation and communication. As we have seen, he was called on to assert the intentions of the United States among the expanding powers, and he had to implement his assumption that the government was a peace-keeper in domestic matters but not obligated to accept any positive responsibility for the welfare or happiness of individuals except as these resulted from a firm and even Administration. His long quarrel with the easy-money advocates was based on his conception of what was "sound." Soundness, order, and industry were his guides.

Cleveland was, in fact, an incredibly simple man to have been President toward the end of that century. The industrial revolution was completing its first phase, and social problems incident to long indifference and neglect were accumulating. Of course equally simple men—Harrison and McKinley—succeeded him in 1889 and 1897; but they were Republicans, carrying an even fuller weight of the conviction that society was really governed in the offices and clubs of the businessmen and that it was the duty of the formal government in Washington to conform to their requirements. There was no difficulty about this except when depression bore down on the economy and the restlessness resulting from unemployment and privation had to be dealt with.

It was beginning to be realized that this conception was hardly adequate as a generalization from the facts. There was the complication that choices sometimes had to be made about the favoring of one set of interests over others. Business was not monolithic. The tariff question had been splitting the nation for fifty years. Generally the Republicans had come down on the high side and the Democrats on the low side; but the writing of every successive tariff act—and there were frequent recastings

—was a sordid exhibition of infighting, with legislators as confused puppets and Presidents as prisoners of commitments to party contributors.

But Cleveland's distinction was that he was not a puppet for anyone or any interest. His beliefs were conservative; he had always operated in and with the going politico-economic system, and he saw nothing the matter with it that simple honesty would not put right—the kind of rugged, industrious, and undeviating honesty that came natural to him. When those virtues were called for he would serve. He would not engage in social adventures, but if order or security were threatened he would set himself against disturbers and aggressors. He could not be frightened and he could not be cajoled. In Buffalo the tag attached to him was revealing; he was known as "the vetoing mayor." As Governor and as President he was just as vigilant to protect the public purse and to curb exploiters of the government as he had been as Mayor.

With these marked characteristics in mind we can see why students of the Presidency are apt to speak of him as the "third sort." It is unlikely that he would have said, as Buchanan did, that he had no power to coerce the states when they threatened to leave the Union; and perhaps he would not have defied the secessionists as Jackson did or have suspended the habeas corpus as Lincoln did. But it is easier to think of him as moving, under provocation, into the definitely "strong" category than to think of him as remaining "weak" if the crisis facing him called for positive assertion.

He was not required to stretch extravagantly any of his constitutional powers, but on at least two occasions we have seen that he did not hesitate to enlarge them. And it is a fair inference that if necessary he might have gone farther. Lincoln was called on to preserve the Union. Cleveland was asked to preserve order and ensure the national influence in the Western Hemisphere. He was a man who usually sat at his desk repelling those who would exploit the government. He had not the imagination to lead his party or his country into the new regions of civilization then opening up. He had a narrow view of government's responsibilities for welfare and even for equity among competing interests. These are the reasons for speaking of him as a "third sort."

Sydney Hyman, struggling to make this distinction clear, has said of Buchanan:

> The Buchanan concept rejects the idea of a President as the political leader of the nation. He is rather, as President Grant expressed it, "a purely administrative officer." This means that the main function of the President is to be efficient, honest, decorous, pious . . . He should not make his own political consciousness—if he has any at all—the source of national political consciousness. He

should never make any great demands on the people. As a model
of self-abnegation, he should diminish his own size in the eyes of the
people.[4]

The possible examples of complete contrast with this are numerous. It
does not fit Washington in one way, or Polk in another; it would incredibly
limit a Roosevelt; Truman would consider it absurd. But Mr. Hyman chose
Lincoln to illustrate the opposite; his conception of duty would begin
where Buchanan's ended; it would be

> political instead of legalistic in emphasis, it is highly articulate,
> highly argumentative, and it has a keen taste of political battle.
> Its view of man is nonangelic. It accepts conflict as a natural aspect
> of life itself. And since it does, it looks upon partisan politics as a
> creative instrument that can define, and to some extent at least,
> resolve things in dispute . . . the Lincoln concept makes the Presi-
> dent himself something more than an administrative officer or a civil
> service reformer or a chief of state or a comptroller of the currency.
> It makes the President the nation's first legislator, the inventor as
> well as the executor of policy, the source as well as the summation
> of the nation's political consciousness . . .

So for the extremes—the cautious, withdrawing, indrawn sort, and the
bold, imaginative policy-maker. But there is, in the variety of American
democratic choices, another recognizable kind, much more numerous, perhaps because genius is rare, perhaps because the processes of selection
operate to prevent such a choice except in crisis or in disillusion. This is
the Cleveland type. It represents a concept that

> shuttles between the other two. Now it seems to say the Presidential
> office is chiefly an administrative one; now it seems to say that it is
> also a political one. Now it talks of leading a march toward brave
> new horizons; now it draws back from adventure. Now it seems pre-
> pared to follow the lead of the Congress; now it seems disposed
> to tell the Congress to mind its own business . . .

This is interesting. It cannot be disputed that as we look back we can
distinguish individuals to fit these categories. But the third—the center
one—really has a spectrum so wide as to lose most of the meaning Mr.
Hyman meant it to have. And Cleveland is an illustration not so much of
a type as of an unusual individual. If he had not had a certain few decisions to make he might be classified with Hayes or Harrison; but in other
circumstances, supplied with a clearly seen vision to embody, he might
have been a Polk. He could not have been supplied with a Lincolnian

---

[4] This and the quotations following are from the article cited earlier.

imagination or Rooseveltian verve. But he might have made the Louisiana Purchase, he might have taken Florida and California, or he might have interposed the might of the United States between the dictators of the 1930s and their victims.

He perhaps serves best to illustrate the effect of the Presidency on a capable and conscientious undertaker of its responsibilities who had not considered their extent or consequences. In the two crises we have used here for illustrative purposes he was so hard at work on other matters that he allowed an aggressive associate to create a situation which, when he became conscious of it, he had to resolve by determination and firm judgment. In both, he strained the bounds of his office when he was shown the way by Olney. He had plenty of courage when it was needed, and if he was not regarded by the electorate with affection, he had the respect he earned by his forthrightness and integrity. He was not a leader; he was a caretaker; but in his caretaking the nation's orderly processes and the respect due it from other nations were perfectly safe.

There have been Presidents who might come within Mr. Hyman's center group of which this cannot be said. Of Van Buren, Fillmore, Grant, Garfield, Harding, and Coolidge, for instance, it cannot certainly be inferred that they would have responded adequately to the demands made by a serious crisis. Fortunately they had none to meet which refused to become resolved by being left alone. Like those of whom Milton spoke, who served by only standing and waiting, Cleveland was a President who made an important contribution by simply keeping the brashly expanding nation from doing things it ought not to have done. The Spanish-American War, which was allowed to happen by McKinley a few years after Cleveland had retired, might very well have happened while he was in office if he had not dampened the development of hysteria. This would have led the nation even earlier into that round of guerrilla warfare, occupation, military government, exploitation, and imperialistic expansion which finally began in 1898 and would not be liquidated until in 1946 the Philippines became independent and in 1952 Puerto Rico became a commonwealth.

It is interesting to see what Cleveland in retirement felt about the Spanish war as it approached. At first, as he wrote to Olney, he could not rid himself of the belief that it would finally be averted. There would be, he said, "infinitely more credit and political capital in avoiding war when so imminent than to carry it on even well."[5] But then he saw McKinley giving in to the Congress when he should have stood fast, and he predicted that "before long there will be an earnest and not altogether successful search by our people for justification." Writing again to Olney in April 1898, he expressed to his former Secretary of State his sad con-

---

[5] *Letters,* ed. by Allan Nevins (Boston, 1933), 497.

viction that it was all unnecessary, with the implication that lack of leadership and firm control was responsible for allowing the crisis to degenerate into war:

> My judgment that we would have no war was predicated upon the anticipation that we would continue to hold a position from which we could honorably and consistently meet any conditions that gave the least promise of a peaceful outcome. It seems to me, however, that we have allowed ourselves to be crowded away from that position and that we face today a sad afflictive war, that our own people will soon look upon as unprofitable, and which, in the sight of contemporaneous judgment and history, may seem unjustifiable . . ."[6]

If Cleveland had been President there would have been no war because he would have felt it the duty of a President to follow his own "conscience and common sense" and not the excited urgings of others.

When he retired to Princeton with his charming wife and still growing family, Cleveland, although not an old man and not destined to die until 1908, was beset with various ills which made him almost chronically unwell. But he spoke occasionally and wrote numerous letters to old associates. He was so inclined to be critical that even those who write about him in sympathy speak of him as "querulous." But in view of what was going on about him, this complaining is not hard to justify. The party had been captured by Bryan, whom he regarded as little better than an anarchist; and the Republicans were in power and having first a war and then an orgy of imperialism. It was a hard time for a man who had so long interposed himself between the people and both Bryanism and Republicanism.

Thinking of Cleveland in his retirement, the student feels a lift of spirits as he reads of a telegram sent to William Randolph Hearst, who, with consummate hypocrisy, was getting up a popular subscription to memorialize the sailors lost in the blowing up of the *Maine*. He had asked permission to add Cleveland's name to a long list of endorsers. The reply sent to that practitioner of yellow journalism was this:

> I decline to allow my sorrow for those who died on the *Maine* to be perverted to an advertising scheme for the New York *Journal*.

He was a strong man as he was also a strong President. We must conclude that the one is necessary to create the other.

---

[6] *Ibid.*, 499. Cf. also his letter to Judson Harmon of July 24.

★ 31 ★

BY A CURIOUS COINCIDENCE, THE HOME CHOSEN BY CLEVELAND WHEN he left Washington was in Princeton, where Woodrow Wilson lived.[1] Neither could have guessed that the younger man would be the next President elected by the Democrats. At the moment—1897—he was professor of jurisprudence at Princeton, no more. He was a very well-known writer—indeed, he already had a national reputation—but he had not yet begun a career of action. His best-known book was the *Congressional Government* which had first been published in 1886 and already had had fifteen editions. It had a significance beyond that of most political essays, and not only because its author was rapidly rising in the academic world; it had met a response, for reasons we shall see, in many minds worried by the apparent inability of government to cope with the increasing complexity of economic and social problems.

Cleveland had not long been a resident of Princeton before the university there began to take notice of his presence. He was soon involved in its affairs and was, in fact, made a trustee. Wilson, as a student of politics and government, had followed the ex-President's career with intense interest. The treatise on government for which he was so well known had been thought out and mostly written before Cleveland had become President, but there is reason to believe that observation of Cleveland's behavior as Chief Executive had induced a change in his thinking even

[1] Cleveland would not return to Buffalo, his home for so long and the scene of his early political successes, because of the resentment he still felt at his treatment during his first presidential campaign by certain prominent clergymen supporting the Republican attack on his private life. The center of this was the allegation that he had had an affair with a Mrs. Halpin and that it had resulted in an illegitimate child. The calm acknowledgment of paternity by Cleveland had stopped the rumors and swung public sympathy to him, so that the effect on the campaign was not decisive; but the clergymen had wrung the last drop of scandal from the affair and Cleveland never forgave them.

while this first work was in process of being published. Considerably later he would publish another study—*Constitutional Government*—which would revise, almost reverse, the main conclusions or suggestions for reform in the earlier work. But when the two met at Princeton the ex-President knew the younger man as a political scientist who had advocated a change to Cabinet government for the United States. Cleveland never commented on Wilson's thesis, perhaps never read it, but the two certainly could not have agreed if indeed they ever discussed such matters.

What is concluded in retrospect about Wilson's suggestions is that as an immature observer he had mistaken the congressional supremacy, and the corresponding presidential debilitation, since—and even before—the Civil War, as a permanent condition. Lincoln was the single great leader in the line from Polk through Arthur, and the circumstances of the Civil War were so exceptional that they hardly affected what seemed to be the rule. Almost before he finished his writing, however, he had had some doubts about the trend his reasoning had taken. These applied more to the conclusions he had drawn concerning the necessary changes than to his critical analysis. The outright advocacy of Cabinet government which he had published in an article the year before was omitted from his book; but it did suggest the need for drastic reform.[2]

By the time Cleveland and Wilson met at Princeton, Wilson's doubts had deepened and he was no longer willing to make the same commitment—largely because he had now seen a President in action who was made of different stuff from Grant, Hayes, Garfield, or Arthur. During their regimes a general longing had set in for the positive principal every democracy must have. He had seen this satisfied to an extent by Cleveland, who was not, perhaps, the chieftain he might ideally have been but who had immensely increased the strength of the Presidency and made it once again the locus of power it was meant to be. This power was mostly exercised in negative ways, but it was invincible.

Cleveland, as a member of Princeton's Board of Trustees, was inclined to even more caution and conservatism than his temperament called for. It was all new to him, and he accepted the advice of his learned neighbors, who happened to be mostly supporters of tradition. When Wilson was made president of the university he had an immediate success in reorganizing the curriculum and in changing the methods of teaching, but he ran full into the whole volume of alumni prejudice when he attempted to change the social environment of the students. To abolish the traditional Princeton clubs and democratize the institutions of undergraduate life were to antagonize those who valued very highly these appurtenances of

---

[2] The article was called "Committee or Cabinet Government" and was published in the *Overland Monthly* for January 1884.

their collegiate years. The trustees, under alumni pressure, were split; and the controversy over the issue became a bitter one.

Wilson had an even worse experience in a prolonged conflict with the dean of the Graduate School and his allies—among them Cleveland—who had ideas about instruction at that level which were at variance with Wilson's. The struggle between Wilson and Dean West's faction became a cause célèbre, with the whole campus polarized and with radiating streams of argument reaching far beyond the campus. Wilson was a good deal more favorably regarded by the relatively uninformed public in this, as in the matter of social reorganization, than he was by the Princeton community. Whether he had the right on his side soon became less important than that massive wounds were being opened in the struggle.

The resultant publicity and the generally favorable attitude of the public made it possible for the New Jersey bosses of the Democratic party to adopt him as their candidate for the Governorship in 1910. It was not very generally recognized that his position at Princeton had become untenable and that the nomination was a kind of rescue to be accepted with gratitude.

So Wilson took off into a new realm of practical rather than academic politics with no kindly thoughts of the man who had changed his view of the presidential system. Cleveland had died in 1908 but while he had lived had given Wilson no encouragement or advice. Nevertheless, Wilson's revised view of the office he would do so much to strengthen in his turn continued to develop in the direction it had begun to follow before the personal quarrel. Cleveland may have been an agent of the academic traditionalism so antipathetic to Wilson, but he had shown what the presidential office could and ought to be. And this was for more reasons than just that he had demonstrated how independence in the Executive could reduce congressional pretensions. He was also a conservative who was yet a strong President, thus breaking up the supposed correlation between conservatism and calculated weakness.

Wilson was a conservative of much the same sort (although he would presently be converted to progressivism), and this, added to the admiration he had for the big, bluff, careful man who had so effectually fixed himself at the focal point of government and resolved the diffusive futility of the many-headed governmental machine, was enough to convince him that the Constitution had not, after all, created a monster of irresponsibility caged within the terms of its directives. It appeared that one of the worst difficulties of the past twenty years had been that none of the Presidents had had any of the tough-fibered resolution exhibited by Cleveland. They had been more than the prisoners of Republican theory; they had been the prisoners of Republican bosses. But no one had bossed Cleveland; he had shown what the Presidency could be even when conservative views of the economy were accepted.

Wilson must also have felt a special interest in one who had succeeded so remarkably in politics in spite of an incorruptible independence. When he had arrived at the Presidency he had had no debts to pay. He had been given the nomination—as he had been given the nomination for the New York Governorship—because the party needed him. Quarreling factions had agreed on him because they could not agree on any of their own number. They had known that they could not expect from him more favors than were necessary to party success, any more than they had expected them in Albany. He would give a vigorous and honest Administration of the office; he would respect its customs—patronage, and so on—as practical devices, within the limits of decency and without lending himself to unseemly raids of deserving Democrats or favor seekers. Altogether he had been a phenomenon not seen in the upper levels of political life since before the Administration of Andrew Jackson, when the Madison-Monroe-Adams decency was in vogue and party extremism had not yet invaded Washington to decimate the Departments and transfer the power over policy to hidden interests. But there was also the added attraction that he had shown how the system provided by the Constitution could be made to work as well as—or perhaps better than—the parliamentary one Wilson had found so attractive when he had been a fellow at the Johns Hopkins.

Professor Link, one of the most careful students of Wilson's career, has indicated the divisions of Wilson's activities as they appear in retrospect:[3] the first, from his Johns Hopkins fellowship to his election as president of Princeton, academic and literary; the second, during his presidency of Princeton, administrative; the third, from his nomination to the Governorship to the end of his life, political. It was during the first of these, with which we are concerned at this point, that he came to his conclusions concerning the need to revise governmental institutions. There were two reasons for his conviction that the American government ought to be changed to resemble that of the British. One was his often-expressed admiration for parliamentary institutions and for their expositors and practitioners—Bagehot, Burke, Gladstone, and their contemporaries; the other was his distressed observation that the going government was helpless before other and stronger forces. It was pulled this way and hauled that way; it was manipulated to suit individual ends rather than public ones, and these ends were not agreed on. There was no direction, no policy, no setting out of objectives. A prevailing feebleness and a recurrent corruption were traceable to the avoidance of responsibility. No one could certainly be held accountable when things went wrong because it was impossible to assess the blame. Likewise, anyone might claim credit even if none was earned.

[3] In *Wilson: The Road to the White House* (Princeton, 1947).

This indictment was very generally held to be true. But with the simplicity of one not too much troubled with practical concerns, Wilson accepted the British alternative; and there not many followed him. It was his view that what was needed was what had already been demonstrated to be successful. An Executive owing his existence to, and drawing his power from, the legislature would supply the lacking responsibility. The confusion and anonymity of standing committees, which were the curse of the Congress, would be ended. The Branches would no longer be opposed; policy-making would be centered in a Prime Minister who could also commit the Legislative Branch; and government so unified could proceed to meet the demands of the increasingly complex world. It was persuasive, but inertia lasted long enough for events to answer his argument for drastic change.

It must be said that Wilson's analysis, even if his conclusions (although, it must be remembered, he was cautious about them in his book) seem to have been somewhat hasty, was a shrewd one; and his exposition had that same eloquence which would mark his state papers as President. His introduction disclosed the premise that the Congress was acceptable "as the central and predominant power of the system."[4] But it should be said by anyone who discusses this—as well as others of Wilson's works —that his intention was not a theoretical one only. He meant to describe and to criticize an actually operating institution. He meant to show, not that it failed to meet the criteria of a political ideal, but that it failed to achieve the necessary minimum ends of any government. He meant to offer, he said, "not a commentary (that is, a treatise), but an outspoken presentation of such cardinal facts as may be sources of practical suggestion." If he lacked experience at twenty-seven, when he was writing this introduction, he did not lack intelligence. Neither did he lack boldness. He had looked closely at Washington, not so far from Baltimore, and had watched what went on with rising concern. The time had come to ring bells, blow whistles, and generally raise an alarm. His book was a very loud effort of that sort.

He had never been abroad to investigate other systems, but he had been introduced to them by his teachers and had followed this by continued reading. He had finally reduced the contrast between what he saw at home and what he read about Britain to the statement in his introduction that there were two striking types of governments. These were not, as was sometimes said, presidential and monarchical; they were congressional and parliamentary. They were distinguished thus:

> Congressional government is Committee government; Parliamentary government is government by a responsible Cabinet Ministry-

---

[4] The references here are to the eighth edition of congressional Government, substantially unchanged from the first of 1886 (Boston, 1891).

. . . semi-independent executive agents who obey the dictation of a legislature to which they are not responsible . . . or executive agents who are the accredited leaders and accountable servants of a legislature virtually supreme in all things.

The choice was—this was what it amounted to—between responsible and irresponsible government.

How this had come to be a fair characterization of the American form he discussed in a chapter devoted to the Executive. This was an exposition of the ways in which policies become blurred and diffused in execution, no matter how plain the intention may have been. The principle of divided power written into the Constitution had been made much worse by the machinery set up to make and execute decisions. The committees of the Congress were many; they operated almost independently of each other and of their parent body, and frequently it was obvious that they had no very clear idea of what they were doing. Their recommendations on legislation were offered, and usually accepted, without adequate analysis; and their supervision of the Executive (which Wilson thought should be very close) in carrying out the laws failed in a welter of misunderstanding and recrimination.

The Cabinet was also puzzling; where everything should be clear and direct, everything was fuzzy and indirect. Were the Secretaries political or nonpolitical officers? They were neither the one nor the other with any certainty. And what were their responsibilities? It seemed that they could not make plans, but they could—and did—wreck those made by others. Their status, being so indeterminate, was a commentary on the system itself.

This chapter on the Executive came to a baffling end. The reason given for this was that an analyst had to deal not so much with the Constitution as with operating agencies and with politicians who created and supported them. Then too, time and events altered the nature of governments and affected the intentions of those who ran them. Nothing was firm enough to bear the weight of a complete descriptive structure. What seemed to have been intended by the framers had been evaded or disregarded:

It is not impossible to point out what the Executive was intended to be, what it has sometimes been, or what it might be; nor is it forbidden the diligent to discover the main conditions which mould it to the forms of congressional supremacy; but more than this is not to be expected.[5]

One deduction from the facts is manifest throughout the essay. This is that the Constitution had failed to give the Legislative Branch the au-

[5] Ibid., 293.

thority it must have. But why it must have this authority is not made clear. A reader can only conclude that he thought it needed in order to make complete the congressional supremacy he had already said did not exist. He seems thus to have argued from a conception of the spirit of our institutions rather than the facts. If congressional supremacy needed to be created it could not already exist. It had not occurred to him that the Congress might already have more power than comported with the intention of the Constitution or that that intention might, if properly implemented, reveal a government with initiative as well as balance. He assumed that its then desuetude resulted from a constitutional defect and not from an abuse of the framers' intentions.

In fact, in his concluding chapter he argued that the separation of powers, so fundamental to the kind of democracy the framers had in mind, was something of an accident—a historical accident. The Convention, he said, had copied a transitory form of the British Constitution. This had soon changed in Britain, but the United States was left with it permanently. And it was as unsuitable as its origin would lead the student to expect. The members of the Convention had been, of course, justified in distrusting the Parliament of that time; it was indeed little more than the creature of the Crown. Perhaps because the framers were in strong reaction against both the King and his legislature, they had felt that by giving a certain independence to both they might prevent either from becoming powerful enough to establish a virtual dictatorship. But the result had been that the legislature, naturally supreme in any democracy, was kept from performing the functions of oversight, the assessing of praise and blame, and the free discussion so necessary to the shaping of opinion and to intelligent governing.

The Congress could legislate, but its legislation was, much of it, ill conceived, largely because of the division of authority among so many standing committees. There was not, and there could not be, any plan or program; no one had the responsibility for shaping or for defending a policy. And this lack of decisiveness was tragic in so complex a world:

> As at present constituted, the federal government lacks strength because its powers are divided, lacks promptness because its authorities are multiplied, lacks wieldiness because its processes are roundabout, lacks efficiency because its responsibility is indistinct and its action without competent direction . . .
>
> Nobody stands sponsor for the policy of the government. A dozen men originate it; a dozen compromises twist and alter it; a dozen officers whose names are scarcely known outside of Washington put it into execution.

This is the defect to which, it will be observed, I am constantly recurring . . . because every examination of the system, at whatever point begun, leads inevitably to it as to a central secret.[6]

As has been noted, when it came to downright advocacy of changes in the constitutional structure, Wilson was a little equivocal in this book. There was, indeed, a certain inconsistency because of this. The last chapter seems something of an anticlimax. But all the argument led to one conclusion: that the remedy for the lethargy and divisiveness which were the curse of American political institutions was the adoption of the later British example as the framers—it is inferred—would have done if their work had been carried out a few decades later. After the Civil War the pressure of events had made reform even more necessary than it had been before. Economic growth was startling, the population was growing and moving, the territory of the states was expanding. More effective government was an urgent need. There had been some improvement because circumstances had forced it; it had, however, not been nearly drastic enough to meet the demands made upon central public agencies. The shape and direction of such change as there was, however, forecast an expansion of the Legislative Branch. It was there that the activists in politics had their sphere of action; it was to the Congress that people looked for the containing framework of the new civilization being built across the continent. Wilson could see no other source:

> The central government is constantly becoming stronger and more active, and Congress is establishing itself as the one sovereign authority in that government. In constitutional theory and in the broader features of past practice, ours has been what Mr. Bagehot has called a "composite" government. Besides state and federal authorities to dispute as to sovereignty, there have been within the federal system itself rival and irreconcilable powers. But gradually the strong are overcoming the weak. If the signs of the times are to be credited, we are fast approaching an adjustment of sovereignty quite as "simple" as need be. Congress is not only to retain the authority it already possesses, but is to be brought again and again face to face with still greater demands upon its energy, its wisdom, and its conscience, is to have ever widening duties and responsibilities thrust upon it, without being granted a moment's opportunity to look back from the plough to which it has set its hands.[7]

If this argument had not been made and this conclusion drawn by a future President, we might regard it as a minor item in the history of American political thought, the analysis and inference of an immature

[6] Ibid., 318–19.

[7] Ibid., 316.

student. But Wilson was to become a President, and no student can afford
to neglect this important early phase of his thought. Also, it has to be
recalled that *Congressional Government* was an unusually well received
essay, widely read within and without the profession of political science.
This reception would indicate that the writer spoke for others as well as
himself in part, if not all, of his thesis.

There were indeed many thoughtful persons who, at the end of the
post-war Republican era, were distressed by the continuing futility of
government while the demands upon it were increasing. It was apparent,
after so long an experience, that Executives chosen by the majority party
could not be expected to offer the necessary leadership and to enforce
the necessary discipline. The Democrats might not be any better in this respect; their concept of Federal power vis-à-vis the states was an even
weaker one than that of the Republicans, and they were no more progressive in their view of industrial control. But they did have in their background the Jacksonian willingness to accept the responsibilities of leadership, and at least the northerners were not proud of Buchanan's
unwillingness to protect the Union in its critical days. The alternative they
offered might not be very clear. But there was a certain closeness to the
people which did offer some contrast with the increasing identity of Republicans and businessmen—the rising elite.

The Republicans had kept the Presidency by doubtful means. The
Hayes-Tilden election they had really lost, and Garfield had not won decisively. It was becoming more likely that in some coming contest their
luck would fail; and it did fail in 1884, just as Wilson was finishing his
book. It was at once apparent that Cleveland was a different kind of
Executive. He was uninformed and unprepared; he was, indeed, scarcely
the statesman type—if such a description may be allowed. Wilson watched
his orientation with fascinated interest and saw him gain confidence
rapidly, and with it a sure control which had not been seen for two
decades. When he challenged and bested the Senate oligarchy, Wilson
could see that national direction was indeed possible even in the system
which provided for a separation of powers.

Until this demonstration opened out he, and others like him, had been
asking a despairing question: how was the vitality to be found which
would mark out and guide the destiny of a people? There were many who
had come to agree with Wilson that it must be found by freeing the
Congress from its constitutional restraints, by allowing it to assume forthrightly the powers it had seized and held by subterfuge, even by illegalities. And it must, along with these powers, be asked to assume the
responsibilities that went with them. This was not done now. Powers
were reached for avidly and hung onto persistently; but they were not
used, because there was no institutional structure through which they
could be used; they were dissipated in the committees. There was only

one solution: the Executive must be made an arm of the legislature, and the mass of standing committees must be abolished.

Nothing, it might be said, could have been more mistaken than this conclusion if tested as a forecast of future development. There was another way. It was being found even while Wilson was finishing his proofs, and before he was done with them he became aware of it. Walter Lippmann, among others, has pointed this out:

> . . . during the summer of 1884, while he was, in fact, finishing the manuscript of this book, Wilson began to undergo a fundamental change in his conception of the American system. Something happened then which caused him to refrain from mentioning the drastic reform—namely Cabinet Government on the British model— which he had advocated publicly shortly before. In the book the analysis of the evils of Congressional government still points toward Cabinet Government as the remedy. But Wilson was no longer willing, as he was a year before, to draw that conclusion.[8]

This, says Mr. Lippmann, was "a critical turning point in Wilson's development." He was moving away from the "constitutional notions of his nonage, and toward those which he acted upon when he became President." What caused this drastic revision? "If I might hazard a guess, it would be that what caused him to see the problem . . . in a new light was the rise of Grover Cleveland."

The rise of Grover Cleveland was a turning point not only for Wilson, it was a turning point for government itself. Wilson only recognized the change. There were others who did not or who would not acknowledge that they did. But there would be a growing preponderance who would follow Wilson's conversion to the belief that there was hope, after all, in the constitutional system devised by the framers, whether or not it had been copied from a transitory form of the British Constitution.

The Congress would not cease making further sporadic raids into Executive territory or abandon the impulse to guerrilla warfare inherent in its make-up, but it would never regain the aggressive confidence shown by the Radicals of Reconstruction days, and it would never again have the successes it had had with Johnson and Grant. There would be other Presidents who would carry with them into the White House the full commitment to Republican theory. In fact, one of these would succeed Cleveland. More curious still, one would be elected as late as 1952 and would, moreover, be given a second term. But there would always be a feeling that these were anachronistic survivals. Their withdrawing from initiative

[8] These remarks were made by Mr. Lippmann in his introduction to the Meridian Books edition of *Congressional Government* published in 1956.

would never extend to the dismantling of the welfare and protective machinery set up in more progressive interludes. They would preside blandly enough over a vastly expanded government, refusing to recognize that anything out of the ordinary had occurred, but refusing, also, to countenance any further such occurrences. Still anyone could see that the cause was hopeless; government was bound to be big and responsible.

Professor Charles A. Beard was one late defender of congressional supremacy, and there were others. But their numbers became fewer and their arguments less convincing. The overwhelming impact of the second Roosevelt would so extend the area of governmental responsibility and demonstrate so convincingly the utility of presidential initiative as to smother opposing theorists. The general approbation of his conduct in office would settle the question of presidential independence once for all.

We shall come later to an account of his contributions to the Presidency. First, however, we have to deal with another Roosevelt—Theodore —who, like Lincoln, fitted so badly the Republican pattern but who was, nevertheless, the successful candidate of that somewhat reluctant party. He was, it is due him to say, the first of the modern Presidents. And then, of course, before a second Roosevelt, there will be Wilson himself, no longer merely a theorist but a President.[9]

[9] The further development of Wilson's political thought will be considered when we come to his Presidency.

THE SENSE OF DEDICATION GOVERNING THEODORE ROOSEVELT'S PUBLIC career was not more genuine than Cleveland's or than Hayes's, but it was of a somewhat different sort. His ambition was a more consuming one and he had a more voracious appetite for public notice. Hayes's conception of the presidential role conformed perfectly with the Whig-Republican tradition; Cleveland, the Democrat, was hardly distinguishable from the Republicans in this. And after Cleveland, when matters of immense importance were being decided, the conclusions were not reached in the White House. Even war—the Spanish-American conflict—failed to exalt the presidential office as every other conflict had, or as future ones would.

If, however, war did not make a hero of McKinley, it did create another —the Rough Rider, the warrior of San Juan Hill. Roosevelt, back from his short military service, almost immediately became Governor of New York and from there moved on to the Vice-Presidency. He had hardly got started in that office when McKinley was assassinated and he succeeded to the Presidency, the youngest of all the line.

There had been more than a suspicion among the Old Guard that Roosevelt was not exactly a model member of the Republican party. The apprehension soon flared into alarmed certainty. It appeared almost at once that he would not be merely a passive occupant of the White House, content to take orders from the party professionals and submissive to the congressional will. He had ideas, somewhat formless and chaotic, but still restless and groping, about the transformation that was taking place in the world of commerce and industry; and obviously he felt that the government could not remain indifferent to the consequences of such events as the steel and oil mergers, the growth and revolutionary activities of labor unions, the vast expansion of the railroaders' empires, and the exploitation by the giant businesses of their smaller rivals, their workers, and their consumers.[1]

[1] Roosevelt, on his accession, made two interesting commitments. He intended, he said, to go on with McKinley's policies: they had made the nation strong and prosperous; he would maintain them. And he asked

The background of the Roosevelt story is that amazing transformation
scene which took place in America as the twentieth century opened. All of
a sudden, it seems on looking back, the trends and tendencies of the old
century came to a climax. There was a kind of coming of age and the
nation was no longer young and immature. It had reached the limits of
its expansion westward; it had achieved an immensely productive industry and agriculture which had only to be properly managed from centers
of consolidation to furnish fabulous profits. It had pretensions to culture.
Its recent stretching of muscles had humiliated one ancient empire and
threatened to humiliate others if it should be challenged. The divisions
of the Civil War were at last healed, so it seemed, and its expansiveness
was backed by unified strength. Its population, about thirty million during
the Civil War, was by 1900 a good seventy-five million; and there were
forty-five states, three of them stretching along the Pacific coast and
developing rapidly.

The President of this mighty nation was a man of paramount importance
in the world. Roosevelt was one to appreciate this and to behave accordingly. The backwoods conceptions of the border Presidents, and
those of the postwar generals who deferred to the political bosses, were
now out of date. There was an assertive man in the White House, and
that Mansion had become the official center of a new and growing
empire.

There were already gigantic figures on the American scene when Roosevelt arrived with his identifying shout at the political center.[2] Rockefeller,

---

the whole Cabinet to remain in office as a kind of guarantee that he would
keep this pledge. But it was not long before he was well embarked on
policies horrifying to most Republicans and using the same Cabinet members in his enterprises. His politician's flexibility was in good working
order.

He also said that he had no intention of being another Cleveland and
doing with the Republican party what Cleveland had done with the
Democratic party. He intended, he said, "to work with my party and
make it strong by making it worthy of popular support." (*Theodore
Roosevelt and His Time* by J. B. Bishop, New York, 1920, I, 150.) It is not
to be doubted that, after his fashion, he meant what he said in these
reassurances to the elders who had lost so complaisant a figurehead in
McKinley. But he *was* a politician; and "working with his party" meant
bending it to his will if that could be done and if it suited his ambitions, as
it very soon did. The elders were very probably not surprised—they were
politicians too—when his determination to set the pattern became apparent.

[2] More accurately, perhaps, scream; by all accounts he had a remarkably high, penetrating voice which rose in pitch as he spoke to large
crowds. And in his day there were none of the aids which have made

Carnegie, Morgan, Harriman, and a few others—with their satellites—were the wielders of economic power at the old century's end and the new one's beginning. They were accustomed to think of politics as a nuisance, but a manageable one, even if expensive, and of the Presidency as an office to be relied on as generally friendly. They controlled the Republican party and possessed a citadel in the Senate—where, indeed, many of their own sort sat—and with these strongholds safe, they could do very much as they pleased.[3] They had been ignoring the rising objection to the uses made of their power. Even the sensational radicalism of the Populists and of the growing labor movement affected their schemes very little. Henry Demarest Lloyd had said in 1894, with what seemed to him evidences of industrial breakdown all around him, that the revolution had arrived,[4] and this too was the period when Bryan and Debs were at the height of their influence; but Lloyd was wrong. The revolution was still to be delayed, and neither Bryan nor Debs achieved enough political support to substitute themselves for more conservative aspirants to the White House. Roosevelt was not regarded by the financiers as an ideal President—he worried them—but, quite rightly, they did not anticipate disaster because of him.

The new arrival did in effect outroar the old bulls, and before he was through he would dominate his era, transferring attention, if not power, from Wall Street to Washington. It would not stay there, but that it had once been there was of immense importance. It was Roosevelt's most significant contribution to the future.[5]

---

campaign speaking somewhat easier for later candidates—beginning with Coolidge. The magnifiers for speakers' voices and the radio reaching out to unseen listeners made a change in campaigning. They made a change, also, in the elected President's ability to reach the public with appeals for support. On the whole, they strengthened him in his perennial contest with the Congress. Franklin D. Roosevelt was the first to make full use of this device for enlarging his influence. His "fireside chats" became famous forerunners of a practice all Presidents would follow. Some would use it more, some less, depending on their theory of the Presidency and on their appeal. That Theodore Roosevelt reached so many without this mechanical magnification of his voice is remarkable indeed.

[3] Cf. W. H. White's illuminating book about the Senate, *The Citadel* (New York, 1958); an older but permanently valuable one is Lindsay Rogers's *The Senate* (New York, 1926).

[4] Address in Chicago, October 6. For a convenient reprinting, cf. *American Radicalism* by C. McA. Destler (New London, 1946), Chap. X.

[5] It was a sign of changing attitudes and a recognition of enlarged presidential responsibility that caused special provision for the President's

The big figure of the McKinley regime had not been McKinley himself but Mark Hanna, his sponsor and mentor. Hanna was a businessman who had picked a handsome politician from the ruck in the Congress and made him President. He had directed campaigns, controlled policies, and, from the Senate, acted as the great friend of the President he had made. Hanna knew very well that when young Roosevelt was nominated for the Vice-Presidency in 1900 (the former Vice-President had died, thus opening the door, which the conservatives would rather have kept closed, to a

---

security to be made for the first time during Theodore Roosevelt's Administration.

Lincoln, Garfield, and McKinley had been shot to death by fanatics, but there had been other incidents only less tragic, and many annoyances that might have been avoided if there had been any protection.

In future the Secret Service would begin a vigil for the President-elect immediately after election that would not relax until he had left office. The security would not be absolute—it could not be so long as there was exposure to crowds—but there was an immense reduction in risk.

Roosevelt, when President-elect, would be fired at in a Miami park; and there would be an attempt to attack Truman in Blair House (where he was living while the White House was being rebuilt); but although the Roosevelt attack would cost Mayor Cermak of Chicago his life because he stood near, and the Truman attack would result in the killing of one guard and the wounding of two others, the Presidents themselves would escape unhurt.

The Secret Service developed an extraordinary talent for spotting potential assailants and for making arrangements, even in the most confused circumstances, that minimized the likelihood of trouble. And Presidents under its care could feel some relief from the physical danger incident to their unique prominence.

That the American Chief of State should have gone for more than a hundred years without protection for his person was due to the Jeffersonian fiction that he was, after all, no one of much importance—a man like others who must live as others must. Something, also, was due to congressional reluctance; the President must not have privileges that Senators and Representatives did not have.

Public indignation that McKinley, who was regarded with affection, should have been shot down without even the excuse of the political fanaticism that had actuated Garfield's assassin, did result in the Secret Service; but it did not change very much the congressional attitude toward the Chief Executive. There would continue to be the most grudging consent to enlargement of his office, to additions of perquisites and conveniences, and, for instance, to provisions for his retirement in dignity and comfort.

A popular account of the work of the Service will be found in *Treasury Agent* by Andrew Tully (New York, 1958).

new choice) something unhappy for the business interests had occurred. It was, to an extent, consoling to reflect that the office was an innocuous one so long as the President lived; but still he shuddered at the thought of "that damned cowboy" being but one life removed from the White House. McKinley himself let it be known that he would like almost anyone for running mate in place of the deceased Hobart except Roosevelt. But Platt, the New York boss, wanted him out of his state, and so, with some apprehension, the Old Guard accepted him.[6]

After Roosevelt had been elected with McKinley, Boss Platt prepared for the inauguration in Washington with open satisfaction; he was going to the capital, he said, "to see Roosevelt take the veil." This was an unprofessional calculation, considering the risks of the Presidency. Roosevelt did not remain in the vice-presidential convent very long. And when he emerged, the doubters soon had cause to know that their reluctance had been justified.

The new President was hardly settled in the White House[7] when he was acting as though he had been chosen as its occupant,[8] and in 1904 he was elected to it. His occupancy of the Mansion, he assumed, made him leader of the party as well as the constitutional head of government. He assumed even more—that the Presidency was the paramount governmental office, not to be subordinated in any way to the other Branches or to be managed in any other interest than that of itself as representative of the whole. His example of active direction went far beyond any Republican precedent, and it would be necessary to go a long way back among Democrats to find a parallel. It surpassed Cleveland's conception of his proper role. He, as we have seen, had not thought it his duty to ensure welfare or prosperity; this was altogether a private realm. But in Roosevelt's view there were no private realms. He was prepared to intervene anywhere if it seemed to be called for, and especially he considered it his responsibility to prescribe standards of conduct for all citizens, the powerful no less than the weak. And if they were powerful because they controlled aggregations of capital, employed many workers, and produced large volumes of goods, their conduct was of more than ordinary concern and must be subject, if necessary, to regulation.

[6] The first account of the McKinley regime is that of Margaret Leech, *In the Days of McKinley,* (New York, 1959). Even so talented an expositor could not manage to make so dull an individual interesting.

[7] This appellation for the Mansion was first made official by T.R. It had long been called that, but now it was put on the presidential stationery.

[8] There was no longer any opposition to the Vice-President becoming the President instead of merely occupying the office on the President's death. Tyler's tour de force had created a permanent precedent.

The new President almost at once raised goose-pimples on financiers' and speculators' flesh by encouraging the prosecution of the Northern Securities case. This serves as a good enough illustration of his attitude, but it also shows an awareness of sharply defined limits to presidential competence. Even this most energetic of Presidents still thought of himself as no more than an arranger for justice to be done. He would support, in every way open to him, the disciplining of the strong in favor of the weak, or the checking of those who exploited the nation's resources; and this was a sensational advance from McKinleyism, but he did not contemplate the acceptance of actual responsibility for well-being. This was not the role of government or a duty of its Chief Executive. The active participation in industrial and commercial affairs which Wilson would undertake a decade later would be initiated in a crisis of War; but Roosevelt had no wars, and if the student of his life sometimes suspects that this was a source of regret to him, still the fact is that he was not called on to go farther with governmental interference than to castigate verbally the "malefactors of great wealth" who were amassing great fortunes and using irresponsibly the power conferred by money. And even the serious depression of 1907 would call out no such Federal attempts at recovery or relief as would mark the regime of a second Roosevelt, who would be faced with much the same problem.

His disciplining of financiers, then, was mostly verbal; but he did insist that the legal devices available be used. When the Northern Securities incident was over, his reading of his own role in such matters was expressed quite clearly in a private letter. In it he said:

> The Northern Securities suit is one of the great achievements of my administration. I look back upon it with great pride, for through it we emphasized in signal fashion, as in no other way could be emphasized, the fact that the most powerful men in this country were held to accountability before the law . . .[9]

If, in this, we read "the President" for "the law," we come close to the Roosevelt view. For it was his insistence and his support which really sustained the legal actions brought by his Attorneys General. They would certainly not have been initiated except for his interest.

The Northern Securities case, if it was to be won, required the Supreme Court to reverse itself. In the earlier Knight case[10] the Court had put an end to Cleveland's motions toward dissolution of the sugar trust and had severely limited Federal regulation. A monopoly of *manufacture*, the

---

[9] To C. B. Cortelyou, August 11, 1904. *Letters,* (Cambridge Mass., 1951–54, 8 vols.) IV, 886.

[10] *The United States* vs. *E. C. Knight,* 156 U.S. 1 (1895).

Court had said, was not a monopoly of *commerce*. Even when a commodity of daily use was controlled and its prices fixed, its production was not in interstate commerce and was therefore beyond Federal reach. Holding companies (trusts) for limiting production might not be regulated or dissolved. The Sherman Act, under which this prosecution had been brought by Cleveland, had been passed in Harrison's time. But the Court's decision was so clear and far-reaching that not one prosecution was started during McKinley's Presidency. The trusts naturally thought themselves safe from the "radicals"; yet it could be seen, looking back, that public sentiment would presently force some sort of action; the abuses were too flagrant, and the results too serious in everyday life, to be ignored. The growing resentment was sensed by Roosevelt, good politician that he was, and he made himself the vehicle for its expression.

Even Harrison, in his first inaugural, had responded with a momentary Midwest indignation and had spoken of "conspiracies" against the public; and it was the conservative Senator Sherman who had sponsored the resulting anti-trust legislation. But even when the Congress and the President gave way before public indignation, the Court held the line for the financiers. The Knight case had seemed for a time irreversible; and when Roosevelt considered renewed attempts to enforce the Sherman Act, only he and his Attorney General, Philander C. Knox, thought success possible. The argument would have to be one from policy: that the government must be able to deal somehow with the monstrous combinations which seemed about to become governments in themselves. The whole country was aroused by the threat they posed. Even the Supreme Court might see the necessity.

The case put to the Court would have to be one that displayed plainly a danger to the public interest. And a satisfactory one soon presented itself in the merger being effected by the formerly warring Hill and Harriman railroad systems. A scheme had been devised for ending their competition with each other and for working together at a mutual profit. But the profit would obviously be gained by maintaining high rates, by using their vast power against other competitors, and by various financial arrangements for mulcting legitimate stockholders. For these purposes the Northern Securities Company would hold the stock of both railroads and provide overhead management for both. The inventors of this device anticipated no legal difficulties. The Knight decision had been so sweeping as to constitute a warning against interference with any arrangement convenient to the financiers.

The Attorney General made his plea not on the form taken by the combination but on the public consequences that were sure to follow. He won a five to four decision—not as satisfactory as could have been wished, but nevertheless remarkable in the circumstances. It encouraged the immediate entering of suits against the Standard Oil Company and the American Tobacco Company, and both these succeeded. The dissolutions ordered were, however, disappointing; before long it was apparent that nothing much had been gained. The trusts simply used other devices, and it was obvious that the ingenuity of their lawyers would continue to allow them as much freedom as they needed.

Because he saw how ineffective these anti-trust attacks were, Roosevelt concluded that a different sort of control over industry and finance was needed. It must be affirmative. Business must be told what it should do as well as what it should not do. This could be accomplished only by setting up permanent agencies for the purpose—such as the Interstate Commerce Commission and the Bureau of Corporations. These he conceived as having "authoritative control." He even felt that there might be instances justifying the setting of ceilings on prices in somewhat the way railroad rates were to be regulated.[11]

So the Roosevelt ideas in this field did seem to have in them hints of something more than the remanding of productive forces to "free competition." He did attempt to think of the nation always as a whole; and industry was part of that whole which ought to behave harmoniously and constructively. Not until another Roosevelt appeared would such ideas have any chance of finding embodiment in policy. But as a forerunner of what must eventually develop T.R. was an important preparer of the way. From his time on a *policy* toward industry was not forbidden. His successors, especially the more orthodox Republicans, Taft, then Harding and Coolidge, might refuse to acknowledge any such responsibility; but it would recur in Hoover's Presidency, even if its appearance was a timid one. Taft, Harding, and Coolidge are marked as comparative failures for this very reason—that they had no policy, or only a negative one, toward

---

[11] He visualized a larger role for the Bureau of Corporations than it ever attained. It was merged in the Federal Trade Commission in 1914 in the renewed progressive surge headed by Wilson. It is interesting to note Roosevelt's comment on this issue after his retirement. Writing to A. B. Farquhar in August 1911 (*Letters*, VII, 326), he said: "I do not myself see what good can come from dissolving the Standard Oil Company into forty separate companies, all of which will remain really under the same control. What we should have is a much stricter governmental supervision of these great companies, but accompanying this supervision should be a recognition of the fact that great combinations have come to stay and that we must do them scrupulous justice just as we exact scrupulous justice from them." In the next year, "the year of Armageddon," he went a good deal farther in the euphoria of the Bull Moose campaign. But what he really felt was probably best described by his favorite word, "supervision."

the formative forces of their generation. The first Roosevelt was hard to live up to, but the bench marks he established could not be altogether ignored.

Bishop tells, in his *Biography*, of J. P. Morgan's coming to the President when he heard of opposition to the Hill-Harriman scheme, in which Morgan was involved as banker, and saying, "If we have done anything wrong send your man [meaning the Attorney General] to my man [naming one of his lawyers] and they can fix it up." "That can't be done," the President replied. And Knox, who was present, added, "We don't want to fix it up; we want to stop it." Then Morgan asked "Are you going to attack my other interests, the Steel Trust and the others?" "Certainly not," the President replied, "unless we find out that they have done something we regard as wrong." When Morgan had left, Roosevelt said to Knox: "That is a most illuminating illustration of the Wall Street point of view. Mr. Morgan could not help regarding me as a big rival operator who either intended to ruin all his interests, or else could be induced to come to an agreement to ruin none.[12]

It was indeed hard for his powerful contemporaries to grasp T.R.'s detachment from entanglements with business. But this was one of his most distinguishing traits. He was indignant that Morgan should regard himself as the equal of the President of the United States. This indignation was an important contribution to the developing presidential tradition.[13] This attitude affected the Presidency permanently. Its complete independence, its refusal to acknowledge special status for anyone, its high conception of the President as head of the government were much needed reminders to his fellow Republicans—and to many Democrats as well— that the government is really one of all the people. They were never forgotten. He came back to the matter in his *Autobiography:*

[12] Op. cit., 185.

[13] We shall see that it was shared by Franklin D. Roosevelt after the abasements before business of the Presidents just preceding him. There was indeed an incident closely paralleling the Morgan interview with T.R. in F.D.R.'s Presidency. The banker in the later incident was Jackson Reynolds, and the argument arose over the draft of a speech to be made to the Bankers Association in 1934. Reynolds was proposing peace between the bankers and the government and made the unfortunate suggestion for a passage in the President's speech which indicated the necessity for a "truce." F.D.R.'s indignation had a kind of epic quality. Its vehemence marked him off from those figures in public life who regarded big businessmen as somehow sharing in the public power and worthy of a special respect. To the Roosevelts they were no better and no worse than other citizens. Cf. Raymond Moley *After Seven Years* (New York, 1939), 295 ff.

> The total absence of governmental control had led to a portentous growth of . . . corporations. In no other country . . . was such power held by the men who had gained these fortunes . . . The power of the mighty industrial overlords had increased with giant strides . . . the Government was practically impotent . . . Of all forms of tyranny the least attractive and the most vulgar is the tyranny of mere wealth, the tyranny of plutocracy.[14]

There are echoes in this of old aristocratic prejudices against "tradesmen." But its usefulness to an expanding Presidency can hardly be denied.

If this was an important contribution, there were several others almost as striking. For instance, Roosevelt went much farther than Hayes or Cleveland had gone in accepting responsibility for the restoration of normal conditions in the virtual warfare that was so likely to develop in the characteristic industrial disputes of that time. It must be recalled that there was no machinery for conciliation and not even any official recognition of the principle of collective bargaining. A strike became a contest of wills and resources, and resort to force on both sides was not at all unusual. Apart from the decision to be arrived at in favor of one or the other of the disputants, there was the interest of the public not only in civic order but in the goods or services whose supply was interrupted. Both Hayes and Cleveland had recognized their duty to the public, but they would not go beyond the preservation of order. Roosevelt accepted the responsibility for supplying the product—at least when it was one so necessary as anthracite coal; but that this was an easily expansible category, anyone could see.

In order to understand the enormity of his departure from hitherto accepted precedent, it has to be realized how safely within the conservative theoretical limits his immediate predecessors had remained. Nothing they had done, even in extreme circumstances, had gone beyond what found acceptance in business circles. The keeping of order is always approved by those who have property to protect and operations to facilitate. Strikes threatened property and closed down operations. Employers themselves sometimes closed their factories or other establishments—in which case it was called a lockout—but even then their interest in order was not less and might be more. In every way the duty of the President to prevent violence, when the authority of local officials was not sufficient, worked to the advantage of the employer and the property owner and against that of the worker, who must in some way ensure that the strike as a weapon— the only one he had—was effective.

In the anthracite strike of 1902 the product was one depended upon by workers and capitalists alike—and by the ordinary householder as well.

[14] *Autobiography* (New York, 1926), 423 ff.

As the stoppage of mining went on from May, when the strike started, into the summer and then into the fall, accumulated stocks were exhausted. Unless production was resumed at once there would be severe shortages during the winter. Suffering from cold could be anticipated among those —and there were thousands of such families—whose homes were equipped to be heated only by anthracite. And this took no account of the industrial uses of coal that would be curtailed. The Mayor of New York, the Governor of Massachusetts—and numerous other officials—spoke with alarm of the prospect. Roosevelt saw that the situation of the eastern states "was quite as serious as if they had been threatened by the invasion of a hostile army of overwhelming force."

But what could a President of Roosevelt's affiliations and convictions do? His dilemma, as the necessity for interference became plainer, is one of the most interesting in the succession of crises calling for presidential action. His duty clearly went well beyond merely keeping order in a civil dispute. Suppression of violence would not heat homes or provide fuel for factories during the coming winter. A calamity threatened. So, although again it was not put into defining words, the Rule of Necessity had to be invoked. What had to be done must be done. The President, as head of the government, as the ultimate civil authority, had in all honesty to acknowledge a responsibility. It was one that devolved upon him because of the growth of industrialization and because of the economic changes taking place in the nation. To see that coal was produced and distributed might never before have been a governmental responsibility; it had now become one. This he saw.

But what means were available to him? They must be ones already in existence. Cold weather was already setting in by the time all his efforts to mediate had failed. He could not wait for legislative authority, as so often Presidents cannot when confronted with crises. He determined to use the army. By conferring with a respected retired general (Schofield) he made sure that his authority as Commander in Chief would be honored. The orders he gave were to seize and operate the properties.

He did something to bolster his constitutional position by arranging, through Pennsylvania's political boss (Matthew S. Clay), for the Governor to invite intervention. But this would of course go only to the question of disorder. It would not legalize seizure. Nothing, actually, could do that. The Constitution, in its enumeration of presidential powers, came nowhere near an authorization for such an action. His designation as Commander in Chief had reference to hostilities with external enemies. It did not say so, but that was a plain inference. The only possible justification was the wording of the preamble, and especially the two phrases "insure domestic tranquility" and "promote the general welfare." But these were used as a kind of explanation for the establishment of government. They were not a directive for any Branch of it. What has to be said, quite simply, is that an exigency had arisen and that authority had to be exercised. No one could do this as well as the President. In fact no one else could do it at all; and if it was held that the President was powerless, then the nation was powerless too—at least until Congress could be assembled and could be persuaded to act; and this would be too late to avert disaster.

It is possible to imagine Cleveland doing just as Roosevelt did, and it is credible that Lincoln would have regarded such an action as justified; but Roosevelt, considering his own situation, thought he was the first President who might have interfered so drastically in a domestic matter. And he may have been right. Both Cleveland and Lincoln were lawyers; and although both responded to the challenge of necessity, Lincoln had the excuse of actual rebellion, and Cleveland stopped at the restoration of order.

It is, however, unrealistic to consider Roosevelt's problem except in the setting of the new industrialism, with its new problems. And the observation is certainly relevant that unless Roosevelt had had an aristocratic detachment from business and a skeptical attitude toward businessmen he could hardly have had the independence to discipline the coal barons as he did. They, with their financial allies, were the bulwarks of Republicanism. They were members of the feared and respected elite of the contemporary economy. This elite until now had had influence in the White House. It is hardly too much to say that the Presidents had been their men—at least since Andrew Johnson—while the latter phase of industrialism was developing.

Roosevelt had been chosen as a Republican—for the Vice-Presidency— and had said he would follow McKinley's ways when he succeeded to the Presidency; but McKinley had been the businessmen's President, and Roosevelt saw that he could not accept this fealty. They had not wanted him and he could not see that he owed them any duty, and certainly no duty that jeopardized the general welfare. His duty was to those who had elected him to the Vice-Presidency and, beyond them, to those who might elect him to the Presidency on his own. If they approved, he could afford to offend the businessmen.

He was aware that the seizure he planned might be attacked not only as illegal but as "socialistic." The legality he could take care of; the emergency would be over before the issue could be brought into court. But the charge of socialism might be serious; it might lose him the verdict in the court of public opinion—the only one a President really need fear. He took precautions to put himself right by loudly and frequently disparaging "socialists" and "anarchists" and presenting himself as their worst enemy. He had, in fact, been making this a policy all along.

His support was soon so secure that the recalcitrant operators softened.

Public opinion had for some time been running against them. They had been arrogantly unwilling to negotiate when the union leaders had agreed to mediation, they had professed a belief that "politicians" would be partial, and they had been insulting to the President himself in his conversations with them. Their position deteriorated rapidly under his pressure; and although they made no graceful retreat when they learned of his plans for seizure, they did give enough ground to allow the start of negotiations. This, in turn, permitted the President to suspend his proposed action. The seizure was not consummated, but under its threat mining was resumed and householders were warm that winter. Incidentally, the operators lost every point of their contention; but, even worse, they acquired a reputation for defiance of public authority and for irresponsible behavior which would haunt all their dealings for a generation.

There is no doubt that Roosevelt would have proceeded to the seizure if the operators had not given in. There is no way of telling what the aftermath would have been. But he himself never doubted that if he had gone ahead he would somehow have been upheld, if not by the courts, then by public opinion. That he felt himself strong because he was on the side of the majority and was detached from those who had to be subdued is clear from many things he said at the time and afterward. But he was not certain how he ought to use the power he possessed. There is, for instance, this letter to Henry Cabot Lodge written September 19, 1902:

> . . . Unfortunately, the strength of my public position before the country is also its weakness. I am genuinely independent of the big monied men in all matters where I think the interests of the public are concerned, and probably I am the first President of recent times of whom this could truthfully be said. I think it right and desirable that this should be true of the President. But where I do not grant any favors to these big monied men which I do not think the country requires that they should have, it is out of the question for me to expect them to grant favors to me in return. I treat them precisely as I treat other citizens; that is, I consider their interests so far as my duty requires and so far as I think the needs of the country warrant. In return, they will support me, in so far as they are actuated by public spirit, simply according as they think I am or am not doing well; and so far as they are actuated by their private interests they will support me only on points where they think it is to their interest to do so. The sum of this is that I can make no private or special appeal to them, and I am at my wits' end how to proceed . . .[15]

[15] *Letters*, III, 332.

On October 13, 1902, he wrote to Joseph Bucklin Bishop, who was another of those in whom he felt he could confide as he felt his way to a
policy. He was making sure that he would not be thought of as a "radical"
when he was stretching his powers to protect the public interest:

> Do you think you are fully alive to the gross blindness of the opera-
> tors? They fail absolutely to understand that they have any duty
> toward the public . . . they and their friends and their allies of the
> type of the *Sun* have been attacking me, just as they attacked me
> about the trust business. Do they find much comfort, not only in the
> speeches of Bryan and Tom Johnson, but of David Hill and of Olney?
> Do they not realize that they are putting a very heavy burden
> on us who stand against socialism, against anarchic disorder? . . .
> If during the ensuing week there comes some heavy riot on the East
> Side of New York, in my judgment the operators, more than the
> miners, are responsible . . . Meanwhile I am sure you know that I
> shall take no step which I do not think can be justified by the sound
> common sense of both of us six months or a year hence.[16]

He must have been relieved at the softening of the situation. The
seizure was an extreme measure, and it seemed more extreme as its actual
use approached. Evidence of this is his volubility at the time. Again and
again he reviewed the situation and worked out his justification. One of
the most interesting of his presidential papers is another letter he afterward wrote to Governor Crane. This ran to many pages and was, in effect,
a complete review of the incident. It will be found in the *Letters.*[17]
In one passage he spoke of absolving his Secretary of War and Attorney
General of any responsibility if they preferred to have it that way:

> Among the trades unions generally . . . there was beginning to be
> ugly talk of a general sympathetic strike, which, happening at the
> beginning of the winter, would have meant a crisis only less serious
> than the Civil War. Even without such a crisis the first long-contin-
> ued spell of weather meant misery and violence in acute form in
> our big cities. I did not intend to sit supinely when such a state
> of things was impending, and I notified Knox and Root that if the
> contingency arose where I had to take charge of the matter, as
> President, on behalf of the Federal Government, I should not ask
> even their advice, but would proceed to take definite action which
> I outlined to them. I explained to them that I knew that this action
> would form an evil precedent, and that it was one which I should
> take most reluctantly . . . but that I should feel obliged to take it

[16] Ibid., 349.

[17] III, 359–66.

rather than expose our people to the suffering and chaos which would otherwise come . . .

The plan was to summon Governor Stone to take action, on the one hand by the use of his troops to put down all violence and disorder, and on the other hand, by calling together the Pennsylvania legislature and getting them to act in any way that was necessary to bring about a reopening of the mines; on the theory that wherever the fault might lie the present management had failed and the needs of the country would brook no delay in curing the failure. Then I would also inform him that if he could not deal with the situation, I could (and to inform me at once), and would. Root told me there were 10,000 regulars I could put in at once, and I had seen old General Schofield and told him that if I put in the regulars I intended at the same time to seize the mines and to have him take charge and run them as a receiver for the government. I do not know whether I have any precedents, save perhaps those of General Butler at New Orleans, but in my judgment it would have been imperative to act, precedent or no precedent—and I was in readiness.

Roosevelt did not speculate further on the possible reactions to his proposed seizure. But he has given us an extraordinarily complete outline of his thinking as he approached the decision to intervene. It constitutes about as clear an appeal to the Rule of Necessity as can be found. Taken in his terms, it would apply to domestic situations of all sorts in which the public interest might be jeopardized by the recalcitrance of the parties to a dispute. But this is the most difficult of situations. It would be easier to take charge in case of natural calamity, of attack from without, or of threatened civil war within. In such circumstances it could not be claimed that intervention had favored one interest against others. It can be seen, therefore, why the Roosevelt plan is so important to any investigation of presidential powers in conditions of stress. One criterion, and one only, is to be used—the public interest; and one judgment, and one only, is to be consulted—that of the President. That, at least, is where Theodore Roosevelt leaves us.

★ 33 ★

THE QUESTION WHETHER ROOSEVELT ACTUALLY ENLARGED THE PRESI-
dency by planning to seize the closed anthracite mines and operate them
by a government agency may be argued. A plan never consummated
had not, after all, had to survive the severe tests of one actually put into
effect. But that an enlargement resulted from other plans which were
translated into action cannot be denied: for instance, by arranging a situation in which a Panama Canal could be built, or by taking charge of the
customs houses in Santo Domingo in order to meet that country's obligations, or by sending the United States fleet around the world on no authority but his own and without an appropriation that would cover its
costs. Of course all these instances were in the field of foreign affairs, more
or less, and Presidents had long been acknowledged to have a special
authority beyond the nation's borders not allowable in domestic matters.[1]
Jefferson, Monroe, Polk, and others had extended the presidential range,
but Roosevelt extended it further. And, as in their dealings with other
Presidents, there was not much that the other Branches could do except to
refuse ratification for treaties or funds for the implementation of policy.

These congressional hindrances—they were no more than that—sometimes caused an Executive severe annoyance[2] and sometimes compelled

---

[1] This could not be said to be a constitutional warrant. The authority
to make treaties and to appoint Ambassadors and consular officials could
hardly be extrapolated to cover the extraordinary dealings engaged in by
Roosevelt.

[2] Secretary of State Hay tried to resign during the McKinley Administration because a treaty—Hay-Pauncefote—negotiated by him was not
ratified by the Senate. This would have superseded the Clayton-Bulwer
Treaty of 1850, then standing in the way of canal construction. The public
desire for a canal had been reinforced by the delay experienced because
the battleship *Oregon*, needed in Caribbean waters, had had to sail all
the way around Cape Horn on her way east from the Pacific. Hay at this
time had referred bitterly to "the power of one-third plus one of the
Senate to meet with a categorical veto any treaty negotiated by the Presi-

him to take the Senate into his confidence during negotiation or, at worst, to withdraw a submitted treaty for revision. There were always galling concessions; consultation involved certain risks of premature disclosure as well as the intrusion of extraneous interests, and withdrawal might involve renegotiation. But any co-operation he might ask of the Senate was at his initiative. There were no rights involved, and neither the President's constitutional position nor the advanced ground by now conceded to him was jeopardized. He could still negotiate without consultation if he wished, and this meant that he could go a long way toward committing the government. If the negotiation resulted in a treaty, it might be repudiated; but this was so unusual as to constitute a notorious incident whenever it happened, in which the recalcitrant Senators were likely to be embarrassed.

Roosevelt, more than any President before him, exploited the possibilities implicit in the advantages won for him by his predecessors. His contributions included especially the creation of situations easily interpreted as involving the national credit or honor, and the taking of Executive action which, strictly construed, ought to have involved consultation with the Senate as provided by the Constitution. These commitments came to be called "Executive Agreements" when they went beyond mere "understandings," and many of them were not distinguishable from the material normal to treaties. They would in future be used more and more frequently, and protests of the Senate were usually ineffectual, since the Senators could never offer any substitute. They were forbidden to "negotiate," and the prohibition was a constitutional one.

The three incidents mentioned here—the Panama Canal transaction, the Santo Domingo receivership, and the use of the fleet for intimidating potential enemies—were not the only Roosevelt initiatives in foreign affairs. He negotiated a treaty with Great Britain that settled the boundary of Canada and Alaska; he faced down the German Kaiser, who showed a disposition to discipline Venezuela; he was the mediator in the negotiations at the end of the Russo-Japanese War; and generally he was, as a convinced imperialist, a free wielder of the new power possessed by the United States as a result of her expansion and prosperity. Since John Quincy Adams no President had been so aggressive and demanding among the world's statesmen. But perhaps the incidents mentioned will serve for illustration of the enlarged presidential area he believed himself called to occupy.

---

dent." His resignation was not accepted, and he renegotiated the treaty. It was then ratified in its changed—and, it was generally admitted, improved—form. It provided that the canal might be constructed either by the United States or by corporations that the government might aid. Also, it did not prohibit fortification, as its first version would have done.

As for Panama, the intensifying demand for a ship-crossing at the narrow isthmus between the continents of North and South America was, Roosevelt judged, strong enough to justify extreme measures to get things going. There had been talk about the project since Polk's time, and the French had tried and failed. This failure had not changed the virtual consensus that there must be a canal, but there had been disagreements about the route, irritations over the existing treaty with the British, and delaying negotiations about buying out the French concern. Finally Roosevelt was exasperated by what he believed to be the blackmailing tactics of Marroquin and his colleagues in Bogotá over the construction rights.

Both the Panama and Nicaragua crossing projects had their advocates.[3] Three commissions had reported in favor of Nicaragua, but by 1902 the New Panama Canal Company, possessor of the French rights, had come down to so reasonable a price for its holdings that it seemed to be the most favorably regarded. Besides, the recent Mount Pelée volcanic explosion had been so catastrophic as to throw doubt on a Nicaraguan route overhung by volcanic mountains.[4] The matter seemed to be decided when Mark Hanna, who was so powerful in the Senate, lent his influence to Panama. A bill had already passed the House providing for the Nicaraguan route, but the Senate amended it to permit the purchase of the Panama Company's assets.[5] But, the bill said, if the President was unable to obtain for the United States a "satisfactory title to the property of the New Panama Canal Company and the control of the necessary territory of the Republic of Colombia within a reasonable time and upon reasonable terms," the President might fall back upon the Nicaraguan route.[6]

[3] McKinley, in his last speech at Buffalo, where he was assassinated, mentioned the canal as a "must," but he spoke of an "Isthmian Canal" to unite the two oceans, and thus avoided favoring either of the two routes.

[4] The Nicaraguan advocates protested that volcanic dangers were no greater there than in Panama, whereupon the Panamanians exhibited triumphantly a current postage stamp issued by the Nicaraguan government with a smoking volcano prominent in its pictured scene.

[5] This company was formed to dispose of the assets belonging to the original De Lesseps concern. The successful engineer-builder of the Suez Canal, in his attempt at Panama, had spent $260,000,000 but had been defeated by tropical diseases and other peculiar difficulties of operating in that locality.

[6] *Acts of the Congress relating to the Panama Canal,* 27. There are various accounts of the affair. There is one story in Roosevelt's *Autobiog-*

It was against this background that Roosevelt began operations. It should be noted, however, that there was more than was at once visible in Hanna's conversion and the passage of the Spooner Act authorizing the Panama crossing. The company, in addition to reducing its price to $40,000,000, hired a lawyer—W. N. Cromwell of New York—who was unusually successful in his dealings with Senators. There may have been no connection between this success and a contribution of $60,000 made about the same time to the Republican party; but there was a striking correlation; and if Roosevelt did not know about it he was more ignorant than seems credible.

Besides Cromwell, the Panama group had an effective representative in Philippe Bunau-Varilla, who had worked as a managing engineer for the French but was now a negotiator for the allied interests who wanted to dispose of their holdings to the American government. These holdings, it has since been contended, were mythical; that is, the company had little or nothing to sell. And if the Colombians delayed and bargained it may have been mostly because they hoped to share in or divert to themselves the $40,000,000 they saw going to the Panamanians. And certainly the company could not dispose of a concession without the agreement of the government of Colombia. Still, Roosevelt chose to be outraged. He called the Bogotá officials "contemptible little creatures" and pictured them as holding up momentous affairs while they maneuvered in the hope of being more generously bribed.

This fury of the President was notice to Cromwell and Bunau-Varilla that another way out of the impasse into which the negotiators had fallen might be agreeable. And in July 1903 there was a meeting in New York, attended by United States army officers as well as Panamanians and agents of the canal company; and it was at this meeting that plans were made to separate the province of Panama from Colombia by revolution. The new government could then execute a lease to the United States for the necessary strip of land across the Isthmus, the company could get its $40,000,000, and the project for a new canal could proceed.

In November the "revolution" duly occurred. The Governor of the province allowed himself to be arrested, the Colombian Admiral departed, and ships of the United States navy miraculously appeared to "keep

---

raphy and it is extended in his *Letters*. Cf. also Croly's *Marcus Alonzo Hanna; His Life and Work*, New York, 1912, Senator George F. Hoar's *Autobiography of Seventy Years, op. cit.* (Thayer's *Life of Hay*), (Boston and New York, 1916, 2 vols.), and various documents. But the facts are not any longer significantly in dispute in spite of the long controversy about the actual role played by Roosevelt and the even longer one as to whether his actions could be in any way justified.

order."[7] Incidentally, they also prevented the landing of a Colombian force which might have interfered with the peaceful proceedings. And when the Proclamation of Independence was read in the plaza by General Huertas, the victor, Secretary Hay at once recognized the new regime.

The government of Panama, as almost its first act, designated Bunau-Varilla as its Washington representative; and Hay proceeded to negotiate with him a treaty leasing in perpetuity a zone across the Isthmus adequate for the canal. It was about this lease that Secretary Knox, when the matter was being discussed at a Cabinet meeting, is said to have remarked, in response to Roosevelt's protestations that all had been in order and that there had been no American participation in any conspiracy, that so great an achievement ought not to be allowed to "suffer from any taint of legality."

If the President of the United States did not participate in arranging the revolution in Panama, he must have connived at it. Perhaps he only lent a benign but silent consent to what he must have known was going on. But he never admitted that it was any of his affair how it was done. When he did protest his innocence, however, he seemed to do it with a wink, at the same time letting it be understood that he had seized an opportunity with vigor and furthered the national interest as a President is bound to do. He liked to say in later years, "I took Panama," which contradicts his earlier protestations and is no doubt nearer the truth.

His resort to the Rule of Necessity was none the less successful because of the criticism he incurred. The volume of indignant comment was formidable at the time and tended to increase as the various deals of Cromwell and Bunau-Varilla came to light and what had been only suspected by critics turned out to be less than the fact rather than more.[8] Later historians would be pretty uniformly condemnatory, so much so that some sort of restitution became an article high on the agenda of the Democrats when they should come to power. And, sure enough, William Jennings Bryan, as one of his first acts when he became Secretary of State

[7] How Roosevelt happened to direct the navy two weeks or more in advance to be present when the transfer of authority occurred, if he knew nothing about the plans, was difficult to understand. The President passed it off, however, by remarking that anyone with sense could see what was about to happen.

[8] James Ford Rhodes, in *The McKinley and Roosevelt Administrations* (New York, 1927), devoted several pages to the contemporary denunciations, beginning with Moorfield Storey's address at the Massachusetts Reform Club in December 1903 and including an article in the respectable *North American Review*, written by L. T. Chamberlain, called "A Chapter of National Dishonor." And in December of that same year, also, a manifesto by a number of Yale professors, protested the treatment of Colombia.

in the Wilson Administration, would negotiate a treaty with the Colombians, offering apologies and a compensation of $25,000,000.

Thus President Roosevelt was rebuked. But it should be carefully noted that the rebuke came after the canal had been built and that the restitution did not take the form of giving back to Colombia the lost province; nor did it affect the lease of the Canal Zone in perpetuity to the United States. Roosevelt in retirement was furious that the alienation of Panama should be thought disgraceful. But by then the issue was a hashing over of old quarrels. The important thing was that a President had acted, that the canal was in operation, and that it belonged to the United States. The lesson certainly seemed to be that following the Rule of Necessity might bring a President criticism and that he ought to be careful to be as legal as possible, but that if he did what he felt he must do and what he did was a success, it would in time be recognized as having had the justification of public benefit. He might be rebuked, he might even be reversed by the Congress or the Court, but the rebuke or the reversal would not come in time to affect the action. It would by then be a matter only of principle. It might exacerbate tempers and cause a political flurry; but if the national interest was involved, nothing would really happen to jeopardize the accomplishment.

★ 34 ★

IF THE CANAL INCIDENT COULD BE DESCRIBED AS HIGHHANDED—AS IT was by Roosevelt's detractors—it was no more so than the other incidents. The establishment of the so-called Roosevelt Corollaries (to the Monroe Doctrine) went even farther and involved the President in much more advanced operations than any such ventures in the nation's past. This benevolent interference in a neighbor's affairs involved not only the enunciation of a wholly new policy for the government but actual physical intervention—on his sole responsibility—to enforce it. Santo Domingo was weak and corrupt, and there was no objection from any other nation—whatever some of them may have thought—but it certainly stretched presidential prerogatives beyond their former limits; and its success was a significant demonstration of their expansibility when used by an impatient and moralistic individual no more afraid to maneuver in the large sphere of world affairs than in the smaller sphere of domestic ones.

It is in such incidents as this that the Roosevelt who was a student of Mahan, who had had the experience of being Assistant Secretary of the Navy, and who thought familiarly in geographic terms, is most clearly revealed. Because of these traits and attitudes and because he was called, as he felt, to enhance the glory and influence of his country, he demanded to be regarded by the rulers of the other nations—the Kings, the Kaiser, the Czar—as one of them. Being one of them, he would enforce the Doctrine of exclusive United States jurisdiction in the Western Hemisphere. More than that, he would see to it that he and his nation were parties to every decision affecting the disposition of rights and influence anywhere in the world. He meant to insist on this position of strength for the United States and he would take any measures necessary to this end. He would assume any risk, and he would ignore any objection if he could, and if he could not he would denounce the views opposed to his own. Meanwhile he would pursue the course that seemed to him necessary. He was a believer in faits accomplis.

Consider, as another instance, his moral intervention in the Russo-Japanese War. During that conflict his sympathies, like those of many Americans, were with the Japanese. There was no better reason for this, apparently, than that theirs was a kind of underdog struggle. The tiny island empire, just finding itself as an industrialized society in the manner of the West, was pitted against the vast reactionary Moloch commanding the Asian heartland. This would seem to be the kind of sentiment ordinary citizens might entertain who had no responsibilities; but a President, it might be thought, could well have been more restrained. He seems to have had no qualms whatever and no intimation that Japanese ego, inflated by victory and by the approval of other nations, might eventually lead to the fantastic challenge in the Pacific symbolized by Pearl Harbor.

Not many individuals have had Roosevelt's magnificent trust in his own judgments, and there have been but two others among the Presidents.[1] Many of these judgments may have been proved mistaken—as they were —but that this unshakable confidence and its accompanying willingness to commit the national power had an enlarging effect on the Presidency, it is impossible to doubt. His successors, for a long time, would continue to be measured by his standard of self-confidence and his estimate of the nation's greatness. The Roosevelt shadow would be as long as those of the strongest in the line of the Presidents.

The assumption of trusteeship in Santo Domingo was in a way a smaller matter, but it was undertaken as a result of the same prideful conception of national importance and the same sense of presidential mission as the intervention in Panama. And it had, in its smaller sphere, the same deplorable long-run consequences, the result, again, of a narrow imagination wedded to an unrestrained ego. It occurred in 1905. It was, therefore, at the beginning of his first term in his own right, although he had had four years in office. During those four years he had shown the kind of reaction to provocation that was so fully displayed in the Santo Domingo incident. There was, for instance, the Venezuela crisis in 1902. At that time Great Britain, Germany, and Italy had been irritated with the current dictator of Venezuela because he would not make any serious composition of debts long owed to their nationals. The Europeans went so far as to set up a blockade and seemed about to invade the country when Roosevelt intervened. The result in this case was the capitulation of the other powers and their consent to the jurisdiction of the Hague Tribunal. How Roosevelt achieved this end is still not entirely clear, but that he was threatening and even truculent seems not to be seriously disputed.[2]

---

[1] Jackson and Truman.

[2] But just how far he went historians are not agreed. In his *Autobiography* (512), he indicated that Germany was the real aggressor and was feebly supported by Britain. Whether or not he threatened to send the United States fleet to the Caribbean within twenty-four hours is disputed. It is suggested by some historians that Germany volunteered to submit to arbitration. At any rate, Roosevelt did intervene.

In his annual message for 1904—the year when he would be seeking nomination and election—he asserted that an extension of the Monroe Doctrine was called for. This was no doubt a popular view, quite in accord with the imperialist sentiments that seemed to seize most Americans in the wake of the Spanish war. Bryan, appealing to Christian and isolationist sentiment, had made an unsuccessful issue of this in the campaign of 1900; and Roosevelt's assertion of national responsibility, which sometimes ran on into something like a mission to the weaker peoples of the world, was neither new nor strange. And the Caribbean was close by; there would be fewer doubts about responsibility for the nations surrounding this "American lake" than about others in more distant places. The invasion of these waters by European navies would be especially resented.

It was only fair, Roosevelt said, and practical, too, if others were to be warned off, to accept the obligations they were not allowed to accept. If the smaller nations permitted themselves to be so badly governed that they could not collect taxes and would not pay their debts they must be required to behave in more civilized ways. If they did not, intervention must be resorted to:

> Chronic wrong-doing or an impotence which results in a general loosening of the ties of civilized society may . . . require intervention by some civilized nation . . . the Monroe Doctrine may force the United States . . . to the exercise of an international police power.

The Roosevelt Corollaries were implicit in this assertion of the right to "international police power." When Santo Domingo, in 1905, was threatened with forcible collection of debts by European governments, he simply sent a Receiver General (backed by marines) to collect customs receipts and disburse them, with 55 per cent being allocated to the payment of external debts and 45 per cent to internal budgetary needs. It has to be said that the operation was a complete success. No one objected except the grafters; and, with corruption suppressed, the income was adequate to the ordinary needs of the government. Roosevelt was able to say with pride years later that the arrangement had "worked in capital style." He went on to say:

> We secured peace, we protected the people of the islands against foreign foes, and we minimized the chance of domestic trouble. We satisfied the creditors and the foreign nations to which the creditors belonged; and our own part of the work was done with the utmost efficiency and with rigid honesty, so that not a particle of scandal was ever hinted at.[3]

[3] *Autobiography*, 509.

This, for Roosevelt, was a complete answer to his critics. Objections, he felt, had come from an impractical and woolly-minded group with nothing to offer as an alternative. A paragraph referring to these criticisms is of interest alike to students of the Presidency and of this particular occupant of the office. It shows how one President, doing what he believed to be his duty, exceeded his writ without compunction; it shows also with what resentment he recognized that not everyone found his justification sufficient:

> Under these circumstances those who do not know the nature of the professional international philanthropists would suppose that these apostles of international peace would have been overjoyed by what we had done. As a matter of fact, when they took any notice of it at all it was to denounce it; and those American newspapers which are fondest of proclaiming themselves the foes of war and the friends of peace violently attacked me for averting war from, and bringing peace to, the island. They insisted I had no power to make the agreement. They were, of course, wholly unable to advance a single sound reason of any kind for their attitude. I suppose the real explanation was partly their dislike of me personally, and unwillingness to see peace come through or national honor upheld by me; and in the next place their sheer, simple devotion to prattle and dislike of efficiency. They liked to have people come together and talk about peace, or even sign bits of paper with something about peace or arbitration on them, but they took no interest whatever in the practical achievement of a peace that told for good government and decency and honesty. They were joined by the many moderately well-meaning men who always demand that a thing be done, but also always demand that it be not done in the only way that it is, as a matter of fact, possible to do it. The men of this kind insisted that of course Santo Domingo must be protected and made to behave itself, and that of course the Panama Canal must be dug; but they insisted even more strongly that neither feat should be accomplished in the only way in which it was possible to accomplish it at all.[4]

The Senators had watched the Santo Domingo protectorate set up with some misgivings; they had, indeed, refused to ratify the arrangement—at least at first. This naturally annoyed the President, although when they finally came around he seemed rather pleased that he had acted without consultation, thus demonstrating the better judgment of the Executive. He was quite certain that those who had opposed him had done so from unworthy motives. Some were under the influence of Wall Street, some

[4] Ibid., 509–10.

were partisan Democrats, some were actuated by an inflated sense of senatorial dignity. When after a first debate on the proposed treaty the Senate had adjourned without voting for ratification, they had exhibited "a feeling of entire self-satisfaction at having left the country in the position of having assumed a responsibility and then failing to fulfil it." He continued:

> Apparently the Senators in question felt that they had upheld their dignity. All that they had really done was to shirk their duty. Somebody had to do that duty, and accordingly I did it. I went ahead and administered the proposed treaty anyhow, considering it a simple agreement on the part of the Executive which would be converted into a treaty whenever the Senate acted.

After about two years the Senate did act, and for our purpose here this is of some importance. The giving in of the Senators was certainly not because they concluded that Roosevelt had been "right" or because they wanted to acknowledge belatedly that he had kept within his powers as viewed by a co-ordinate Branch. It was because the tour de force was an obvious practical success and refusal to approve it would have seemed ridiculous to a public convinced that the President had done the right thing and not inclined to cavil at the method he may have used—and even less inclined to examine the hurt feelings of the Senators. If he had gone on to annexation, as his critics said he intended to do, he would undoubtedly have had support for that too. The combined imperialist and missionary sentiment of the time was very pervasive, and by now the disposition to regard the President as mentor and leader was impervious to the objections of the "philanthropists" upon whom he poured a scorn he otherwise reserved for the "malefactors of great wealth." But he happened to feel about such an addition to the territories as another Roosevelt would feel about the British West Indies during World War II—that the obligation would be more costly than would be warranted by any possible benefits. He wrote to Bishop that "as for annexing the island, I have about the same desire to annex it as a gorged boa constrictor might have to swallow a porcupine wrong-end-to."[5] So the presidential power of annexation without the benefit of legislative sanction was not tested.[6]

---

[5] Op. cit., 431.

[6] It may be noted that years after leaving the Presidency, when he was traveling in South America, he modified considerably his stated attitude on the Monroe Doctrine. At that time he urged that it should be regarded as a mutual responsibility. He put it this way when the President of Uruguay toasted him as the defender of the Doctrine: "As soon as any country in the New World stands on a sufficiently high footing of orderly liberty and achieved success . . . it becomes a guarantor on a

The final illustration of the Roosevelt impact on the Presidency, chosen here as representative, is the sending of the United States fleet around the world to "show the flag." Taken at its surface appearance, this may not seem so notable an extension of the constitutional duty of the President as Commander in Chief. Actually it was a novel and audacious commitment for the nation from which retreat would have been difficult if not impossible. That commitment was to a place of power, backed by naval strength, defined by the President and to be defended by him if necessary. At the beginning it was represented as no more than a move into the Pacific for the fleet. Even about this there was apprehension:

> There were various amusing features connected with the trip. Most of the wealthy people and "leaders of opinion" in the Eastern cities were panic-struck at the proposal to take the fleet away from Atlantic waters. The great New York dailies issued frantic appeals to Congress to stop the fleet from going. The head of the Senate Committee on Naval Affairs announced that the fleet should not and could not go because Congress would refuse to appropriate the money—he being from an Eastern seaboard state. However, I announced in response that I had enough money to take the fleet around to the Pacific anyhow, that the fleet would certainly go, and that if Congress did not choose to appropriate enough money to get the fleet back, why, it could stay in the Pacific. There was no further difficulty about the money.[7]

So the expedition, which was a really formidable one for the fleet, was planned in some secrecy and without consulting the legislators. It was also planned, as afterward appeared, without consulting the Cabinet. The President, with the naval commanders, made the elaborate arrangements necessary for coal-burning vessels; he himself, overruling the admirals, decided that the smaller ships of the torpedo-destroyer class should go along; and the sixteen-month adventure was begun.

It was, it will be seen, pure President, and intended to be so. As Roosevelt said:

---

footing of complete equality." (*Letters*, VII, 756, *note*.) Somewhat later he explained more fully in *Outlook* articles. This revision was in accord with the position taken by Mahan ten years earlier, and of course anticipates the Good Neighbor Policy of F. D. Roosevelt, first stated in 1928 before he became President but when he was anticipating his candidacy. Truman's Point Four policy of outright assistance would be a further extension of the same trend. For our purpose here it is important to note that presidential initiative operated over this considerable period, consistently and without effective opposition.

[7] *Autobiography*, 552–53.

I determined on the move without consulting the Cabinet, precisely as I took Panama without consulting the Cabinet. A council
of war never fights, and in a crisis the duty of leader is to lead and
not to take refuge behind the generally timid wisdom of a multitude
of councillors.

This may have been ingenuous. The fleet was not going to fight. He intended that there should be a recognition abroad of the new American
position, and he intended to demonstrate a readiness to enforce that recognition. The President, as the chosen head of the nation, had at his disposal
the means necessary to his obligations.

One student of the Roosevelt career has put it this way:

> . . . Roosevelt sought security and peace in concepts of power in
> Europe and Asia and in power applied to discipline disorder. His
> was not a legalistic system. Nation states themselves decided, as
> they interpreted their interests, how best to canalize their force.
> Although from each he hoped for courteous restraint, to ensure that
> quality he relied not upon a world league of laws but upon con-
> sciousness by each great nation of counterbalanced power. . . .[8]

American power should be on exhibit continuously so that there should
be no mistake on the part of any other nation. The chosen weapon, available for ready use in waters anywhere, was the navy. Let the world see
the fleet in being; in particular, let the Japanese see!

For he had noted in conversations with Japanese diplomats an under-
tone of truculence. They had been emboldened by victory over Russia;
they were infected with the samurai spirit. They might, he considered,
"enter into a general career of insolence and aggression." The best way
of damping down any enlarged ambitions the Japanese Empire might
have would be for them to have a good look at the United States fleet
in the Pacific and in their own harbors.

The anticipation of a certain resentful aggression on the part of the
Japanese was logical. They had been, and continued to be, offended by
the exclusion of their nationals from the United States, and their protests
against it had been increasingly irritable. The Pacific coast, where the "yellow peril" was most talked about, was completely intransigent. There was

_____

[8] John Morton Blum in *The Republican Roosevelt* (Cambridge, Mass.,
1954) Chaps. VIII and IX, in which there is also this illuminating characterization: "He savored entrances upon a vast, well-lighted stage. In any
hour he liked to strut. The possibilities of war that caused even the brave
to pray stirred in his heart a disquieting delight. These dreadful temperamental traits, however, made his understanding of national interest no less
sure . . ."

absolute refusal to recognize any larger interest than the competition offered to farmers and laborers by the Orientals who had been drifting into
most occupations and businesses for a generation. Continual agitation, accompanied by embarrassing talk and action, posed a problem in foreign
relations. The President sought compromise and reasonableness. But he
had little luck. The Japanese gave way to California insistence, but it
could be seen that the injury to oriental pride would someday be revenged
if it became possible.

The navy was excellent for its time. Ever since Roosevelt's accession
he had been urging the Congress to provide more and better ships, and
he had devoted himself personally to raising the efficiency of operations.
When the Second Hague Conference in the summer of 1907 ended without agreement on naval building, he felt that it would be most unwise
to set a unilateral limit. The navy was needed, because only by destroying any foreign force that threatened could the country's coasts be really
protected.[9]

The threatening navy Roosevelt had in mind was that of Japan. Looking at California and talking to the Japanese, he saw a real prospect of
trouble. Letters written in July of 1907 make it quite clear that it was
this trouble he hoped to stifle by the fleet's appearance. No one knew as
yet that he intended it to visit Japan and then extend its voyage around
the world. Such a project, he knew, would be considered fantastically
risky. The moving of a fleet for long distances was extremely difficult, as
the Russian experience in bringing one around from the Baltic to the
China Sea had recently shown. He was convinced of the superior technical
abilities of the American commanders; but, good as the navy was, extended maneuvers would make it better. Even to his confidant, Lodge,
he spoke only of this need for experience:

> It became evident to me, from talking with the naval authorities,
> that in the event of war they would have a good deal to find out
> in the way of sending the fleet to the Pacific. Now, the one thing
> I won't run the risk of is to experiment for the first time in a matter
> of importance in time of war. Accordingly I concluded that it was
> imperative that we should send the fleet on what would be prac-
> tically a practice voyage. I do not intend to keep it in the Pacific
> for any length of time; but I want all failures, blunders, and short-
> comings to be made apparent in time of peace and not in time of
> war. Moreover I think that, before matters become more strained,
> we had better make it evident that when it comes to visiting our
> own coasts on the Pacific or Atlantic and assembling the fleet in

[9] Messages to Congress, 1906 and 1907.

our own waters, we cannot submit to any outside protests or interference. Curiously enough, the Japs have seen this more quickly
than our own people.[10]

But to Secretary Root, who must be made aware of what he intended,
even if he was not asked for advice, the President was writing as follows:

> I am more concerned over this Japanese situation than almost any
> other. Thank Heaven we have a navy in good shape. It is high
> time, however, that it should go on a cruise around the world. In
> the first place I think it will have a pacific effect to show that it can
> be done. . . .[11]

The rest of this letter was divided between a denunciation of those who
were opposed to his policy and an account of a visit to his home in Oyster
Bay of the Japanese Ambassador and Admiral Yamamoto. He thought
the influential Admiral hopelessly misunderstood the problem of Japanese
immigration, and he was quite sure that he had not had much success
in explaining it. The fleet in Japanese waters would be the only lesson he
and others like him would understand.

In other letters he said that he had become convinced of something
else—that the Japanese "thought he was afraid of them," something intolerable to his perpetually adolescent nature. When he returned from
seeing the fleet off he announced from the White House that it would go
on to the East. The furor following this announcement, he simply ignored.

Later, in writing his *Autobiography*, he ventured the opinion that his
most important contribution to peace had been the orders given for the
world-circling cruise:

> I made up my mind that it was time to have a showdown . . .
> many persons publicly and privately protested against the move on
> the ground that Japan would accept it as a threat. To this I an-
> swered nothing in public. In private I said that I did not believe
> that Japan would so regard it because Japan knew my sincere
> friendship and admiration for her and realized that we could not
> as a nation have any intention of attacking her . . .

But in a later passage he seemed not quite so certain. He spoke of hearing,
in 1910, when he visited Germany, that the naval authorities there had

[10] July 10, 1907. Even late in August, when the announcement was
made of the voyage to the Pacific coast, nothing was said about a voyage
to Japan or further. For a full treatment of this and other Roosevelt
actions vis-à-vis Japan, cf. Bailey, *Roosevelt and the Japanese-American
Crises*, especially Chap. X.

[11] These communications will be found in *Letters*, V, 709, 717.

expected the Japanese to go to war rather than accept the humiliation implied in the fleet's visit. He told them, he said, that he had not expected war but also said that he had told the officers to take every precaution. If the Japanese had been hostile "it would have been proof positive that we were going to be attacked anyhow and in such event it would have been an enormous gain to have had three months' preliminary preparations which enabled the fleet to start perfectly equipped."

As it turned out, the voyage was a tremendous success in all the ways the President had hoped it would be, and he continued to be proud of it as long as he lived. When the fleet arrived in Japanese waters the highest honors were paid its officers and men and they were overwhelmed with entertainment. The Orientals knew how to speak softly, too, at least until they had acquired a big stick. There was afterward more reason to doubt that the visit of the fleet contributed to the long-run peace of the world than Roosevelt had when he was writing his *Autobiography*.[12] But whatever the results, they were presidential ones. No one had shared in the decision, and no one else need share any blame or was entitled to any credit.

[12] The self-congratulations will be found at pp. 592 ff.

★ 35 ★

IN ONE WIDELY READ STUDENT'S HISTORY OF THE UNITED STATES THERE are several paragraphs devoted to Theodore Roosevelt's weakness for making a noisy disturbance about moralistic issues but never coming to any workable program for correcting abuses and punishing miscreants, and the authors'[1] opinion seems to be common to most historians. Roosevelt is said to have been superficial and, because of this, to have failed in offering the plans necessary if the nation was to master, when it should have done so, the anarchic forces of free enterprise. It is granted that his hold on the electorate was remarkable; but this was because of his attractive personality and his extraordinary energy, not because of wisdom or foresight. Because his popularity seemed to have no depth, no real reason for being, the following he continued to command is puzzling. It cannot be denied, yet it seems to have been so little deserved that historians hardly know how to account for it when they try to sum up his political career.

This was not unforeseen by his contemporaries, and some of them were amused by the prospect. William Allen White, the shrewd journalist of Emporia, Kansas, was one of these. He was amused, but he also thought it a little too bad that something of the vitality and bubbling enthusiasm of the man, as they communicated themselves to his followers and, indeed, spread readily to ordinary citizens, could not somehow be captured and preserved for the future. If this could be done, later generations would look back with less chilling cynicism to Roosevelt's admiring contemporaries. They were not so simple, White said, as it would seem. The delight of the crowds who listened to and voted for T.R. was a genuine phenomenon. Even when his performances were bombastic, ridiculous, or even contradictory, they possessed a kind of political magic that students of democracy cannot afford to disparage. Historians acknowledge this with

[1] Samuel Eliot Morison of Harvard and Henry Steele Commager of Columbia, in *The Growth of the American Republic,* 2 vols. (New York, 1942).

some reluctance. Communication about personal magnetism, the sense of solidarity between leader and led, from one generation to another, is very difficult, however, and they do not rate Roosevelt high in any category.

We, of course, for our purpose here, must demur. That very magic, so elusive and yet so real, is something the student of the Presidency must accept as important. And it is truer than the historians readily grant that Roosevelt was one of the superior Presidents. He was abashed in the presence of no one. He did not understand the powerful men of his time in economic affairs, but he refused to become their servant. He may not have affected very much the relations between government and business, but he checked the trend toward control of the government by businessmen. He gave an example of independence, at the very least, and sometimes, as we have seen, he interfered with vigor and determination.

Roosevelt has suffered, it must be admitted, from close examination of his record. There is in it more talk than action. And discovery of this, along with a certain tendency he had to improve it after the fact, has shadowed his reputation. There are certain incidents which seem not to have happened exactly as they are related in his *Autobiography* or in his letters. And it cannot be denied that the alterations have the effect of improving the author's performance. But his followers seem to have known all about these and other weaknesses and to have regarded them as faults linked to the virtues they delighted in. Elihu Root is quoted as having said of T.R. that he imagined he had discovered the Ten Commandments; but surely Root said this and other things a little tenderly and forgivingly. Strict moralists were not sympathetic; they thought him hypocritical. But urbane and wise men like Root knew they were watching a superb performance of a sort they themselves would have been utterly incapable of staging.

But the historians remain skeptical; they say of him:

His morality was positive, but not subtle; he was never in doubt as to the right or wrong of any question, and he regarded those who differed with him as either scoundrels or fools. . . . He was a man of fixed convictions and implacable prejudices . . . He was an ardent nationalist, but his idea of nationalism was to a large extent a matter of flags and martial airs. He was a faithful Republican, looked upon Democrats with deep suspicion and, until he himself bolted his party in 1912, looked upon bolters with positive loathing. He was a sincere progressive, but his progressivism was circumscribed by a limited understanding of economics . . .

He advocated 'trust-busting' but his moral sense led him to distinguish between 'good' trusts and 'bad' trusts, and actually the trusts were more powerfully entrenched when he left than when he entered office. . . . He denounced 'malefactors of great wealth' but was critical of the 'muckrakers' who exposed their malefactions, and took no positive steps to curb individual fortunes or to secure a more equitable distribution of wealth through taxation. . . . His chief service to the progressive cause was to dramatize the movement and make it respectable. Yet Roosevelt's dramatics often distracted attention from big tent to side shows, and his respectability required a conformity that seriously impaired the integrity of a reform movement. After the seven years of tumult and shouting had passed, many reformers came to feel that they had been fighting a sham battle and that the citadels of privilege were yet to be invested.[2]

This doubting of the twenty-sixth President may be too insistent. Perhaps the historians miss the intention of his bizarre behavior—that is, beyond the getting and keeping of a position: every politician has this as a primary ambition; it serves to start him and keep him going. The myth of the reluctant citizen upon whom office is thrust may occasionally have a materialization in real life, but it is seldom indeed an appropriate characterization of anyone who has got so far as the Presidency, and especially it cannot be said of the "strong" ones; all of them, with one exception, attained office by striving and scheming, by using others ruthlessly, by accepting necessary but repulsive duties, by compromising and pretending.[3] All this was characteristic of Roosevelt. His equivocal relations with the bosses of his party he concealed as best he could, but they eventually came to light. There were many passages in his career that he cannot have looked back on with pride. As a conservationist of natural resources, however—especially the forests—he deserves enormous credit; more, perhaps, than any other single individual except Gifford Pinchot, who was his mentor. And he did get enacted, against the fiercest opposition, a Food and Drug Act which gave at least some protection to formerly helpless consumers. These were mountains of accomplishment in the long struggle to preserve the public interest against the depredations of private profit seekers. No other leader following him, even the second Roosevelt, would stand as he did against the pressures of the patent-medicine, the meat-packing, the grain-milling interests. But what has to be noticed about these issues is that they were simple and moral. It was wrong to destroy the

[2] Ibid., II, 386–88.

[3] The exception, of course, was Washington, as has already been explained. But his situation was one not likely ever to recur in a democracy. Other generals might be cited as having been overcome with presidential ambitions, but only at a quite late stage; and none of them has been strong. Most of them were discovered by party insiders who took advantage of their military reputations, with deplorable results for the country if not for the party.

forests for profit; it was wrong to poison people or deceive them. There was crusading material in such issues, and he seized on it with his unmatched flair for dramatization and whipped his enemies with righteous zeal.

He tried to see in more crucial issues the same moral positions, unassailably right and simple enough for the demagogic exposition he had at his command. But when it came to economics—finance, the tariff, business regulation—he found the complications confusing. When he had to distinguish between good and bad trusts he was lost. This may have annoyed him, because he liked to think of himself as an all-round man, competent in many fields and really ignorant of none; but he probably would not have admitted that this was a disqualification for the Presidency. In his view the President had a broader writ than to be Chief Executive, Commander in Chief, or even policy-maker. He was an educator, an admonisher, an enforcer—not merely a setter—of moral standards. This was a new role for the President. It was one future Presidents would have to accept or be criticized for not accepting.

It was a President's business, in the Roosevelt view, to know right from wrong in every activity and to see to it that the right was rewarded and the wrong punished. But the rewarding and punishing could not be too condign except in the clearest cases. The people had to be brought to see the issues too. Presidents had to have support, unmistakable support in vast volume, when it was called for; and above all they had to be elected and re-elected. They therefore had to educate their constituency. But education can be a long process, and until the conviction of rightness and wrongness had spread, action would be premature; it might even fail.

This was an educator's excuse for not doing everything that needed doing. It helped also, it must be said, to cover indecision. Roosevelt knew that certain business practices of Standard Oil were bad and that the railroad financiers were engaged in skulduggery. But did that mean that Standard Oil must be abolished or railroad consolidation blocked? It did not take much knowledge to know that this was too easy an answer; and anyway it was probably a wrong one. Corporations, like people, must stop doing bad things. They must be punished. But, like people, there was a reason for their existence. He did not agree with those who thought their existence was owed to their sins and that they must be destroyed to get rid of the sins.

Roosevelt in a way was representative of transition in America. The rural way of life was giving way to urbanism; and he was urban, really the first of the city Presidents. He had been born in New York City of a wealthy family, one also with a claim to aristocracy. The Roosevelts went back a long way in the history of New York, and from the first they had been respectable, often prominent, people; and his mother was a Georgia Bulloch, which meant much in the South. He was as far from the log-cabin tradition as he could well be. Yet he had that interest in the wide West which was so well publicized. His experience in the plains states as a rancher, a hunter, and a horseman gave him a different background than was possessed by most natives of New York with a Harvard education. And no one could have made more than he did of the Rough Riders —the regiment he had raised for the Spanish-American War. They had fought gallantly in Cuba with him at their head; and as veterans they afterward became a regular feature of his political campaigns—this was why Mark Hanna shuddered at the thought of "that damned cowboy in the White House." He worried the business interests. They were never sure how much he meant of what he said or how far he would actually go to implement his threats. They gradually learned that he was much less dangerous than he sounded. He meant to enforce the anti-trust laws —within reason; he meant to regulate destructive competitive practices —also within reason. He meant to lower the tariffs—but could be argued with.

As his critics continue to say, he got little done of the agenda he professed to be guided by. But there was a vast educational enterprise involved in his doing nothing. After him, Americans were dissatisfied with Taft; and Wilson's accomplishments were easier because T.R. had prepared people's minds. He helped them to understand that the nation and its various affairs were vast in scale and significance, that bigness was necessary to the productivity of industry, and that there was nothing to be afraid of in the apparent power of the financiers and big businessmen; they simply had to be cut down to size by a capable political leader. All the time he fulminated against socialism, however, often speaking of it as though it could not be distinguished from anarchism. This was no way to clear people's minds, but since there was no danger that either philosophy would gain much hold, it was a harmless exercise. His opponents were always trying to label him as something of a socialist, and his disclaimers were needed to keep him respectable.

Nevertheless, Roosevelt was always very much aware of progressivism, which may have been more of a temperamental than a philosophic matter. What he could not stand about the Old Guard was its "stand-pat" character. He was full of life, always on the move, even when he was not going anywhere very much. His vigor and compulsive activity were notable traits. But he was also conscious of belonging to an elite with privileges. This transferred itself to the nation; it also belonged to the elite, and it too had privileges. The leveling nature of much advanced social thinking repelled and enraged him. He could not have been a Democrat, and he remained a regular Republican without misgivings until his break with the party leaders in 1912, four years after he had left the Presidency and, in effect, turned it over to William Howard Taft. But in a sense he had been a Progressive even when he had been a Republican, which was one reason why he was so annoyed with Taft's performance as his successor. Taft was reactionary and so were his policies.

It must be recalled, however, that many respectable Republicans agreed with the Progressives about some matters, such as the anti-trust laws, for instance, and were angered by the machinations of their contemporaries in Wall Street and its vicinity. The Sherman Act was named for a Republican Senator from Ohio and was signed by a Republican President—Harrison, from Indiana. There were differences, destined to continue and intensify, among the conservatives. Particularly those from the Midwest often did not agree with easterners.

But if midwestern Republicans did not get along with the Wall Streeters, it was for more reasons than that big business had its managerial seat in New York. The Midwest was also isolationist and anti-imperialist and the financiers were apt to be internationalists. Roosevelt, in this confusion, did not always find it easy to organize and maintain support for his imperialism on the one hand and his inclination toward domestic progressivism on the other. His way out was to impose his combination of policies on the Republican party and to ignore charges of inconsistency. But he created a grave handicap in his stated intention not to be a candidate again in 1908. This caused his prestige to decline steadily with the party leaders during his last years in the White House. But why he decided on Taft as a successor remains a puzzle. It must have been that, as usual, he failed completely to understand another individual, or even, perhaps, to try. He was so vocal, so active, that he was careless and superficial in listening to and judging others. Taft's acceptance of his orders in various administrative posts was assumed to involve agreement in philosophy.

It was only when he was forced to listen and watch from retirement that he began to comprehend what a colossal error he had made. He had not remade the Republican party and he had given it a President who would carry it backward rather than forward. In his annoyance he determined that he must run again, so he tried to recapture his party position and become the presidential nominee in 1912. Until then he had ascribed the lowest motives to any politician who would even think of such a thing as revolt. But when he was rejected, he accepted the Progressive nomination and started out on a new campaign of exhortation under the sign of the Bull Moose. If he had been elected in that year he would have absorbed the Republicans again, if he could, during his Presidency. As it was, he captured a good many of them—enough to split the party and enable the Democrats to elect Wilson. But, although it was a glorious campaign, in the best Roosevelt manner, it not only did not elect him President, it ruined the burgeoning Progressive movement. The Republicans had refused to become a Roosevelt party, but the Progressives did not refuse, and when Roosevelt's enthusiasm died and he no longer saw in the new party a possible vehicle for a return to power he abandoned it. The enthusiasts were left leaderless and bereft. Their betrayal was complete.[4]

Roosevelt was voluble all his life. Looked back upon as a whole, his output of words seems incredible for a person who was, most of the time, a politician. In his bibliography there are books, articles, memoranda, and letters in amazing quantities. He seized every opening for speeches and other pronouncements; and while he was an official in city, state, and nation, he left a wide and continuous trail of utterances having an astonishing variety. In a way this corpus of words is more the real Roosevelt than his actions; and it may well be that he regarded them as his most valuable legacy to the nation, although he was not one to underestimate the value of his administrative achievements. Even his *Autobiography*, which is a long justification of his official behavior, has the character of a tract for young men aspiring to a political career. It may even be that this earnest moralizing, rather than an unprincipled attempt to glorify himself for posterity, accounts for the passages of doubtful accuracy which give him all the best of the possible interpretations of his actions and sometimes go so far as to falsify the record. He would have future generations believe the story of Washington and the cherry tree whether or not it was fiction, and he would have them think of himself as standing at Armageddon and battling for the Lord rather than as a practical politician who had to get along with Boss Platt at considerable expense to his principles, who compromised with J. P. Morgan and with Mark Hanna, who conspired for revolution in Panama, and who betrayed La Follette.

There are eight large volumes of *Letters* in the collected edition; there are, in any library of size, a shelf of the most varied books, whose contents

---

[4] This was a terrible tragedy for Robert La Follette, especially, who had spent his whole life in creating and leading the movement from Wisconsin. He was casually displaced by Roosevelt, who wished only to use the party for his own purposes; but with this we are not concerned here, except to note the effect on the Presidency and its occupants of knowledge long in advance that the office is to be given up. This deprived Roosevelt of power and led to his candidacy in a third party. It led also to the selection of a minority President. That President may be said to have acknowledged his debt to Roosevelt by becoming a Progressive himself and adopting most of the projects on the Progressive agenda. Perhaps also it was in a way acknowledged by appointing another Roosevelt to a position in his official family—Franklin, as Assistant Secretary of the Navy. Wilson may or may not have known of the coolness between the two branches of the family. If he did, he must have had a certain sardonic pleasure in paying his debt in this way. The younger generation of Oyster Bay Roosevelts would have to wait for preferment until the Republicans again captured the Presidency.

range from accounts of outdoor life and exploration (*American Big Game Hunting, The Wilderness Hunter, Through the Brazilian Wilderness, African Game Trails,* etc.), biography (*Thomas Hart Benton, Gouverneur Morris,* etc.), to history (*The Naval War of 1812*) and homilies on morals (*American Ideals,* etc.). And this is not to mention the hundreds of essays, notes, comments, and argumentative articles published in magazines and newspapers. Some of his letters, now published, run to article length and are expositions of his policies, attitudes, or actions, written sometimes to supporters and sometimes to critics. They are always verbose, frequently pungent, and are generally written in a style that is far from distinguished, often careless, and sometimes regrettable. He was apt to be defensive, but he never admitted to having been mistaken; and those who disagreed with him or ventured to criticize were likely to be written off as ungrateful, wicked, or idiotic.

His certainty, his rigid opinions, his conventional standards, linked with his ambition and his sense of inevitable rightness, made him a dangerous character in the opinion of many contemporaries. It was not only Hanna and other big businessmen who were afraid of so irresponsible and self-righteous a person in the Presidency. There were thoughtful and disinterested people who were afraid not only of what he might do in domestic affairs but of his possibly provocative attitudes toward foreign nations. But his very certainty and simplicity, the lack of doubt that made him so furious an opponent or so enamored an advocate were political assets. On the hustings he could swing his arms, shake his fists, scream in his half-falsetto voice, and carry conviction to the immense crowds he always attracted. He had a following seldom equaled in American political history. When he ran with McKinley for the Vice-Presidency, McKinley stayed at home and conducted a dignified front-porch campaign; but Roosevelt, with complete unrestraint, spread himself as widely as transportation facilities would permit over the whole country. "On one tour alone, toward the end of the drive, he visited twenty-four states and made 673 speeches in 567 towns and cities. He traveled 21,209 miles and 3,000,000 people saw and heard him."[5] In fact, he made rather more noise and received rather more attention than McKinley himself.[6]

There is, indeed, some reason for saying that he was the inventor of the modern presidential campaign as he was the inventor of the modern Presidency. Both these claims have about them a certain exaggeration but

[5] *Theodore Roosevelt* by H. F. Pringle (quoting a compilation in the New York *Times*) (New York, 1931), 225.

[6] A technique to be copied by a younger Roosevelt in 1920 when running with Cox on the Democratic ticket.

also a kind of truth. James G. Blaine did not follow the Republican precedent; he made a speaking tour, but it was generally agreed that it did
him no good. He was not elected anyway, and if he had followed advice
and retreated to his Maine home during the campaign's last stages, his
fatal mistake in New York would not have occurred and Cleveland might
not have carried that important state. Bryan was an orator who could
not resist any opportunity to use his magnificent voice; he rampaged up
and down the country in all his campaigns, but he too was never elected.
McKinley's return to the dignified custom of making an acceptance statement and from then on staying at home was modified by an elaborate
organization of visiting delegations to whom the candidate spoke from his
"front porch," thus getting his views effectively before the country and at
the same time maintaining the decorum of a statesman; but still the fiction
of dignified withdrawal was maintained.

On form, it paid better to follow McKinley's example. Elections were
pretty clearly not won by speeches and all the other accompaniments of
the traveling campaign. The speechmakers uniformly seemed to lose. But
as a vice-presidential candidate Roosevelt was not held to any customary
limitations, except that the second man on the ticket was not a highly
regarded expositor of party principles, having been chosen, usually, for
some reason of convenience rather than for his position of leadership in
the party. At any rate, Roosevelt was about as active as it was possible
for a human being to be. He spoke everywhere and about everything.[7]

Roosevelt having made that kind of approach to office, and done it
to everyone's satisfaction, especially his own, it was not strange that he
should make the same kind of campaign when he came to run for the
Presidency on his own in 1904. By now there were transportation and
communication facilities not available in such rich array before. The railroads had spread a comprehensive network, there were telegraph and
telephone connections to every village, and there were numerous organs
of opinion, especially the small-town and rural newspaper, to carry propaganda into many homes. Besides, T.R. was well aware that he excited the
electorate. There was about him a magical ability to attract attention
that successful leaders know so well how to use. It was not true that a
man must have it to become President; there had been a whole line of

---

[7] Here again the precedent for Franklin Roosevelt in 1920 is too obvious to be overlooked. Each had the problem of emerging from the
obscurity of the Vice-Presidency—or the candidacy for the Vice-Presidency—to a position of party prominence. Each thought that by an earnest
and industrious campaign the party leaders all over the country might be
impressed for the future. And they were right. Their vice-presidential
campaigns were important for their future preferment in the party.

them who had altogether lacked it. They had been dull and inarticulate, stiff and unexciting. The most that could be said of them was that they could be made to represent the father-image so significant in democratic societies with a largely ignorant and illiterate electorate. But these were Republican party front-men, almost puppets; and Roosevelt was making his way upward in spite of the party elders. There were not many politicians who possessed the talent of the Roosevelts, but those who did succeeded in spite of any opposition or any difficulties. This was something that Jackson had, and Lincoln. But even those artists had it in no greater degree than T.R.

The point has been made that Roosevelt was articulate, even loquacious. It would be remarkable rather than otherwise if so voluble a man had not had something of interest to say about the office under inquiry in this study. And he did. In his *Autobiography* there is a passage defining his attitude. It was soon labeled the "stewardship theory." It put into words—rather defiant ones—the duty of Presidents to assume power in national emergencies; and emergency, of course, was to be defined by the President himself:

> The most important factor in getting the right spirit in my Administration, next to the insistence upon courage, honesty, and a genuine democracy of desire to serve the plain people was my insistence upon the theory that the executive power was limited only by specific restrictions and prohibitions appearing in the Constitution or imposed by the Congress under its Constitutional powers. My view was that every executive officer, and above all every executive officer in high position, was a steward of the people . . . I declined to adopt the view that what was imperatively necessary for the nation could not be done by the President unless he could find some specific authorization to do it. My belief was that it was not only his right but his duty to do anything that the needs of the nation demanded unless such action was forbidden by the Constitution or by the laws. Under this interpretation of executive power I did and caused to be done many things not previously done by the President and the heads of the Departments. I did not usurp power, but I did greatly broaden the use of executive power. In other words, I acted for the public welfare, I acted for the common well-being of all our people, whenever and in whatever manner was necessary, unless prevented by direct Constitutional or legislative prohibition. I did not care a rap for the mere form and show of power; I cared immensely for the use that could be made of the substance.[8]

[8] 388–89.

Just before he left the Presidency he referred to the incidents he felt ought to be cited as showing his view of the President's powers and duties:

> While President I have *been* President, emphatically; I have used every ounce of power there was in the office and I have not cared a rap for the criticisms of those who spoke of my "usurpation of power"; for I know that the talk has been all nonsense and that there has been no usurpation. I believe that the efficiency of this government depends upon its possessing a strong central executive, and whenever I could establish a precedent for strength in the executive, as I did for instance as regards external affairs in the case of sending the fleet around the world, taking Panama, settling affairs of Santo Domingo, and Cuba; or as I did in internal affairs in settling the anthracite coal strike, in keeping order in Nevada this year when the Federation of Miners threatened anarchy, or as I have done in bringing the big corporations to book—why, in all these cases I have felt not merely that my action was right in itself, but that in showing the strength of, or in giving strength to, the executive, I was establishing a precedent of value.

This was in a long letter, written to Sir George Otto Trevelyan after the convention of 1908 was over and Taft had been nominated according to his wishes. It opened with an endorsement of Taft, who, he predicted, would "rank with any other man who has ever been in the White House," Washington and Lincoln excepted. It went on to an interesting argument with himself as to whether he had done the right thing in making the announcement, just after his election in 1904, that he would in no circumstances again be a candidate. There was an obvious reluctance to give up the office. He had, he said, been a little uncomfortable as to whether his announced decision had been wise. There was much to be said in favor of "the theory that the public has the right to demand as long service from any man who is doing good service as it thinks will be useful." During the last year or two, he confessed, he had "been rendered extremely uncomfortable both by the exultation of my foes over my announced intention to retire, and by the real uneasiness and chagrin felt by many good men because, as they believed, they were losing quite needlessly the leader in whom they trusted, and who they believed could bring to a successful conclusion certain struggles which they regarded as of vital concern to the national welfare." There was more of this; he spoke of "ugly qualms" and hinted strongly that if he had known, when he made his original announcement, that his following after four years would have regarded him as "the man of all others whom they wished to see President" he might have decided differently.

He really did feel that he had been a Lincoln-like President, and he expanded on this theme:

> Above all and beyond all I believe as I have said before that the salvation of this country depends upon Washington and Lincoln representing the type of leader to which we are true . . . I may be mistaken, but it is my belief that the bulk of my countrymen, the men whom Abraham Lincoln called "the plain people"—the farmers, mechanics, small tradesmen, hard-working professional men—feel that I am in a peculiar sense their President, that I represent the democracy in somewhat the fashion that Lincoln did, that is, not in any demagogic way but with the sincere effort to stand for a government by the people and for the people.

He was leaving the Presidency, he indicated, in spite of his reluctance, because he had a feeling that he ought not to shatter the belief in his integrity held by so many of these followers. His leaving, after making a commitment to do so, was tied to his defense of the stewardship theory. His integrity must be beyond question; only such an individual ought to have the powers he believed a President must have at his disposal in case of necessity. Just as no one should question a President's right to act as the nation's steward, no one should be able to say that he wanted the stewardship for his own aggrandizement. It was a pure impulse; it must not be sullied.[9]

He was like a comet in the skies, brilliant while in sight, but leaving the scene emptier when he had gone. The temporary effulgence had been merely temporary. Still it is known that when a younger Roosevelt assumed the office some twenty-four years after the older one had left it, he definitely had in mind the performance of "Uncle Ted"; he hoped to outdo the old master. Perhaps in this his example had the value of inspiration and so was still another contribution to the Presidency.

[9] *Letters*, VI, 1085–90.

★ 36 ★

ROOSEVELT SAID, IN THE SAME LETTER TO SIR GEORGE TREVELYAN IN which he discussed his theory of the Presidency, that he would have been more reluctant to leave the office if his leaving "had meant that there was no chance to continue the work" he was engaged in and which he deemed "vital to the welfare of the people." He had, he said, "ready to hand a man whose theory of public and private duty" was his own and "whose practice of this theory" was like his own. "If we can elect him President," went on T.R., "we achieve all that could be achieved by continuing me in office, and yet we avoid all the objections, all the risk of creating a bad precedent."

This was surely as grievous an error as any politician, substituting wish for judgment, ever allowed himself to make. For actually Taft's views were precisely the reverse of Roosevelt's. When he came to state them years later, he spoke heatedly of the mistaken notion that the President had any constitutional warrant for acting as a "Universal Providence." On the contrary, "the true view of the executive functions," he said, was that the President could not legally do anything which could not "be fairly and reasonably traced to some specific grant of power or justly implied and included within such express grant of power as proper and necessary." He proceeded to speak of Roosevelt as believing in a "residual executive power." This he regarded as thoroughly "unsafe."[1]

President Taft was one of the line whose thoughts about the office have for the student almost as much interest as his behavior. His actions may have classed him among the more passive Executives, but they were deliberate. He understood the tensions imposed by the Constitution, and

[1] The references are to lectures at Columbia University, published by the University Press in 1916. It has been suggested that Roosevelt's mistaken estimate of Taft as a successor was formed in the years before 1908 when Taft was a subordinate in various administrative positions, including the Secretaryship of War and the Governor-Generalship of the Philippines. In those positions he would have had no occasion to state— or perhaps even to formulate—a theory of presidential power.

it would be difficult to find anywhere a more lucid explanation of the Rule of Restraint than is found in *Our Chief Magistrate and His Powers.* Quoting Jefferson, Jackson, and Lincoln in famous instances of differences with the Supreme Court, he put the case for the Justices as against the President with some persuasiveness by saying that the Court was a permanent body and that it respected precedent and sought consistency. Because of this, he argued, its view of the Constitution was likely in the long run to prevail. But this was not inevitable; it had no enforcing power:

> While it is important to mark out the exclusive field of jurisdiction of each branch of the government, Legislative, Executive, and Judicial, it would be said that in the proper working of the government there must be cooperation of all the branches, and without a willingness of each branch to perform its function, there will follow a hopeless obstruction to the progress of the whole Government. Neither branch can compel the other to affirmative action, and each branch can greatly hinder the other in the attainment of the object of its activities and the exercise of its discretion. The judicial branch has sometimes been said to be the most powerful branch of the government because in its decision of litigated cases it is frequently called upon to mark the limits of the jurisdiction of the other two branches. As already noted, by its continuity and the consistency of its decisions, the Court exercises much greater power in this regard than the other two branches. But it has no instruments to enforce its judgments, and if the Executive fails to remove the obstructions that may be offered to the execution of its decrees and orders, when its authority is defied, then the Court is helpless. It may not directly summon the army or the navy to maintain the supremacy of the law and order. So if the judges of the Court were to refuse to perform the judicial duties imposed by the Congress, the object of Congress in much of its legislation might be defeated. And if Congress were to refuse to levy the taxes and make the appropriations which are necessary to pay the salaries of government officials, and to furnish the equipment necessary to the performance of their duties, it could paralyze all branches of the government. The life of the government, therefore, depends on the sense of responsibility of each branch in doing the part assigned to it in the carrying on of the business of the people in the government, and ultimately as the last resource, we must look to public opinion as the moving force to induce affirmative action and proper team work . . .[2]

When, as an ex-President, Taft was saying these things at Columbia in 1915, he had before him the remarks of ex-President Roosevelt to the

[2] Ibid., 138–39.

effect that necessity is a justification for presidential acts of almost any sort, and his dissent took on the interest of high-level debate. Since this difference concerned the scope of the presidential powers, we may well quote him further. His reference was to the anthracite strike of 1902 and to T.R.'s plan for the seizure and operation of the mines.

> Now it is perfectly evident that Mr. Roosevelt thinks he was charged with the duty, not only to suppress disorder in Pennsylvania, but to furnish coal to avoid the coal famine in New York and New England, and therefore he proposed to use the army of the United States to mine the coal which should prevent or relieve the famine. It was his avowed intention to take the mines out of the hands of their lawful owners and to mine the coal which belonged to them and sell it in the eastern market, against their objection, without any court proceeding of any kind and without any legal obligation on their part to work the mines at all. It was an advocacy of the higher law and his obligation to execute it which is a little startling in a constitutional republic . . . The benevolence of his purpose no one can deny, but no one who looks at it from the standpoint of a government of law would regard it as anything but lawless. . . .[3]

This exchange between two ex-Presidents shows as well as it could ever be shown how deep the differences are about the scope of Executive power. It might even be said from the character of their remarks that Roosevelt was a natural President and that Taft was a natural Judge. Roosevelt was a strong President, and Taft was a competent Justice of the Supreme Court. Maybe it should be concluded simply that first Roosevelt and then the American electorate made a mistake in choosing Taft for the Presidency.

At any rate, Taft's belief in judicial supremacy stands out even in his remarks in praise of restraint; and he did prove to be one of the weaker Presidents—although it should be noted that he was exactly the sort approved by the conservatives. He was also, however, a kind man who possessed a sense of humor; in the same Columbia lecture he told a little story which carries more conviction as a commentary on T.R. than the weightiest aspersions on that ebullient Executive's excesses:

> Mr. Roosevelt, by way of illustrating his meaning as to the differing usefulness of Presidents, divides the Presidents into two classes, and designates them as "Lincoln Presidents" and "Buchanan Presidents." In order more fully to illustrate his division of Presidents on their merits, he places himself in the Lincoln class and me in the

[3] Ibid., 146–47.

Buchanan class. The identification of Mr. Roosevelt with Mr. Lincoln might otherwise have escaped notice, because there are many differences between the two, presumably superficial, which would give the impartial student of history a different impression. It suggests a story which a friend of mine told of his little daughter Mary. As he came walking home after a business day, she ran out from the house to greet him, all aglow with the importance of what she wished to tell him. She said, "Papa, I am the best scholar in the class." The father's heart throbbed with pleasure as he inquired, "Why, Mary, you surprise me. When did the teacher tell you? This afternoon?" "Oh, no," Mary's reply was, "the teacher didn't tell me —I just noticed it myself."[4]

This bit of geniality shows Taft in a very becoming light; he might have made his point in a far more cutting way. Roosevelt by then had made himself a little ridiculous. He was querulously unhappy; the habit of carping was growing on him as his exasperation with his impotence in retirement increased. Intemperances of expression and futile reaches for power tended to reflect on his behavior in former days as President, making people wonder why they had once held him in such esteem. But what Taft was inclined to ridicule was nevertheless true. In general Roosevelt *had* been a Lincoln sort of President; and equally Taft *had* been a Buchanan sort.

There were others involved, even if indirectly, in this debate—for instance, Wilson, who, as Taft spoke, was the incumbent President. But then Wilson seems to have been carrying on a debate with himself from his student days; and its outcome, since he had become President, would be important even if no other thinkers had been involved. He was about to lead the nation into and through a war and was at the moment presiding over the most momentous assumption of governmental responsibility in the nation's history.

Wilson did not allow himself to admire Roosevelt. This contrasted with his feeling about Cleveland, yet he must sometimes have been conscious that he owed a good deal to his Republican predecessor. And one remark is recorded which shows that he was very much aware of the debt. It was just after he had re-established the custom, in abeyance since the Presidency of John Adams, of addressing the Congress personally instead of by written communication that he remarked to his wife, "Yes, I think I put one over on Teddy."[5] The likeness 'was not one of outward ap-

---

[4] As Mr. Dooley did, perhaps, when he suggested an appropriate title for Roosevelt's account of his experiences in the Spanish-American War. It might well be called, he said, "Alone in Cubia."

[5] R. S. Baker, *Life and Letters*, 8 vols. (New York, 1927–39), IV, 123.

pearance or of temperament; no two individuals could have been more in contrast; but concerning the office of President their attitudes were unmistakably similar.

But Wilson had not come easily or quickly to the view he professed when his occupation of the office was in prospect or after he arrived there. We had better follow him briefly through this evolution. To do so we may first list the references along the way:

1. "Cabinet Government in the United States," *International Review* (1879). Cf. also *The Public Papers of Woodrow Wilson,* R. S. Baker and W. E. Dodd, eds. (New York, 1925–27).
2. "Committee or Cabinet Government," *Overland Monthly* (1883). Cf. also *Public Papers,* op. cit.
3. *Congressional Government* (Boston, 1885).
4. *The State* (Boston, 1889).
5. "Mr. Cleveland's Cabinet," *Review of Reviews* (1893). Cf. *Public Papers,* op. cit.
6. "Mr. Cleveland as President," *Atlantic Monthly* (1897). Cf. *Public Papers,* op. cit.
7. "The Making of the Nation," *Atlantic Monthly* (1897). Cf. *Public Papers,* op. cit.
8. "Leaderless Government," Virginia Bar Assn. address (1897). Cf. *Public Papers,* op. cit.
9. Preface to the fifteenth edition of *Congressional Government* (1900).
10. *Constitutional Government in the United States,* Columbia University Lectures (1907).

In all of these articles, books, and speeches he said something about the Presidency, showing that throughout the stretch of years he continued to think about the office and its responsibilities. All of these comments antedated his own Presidency. The last of them, however, may possibly have been influenced by hints that he might be considered for candidacy and so may have been less purely academic than the others. This is suggested by Professor A. J. Wann, and it may be fact.[6] At any rate, it represents a drastic change from the views in *Congressional Government* to which we earlier gave some attention.

Following the first two articles and *Congressional Government,* which praised so highly the British system and suggested revisions of American institutions to achieve a similar integration of policy-making and of administration, there began a gradual change which resulted, some twenty-

[6] The suggestion was made in "Woodrow Wilson's Theory of the Presidency," in the volume generally titled *The Philosophy and Policies of Woodrow Wilson,* edited for the American Political Science Association by Earl Latham (Chicago, 1958).

four years later, in the admission that the constitutional provision for leadership was adequate as it stood if the President should aggressively assume the role required by his office. That role had been illustrated in the behavior of Cleveland, perhaps also in that of Roosevelt—although Wilson did not say so. He seemed by then to feel that no constitutional change was imperative.

In the early appraisal Wilson was not certain, apparently, whether the decline in American leadership should be charged to the failure of Presidents to defend their prerogatives or to the discovery by the Congress of its potential strength. Both were really phases of the same phenomenon. He felt that one congressional invention was largely responsible—the system of standing committees. These had attained more and more control over legislation as the House, particularly, had increased in numbers. They had decided what should be acted on and what should not; they had gone further; they had interfered with the Executive and had even usurped many administrative functions. It could be said generally that they had taken over "all the substantial powers of government."

There was another cause for presidential decline—this was the substitution of the party convention for the congressional caucus as a presidential nominating device. The caucus had been more likely to select nominees who had won their way to the top of their party's councils and who therefore had more influence when in office. Then there was the consideration that the convention was not a continuing body. It nominated and then dispersed. It could have no further control over the candidate it had selected. This contrasted unfavorably with the British system, in which the Ministers continuously reported to the party and to Parliament.

The whole, it seemed to Wilson, worked to diffuse authority, to smother initiative, and to make government ineffective. It was to bring together responsibility and power that he suggested formal subordination of the Executive to the Congress.

It has been noted that Wilson was already having second thoughts as he revised his proofs in 1884. But his next book, one of the earliest on comparative government written in the United States, was not published until 1889. It was strictly a descriptive text and allowed no space for consideration of such constitutional changes as he seemed to have been suggesting previously. There was no comment on the convention system of nominating and no adverse discussion of the standing committees. They were merely described.[7] But there was a paragraph concerning Executive communications to the Congress which has a certain theoretical interest:

[7] Although, in discussing the committees of the House, the remark was made that the House must depend, just as the Senate must, upon its standing committees "for information concerning the affairs of the government and the policy of the executive departments, and is often just

Washington and John Adams interpreted the clause [Art. II, Sec. 3] to mean that they might address Congress in person, as the sovereign in England may do . . . But Jefferson . . . being an ineffective speaker, this habit was discontinued . . . Possibly, had the President not so closed the matter against new adjustments, this clause of the Constitution might legitimately have been made the foundation for a much more habitual and informal, and yet at the same time much more public and responsible, interchange of opinion . . . Having been interpreted, however, to exclude the President from any but the most formal and ineffectual utterance of perfunctory advice, our federal executive and legislature have been shut off from co-operation and mutual confidence to an extent to which no other system furnishes a parallel.

Since this was a book on comparative government and had already described, even if only briefly, the British system as well as others, Wilson evidently thought it proper to go on to the following remark:

In all other modern governments the heads of the administrative departments are given the right to sit in the legislative body and to take part in its proceedings. The legislature and executive are thus associated in such a way that the ministers of state can lead the houses without dictating to them, and the ministers themselves be controlled without being misunderstood—in such a way that the two parts of the government which should be most closely coordinated, namely the part by which the laws are made and the part by which the laws are executed, may be kept in close harmony and intimate cooperation, with the result of giving coherence to the action of the one and energy to the action of the other.[8]

During the next period of his career Wilson was a busy scholar at first and then was president of Princeton University. As a writer he reached an extraordinarily large audience and attained unusual prestige among political scientists. The articles and the address (listed above) reveal a changing attitude. He seems to have felt the weight of his position and to have become definitely more circumspect. The first two articles were actually comments on the Cleveland administration. In them

---

as much embarrassed because of its entire exclusion from easy, informal, and regular intercourse with the departments. They cannot advise the House unless they are asked for advice; and the House cannot ask for their advice except indirectly through its committees, or formally by requiring written reports." But this stops short of suggesting that the committees have usurped executive functions. (*The State*, 554.)

[8] Ibid., 565–66.

the point was somewhat labored that Cleveland was not really a party leader. Wilson definitely approved the President's conduct; it had been, he said, direct, fearless, and practical; it had "refreshed our notion of an American Chief Magistrate." It was also noted that Cleveland had changed while in office. He had at first not considered himself to be responsible for policy but only for administration. In spite of himself, however, he had been unable to keep to that function. And in his second term he had really risen to the challenge and had become what the President should be—a policy-maker and a shaper of opinion.

Yet that Cleveland was an exception, Wilson still believed. In "The Making of the Nation" and in "Leaderless Government" he still insisted that only in exceptional circumstances would the structure allow adequate initiative to be exercised. For the most part there would be a fatal diffusion of responsibility. But he did not advocate a change to Cabinet government; instead he rather evasively urged that the parties reform their habits. They ought, he said, to nominate tried and tested politicians so that the President would at least have the strength of his party behind him in formulating policy.

But when *Congressional Government* had run through fourteen editions and was about to have another, and its author was no longer an aspiring student but the most influential of American political scientists, his opinions had become so consequential that his old theses could not be republished without explanation. In the new introduction he asked future readers to remember that the book had been written in 1883–84 and that its description of the government was "not as accurate now as I believe it to have been at the time I wrote it." Because of the war with Spain the President had been given increased power; his relative importance had grown. Wilson came then to the statement of his present belief, an almost complete reversal if the text of the book is consulted:

> It may be . . . that the new leadership of the Executive, inasmuch as it is likely to last, will have a very far-reaching effect upon our whole method of government. It may give the heads of the executive departments a new influence upon the action of Congress. It may bring about, as a consequence, an integration which will substitute statesmanship for government by mass meeting. It may put this whole volume hopelessly out of date.

He knew very well that the volume was already out of date in the sense that its conclusions were not ones he would now defend. But its opinions were to be made even more obsolete by the performance of the first Roosevelt now about to begin. After watching the presidential behavior of T.R. there could no longer be any doubt in an analyst's mind of the potentialities of the office. What had been lacking had been competent

Presidents, not constitutional directives; political courage, not govern-mental devices.

Constitutional Government, a wholly new treatment, written soon after this apologetic preface, showed quite clearly that its author was a more mature student who had become conscious of his authoritative position. Since its ideas were those Wilson publicly professed as he assumed the Presidency, we ought to look at them with some care.

That the enlargement of the Presidential office was now actually in proc-ess Wilson had no further doubt. He still felt that the Constitution had intended only that the President should be the government's administrative head, faithfully executing the laws; but circumstances had required more of him and there had been a significant extra-constitutional response. If the Presidency had in this way come to mean a great deal more than had been intended, the reason was not obscure: it was sheer necessity. There must be a close synthesis of active parts in any work-ing government, and some active agency at the center must bring it about. The unifying force in our complex system had to be the Presidency. From generation to generation the emphasis on this central responsi-bility had become more notable. Presidents had differed considerably in their willingness to accept, but the duty to do so had become more and more customary. It was now expected.

The earlier contention, expressed several times, that the President's handicaps in any effort to become the national exemplar were more than he could overcome, was abandoned. Wilson was now quite certain that the President must necessarily be the party's head because he had been nominated by the party's convention; and if the Cabinet should consist of its prominent members, the ties between the Executive and Legislative Branches would be greatly strengthened; there would indeed be a general willingness to allow the President adequate initiative.

But even if the Cabinet members were recognized politicians, they should be competent administrators. The government was now too large, and its duties too complex, for the President to act as its real adminis-trative head. He must have time and energy for planning, for developing legislation, and for the marshaling of public opinion. There had been a noticeable change in this. Early Presidents had picked their Cabinets from among the strong men of their party; it was a group competent to advise but very often not competent to manage. Cleveland and Roosevelt had been examples of the more modern practice. They had definitely regarded the Cabinet as a group of administrators and had picked them for having demonstrated ability in private life rather than for being prominent in politics.

The extreme separation of powers in the American system which had so worried Wilson in earlier discussions no longer seemed to concern him. The congressional aggressions which had diminished the Executive and enhanced the Congress, where responsibility was dispersed into the standing committees—and was therefore hardly responsibility at all—had been repelled by the latest Presidents. What was needed was Presidents of positive views who would continue to dominate the Legislative Branch. When such men occupied the office the apparent difficulties disappeared.

That so important and widely recognized a theorist should have changed his views so radically has been the source of a good deal of speculation among political scientists. Wilson never expressed any embarrassment at having been so mistaken in his early essays except for remarking that circumstances had changed; and it is true that they had changed. The government was a very different affair in 1907 from what it had been in the eighties of the nineteenth century. It had expanded during the Spanish-American War, although without resorting to the novel devices the next war would stimulate. The war with Spain had been badly managed, especially in matters of procurement and supply, but the attempt to solve its problems had resulted in more modern machinery. Furthermore, Wilson had seen the Civil Service gain recognition. That Roosevelt had been a Civil Service Commissioner on his way to the Presidency had ensured his support of the merit system when he was in office and while the bureaucracy was rapidly expanding. And the struggle with the problems of financial and business control had resulted in new devices under the influence of anti-trust theory. The progressives in the United States were committed to free competition under governmental rules, and Wilson was adopting the progressives' attitudes. He had not yet thought very much about these new responsibilities. He realized that they were very complex and that they made new demands on everyone involved, especially the President, but he did not doubt that any strong man would be able to meet the heavy and complicated requirements.

It has been suggested that in *Constitutional Government* Wilson was really talking about the Presidency as it would be if he had the responsibility for it. When he reconsidered the weaknesses he had pointed out in other years, he realized that they were ones he could overcome. He knew how it could be done, and he explained how in this book. It is possible to think of it thus as his earliest bid for the office.[9] In all the literature about the office there is no discussion more wise, restrained, and yet eloquent than Chapter III of this book. The straining for effect, the literary elaboration, and the reader's sense that the writer was not very sure of himself —all characteristics of *Congressional Government*—had disappeared. The President emerged, in Wilson's exposition, as a live and operating person,

[9] Cf. "Woodrow Wilson's Theory of the Presidency," 65: "There may well have been a tendency for him to think in 1907 not merely as a political scientist but as a man who was being talked about as a potential President . . ."

harassed, but not inescapably so, and with potentialities he might realize
by adopting the behavior appropriate to his duties. It was no longer contended that because he was selected by a convention he must be inept and
unresponsive; rather it was argued that because he had been selected so
deliberately by the party machinery he had a better chance to become an
effective leader. He put it this way:

> What is it that a nominating convention wants in the man it is to
> present to the country . . . ? A man who will be and will seem to
> the country in some sort an embodiment of the character and pur-
> pose it wishes its government to have—a man who understands his
> own day and the needs of the country, and who has the personality
> and initiative to enforce his views both upon the people and upon
> Congress. It may seem an odd way to get such a man. It is even
> possible that nominating conventions and those who guide them do
> not realize entirely what it is that they do. But in simple fact the
> convention picks out a party leader from the body of the nation . . .
> It cannot but be led by him in the campaign; if he be elected it can-
> not but acquiesce in his leadership of the government itself . . .[10]

So the President must dominate the party. He is, in fact, the only one
for whom the whole country votes. Legislators represent localities; he
represents the nation. And this representation clothes him with responsibility; he is "not so much part of party organization as its vital link of
connection with the thinking nation":

> For he is also the political leader of the nation, or has it in his choice
> to be. The nation as a whole has chosen him, and is conscious that it
> has no other political spokesman . . . Let him once win the admira-
> tion and confidence of the country, and no other single force can
> withstand him, no combination of forces will easily overpower
> him . . . When he speaks in his true character, he speaks for no
> special interest. If he rightly interpret the national thought and
> boldly insist upon it he is irresistible; and the country never feels
> the zest of action so much as when its President is of such insight
> and calibre. It is for this reason that it will often choose a man
> rather than a party. A President whom it trusts can not only lead
> it, but form it to his own views.

He noted that there have been Presidents who have refrained from
developing their powers because they were "more theorists than statesmen." They held strictly to the separation of powers and acted "as though

---

[10] This and succeeding quotations are from Chap. III of *Constitutional
Government*.

they thought Pennsylvania Avenue should have been even longer than it is." But under the Constitution such an attitude is not necessary, and in fact it is pedantic and impractical:

> The President is at liberty, both in law and conscience, to be as big a man as he can. His capacity will set the limit; and if Congress be overborne by him, it will be no fault of the makers of the Constitution—it will be from no lack of constitutional powers on its part, but only because the President has the nation behind him, and Congress has not . . .

To emphasize, as Wilson did, the President's duty to plan and to dominate was to impose on him vast, almost terrifying, burdens. Obviously to carry them he must give to the task intense efforts and unremitting attention. What, then, became of his elementary constitutional duty to be the nation's Chief Executive? This was obviously a major theoretical difficulty which must be met. Wilson disposed of it by citing the practical possibilities disclosed by recent history. What Cleveland and Roosevelt had done were what Presidents, faced with modern difficulties, could do if they would.

It might be put shortly by saying that the "Chief" in Chief Executive was emphasized. The executing should be left to the heads of Departments, who made up the Cabinet: "Mr. Cleveland may be said to have been the first President to make this conception of the Cabinet prominent in his choices, and he did not do so until his second administration. Mr. Roosevelt has emphasized the idea." This would eliminate those who might be expected to give political advice and support, but this might not turn out to be so bad. Like so much else, it depended on the individual in office:

> He may be like his cabinet or he may be more than his cabinet. His office is a mere vantage ground from which he may be sure that effective words of advice and timely efforts at reform will gain telling momentum. He has the ear of the nation as of course, and a great person may use such an advantage greatly. If he use the opportunity he may take his cabinet into partnership or not, as he pleases; and so its character may vary with his. Self-reliant men will regard their cabinets as executive councils; men less self-reliant or more prudent will regard them also as political councils, and will wish to call into them men who have earned the confidence of their party . . .

But it is clear that Wilson believed and hoped that the nation would thenceforth have the self-reliant sort in the Presidency—those who made policy, persuaded the public that it was good, and through their prestige with the electorate translated it into accomplishment.

There is one more note to be made about this pre-election discussion —its concern for the burdened President. As we know, Presidents had often complained of their confining duties and of the harassment of office seekers. It had recently become obvious that the sheer burden of work was beyond human capability. It would have to be lightened. Fortunately, as Wilson knew, the arts of administration were paralleling the advance of many techniques in the expanding nation; but if the President was to be all that Wilson said the nation demanded of him, some drastic over-hauling of his specific duties as well as of his methods of working was indicated. Otherwise he would break down. Or, if he did not, he would be less effective than he ought to be; but:

> He can secure his own relief without shirking any real responsibility. Appointments, for example, he can, if he will, make more and more upon the advice and choice of his executive colleagues; every matter of detail not only, but also very minor matters of counsel or of general policy, he can more and more depend upon his chosen advisers to determine; he need reserve for himself only the larger matters of counsel and that general oversight of the business of the government and the persons who conduct it which is not possible without daily consultations, indeed, but which is possible without attempting the intolerable burden of direct control. This is, no doubt, the idea of their functions which most Presidents have entertained and which most Presidents suppose themselves to have acted on; but we have reason to believe that most of our Presidents have taken their duties too literally and have attempted the impossible. But we can safely predict that as the multitude of the President's duties increases, as it must with the growth and the widening activities of the nation itself, the incumbents of the great office will more and more come to feel that they are administering it in its truest purpose and with greatest effect by regarding themselves as less and less executive officers and more and more directors of affairs and leaders of the nation—men of counsel and of the sort of action that makes for enlightenment.

This will have to do for a discussion of Wilson the theorist. We have seen him begin as a doubter; as one who thought that nothing less than a copying of the British plan for meeting the problem of separated Branches would do; and we have seen him develop an appreciation of American institutions as they had been shaped by practical men, within the very flexible limits of constitutional tolerance. He had ended as an optimist, feeling that nothing more than an improvement in men themselves was needed—in politicians, who must pick the candidate; in the candidate, who must dominate the party and explain it to the nation; and in the President, who must assume direction of the nation's policy, explain it, defend it, and see it implemented. We cannot escape the feeling that he may well have been outlining the course he himself would follow if given the chance. And of course he was given the chance.

It may be appropriate, leaving Wilson the theorist, to quote another wise and tolerant observer. Lord Bryce's *American Commonwealth* was published in 1888 and must have been written about the same time as Wilson's first essays. He was somewhat pessimistic too; in fact, he had the same kind of reservations as Wilson after observing the American scene since the Civil War. It is interesting to quote his appraisal of the President in office:

> His main duties are to be prompt and firm in securing the due execution of the laws and maintaining the public peace, careful and upright in the choice of the executive officials of the country. Eloquence, whose value is apt to be overrated in all free countries, imagination, profundity of thought or extent of knowledge, are all in so far a gain to him that they make him a "bigger man," and help him to gain a greater influence over the nation, an influence which, if he be a true patriot, he may use for its good. But they are not necessary for the due discharge in ordinary times of the duties of his post. A man may lack them and yet make an excellent President. Four-fifths of his work is the same in kind as that which devolves on the chairman of a commercial company or the manager of a railway, the work of choosing good subordinates, seeing that they attend to their business, and taking a sound practical view of such administrative questions as require his decision. Firmness, commonsense, and most of all, honesty, an honesty above all suspicion of personal interest, are the qualities which the country chiefly needs in its chief magistrate.[11]

Bryce and Wilson—as well as others—were of the same opinion about one thing put by Wilson in a characteristic phrase. He said, "You cannot compound a successful government out of antagonism." In other words, the separation of powers must somehow cease to be an effective principle. And Wilson had come to have the view that the divisiveness might be healed and unity gained by presidential leadership. This seems to be the same sort of President Bryce was describing, one who could choose good helpers and who had "firmness, commonsense, and . . . honesty."

[11] *The American Commonwealth*, 2 vols. (London, 1888), I, 76.

★ 37 ★

TAFT'S REVERSION TO REACTION—TOGETHER WITH HIS OWN RECURRING ambitions—led Roosevelt to repudiate his former protégé and attempt to take for himself the Republican nomination in 1912. He was unsuccessful; but his agitation engendered in him such a sense of righteousness that he was unable to control its expression. There was ready to hand a militant group of Progressives who were as disillusioned with Taft and the Old Guard of the party as he had become. He accepted their nomination and, forgetting the principle of regularity which had seemed so worthy in 1908, campaigned up and down the land for another term.[1] He succeeded only in splitting his party and allowing the Democratic candidate to win. This was at least interesting to students of the Presidency, because, although Taft had been among the less notable of the line, Wilson became and remained one of the strongest. We have attended to the pre-presidential ideas of the political scientist. It remains to review the same individual's performance as the President he had sketched before assuming the responsibility himself.

It is obvious that from the outset he followed his own generalization about being as big a man as capacity allowed. He was not a modest person. All his life he had studied the office he now occupied, with the idea growing in his mind that he might sometime wield its powers; consequently he was prepared to exploit them fully. In retrospect it would

---

[1] Whether it would have been a third or a second was subject to argument. The wording, later, of the Twenty-second Amendment would seem to define it as a third: "No person shall be elected to the office of the President more than twice, and no person who has held the office of President, or acted as President, for more than two years of a term to which some other person was elected President shall be elected to the office of the President more than once." But this whole amendment soon fell into such disrepute as a product of partisan spite that, although it had to be respected as part of the Constitution, it was still perhaps the most deplored of all that document's provisions.

be difficult for historians to point to any particular incidents—as they could in the case of his "strong" predecessors—as advanced beyond the *constitutional* limits of the office. But he certainly went far beyond the *traditional* limits, thus giving the Constitution's provisions new meaning. This enlargement would, of course, not be accepted by strict constructionists any more than other enlargements had been, but it would be a guide to Presidents yet to come.

His bigness in the Presidency would not seem to be warranted by his mandate. He had been nominated by the 1912 convention in Baltimore only after a long and bitter struggle. The professionals of conservative persuasion had been determined to have one of their own in a year when it appeared that *any* Democrat could be elected;[2] and Wilson finally owed his nomination to the Bryanites, who feared the "money power" discernible behind his rivals. They had no particular reason to support Wilson except that he was an independent alternative. Bryan, who had been nominated three times and defeated three times, was still influential —Josephus Daniels, for instance, was one of his followers—and his preference was, in the end, respected. But it had been a close decision, and many angry words had been spoken. The Democrats seemed almost as divided as the Republicans had been after Theodore Roosevelt had bolted.

The divisions showed up in the election. Roosevelt reduced Taft's vote to less than his own, but Wilson's was considerably less than the total of the other two.[3] He was, therefore, a minority President. In fact, two and

[2] The rule about this is that the professionals of the party, knowing themselves not to have any reliable popularity with the electorate, and knowing its preference for "independent" heroes, will risk nominating one of their own number, or one they can completely control, only in years when the party seems fairly certain to win. In doubtful circumstances they will select a less trustworthy candidate with more popular appeal. If he should win they will get something even if they have to allow him to assume authority, and if they lose they will still be in control of the party.

Following this rule, the Republicans nominated Lincoln over Seward in 1860 and Eisenhower over Taft in 1952. They violated it and lost in 1912; but it is always hard to deny the renomination to an incumbent, and Taft had served them well.

So, also, the Democrats allowed Stevenson to batter himself against the popularity of a hero-opponent in 1952 and 1956; but, being a loser, he acquired only a limited influence within the party.

[3] And was still less if that of Debs, the Socialist, who in that year had almost a million votes, was added. Wilson actually had 6,286,214; Roosevelt had 4,126,020. Taft's total was 3,483,922.

a half million more had voted for others than for him.[4] So he was neither
the enthusiastic choice of his party nor the majority choice of the electorate, and it might have been expected that he would enter on his duties
tentatively and with a modest hope of finding support by conciliation. His
behavior was exactly contrary. It is true that he accepted the obligation to
Bryan by appointing him Secretary of State and by appointing Daniels
Secretary of the Navy and Burleson Postmaster General. He must have
had misgivings about Bryan, but it can be imagined that they were miti-
gated by his forecast of quiet on the foreign front. His agenda called
for domestic reform but not for any foreign adventures.

That this turned out to be a mistaken estimate is well enough known.
The man who had prepared himself, as he thought, for progressive
changes at home would be faced with crises abroad calling for the most
sophisticated understanding. But for this he would be given a little time.
He began at once to take advantage of a President's honeymoon prestige
to fulfill the reformist hopes of those who had been his sponsors.

In the end he would enlarge his office in two respects—first, by making
energetic attacks on accumulated problems; and in this what Wilson
actually accomplished was what Roosevelt had always seemed about to
accomplish but never had. In doing it he exerted the power of his office
without stint; he cajoled, he bargained, he argued, and he created climates
of supporting opinion. His success was amazing; and, considering that
he had been rather reluctantly accepted as his party's nominee and had
attained office only because of a split opposition, it was much more
amazing.

His second contribution was even more unexpected. He brought to bear
the power of the United States on a decision affecting the whole world
and, by the use of superb powers of persuasion and a wonderful exhibition
of eloquence, made himself leader of all the democratic forces aligned
against totalitarianism. In the end he became the accepted mentor not
only of the United States but of the world. It is true that at the last he was
thwarted in establishing the international institution he believed would
ensure a permanent peace. For this, interesting technical reasons can be
adduced. But it must also be said that he was precisely right in predicting
that failure to accept his solution would result in another world war within
a generation; a League of Nations joined by the United States might not
have prevented that second war, but it might at least have gained some
time. Another President, who was then "going to school to Professor
Wilson" (as Assistant Secretary in his Navy Department under Josephus

---

[4] This includes not only Debs's vote but that of Chafin, the Prohibition
party candidate, who had 208,923. It was guessed that many Democrats had voted for Debs.

Daniels) would have to deal with that crisis. He would be instructed by Wilson's failure as well as by his successes.[5]

As President, there had never been a more resourceful virtuoso than Wilson. He used to their capacity all the means available for getting things done; but it is at once apparent that his own tenet for Cabinet selection had been ignored. For instance, he abandoned his own rule that members should be executives who would free the President for the more important duties of leadership and education. Altogether during his Presidency he made twenty such appointments. Of the original ten, three served throughout his two terms—these were Daniels, Burleson, and Wilson (Labor)—and none was noted for executive ability. Yet their Departments were conducted satisfactorily; and the expansion of the Navy to meet the demands of war and its operations during the war were so well carried out that determined Republican investigations afterward were unable to turn up any politically useful material. The War Department's problems of transforming civilians into soldiers and shipping them overseas to fight were solved with similar efficiency. When Baker replaced Garrison as Secretary in 1916, there were howls of disapproval from those who said that he was an intellectual, a pacifist even, and quite without qualifications for the duties of the Department. But he proved to be efficient, wise, and determined. No better choice could possibly have been made. But it was not made according to Wilson's rule. He was getting a like-minded colleague, he knew; but he did not know that Baker would be an unexceptionable administrator.

The other Departments were, in the circumstances, less important. Lane, in Interior, was a notable defender of the public interest, which is always a first requirement in that post, and a man whose reputation grew; the same was true of Houston in Agriculture.[6] McAdoo, in the Treasury, was a fortunate combination of politician and man of large affairs. He also performed prodigies in office, not the least of which was the taking over and running of the entire railroad system of the country; the financing of the war expansion, too, was no small endeavor, and it was well done.

Wilson from the first took charge of foreign affairs. Bryan, as he saw war coming, left his post in a kind of pacifist protest which had in it a good deal of midwestern isolationism. Lansing, who succeeded, was a departmental technician. He served Wilson less well than any other Cabinet member and, in the end, was dismissed; and he was one who was chosen as an expert and not at all for political reasons. Wilson's rule

[5] I borrow the phrase from Frank Freidel's careful study of Roosevelt's naval years in Vol. I, *Franklin D. Roosevelt: The Apprenticeship* (Boston, 1952).

[6] Both were replaced late in Wilson's term, but only after the war, as was Redfield in Commerce.

seems not to have operated with any considerable effectiveness or even to have been a guide when selections had to be made. His political choices proved satisfactory as departmental managers, and his one or two managerial choices were less satisfactory than he anticipated.

But even if his guide to Cabinet selection did not work, the business of the government was carried on with notable efficiency during his Presidency. As to another of the generalizations in *Constitutional Government* —that the President must become the political leader because of his selection by the convention—there was more validity. He himself had certainly not been a considerable party figure before his nomination; but, once in office, he dominated its councils without serious challenge for at least six years. He was, however, held to be responsible for Democratic defeat at the mid-term congressional election in 1918; and from then on his dominance diminished. But on the whole his expectation was met. So long as he offered positive leadership and was accepted by the electorate, he could dictate party policy.[7] It probably should be said that Wilson neglected an important phase of the leadership rule. The party would follow only as long as the President had the support of the voters. It had to follow that far; but it would follow no farther.

The political scientist who had sought unity and synthesis in his earliest writings by making the President the Executive arm of a controlling legislature always refused to accept the full implications of separated powers. He still thought it necessary to achieve common purpose and accelerated motion rather than balance and check; but he had changed his view of the way to achieve it. Because the President had the support of the electorate —the whole nation voting—he could dominate the Congress, if necessary disciplining it by appeals to the public, but preferably by reasoning with its members and by rewarding co-operativeness. Thus the British synthesis was to be achieved, but by reverse means, the Executive leading instead of the Legislative.

This could succeed only if the President divined and sought to execute the wishes of the electorate. The voters might very well not know what

[7] The demoralization following strong leadership and its eventual failure was well illustrated at the party convention at San Francisco in 1920 when Cox and Roosevelt were nominated. Cox was chosen largely because, as Governor of Ohio, he had been entirely dissociated from the Wilson Administration in Washington. If the electorate was tired of Wilson, the party was even more so. The selection of F. D. Roosevelt to run with Cox was a slight gesture of respect to the Administration; but actually Roosevelt was not in Wilson's good graces. The gesture was not one that the ailing President would accept as authentic. His power, he must have realized, had completely evaporated.

they wanted. It was his obligation to tell them. Once they had accepted his definition he must keep them persuaded. Not only that, he must also translate the policy into measures and actions, and he must explain over and over that these belonged to him and to them. This complicated and exhausting process was what a President must do to be the kind of one Wilson believed in. He proceeded to do it. And by succeeding he gave the Presidency a really new dimension.

What was the place of the party in this conception? It was not the one assigned to it by the political scientist. It really became an organ of the man in authority. Its duty was to organize support for his measures, to punish and reward as the members deserved—in the President's judgment. It was not foregone that the party chiefs would take kindly to this practice. They might submit to being disciplined, but they could not be made to like it, and when it became possible they would revolt. The Republican chiefs had accepted T.R. for one term of his own because they must; but when after an interval he offered for another, they chose certain electoral defeat rather than submit further to his personal domination. In this the Democratic politicians were no different. The professionals who chose Wilson as the party candidate had no idea that such an ordeal as they were about to undergo was in store for them. And, in fact, they had chosen him in an inter-party battle, one faction prevailing over the other. The winning faction was the one whose commitment was to progressivism. This was congenial to Wilson, who from being conservative in public policy had rather quickly become liberal. This was the first indication, really, of his quality as a statesman. He divined, before the public knew it, what was to be demanded and put himself at the head of a still-unfocused movement. Roosevelt had broken the crust, but he had been repudiated by the Republicans. Wilson, backed by the Bryanites, offered the people progress in economic and social affairs. They would choose him, rather than Roosevelt running on a third-party ticket, to attain their ends. The Democrats had Bryan in their background. His offerings had been more appealing to the small farmer than to the urban worker, but they had had a welfare orientation. Contrast with Republican conservatism was complete. Wilson could accept and redefine the tradition.

This is what he did. Seizing control in accordance with his theory, using the party as a source of persuasion and discipline, and formulating a progressive agenda now felt to have been too long delayed, he gave a convincing demonstration of what a President could be who understood his country, his responsibilities, and his powers.

It has to be said that the office was not modernized in his time. It acquired very little of the apparatus which the specialists in administration would soon recommend and see installed. He got along with the simplest organization possible; and this was only partly because he would have had difficulty in getting appropriations for expansion—although that was true; it was even more because this was for him a natural method of operating. His was a highly personalized leadership. When he spoke of bigness, he did not mean a multiplicity of assistants or complex controls; he meant greatness in an individual expressed directly.

Day after day, as we learn from studying the Baker chronology of his Administration, he began by spending several hours "in his study." During that time he was really doing research, thinking, and writing. He made notes in shorthand; he wrote memoranda, messages, and speeches on his own typewriter; he came to decisions in solitude. Ghost writers were of no use to him, and he had none. After his hours alone at his reading and writing, he "saw people" in the West Wing office he owed to Roosevelt, or held conferences there. Sometimes he went to others' offices for information or for meetings or just to look around and see how work went on.

This personalized concept of the Presidency would soon seem antiquated to students of the office. In the course of discussions at the University of Chicago in 1956, celebrating the centennial of Wilson's birth, this method of management caused one expert in administration to ask of another who had studied the matter:

> Woodrow Wilson was President before any of the modern apparatus for being President existed. There was no Bureau of the Budget; the Civil Service Commission was off to one side and not thought of as the personnel arm of the President . . . how could he be an administrative head of the Government in these circumstances? And did Wilson, despite the lack of machinery, succeed in being an effective administration head?[8]

The answer was that Wilson failed even to develop what was already around him or to make use of it effectively. He did not make much of any attempt to set up the machinery he might have used to advantage; but going on, the answerer made an interesting comment:

> I think part of the explanation is that the politician was stronger in Woodrow Wilson than the administrator . . .[9]

[8] The quotations here are from "Lectures and Seminar" (Chicago, 1956), 287 ff.

[9] The questioner here was Professor L. D. White, and the answerer was Professor A. W. Macmahon. This commentary went further and was joined in by Louis Brownlow. White's wonder was doubtless the greater for his knowledge of Wilson's own theoretical interest in administration; he was one of its earliest students in the United States.

On the whole, the assessment was, even when the apparatus of the war was taken into account, that we must

> remember this episode in history as a situation where the Presidency was in transition, the scale of the operations gigantic, and the imprint of Wilson forever on the institution. At the same time there were no important immediate beginnings of the developments that were to follow in the executive office.

If it seems incredible, considering the accomplishments of the Wilson Administration in domestic reform, the immensity of the war burden, and the comparative success throughout in maintaining a high level of administrative effectiveness, it is nevertheless exact. It may not have been an advantage to Wilson that he had so little of the assistances that experts in public administration would soon put at the disposal of Presidents, but it is clear that he felt no need for more elaborate administrative devices. Whether because of this or in spite of it, he did make of the Presidency something grander than it had ever been before.

We ought to see more in detail how he achieved domestic reform and how he led the nation into and through the first war of world proportions.

★ 38 ★

WILSON'S APPROACH TO A PROGRAM OF DOMESTIC REFORM, DISCLOSED,
when he became President, had been a late one. He had neither written
nor spoken much about such matters until his campaign for the Presidency.
This has led to some suspicion that his conversion was a purely political
one, influenced by his need to conciliate the Bryanites, and perhaps by
a perception that progressivism was to attract an American majority. But
some studies of his student years have indicated that his economic education was not so truncated as has sometimes been assumed. He undoubtedly made a deliberate and significant choice, but it was not an
unconscious one.

Professor Marshall E. Dimock, relying on his own researches and those
of some others, has insisted that Wilson's reforms came from a long schooling in economics as well as politics and that this was the reason he was
so successful in what he undertook. At the Johns Hopkins, as a student,

His chief interest was in politics . . . But also he became well-
grounded in economics, because at that time, as for many years
after Wilson was a student there, candidates were required to emphasize history, political science, and economics equally. He was a
student of Ely in economics and of Adams in history and politics;
and at one time he lived in the same house with Turner when the
latter was a student and Wilson himself was a young lecturer. He
actually set out to read all of Adam Smith in preparation for a
lecture in one of the seminars, for which Hopkins was then famous.
Fresh from the German universities, Ely probably helped to infect
Wilson with an interest in public administration and with a zeal
for municipal reform. So interested did Wilson become in economics
that during this Hopkins period, in collaboration with Ely and
Davis R. Dewey, he set out to write a history of American economic
thought, which was never published.[1]

[1] "Wilson the Domestic Reformer," in the Chicago seminar volume
previously cited, 312.

Another paragraph pursues the question of Wilson's economic ideas somewhat further:

J. F. Jameson, looking back on Wilson's Hopkins career, has averred that when Wilson arrived there after an unsuccessful attempt to practice law in Atlanta, his economic opinions were "pretty much of the old Manchester school"—to the right of John Stuart Mill. "The Wilson who left Hopkins was not the Wilson who entered the Baltimore University in 1883," concluded one of his academic biographers. When he arrived he had brought with him Calvinism, the South of the Confederacy, Burke and Bagehot, Smith and Cobden. But at Hopkins new men and new ideas broadened his horizon and added new elements to his intellectual equipment. He seems to have been weaned away from a strict Manchesterism and headed towards an historical inductive economics.[2]

But Wilson did not become an economist or acquire much interest in economic theory; and the traces of those older ideas he was supposed to have lost at the Johns Hopkins are quite obvious in the reforms he proposed as President. It was evidently a range of subject matter he simply did not consider deeply. We know that the radicalism of Bryan was distasteful to him until the very moment when he was required to compromise with it and dissemble his doubts. But Bryan was nothing of a socialist, although the agrarian radicals with whom he was allied did advocate certain ventures into public ownership and operation—for instance, of common carriers and public utilities. He was much more the champion of the farmer and small businessman. His attacks on big business and the money power were directed against the bigness and the power rather than against the business and the money.

Wilson followed in this general tradition, taking advantage of the immense momentum built up by the radical movements of past decades and the bitter frustration felt by vast numbers of people. There are no more eloquent statements of the intention embodied in the original Sherman Act, and perpetuated in the Clayton Act, than are to be found in some of his speeches. One of these is quoted by Dimock. It is taken from *The New Freedom:*

There has come over the land that un-American set of conditions which enables a small number of men who control the government

[2] Besides Jameson, the others relied on here by Dimock were Davis R. Dewey and William Diamond, the latter of whom wrote a doctoral dissertation, *The Economic Thought of Woodrow Wilson*, which was published as a University Study in Historical and Political Science by Johns Hopkins University Press in 1943.

to get favors from the government; by those favors to exclude their fellows from equal business opportunity; by those favors to extend a network of control which will presently dominate every industry in the country, and so make men forget the ancient time when America lay in every hamlet, when America was seen in every fair valley, when America displayed her great forces on the broad prairies, ran her fine fires of enterprise up over the mountainsides and down into the bowels of the earth, and eager men were everywhere captains of industry, not employees; not looking to a distant city to find out what they might do, but looking about among their neighbors, finding credit according to their character, not according to their connections, finding credit in proportion to what was known to be in them and behind them, not in proportion to the securities they held that were approved where they were not known . . . That is dependence, not freedom.[3]

Wilson may have been a political rather than an economic philosopher, but he saw that if freedom was to be restored in his time, it was economic freedom that was most in jeopardy. It was being circumscribed by big businessmen and financiers. It never occurred to him—as it did not to the orthodox Progressives—that this strangulation might be relieved in any other way than by loosening the tentacles and re-creating the conditions in which equal opportunity again prevailed and competition was again restored.

This approach comported with his political and moral ideals. And there is much less of economic realism in his utterances than of appeals to democracy, fairness, justice, and trust in the common man. The broad reaches of political philosophy were where he was really at home, and he was happier as a teacher than in any other role. It was, however, a special kind of teaching; it had a heavy content of morality, and there was in it a kind of certainty which a skeptical generation accepted for a time and then found too harsh. The disciplines of freedom seemed a contradiction in terms. Easygoing Americans wanted more obvious and immediate liberties. They wanted to do what they liked, and they preferred politicians who would promise them those liberties without any duties—in the Jackson manner.

In a way, it is to be supposed that the policy-bent of progressivism resulted from this unwillingness to accept duty and discipline as the corollary of benefits. Collectivism would presuppose a concept of the whole in which individuals would find their contributions more or less

[3] A collection of the new President's speeches and other papers (New York, 1913).

designated for them. Americans preferred, and the progressives accepted, the guidance of initiative springing from individual impulse. The only recognition of the completeness of society was a post-recognition. The activities of individuals would sometime be added up. But it was not envisaged that the whole—represented by the state—would ever say to individuals: "You must do this or that because society needs it done, because it is necessary to the social organism."

Wilson's acceptance of the individualist approach is a very important matter in American history. A man of his intellectual bent, with an orderly and practiced mind, skilled in disquisition, might very well have taken the other approach. It would seem more consonant with his habit. He might have begun to consider how society could meet its responsibilities better instead of how individuals could have more freedom. He might have found the exploitation at the root of competitive enterprise repugnant instead of being exclusively irritated by the unfairness of big businessmen to small ones.

Why the one way was chosen instead of the other, we can only guess. And the guess can be substantiated only by circumstantial evidence. Besides his long acceptance of liberal British political and economic thought, there was also the knowledge that progressivism in the United States had its deepest roots in populism. Also, it is probably not irrelevant that the tenet of free competition was sacred among the American economists whom he admired. It is apparent that if he had progressed beyond the Manchester school he had not progressed beyond John Stuart Mill; and Mill's program had been one for a much simpler age. It is not extreme to say that the New Freedom was obsolete from its inception—that is, in its relevance to the ends he himself envisaged. It was, however, as he had anticipated, popular enough politically. Could he have adopted the collectivistic philosophy and yet have been elected? It seems just possible that he might have brought it off. The Democratic differences in 1912 were not so damaging as Republican ones; and a Democrat of any persuasion could probably have won. There is more reason to doubt whether, after he had won, he could have initiated and carried out a program of collectivization—ownership of railroads and utilities, strict control of heavy industry, and forthright limitations on prices, and all this accompanied by nationalization of financial institutions. Something of this sort would have been required. He might or might not have been unsuccessful in persuading the public and the Congress to accept it. But, as we know, he chose the less difficult line.

His adoption of progressivism of the orthodox sort allowed him to speak from very high ground in pressing for "freedom"; and it allowed him, as well, when he did formulate a program, to make it one which would rally to his support a host of followers. He could even say to those who were more conservative and doubtful that what he proposed was what they professed to believe in. It was true that their expressions were mostly insincere, but individuals confronted with their professions are at a disadvantage in opposing a program to make them actual. So Wilson had startling success in his honeymoon period. No American President had equaled the record he established. In fact, no American President had until then so fully accepted the responsibility for the nation's welfare and the prosperity of its business, and certainly none had accomplished so much; T.R.'s record, for instance, was slight by comparison.

Wilson's achievements may be partially catalogued as follows:

1. The Federal Reserve System
2. The Clayton Act and the Federal Trade Commission Act
3. Tariff reduction
4. The Federal Farm Loan Act and other agricultural legislation regulating speculation and improving the Extension Service
5. Labor legislation: the Adamson eight-hour law for the railroads and laws protecting seamen and miners
6. The setting up of a separate Department of Labor

There were also contributions to conservation, to a more just immigration policy, and an enlightened program of territorial administration—especially in the Philippines and Puerto Rico.

Whether or not it is agreed that Wilson took the right road in national policy, it must be admitted that he took a decision concerning direction and accepted the obligation of pursuing it with vigor and with no apparent doubts as to its efficacy. It was comprehensive; and the fact that it was gave him an opportunity to try to the full his theory of responsibility. It remains to be said that in this, for a stubborn and rather narrow Presbyterian moralist who did not easily tolerate opposition, he showed an amazing flexibility and practicality in his relations with the legislature, something not always appreciated. His final stubbornness and failure with the Senate over the peace treaty have tended to obscure previous years of success. This is illustrated very well in the formulation and the passage of the Federal Reserve Act. We may consider it as offering an example of the Wilsonian method at its best.

In his clear and judicious account of the proceedings leading up to the passage of the Act, Professor Link has emphasized two incidents of symbolic significance, one at the beginning and one at the time of final decision.[4] The first was late in December of 1912, shortly after the election; and the second was in June 1913. The bill did not become law until another December. Just a year passed while the discussions, the maneuvers,

[4] In *Wilson: The New Freedom* (Princeton, 1956), VII.

the compromises, and the dealings went on. But on both symbolic occasions Wilson interfered in a creative way. He acted as a President should who had a sense of responsibility to the nation, to his party, and to the office he occupied.

Wilson must have known—any citizen would—that something would have to be done in the field of money and banking. No one was satisfied with the system, or lack of it, that existed. But there were various fiercely held opinions as to what should be done. The Bryanites wanted a politically controlled currency and at least governmental supervision of the banks. The bankers wanted a central institution owned by themselves. There were believers in modified versions of each extreme scheme, but the moderates were as usual not nearly so vocal as the fanatics.

What Wilson knew and what he believed were not the same thing. He knew that something would have to be done, but he had no firm belief that it must be any particular sort of action. Link is of the opinion that he thought Wall Street had acquired a dangerous monopoly of both currency and credit and that it must be broken up. This would be consistent with his general theme of freedom. But what should be substituted for the Money Trust? Some sort of institutional structure must be created which would meet both the tests of freedom and of practicality. It can be imagined that this was a very real difficulty for Wilson. Without knowing anything at all in the technical sense about either money or banking, he must still arrive at some way of judging what to choose out of the competing proposals he was certain to meet as the radicals and the conservatives clashed. To the radicals he owed much; to the conservatives he still leaned by temperament.

He must have concluded that the "freedom" of the progressives was not meant to be bankers' freedom; it was businessmen's freedom; it was for banking to facilitate but not to control business. At the same time politicians were not capable of managing the fiscal system. They would have to have the help of practitioners. So he would agree to the breaking up of the Money Trust, but he would insist on keeping bankers as managers. With this much firmly in mind he was in a position to guide the contenders toward a compromise.

The Senate and House committees destined to have charge of the legislation were headed, respectively, by Senator Owen and Representative Glass. Glass was the first to move, having at his side an able but stubborn academician, H. Parker Willis. Glass was a Virginian who feared and detested the radicals, of whom Owen was one. Willis had drafted a bill for him, and he sought to seize the initiative by getting the President-elect to approve it. This was the occasion of a Princeton meeting in the December after the election. It was deep winter, and Wilson is described as being in bed, confined because of a cold, propped up on pillows and probably not at his most alert. We have Glass's own account of the two-hour interview:

Toward the end, Mr. Wilson announced it as his judgement that we were 'far on the right track'; but offered quite a few suggestions, the most notable being one that resulted in the establishment of an altruistic Federal Reserve Board at Washington to supervise the proposed system. We had committed this function to the Comptroller of the Currency, already tsaristic head of the national banking system of the country. Mr. Wilson said he was for 'plenty of centralization, but not for too much.' Therefore he asked that a separate central board provision be drafted, to be used or not, as might subsequently be determined.[5]

Glass saw him again in January, by which time his colleague, Willis, had made a more acceptable draft. But Wilson did not commit himself beyond encouraging words; and even when the special session of the Congress met shortly after his inauguration, he refused to say anything about money or banking legislation except that it would be considered presently. Other matters, in his judgment, came first. One was the tariff, which could as well be used as an example of Wilson's leadership, except that it was a simpler issue. When this was well under way he reverted to the more complex subject of finance.

Glass, as much as the radicals, wanted to break up the Money Trust, but he meant to substitute numerous trusts for one big one. The regional system he favored would still have been a bankers' system. He and Willis had therefore been aghast at the Wilson suggestion of an overhead board. This, they saw, would be governmental and therefore political. But they gave way, and the suggested draft submitted to Wilson in January provided for fifteen regional banks owned by its members but controlled by a national board with six public members and three bankers. This seemed to please the President-elect, and Glass felt that he had what would become the Administration bill. There was, however, much more to come from both sides—as Wilson undoubtedly anticipated.

The Glass production did not seem so dangerous to the bankers, but the radicals thought it not much better than the Aldrich plan—the hated scheme which had resulted from the investigations and discussions following the "panic" of 1907. This financial disturbance had been much like others in the seventies, eighties, and nineties; and it was these which had resulted in the demand for easy money and the resentment against those who had caused it to be so tight—the bankers. The Aldrich-Vreeland Act of 1908 had been the only congressional response hitherto, and it had provided only for an awkward emergency currency. Otherwise it had avoided the issue by authorizing an investigatory commission. From 1908

[5] *An Adventure in Constructive Finance,* (Garden City, 1927), 81–82.

to 1912 this commission had operated and had finally reported. One of its recommendations had been for a central bank—a National Reserve Association—with fifteen branches in various parts of the country. It would have had a board of directors consisting mostly of bankers and businessmen.[6]

This was what the bankers wanted and what they were going to get if they could find any way to do so. They were well organized and financed and were close to the Congressmen who would be most influential. Even among the new Democrats they had numerous representatives. They had argued long with Glass but had not been able to win him away from decentralization. It was on this point that Wilson had intervened with the suggestion that there should be some, but not too much, central control. The bankers had evidently reached him with their arguments.

Aside from the question of how much centralization, there was the question of who would hold the central control if there should be any. Here there can be distinguished two shadowy but undoubtedly influential figures moving in the background. Colonel House was already at work *for* Wilson. It appears that he was also working *on* him—in bankers' interest; and it seems not unlikely that he may have been responsible for Wilson's dictum that there must be a Reserve Board. On the other hand, there was Louis Dembitz Brandeis, who was just beginning his long career of interference in public policy. He was much respected by Wilson and he was a very determined advocate. He believed in smallness and competition. He had no faith at all in the benevolence of anyone or any organization big enough to control the behavior of others. When they reached that size, he would break them up and would see that thenceforth they should compete on equal terms with others and among themselves. This was a whole policy; it was enough. He believed in it with a missionary's fervor, and there were not many means he would not use to gain his ends.

The interference of House came at an early stage, that of Brandeis at a later one;[7] but it was Brandeis who had the most respectful hearing. He was appealed to when Wilson began to fear that he might not be able to reconcile the intransigent factions. This was in June 1913. Senator Owen had introduced a bill of his own; Bryan was politely but firmly threatening to resign; and Secretary McAdoo, stepping into the contro-

[6] This movement is described in H. P. Willis's *The Federal Reserve System, Legislation, Organization, and Operation,* (Garden City, N.Y., 1915). This book also contains Willis's version of the negotiations leading to the passage of the Act.

[7] There is a good deal about both in Baker's *Life and Letters of Woodrow Wilson,* 7 vols. (New York, 1927–1939), IV.

versy, had tried to find a middle ground, only to make matters worse.[8]

The McAdoo scheme almost demoralized Glass and Willis, but when they caught their breath they fought back and finally persuaded McAdoo to withdraw. He was, however, very much involved from then on—as Secretary of the Treasury and as a party man, he had to be. When Wilson felt the time had come to reconcile differences and called a conference at the White House among Glass, Owen, and McAdoo, the atmosphere crackled with enmity. But if the hostility of the opponents had not lessened, the differences were by now narrower than they had been. It was accepted that there was to be a regional organization with a central board; but Glass still insisted that this should be composed of bankers, and Owen was just as insistent that it should have only public members. And behind Owen was the shadow of Bryan, who could embarrass the President by resigning. At the same time the bankers, through House, were insisting that the result of such a scheme would be chaos; the system must be operated by experts who knew the intricacies of finance. Wilson felt the force of this the more because of his own ignorance, but he had to decide and then to use his office and his powers to implement the decision. The time had come.

It was at this juncture that Brandeis appeared. He was the one man known to Wilson who was public-minded and yet to whom the intricacies of finance were not mysterious. After talking with him a few days after the acrimonious disagreement among the leaders, Wilson informed Glass that the board must be public. He also added that the notes to be issued by the Federal Reserve Board must be obligations of the United States, something the radicals insisted on. This was the worst crisis, and this was the way Wilson met it. How uncritically he accepted Brandeis's advice can be seen by reading the follow-up letter Brandeis wrote after their talk:

> The power to issue currency should be vested exclusively in Government officials, even when the currency is issued against commercial paper. The American people will not be content to have the discretion necessarily involved vested in a Board composed wholly or in part of bankers; for their interest may be biased by private interests or affiliation . . . the conflict between the policies of the Administration and the desires of the financiers and of big business, is an irreconcilable one. Concessions to the big business interests must in the end prove futile.[9]

[8] McAdoo's National Reserve plan would have set up a central bank in the Treasury Department with a board of political appointees. It would also have established a National Currency Commission having powers to issue money with a backing of gold and commercial paper. He appears to have conferred mostly with the dissenting Democrats but also with a few bankers.

[9] Quoted from Link, op. cit., 212.

During the next six months there took place one of the most interesting struggles in the history of the Presidency. What had to be determined was not so much whether the Federal Reserve System should be of one or another sort as whether the presidential leadership would be accepted. It was not an issue made by Wilson; it was one of the oldest in American politics. Democrats since Jackson had been suspicious of bankers and recurrently agitating for a loosening of the restrictions on currency. Cleveland had let them down in this respect, but Bryan had made this one of his chief issues ever since he had been nominated in 1896 in the enthusiasm following his Cross of Gold speech. But Wilson was now the President. He had made up his mind. To prevail he must use every weapon he possessed, argue endlessly, conciliate those who dissented violently, and convince the public generally that what he had decided was in their interest.

This last he believed he could do after Brandeis had assured him that it was right to exclude the bankers. And he did. As the months of agitation passed and independent counterproposals appeared, there was a growing support for his position—not so much for his position, perhaps, as for him. The feeling was that he was a man to be trusted.[10] If he said it was right, then he should have what he asked for. Wilson knew very well that this was his ultimate resource; having it, Presidents have everything; lacking it, they have very little. They can win battles with it; but if the opposition senses its loss, congressional opportunists close in like wolves for the kill. They did this to Tyler and to Johnson. They were to do it to Hoover. Wilson had both the confidence of his conviction, once his mind was made up, and the sense of embodying a tradition of his party; and he made good use of both. He told the party leaders that there must be legislation and that it must be constructive. It must establish an institution that would at once free business by providing it with credit not controlled by metropolitan bankers, and see to it that currency was responsive to economic needs and not restricted by private interests. It would be decentralized and democratic, but it would be held together as a system and be guided by rules recognizably in the public interest.

So he first called into conference, in the humid heat of Washington's summer, the House Committee on Banking and Currency. For two and a half hours the former professor instructed the committee members. He saw that they understood every detail of the bill, but he also left no doubt in their minds of his determination that it should be passed. One member is said to have displayed a little ill temper; the Congress was not being asked for anything more than advice on tactics; the bill was already written; and he, among others, was restive in these circumstances. On

---

[10] It was shown in many ways, but it was reflected unmistakably in the President's correspondence.

the whole, however, Wilson's visitors, if not won over, were at least impressed.

Getting to this point had not been easy. Brandeis had shown him the way to Bryan's confidence; and the Secretary of State, who was also the party's recognized elder statesman, gave it generously. With it went the support of Owen, chairman of the Senate committee. But the bankers were a different matter. They stood to lose their monopoly of credit and of currency issue; and their long and successful campaign to create and embody in law the Aldrich plan for a banker-owned central bank was now to be defeated by politicians they despised. Glass was bad enough, but they could deal with him. Wilson was not so easy as House had thought, but they might convince him. They had their chance in a White House interview, told about by Glass, who came along with them.

Glass had told the President that he could expect a stormy interview. The bankers were furious; they did not yet understand very well the details of the bill, but they knew that there was to be a public board controlling it. This they preferred to call "political," and such an epithet to them was the ultimate in derogation. Glass told about the interview:

> Forgan and Wade, Sol Wexler and Perrin, Howe and other members of the Currency Commission of the American Bankers' Association constituted the party. The first two, peremptory and arbitrary, used to having their own way, did not mince matters. They were evidently not awed by 'titled consequence,' for they spoke with force and even bitterness. Sol Wexler and Perrin were suave and conciliatory. The President was courteous and contained. These great bankers, arbiters for years of the country's credits, were grouped about the President's desk in the executive office adjoining the cabinet room. I sat outside the circle, having already voiced my own dissent from the President's attitude. President Wilson faced the group across the desk; and as these men drove home what seemed to me good reason after good reason for banker representation on the central board, I actually experienced a sense of regret that I had a part in subjecting Mr. Wilson to such an ordeal. When they had ended their arguments, Mr. Wilson, turning more particularly to Forgan and Wade, said quietly:
>
> 'Will one of your gentlemen tell me in what civilized country of the earth there are important government boards of control on which private interests are represented?'
>
> There was a painful silence for the longest single moment I ever spent; and before it was broken Mr. Wilson further inquired:
>
> 'Which of you gentlemen thinks the railroads should select members of the Interstate Commerce Commission?'

This was indeed, as Glass appreciated, one of the high moments of the Presidency. In a single pithy sentence the President had asserted the paramountcy of the public interest and his own identity with it as against any private interest, however powerful. This did not mean that the bankers would give up; for the next six months they used every device they could think of and brought every conceivable pressure to bear. They did not surrender until the very end, and then far from gracefully. But it was Wilson who had undermined their moral position.

It was past the middle of September before the bill passed the House. There had been several months of hectic activity, the Congressmen on both sides resorting to every subterfuge that their wily minds could conceive to escape the presidential pressure and discredit the compromise demanded of them. The main attack came from the radicals, who not only were more politically minded and cruder but believed they could successfully represent to their constituents that the bill was a bankers' measure and that Wilson had been taken in by them. A caucus on the measure lasted for a week, something never known before; and the opposition collapsed only when Bryan called a halt. He wrote Glass saying that the bill had his full support and that it was the duty of good party members to stand by the President. So the bill finally passed the House and went to its ordeal in the Senate.

What happens to a man who is at the center of such a struggle, brought on by his own initiative, shaped according to his understanding of the issues, and conducted with the means regarded by him as suitable? For one thing, there was clearly a sense of exuberance. Wilson was acting as he had always believed a President should act, and he was demonstrating that he had been correct. An old professional, Chauncey M. Depew, watching the performance from New York, predicted to the St. Nicholas Society in early fall that Wilson would have his way before Christmas:

> For the first time in the history of the country we have got a man as President who had not been in politics for more than two years before he was elected. He is working on theory, and every man wants his theories to succeed. This man who was regarded as a pedagogue, a theorist, is accomplishing the most astonishing practical results.[11]

This may not have been very accurate as history, but it was an appreciation from an expert. It was called out by the virtuosity of the performance. Wilson missed no opportunities; he gave no unnecessary ground; he whipped on his own cohorts; he discredited his opponents. No Presidents

[11] Quoted in Baker, op. cit., 195.

except Jackson and Roosevelt had done anything like it before, perhaps because none had had such supreme confidence. The retired President watched from Oyster Bay with hardly concealed jealousy. He was being outdone.

★ 39 ★

SINCE WILSON WAS THE MOST COMPLETELY CONSCIOUS OF ALL ITS practitioners we must give special attention to his leadership. It can be said first of all that it was infused with a kind of euphoria. This increased as his struggles became heated, and it became most intense when the difficulties seemed most intractable. It operated both to reinforce his courage and to intensify his effort. It also obscured any possible doubt. When it stimulated him most it was manifested in humor, in an almost boisterous good nature, and rarely in a tight-lipped anger. Captaincy was natural to him; he gloried in its opportunities, he rose to its challenges, and he was impervious to the barbs of criticism that came his way. This is not to say that he did not become fatigued or that, like other Presidents, he did not complain. He had moments of impatience and irritability, and he sometimes voiced them. It had become almost a convention of the Office that Presidents should speak of themselves as put upon and harassed; but, as we have seen, they had usually asked for it, and hardly ever had they done anything to lighten the load they thought so heavy.

This was especially true of Wilson, who worked everything out for himself and asked no one—except Brandeis—for any advice of a substantive sort. He saw many people, all kinds of people, and he got information from them, more than they knew they were giving; but this was only the material for his decision-making; it was not guidance. He thought of most people around him—and this included the Democratic legislative leaders—as available to carry out his directives. His conferences with the committees who were entrusted with legislation were briefing sessions. He told them what he wanted, assuming it to be what they must want too, because he spoke for the country and for the party. They seem to have accepted it remarkably well, on the whole, considering that they *were* legislators and that his party credentials were rather weak. He was not an intellectual for nothing; he knew precisely what he was talking about and how to marshal his material. As to tactics, that was different. It was their province, and unless there were delays he deferred to them. But there were many times when he made suggestions about obstacles and the handling of objectors, and many times when he showed his impatience.

All that year of 1913 he was a President in a hurry. It was as though he knew very well about honeymoons—that they did not last and must be taken advantage of, every minute of them. It was not only the financial system that he had on his mind at that time—the one we have chosen to inspect for an understanding of his method. Much else was in train. There was, for instance, as has been noted, the tariff; but he got that out of the way, after some disgusting trouble with Senators who represented special interests, by early fall.[1]

Then the legislators wanted to go home. They were weary, and Washington was sunk in that lethargy which comes with September heat and humidity (there were still no devices for air conditioning), and they were tired of being pushed from one side and blamed from the other. For no legislative action suits everyone, and those who are annoyed are much more in evidence than those who are pleased. And this was especially the case with the tariff, that perennial magazine of special privileges.[2]

Throughout the long months not only the legislators were in session, but the bankers all over the country were having emergency meetings, telling each other of the dangers and outrages involved in the proposed financial legislation. Every time a banker spoke, some Congressman quivered and hunted an excuse for equivocation; but at the same time he knew, with that sense politicians have for such communications, that he was caught in a vast demand for action. The measure was what the President said was needed. That was enough for the public. People were rising to his will in spite of opposition well represented in the press.

---

[1] There was also a crisis in Mexico that he was puzzled to know what to do about and that would presently turn into intervention; there were problems in the Pacific; and there were the hungry Democrats—all the party faithful clamored to be rewarded, and this sort of thing was not easy for Wilson.

[2] Wilson's victory on that issue was his first, and in many ways his most notable since it was his first. He learned much from it. That it was his own, there was no doubt in anyone's mind. Link, for instance, quotes the London *Nation*, which, viewing the affair from a distance, wrote:
This is Dr. Wilson's tariff in no conventional sense. He called the Special Session, himself framed the Bill, cooperated directly with the legislators of his party in the House and in the Senate, routed and exposed the audacity of the lobbyists who sought even this year to renew their customary attacks upon the virtue of Congress, and carried the measure to a triumphant issue without mutilation or considerable concession. It has raised him at a single stage from the man of promise to the man of achievement.
This quotation was from the issue of October 11, 1913. In Link, op. cit., at p. 197, references to other comments on the tariff victory will be found.

Glass knew well enough that it was no laissez-faire measure they had in hand. It had ceased to be that at Wilson's decree. If Wilson was clear about the freedom principle—and he seemed to be—this was attaining freedom for some, for many, by abridging and limiting it for others, a few; but progressivism had always been practical in this sense. The main thing was, as the westerners said inelegantly, "to get the bankers off the business-men's and farmers' necks." If the government had to do it, then that would have to be accepted. Wilson had come to see that he was dealing here with one of those leverages in the economic system which are too crucial to be left to the control of those who had some other interest in it than that of keeping it operating fairly. Banking was a profit-making enterprise. It might or might not, if uncontrolled, result in economic good and fairness. There had been many times when it had not, and those times had been terrible ordeals for the nation. They must be made impossible in future. Wilson was told that the Federal Reserve scheme would do it; it em-bodied a nice combination of public control and banker expertness. This was also a good political compromise. He would drive it through.

Late in June, after briefing the relevant committees, he himself went to the Capitol to start the legislation on its formal route. This was his second such appearance. His inaugural had been thus read in person. Dis-continuing this practice had been one of Jefferson's unspoken ways of giving notice that Presidents were not kings.[3] But Wilson felt himself, in spite of Jefferson, king in a very special democratic sense. Being chosen of the people, gave him a privileged position as their representative, and he accepted it with all its implications. It was not at all for him, Wilson, that deference might be demanded. It was due, and must be paid, to the symbol of Union, the President. He chose to emphasize this concept of

---

[3] Another was his casual appearance in riding clothes and with muddy boots on the customary day for the levee at the President's house, when Washington society had gathered on the assumption that the practice of select receiving was an unchangeable institution. There would be no more such gatherings, said Jefferson; the President would thenceforth be avail-able to everyone, and the doors of his house would always be open. It may have been more hypocritical than sincere, and it may not have worked in practice, but it was good politics. If it made continuing difficulties for Presidents for a hundred years, that would probably not have worried Jefferson overmuch. The hand-shaking days would not be wholly aban-doned until the great wars came along and security regulations were put into effect. There was a gradual reduction, but Theodore Roosevelt was said to have shaken several thousand hands at the New Year's reception in 1902. And all the Presidents down to his time lived in a House as open to the public as any other public building. And none had ventured to address the Legislative Branch in person. These matters were less difficult for Wilson, but he still suffered from Jefferson's precedent.

the position by going in person to tell the legislators what was needed by the nation whose voice he was. It was for them to listen; it was for him to speak.

What he had to say, he worked out with a professor's care. On one sheet of paper he made his notes, partly in shorthand. He then, again in shorthand, wrote a text. This he transcribed on his own typewriter, afterward making corrections and enlargements. It was not long, as it might have been if dictated; nor was it discursive. It was compact and economical. It required exactly nine minutes to read, and he read it as one who knew it by heart. He told the Congress that he knew they wanted to go home, but he also told them they would have to stay. They had a duty they would have to see through. His main text was pure Brandeis. It was absolutely imperative, he said, that the businessmen should have a financial system by means of which they could make use of the freedom of enterprise which was about to be more fully bestowed on them. He took only one paragraph to summarize the essentials of the bill. Then he concluded by saying simply that he had come to them as the "head of the government and the responsible leader of the party in power, to urge action now . . ."[4]

It was a perishing day in Washington, but all the notables were present, including the President's own family. Altogether it was an occasion only less formally impressive than the inaugural in March which had broken with the Jeffersonian tradition. When a few days later the bill itself made its appearance in both Houses, it clearly carried the official brand. It had come from the President; it was to be passed by the legislature. There was no pretense that he had not sponsored it, none of the familiar fiction that it was, after all, the Congress's responsibility to make policy and to write legislation and the President's to execute it. It was a White House measure.

That the way had been so far cleared that it seemed safe to start the bill on its legislative route did not mean that there would be no further opposition. Wilson knew well enough that, even though he had got together the opposing groups within the Administration and had in some sense made it a party measure by establishing a compromise between Glass and Owen, with Bryan giving his very necessary blessing, there were those among the radicals who were not yet satisfied; and then, also, there were the bankers who had worked themselves into one of those frenzies which even the most sensible people can achieve on occasion. The hysteria among the financial elite seems now to have been so ridiculous as to be incredible. But that there were predictions of doom and disaster, and that what later seemed a most conservative measure was called socialistic, communistic, and any other damning epithets the excited opponents

4 *Public Papers*, III, 37–40.

could think of, we must recognize from the record. These bouts of fever are recurrent. They had happened before and would again—as in 1933–34 —but they made a problem for Wilson. How would he behave toward these hysterical folk?

Perhaps he did the best thing by virtually ignoring them. When they sent an envoy in the person of Roland Morris, a well-intentioned Philadelphia lawyer who had been a Wilson supporter, he gave it to him straight. Morris was worried. He wanted Wilson to "see the bankers again." The President listened with his usual courtesy, then he said with that chilly smile which was becoming familiar:

> Morris, I *have* seen those men. They came down here with a long brief. The essence of their case was that nothing whatever should be done. They asserted that the time was inopportune. I told them that so far as their principal contention was concerned the case was decided. It was *res adjudicata*. Something was going to be done. I told them I would be glad to have them suggest changes or criticisms based upon their intimate knowledge of conditions to help me in making a better law. They went home and afterwards sent me down a long brief which I considered carefully. I found that in its essence it was only a repetition of their former contention, really an argument to do nothing. What is the use of my seeing them again? I will not. You can tell them exactly the reason why . . .[5]

On a later occasion, when the bill was in the Senate and diversionary tactics were being used, he again refused to see the bankers. This was when the Vanderlip proposal was introduced with a considerable hoorah in the newspapers. It was an entirely new bill; it had the backing of the Morgan group and of Benjamin Strong of the Bankers Trust Company, and the recalcitrant conservatives in the Senate were disposed to accept it. But actually it was no more than a delaying tactic, and the President recognized it as such, so that when Vanderlip requested an interview he got the answer he might have expected if he had known Wilson better:

> I am at a loss to understand how you can have come to think of the bank plan which you proposed to the Senate Committee on Banking and Currency yesterday as 'being along the lines of my own thought.' It is so far from being along the lines of my thought in this matter that it would be quite useless to discuss it with you . . . I could in no circumstances accept or recommend it . . .[6]

This was late in October, and he could smell victory. For all the months since June—and with much preparation before—he had shepherded his

[5] Baker, op. cit., 188.

[6] Ibid., 193.

bill through the House and into the Senate. He had no patience with attempts to divert him now. But he was clearly invoking the Rule of Restraint with the Senators. It would have been thought, from what he said and wrote to the most troublesome of them—such as Reed, O'Gorman, and Hitchcock—that he was tolerance itself. To Hitchcock, for instance, who refused even to be bound by the invocation of a caucus, most unusual in Senate procedure and resorted to only in desperation, he wrote:

> I am sincerely obliged to you for your letter explaining your position on the currency bill. I think you must know from our conversation that I have no jealousy . . . in all these matters I feel that successful action depends upon the yielding of individual views in order that we may get a measure which will meet the well-known principles of the party and enable us by *common* counsel, to arrive at what I may call a corporate result . . .[7]

Even before this, things had begun to turn his way. Like a general disposing his troops, he sent Bryan, McAdoo, and others into the battle. House saw Reed and perhaps did no good, but he was at least working for what Wilson, rather than the bankers, wanted. For that strange, wild man, Reed, the President had a gentle word:

> I want to thank you very warmly and sincerely for your statement made through a New York newspaper. I have felt all along the sincere honesty and independence of judgment you were exercising in this whole matter; and you may be sure that there has never been in my mind any criticism . . . I feel that from this time out I can count on you to play a leading part in bringing this whole matter to a successful issue . . .

This was restraint, but it was not candor. Reed could be counted on for nothing, then or any other time, and Wilson knew it very well. Still, it was his method to consolidate his forces, encourage friends, disarm enemies or warn them off, and finally to have his way. This he defined as the party's way, and when this battle was over it was accepted as such.

It was an exhausting summer and fall. He sent his family off to a New England resort and went to visit them occasionally, but there was never an hour when his restless mind was not playing with the affair he had left in process back in the heated capital. By telephone, by letter, by messenger, he encouraged his friends, suggesting new moves, watching the opposition, and taking advantage of every opening. It must have been obvious, for instance, that the bankers of the West would sooner or later understand that the proposed regional system would enhance their power at the expense of the New York financiers. And presently there was indication that

---

[7] Ibid., 196.

this was so. Moreover, the usually unimportant off-year elections in November were very strongly indicative of support for the President, something the legislators had been feeling for some time.

From this time on it was a question of overcoming delays and diversions. Not until Thanksgiving did the bill finally reach the Senate for debate. On December 19 it was passed, after a flood of speeches and a nearly successful demand for recess until after Christmas. He had held the Congress sternly at its work since April. He now demanded that it finish, and demanded it without apology.

When it was all over and he was signing the bill in an office ceremony, he was all gracious affability. He presented pens to Glass, Owen, and McAdoo; he made a little speech of thanks. This he followed with a letter of thanks. And now the whole country was disposed to recognize the President's achievement. He might seek to share it with others, but no one was fooled; a hard, bright, implacable authoritarian had won a victory. Hardly a one among the others had not either opposed him or sought to modify his position. But after he had seen where he was going, in relation to his whole theory of freedom, and had made his judgment of the essential compromises, he had been inflexible and determined. He had demanded submission, even if he had made it possible for the yielding to be graceful, and in the end he had had his way.

We are not here concerned with the sufficiency of the Federal Reserve Act either as a measure consonant with the New Freedom or one capable of facilitating the economic processes of American capitalism. We are concerned only with the achievement. It was a notable conception and a tremendous victory. This was a President in the great tradition.

WE ARE READY NOW TO SPEAK OF A THIRD PRESIDENTIAL RULE TO BE added to those of Necessity and Restraint referred to here so often. This is the Rule of Responsibility.

It could not quite yet be said that Wilson's wonderful ability to grasp and to project the concepts, otherwise so unfocused and inchoate, of party and people would be an always respected standard for future Presidents. The people still chose, and their reasons were mixed and various. They were not by any means so impressed with sheer intellect that they would yield to the candidate who demonstrated his possession of it. They would choose those in whom they saw other admirable qualities and they would sometimes be sorry; and they would still make the same mistake again. After Wilson there would be Harding, of all possible persons, who offered nothing, nothing at all but relief from the disciplines to which Wilson had put the democracy. People were obviously tired of behaving well, of being required to follow good impulses, of being led, even, and they certainly got a change when they elected Harding. He was not likely to require anything serious or difficult of anyone. That seemed to be his advantage over Cox in the voters' estimation.

Nevertheless, a standard *had* been set. The Presidency never again would be quite what it had been. The man in the White House would henceforth be expected—even if he had not been chosen because of such a qualification—to grasp and project, as Wilson had done, what was necessary to secure the nation's future—its well-being as well as its position in the world—and to drive the Congress to its implementation, meanwhile explaining and persuading, carrying with him the mind of the majority. Thus he must accept the duty of embodying in institutions the devices and arrangements necessary to the well-being he was asked to achieve and preserve. He was not to be excused, either, from running the machine. He must still be the First Administrator as he must also be the First Legislator. In sweeping all this responsibility into the presidential orbit, Wilson had undoubtedly added to an already almost impossible burden for one individual to carry. Perhaps it could not be carried by one person, and especially by a separate worker such as Wilson was. Luckily, the whole range of *expertise* in administration was on the verge of advance, becoming the subject of study and analysis. Young people were being trained in its various techniques. The administrative bureaucracy would be so remade during the next generation as to be almost unrecognizable to old-style politicians. They would be inclined to belittlement, speaking scornfully of "intellectuals," but the scorn would be a little queasy. Some of them rightly suspected that they themselves were accumulating the mold of obsolescence; and, sure enough, in that other generation there would be in the Congress itself quite a collection of Ph.D.s—the higher degree which must be earned—and only a few would be left with no degree at all. Even politics was a changing profession.

A Legislative Branch with such an infusion of intelligence would be more understanding and it might well be more responsive to presidential direction. But the old strain caused by the divergence among the Branches would be hard to dissipate; it would recur with discouraging effect many times in the future. Wilson had shown how to overcome the divisiveness in an important instance by making himself, who was not a professional at all, head of the party and of the unvoiced people; as such he could exert a leverage which stifled dissent and forced action. Presidents would never again be quite excused from this duty. The Rule of Responsibility was laid upon them even if not all would acknowledge its implications.

There was just then a young man in the Navy Department, serving under Josephus Daniels and entrusted with extraordinary administrative discretion because Daniels was so much needed by Wilson for other matters, who, it appeared afterward, was watching and learning, even though it did seem at times that he was too obtuse to learn much of anything. Franklin Roosevelt had an uncontrolled admiration for admirals, and just now he was very much taken up with their campaign for a bigger navy. He had a very limited appreciation for Wilson's leadership in a dangerous world ruled by power politics. He thought the President close to being a pacifist. As for Daniels, with his square-toed shoes and string ties, he had the sniffy disapproval to be expected of an old Grotonian. Still, he was learning to be a politician and, in spite of himself, he must have respected the older man's ability to get along with congressional committees; the navy did very well, financially speaking, with Daniels to shelter it. Following his political bent, Franklin Roosevelt tried to escape into the arena of New York State politics about once a year, only to be either rebuffed or actually defeated. And his respect grew for those who succeeded better. He even made peace with some peculiar characters in Tammany Hall after they had shown him how well it might pay.

This is mentioned because it was this young man who was to be, after

Wilson, the next President so seized of Responsibility. He would arrive at the White House by devious means and after a hard education; but anyway he would arrive and, having got there, he would very obviously, in this respect, be just such another as Wilson—not so powerful in intellect, but much more charming and quite as willing to take his full part and more. But also he would—because of experience—follow with uncanny sureness the Rule of Restraint which Wilson tended to neglect, even to ignore.

Looking back along the line of the Presidents, we can see that Responsibility, in the Wilsonian sense, was not something new; it merely came to a kind of maturity with him. It emerged, so clearly and recognizably, partly because the situation of the nation at that point in history demanded it, and partly because Wilson was a man to meet obligations without evasion and with the whole devotion of his mind and heart. What this amounted to, how it rose above personal sorrow and transcended ambition, we have a chance to see in Baker's account of his behavior at the time he lost his wife, close companion of many years, just when the war in Europe was beginning and a whole new policy for the United States had to be worried out. He saw the President, Baker said, a few weeks after Mrs. Wilson's death—it was in September 1914—and he recorded this:

> He looked very well—clear-eyed, confident, cheerful—a neat gray suit looking as though it was just from the tailor—a black band on his left arm, a dark tie with a gold ornament. His desk was extremely neat, with a bouquet of roses upon it . . .

And, writing a little later of the same occasion, he tried to convey the sense of easy power he felt coming from the man:

> At the end of a hot and wearing summer, with scarcely a day of vacation or of rest, with great questions crowding for settlement, with a domestic affliction which in itself might well be overwhelming, the President remains one of the steadiest, clearest, most cheerful men in Washington . . . There has not once been a sign of wavering, or of weakness, nor has Mr. Wilson allowed his personal sorrow to interfere for a moment with his efficiency . . .

Yet, at almost the same moment, the President was writing to Mary Hulbert, cousin and friend:

> My loss has made me humble. I know there is nothing *for me* in what I am doing. And I hope that that will make me more serviceable. I have succeeded so far, I believe, only because I have not sought my own pleasure in the work or in the office, and have . . . devoted my entire time and energy, alike of body and of mind, to

the work of administration and of leadership to be done from day to day. And now self is killed more pitilessly than ever—there is *nothing but the work* for me.[1]

We have not seen this remarkable abstraction from personal pressure in many of the Presidents—only, perhaps, in Lincoln, who day by day seemed to become refined by the slaughter and bitterness over which he presided. The more there was cause to hate, the more he pitied and forgave. Wilson's grief seemed also to be a refining agent; and that it came just when momentous international issues had to be thought out was rather contributory than otherwise to his solitary deciding. Anything, apparently, that sharply reminds Presidents of the perspective in which they function and takes them out of the wash of daily influences deepens their sense of responsibility and tightens its demand.

No more serious crisis had ever confronted the nation than was coming into view as the European war began, and Wilson was almost totally unprepared to meet it. He was in the midst of a fight for domestic reform; it had engaged all his attention since he had become President, and before that he had given little real attention to international matters. But he saw at once that the United States would be involved. It would not, he hoped, be a military involvement; still, a war spreading throughout Europe and across the seas would touch and even shake every nation. And one with a vast commerce and close relationships could not be immune. Choices would have to be made, but what they must be was not at all clear. We see him, in Baker's remarkable description, at the very beginning of his ordeal, grappling with his new problem:

> The matters he had to consider were . . . nothing less than a world war in which, inevitably, his own decisions would be of conspicuous, if not determining, importance.
>
> We find him, therefore, sitting for hours alone in his study poring over the documents relating to the war which gathered steadily, in unrelenting piles, upon his desk. All of the important reports that came into the State Department were forwarded by his direction to the White House—not in digests, but in their original form or in verbatim copies. His attitude was that of the thoroughgoing scholar, impatient to see everything that would contribute . . .
>
> It was thus a hodge-podge of fevered cablegrams, reports, letters . . . Few of them were accompanied by any explanatory memoranda to make them more intelligible. To make matters worse, a flood of high-keyed and excited admonitions and suggestions poured in from American sources, including a deluge of articles, editorials, books, dealing—who could say with what authority—with complex foreign

[1] *Life and Letters*, V, 138–39.

problems which the oncoming conflict had thrown into high relief
. . . One who looks back years afterwards into this clamorous mass
of papers wonders how any human mind could have drawn any
dependable conclusions from them. And yet the President must have
felt the responsibility, indeed the necessity, for deciding what the
American attitude toward the war should be. He must consider such
questions . . . as those relating to the origins of and the responsibility for the war. He must reflect upon the consequences of victory
for either side, and finally, he must not fail to venture some visions,
however vague, of what the final settlement might involve for America and for the world.[2]

Again and again in all the accounts of Wilson's life in the White House
he is pictured thus alone, studying, pondering, weighing what was best to
be done. And it is interesting that in all his correspondence, a voluminous
one, with House there is no actual intimacy of thought. He sends affection,
he is grateful for assistance, he congratulates, but he never asks for
guidance. There is a clear demarcation between the tasks he must do
and those that others can be allowed to do for him. He must himself
conceive policy. He must embody the national ethos. And, doing so, he
must see what the requirements are in lawmaking, in Executive action,
in persuasion and leadership. And he must see that others carry out his
directives. That is what it was to be President: with Wilson it was not
something others could share to any degree whatever. They might bring
him facts and give him argument; many of them urged and plotted; some
ran errands or maneuvered in his behalf. That was their part. And
the Departments ran the affairs of government, the Secretaries presiding
under his supervision. But it was he who stood over all, thinking, concerned, responsible, alert.

This the Republicans had rejected as the desirable presidential con-
figuration; and there were many Democrats who agreed, but not, usually,
it should be noted, the southerners. Really, they ought not to have favored
such a President. They had fought and bled for states' rights; yet Wilson,
the strong President, was a southerner born and bred, and his being the
sort he was did not make him less one. What he was just went to show
that it had not been strict construction *of the Presidency* that had moved
the South to secession and civil war. It had been a sense of outrage, something of arrogance, and having to make good a bluff. Southerners were
with Wilson more solidly than they would be with any President, even
Democratic ones, in the foreseeable future or than they had been with any
in the past back to Buchanan, who had been a good deal their man but
whom they had despised for his weakness. It was the lordly new industrial

[2] Ibid., 58–59.

rulers and the rich financiers who wanted a puppet President and who sought to control the Republican party in that interest.

But the responsible President was to be. Without him the nation had no mind in its crises. And we can see, looking back, that the accreting responsibility was inevitable as the nation became an organism that must function as a whole, with purpose and design. It had been fated from the victory of Union in the Civil War. The people had fought for that Union; it was sacred to them as only something gained with blood can be. But the big businessmen wanted it weak at the center so that they should not be interfered with. And so long as they could keep the President in subjection they would have it their way. They had succeeded, we have seen, by playing at first on patriotism, then by representing their policies—especially the high tariff—as responsible for the "full dinner pail." Theirs, they claimed, was the party of prosperity.

Wilson saw that he must break these connections in peoples' minds; and this was why, when he had thought it out, he made freedom the theme of his first campaign, and the "new freedom" he spoke of was emancipation from thralldom to special interests. He decided then, for the nation, against big business. He decided also—a matter of importance—against a politically directed collectivism as its alternative. But it was he who decided and he who took the responsibility. He began at once, when his mind was clear, to exhort and argue, so that he might carry the electorate with him. And as soon as he was in office he began to implement what he had offered and what had been accepted.

There was a flaw in this philosophy which went to its very heart. It was those business captains and the financiers who had made America economically one. They had done it for their own reasons and purposes, and they had done it ruthlessly. This selfishness left them open to radical attack, and they were vulnerable to such denunciations as Wilson used in his progress toward political success; but it was illogical of him—politic, but in the long sense unwise—to advocate their destruction rather than their reform. In fact, the whole freedom concept was a denial of history and, so far as Wilson was concerned, worse than that. For the Rule of Responsibility implied a national organism for which to be responsible. If he was to regionalize the financial structure, break up the trusts, and enforce competition—not merely set standards for it where it existed—he ought not to have taken charge in a commanding way as he did. The United States to him was one society, one people, one electorate—but he would not have it one economy. And the two would not be separated without violence, waste, and ultimate retreat.

The immediate influence determining this policy in his mind may have been the progressivism which trailed behind him into the past. It came to him in the support of Bryan and the Bryanites of the party. It rather gained strength when the Republicans repudiated it as they defeated

Theodore Roosevelt. When he did come to the Presidency, at any rate, he seemed to have no doubts whatever, though occasionally there were hints of alien intrusions into the Brandeis paradise of small people all plotting and squirming to get the better of one another. There was a proposal, stopped before the operative stage, to nationalize the telegraph systems which might easily have extended to all communications.[3] And one of the first actions to be taken as the war organization took shape in 1917 was the nationalizing of the railways. But then it could be said that the whole war administration was a negation of the New Freedom—just as it could be said of that devised for Roosevelt's later war.

So it would have been more logical for Wilson, the consolidator of the nation, the leader who gave it one purpose and who disciplined its re-calcitrant parts, to take over for the government the co-ordinating functions of business and finance rather than to attempt their destruction and to punish their creators. It could hardly have been expected of T.R., who was no philosopher, to be guided by so considered and homogeneous a policy. For him to have done what was expedient, what the progressives promoting him wanted, was to be expected. He seldom saw below the surface of affairs, although he was extremely sensitive to movements on that surface; but Wilson might very well have been expected to achieve the synthesis he either avoided or did not see.

It may have been that, aside from the same political expediency that moved Roosevelt, Wilson was so steeped in English liberalism as not to con-sider any other economic policy than the automatism of laissez faire. But there is another philosophic consideration to be taken account of which seems inconsistent too. This is his insistence that the government of separated powers was inferior to the wholeness achieved in the parlia-mentary or Cabinet system. He spoke of the impossibility of building a government on antagonisms and of the necessity of achieving one purpose under one leadership. And that was what he intended to give the nation and what, in a way, he did give it. But the purpose throughout is clearly inconsistent with the method. Even the war, as he approached it, was pictured by him as one for freedom and "self-determination," a principle as obsolete as the breaking up of the trusts, and of the same nature.

What we must say is that his conception of the Presidency, his accept-ance of the Rule of Responsibility, was something he came to as the result of his instinct for taking charge. It was also his way of setting up, within a defective structure for the purpose, political unity. In earlier days he said

[3] He wrote to Burleson, the Postmaster General, in January 1914, with the Federal Reserve legislation just out of the way, that he had long "thought that the government ought to own the telegraph lines of the country and combine the telegraph with the post office." *Life and Letters,* IV, 212.

this could never be done with the Branches set against one another and constantly checking each other in operation. But he had seen that this defect could be overcome by talented exertion at the center—that is, in the Presidency. For this purpose, primacy in that office had to be acknowledged. He demanded it daily and, for the most part, successfully. It is an unaccountable mystery that his political theory and his economic theory never came together.

But it seems less strange when it is observed that this was an inconsistency which generally afflicted American economic and political thinking. A whole generation of American economists and political scientists had had their training in German universities and had come back to teach and write at home; but what they taught and wrote was not the German organismic or nationalistic social theory they had learned. It was that of the English liberal school stemming from Smith, Bentham, Ricardo, Bagehot, and others, and having its apotheosis in Mill. Almost the only exception to this was Simon Nelson Patten, who founded the Wharton School at the University of Pennsylvania in the eighties. Patten had watched with growing concern the going over of American economists to laissez faire and had pointed out its inappropriateness in a land of organizational talent expressed in vast business agglomerations. And he had spoken of the German philosophy as a living and growing one, accepting man's capacity for development and his genius for the management of large affairs. The British alternative, he said, was reactionary. Its thesis was that growth was evil and must be prevented. What was large was necessarily bad and must be destroyed. It was never considered that it tended to grow to serve man because it served society better in its comprehensive phases and that the problem was to master it rather than to prohibit its elaboration.

Wilson, with the Federal Reserve System in being, had now had his first taste of victory in the interest of the New Freedom. He was applauded as a master of tactics. And since he had succeeded, he was assumed to have been right in strategy. His acceptance of the Brandeis economics was considered a virtue in progressive circles, and even from overseas the echoes of praise came to his ears. They were the sweeter because of his long devotion to the English theorists. Bagehot would have approved what he had done. So might even John Stuart Mill, although that philosopher had tended to develop toward collectivism as Bagehot never had.

The tariffs were revised, and the financial system had been decentralized. As the President rested at Pass Christian on the Gulf that January of 1914, his mind was restlessly searching for new projects logically belonging to the system he was developing. He thought not only of nationalizing the telegraphs and of a government-owned steamship service but of conservation, of labor legislation, and of other "welfare" measures, and again, somewhat inconsistently, of making his administrative management more effective through a budget system. As to this last, he said that ever since he was a youngster he had "insisted upon the absolute necessity of a carefully considered and wisely planned budget," and he meant to put such a movement in hand at once.[4]

He had no doubts. If he had had one of those deep and silent struggles his biographers speak about over the progressivism he had accepted, it was far in the past and buried. It was obvious from his success that he had been right. He would now go on, not only to lesser items on the progressive agenda, but to the breaking-up process itself. The trusts had too long evaded the fate of the wicked. He would not only prosecute them, he would set a policeman over them. He had the Federal Trade Commission in mind. And in this project, too, he succeeded.

[4] Ibid., 216.

★ 41 ★

WE NEED NOT, FOR OUR PURPOSE HERE, FOLLOW THESE MATTERS further. They were consummated. They proved again that a determined man in the Presidency could shape a nation's fundamental policy and could see that it was implemented. But a test of a different order was to come. It was something that would overtake him almost unawares. And he would have to retreat again into those solitudes where he found his strength and emerge with a plan for war and peace. We have spoken of the beginning when he was doing this, papers piling up on his desk, his light burning far into the night, and he finding his way into a strange country of international intrigue.

Would he be guided by principles he already had at his disposal, from which he had until now derived his strength? Would he be a progressive in foreign affairs too? Or would he assess the new crisis as a fresh and different problem requiring new solutions? We know, of course, that ultimately he went the way he must. He had trouble with the annoyances thrown up by the British, but he was too much their intellectual partner to have allowed such things any real part in his deciding. And the Germans were accommodating. They furnished good excuses. It is our interest here to see how, differently from Lincoln, and even more differently from McKinley, he conducted his war.

What can be said with the perspective of the years is that in 1917 the New Freedom went to war with German collectivism, just as English liberalism had gone to war with it three years earlier. No one at the time saw the issue as being as simple as this. By then the Germans were convicted of having committed atrocities of such bestial sorts as to warrant any punishment civilized men might devise; also, they had broken treaties, ignored international law, and threatened unlimited sinkings of neutral shipping—a threat finally consummated in the sinking of the *Lusitania*. The nation was quite ready for the war. The President had made up his mind to it sometime before in those withdrawn chambers of the mind where his deciding processes were located. He was not convinced of its necessity, as so many others were, by the tremendous

propaganda operation staged by the British; he saw it as a struggle between democracy and absolute monarchy. And it was toward the ideal
of world peace through the co-operation of independent nations that he
looked. Even a war could be justified in so glorious a cause.

It had not been easy. During the period of neutrality, lasting from the
outbreak of war among the Europeans in 1914 until it began to be plain
that the United States would be actively involved, he had been almost
as annoyed by the effrontery of the British in ignoring American rights at
sea as he had by the German submarine threat. He was also troubled by
the machinations he knew of, and more that he guessed at, being carried
on by the Allies. They were promising themselves spoils of unprecedented
richness at the expense not only of their enemies but of bystanding neu-
trals, and this contradicted every protestation of altruism he was so
eloquently declaiming. Against this he had certain defenses. The Allies
needed the United States. Their war had about come to a stalemate. So
vast had been the slaughter that victory depended on the infusion of fresh
strength from the only source available. That was the United States. And
Wilson's price was to be a world made safe for democracy through the
principle of self-determination. He foresaw an international organization
for keeping the peace. But he had no illusions about the indifference to
this idea of France, Britain, and Italy. They were deep in self-interested
machinations, and their statesmen had no intention of giving way to the
nonsense of world organization.

There was one chance that he might prevail. The fresh military rein-
forcements he could bring to bear might be so great as to make the difference between stalemate and victory, and might even be powerful
enough to dictate the terms of the peace. As it accumulated and was
brought into the field, he might, by expressing a new and radiant intention,
undermine the selfish and cynical leaders of old Europe. American
soldiers were not to fight just to defeat an enemy; they were to establish
a renovated world in which war was outlawed and the processes of peace
were secure. There came in succession, during the years of neutrality and
of tentative preparation for defense, a series of statements, usually
speeches, so eloquent and moving that no comparison with them may
be made—in our history—except those spoken by Lincoln as he defined
the issues of the approaching Civil War. A President was showing the way.

There was a certain irony in this. Wilson's struggle with himself to
achieve a clear domestic policy had been so formidable a one and had
occupied him so exclusively, in its formulation and execution, that he
had considered only tangentially the defining of an American position
among the nations. He was far from being provincial—he had traveled
abroad, he had studied foreign affairs, and he was interested in their
conduct—but it had seemed to him that the possibilities of major disturbance were very slight. He had said so, but he had also remarked to a

Princeton friend before going to Washington that it "would be the irony of Fate" if his Administration had "to deal chiefly with foreign affairs."[1]

It was certainly not within the farthest stretch of his imagination that he would have to conduct a war as its Commander in Chief or find for himself the proper behavior of a President in wartime. Reading about him as the possibility of war became more real, it is interesting to see the student of public administration emerge and traditional progressivism loosen its hold on his mind. He soon saw that war, if it did come, would be unprecedented in scale and that it would involve a mobilization of all the nation's resources. This, in turn, would involve some sacrifices and disciplines hard for a free people to accept. But he seems to have had no doubt of his ability to persuade them of the necessity and to gain compliance. This was rather strange, because his first venture in interference abroad had had such an unfortunate course. It had seemed to illustrate every conceivable awkwardness. The principle was mistaken, the means used were the wrong ones, and the execution was deplorable. This was the Mexican affair which arose out of his detestation of the dictator Huerta and his conviction that it was his duty to curb excesses that disgusted him.

It is still not very well understood why Wilson was so eager to take personal charge of foreign affairs from the very beginning. It may have been because he distrusted Bryan; it may have been, also, that he distrusted even more the bureaucracy of the State Department. At any rate, he centered in himself every phase of these dealings. And almost at once he got himself into the Mexican mess. It is described by Link:

> In the areas that he considered vitally important—Mexico, relations with the European belligerents, wartime relations with the Allied powers, and the writing of a peace settlement—Wilson took absolute personal control. He wrote most of the important notes on his own typewriter, bypassed the State Department by using his own private agents, ignored his secretaries of state by conducting important negotiations behind their backs, and acted like a divine-right monarch in the general conduct of affairs.

Mexico was the first example of this compulsion to take charge:

> Ignoring the men in the state department who knew anything about the subject, the American ambassador and the chargé in the Mexican capital, and the consuls in the field, Wilson proceeded to make a Mexican policy in his own way, as follows: He first sent a journalist to Mexico City to investigate. Accepting this reporter's recommen-

[1] A. S. Link in "Wilson the Diplomatist," from *The Philosophy and Policies of Woodrow Wilson,* Earl Latham, ed. (Chicago, 1958), 147.

dations, Wilson next sent a former governor of Minnesota, who had neither experience in diplomacy nor any knowledge about Mexico, to present certain proposals for a solution to Huerta. Then, after the dictator had repudiated the President's right to interfere, Wilson pursued a relentless personal campaign to depose Huerta, one that culminated in armed intervention and Huerta's downfall.

And, added Link:

Time and again Wilson used the same methods and almost always with the same results: the formation of a faulty policy through sheer ignorance, men working at cross-purposes, confusion in the state department and in the embassies and legations . . .[2]

The biographer is quite right. This was a small exercise of the same sort as the tremendous one which was to end in American intervention across the Atlantic. If from the recorded results it should be concluded that the Rule of Responsibility monopolized by one individual is extremely dangerous for the nation, that is something we shall have to deal with. It cannot be ignored. But that must come later. We are here interested in its operation as managed by a practitioner who happened to have a distinctive approach. We shall see that Hoover, F. D. Roosevelt, Truman, and Eisenhower, who were to follow, had their own ways of operating too; and we shall ask whether they were any more successful and, if not, whether any possible variation could succeed.

At any rate, Wilson's personal diplomacy and the ascendancy he achieved over American impulses—and so the Congress—brought him eventually to the sending of American armies across the seas to enforce his views. Of course he conceived these views to be inevitable truths, and he had no doubt whatever that their establishment by force was essential to the future of civilization; but the method was the same from beginning to end. If his embracing of the Rule of Responsibility constituted a monstrous enlargement of the Presidency which no one's personal competence could possibly comprehend, the results were registered not only in the formation of policy and in its implementation by mustering opinion and creating law, but in an expansion of the Executive mechanism. And these last are not the least interesting of the innovations into which he was forced by the momentum of events once they had been set in motion.

The New Freedom, as a philosophy, had relied on the initiative of individuals to supply the economy with goods and services. There were to be certain rules, but they were completely negative. They did not stimulate, or encourage, or direct, or even counsel. They merely told those who were impelled by inner propensities what they must not do to each other

[2] Ibid., 160–61.

under the urging of their instincts to be active. But when the President was compelled to consider the situation of the nation as it prepared for war, it was obvious that there was something lacking. The rules of freedom did not even go far enough in a negative way. They did not, for instance, forbid one producer to buy up the whole supply of a raw material no matter what its effect on others who might need it in their operations. And there was no distinction between, say, the manufacturers of sporting goods or those of munitions; either might draw on scarce stocks. This immediately became intolerable. And how easily the necessary modifications led on to more positive interferences can be seen by the most casual look at the administrative changes of the year or two preceding the war and the months of the war itself. By the time it was over the system that had been elaborated would have given satisfaction to the most convinced state socialist. Not only were the numerous necessary prohibitions implemented by an enlarged bureaucracy, but positive directions were being given all through the economy. There was no one who was not being told what to do, as well as what not to do.

It must have amazed Wilson to see how quickly the big businessmen he had so recently been denouncing with a fervor only to be described as demagogic could bring the productive system into orderly control, managed from the center, and happily co-ordinated in all its parts.[3] It must be said that the results achieved brought into the severest question the appropriateness, under American conditions, of the Brandeis theories on which Wilson had been operating. It was possible, with the loose affection

[3] And this led on to lessons in the businessmen's supposed incapacity for direction:

The theory that the men of biggest affairs, whose field of operation is the widest, are the proper men to advise the government is, I am willing to admit, rather a plausible theory. If my business covers the United States, not only, but covers the world, it is to be presumed that I have a pretty wide scope in my vision of business. But the flaw is that it is my own business that I have a vision of and not the business of the men who lie outside the scope of the plans I have made for a profit out of the particular transactions I am connected with. And you can't, by putting together a large number of men who understand their own business, no matter how large it is, make up a body of men who will understand the business of the nation as contrasted with their own business interest.

This was written during the interlude between his election and inauguration (and published in *The Fortnightly Review*. It is to be found in *Public Papers*, I, 7 ff.) It did not suggest that central direction or even a mechanism for co-ordination was needed. It suggested that policies should be made without the interference "of these business leaders," and that they themselves should be reduced to non-leadership. This was the anti-trust policy.

of politicians for specious logic in the service of their constituents' conceptions, to make a distinction between what was allowable in peace as
contrasted with war. But there must have been many to whom this seemed
a false distinction, and it was. Nevertheless, it was made. And the enlargement of the Presidency represented by Wilson's war organization remains
a specimen to be studied in isolation. It was abandoned abruptly when
the armistice was signed in 1918—when it was just coming into really
smooth operation after several reorganizations and changes of direction.
This was one sector of his responsibility that operated with acknowledged
success, and it was the businessmen who were in charge. He interfered
with it very little, being somewhat defeated by its strangeness and intri-
cacy; besides, there was much content with it. He left it alone.

In the second year of his Administration, and the year war broke out in
Europe, it began to be all too apparent that something would have to be
done to strengthen the military posture of the United States. With a peace-
time navy and an army of little more than a hundred thousand behind
him, his voice would not be heard very clearly in the thunders of conflict.
The National Defense Act of 1916 recognized this need and doubled the
army. And the navy, Daniels suggesting the need to the Congress, was
put in the way of enlargement; but these were simple and traditional
measures. What was not so usual was the provision for a Council of National Defense. This was something which had been germinating in Wilson's mind for more than a year.[4] Obviously it had not been given that
intense probing he was capable of; it was more a sketch than a structure.
But it constituted a beginning of something destined to be an important
innovation.

This and the companion measures following—indeed the whole system
of devices for conducting the war—do not illustrate the Rule of Necessity
in the same sense that Lincoln's first war measures did. They were all
given the approval of the Congress. They did not legally enlarge the presidential powers. But there was about to occur, nevertheless, the most fantastic expansion of the Executive known to American experience. No President had been so big a man as Wilson, if for no other reason than that
no other President had had a comparable task to perform. Presidential
expansions do not have to be extra-constitutional; they may grow out of
the phrases of Article II. During the next few years many Acts would be
passed in which delegations of power were made. They would say "the

----

[4] In his message of that year he had spoken of the need for creating
"the right instrumentalities by which to mobilize our economic resources
in any time of national necessity." He spoke of the co-ordination of transportation and the securing of manufacturers' co-operation, by compulsion
if need be. There must be complete integration of military and industrial
functions.

President may" or he is "authorized to" do many things jealousy refused him in the past. And it is not irrelevant to mention here that Wilson was able to prevent the setting up of a congressional committee on oversight such as tormented Lincoln throughout the Civil War. He had difficulty about it, but he prevailed. And this in itself was an achievement.[5]

The Council of National Defense consisted of six members of the Cabinet: War, Navy, Interior, Agriculture, Commerce, and Labor. It was authorized in the Army Appropriation Act of 1916 as an advisory body, but it was to co-ordinate industries and resources for "the national security and welfare"; and there was also an Advisory Commission to consist of seven persons, each of whom should be especially qualified in some field of peculiar value. Both bodies were brought into being in October 1916, the Secretary of War being designated to be chairman of the Council. Provision had been made for a director and a secretary, and meetings among them began at once.[6] Nothing happened at once. There were discussions, but that was all. Still, it was a useful period; the members were exploring possibilities and making ready to recommend procedure. They were in touch with the administrative elite of industry not only in America but abroad, where experience was accumulating. And presently they were ready to define their own purpose and to suggest a way of implementing it.

A note to this early stage of preparation for converting the productive facilities of the nation into an organism very different from the confused world of the anti-trust laws is suggested by the President's words addressed to the Council at the time of its appointment. He told them that they were to unite the forces of the country "for the victories of peace as well as those of war." Whether this meant such a reversal of progressive tenets as it seemed to imply cannot be known. When the war was over, Wilson was a wreck and the country was going back to "normalcy" so rapidly that nothing more of a creative sort would be allowed to happen. But it hints at a sophistication Wilson had not otherwise revealed; the author

[5] Besides the *Life and Letters* and the *Papers* referred to here, Clarkson's *Industrial America in the World War* (Boston & New York, 1923), is helpful for the management phases of the war effort. There is also Baruch, *American Industry in the War* (New York, 1941). It was briefly summarized afterward by the present author in "America's War Time Socialism," *The Nation*, April 6, 1927.

[6] This Advisory Commission had a distinguished membership, mostly industrialists: Daniel Willard, Hollis Godfrey, Howard E. Coffin, Bernard Baruch, Dr. Franklin H. Martin, Julius Rosenwald, and Samuel Gompers. The director was Walter S. Gifford, and the secretary was Grosvenor B. Clarkson. These names will have significance for any student of American industrial history.

of the New Freedom, in defeating the German collectivism, may have learned something from the rival system; but how much we cannot be sure.

Wilson's part in subsequent developments affecting the Presidency was not especially significant. The experts had been called in, and he could devote himself to diplomacy and to the tasks of legislation and public leadership. The proliferation of central management devices occurred without any particular effort on his part. But the war organization as it stood at the time of the armistice in 1918 was a formidable structure with an immense reach.

Early in 1917 the Council of National Defense had set up the Munitions Standards Board and the General Munitions Board; the one, as its name implies, was to fix standards; the other was to supervise the purchasing of munitions. This was followed by the appointment of numerous committees whose functions were to prevent the development of shortages and to stop the spiraling of prices. They were unsuccessful, and subsequent profiteering and confusion led directly to the creation of the War Industries Board. This was still subordinate to the Council of National Defense, which had only advisory relations with the government and with industry. During the summer and fall of 1917 several other agencies were authorized in congressional Acts: the Food, Fuel, and Railroad Administrations, the Shipping Board, and the War Trade Board. But the War Industries Board struggled with its difficulties for the better part of a year before it was reconstituted, with enlarged powers deriving directly from the President himself by Executive Order. This was made possible by the passage of the Overman Act giving the President more freedom than any of his predecessors had ever had in disposing the Executive establishment to suit himself. Even under the pressures of war the Congress held onto some of its prerogatives; no agency could be abolished without the permission of the Congress, thus protecting the Democratic protégés now so well distributed among the Departments; and the granted powers were to end six months after the coming of peace. Still, the President could expand and manage the administrative staff pretty much as he pleased. And under grants of power in other Acts he could approach the manipulation of priorities and the control of prices, the two most needed actions. Some effect could be got by fixing prices for government purchases, and when its various agencies could be persuaded not to compete, a priorities system was possible for these. But there was not then or later any grant of authority for fixing prices of civilian commodities or for actually directing production. Such effect as there was came from voluntary or indirect regulation.[7]

---

[7] Price fixing was recognized as a difficult constitutional question by the elite of business, gathered to win the war. R. S. Brookings, who was made chairman of the Price Fixing Committee, said afterward to Baker

The War Industries Board had more to do than price fixing; it had to arrange production. A chart of its functions, as it shaped up after its final reorganization in 1918 when Baruch became its chairman, showed a Priorities Board, a Requirements Division, various industry sections, a Labor Division, Steel and Chemical Divisions, and a Conservation Division, as well as a Price Fixing Committee. There were, besides, certain staff divisions, such as legal, planning, and publicity. But getting production straightened out was its chief problem. This it did through its various industry sections and committees. In these the more important manufacturers and traders met and came to voluntary agreements, aware that there was no force that could be used against them if they did not comply, but aware, also, of the attraction exerted by the enormous volume of government purchases. Added to this was what pressure the President could muster from a public which naturally resented rising prices and shortages of goods unless it could be demonstrated that these were necessary and fairly shared.[8]

The impression from Baruch's account might be that this mobilization was something Wilson paid close attention to and had very much on his mind. That impression, however, is not borne out by following his daily activities in *Life and Letters*. Only very occasionally did he deal with some problem brought to his attention by the industrialists, and then with a certain superficiality, such as when he objected, for no good reason, to an expansion of the Price Fixing Committee. It is more realistic to conclude

---

(op. cit., VIII, 22), "As we were compelled to fix prices for the civilian population as well as for our war needs there was some question as to our legal authority, but the President assured me that as his personal representative I would be supported by all the authority which he had not only as President, but as Commander in Chief with the nation at war . . . I have taken every opportunity to testify to the unyielding support which he gave me through the trying period during which my committee fixed prices on more than 30 billion dollars worth of goods." Wilson, of course, had no such authority either as President or Commander in Chief. It was only the Rule of Necessity—unchallenged—which permitted so gross a violation of constitutional boundaries. It is a case—the clearest case during World War I—of doing what needed to be done in deliberate disregard of legal limitations. Like most appeals to this Rule in national crises, it succeeded so well as to go almost unnoticed into the record of the Presidency.

[8] The chart mentioned here may be found in Baruch's *American Industry in the War*, op. cit., 14. In that book will be found also descriptions of the various activities referred to, and a series of appendices showing the enabling acts, the Executive Orders, and the directives under which the Board acted.

that Wilson at this time deliberately relegated much of the administrative work of his office to subordinates. He had larger affairs to deal with, ones affecting the nation and the world, then and for the future.

All those who had any part in the economic effort were always afterward very proud of it, and many of the individuals went on to later careers of importance. Some even survived to have a part in the similar organization that would become necessary for World War II. What can be said is that it sufficed for the short but intensive drive to move an expeditionary force overseas and supply it with munitions, meanwhile going on with the supplying of the Allies.

Wilson himself, surrounded by an array of Executive agencies of unprecedented scope, was finally at the center of an organism no man, however vigorous, could in any real sense direct. It was during this period that the limitations of a one-man Presidency began to appear so serious as to call in question the whole institution. With a tremendous administrative machine operating at velocity and penetrating every area of economic and social life, the President was still a single individual, subject to all the ills of aging men. If he was ill or fatigued, there were still decisions affecting millions to be made. He had no substitute, no second, no assistant who shared his presidential powers. He might delegate, but that did not make his delegate part of his own person. The constitutional Executive was still not a Presidency; it was a President. Wilson had done his best at enlargement. It was a memorable achievement within the individualist tradition. But without a staff the office did not—could not—exceed the limitation of one man's mind and energy.

42

THIS, THEN, IS A GOOD PLACE TO PAUSE AGAIN AND LOOK AT THE PRESI-
dent in his House and his place of work—one man now in charge of far
vaster concerns than had been true during the nineteenth century. His
potential had been immensely increased by the simple changes in his
environment made by Theodore Roosevelt. Best of all, he no longer had
his offices on the second floor of the White House. The living rooms of
the presidential family were also on that floor, and at any time after
additions to the clerical staff had begun to be made the mixture of the
two activities had been both unpleasant and inefficient. By Fillmore's time
there had been some six clerks and a messenger or two, and all of them
had used the same upper hallway as the family and guests; and any callers
who came to see the President had to be ushered upstairs. The President's
offices and his Cabinet room occupied five chambers. If the family included a child or two, or a relative, there were almost no extra accommodations. And of course the entire first floor was ceremonial and always
open to public viewing.

Continuous hard use had made frequent refurbishing necessary merely
to maintain a decent appearance, and these occasions were embarrassing.
The Congress was always reluctant to appropriate funds, and their expenditure was the subject of jealous comment. In spite of the risks, there
had been several fairly thorough interior rebuildings. They had not always
been thorough enough, however; as modernizations became available or
as fashions changed, fixtures, pipes, or wires were hung from ceilings, and
furniture was moved onto already overweighted floors. Tyler, Grant—and
later Truman—experienced actual collapses, and such accidents were narrowly escaped at other times. The emphasis was seldom on needed
structural changes. What seemed large amounts were spent at various times
on redecoration and refurnishing. For instance, Grant's ebullient party
colleagues in the Congress allowed him a sufficient sum to discard all the
fine French furnishings surviving from the Monroe period and to install
the gloomiest of heavy Victorian drapes, buffets, sideboards, armoires, and

sofas. The victorious General was well treated in other ways too; his salary was raised from twenty-five to fifty thousand dollars, and outside the House new stables were built and terraces were regraded and planted. This last was part of a post-war program for Washington, whose few cobbled streets had been ground to dust and sunk in mud under the hoofs of cavalry horses and the wheels of army wagons. Pennsylvania Avenue was repaved, and, best of all, the notorious Tiber River was roofed over and its surrounding marshes filled in. This relieved a health hazard and did something toward making Washington more a city and less a country village.

Jackson had brought the first water into the House through iron pipes, but not until Fillmore insisted was central heating installed—which was part of the reason why the floors fell in on the Grants. Buchanan was an elegant old bachelor and made the contribution of a greenhouse on the west terrace to furnish fresh flowers—something all future Presidents would have, although not from the same greenhouse. What was of more practical importance, Hayes installed the first bathtubs with running water. There was some commotion about this; besides the extravagance, the medical profession was of the opinion that these contraptions were a hazard to health.

Occasionally new china and silver services had to be bought. Their cost ran into thousands of dollars on each occasion since state dinners grew larger and the numbers to be received multiplied. Presidents could not make public the considerable losses from pilfering, but if there were to be any social occasions there had to be new purchases of plates, glasses, and silverware. They disliked these bouts of refurbishing because of the publicity; but their wives were more innocent politically and more ambitious socially, and so they insisted, when neglect went far enough, on attention to household needs.

The House planned by the architect Hoban, who supervised its building during some twenty worrisome years, and then rebuilt after the burning in 1814, was considerably changed in appearance by the addition of Latrobe's North Portico during Jackson's regime. This had the effect of turning the House around, and after that the main entrance was from the north. The south meadow, whose lawns had run off into rough pasture and marsh, was now more secluded and more plainly grounds for a House. Jackson, the rather ostentatious Democrat, in fact left a comparatively pretentious establishment to Van Buren. And that wispy widower soon had the reputation of trying to return to the regality of the Virginia gentlemen. But he was not to be for very long the incumbent, and his gold and silver accumulations were soon dissipated in the less ambitious regimes to come.

It is impossible to think of Lincoln being concerned with the paraphernalia of living, but Mary Lincoln was; and before the war made them inappropriate, the social occasions of the Illinoisans were as notable as those of their predecessors. Coming to Grant, and then to Hayes, and to others down to Theodore Roosevelt, the House was several times drastically overhauled inside, and the coats of paint and layers of wallpaper accumulated. But when the Theodore Roosevelts surveyed the prospect of life for their large and lively family in what had become not only a gloomy and shabby but rickety structure, they revolted. It was positively dangerous. Fillmore's heating devices and modern plumbing were likely at any moment to fall through the floors. They demanded a reconstruction.

The insecurity had been made factual by a report from the noted architectural firm of McKim, Meade and White:

> The preliminary examination of the White House shows that the portion devoted to the President's offices is in an unsafe condition, and that radical steps should be taken to relieve the beams from the weight they have carried too many years . . . The original house was built simply, and well built, considering the limited amount then available for public buildings in Washington . . . The original plans for the White House show porticoes on the West and on the East, extending 150 feet from the main building. These porticoes contain servants' quarters, the laundry, store rooms and house offices generally . . . The restoration of the West Portico to its original uses and the replacing of the East Portico will relieve the main building of a number of domestic offices and make available for public purposes more than half of the garden floor . . .
>
> The elimination of the executive offices from the White House gives an opportunity to rearrange the house as a residence for the President. The President retains a room in which he would see callers at hours when he is not in his office. The main hall becomes a spacious and dignified reception room . . .
>
> Of the floors of the first story those under the main hall, private dining room, and the pantry were found to be in good condition. The floor under the central portion of the East Room showed a marked settlement due to overloading and to hanging heating coils to the ceiling underneath. The base of the room gave evidence of the settlement of the room, and the same was true in the Green and Blue Rooms. The floor of the State Dining Room, while not showing settlement, was so insufficiently supported as to cause the dishes on the sideboard to rattle when the waiters were serving, and the plastering below was badly cracked from vibration.
>
> At larger receptions, when potted plants were brought in from the greenhouses and when the house was filled with people, it was the custom to put shores under the floors of the East Room, the State Dining Room and the Main Hall at both ends for safety . . .
>
> The second floor showed such a degree of settlement as to make

an entire new floor necessary . . . The attic occupied by servants was reached only by elevator . . . a most dangerous arrangement in case of fire . . .

The electric wiring was not only old, defective and obsolete, but actually dangerous, as in many places beams and studdings were found charred for a considerable distance about the wires where the insulation had worn off . . .[1]

So at this time there was a reconstruction of the interior from basement to attic and a rebuilding of the east and west terraces found on the plan drawn by Latrobe in 1807. This whole area had been cluttered with workshops and greenhouses. The east terrace, in fact, had disappeared under rubble. When this was cleared away the old foundations were discovered. A porte-cochere erected there now became the entrance to the house for such occasions as receptions and large dinners. The removal of the greenhouses restored to the south front of the building that spacious dignity which had been hidden for some forty years by the various careless encroachments, and since it could be seen across a field of green, its serene beauty was fully revealed.

This was substantially the environment in which Wilson lived and worked during the era of domestic reform and the World War. For so confirmed an individualist it was not at all a bad situation. So far as administration was concerned, the West Wing offices were sufficient. Wilson was a departmental man anyway—that is, he did not use staff to supplement the Department heads or to maintain liaison with them. And the war agencies were similarly independent, just as though they too had been Departments. And when he wanted to be alone to study or write, or when he wanted to confer with friends, he had the Oval Room, looking out to the south, one of the most beautiful rooms and one of the loveliest prospects imaginable.

Wilson evidently had a feeling for landscapes; his favorite recreation was an afternoon drive, although he did play a good deal of amateurish golf for the exercise. Time and again the notes of his daily life record outings of this sort. They were, however, routinized, according to Ike Hoover, the Chief Usher. He had only to tell the chauffeur to follow Route 1 or 2, and the familiar scenes of the Maryland or Virginia countryside were unrolled before his tired eyes. They never failed in their soothing purpose. The President knew his own capacity and he rationed his strength carefully, so that all through the stormy scenes of his first years, in spite of personal loss and then of newly married euphoria, he is pictured as firm and collected. He was a sane and healthy man. It was only in the stress of world leadership and the frustrations he suffered, first abroad and then at home,

[1] S. Doc. 197, 57th Cong., 2d sess., February 1903.

that he allowed his capacity to be overused. His collapse then was tragic and complete.

The White House never had a more seemly occupant than Wilson. He was the presidential model par excellence, always in complete charge, never confused, offering the symbol of correctness and turpitude. He may have become, as time passed, just a little over-righteous, somewhat too sure and inflexible; but during his best years he gave the American people reason to be extraordinarily proud of their President.

We come naturally to linking up the kind of place the White House had become with the kind of Presidency which had evolved and which would last through the individualist period, expanded here and there and modified to suit the habits of different persons, but essentially remaining the same. It will be noticed, as we go on, that this stage lasted until the time of the second Roosevelt, when there was an administrative reorganization; but how effective a one, and how much it changed the Presidency, we shall have to see.

Wilson continued to be a one-man Executive as he was a one-man political leader and all the rest. It has been mentioned that he was one of the early commentators on administration as an activity worth special consideration.[2] He had said that he thought it curious that the English race had been so long engaged in studying the art of curbing Executive power "to the constant neglect of the art of perfecting executive methods." As Professor Macmahon has pointed out, there was, in his 1887 article, "the core idea of executive integration," but the structural and procedural corollaries were not worked out.[3] And this might serve for commentary on all his life as an administrator. The core ideas were there but were never very fully developed, and he never used them in practice. It does not seem strange that his immediate successors should have neglected these possibilities; they accepted them as a matter of belief; but that Wilson did shows a real conflict between his theory and his practice. He simply could not work as he would have said administrators ought. Because of this, his daily activities were carried on almost as though there were no bureaucracy at his command, and he made none of the administrative improvements he might have made.

Consider as an example the fate of the proposal for an Executive budget. It was no longer a new idea that there should be developed a presidential estimate which, when sent to the Congress, would be treated as one whole, bringing all the functions of the government into focus and making it possible to relate expenditures to income. Such an achievement would

[2] "The Study of Administration," *Political Science Quarterly*, June 1887, 197–222.

[3] "Wilson: Political Leader and Administrator," in *The Philosophy and Policies of Woodrow Wilson*, op. cit., 113.

make administrative management really possible for the first time. Wilson, by his own profession, ought to have been enthusiastically for it. But the fact is that it had a miserable history during his Administration, as it had had in Taft's, and went down before the fierce determination of the congressional committees to keep all such matters in their own untidy care.[4]

So it was with other matters having to do with administrative reorganization, including the presidential staff. He would not have known what to do with a larger one than that assembled by his faithful secretary Tumulty. He did get around, a few months before the armistice, to requesting that an organization be set up within the War Industries Board to provide a "conspectus" of war activities and thereafter a periodical checking up of operations. This resulted in a Central Bureau of Planning and Statistics. Directing this work was Edwin F. Gay, who also was in charge of divisions of this sort for the Shipping Board and the War Trade Board.[5] And this was one of the useful devices which would be re-created by Franklin D. Roosevelt.

But, having in mind the elaborate modern services for information available to a President, Wilson seems to have had amazingly little interest in this sort of thing. He continued to be a family man who worked in his private study in the morning and, when he had to, in the evening, although he frequently went to the theater, and who otherwise preferred the society of wife and daughters or cousins. He was, as Link points out, an intellectual in one sense but not in another. He had a brilliant mind, easily brought to bear on the problems it was required to face. But he was not interested in literature or the arts and, after his professional interest ceased, was neglectful of progress in the social sciences. Being thus limited and not having reading as one of his pleasures, he was not likely to reflect a knowledge of contemporaries or their thoughts in his conversation.

So in his case the White House was important as a home, and he was not a traveler for recreation as many Presidents have been. On the other hand, neither he nor his family made any additions or total refurnishings such as we have read about. After his modest Princeton home, the White House probably seemed more than adequate, and he must often have thought it luxurious for the son of a Staunton minister. But then Wilson was not a builder or planner in the physical sense. He was not concerned to improve Washington or to beautify other American cities. He had no interest in providing more facilities for governmental business.

[4] Ibid., 121–22. The Democratic platform of 1916, over which Wilson ought to have had some control, spoke of the budget function as a congressional rather than a presidential one. And he did not carry the matter farther.

[5] Ibid., 115.

His habits and preferences owed something to his being a southerner, even if he had spent nearly a lifetime in the North. The food on his table was by preference prepared by Virginia cooks, and the soft accents of the South were never quite eliminated from his speech. His second marriage, too, was to a lady who belonged to the "cave dwellers" of Washington. These families are the permanent core of capital society. They watch newcomers settle in, and somewhat later depart, with the detached air of sophisticates. New brooms, they are apt to say, soon fray, and house cleanings come to an end. They themselves are unaffected. Mrs. Galt was one of these. She gave the President repose and brought him accustomedness to the Washington scene. The White House, under her management, was more a home than ever in the upper-class tradition of the South. And that was what Wilson wanted most.

There would be a sharp change when Harding moved in. The Roosevelts and Tafts had had children and extensive family circles. But after Wilson, the shady Harding menage really demeaned the House for almost the first time in its history. Even the Grant entourage of camp familiars had not been given to barroom manners and gamblers' morals. Coolidge returned the environs to strait-laced behavior but not to the subdued and lustrous gaiety of the better regimes. Hoover meant to do his duty as he saw it, but he was a dour man and his wife not inclined to expansiveness. It was not until the second Roosevelt family assumed charge that the White House again seemed to release its charm and to glow with the air that Hoban and Latrobe—and Theodore Roosevelt—had intended.[6]

[6] Something more about these matters can be learned by the reader who cares especially about them by reading various memoirs and intimate histories. Charles Hurd's *The White House, a Biography* (New York, 1940) tells in a sketchy way of the various changes made by successive Presidents. Ike Hoover's *Forty-two Years in the White House* (Boston, 1934) is the notes of an usher who served in ten presidential regimes, beginning with Harrison's. Mrs. Nesbitt and Mrs. Helm of the F. D. Roosevelt entourage and Starling and O'Reilley of the Secret Service have written of their experiences. There are many accounts of the sort. What is to be got from them is nothing very perceptive, mostly surface observations and descriptions the significance of which was not understood. The reader who really wants to know about T.R. must read Pringle, about Wilson must read Link, about Coolidge must read White, and so on. There is no substitute for scholarly depth.

43

IT MAY BE ALLOWABLE TO SPEAK AGAIN OF THE SHATTERING INCON-
sistency that runs as a kind of geological fault through Wilson's politico-
economic theory. It was not his alone; he shared it with most of a generation of American intellectuals. This was the conception on the one hand
that government must not rest upon conflicts and antagonisms, but ought
to have an integrated form—like the British system—in which conflicts were
resolved and positive action made possible; but, on the other hand, that
the fractionalization of enterprises throughout the economy must be forced
—by the same government that must itself be integrated. The principle
on which government should be founded was abandoned for its complete
opposite in the economic world. Of course the integration principle in
government was not approved by many of Wilson's contemporaries any
more than it had been by Adams, Jay, Madison, and others in the Con-
stitution-making period. If they were mistaken, they were at least consistent. Brandeis put the matter succinctly:

> The doctrine of the separation of powers was adopted by the Con-
> vention of 1787 not to promote efficiency but to preclude the exer-
> cise of arbitrary power. The purpose was not to avoid friction, but,
> by means of the inevitable friction incident to the distribution of
> the governmental powers among the three departments, to save the
> people from autocracy.[1]

Brandeis spoke for most contemporary progressives.

It was this about the Constitution that Wilson had always believed so
strongly to be a fault; he could not bring himself to accept the theory
that friction was more desirable than co-operation. Yet it was Brandeis

---

[1] In *Myers vs. United States*, 272 U.S. 52, 293 (1926). This Brandeis
statement was an echo of Madison in *The Federalist* (No. 47):

*The accumulation of all powers, Legislative, Executive, and Judiciary in the
same hands, whether of one, a few or many, and whether hereditary, self-
appointed or elective, may justly be pronounced the very definition of tyranny.*

who became his most trusted adviser in economic matters. There is no way to reconcile this inconsistency.

It is apparent, also, that Wilson never really surrendered his theoretical position concerning government. He temporized as he approached the Presidency, as we have seen, and seemed to have modified his views. Yet he was soon stating them again. There is, for instance, the note made by House of a conversation in 1917. The President was speaking of his retirement. He intended, he said, to write about some things that were on his mind—not anything about his Administration, but something again about government:

> I thought that if he would bring out clearly the necessity for a more responsible form of government and the necessity for having Cabinet members sit in the House of Representatives it would be worth while. He agreed that if the Cabinet members sat in the House, the outcome would be that the President would have to take his material for the Cabinet from the Congress. This, in the end, would give the Cabinet more power, and would have the further effect of bringing into the Congress the best talent in the country. It would eventuate in something like the British system.[2]

This is not accepted as dependable evidence by Professor Macmahon who has pointed out, in commenting on it, that House was obviously leading the conversation; but that it has a likeness to the ideas of the *Congressional Government* is undeniable.[3] And even if his belief in synthesis rather than continued separation did not survive his experience in office as House thought, there is sufficient evidence of his continued acceptance of the Rule of Responsibility which implies a holistic philosophy. And he was intolerant of any suggestion that would in any way restrict his freedom to accept that Rule. Consider, how emphatically he reacted to A. Mitchell Palmer's inquiry concerning the limitation of presidential tenure to one term of six years, a plank in the platform on which he presumably had just been elected. The reply was made early in February of 1913; in it he repudiated the party commitment, saying that if a President "was not a true spokesman of the people" four years was too long a term; and if he was, four years was too short a one. He went on to say that an increase to six years would increase the likelihood of its being too long, without assurance that it would, in happy cases, be long enough. It seemed to him, he said, that the people should decide by their votes. They ought not, in fact, to be deprived of the right to decide, and he

[2] *The Intimate Papers of Colonel House,* arranged by Charles Seymour (Boston, 1928), III, 47.

[3] University of Chicago Seminar, op. cit., 212 ff.

would pledge himself to abide by their decisions. Then he came to a passage which shows that he still looked for a means of Legislative-Executive merging:

> It must be clear to everybody who has studied our political development at all that the character of the Presidency is passing through a transitional stage. We know what the office is now and what use must be made of it; but we do not know what it is going to work out into; and until we do know, we shall not know what constitutional change, if any is needed, it would be best to make . . .
>
> He is expected by the Nation to be the leader of his party as well as the Chief Executive officer of the Government and the country will take no excuses from him . . . he must be Prime Minister, as much concerned with the guidance of legislation as with the just and orderly execution of the law, and he is the spokesman of the Nation in everything . . . Why, in the circumstances, should he be responsible to no one for four long years? All the people's legislative spokesmen in the House and one-third of their representatives in the Senate are brought to book every two years; why not the President . . . ?
>
> Sooner or later, it would seem, he must be made answerable to opinion in a somewhat more informal and intimate fashion—answerable, it may be, to the Houses whom he seeks to lead, either personally or through a Cabinet, as well as to the people for whom they speak. But that is a matter to be worked out—as it inevitably will be—in some natural American way which we cannot yet even predict . . .[4]

There are two matters, relevant to our interest here, touched on in this statement. The first has to do with the strong Leader-President, answerable to the people, not to the politicians, and not further bound by constitutional restrictions than those already established. It is evident that what he had in mind by speaking of the office as "transitional" was that it would gain rather than lose in strength. This is hardly consistent with the moves to reduce both presidential and government powers that would follow from the economic policy of both the progressive and the Republican traditions. In that theory, as we know, the government would be a policeman, setting standards and enforcing competition, but not planning and directing.[5]

[4] This letter also contained a commitment to the direct primary for presidential nomination, something he did not further pursue. *Public Papers: The New Democracy*, I, 21 ff.

[5] Elihu Root, one of the ablest and most honored of Republican conservatives, once said (in an address at Harvard University in 1909, pub-

The second matter has to do with the separation of powers. He was again reverting to the suggestion that the President ought to be, with his Cabinet, answerable to the Congress; and this is where he had started from, as we have seen, in his student days.

But the inconsistency of his political and economic views is a glaring one. And it does not become less so as the policies of his Administration are studied. For after the Federal Reserve Act there came a tightening of the anti-trust laws and the establishment of the Federal Trade Commission. And these were subtractions from presidential power of a most serious sort. This erosion, of course, had been going on for so long a time as to have become traditional—a concomitant of the capitalist system; one, as the progressives said, that made it tolerable. It was also, Wilson might have said, no more inconsistent than the British liberal system of responsible government and their economic laissez faire. But the British were on their way to socialism, as was soon to appear; and their laissez faire was on its last stretch of acceptance. In the United States, socialism was not contemplated by major political personages, and it certainly was no part of Wilson's anticipation.

But that this philosophical dichotomy was doing deep damage to the Presidency, Wilson did not recognize, any more than his predecessors had who had acquiesced in the independent-offices development. Already, when Wilson came to office, there were several such agencies; he was to create more; by F. D. Roosevelt's time there would be twenty, and they would go on multiplying with his active concurrence.[6] We must examine

---

lished by the University Press in 1916) as he expressed alarm at the growth of government even before World War I:

There are two dangers . . . One that the national government will break down in its machinery through the burden which threatens to be cast upon it. This country is too large, its people are too numerous, its interests are too varied and its activity too great for one central government at Washington to carry the burden of governing all the country in its local concerns, doing justice to the rights of the individual in every section, because that justice can be done only through intelligent information and consideration. The mass of business that is now pressing upon the legislative, executive, and judicial branches of our Government in Washington seems to have come about to the limit of their capacity . . .

The other danger is that of breaking down the local self-government of the states.

This might as well have been said by Brandeis himself. I am indebted for this quotation to J. M. Gaus, whose *Reflections on Public Administration* (Tuscaloosa, 1947) I, like many others, have read with so much profit.

[6] The Interstate Commerce Commission dated back to 1887 and the Civil Service Commission to 1883. There was a hiatus until the Wilson

their relation to the constitutional system in which the Presidency was one of the co-ordinate but separate Branches.

The independent offices, most of them, represent the obeisance paid to developing capitalism by a society unable to determine what the policy about it ought to be. Politically, democratic representatives trying to do what they believed their constituents wanted—when they were not serving the special interests whose support seemed to them indispensable—were forced to attempt the impossible: to prevent the growth of concerns powerful enough to injure their competitors, yet leaving the way open for those same constituents to advance into the big-money company themselves. The regulation of business, as pictured by the politicians, is the guarantee of life for the "little fellow." There have been, ever since New Deal days, Small Business Administrations in Washington with the purpose of giving special help and consideration to concerns under a certain size, another unrealistic attempt to stem the tide of expansion. The evolution of industrialism has been toward larger and larger scale. The elaborate and incredibly costly arrangements devised to prevent this evolution from occurring have proved to be no more than nuisances. Big businesses have dealt with them as required—usually with a certain contempt, tempered by political wariness. The suborning of the regulatory agencies became expense deducted from taxes and so paid for by government itself as, one after another, they became informal appendages of the industries they were set up to regulate.

The usually subtle and hidden, but sometimes flagrant, corruption of the regulatory authorities and their failure to modify the evolution they were supposed to prevent are not our thesis here. But we have an interest in the Presidents—strong ones too—who acquiesced in this hypocrisy and who either assisted in its invention or embraced it with the zeal of desperate converts. Wilson, a convert, for instance, was as convincing in his eloquence as Theodore Roosevelt at his best. No one can doubt this who reads such indignant outbursts as his "Freemen Need No Guardians."[7]

Administration; then there came the Tariff Commission, the Federal Reserve System, the Federal Trade Commission, and the Federal Power Commission. There were also certain war agencies: the Fuel and Food Administrations, the Maritime Commission, etc. Hoover set up the Reconstruction Finance Corporation and the Federal Farm Board; there followed the New Deal agencies such as the Securities and Exchange, the Federal Communications, Civil Aeronautics, etc., Commissions, and various Banks and Corporations. In Eisenhower's time it continued—for instance, in the Aeronautics and Space Administration. It was thus a continuing and consistent policy.

[7] An interview published in *The Fortnightly Review* for February 1913, 99, 209–18, republished in *Papers: The New Democracy*, op. cit., 7 ff.

One passage is quite sufficient to show his enthusiasm—a recently acquired one on this subject, but genuine for all that:

> The hypothesis under which we have been ruled is that of government through a board of trustees, through a selected number of the big business men of the country who know a lot that the rest of us do not know, and who take it for granted that our ignorance would wreck the prosperity of the country . . .
>
> Mark you, I am not saying that these leaders knew that they were doing us an evil. For my part I am very much more afraid of the man who does a bad thing and does not know it is bad than of the man who does a bad thing and knows it is bad; because I think that in public affairs stupidity is more dangerous than knavery, because harder to fight and dislodge . . . These gentlemen, whatever may have been their intentions, linked the government up with the men who control the finances . . .
>
> I tell you the men I am interested in are the men who, under the conditions we have had, never had their voices heard, who never got a line in the newspapers, who never got a moment on the platform, who never had access to the ears of Governors or Presidents or anybody who was responsible for the conduct of public affairs, but who went silently and patiently to their work every day . . .
>
> America is never going to submit to guardianship. America is never going to choose thralldom instead of freedom. . . . There are tasks awaiting the government of the United States which it cannot perform until every pulse of that government beats in unison with the needs and the desires of the whole body of the American people . . .

The heart of the government Wilson was about to take charge of did beat strongly for the little fellow; and this sympathy resulted in a considerable further development of independent agencies to shackle and curb the big businessman and the banker—who were, as it turned out, rather better off for the curbing and the shackling, at least after a little time had passed and their lawyers had gone to work. What Wilson's conclusions were at the end of his futile labors of this sort, we do not know. He was too deeply engaged in other matters having to do with war and peace to say. But his acceptance of the widening breach between profession and performance in controlling industry left some problems for the future which were worse because of the line he follówed.

One of these problems was constitutional. When the advocates of laissez faire desired to regulate business they would not trust the President, and the Congress had neither the expertness nor the courage to do the job itself. It was hoped that an agency removed from the pressures of politics could be established which would act for the government—not for any Branch but for all Branches. This was a gross violation of the separation-of-powers principle and ignored completely the intent of the "distributive clauses" of the Constitution.[8] Nevertheless, it became a fixed policy. It is only necessary to refer again to Justice Brandeis's flat statement of the reason for the separation—it was, he said, to "save the people from autocracy"— to understand that the policy was indeed a violent departure from constitutional principle. Yet the fact had to be dealt with that Brandeis was also a principal promoter of the violation represented in the delegations made to the independent agencies. Was it that Brandeis and Wilson were practical men and thought results more important than a theory or even than the Constitution? Then another fact has to be dealt with: their practical way of dealing with industry was a failure. They might have argued, if they could have been persuaded to argue this point, that the regulation imposed was never faithfully administered; but that surely was a weakness which was inherent and bound to happen; it could not have been avoided except in Utopia. With Wilson it might be guessed that this was not a subject on which he had thoughts of any depth, that he relied on Brandeis and others, and that he was mostly aware, anyway, that this was the politically feasible way to go. That is at least an explanation. But how account for the zeal of Brandeis in pursuit of an impractical and unworkable theory? He was, after all, a lawyer, and he became a Supreme Court Justice. Why would he not only embrace an unworkable theory but be willing to connive at a gross violation of the Constitution in pursuit of it —and a part of the Constitution he had been at pains to defend and obviously felt to be fundamental to its integrity?

Could it be because it left the Court in a stronger position and the Congress and the President in a weaker one? For it is true that Congress delegated important powers of its own to the commissions, and it is true that many of their duties were Executive and that the President had— after the Humphrey decision[9]—no control whatever over them. And it is also true that the Court reviewed their actions. It thus exercised the oversight that was otherwise lacking, and brought into the Court's orbit the course of industrial evolution, at the same time excluding it from the control of the other Branches. Whether or not this was intended, it was the result.

It is not possible in an essay on the Presidency to give this matter the attention it deserves. But it is relevant to note that congressional delegations of power have increased as industrial society has expanded and that

[8] Art. I, par. 1, clause 1; Art. II, par. 1, clause 1; and Art. III, par. 1, clause 1.

[9] *Humphrey's Executor vs. The United States*, 296 U.S. 602 (1935). This decision, reversing the Meyers opinion, held that the President had no removal power.

many of them have been made to independent agencies. To the extent that these delegations are of legislative functions, we are not required to comment on them further than to remark that the Supreme Court, in reviewing them, has discriminated to the disadvantage of the Executive. It has approved delegations to independent agencies which it would not allow to the Executive.[10] But it has also allowed admitted Executive functions to be delegated by the Congress to the independent agencies, thus reducing the President's powers. This is so patently unconstitutional that Presidents might have been expected to resist. That they have not—although they have not hesitated to resist the Court in the matter of removal—shows that they are as caught up in the confusions of laissez faire as are others.

On this it is relevant to quote Professor Cushman's conclusion:

> Congress has not . . . hesitated to give to the independent commissions any jobs which could be conveniently dumped upon them. The Interstate Commerce Commission has the executive task of enforcing the Safety Appliance Acts. No one claims this work is quasi-judicial or that a separate body could be set up for its exclusive administration. The Maritime Commission has important managerial and executive duties in respect to construction, operating subsidies, and the leasing of government-owned vessels. It is believed that the giving of major executive duties to commissions which lie out of reach of the President's discretionary removal is unconstitutional.[11]

It will be seen that this argument turns on the issue of the President's power to remove, which, it is considered, would give him control over the commissions. That it would give him complete authority is not true, but it would give him a certain influence; so that, although this does not go to the heart of the issue, it explains why this has been the presidential sticking point even when the commissions themselves have not been objected to. Examining this, Professor Cushman believes that the Congress may place the performance of legislative and quasi-judicial functions beyond the President's reach through removal but that it cannot constitutionally withdraw from his control agencies performing Executive functions.

But in the Humphrey case President F. D. Roosevelt was forbidden to remove a Federal Trade Commissioner, and the language of the de-

[10] On this point see the thoughtful discussion in *The Independent Regulatory Commissions* by Robert E. Cushman (New York, 1941), 428 ff. Cases to be cited are, among others, *Schechter* vs. *United States*, 295 U.S. 495 (1935), and *Isbrandsen-Moller Co.* vs. *United States*, 300 U.S. 139 (1937).

[11] Ibid., 459.

cision made no such discrimination as is suggested between one and another kind of function. It may have been that this brought one President to see where a policy was tending which, like his predecessors for some time, he had been approving. He was not one to let power slip out of his hands and escape into that of the Supreme Court without protest. The Humphrey case, denying his power of removal from the independent agencies, and the Schechter decision, saying that he could not exercise such powers as had been delegated to him under the National Industrial Recovery Act, both coming in one year, induced a violent reaction. There followed his attempt to punish the Court in a reorganization plan. The result of this contest between President and Court was, for several reasons, inconclusive. The President failed to persuade the Congress that his law ought to be enacted; but, on the other hand, he induced a new caution on the part of the Justices which went some way toward re-establishing his position antecedent to the aggressions of the Court. But the loss was more permanent than it may have seemed. The steady inroads of the Judicial Branch upon the Executive as well as the Legislative Branch were set farther forward by the so-called liberal Justices appointed by Roosevelt than they had been by the admitted conservatives of all the past generations. To this we shall recur.

But we may note here that Justice Brandeis, Wilson's chosen economic adviser, concurred in limiting the Executive power and seizing new territory for the Court. He more than concurred; he was the particular designer of the policy.

★ 44 ★

BETWEEN WILSON AND THE SECOND ROOSEVELT THE PRESIDENCY neither expanded nor contracted in any startling way. There were mild engagements with the other Branches and a few enlargements of the administrative machinery—notably the Bureau of the Budget. But the most important change was the addition by the Republicans of several independent agencies in the attempt to meet the problems of the economic crisis—particularly those of agriculture and finance.[1] This was more and more becoming an accepted way of expanding governmental responsibilities without assigning them to the Executive—accepted because approved by the Court.

Even before Hoover there had been a minor flare-up in the area of twilight among the separated Branches. President Coolidge, usually as passive as it was possible to be, attempted to discipline the Tariff Commission. Far from feeling that the Commission represented a subtraction from presidential powers, he was annoyed because it seemed to be passing on to him a responsibility he had no liking for. Tariffs were warm issues, and he was not one to handle warm issues if he could avoid them. Professor Herring has told about the incident:

> President Coolidge felt that the Commission had failed in its duty because of its inability to reach an agreement as to schedules. He was angered by the long complicated reports he was expected to plow through. He could not read such a mass of material. He felt that if the Commission could not agree upon its findings it should be reconstituted. He resented this direct shifting of responsibility to the President. The Commission was disrupted by deep personal animosities. The writer has it upon the authority of the President's secretary, who was directly in touch with the situation at the time, that a desire to restore harmony in the Commission was a leading consideration in the President's mind.

[1] The Federal Farm Board and the Reconstruction Finance Corporation, for instance.

Whatever the President's motivation may have been, his efforts were directed toward "restoring harmony" by removing those members who insisted upon the judicial character of the Commission. He tried to break up the Lewis-Culbertson-Costigan trio, which was trying to lower tariffs and which objected to Presidential interference. These men were Wilson appointees. Coolidge offered Culbertson a place on the Federal Trade Commission (which was refused) and finally sent him off as minister to Rumania. Lewis, when the time drew near for his reappointment, was requested by Coolidge to leave an undated letter of resignation at the White House. When he refused, he forfeited the renewal of his appointment. Costigan continued the battle a few years longer, but finally resigned in 1928.[2]

It was sometimes difficult to decide—if anyone should be required to decide—what of the duties delegated to the various agencies were legislative, what judicial, and what Executive. Apologists often retreated, when under some sort of attack, to the claim that they were semi-judicial and, since their findings were reviewable, that this was an assistance to, rather than an impairment of, the judicial function. But that their numerous regulations, issued in the most formal fashion, were legislative in nature was obvious. The question about them came to turn on the nature of the delegation. And this would be one of the grounds for declaring certain of the New Deal laws unconstitutional. In those cases the Court would profess concern because the Congress had delegated its powers too freely not to independent agencies but to the Executive. This was inadmissible.

But the deeper problem was not the one that appeared on the surface. The imperious question was whether the economy was to accept direction from the public as represented by the government, or whether it was, in another convulsion of destruction, to be broken up again into small and competing units. This would remain the tormenting and unanswered question throughout the New Deal and would go on and on into the future. Presidents hated to be brought face to face with this issue. And even Roosevelt, who seemed at first to have an answer he would stand by in NRA, found himself out of his depth and merely gave up.[3] He too accepted the breaking-up program, and went on, as others had, proliferating independent agencies for controlling the uncontrollable.

But his first efforts precipitated the conflict to be expected when a strong

[2] E. P. Herring, *Public Administration and the Public Interest* (New York, 1936), 95–96.

[3] The "self-government for industry" principle outraged the progressives, and "partnership with government" was weakly administered, so that government lost control.

President appeared and accepted responsibility in time of crisis. There was at first submissiveness; then presently there was revolt. Responding to the Rule of Necessity, he took, or caused to be taken, such measures as seemed to him necessary to induce recovery. After an interval, passionate objection was forthcoming from conservatives, who were willing enough to condone emergency actions for this purpose but who detected an alarming odor of reform about many of the New Deal proposals. When the election of 1936 approached there arose a Liberty League, whose members were among the wealthiest and most powerful individuals of the industrial elite together with their lawyers. The burden of their complaint was that the Congress had become a "rubber stamp" for a dictatorial President and that the hard-won freedom of Americans was in immediate jeopardy. When President Roosevelt inquired just what liberties the heads of Du Pont and General Motors had lost, there was an embarrassed silence; but the well-financed propaganda did not cease for all that. It was not very effective. The election was a rebuke of dimensions seldom before known. It seemed to President Roosevelt a complete democratic answer to a Supreme Court which had declared several of the most important New Deal measures to be unconstitutional. He presently undertook to discipline the Justices by reducing the Court to amenability. If it could be enlarged by a certain number of Justices of his own choosing its decisions would be less likely to be adverse.[4]

The measures most in question had admittedly a certain experimental quality. No one knew certainly how to meet successfully the complex problems of a nation in deep trouble. But there were guides of a sort, and Roosevelt was determined to exploit every possibility. The one thing he would not be forgiven for—as Hoover had not been—was supineness. The complaint about Hoover—and his defeat in 1932 had been his punishment for it—was that he had been unwilling to meet the crisis with adequate and appropriate resistance. It was undoubtedly true that the means he was willing to use were *inadequate,* but a number of them were *appropriate,* so much so that they were merely amplified for his successor's purposes. This was generally overlooked at the time, but there is no doubt that Hoover knew what to do, within the capitalist rules, and that he did it. If his efforts were halfhearted and insufficient, it must be recalled that he was a Republican President, following two Republican predecessors, and that his views of governmental and presidential responsibility were well known and had been until then approved by the public. It was when both his and their energies failed and fright took hold that an ungrateful electorate chose to punish him.

---

[4] There were other provisions in his reorganization plan, but the addition of Justices was the one seized on by his opponents; they called it "packing."

Neither Hoover nor those who formed his circle of assistants and advisers could bring themselves to accept fully the logic of their situation.
They knew that there ought to be a sequestration of gold and an attempt
at stemming the decline of prices, if not a forthright attempt to raise
them. They knew that unemployment had plunged the nation into such
miseries as no civilized people would bear without frantic efforts to escape
them. They knew that the failure of banks, businesses, and individuals,
consequent on the stagnation of commerce and the paralysis of the productive system, might be relieved by massive government action. But,
knowing all this and knowing the remedies, or some of them, they were
still bound by the conviction that the means resorted to ought not to be
primarily governmental. It was a capitalist system; and private enterpris-
ers, shown the way, ought to lift themselves out of the trough into which
they had fallen. So they tried to relieve suffering with private charity, to
lay the burden of providing public employment on state and local governments already drained of resources, and to stop the flood of bankruptcy
by saving the largest of the banks and other enterprises on the theory that
they in turn would help the smaller ones.

There was a complication in the world-wide nature of the cataclysm
which Hoover sought to meet also in a characteristic way—by forgiving or
postponing payment of the intergovernmental debts so that the ones held
by the large private banks could be met. And as his term ran out in an
agony of spreading paralysis he sought to involve his incoming successor
in this policy; it was necessary, he said, to the re-establishment of confidence and the resumption of commercial relations. But he was unwilling
to take the country off the gold standard so sacred to the international
bankers and thus free it from the influence of those financial interests
abroad and at home who took advantage of falling values as gold remained
rigid.

He afterward claimed that the actions he had taken and others he had
proposed to his successor would have been sufficient and that the depression had in fact been conquered. The panic at the time of the change-over,
he said, was a crisis of confidence; businessmen were so frightened of
Roosevelt in prospect that they would make no ventures; consequently
there was a further slackening of business and a rise in unemployment.
Presently debts could not be paid, and this involved the banks; in spite
of the efforts to stave off their bankruptcy, on inauguration day in 1933
every bank was in trouble and most were closed. Roosevelt succeeded to
the Presidency of a country frozen and frightened; in spite of its magnificent productive apparatus it was brought very nearly to a standstill.

This seems almost inexplicable to the historian who studies Hoover's
contributions. He had been one of the few able members in the Cabinets
of Harding and Coolidge; and after the minor post-war depression in 1921
he had persuaded Harding to call a conference on unemployment. A com-

mittee of this conference had sponsored an investigation "of methods of stabilizing business and industry so as to prevent the vast waves of suffering which result from the valleys in the so-called business cycle." Such terms of reference were at that time very significant. There was still a popular impression that recurrent depressions were visitations of nature. But the study of their phenomena had been going on in academic circles for a generation even if its results were not known at all widely; and students had long since come to the conclusion that there was a regularity and progression in them which made an attack on their causes possible. The best known of the investigators in this field was Professor Wesley C. Mitchell, and it was he who was chosen—associating with him the National Bureau of Economic Research—to lead the study.

In the end, in 1923, the group published a substantial volume containing a report and certain recommendations. It was thorough and convincing.[5] The business system had to be supposed to be unchanged, and there was an obvious caution about involving government in prevention or cure; but these were the assumptions of the time. Within these limits the proposed remedies were these:

Control of credit expansion by banks generally.
Possible control of inflation by the Federal Reserve.
Control by businessmen of the expansion of their industries.
Control of public and private construction.
Construction of public works during depression.
The building up of unemployment reserve funds.
The establishment of Federal and state employment bureaus.

Each of these recommendations was elaborated and the business community was, in effect, told what it must do to avoid further depressions and what it must do to recover if they should nevertheless occur. It will be noticed how restricted the program seems from a later point of view, but that is because so much has been learned since then from hard experience as well as because of the limits within which the study was confined. The phenomenon being studied was called a *business* cycle, with the slight intimation that in any other than a system of free enterprise it would not occur. The analysis bore this out. It was as a result of many unco-ordinated decisions to undertake or not to undertake enterprises, to increase or cut down manufacturing commitments, that booms and depressions occurred. Presumably activities could be smoothed out if activity could be restrained at appropriate times and encouraged at others. It was hoped that businessmen, if they were better informed, would do this. And if they did not, then it might be necessary to plan public

[5] *Business Cycles and Unemployment* (New York, 1923).

work so that it would be less when other activities were at their peak and would increase when stagnation threatened.

That this was a naïve and insufficient approach to the kind of cataclysm that would shake the economy of the whole world a few years later, no one needs now to be told; but it did not seem so in 1923, even to such students as Mitchell and his colleagues, who had studied carefully the numerous depressions of former years. These could usually be traced to some precipitating cause such as speculation (land, canals, railroads, mining, and so on) or rapid expansion. And the latest, that of 1921, was attributable to the readjustments after the war. That war had not yet registered all its consequences, and there was a continuing deflation of agriculture which was having effects on industry, but the seriousness of these disturbances was not apparent at the moment. In fact, the vast boom of the twenties was just getting under way and it seemed like borrowing trouble to think that anything so uncontrollable as the Great Depression of the thirties might occur.

At the very least, it should be said that the *Report*, issued under the auspices of the Secretary of Commerce, who would soon become President, was a genuine contribution to the self-knowledge of a nation grown too big and too complex to go on in the old carefree way. That he had turned to the most reliable of scholars for this work was also a precedent of some importance. It was one that he reinforced presently with another similar survey, even broader in scope and even more significant in its implications. This was the study issued as *Recent Social Trends*. Wesley C. Mitchell was chairman of the committee for this study, but the director of its research was Professor William F. Ogburn, the eminent sociologist.[6]

It was an undertaking of such scope as to be literally appalling; but that it was necessary, every subsequent event proved. And that it helped to meet the problems of the terrible period just ahead, everyone involved was well aware. It was more than an appraisal; it pointed to necessary changes; and, above all, it insisted that the nation must be studied and understood as an integrated interacting society of the most intricate sort; this, in fact, was said in the introduction to the first of its volumes:

> The first third of the twentieth century has been filled with epoch-making events and crowded with problems of great complexity. The World War, the inflation and deflation of agriculture and business, our emergence as a creditor nation, the spectacular increase in efficiency and productivity and the tragic spread of unemployment and business distress, the experiment of prohibition, birth control, race riots, stoppage of immigration, women's suffrage, the struggles of the

[6] *Recent Social Trends*, 3 vols. (New York, 1933), with various other vols. of supporting data.

Progressive and the Farmer Labor parties, governmental corruption, crime and racketeering, the sprawl of great cities, the decadence of rural government, the birth of the League of Nations, the expansion of education, the rise and weakening of organized labor, the growth of spectacular fortunes, the advance of medical science, the emphasis on sports and recreation, the renewed interest in child welfare—these are a few of the many happenings which have marked one of the most eventful periods of our history.

There was one thing not mentioned in this comprehensive listing. That was the academic expertness now arriving at maturity which made such a study possible. Ogburn was able to call on the resources of hundreds of helpers from many institutions of learning. A good many of these had had an unspectacular but steady development over the past two generations, spreading into fields where formerly rule of thumb had been relied on and where charlatans had prospered. In 1880, to have regarded the subject matter of modern sociology or political science as proper academic studies would have shocked the educator who relied on Latin, Greek, and mathematics as "mental disciplines." Most universities had only recently struggled out of the confines of denominational religion. But they had emerged and been joined by the growing state universities; and it was a significant recognition of the importance of factual study and scientific method that a President should have asked for such assistance in meeting his responsibilities. For practical politics was still in a much more primitive phase. The spittoons had not yet disappeared from congressional committee rooms, and demagoguery was still the main reliance of the Representative.

Another paragraph of the introduction to the *Report* must serve as the summary of this vast work, in which our specific interest, after all, is only that it represents so important an act of imagination on the part of a President usually considered to be one of the stodgier and less enterprising of the company:

> If, then, the report reveals, as it must, confusion and complexity in American life during the recent years, striking inequality in the rates of change, uneven advances in inventions, institutions, attitudes, and ideals, dangerous tensions and torsions in our social arrangements, we may hold steadily to the importance of viewing social situations as a whole . . . What seems a welter of confusion may thus be brought more closely into relationship with the other parts of our national structure.

What the academicians said was not exaggerated. To look back along the last few decades from 1930 was to view a panorama of events impossible for the citizen of 1900 to have imagined. During that time new inventions, new institutions, and new relationships had replaced so many of the old as to constitute in effect a new world. And it was a world which, in spite of theories and of efforts to prevent it, was knitting together in innumerable ways. To touch any part of the social fabric now was to cause reverberations in its further reaches. This was hard for the believers in individualism to accept, and their failure in economics and in politics was due to their stubborn unwillingness to admit the fact. There was a strange condition in which the financiers, businessmen, and others were creating larger and larger-scale institutions and were setting up regular institutional relationships among themselves at the same time that they were refusing to recognize the need for adapting social institutions to these changes. "Rugged individualism" became a Hoover slogan as he sought to combat the ills of depression after 1929 with only the weapons suggested by the economists in 1923. But the slogan quickly turned to a phrase of ridicule as the rush of events overwhelmed him. Hoover should have known that the "whole society" spoken of by the social scientists must have direction and that the direction must come not from a cabal of big businessmen but from the President in the White House. He sought to relieve the miseries of unemployment first by relying on private charity—setting up local committees, exhorting the well-to-do to give generously, and so on—then by depending on city and state funds, which soon ran out; and finally by lending Federal funds to the states. One after another the available resources were exhausted. And finally the desolation was complete. Even then Hoover would not give in. Deflation must run its course. Business would sometime resume. Then all would be well.

Long before this could happen Hoover was replaced and Franklin D. Roosevelt, who had learned from Wilson—if he needed to learn at all—had offered to accept the Rule of Responsibility. It had been defined for Hoover, but something in him and in the Republican party had made it impossible for him to accept its challenge.

★ 45 ★

BEFORE WE CONSIDER THE SECOND ROOSEVELT WE OUGHT TO SPEAK OF certain developments affecting the Executive establishment itself. The office came down to him, as we have noted, still an extremely personal, meagerly staffed operation. The President, not the Presidency, was the object of the people's interest. For more and more of what happened in the nation he was given the credit or the blame; and there had been a growing tendency, reluctantly accepted until his time, to extend this to economic well-being. The Republicans had long claimed that high tariffs and sound money were responsible for progress and prosperity, thus connecting party policy with employment, wages, and profits. And their Presidents had been involved in struggles over tariff bills, monetary questions, and other economic issues. They did not really believe in letting matters alone. Wilson, for the Democrats, had seized the initiative in the reorganization of the banking system and had captained a campaign to reduce tariffs. So both Republicans and Democrats, although their policies were somewhat different, had gradually accepted the idea of a certain governmental responsibility in the economic field.[1]

This was an immense extension of presidential responsibility, one the Republicans deplored even while they argued that their policies contributed to prosperity. And it was one whose implications Harding and Coolidge would not accept. They would take the credit but not the blame. Hoover agreed in theory, yet his activities both as Secretary of Commerce and as President were calculated to stimulate business and to extend the influence of businessmen. His ambivalence was torture for so intelligent and experienced a man.

With the expansion of these responsibilities it became more and more necessary that the capabilities of the person in the White House should be increased. Wilson had succeeded in managing a reform program and a war without much change in the office itself, but it was a feat not many men

---

[1] In fact, their policies were not *very* different, but they were made to seem so for political purposes.

could have accomplished. And his substitute for an enlarged staff had been the creation of numerous agencies to supplement the Cabinet. These had somewhat the same effect. But that he was an oversolitary man who was badly served with information necessary to decisions, and with the means for executing and publicizing them, was obvious. Once the war was won, the general impatience with discipline caused the almost instant abolition of these agencies, and there was a return to laissez faire—so far as the government controls was concerned. Needless to say, this did not apply to business. The expansion of the war years had immensely increased the scale of operations in industry and the power of the financial interests controlling it. The government returned to its former position, but Gargantua was now astride the nation's economic system, holding it in subjection. This seemed to conservatives an ideal situation. But what must happen as a result was soon made known. The Great Depression occurred because the enormous concentrations of economic power had no central governance and no obligation to the organism as a whole. There was no direction for productive activity, no way to maintain balance and co-ordination. There was not even an official awareness that such a disaster as closed the New Era of prosperity impended, although academic economists had been warning of certain trouble for some time. The boom of the twenties had exceeded all bounds, debts had outrun resources, consumers had been deprived of that percentage of income which would have been necessary to take off the market the margin of goods made by newly speeded up industrial processes. When the paralysis came it was as complete as it was unexpected. And there were no adequate means for meeting the crisis it imposed.

The studies of the Conference on Unemployment, as we have seen, had made certain recommendations, most of them having to do with the behavior of businessmen. It was apparent that if the businessmen had known of these they had not carried them out on any sufficient scale. It was the first recourse of Hoover, upon whom the disaster descended only a few months after his induction, to follow the design offered in the economists' report. He was ready with a certain number of public works projects planned by a small staff he had caused to be organized. But it was soon obvious that this was a remedy of such slowness that its effect would be delayed beyond the time when it would do any good, and that anyway the scale of a ready shelf of such works could not possibly compensate for the decline in private activity.

Hoover called together the nation's business heads. He exhorted them to do this and do that in the national interest, but businessmen must try to make profits and avoid losses, not to manage their affairs in the public interest. They were appointed on numerous committees to collect funds for private charity, and large sums were actually given; but in comparison with the need they were infinitesimal. Before the volume and speed of the rushing recession, all the preventives and remedies were exposed as hopelessly inadequate. And presently Hoover was abandoned even by those who had been most insistent on the policies he had followed. These were not successful, and he must take the blame.

In contrast Roosevelt accepted—as Hoover never really had—the duty of organizing the nation's resources, governmental as well as private, to meet the crisis. He was not too clear about what he would do with them, but that he promised action on a scale commensurate with the need was his most telling appeal. Also, he extended his theory of duty beyond that of Hoover. He said that the government must either provide employment or give relief to those who were unemployed; and he meant the Federal government, not the local governments called to this responsibility by Hoover. This put the Democratic party and its nominated candidate in a strange new position. Not all the Democrats were happy about this commitment to expanded governmental responsibilities. But their reservations were temporarily suspended as the crisis deepened. And when on inauguration day in 1933 almost complete paralysis was reached, they were willing to accept any suggestion the new President might make. If they had not they would, if they were legislators, have heard loudly from their constituents, who were in a mood to support the new national leader with any necessary action.

We shall need to survey with such brevity as can be managed the unusual actions taken by this new President who had once served in the Wilson Administration and had recently been Governor of New York. But first we must look at the office he inherited and with which he would have to function as he began his fight on the depression.

He was at once aware that the physical arrangements were inadequate, that he had insufficient assistance and that the staff agencies needed improvement. About none of these could he do much at first. The emergency was such that it had to be met with the means at hand; only later could attention be given to improving the Executive for the kind of program he meant to undertake. He did have three secretaries, one for press relations; and there were clerks for disposing of correspondence and for seeing to it that official papers were handled correctly and on time. There were now a Civil Service and a Budget Bureau; but the Civil Service was not an administrative personnel office, and the Bureau of the Budget was not much more than a correlating center for departmental estimates with the duty of reducing them in conformance with presidential policy.

Within a short time the quarters in the West Wing would be enlarged and modernized; in a somewhat longer time staff enlargements would follow, and there would be a transformation in personnel and budgetary policies. We must give some attention to their growth before Roosevelt had occasion to depend on them in depression and then in the vaster emergency of war.

We have noted the beginning of the Civil Service with the passage of the Pendleton Act in 1883.[2] By 1930 it had been supplemented by several other measures, but it had not been much amended. The Commission had been authorized to make rules and regulations, and Presidents had extended its scope by Executive Order. Its operations had been widened with the most reluctant consent of the Congress; patronage in the Federal Departments was held onto by the legislators with stubborn and un-ashamed doggedness. The Post Office Department, the Treasury, and the Department of Justice still had thousands of exempt personnel, some of very doubtful quality; the resistance of the legislators was still very difficult for the advocates of the merit system to breach. The Roosevelt expansion would not affect this order of things, and in fact the lower classes of the service in the many emergency agencies would be very largely at the disposal of deserving Democrats, deployed into the De-partments by genial Jim Farley, Postmaster General and party chairman. This would add to the despair and rage of the exiled Republicans, which rage and despair would not be lessened when President Roosevelt later on "covered in" to the Civil Service many of those appointed by patronage methods.

For our purpose here it is necessary only to note that the merit system included more than 425,000 out of some 600,000 Federal employees. If a surprising number of these were Republicans, as it seemed to the incoming Democrats, that was because the "covering-in" procedure had long since been found to be a way of keeping jobs once they were captured. A Congressman's protégés might in this way have a longer term of employ-ment than he himself. And to supplement the covering-in, there was by now some protection against summary dismissal; a statute of 1912, amended by later ones, set up these defenses. They seemed by now, even to the most enthusiastic reformers, to give rather more protection than was required, and there undoubtedly was a tendency to keep the mediocre employees and to lose the better ones who could get jobs else-

---

[2] "Beginning" is not really an accurate word in this connection. There was an admirable small service in the years before Jackson. It was largely washed out in the Democratic deluge but had a tendency to re-establish itself even in the worst era of patronage. In 1853 certain examinations were inaugurated, dividing employees into four classes and providing that appointments were to be made after a Chief of Bureau and two other selected clerks had approved. But the reform did not stick. In 1871 the Congress authorized the President to make rules and regulations for ad-mission to the service, and President Grant appointed a Commission. It did not function long; the Congress refused further appropriations after two years, and it quietly disappeared. The Pendleton reform was the first to persist and to form the nucleus of later growth. In this sense it was a beginning.

where, but without them a merit system could not survive political overturns.

There had been, besides, a classification statute, passed in 1923, which fixed categories of employment and allowed wage scales and other conditions to be standardized throughout the service. On the whole, the laws, together with the Commission's regulations, had firmly established a dependable bureaucracy in all the regular Departments, now numbering ten, and in the numerous independent agencies; but there were an indeterminate number of unclassified positions remaining at the disposal of the patronage chief.[3]

The emergency agencies—the AAA, the NRA, the FERA, and all the rest—were, by the laws or the Executive Orders setting them up, exempt, which meant that their ranks from top to bottom were filled by patronage, with some few key organizers and administrators chosen specifically for the jobs they had to do by those who would be responsible for the performance of the agency. This was one of the means Roosevelt used to get his way with the Congress, and he managed it with ruthless discretion. Farley administered his favors in return for the support of party measures, and together they got through the first years with a record of accomplishment equaled only by the similar honeymoon period of

[3] Concerning the Civil Service and the budget, discussion of which follows immediately, there was by 1930 a formidable literature. There had been intensive independent study of all phases of Federal administration, and courses were being given in several universities which were furnishing a growing body of trained students. These, making their way into the public services or remaining as teachers to train others, were transforming the bureaucracies of city and state governments as well as of the Federal government. The interested reader, by beginning with the pioneering works of Leonard D. White (*Introduction to the Study of Public Administration* [New York], first published in 1926 but having several subsequent editions before his death in 1958), of W. W. Willoughby, Director of the Institute for Government Research, and of others in universities as well as the Institute, will learn how each advance in good government was prepared many years in advance by the earnest work of devoted scholars and publicists. The purpose of this book does not allow adequate treatment of these various movements and bodies of literature. We confine ourselves here to their effect on the presidential office and shorten our account of that because of the merger into common use of many devices and arrangements which in earlier years were regarded as innovations, and sometimes as doubtful ones, especially by the politicians. We accept these benefits as we do the telephone and wireless communication, together with other advances, as nothing to exclaim about, forgetting how recently Presidents and others alike had no such apparati at their disposal but had to make do with written messages, horse transportation, and other appurtenances of the primitive days, say of 1880.

Wilson's Administration. The execution of the New Deal laws left a good deal to be desired in most cases, but when they became more permanent, if they did, their employees were also covered in and gradually achieved the efficiency of the regular bureaucracy.

Roosevelt, having served more than seven years in the Navy Department, knew all about the possibilities of the government service; and as time went on, although he used patronage freely at first, was responsible for more advance toward a full career service than any President before him—as he should have been, having more than three full terms. When he finished, the half million Federal employees of 1932 would have grown to some two and a half million as a result of the war and the depression; and, in spite of the expansion, the quality would have improved, as most observers believe, because of the advances in selection procedure and better supervision of work, and many more would have come under Civil Service.

The Bureau of the Budget was an even more important resource than the Civil Service, being a more specific agency of the Executive. By 1933 it was twelve years old and had begun to be grudgingly accepted by a Congress which had hated to pass the original enabling Act (the Budget and Accounting Act, 1921) and had sabotaged its operations steadily ever since.

In spite of this congressional reluctance, Professor Willoughby in 1927 was moved to say of the provisions of the Act that they had brought about "the greatest change in the character of the office of the President since the first organization of the government," and, although this statement owed something to the enthusiasm of one who had devoted many years to the accomplishment represented by the legislation, there was a certain truth in what he said. The change implied by the existence of an Executive budget in the relations of President and Congress was in fact a profound one—to realize how important, it is only necessary to recall what the old procedure had been.

In December of each year, when the Congress met, the Treasury Department prepared an estimate of the expenditures for the next fiscal year (beginning the following July), but this was merely a compilation of departmental requests; it assumed that the Secretary was precluded from examining or revising them except to put them into convenient form as prescribed by various laws.[4] And there was no suggestion that the

[4] This was not the original intention. When the Treasury Department was established the Secretary had been directed "to prepare and report estimates of the public revenue and public expenditures"; and a supplementary Act in 1800 had required him "to digest, prepare, and lay before Congress . . . a report on the subject of finance, containing estimates of the public revenue and public expenditures, and plans for improving or

President should play any part in making these estimates. Whether or not he approved the requests of the Departments was completely unknown. When these demands reached the Congress they were distributed among the various committees having an interest in the Departments and were considered without any relation to each other or to any whole. There was, moreover, no machinery for bringing them into relationship with expected revenue, so that if there were funds to meet appropriations it was wholly by accident. As a result, numerous appropriation bills, sponsored by different committees, were passed. They were sometimes months apart and they were frequently amended; also, they might be changed in conference when reconciliation of House and Senate measures was undertaken.

It was so indefensible a process that it would afterward seem impossible that it should have persisted until 1921 and even through World War I with its mammoth expenditures. But the Congress was very determined in its defense, and any suggestion for reform was choked off with an energy worthy of a better cause.

But even Congressmen defending their prerogatives have their careless moments, and one of them occurred when a clause was inserted into the civil appropriations bill for 1911 (signed in June 1910) giving the President $100,000 to investigate the organization and operations of the Executive Branch. This, it may be noted, initiated the first of several such investigations, the Congress always being willing to see the Executive brought under scrutiny. What was not realized was that the matter of appropriations was sure to arise and that any scrutiny of this subject would find the trail leading directly into the Congress itself.

President Taft appointed a Commission on Economy and Efficiency. Its membership included several well-known experts who had for years been studying government administration and who had long since concluded that a thorough overhaul was needed.[5] It was active from 1910

---

increasing the revenues . . ." Hamilton had assumed that he was to examine and revise the requests from the Departments and submit a document which would represent his judgment. He was, however, prevented from doing this by the jealousies that soon arose among the Branches. Gallatin tried later to do the same thing, but his efforts were also defeated. Cf. Willoughby, op. cit., and the discussions of Henry Jones Ford in *The Annals* for November 1915, and of Henry Adams in his *History*, I, etc. The history and a compilation of the various laws were included in the *Report* of Taft's Commission on Economy and Efficiency, H. Doc. 854, 67th Cong., to be referred to again.

[5] Frederick A. Cleveland was chairman—he was the Director of the New York City Bureau of Municipal Research. The movement for city reform, following the muckraking period, preceded that for reform of the Federal government by something more than a decade. Other members

to 1913. It made many suggestions for administrative change, but its most determined stand was taken on the matter of the budget. Nothing else was much worth doing, it insisted, until a system relating estimates and expenditures was adopted.

It is impossible to embarrass a body of several hundred members because no individual who has taken some care to retain his anonymity can be exposed as culpable; but if any congressional shame could have been evoked it ought to have resulted from the *Reports* of this Commission.[6] What emerged at once, however, was a whooping roar of defense. In an appropriation Act immediately following, a provision was inserted which said that persons charged with the duty of preparing estimates should do it "only in the form and at the time now required by law, and in no other form, and at no other time." The chairman of the Appropriations Committee emerged from the meetings of that committee to say that the Congress knew best the character and extent of the information it wanted, and it would be very unwise to give up its prerogative. So reform died aborning. President Taft was by now on his way out, and the matter could be ignored without penalty.

Curiously enough, President Wilson did not raise the issue until after the war. By that time a congressional renegade, who is given merit marks by his contemporaries for earnest work, had become convinced that a mistake had been made. He was, moreover, chairman of the Appropriations Committee of the House and so in a position of influence. His procedure was to have an investigation by a Select Committee of the House itself, at the end of which a bill was reported. The House passed this bill, but the Senate ignored it. Then President Wilson, in his annual message, finally recommended that a budget system be devised. The war was over, large debts had been incurred, the burden of taxation was regarded as heavy, and reduction of expenditures was a popular consideration. It was, in fact, largely as an economy and efficiency measure that the budget was finally established. But it was not done in Wilson's time. He felt forced to veto the bill agreed to in 1920, because the Comptroller General it created had been put beyond his power of removal.

The Budget and Accounting Act of 1921 is thus credited to Wilson's successor, Harding. The objection of Wilson was not met, and the

---

were W. W. Willoughby, Director of the Institute for Government Research; W. W. Warwick, Frank J. Goodnow, Harvey S. Chase, and Merritt O. Chance. Political scientists recognize these as names belonging high on their roll of distinction.

[6] Transmitted by the President: H. Doc. 854 and S. Doc. 1113, 62d Cong. Cf. also Willoughby, op. cit., Chap. 3.

Comptroller General would become a serious limitation on the presidential power, a nuisance matched only by the Committee on the Conduct of the War which had so harassed Lincoln. The continuing emergency of depression and war lasted for Roosevelt even longer than Lincoln's ordeal, and the carelessness of Harding in agreeing to an auditing officer beyond his control was paid for by many man-hours spent in conference or in paper work to conciliate a captious congressional representative.

It was a rather unexpected feature of the Budget bill that the Comptroller General should have been given so much power. In fact, the budget reformers seem not to have realized at once what had been done. It was a good principle that the Congress should scrutinize Executive performance; and the Comptroller General was thus made an officer responsible to the Congress, with the duty of reporting on the use of appropriated funds. What was not expected was that the enormous power of an irremovable official would be used to establish a system of pre-audits which, in effect, could seriously limit the President's constitutional duty to see that the laws were faithfully executed. McCarl, the first Comptroller General, took it upon himself to say what might and might not be done with appropriated funds. He demanded to be satisfied with the Executive's *intentions* and would approve no warrants until he had looked into the elaborate submissions he demanded. The infinite delays and the infinite personal prejudices of McCarl became a New Deal legend and infuriated a harassed military. It is not strange that he was the special object of attack when President Roosevelt's first study group on administrative organization reported.[7] Nevertheless, the Congress refused to limit his activities and the harassment of the Executive establishment continued. It was one of the most serious losses sustained by the Presidency in all its history.

[7] Report of the Committee on Administrative Reorganization, 1937.

★ 46 ★

IT HAS BEEN SUGGESTED THAT THE PASSAGE OF THE BUDGET AND
Accounting Act of 1921, in spite of opposition owing to ingrained congressional distaste, may have been because of a post-war demand for economy. This was largely true, although it ought not to be suggested that the earlier efforts of the reformers did not play an important part. They did. Years of earnest work had gone into the forming of a favorable opinion as well as the perfecting of an effective device. But propaganda had been based largely on the obvious inefficiency of the old system and on the promise of economies if a budget should be introduced. Indeed, the argument seems to later students of the government's operations a strangely narrow one. For the budget, as an instrument, soon came to have a tremendously expanded significance. It became in F. D. Roosevelt's time and later a means for central planning, for maintaining the economy in full running flow, for continuing improvement of operations, and for helping to make and enforce many decisions of the presidential office. This did not happen at once. It was not even envisaged as Roosevelt entered on his duties in 1933; but as the efforts for recovery and then for advance toward a posture of defense intensified, the budget as an instrument became more important with every passing year.

But the early reformers were not concerned with such matters as this. They were thinking of what they called "the *business* of the government," thus appealing to the prestige of private endeavor. The Bureau provided for in the Act was to formulate a financial plan for the fiscal year just ahead, no more. It was placed in the Treasury Department, but it was made clearly subordinate to the President, and its Director was made responsible to him. In each Department there was to be a budget officer who would submit estimates to the Bureau. The Bureau's investigators would hold hearings to determine the validity of the requests and, in the light of the President's policy, would reduce the whole to one document. This constituted the request of the money-spending Branch to the money-granting Branch.[1]

The President now had a preview of Executive operations for a year ahead, and so did the Congress. The theory was that if the Congress insisted on ignoring it the responsibility for the departures would have to be accepted. Unfortunately the Congress had no sense of responsibility. Its committees did not hesitate to reshape the presidential estimates, and they had no respect whatever for the President's cautions concerning revenues to cover expenditures. This part of the hoped-for reform was only very gradually, and with groaning reluctance, accepted. For many years the committees continued to behave much as they had before the Budget Act had been passed. But the President did have a noticeably better control over the Departments under his supervision. The Bureau began to act as his eyes and ears in finding out what was taking place and in modifying or changing administrative actions. And slowly some order did creep into congressional deliberations.

From the reformers' point of view, the budget accomplished at once only a small part of what had been hoped, and it was not long before suggestions for a further reform were being made. None found favor, and the system inherited by Roosevelt was not much changed from that of the first few years. But he understood it thoroughly and even before he took office was scheming to reduce congressional inroads on the budget as submitted. One of the reasons he felt this to be important was his belief that a balanced budget was necessary to the plan for recovery he had in mind. Only if expenditures were brought under control could inflation be checked, taxes reduced, and business confidence restored—this was what he had been told by such advisers as Bernard Baruch and conservative financiers, and it was what he at first appeared to believe. If businessmen regained confidence they would resume their activities, now restricted, and would again provide employment. This was the theory, and it could be carried out only by the strictest control of expenditures. It was for this reason that Lewis W. Douglas was chosen to be Budget Director. It was illustrative of his attitude that he persuaded Roosevelt to sign a stop order which brought to a halt such public works as Hoover had begun. The effect, naturally, was to make matters already desperate somewhat worse, and the new President soon had to reverse his "confidence" policy and adopt one of expansion. But his respect for the Budget Bureau and his support of

---

[1] The budget messages soon assumed a regular form, having two parts. The first had to do with the general financial condition of the government (income and outgo), and the second with proposed expenditures.

its functions were not affected. And it was in his Administration that its usefulness in a larger role was gradually extended.

The budget need not always restrict and reduce; it might also show the way to larger responsibilities. When Douglas had left the Roosevelt Administration in anger because of the reversal of the "confidence" policy, he was succeeded by more amenable Directors,[2] whose enterprising minds understood these possibilities. The Bureau really became in Roosevelt's later years his most effective administrative arm. He needed one. The expansion of the emergency agencies required the spending of large sums beyond the revenue resources of the government, and there were possibilities in this that the politicians were not slow to understand. To furnish relief, finance vast public works, undertake new enterprises and projects, and yet maintain some sort of central control was a tremendous task; considering its size and the need for haste, it was not at all badly done.

When the President got around to a more thorough reorganization of the Executive Branch than he had been able to carry out in his first term, his committee of experts was critical of the budget.[3] But it was also critical of the whole Executive Branch. And its recommendations constituted an indictment of considerable severity. We cannot consider the *Report* of this committee at the length it deserves. It can be summarized, however, by quoting the President's letter of transmittal when he sent it to the Congress; from it something can be learned, as well, of Roosevelt's quality in the role of administrator:

> I address this message to the Congress as one who has had experience as a legislator, as a subordinate in an executive department, as the chief executive of a State, and as one on whom, as President, the constitutional responsibility for the whole of the executive branch of the government has lain for four years . . .
> The executive structure of the government is sadly out of date . . . Theodore Roosevelt, William H. Taft, Woodrow Wilson and Herbert Hoover made repeated but not wholly successful efforts to deal with the problem. Committees of the Congress have also rendered distinguished service through their efforts to point the way to improvement . . . The opportunity and the need for action now come to you and to me. If we have faith in our republican

[2] The first of these was Daniel W. Bell, a Treasury official, who presently was succeeded by Harold D. Smith, one of the most important figures in the later Roosevelt Administration. He was a wise and liberal adviser. Something of his caliber can be gathered by reading his small book, *The Management of Your Government* (New York, 1945).

[3] Charles E. Merriam, Louis Brownlow, and Luther E. Gulick. It was called the Committee on Administrative Management.

form of government, and in the ideals upon which it has rested for 150 years, we must devote ourselves to making that government efficient . . .

The Committee on Administrative Management (appointed over a year ago) points out that no enterprise can operate effectively if set up as is the Government today. There are over 100 separate departments, boards, commissions, corporations, authorities, agencies, and activities through which work is being carried on. Neither the President nor the Congress can exercise effective supervision and direction over such a chaos of establishments, nor can overlapping, duplication, and contradictory policies be avoided.

The Committee has not spared me; they say, what has been common knowledge for twenty years, that the President cannot adequately handle his responsibilities; that he is overworked, that it is humanly impossible . . . for him fully to carry out his constitutional duty as Chief Executive because he is overwhelmed with minor details and needless contacts arising directly from the bad organization and equipment of the Government. I can testify to this . . .

The Committee does not spare the Comptroller General for his failure to give the Congress a prompt and complete audit each year, totally independent of administration, as a means of holding the Executive truly to account; nor for his unconstitutional assumption of executive power; nor for the failure to keep the accounting system up to date . . .

The Committee criticizes the use of boards and commissions in administration, condemns the instrumentalities, and points out that the practice of creating independent regulatory commissions, who perform administrative work in addition to judicial work, threatens to develop a "fourth branch" of the government for which there is no sanction in the Constitution. Nor does the Committee spare the inadequacy of the Civil Service system.

To meet this situation the Committee presents a five point program . . . :

1. Expand the White House staff so that the President may have a sufficient group of able assistants in his own office;

2. Strengthen and develop the managerial agencies of the Government, particularly those dealing with the budget and efficiency research, with personnel and planning, as management arms of the Chief Executive;

3. Extend the merit system upward, outward, and downward to cover practically all non-policy-determining posts; reorganize the Civil Service system as a part of management under a single, responsible, Administrator . . .

4. Overhaul the one hundred independent agencies, etc., and place them by Executive Order within one of the following major executive departments: State, Treasury, War, Justice, Post Office, Navy, Conservation, Agriculture, Commerce, Labor, Social Welfare, Public Works . . .

5. Establish accountability of the Executive to the Congress by providing a genuine independent post-audit of all fiscal transactions by an Auditor General, and restore to the Executive complete responsibility for accounts and current transactions.

As you will see, this program rests solidly upon the Constitution and upon the American way of doing things. There is nothing in it which is revolutionary, as every element is drawn from our own experience either in government or large-scale business. . . .

In placing this program before you I realize that it will be said that I am recommending the increase of the powers of the Presidency. This is not true. The Presidency as established in the Constitution has all of the powers that are required.

In spite of timid souls in 1787 who feared effective government the Presidency was established as a single strong chief executive office in which was vested the entire executive power of the National Government, even as the legislative power was placed in the Congress and the judicial in the Supreme Court.

What I am placing before you is not a request for more power, but for the tools of management and the authority to distribute the work so that the President can effectively discharge those powers which the Constitution now places upon him . . .

What followed this request was one of those farcical performances which are so often incident to the recovery of congressional aplomb after a period of abasement. The President had just won the election of 1936, after dominating the events of the four years preceding, and, presuming himself to be at the height of his prestige, had demanded of the Congress the Court reorganization plan—the same Congress, more or less, that had delegated to him so many powers in the past. This request, however, occasioned a first-class uprising among the outraged conservatives who by now regarded the Court as the special—and almost only—bulwark of their privileges. Four years of the New Deal had frightened them to the depths, but some recovery of their initiative and their incomes had given them the courage to oppose any further inroads on their privileges. The source of the evil they fought was clearly enough in the White House. They were not disposed to allow it any more power than it already possessed.

Reorganization of the Executive could have as its intent either the enhancement or the diminution of Executive power. When the Senate conservatives heard that the President had appointed a Committee on Administrative Reorganization, they were glad to have the Senate adopt a resolution for the investigation of the Executive agencies "with a view toward co-ordination." The President suggested it, obviously not expecting a hostile committee. But when Senator Harry F. Byrd of Virginia was made chairman, Roosevelt must have realized what was coming. Byrd was by now at the forefront of the anti-Roosevelt movement and the spokesman for the anti-New Deal bloc. The Brookings Institution, once a source of plans for government reform but then a kind of research organ for the conservatives, was given the task of preparing recommendations. And a series of such suggestions were made.

Nothing came of all this during that year of fuss and fury. The President had rightly anticipated that he would be said to be reaching for more power, but he had obviously not expected that the opposition would generate such violent energy. He was called dictator in a hundred different variations by ingenious orators. The reorganization bill was associated with the furious rejection of the Court reorganization bill, and the session ended with nothing having been done.[4]

The President's own note about this affair and the subsequent approval of an amended bill appears in his *Papers*.[5]

The most irrational arguments imaginable were advanced against

[4] All this was the more farcical because it was so generally conceded that reorganization was badly needed, though there was disagreement, as would be expected, about some of its detail. In fact, other Presidents, including Hoover, had asked for, and got, certain changes; and under the Economy Act of 1932 Hoover had been given freedom to reorganize. In December of 1932 he had sent a plan of reorganization to the Congress for approval; but by then he had been defeated and it was said that the new President ought to have the opportunity to do his own reorganizing. In the Treasury appropriation bill of 1933 a two-year power to transfer or abolish agencies and functions had been granted Roosevelt. But he had not been able to make up his mind in the midst of so much activity. He had, however, been pressed, particularly by the members of the National Resources Committee, and had finally appointed Merriam, Brownlow, and Gulick. At the same time he had suggested the collaborating congressional committee, and it was this that had turned into the Byrd-Brookings rival of the President's group.

[5] *The Public Papers and Addresses of [President] Franklin D. Roosevelt*, 13 vols., compiled by Samuel I. Rosenman (New York, 1941), IV (1938), 180 ff.

the bill, the most frequently stated of which was the bland assertion that the proposals were unprecedented and dictatorial, and involved an abdication by the Congress of its constitutional legislative functions.

Few of the opponents of reorganization knew, or were willing to admit, that practically all the proposals of the President's Committee had been either recommended or put into effect for brief periods under previous administrations. Recognizing that reorganization can best be accomplished by the executive, the Congress in 1903, 1912, 1917, 1919, and 1932 had vested power in the President to transfer governmental agencies by executive order . . .

A barrage of telegrams descended upon the members of the Senate and the House. The charge of "dictator," which at first seemed such a flagrant distortion of the facts as not to justify recognition, soon was conjured into a real fear in the minds of many people. Some radio orators, demagogues, a large part of the press and many of the pernicious Congressional lobbies served to deluge Congressmen with telegrams. What these people were really seeking to accomplish was not so much to block this particular legislation, as to try to discredit the administration so as to block any further thought of social reform, and, incidentally, reduce the effectiveness of its reform program by preventing efficiency generally in government. . . .

After the tumult and the shouting of the 1938 fight had died, the reactionary opponents of administrative reorganization apparently felt that their purpose had been accomplished. When a very similar reorganization bill was proposed in 1939, it passed with little opposition . . .

But in a later note in the same volume, rather serious changes from the original bill were noted:

The Act did not embody several of the original recommendations . . . It failed to include any provisions for developing the General Accounting Office and the Comptroller General into an independent post-auditing agency. It exempted a number of independent agencies from the terms of the Act. It did not touch upon the suggestion that a single headed administrator be established to direct the Civil Service Administration. [The recommendations of the Committee regarding civil service were later carried out, however, through the establishment of the Liaison office for Personnel Management.] Finally, it made no provision for the addition of Departments of Public Works and Social Welfare . . . However, the Act did authorize the appointment of six administrative assistants as recommended . . .

During 1939 and 1940 I submitted five reorganization plans, all of which became effective when the Congress defeated moves to vote them down.[6]

It may be as well to pursue this matter to the point of seeing what these reorganization plans amounted to before going back to a consideration of the New Deal itself as an example of the Rule of Responsibility. It is obvious that the President did not get nearly all the freedom for reorganization that he asked for. The pre-auditing nuisance was not abated; and special-interest groups successfully protected many of the independent agencies, either in the law or by unwritten agreement. Still, he was able to improve his own office.

During the few months after passage of the Act he sent to the Congress the first of the several proposals mentioned in his note. By the end of the year his office had a new and much more effective organization. For the first time the Presidency, as an operating mechanism, was something more than an informal group of assistants surrounding a principal. What was done, in effect, was to set up an Executive Office with a formal organization of its own and to transfer to it three management arms: (1) Budget and Administrative Research, (2) Planning, and (3) Personnel. Budget he transferred from Treasury, and Planning from Interior (where it had been growing under Secretary Ickes's guidance). Personnel was difficult. It was one of those exempted from the effect of the Act. He had to be content with appointing an assistant to deal with the Civil Service Commission. In addition to this, he established three new agencies which obviously were intended to become full-scale Departments: Security, Works, and Loans. These, he explained, had become necessary because of multiplying responsibilities centered in the Federal government but scattered among many operating divisions. That duties had multiplied was no exaggeration, as everyone knew who had lived through the years just past and seen the New Deal burgeon in many-faceted immensity.

The Executive Office of the Presidency now began to have its locus in the old State, War, and Navy building next door to the White House on the west. Its personnel had outgrown any possible expansion of the West Wing and would, in fact, soon be too large for its new home. From this time on it could be seen how important the work of the Budget Bureau could be. Several years before (in 1935) the Bureau had begun to have a small research and investigation unit. There was added a new Division of Administrative Management, divided into four sections whose names convey an idea of their duties: Management Counsel, Administrative and Fiscal Reorganization, Investigation, and

[6] Ibid., 207.

Defense Organization. None of these was intended to reach decisions on policy. They were to co-ordinate, to give advice, and to furnish information to the President.

The transfer to the Executive Office of the planning function under the name of National Resources Planning Board was another move in that agency's unhappy history. Its members—and the President—had never been quite clear about its place in the government. It had at first been an adjunct of the Public Works Board, then had gained more autonomy as the National Resources Planning Committee. It had carried out some useful surveys in the conservation field, had sponsored planning units in the state governments, and had made cautious suggestions concerning policy. But it had not ventured into the fiscal field and had tried to conciliate both Executive Departments and the Congress. It never possessed the necessary independence and review authority for genuine planning, and it was always feeble and insecure. It was strangled a little later by an impatient Congress (in 1943), to almost no one's regret.[7]

But the general effect of the reorganizations of that year was to advance the Presidency, in its administrative phases, into entirely new territory. The active contacts the Executive must somehow maintain were reduced to a realistic number; he was given assistance for better supervision over the old Departments, and the information coming to him on which his decisions could be based was considerably augmented.

It remains to be said about this that President Roosevelt was the kind of person who could make use of these instruments with immense effectiveness. It had been a notable characteristic of Wilson and his successors that they had almost no interest in the face of the land or in changing the nation into an organism competent to match its promise and meet its responsibilities. Roosevelt was interested in everything to be seen—the design of its post offices, its roads, its hospitals and power facilities (these, especially, since from the days of his Governorship he had carried on a feud with the private power interests)—and had a great fondness for its forests, its parks, its rivers, and its plains. To him the land he called his own was one vast home area, to be

[7] It could be said, as will be noted, to have been succeeded by the Council of Economic Advisers and a Joint Congressional Committee on the Economic Report provided for in the Full Employment Act of 1946. This too had only advisory functions. The author's views about this effort were summarized in "The Utility of the Future in the Present," *Public Administration Review*, VIII, 1948, and (with E. C. Banfield) "Government Planning at Mid Century," *Journal of Politics*, May 1951. Cf. also *The Place of Planning in Society*, San Juan, 1945.

improved and beautified, to be given to another generation in the condition he had dreamed for it. And the means for care and improvement of all this vast estate were perhaps his deepest concern.

He was an outward-turning man, but one of firm convictions; he had none of the theoretical interests of Wilson, but he had as firm a grip on the presidential powers and as exalted a view of his duties. He meant to make his visions materialize, and, on the whole, they were ones that could materialize. What he did for the nation in a physical way—with the use of the vast public works funds at his disposal and his improved administrative machine—was, if it could all be visualized at once, gloriously immense. That was the part of the New Deal in which his gusto was most evident. He had genuine joy in the work of forest improvement, in the vast number of water and sewer systems made possible for communities large and small, in the roads and bridges built, and in the ponds for conserving water scattered all across the short-grass country where the droughts struck so devastatingly, as well as in the vast spectacular power and waterway projects which were better known.

But even these were not the heart of his concern. That was the people of America, hard hit by depression and not in too affluent circumstances even before the hard times had arrived. The common folk had not shared in the booming prosperity of the New Era. During all the Republican years since Wilson, when the productivity of the industrial machine was increasing and financial speculation was so much the center of attention, real wages had been standing still or dropping, and living conditions in cities and on the farms had worsened rather than bettered.[8] He had pondered these things. When he came to the Presidency, he had not known what to do about all or even many of the ills besetting the nation. But he meant to find out if he could, and at any rate he meant to try something. His trying constituted the New Deal.[9]

[8] He learned a great deal from his stays at Warm Springs in western Georgia, where he went often between 1924 and 1932 for treatment of his crippled legs. That country was suffering not only from the disadvantages of all agriculture at that moment but also from the terrible visitation of the boll weevil. He got about the countryside there and came into close communication with farmers who were ready to instruct him in their troubles. He was much moved.

[9] For his own account of the preliminaries to the Reorganization Act of 1939, see various passages in *The Public Papers*, 1938 and 1939 vols. The reorganization of the Executive Office is fully covered in Item 125 of the 1939 vol. at pp. 490 ff.

★ 47 ★

WE COME NOW TO THE NEW DEAL AND TO FRANKLIN D. ROOSEVELT, who burst the bonds of the Presidency as none of his predecessors had been able to do and who strengthened it immensely for its new obligations to the nation—and even beyond the nation to the world.

We must do our best, in considering the Roosevelt contributions, to keep in mind our restricted subject here. He becomes, as he is studied, so refulgent a personality that confinement in any matter he touched is difficult. Wanderings from our purpose could be almost endless. And this is the more true because his influence on the Presidency was not so much formal, not registered so much in describable change, as the sort of enlargement that comes from enhancement, now capturing a people's trust. It was already, because of his strong predecessor Presidents, the cynosure of American eyes; it became immensely more so during his tenure. He was a kind of sun, lending light to duller objects around and spreading energy throughout the society he illumined. But this we must take for granted and describe in more pedestrian terms where he reshaped the office and to what pattern. When we try to do this, we at once find ourselves making categories. They may not be very satisfactory, but they somehow help us to think, as we must, in specific terms. So the list might run: recovery, reform, welfare, habilitation, war, and peace. Such divisions are not very satisfactory; they tend to intermingle and they do not correspond precisely with any chronology. Yet they may help in understanding what Roosevelt felt he had to do. They are, in a way, the measure of the Rule of Responsibility any President would afterward have to accept and which this one assumed with no hesitation or reservation.

For recovery there were the fiscal measures—for instance, "going off gold," for which it was necessary to prohibit transactions in the metal and require all of it to be deposited in the government's keeping, and later the buying of gold to raise the prices of other goods in relation to it; and there were the rescue measures, such as loans to banks with "frozen" assets, to businesses, to home owners, and to farmers. For recovery and welfare combined there were the relief and public works undertakings. For welfare and habilitation combined there were the Civilian Conservation Corps, the Tennessee Valley Authority, and many of the public works, such as housing and municipal projects. For welfare there was the Social Security system. For habilitation there were the conservation measures and all the extensive betterments of the national plant —roads, water and power projects, parks and forests. Then for war and for peace there were the vast expansions of army, navy, supply facilities, and later on the measures of assistance to the Allies and preparations for the United Nations.

This whole undertaking was not so different in kind from Wilson's; but its scope and intensity, as well as its prolongation, were far in excess of his. The New Deal and the New Freedom had likenesses; they were out of the same philosophy; but the later one had to be measured to a nation grown beyond its old confines and speeded up by invention and ingenuity. It was this that underlined so vividly both Roosevelt's courage and dash and his uncertainty of direction. For the dichotomy of Wilson's dependence at once on a strong centralized Presidency and an industrial system running itself to suit itself was projected now into a far more difficult situation. Wilson had had no depression on his hands when he came to office, only a calendar of reforms to be accomplished. Roosevelt had the worst industrial paralysis of all time to cure as well as an agenda for reform to get through—and sometimes they conflicted.

For instance, the "confidence" so insistently demanded of him by business leaders and by many of his business-minded associates was inconsistent, to say the least, with the legislation demanded by the Brandeis followers who had his ear. He opted to change the rules for bankers and the purveyors of securities while the recovery was still not by any means secure. About this he had fewer qualms than about the principles involved in the National Industrial Recovery Act and the Agricultural Adjustment Act (one part of it). For these were measures which projected a new relationship between the industrial world and the world of government, one in which there was an intermingling of powers and a conception of the national productive apparatus as a functioning whole. And this was anathema to the Brandeis progressives. The old Justice was, in fact, furious and let his displeasure be known.

In this matter Roosevelt simply retreated, pretending, like a child caught with his hand in the cookie jar, that the whole thing had been a mistake.[1] And although some parts of the outlawed recovery program

---

[1] For an account of the New Deal period and the various measures undertaken and carried through, together with some assessment of successes and failures, the reader may care to consult the author's *The*

were subsequently re-enacted in forms more acceptable to the Court—or possibly, it might be said, acceptable to a chastened Court—the "partnership between business and government" which was at the heart of NRA was abandoned. The period following—roughly that after 1935 —has been called, with good reason, the "Second New Deal." It characteristically concentrated on welfare. To this there might be conservative objection on moral grounds—it would ruin the workers' characters, and so on—but not on constitutional ones. The power to tax and the power to spend, so long as they were not intermingled (thus making the tax fall on some specific individuals for the benefit of others), could not be questioned. On this principle the Roosevelt economy became a very different one from that old one of unmitigated exploitation which even Wilson's efforts had not changed much. It began really to honor the principle of equality; it did give its citizens security—which, the conservatives insisted, took from them all incentive to produce—and in doing this it gave the economic system an incidental stability. It made sure that consumers would never be entirely without the incomes necessary to the support of the industrial system. But it did not move toward collectivism.

Franklin D. Roosevelt may have been a confused and uncertain economic philosopher, but he was firm and direct enough about the intention to build into the system the security and fairness it had never before possessed. He had been clear about this ever since, as Governor, he had been faced with the problems of depression in one state. He had learned that there was not much that a Governor could do; what there was to do, he did; but in weighing his responsibility he was forced over and over to consider the scope of government. He refused to accept a narrow definition; and, as the role of presidential aspirant became more immediate, the definition tended to widen. As a nominated candidate, he castigated his opponent for not using the powers of his office to overcome the crisis and promised, if elected, to use them himself to the full.

Representative of his mood as he approached candidacy was his message to the state legislature in 1932. Speaking of the problems of depression, he mentioned specifically unemployment, the risks of old age, the need for banking reform and several labor measures, such as

---

Democratic Roosevelt (New York, 1957), Arthur M. Schlesinger, Jr.'s *The Coming of the New Deal*, Basil Rauch's *History of the New Deal* (New York, 1944), etc., or various other books. There are many of them, written from many points of view. Again it must be recalled that the purpose here is a special one, not historical; and a general knowledge of events is assumed.

the minimum wage and workmen's compensation. And he denounced the political leaders who had allowed the crisis to develop:

> In the field of private endeavor we have retained in large degree, perhaps, the personal liberty of the individual; but we have lost in recent years the economic liberty of the individual—this has been swallowed up in the specialization of industry, of agriculture, and of distribution, and has meant that the cog can move only if the whole machine is in perfect gear. We thus see on one hand an overproduction of food and clothing and close by many millions of men and women who lack the medium of exchange—money—with which to ward off starvation and nakedness . . .

It can be seen that it was not too long a jump from this kind of perception to the conclusion that the money to "ward off starvation and nakedness" had to be provided somehow; and, if it was, the "whole machine" would again be "in perfect gear." And that is where the New Deal excelled—in keeping firmly in mind, throughout all the vagaries of reform and of fiscal experiment, the principle of the English economist Hobson, and of some Americans, that underconsumption and underprivilege were at the root of the recurrent economic troubles. Roosevelt was much more certain at first that measures to remedy lack of income were necessary to relieve individual hardship than that they were necessary to the continuous and efficient operation of the "whole machine"; but he came to the theory of stable relationships quite logically, and his later policy of government spending to meet the deficit of private spending was vigorously pursued.

But it is clear that even so early he accepted for government, and for himself as Chief of a state government and prospectively as Chief of the national one, the responsibility of remedying the incapacity of the individual. This acceptance had at its heart the conception that if government represented all citizens it represented the disadvantaged ones too and that Governors and Presidents had a first duty to those who most needed their intervention.

In this same message he went on to say that an increasing concentration of wealth and of the power that wealth controls did not guarantee an intelligent or fair use of that power. He had no wish to condemn any of those who were harassed by contemporary problems. Many of those who had "run after false gods—many of the leaders of American thought in government and in business"—appreciated the errors of their teaching:

> Nevertheless, more than two years have gone by and these leaders have as yet shown us few plans for the reconstruction of a better ordered civilization . . . the public asks that they be

given a new leadership which will help them and at the same time give definite recognition to a new balance based on the right of every individual to make a living out of life.

If this seems a little inchoate, that is because the speaker's ideas were not yet clear. Nor was he certain how far he ought to go in asserting the responsibility he obviously believed the government should assume. It will be noticed that he spoke not only of recovery but of "a better ordered civilization," and he returned to this in a later paragraph:

> The times and the present needs call for a leadership which insists on the permanence of our fundamental institutions and at the same time demands that by governmental and community effort our business and industry be nourished and encouraged back to a basis made more sound and more firm by the lessons of the experience through which we are passing. Let us seek not merely to restore. Let us restore and at the same time remodel.[2]

The passages from this message are representative. There is a steady building up of a firmer and clearer conception as time passes and preparation for the Presidency becomes more imminent. It should have been no surprise to anyone that, as President, his understanding of governmental responsibilities and of his own was well considered. When he spoke to the nation in his first inaugural, with the depression at its deepest stage, he went the whole way. He accepted responsibility for recovery. Also, beyond that, he indicated his awareness of the need for reconstruction. This address is certainly as famous among state papers as any presidential pronouncement; and this is not only because of the reminder that the nation had not been stricken by any plague of locusts and that its productive power was really unimpaired, but because it offered to take action—action of whatever sort should seem appropriate—to overcome the crisis. This immediate and uncompromising invoking of the Rule of Necessity was notice to the Congress that it must keep out of the way and let the President get to work:

> It is to be hoped that the normal balance of Executive and legislative authority may be wholly adequate to meet the unprecedented task before us. But it may be that an unprecedented demand and need for undelayed action may call for temporary departure from that normal balance of public procedure.
>
> I am prepared under my constitutional duty to recommend

[2] *The Public Papers of [Governor] Franklin D. Roosevelt, 1932* (Albany, 1932), 29 ff.

the measures that a stricken nation in the midst of a stricken world may require. These measures, or such other measures as the Congress may build out of its experience and wisdom, I shall seek, within my constitutional authority, to bring to speedy adoption.

But in the event that the Congress shall fail to take one of these two courses, and in the event that the national emergency is still critical, I shall not evade the clear course of duty that will then confront me. I shall ask the Congress for the one remaining instrument to meet the crisis—broad Executive power to wage a war against the emergency, as great as the power that would be given to me if we were in fact invaded by a foreign foe.[3]

But instead of beginning to act before calling the Congress into special session, as Lincoln had done, he convened a meeting for five days later. It is true that he issued an important proclamation even before that, declaring a bank holiday and prohibiting gold and silver exports as well as foreign-exchange transactions; but these actions were ratified immediately when the Congress met. There was no long wait for legislative support.[4]

During the special session of the Congress running from March 9 to June 16, usually spoken of, with only slight inaccuracy, as "the hundred days," the Congress behaved as every Chief Executive always hopes it will behave—but as it seldom does. Not all the legislation asked for was passed in the exact form requested; not quite all of it was even passed at all; but there was amazing compliance with the President's demands. During that period both NRA and AAA were enacted; the TVA and the CCC were established; relief and public works were begun. And on his own the President announced a new "Good Neighbor Policy" and entertained a parade of foreign statesmen, in preparation

[3] *The Public Papers and Addresses of* [*President*] *Franklin D. Roosevelt*, 1933 vol., 11 ff.

[4] This was fortunate, because the gold action was based on an Act of 1917 which had been in part repealed; and it was not certain whether the authority appealed to was still in effect. The reference to consultation with Senator Walsh, who was to have been Attorney General, appended to the proclamation in the *Papers,* describes the matter more confidently than was warranted. There was, in fact, a good deal of doubt. That the action was nevertheless taken does not seem to me to need concealment. But it is clear that the President preferred afterward to have it seem that he had acted altogether legally rather than by invoking the Rule of Necessity.

for an international economic conference.[5] In most of the Acts, the one notable common characteristic was the delegation of broad powers to the Executive. When the Congress went home in June, practically everything except authorization remained yet to be done; the Executive now must proceed with organization and administration. The President had asked for power and it had been given. The responsibility was his.

Nothing like it had ever happened before; and, in spite of general acknowledgment that also there had never before been a comparable crisis, there were some murmurs of discontent. These would before long rise to howls, widely heard because the owners of newspapers would be, if possible, more disaffected than other privileged characters who feared for their prerogatives. But for the moment the relief from the devastating fears of early spring was so general that dissent was smothered. Besides, Roosevelt at once began to demonstrate that he understood the Presidency in all its phases as very few of his predecessors had done at the beginning. Usually a period of learning had been necessary, sometimes very costly if the honeymoon was allowed to pass without accomplishment. But Roosevelt used every moment of his privileged time.

The first "fireside chats" and the first press conferences established the new President as more than the man of action he had held himself out to be in his inaugural. He was also aware of the need for communication with the electorate, and he began at once an "educational" effort which lasted throughout his Presidency. He proved to have a special talent for this. Whether he spoke over the radio or used the press, his ideas gained the widest possible circulation; and, in spite of publishers' opposition, his rapport with White House reporters was such that his access to print could seldom be blocked. The result was a continuous stream of propaganda reaching directly those who were affected by the policies of the Administration. There was such a response as had been known before only in the first Roosevelt's Presidency.

That the new President had from the first been aware of the wide responsibility a modern Executive must accept surprised many observers who regarded themselves as experts. There had been some question about his quailing before Tammany while he was Governor; he had seemed to equivocate during the campaign; and many of his policies were inconsistent with others. All this seemed to indicate a confusion of mind. But it could now be seen that what had gone before was the behavior of a professional gaining the Presidency. And since he was a professional, he knew exactly what was called for both before

[5] Scheduled, before his inauguration, to take place in July. It was an unhappy event from which he extricated himself rather ungracefully. It is described in Moley's *After Seven Years*, op. cit.

and after gaining it. He was cautious in his bid but bold in office. His fireside chats went straight to the minds and hearts of a worried people; and his news conferences were handled in a manner so confidentially informal as to constitute almost a new medium of presidential expression.

He himself spoke just after his first election of this wide interpretation:

> The Presidency is not merely an administrative office. That is the least of it. It is pre-eminently a place of moral leadership.
>
> All of our great Presidents were leaders of thought at times when certain historic ideas in the life of the nation had to be clarified. Washington personified the idea of Federal Union. Jefferson practically originated the party system as we know it by opposing the democratic theory to the republicanism of Hamilton. This theory was reaffirmed by Jackson.
>
> The great principles of our government were forever put beyond question by Lincoln. Cleveland, coming into office following an era of great political corruption, typified rugged honesty. Theodore Roosevelt and Wilson were both moral leaders, each in his own way and for his own time, who used the Presidency as a pulpit.
>
> That is what the office is—a superb opportunity for reapplying to new conditions the simple rules of human conduct to which we always go back. Without leadership alert and sensitive to change, we are bogged up or lose our way.[6]

And it was obviously with this conception of the office in mind that he faced the emergency he inherited. It could be argued that he had learned from both Theodore Roosevelt and Wilson; it was their ideas that he seemed to personify. But, if so, he enlarged those ideas almost beyond recognition. The delegations of power for which he asked, and which were given, were so extensive as to suggest the substitution of Executive for legislative lawmaking. This was especially true of NRA and AAA.

In the NRA it was provided that he might approve "codes of fair competition" to be proposed by industries themselves. These, when written, seemed to embody the privileges industrialists had long been denied. The very conspiracies in restraint of trade aimed at by the anti-trust Acts since the nineties were now legalized. Prices could, in some instances, be fixed; markets could be apportioned; and cost-cutting practices could be outlawed. It was true that concessions were made to labor. Through the operations of clause 7(a) child labor was

---

[6] The New York *Times,* November 13, 1932.

abolished, women's employment was regulated, and collective bargaining was legitimized. But there were many, even of those who had voted for the law, who were aghast at the content of the codes. This included, of course, all the old progressives, who saw in these new administrative provisions the defeat of their long struggle against big business. Perhaps they might not have objected to the making of law by the Executive if it had appeared to be a different kind of law—the kind they understood Roosevelt to have promised. But as the codes were formulated, they seemed to them a confirmation of their contention that business could certainly not be trusted to govern itself, and also that the Executive could not be trusted to legislate in the public interest. He would always bargain for what seemed to him important—in this case labor gains—and would trade away what seemed less important—in this case regulations against the restraint of trade.

When in 1935 a unanimous Court declared NIRA to be unconstitutional, it was noted that one of the Justices was Brandeis. This was the progressive protest. The opinion was written by Justice Sutherland, who with McReynolds represented extreme reaction. This uniting of progressives and conservatives against Roosevelt was so formidable that, although he muttered darkly about "horse-and-buggy" thinking among the Justices, he did not attempt to have the law rewritten, as it might have been. Even the businessmen who gained most from the codes were by now so disaffected by other phases of the New Deal that they could not be counted on for support. It was clear that the day of blanket delegations to the President was over. He was not giving up, however; he was only biding his time. His answer to the Court would be made after another election had shown the Justices who had the nation's approval.

The AAA was also struck down by the Court, but for a different reason which did not go to the constitutionality of extending help to farmers in distress; and it was repassed in more acceptable form. The legislative delegation in this instance had taken an interesting form which ought to be noted. It amounted, in effect, to allowing the Executive a choice among several proposals for farm relief. These had been the subject of acute controversy for more than a decade, a controversy which had hardened into opposing crusades among contending farm organizations. Because of the fighting among themselves the farmers' representatives had never mustered the strength to pass and get approved legislation necessary to agricultural recovery. Even when bills had been passed they were vetoed by Coolidge and Hoover.

Roosevelt had demanded of the farmers' organizations that they agree on legislation as the price of his approval. This seemed impossible, so the device was hit on of writing into the law permission for the Secretary of Agriculture to use any one of several devices at his own discretion.

This amounted to passing to the Executive Branch a controversy that had tormented the Congress for years. The Congress was glad to get rid of it in this way. But it removed to the Department of Agriculture a bitter controversy which within a year caused a sensational explosion; the repercussions of this continued for some time.

The public generally was not much interested in these troubles. In fact, the President's careful cultivation of support, and his repeated explanations by radio, especially, turned them to good account. He was a vigilant leader trying his best, amid difficulties, to achieve recovery and reform. And sympathy for his effort registered itself in the election of 1936. There should have been a falling off in his majority after four years of controversial action and, to tell the truth, not too much recovery, but instead his popular majority increased and actually his party carried every state but two.[7]

Nevertheless, the Congress had recovered from its depression fears. Roosevelt's command of the electorate was difficult for legislators to swallow. And it was obvious that the conservative leaders—Democratic as well as Republican—smarted under the now-familiar taunt that they were "rubber stamps." It might have been predicted that an assertion of independence at almost any cost would be made at the first good opportunity. It was careless of Roosevelt to furnish that opportunity in the bill he sent to be passed reorganizing the Court—or "packing" it, as his opponents at once said.

[7] Maine and Vermont. The Roosevelt majority in 1932 was about seven million and in 1936 was about eleven million. The electoral vote in 1932 was 472 to 59 and in 1936 was 523 to 8. This second-term gain was unique in the history of elections.

★ 48 ★

THE ROOSEVELT SCHEME FOR REFORMING THE COURT HAS IMPOR-
tance for our study here not only because it represents an unusual presidential aggression but also because of its immediate catalyzing effect
in uniting all his potential enemies in one angry spasm of opposition
to show him where actually the weight of governmental power rested.
It was meant to reduce him to normal size as he had meant to reduce
the Court to what he regarded as its proper dimensions.

For a generation the Court had had two members who were said
to be "liberals": Holmes and Brandeis. Actually their philosophies were
in complete contrast. Brandeis became a consistent dissenter, but not
on the ground that the Court was incompetent to establish a philosophy
and to enforce it. This last was Holmes's point of view; he felt that a
changing society could not be held within the rigid bounds of a literally
interpreted Constitution but that it was for the legislature, and not the
Court, to determine what accommodations must be made. He was
scrupulously determined not to impose his ideas through Court interpretation; Brandeis, on the other hand, was determined that he would
impose his ideas if he got the chance. They were both dissenters, but
for opposing reasons.

The Court that rejected the New Deal legislation in Roosevelt's first
term still had Brandeis as a member, but it did not have Holmes; he
was only a memory. The Chief Justice was Charles Evans Hughes, who
had Holmeseian moments and who, as Roosevelt soon found out, was a
superb tactician in the upper reaches of governmental maneuver; there
were, besides, Stone and Cardozo, who were genuine liberals, and Roberts, who was hard to place; the rest[1] were so conservative as to be generally called reactionary. Roosevelt's opponents made a majority, and
most of them were aged—which the President used as a point of attack.
They were, he implied, too old to appreciate the problems of the modern

[1] Van Devanter, Sutherland, McReynolds, and Butler.

world. He proposed that they be allowed to retire on full pay and that for those who were over seventy and would not retire a coadjutor be appointed. He proposed a good deal else as well, but it was made to appear that he was attacking the "nine old men," several of whom were genuine liberals. It is not at all certain that the President did not have popular support for his proposal; but election was at the moment as far away as possible, and if his opponents were ever to humiliate him, this was the time. Even if he appealed for and got public support, it could be ignored.

The fight was for them advantageous. The well-fostered tradition of judicial dignity by now had the effect of making decisions seem to come from on high, to originate in a remote monopoly of wisdom and justice, not subject to question by ordinary men. It was this sanctity that the President invaded. All the congressional lawyers felt the outrage, and their colleagues elsewhere felt it just as strongly. Their fury was that of a respected institution threatened by revolution.

The sentiment might be that of a profession scorned, but the effect was to bring into immediate conflict again—as so often had happened in the past—the three Branches of government. This was the first serious struggle among them since the days of Reconstruction. But before we speak of the battle itself we must recount briefly the events leading up to it, and especially the aggression of the Court—as the President believed it to be—and its effect on the program for recovery and reform.

When on January 7, 1933, the Court decided adversely the "hot-oil" case, the whole structure of welfare legislation was brought into jeopardy.[2] Directly involved was Section 9 (c) of NIRA,[3] which gave the President authority to reduce the amount of oil in interstate commerce in conformance with the general purpose of the Act. It was unconstitutional, said the opinion, because it was a delegation of power belonging to the Congress without adequate controls or standards. Cardozo dissented in an opinion which, together with certain suggestions of the majority, made it seem that a few revisions would satisfy the Court. Administration lawyers at once undertook this rewriting, but opponents of the New Deal in the Congress succeeded in delaying action until the Court

[2] This included not only the National Industrial Recovery Act and the Agricultural Adjustment Act but also the Social Security Act, the laws subjecting public utility holding companies to Federal regulation, the National Labor Relations Act, etc., etc. Some of these were as yet only projects, such as the Social Security Act, but all that Roosevelt had in mind seemed to be jeopardized.

[3] This refers to the National Industrial Recovery Act, under the authority of which the National Recovery Administration (NRA) was established; the two sets of initials are sometimes confusing.

decided a case involving the whole Act. The Schechter decision came in May. For the remainder of the session the war between the President and the Court was an active one, with the Congress as the scene of action.

Matters were somewhat confused when the Court proceeded to uphold the abrogation of gold payments for private and public debts; but presently the Railroad Retirement Act was invalidated as not conforming with the "due process" clause of the Fifth Amendment.[4] Also, in a second objection, the Court found that there was no relation between pensions for workers and the safety of interstate commerce. These, like medical attention, education, and housing, were "really and essentially related to the social welfare of the worker, and therefore remote from any regulation of commerce as such."[5] But to this Chief Justice Hughes dissented and was joined by Cardozo, Stone, and Brandeis. Hughes thought pensions did have a relation to interstate commerce, and anyway, the Court had in other times held that employee compensation regulations were permissible, and these were indistinguishable from those now in question. Furthermore—and this was important—he felt that it was not the duty of the Court to pass on the wisdom of particular regulations of commerce by the Congress. But the majority decision did prevent railroad workers from receiving the benefits of the Act, and it seemed to indicate that any Social Security legislation would probably be rejected.

This was an affront to all those who were interested in the welfare of the workers, and because of this the President could count on support for circumventing it in some way.[6] But on May 27 another decision of especial significance to the Presidency was handed down. When in October 1933 the President had removed William E. Humphrey from the Federal Trade Commission, he had, the Court said, exceeded his

[4] Which said that no person "shall . . . be deprived of life, liberty, or property, without due process of law; nor shall private property be taken for public use, without just compensation."

[5] The cases referred to here begin with *Panama Refining Co.* vs. *Ryan*, 293 U.S. 388, and continue through *Railroad Retirement Board* vs. *Alton Railroad Co.*, 295 U.S. 330; *Humphrey's Executor* vs. *United States*, 295 U.S. 602; *Louisville Bank* vs. *Radford*, 295 U.S. 555; *Schechter Corporation* vs. *United States*, 295 U.S. 495; *United States* vs. *Butler*, 297 U.S. 1; *Ashwander* vs. *TVA*, 297 U.S. 288; *Carter* vs. *Carter Coal Co.*, 298 U.S. 238; *Morehead, Warden* vs. *New York ex rel. Tipaldo*, 298 U.S. 587.

[6] As actually happened. The railroads installed a voluntary universal plan before two substitute laws, enacted to replace the original Retirement Act, could be tested in Court. In 1937 new legislation of undoubted constitutionality was also passed.

powers. This case has been spoken of before as having significance in the history of the independent agencies; it had a special one in the context of New Deal events. The Federal Trade Commission, during the previous Republican Administrations, had practically ceased to serve the function assigned to it in the progressive philosophy and delegated to it by law. It was meant to secure compliance with the antitrust Acts and generally to ensure fair competition; it had, in fact, become a kind of appendage to the business system, engaged mostly in promoting the acceptance of codes of fair practice of the sort approved by big business. Moreover, the Securities Act of 1933 had given it the duty of supervising certain transactions, and the Recovery Act had provided that appeals from decisions of Code Authorities should go to it.

President Roosevelt requested Humphrey's resignation. It was not forthcoming. But a vacancy was needed to secure a Democratic majority.[7] Humphrey was a notorious reactionary, appointed by Hoover in 1931, and it was he who was picked for sacrifice. He refused, however, to admit that his unwelcome opinions could be equated with the "inefficiency" spoken of in the law as ground for removal, and insisted that he was still a member. He soon died and his executor sued for his back pay. The Court's opinion held that the Commission was an agent of the Congress and that its members could not be removed except for designated causes.

The President understood only too well the contribution this decision made to the already dangerous power of the Court; it was not the Congress which was being protected; it was the Court, determined to have the exclusive privilege of setting regulatory policies through review. But there were two more decisions on that same day (May 27, 1934). One invalidated the Frazier-Lemke Farm Bankruptcy Act, and the other the NIRA. The first refused recognition of the emergency as an occasion for suspending the operations of the "due process" clause of the Constitution. A bank might foreclose a defaulting farmer's property; otherwise it was unjustly deprived of its rights. The second was the sweeping rejection of the Recovery Act, which constituted the real declaration of war with the Executive.

This last opinion turned mostly on a principle that had a rather tenuous relation to interstate commerce.[8] The Congress could not regulate, the Court said, unless there was a *direct* relation between the behavior regulated and interstate commerce; an *indirect* relationship was not enough; if it were, "there would be virtually no limit to the federal

---

[7] Under the law not more than three of the five members could belong to one party.

[8] Although excessive delegation was also cited.

power and for all practical purposes we should have a completely centralized government."[9]

During the following week the President held three press conferences. In them he related at some length the pressure that was coming on him from those who wished to keep NRA in existence. He spoke more in sorrow, he intimated, than in anger. The lowering of wages and the increases of hours sure to result from uncontrolled competition would be inhuman.[10] He pointed out that the Court had been inconsistent too. When, for instance, injunctions against striking miners had been sought, the commerce clause had been broad enough; but when miners' wages and hours were being regulated, it was found to be very narrow. He said that turning back to the states control over the complexities of modern industry would create "a perfectly ridiculous and impossible situation." If this attempt prevailed, the nation would have been relegated "to horse-and-buggy definition of interstate commerce."

In this last phrase he had, as he at once recognized, a wonderfully effective slogan, the kind of weapon that might win his battle if he did not press it too hard. When the correspondents asked him to say what was "the way out," he refused to specify and changed the subject. They themselves spoke of historic conflicts among the Branches—that precipitated by the Dred Scott decision particularly—and asked whether a constitutional amendment would not be necessary. He would not say. But it was obvious that feverish consideration of means to meet the Court's aggression was going on in New Deal circles. There were those who felt it imperative to initiate an amendment giving the Federal government specific powers to regulate economic activities. Roosevelt must have considered, but he never acceded to, this solution. What way his mind was turning became apparent soon to those about him; but the actual preparation of the Court reorganization bill was left to the Attorney General, Homer Cummings, and its introduction was delayed until after the election and after the Court had offended further by

[9] The obvious embodiment in this of the sentiments of the author of *The Curse of Bigness* was noticed at once. It was a special blow to the President, who was known to be turning as rapidly as he could toward the Brandeis position and had, in fact, been trying to rush through the Congress curative amendments before the Supreme Court should deliver this blow.

[10] The pressure was not actually very intense, and, as we know, Roosevelt was in all probability relieved to have NRA eliminated at a time when he was making his economic turnaround, from a policy of "collectivization" to one of renewed "trust busting." He made no effort to have NIRA repassed in acceptable form, as was done with AAA.

handing down several more adverse decisions, including one invalidating the Agricultural Adjustment Act.

This opinion said that the Congress had "no power to enforce its commands on the farmer to the ends sought" by the Act. It followed that it could "not indirectly accomplish those ends by taxing and spending to purchase compliance." In this case Justices Stone, Cardozo, and Brandeis dissented. Brandeis may have felt that farmers, being small, were different from businesses, which might become big; and Stone wrote a dissent that seemed, in retrospect, more convincing than Roberts's opinion for the majority. Roberts's argument seemed somewhat defensive, an answer, perhaps, to the "horse-and-buggy" allusion which by now had passed into the list of metaphors so familiar as almost to be clichés:

> It is sometimes said that the Court assumes a power to overrule or control . . . the people's representatives. This is a misconception. . . . When an act of Congress is appropriately challenged in the courts . . . the judicial branch . . . has only one duty—to lay the article of the Constitution which is invoked beside the statute which is challenged and to decide whether the latter squares with the former. . . . This Court neither approves nor condemns any legislative policy . . .[11]

In 1936 a Soil Conservation and Domestic Allotment Act was passed as a substitute for the AAA, and the President signed it without comment about the Court; but the Democratic platform of that year said that if the problems of welfare—monopolies, child labor, minimum wages, relief for sufferers from disaster, etc.—could not be solved within the Constitution, the party would seek clarifying amendments such as would "assure to the legislatures of the several states, and the Congress of the United States, each within its proper jurisdiction, the power to enact those laws . . ." This might have been thought to be an opening for the President. During the campaign he might well have condemned the Court as the enemy of progress and have ended by asking for a mandate. But he did nothing of the kind. He ignored the platform and held the whole matter in abeyance until, in the full assurance of personal support, presumably for all his policies, he sent his bill to a surprised Congress in January 1937.

There had been a peaceable enough opening of the new session. The annual message had spoken of the Constitution, saying that it ought to be more widely studied and that if it were the discovery would be

---

[11] But a number of Justices had said that their colleagues did just that. Stone had recently said so; Holmes had always contended that it was a vice of the Court; and Cardozo had deplored the tendency.

made that it "could be used as an instrument of progress, and not as a device for prevention of action." Of the Judicial Branch, he said that it was "asked by the people to do its part in making democracy successful." This was interpreted as a kind of warning. There were before the Court more laws of the Second New Deal[12]—including the Labor Relations Act and the Social Security Act—and it was thought that the President meant to remind the Justices of the election results. It seemed to be a plea for restraint and co-operation.

But on February 5 his Judiciary Reorganization Bill was submitted for consideration along with a special message reminding the Congress of its powers over the judiciary. He spoke of the changes in other times in the number of Justices, of the need for an overhauling of the rules of procedure, and of his own duty to recommend such measures as he judged "necessary and expedient."[13]

The President was very evidently intent on a showdown; he had not forgiven the challenge to his leadership represented by the invalidations of the years just past. He meant to make it impossible in future for the Court to reject measures agreed on by the President and the Congress. But before long an important section of the Congress had made common cause with the Court. It soon seemed to be a struggle between the Presidency and the other two Branches. Roosevelt became stubborn; his liaison with Administration leaders in the Congress was careless, and more and more defections were announced. First to declare themselves were naturally the Republicans, then the conservative Democrats, and finally many of the liberals. The two worst occurrences were the volunteering of Senator Burton Wheeler for the leadership of the opposition[14] and the death, in the midst of the battle, of Senator Robinson of Arkansas, the Senate leader, who, tempted by the promise of one of the Justiceships to be opened up by the bill, had gone against his conservative preferences and was managing the fight for the bill in the Senate.

By March it had become probable that the President would fail to carry his measure unless something extraordinary was done. He did what other Presidents before him had found uniformly successful—he

[12] For the distinction to be made between the "first" and "second" New Deals, see the author's *The Democratic Roosevelt.*

[13] *Public Papers,* V (1937), 639 ff.

[14] Wheeler was so famous a progressive that he had been a running mate of La Follette in the presidential campaign of 1924, and he had been known for his courageous battle with the industrial interests in Montana against whom labor had an old grievance for outrageous exploitation. But for some time he had resented what he felt was Roosevelt's neglect.

went to the country. On March 4 he made a radio address to numerous Democratic gatherings holding victory dinners. In it he accepted the terms of battle as his enemies were defining them. "There is," he said, "as yet no definite assurance that the three-horse team of the American system of government will pull together." A few days later he made a fireside chat in which, after speaking of the welfare legislation jeopardized by the Court and describing his proposals in simple terms, he ended by saying:

> During the past half century the balance of power between the three great branches of the Federal Government has been tipped out of balance by the Courts in direct contradiction of the high purposes of the framers of the Constitution. It is my purpose to restore the balance. You who know me will accept my solemn assurance that in a world in which democracy is under attack, I seek to make American democracy succeed.[15]

But in the end his fight was lost, or at least his attempt to reorganize the Supreme Court so that it would be more amenable to democratic leadership. He did not admit that more than the immediate battle had been lost; he always afterward contended that the Court had given way so spectacularly as to make the reorganization seem unnecessary. But the fact was that the Rule of Restraint, recognized by the Chief Justice and also by Justice Roberts, thus making a majority for moderation, had defeated the President. The Court emerged with its prestige enhanced, even if with its powers impaired. The President said it would not have restrained itself if he had not forced the issue, and he was probably right; but the retreat of the judiciary left still unmarked the limits of judicial prerogative and the possibilities of presidential leadership.

In his later argument[16] he shifted his ground somewhat. He spoke as though, all along, he had been struggling to enhance the powers of the Congress, not of the Presidency:

> Whatever doubts were created by the old Court before the elections of 1936 have been practically all removed. There has been a reaffirmation of the ancient principle that the power to legislate resides in the Congress and not in the Court; and that the Court has no power or right to impose its own ideas of legislative policy, or its own social and economic views, upon the law of the land.

---

[15] *Public Papers and Addresses*, 1938, vol. 133.

[16] Particularly in the Introduction to the 1937 volume of the *Public Papers*.

But this was an overoptimistic estimate. Restraint had been used; but later Courts would go right on imposing their views by way of judicial review, their only guide being exactly that used by the other Branches —what they judged they could get away with, the time and circumstances being what they were.[17]

That this was destined to be an unchanging, although constantly varying, rule was made certain by the structure of the Constitution. We have seen that structure time and again impose upon overaggressive Branches the Rules of its architecture, but we have seen also that the one duty the Branches may not neglect is that of keeping a proper pressure on each other. This was not always understood. Hamilton, who had no very great part in the writing of the document and no very strong faith in it either, showed how he misunderstood its imperatives by saying in *The Federalist* (No. 78) when duty required him to invent arguments for ratification:

> To avoid any arbitrary discretion in the Courts it is indispensable that they should be bound down by strict rules and precedents, which serve to define and point out their duty in every particular case that comes before them.

Speaking of this passage, and reflecting on the nature of the judicial process, Professor Pritchett thought the Justices would always make law:

> If this view of the judge as automaton and of the judicial process as a ministerial function involving nothing more than the applying of agreed-on rules and precedents to individual situations were accurate, there would be no need to examine into the question of judicial alignments and motivation. It is true that for subordinate tribunals, in stable times, and in settled fields of law, the Hamiltonian statement is not too wide of the mark. But for a Supreme Court, operating in times of crisis, whose grist is almost entirely the hard cases, the difficult problems, the fields where new legislation needs interpretation, the areas of the law where precedents conflict or are nonexistent—on such a Court decisions must inevitably reflect the values of the Justices who make them . . .[18]

[17] Anyone who doubts that this is so is asked to examine *The Roosevelt Court* by C. H. Pritchett (New York, 1948). The later views were different ones, but they were imposed just the same.

[18] Ibid., 239. This generalization is given significant body by the studies of opinions, reduced to classification, to be found in Professor Pritchett's chapters.

★ 49 ★

IT WAS SAID EARLIER THAT ROOSEVELT'S PROGRAM MIGHT BE DI-
vided without too much straining into efforts for reform, welfare, habilitation, war, and peace. The failure of his attempt to restrict the latitude
of the Judicial Branch brought nearly to an end the period of reform,
welfare, and habilitation. There were some delayed successes. A developing recession in 1937 had to be checked by renewed spending, and
this resulted in more internal improvements. Also, the important Fair
Labor Standards Act was passed in 1938.[1] Generally, however, the relations between President and Congress were unfriendly and unco-
operative. There had coalesced a majority bloc made up of Republicans
and southern conservatives, and its members lost no opportunity to humiliate the President. As he moved into a new phase of policy, he had
to find the means to break up this union. His sense of urgency, after
the war began in Europe in 1939, was responsible for many compromises; but he found that southerners would support his defense measures if he would sacrifice the New Deal measures they so disliked.
And this was what he did. One after another the welfare measures
were dismantled or reduced in effectiveness, until finally only certain
labor measures, the Stock Exchange regulations, the banking laws, the
Social Security system, and a few others were left.

Until American participation in the war became imminent there was
no renewal of delegations such as had taken place in 1934 and 1935.

[1]But not without another outbreak of acrimonious criticism. No less
than seventy-two amendments were offered to the bill as drafted by Administration lawyers. And the Congress was hospitable to the arguments of
lobbyists for industries asking exemptions; also to the contention that
lower standards should be established for the South than for the North.
Chairman O'Connor of the House Rules Committee almost succeeded in
bottling up the bill in his committee, and only open denunciation by the
President brought it to a vote. The struggle made the already unhappy
relations between the Branches much worse.

There was one notable incident usually counted as a loss for the Presidency even in a period of generally eroding prestige. This was the so-called "purge" failure in 1938. There is some reason for thinking that the loss was perhaps a gain. Writing some years afterward, the President himself made an able justification of his interference in the primary election that year:

> . . . in a representative form of government there are usually two general schools of political belief—liberal and conservative. The system of party responsibility in America requires that one of its parties be the liberal party and the other be the conservative party. This has been the division by which they have identified themselves whenever crises have developed . . . In Jefferson's day, and Jackson's day, and in Lincoln's and Theodore Roosevelt's and Wilson's day, one group emerged clearly as liberals, opposed to the other—the conservatives . . .
>
> There can, of course, be no quarrel with anyone who sincerely subscribes to the principles of liberalism or conservatism. The quarrel in 1938 was with those who said they were liberals, but who, nevertheless, proceeded to stand in the way of all social progress by objecting to any measure to carry out liberal objectives. He says, "*yes*"—that he is in favor of the end; *but* he objects to the means—at the same time offering no alternative, and seldom, if ever, raising a finger to try to obtain the ultimate objective. I have frequently referred to this type of individual as a "yes, but—" fellow . . .[2]

The President went on to argue that the Democratic party had become the liberal party and that those who were elected under its aegis had a duty to behave as liberals should. Those who refused ought to be made to present themselves as conservatives. The group which had allied itself with the Republicans to harass him and to defeat his measures since the earliest days of the New Deal, he thought, ought not to run as Democrats; and he sought, by appealing to their constituencies, to prevent them from doing so. The results were not wholly encouraging any more than they had been for Wilson when he had attempted the same thing. Some of those he favored were nominated; some were not. That he had much influence on the actual primaries may be doubted. If what he wanted, however, was further demonstration, after the defeats of 1937 and 1938 (in the Court fight and in the attempted primary "purge"), that he was still the champion of those groups whose situation he had undertaken to improve, the incident was a success. What is sometimes missed is that he had a way of gaining

[2] *Public Papers*, 1938 vol., Introduction, XXIX.

as much by ostensible defeat as by victory; his defeat underlined his affiliations. There was no hard struggle in all his more than three terms that did not arouse sympathy among a majority whether he won or lost. This resulted in the tremendous election victory in 1936, a lesser but still impressive one—because it was for a third term—in 1940, and a still more remarkable one in 1944. In every one of these he had nearly all the press, as well as the other propaganda media—such as the radio, whose commentators were now very voluble—actively opposing him. It was the mark of his genuine political genius that he made the opposition count in his favor.

This underlines a technique that cannot be said to have been invented by Roosevelt but that was used by him with enormous effect. He had a disconcerting way of joining movements for reform or for the redress of grievances and of becoming their spokesman and leader. He expected—and got—political support in return. This did not always please the organizers of these movements, who were politicians too, but they could not often say so. His hold on the rank and file was such that to oppose him was to ask for loss of influence, even to risk being discarded. This was true of the farm leaders, of the labor organizers, of the big-city bosses, and of many other lesser men who had risen to the top in their own organizations.

A good example of this technique was the capture of the farmers' vote in 1932, some of which was lost as campaigns succeeded each other, but which continued to be remarkable, considering the traditional Republicanism of rural America. The years of struggle for farm relief had developed as prosperous a crop of organization politicians as ever functioned in the United States. There were a half dozen farmers' associations with large memberships and considerable voting solidarity. There was, in response, a "farm bloc" in the Congress, and it did the bidding of the association lobbyists without demur—except when they disagreed. But they disagreed very often. One group believed in subsidized exports, another in the domestic allotment plan, another in outright price fixing, another in inflated prices—and so it went. The divisions had grown deeper with the passing years, and adherence to different policies had hardened until prestige was intimately involved in the acceptance of plans for relief.

When Roosevelt was approaching nomination in 1932 he let these quarreling leaders know that he was ready to sponsor a measure for farm relief but that he would not involve himself in the argument. They must agree, he said, on one concerted scheme. When they did he would support it, whatever it was. This was the unhappiest day of their lives for the organization politicians. How could they persuade their constituencies that a plan different from the one they had committed themselves to so vehemently was one they had urged on the candidate? Yet they had to do it, for Roosevelt was going to be nominated, and to win, as appeared more clearly with every passing spring day.

Some of the strangest meetings in American history took place in various hotel assembly rooms both before and after Roosevelt's nomination. The leaders were under compulsion to agree on something, but they maneuvered to the last for their own prestige. Each knew what the others were trying to do, and each was intent on gaining the appearance of having prevailed over all of them. They had a kind of sympathy for each other, because all were in the same kind of difficulty, but they could afford only a minimum of co-operation.

Roosevelt and his assistants continued to insist and even suggested face-saving formulas. In time the leaders took these back to meetings of their constituents with explanations and confessions, and a kind of compromise was reached which resulted in the speech Roosevelt made in Wichita during the campaign. From the carefully tailored phrases of that address no very hard-and-fast line could be deduced. But farmers were convinced that something would be done and that their lot was at last to be bettered. Roosevelt would see to it.

When it came to passing legislation, Roosevelt, now President, insisted on the same formula—there must be agreement. There was another series of meetings with much the same maneuvering and suspicious co-operation. When the legislation was finally written that all agreed to help push through, it embodied no less than four separate and quite distinct plans for relief—only the radical price-fixers were left out. All the old quarrels were to be deposited in the lap of the Secretary of Agriculture. But Roosevelt was the farmers' man no matter what measures prevailed. He had made himself their super-leader, and every one of the organizers was thenceforth conscious of having to subordinate himself to a superior to whom his constituency's real loyalty went.

The same method, exactly, made labor cleave fiercely to Roosevelt as friend and champion. And union politicians were helpless in the grip of this sentiment. But this technique almost inevitably exhausts itself. When objectives are gained, older loyalties reassert themselves and more permanent sentiments take charge again. It was so with the Roosevelt followers. He lost many of the farmers once they had regained a certain prosperity; they went back to their traditional Republicanism. And even labor forgot to whom its gains were owed and could no longer be counted on. In the end only the city bosses remained dependable, and that was because they had continuing interests to be served by having a friendly President in the White House.[3]

---

[3] The evidences of municipal corruption and the sinister rule of gangsters that were turned up in the Kefauver investigations a few years later were the real price paid for the co-operation of the bosses. It will be re-

His ability to command support became very important to Roosevelt during his second term. For several years before the war he was trying to lead the nation in a direction it was manifestly reluctant to go. Isolationism was strong. There was still a feeling that World War I had resulted in gains for the European powers but not for the United States. American intervention had been a mistake. The sense of disillusion that had defeated Cox and Roosevelt in 1920 still lingered, and another adventure of the same sort was the last thing most Americans wanted to contemplate. Roosevelt was determined that they should. Totalitarianism was a menace; its leaders meant it to dominate the world; and it must be checked. He felt that Wilson had made too early a peace before; if he had insisted on punishing the Germans they would not have been encouraged to try again. There was another thing: they might not try this time if it was made perfectly clear that America would intervene. This the President wanted to do. But the Congress, with undoubted support from the country as a whole, insisted on a neutrality calculated to encourage aggressors because they were not opposed. Two years were spent in overcoming resistance to any moves for defense—that is, to put limits to the dictators' expansion.

In the end it was less presidential insistence than brutal behavior on the part of the Fascists and Nazis that won the argument. Isolationism died hard, but it began to lose strength in 1940, and by 1941 the President felt able to take certain measures he would not have dared to take a year earlier. Even in 1939 the shock of actual war in Europe enabled him to secure the repeal of the arms embargo which had been a feature of the neutrality legislation passed in 1935 and later extended. The rigidity of the embargo had been objected to violently by the President, but in the regular session of 1939 he had been unable to persuade the Senate to make any change. When war was declared in Europe, however, he called a special session, which passed a bill giving him a certain leeway. It had been a long and arduous struggle, not yet over, by any means. Not long before Pearl Harbor the Selective Service Act nearly failed of extension.[4]

The new neutrality measure of 1939 (Public Resolution No. 54 of the Seventy-sixth Congress) resorted to a device having some relationship to the former delegations of power but making them dependent upon

---

called that they were responsible for the ditching of Wallace as vice-presidential candidate in 1944 and the nomination of Truman. When he succeeded to the Presidency within a few months, patronage and favor-giving were safely within the bosses' control.

[4] After a vote of 45 to 30 in the Senate and 203 to 202 in the House, the Act was signed on August 18, 1941. The objection was largely to extending the period of active service to 18 months from the former 12.

the acceptance of presidential responsibility for finding facts. The President now had not only to affirm that a state of war existed before he could proclaim neutrality, but also to find that putting it into effect was "necessary to promote the security or preserve the peace of the United States, or protect the lives of citizens."

Once having proclaimed neutrality, however, the President could go on to declare further that the state of war imposed certain duties "with respect to the proper observance, safeguarding, and enforcement of such neutrality." His first such proclamation (September 8, 1939) established a "limited emergency," but a later one (May 27, 1941) recognized an "unlimited" one. These declarations were assumed to be authorizations for almost any measures judged to be necessary. They opened the door to the tremendous expansion of the next few years.[5]

In one of his most effective radio addresses the President spoke to the nation on the evening of the issuance of his later proclamation. In it he spoke of the policy of "aid to the Democracies" as now fixed, and said that it had become obvious that American independence was "bound up with the independence of all our sister Republics." He reviewed the deepening crisis and the measures already taken—they included, by now, not only the destroyer-bases deal, presently to be discussed, but also the Lend-Lease Act—and said that they were strictly matters of self-interest:

> I have said on many occasions that the United States is mustering its men and resources only for purposes of defense. I repeat the statement now. But we must be realistic when we use the word "attack"; we have to relate it to the lightning speed of modern warfare . . .
>
> It does not make sense to say, "I believe in the defense of all the Western Hemisphere," and in the next breath to say, "I will not fight for that defense until the enemy has landed on our shores" . . . It is time for us to realize that the safety of American homes even in the center of our country has a very definite relationship to the continued safety of homes in Nova Scotia or Trinidad or Brazil. . . .

[5] "Emergency" was by then a familiar term. The President had used it frequently in New Deal days, and it had numerous statutory recognitions. A digest of these will be found in L. W. Koenig's *The Presidency and the Crisis* (New York, 1944). But the "limited emergency" was a creature of Roosevelt's imagination, used to make it seem that he was doing less than he was. He did not want to create any more furor than was necessary. The qualifying adjective had no limiting force. It was purely for public effect. But the finding that an emergency existed opened a whole armory of powers to the Commander in Chief, far more than Wilson had had.

He went on to draw the conclusion that defense meant giving every possible assistance to Britain; it meant enlarging the army and navy; it meant patrolling the Atlantic against the submarine menace; it meant, also, certain domestic disciplines—the stopping of labor disputes, limitations on profits, a system of priorities in production, and all the other controls necessary to a posture of readiness.

With respect to some of this he was in a better position than might have been expected. He had always advocated a large navy; and since the early days of his Presidency, when he had diverted emergency funds to the building of ships—for which he was rebuked by the Congress— he had been enlarging it and pressing for more efficiency. He had also supported General MacArthur, who, as Chief of Staff, had pushed the mechanization of army forces. But his best preparation for the burdens now falling on him as Commander in Chief was the reorganization of the White House staff, and particularly the existence of the unused Office of Emergency Management.

Lincoln had managed the Civil War with a White House staff of half a dozen, partly borrowed from the navy; Wilson had had hardly more assistants immediately around him during World War I, although there had been a tremendous sudden expansion of emergency agencies —such as the War Industries Board and the Food and Fuel Administrations. Roosevelt was to be much more elaborately served. As the delegations widened, and especially after Pearl Harbor, when he was Commander in Chief of a nation at war, he had need at once of the means for controlling the immense civilian organization which had to be brought to the support of the forces in the field. Success was, as never before, dependent on the efficiency of this organization, and especially for a President who had gained his authority over public opinion by promising to improve the well-being of common folk. He must prevent profiteering either in military procurement or in civilian trade.

The Executive Order setting up the Executive Office of the President, under the statute finally passed in 1939, read in part:

> There shall be within the Executive Office of the President the following divisions: (1) the White House Office, (2) the Bureau of the Budget, (3) the National Resources Planning Board, (4) the Liaison Office for Personnel Management, (5) the Office of Government Reports, and (6) in the event of a national emergency, such Office for Emergency Management as the President shall determine.

Within this scheme, an Executive Order early in 1941 defined the status and functions of this last office, now become appropriate. There was, by proclamation, an emergency; there was, by Executive Order, an Office of the President; there was now to be a comprehensive implementation of that office to contain the agencies created in the coming expansion. One of them, in fact, was created on the same day. This was the Office of Production Management, which would have several transformations but which was now to have divisions of production, purchases, and priorities but was not yet to have the authority it would later need to bring about wartime discipline in industry and transportation.[6]

The OEM, when first set up in May 1940, was given only advisory and liaison duties; the intent of the later order was to make it a "coordinating" body. There now existed not only the new OPM but a Defense Communications Board and a Council of National Defense, and this last, it was anticipated, would itself have many subordinate bodies or divisions. There would presently be added, under the OEM, the Central Administrative Services, the National Defense Mediation Board, the Office of Price Administration and Civilian Supply (these took over from the Advisory Commission to the Council of National Defense the Divisions of Price Stabilization and Consumer Protection and the Office of Civilian Defense).[7]

This is the way the organization appeared in the spring of 1941. A note appended to the description in the *Papers* might almost—in view of later developments—be taken as presidential humor. It said:

> It is, of course, expected that there will be changes in the administrative organization of the various defense agencies as new developments arise . . .[8]

These "new developments" can be imagined even by one who has not followed the administrative history of the Executive Office. To detail the changes implied by them in the years following would be both tedious and, for our purpose, unnecessary. We ought, however, to understand their general purpose and to speak of their no more than moderate

---

[6] Copies of these orders will be found in the 1939 and 1940 vols. of the *Public Papers*, and an explanatory note is appended to the OEM Order at p. 695 of the 1940 vol.

[7] There remained in the Advisory Commission to the Council of National Defense the Agricultural Division, the National Defense Research Committee, the Office for Coordination of Health, Welfare and Related Activities, the Office of Coordinator of Commercial and Cultural Relations between the American Republics, the Division of State and Local Cooperation, the Division of Transportation, the Division of Defense Housing Coordination, etc. Cf. the chart of these at p. 701 of the 1940 vol. of the *Public Papers*.

[8] The Office of Emergency Management proved to be available as an amazingly comprehensive catchall. Cf. W. McReynolds "The Office for Emergency Management," *Public Administration Review*, 1941.

success. The purpose was to get and retain control for the President of the vast administrative machine now his sole responsibility. Not much attention was paid to the other presidential problems. Political scientists were speaking by this time of the presidential office in suitably complex terms. They realized that its occupant was more than an administrator. He was, for instance, party head, ceremonial chief, legislative leader, shaper of opinion, moral symbol, planner of the nation's future, economic stabilizer—and, of course, Commander in Chief, with all the widened implications of this title. Some of these functions were becoming vital in a sense never imagined before and still not very generally recognized.

The nation's expectation of survival and prosperity might very well depend far less on effective administration than on research in the most esoteric areas of pure science, something to be underlined with shocking violence by the advent of the atomic bomb then in the making. And others of the implied presidential duties, such as maintaining national unity and purpose by constant and careful cultivation of opinion, were of imperative importance. They ought to amount to a running education accustoming the public to the advances crowding each other as they burst into view. And the whole broad field of economic knowledge and policy, so recently the private preserve of the businessmen, had to have an understanding it was unreasonable to expect in one individual. Even this was not the entire list. Foreign policy, traditionally the peculiar province of Presidents, had become a baffling complex of interpenetrating forces and conflicting interests. The thread of policy to be followed as the billowing clouds of national jealousy obscured the future and the released energies of nationalism broke up the old empires and re-formed the new alliances of race and ideology—often defying the realities of geography—had to be one that would bring the country safely through the dangerous years. It was indeed much more than an administrative task.

Yet the technique of reorganization which was applied to the presidential office and was represented in the Act reorganizing that office in 1939 took little note of any but the administrative job. It would not be true to say that this was the least of a President's duties—the government now had complex economic responsibilities as well as the traditional ones and a personnel running upward rapidly to two million—but it was not more important, certainly, than the others. If the administrative machine ran badly, there were costs, wastes, delays, failure to achieve goals, and even, sometimes, intrusions of disgraceful nepotism, amicism, and occasionally corruption; but of these diseases the nation did not die; in a way, they were self-curing. There were now trained administrators finding their way into the Federal service. It was impossible to ignore their protests and to stifle their knowledge. The various services did improve in spite of indifference or hostility on the part of politicians and an undeniable prevalence of incompetence among the employees sponsored by them. And the Civil Service was building up against congressional opposition. The New Deal had brought in a flood of deserving Democrats; but it had brought in, too, a not inconsiderable number of intelligent and energetic novices who saw in government an opportunity to be of service. No other generation of young people since Jackson had been so inspired by the public philosophy.

The authors of the Reorganization Act were the same three advisers who had been responsible for the *Report* of 1937. They were experts in public administration. They were more familiar with cities and states than with the Federal government, and it is impossible to escape the impression that they saw the Presidency as an enlarged Mayoralty. And, to make the worst criticism at once, there is the impression to be got from their advice during the whole Roosevelt regime—for their influence did not end with the writing of the *Report* or the passage of the Act; they were around to advise about staffing, about the expansion of the Office of Emergency Management, and about the management of the mobilization—that they had in mind the picture of a big businessman, master of his organization, served by an efficient staff, running a taut organization, and getting well-defined jobs done in good time.

These are very possibly unfair comments; yet it is true that from their revised organization of the White House the emphasis was on better operation of the administrative machine and that there was very little attention paid to relief or assistance for the President in the other fields of his responsibility. This may have been because this was not what they were asked to do, or it may have been because the other fields were not recognized—were, in fact, very strongly resented—and could not have been implemented in any reorganization authorized by the Congress. That body still held strongly to the theory of congressional policy-making if not exactly, any more, to that of complete congressional supremacy. It favored more efficiency in the Executive—if it did not interfere with legislators' own claims for patronage and favors—because their business friends were always talking about economy and efficiency. But that the President was all those other things the common people demanded he be and that the fate of the nation depended on, they were not ready to acknowledge. Far from it. They resented presidential bigness, grudged him staff, made no provision for his retirement, pinched his budget, and generally showed the same traditional hostility we have by now become so familiar with. A suggestion for recognizing the President as leader, preserver of unity, maintainer of morale, guardian of security, and creator of a better future would have been received with sarcastic hostility in the Congress of Roosevelt's later terms. And this was true even when war was imminent and when it was going on.

At any rate, these phases of presidential responsibility remained largely extra-official, so to speak. If the President fulfilled the expectations of his vast constituency, it was not with the approval of anyone with constitutional powers to check him or to co-operate with him. He got very little co-operation and plenty of checking—so much that a distressing proportion of his time and energy had to be devoted to circumventing congressional maneuvers, to overcoming the inertia of the bureaucracy infiltrated with hostile appointees, and to blocking the machinations of those determined to make a good thing out of the nation's agonies. And the truth is that much had to be neglected in order to get the essential things done. There had to be a constant process of selecting what was most important to do at the moment, since everything could not be attended to. There were repeated occasions when those whose claims on the Chief Executive's attention were imperative had to be put off. Decisions were delayed, undertakings were stillborn, wrong directions were persisted in. The President could not do everything; he must choose what seemed to him vital, and often matters of moment never came to him at all but were lost on the desks of lesser officials.

This trouble was intensified and made conspicuous by his terrible and inescapable ordeal as Commander in Chief in war. It had been true before, but only to a degree that could be ignored by those who preferred not to see it. The confusions and wastes of the defense and war efforts were scandalous, and not a small part of them existed because the President could not get around to straightening them out. He had been given formally the status of big businessman at the head of the biggest of all businesses; but he still found, as any politician would, as any natural leader would, that his first and most important duties were not those of administration. They were those of maintaining morale, shaping strategy, winning the conflict—and being forehanded in creating the institutions of peace.

When victory came into sight the problems of peace blotted out the transient ones of war. There had been many efficient and devoted administrators down the line from the President who had got things done somehow. But they had had to operate very largely without the directives they should have had. There were Cabinet members who did not see the President for months at a time, in one case more than a year.[9] And there were heads of other agencies, supposed to report directly to the President, who never saw him at all. This was no one's fault. It

[9] This was perhaps an exaggerated instance. There may have been reasons other than crowded time why Ickes was excluded from the office for so long. Cf. his published *Diaries*, incomplete in three vols. (New York, 1953, *et seq.*).

was just that first things had to come first, that the President was one man, and that so many matters waited for his decision, not the small ones of former days, but yet all those that fell finally within his vast responsibility. Not even a genius with unlimited energy could have met the need. Something had gone wrong with the Presidency, even the reorganized office of the experts; and it was a wrong that could be righted only by some sharp and novel correction. This was true not only in war; it was true during the uneasy peace that followed and in succeeding presidential regimes.

★ 50 ★

AS ROOSEVELT, DURING THE YEARS OF THE WAR, GAINED IN APPARENT power and prestige, he steadily lost control over the Congress and over the civilian operations carried on by the government. He was at the head of the mightiest force ever assembled under one direction, and the whole world gradually became his constituency as the leader of democratic peoples. In the end he achieved the same position as Wilson had held in the general regard and, with more political foresight, he brought into being the institutions he believed would ensure a durable peace. It was paradoxical that the same Chieftain who was participating in the strategic direction of a world war and achieving an almost adulatory regard abroad because of his definition of the war's aims, should have been embroiled at home with a rebellious Congress and should have been suffering a diminishing popular support. He was lucky indeed to have won the 1944 election; if it had not been for his opponent's unhappy faculty of appearing arrogant and unfair, he would certainly have lost. The war involved civilian disciplines, and impatience with them was easily exploited.

The erosion of his influence with the electorate and his loss of control over the Legislative Branch must be laid in large part to the impossible demands made upon him. He had not lost his ability to explain his policies in ways calculated to arouse approval; and he had not lost, either, his cleverness in maneuver or his understanding of congressional psychology. He simply did not have time for such things—and perhaps he thought wearily that a President with such a burden of responsibility in great affairs ought to be spared that in lesser ones. The difficulty with this was that both Constitution and custom had laid them upon him and that his attempts to shift them to others did not succeed.

A climax to his tragic differences with the Congress came when in February 1944, in the midst of war, he vetoed a revenue measure. This had never been done before in the nation's history,[1] and to underline

---

[1] For this, Professor Corwin is the authority, *President: Office and Powers*, op. cit., 325.

the nature of his unprecedented act, he wrote and sent to the Congress an angry message of reproof. It was, he said, a bill for the relief of the greedy, not the needy. This caused the Majority Leader, Senator Alben Barkley, who had worked out what he understood to be an acceptable compromise, to resign his Senate post. He was promptly re-elected, and this rebuke to the President was notice that he was no longer recognized as undisputed party chief and spokesman. The Legislative Branch was in full revolt, and it never again returned to good relations.

The tax-bill veto was not the only incident in the conflict between the Branches. Only a week previously a bill extending the life of the Commodity Credit Corporation had been disapproved. The accompanying message had practically accused the Congress of plotting with profiteers to gouge consumers; if the bill should be passed, the message said, the whole retail price index would rise immediately not less than 7 per cent; in effect, it repealed the indispensable Stabilization Act and would result in increased costs of production for farms and factories. It did, in fact, affect the whole conduct of the war. In this case the veto was narrowly sustained, and the President was able to speak of it in a note to the *Papers* (1944–45 vol., 75) as a victory "against the special interests who had tried to break through the line." Interestingly, he blamed the agricultural bloc; it was, he said, "the last of a long series of efforts to kill subsidies and undermine . . . stabilization strategy."

This farm group, with whom he had once been allied and for whose benefit he had used his influence unsparingly, repudiated the alliance almost at once when their incomes were increased. Political marriages are ones of convenience only; and once their usefulness to either contractor is past, the alliance is abandoned without notice. But the farm bloc was so sizable a fraction of the Congress that its defection made a serious problem for the President as legislative leader. Added to the Republicans and the dissident Democrats, its members made a majority. And throughout the whole period of the war, his measures, when not directly concerned with the armed forces, were passed only when they were approved for themselves by a congressional majority; and this was almost never.

This crippling of Roosevelt as Chief Legislator makes it all the more remarkable that, in contrast with Wilson, who had fallen into the same bad relations with the Congress, he was able to get approval for his comprehensive plan for peace. This was undoubtedly because of the care he gave to the preparatory moves, although he was fortunate—as Wilson had not been—in having the Republican leader, Vandenberg, on his side. Henry Cabot Lodge and his "dozen willful men" had repudiated Wilson's League of Nations for reasons strongly tinctured with pique and partisan annoyance; but many of the Republicans co-operated with Roosevelt, and although it is doubtful whether there was any considerable favorable public feeling, the Senate ratification of the United Nations treaty was by a vote of 89 to 2. The price for this had been the actual establishment of a bipartisan group which was consulted from the first and was represented in all stages of the preparation. This went farther back than the writing of the peace. At the very beginning of the war two respectable Republicans had been brought into the Cabinet—Stimson and Knox—in the vital posts of War and Navy, and throughout there had been no partisan tests for employment in the upper levels of the war machine. Secretary Hull, in the State Department, had helped to hold together the southern representation—well disposed for the support of international co-operation, not for domestic programs—and, as a result, the very smoothly working Republican-southern conservative alliance was favorable to the UN. Also it should not be overlooked that the President did actually trade away the most disliked New Deal agencies.[2]

Then too, he was conciliatory to the point of being humble, recalling, as he did so vividly, Wilson's experience. On his return from Yalta his address on March 1, 1945, contained the following paragraphs:

> A conference of all the United Nations of the world will meet in San Francisco on April 25. There, we all hope, and confidently expect, to execute a definite charter of organization under which the peace of the world will be preserved and the forces of aggression permanently outlawed.
>
> This time we are not making the mistake of waiting until the end of the war to set up the machinery of peace. This time, as we fight together to win the war finally, we work together to keep it from happening again . . .
>
> The charter has to be—and should be—approved by the Senate of the United States, under the Constitution. I think the other nations know it now. I am aware of that fact, and now all the other nations are. And we hope that the Senate will approve of what is set forth as the Charter of the United Nations when they all come together in San Francisco next month.
>
> The Senate, through its appropriate representatives, has been kept continuously advised of the program of this government in the creation of the International Security Organization.

[2] For instance, the House in 1943 refused to appropriate funds for the planning agency in the President's own office. The President accepted the rebuke in the interest of other measures he needed more urgently. That he did, disposed the conservatives to accept his war measures and his proposals for the peace, especially when they were admitted to the processes of formulation.

The Senate and the House of Representatives will both be represented at the San Francisco Conference. The Congressional delegates will consist of an equal number of Republican and Democratic members. The American Delegation is—in every sense of the word—bipartisan.

World peace is not a party question . , . I think that Republicans want peace just as much as Democrats. When the Republic was threatened, first by the Nazi clutch for world conquest back in 1940, and then by the Japanese treachery in 1941, partisanship and politics were laid aside by nearly every American; and every resource was dedicated to our common safety . . .[3]

There was in this some of what the President was accustomed to call "buttering up," but there was also a justifiable reminder of favors calling for reciprocation. It must be recalled that Roosevelt died less than two weeks before the San Francisco conference and that the meeting there had to be held in the shadow of his passing. The Republican role was more than ever important when his influence was removed. Perhaps, also, there was the difference from the time of Wilson that the grasping empires were in decline and that the suspicion of secret treaties to gain a further hold on defenseless territories in Asia and Africa did not have to be contended with.

On the whole, it is not difficult to explain Roosevelt's success with the peace, even though it represents an exception to the general hostility and unco-operativeness of the Legislative Branch in the later years of his Administration. How strong the feeling was against him in professional political circles is perhaps indicated by the relatively swift adoption of the Twenty-second Amendment to the Constitution. The resolution submitting it to the states was passed in 1947 and it was ratified by 1951. This too was a remarkable instance of pique continuing even after the death of a hated opponent. It is to be suspected that most of those who voted for it knew it to be unwise, and certainly most were soon willing to admit regret. Especially the Republicans, in view of their hold on the Presidency through Eisenhower, soon realized how childishly impetuous they had been.

The President's loss of control over the administrative machinery of government was, of course, quite another matter. Yet it had the same source—sheer inability to do what the responsibilities he had asked for and got required of him. His efforts to remedy his failings as an Executive caused him to resort finally to desperate measures. He relied to an extent unknown, except in Wilson's case, on an unofficial alter ego—Harry Hopkins—which was not so novel except in its unusual intimacy; but

[3] *Public Papers*, 1944–45 vol., 578.

also he had to create what amounted to an Assistant President for civilian affairs and to appoint no less a person than a Justice of the Supreme Court in the effort to provide the office with prestige enough to impress officials who felt themselves entitled to directives from himself alone. It cannot be said to have been much of a success, and it was not continued; but similar efforts would be made by his successors, and for the same reason—that the Presidency had become too tremendous for one mere man to hold, a man with only the constitution of the aging and only the intelligence granted to most politicians, even those of undoubted genius.

It was not new for Roosevelt to experiment with possible solutions to this most puzzling of problems for a Chief Executive. At the beginning of his first term, when the full weight of the recovery agencies began to fall upon him, he had asked for—but had not much used—the right to rearrange the Executive establishment. Later, as has been noted, he had sponsored, and finally got passed, the Reorganization Act of 1939. Another attempt was represented by his Executive and emergency councils, made up of the heads of the new agencies—NRA, AAA, FERA, CCC, HOLC, RFC, etc.—together with the Cabinet. He hoped that regular meetings of these groups would make it less necessary for those who must otherwise come to him for directions to make demands on his time. The repeated appearance of Frank Walker, who was a person respected and trusted by everyone, in the role of secretary to or chairman of successive groups of this sort went as far to make them successful as could have been expected. But this was not far enough. The burden was still fantastically heavy and complex. And in spite of Walker's devotion and popularity, this kind of device was gradually abandoned as not worth the trouble.

Another interesting attempt of a similar sort was that of setting administrative boards over such agencies as NRA and AAA. The administrators were supposed to report to these boards and they were to meet regularly for the discussion of policy and to give directions. They did not succeed because the administrators insisted on going over their directors' heads to the President, an irregularity tolerated by Roosevelt; probably he considered the policy matters involved to be ones he could not afford to delegate in the circumstances. These boards were not usually made independent by law; they were established by Executive Order; when this was the case they soon disappeared altogether or became moribund.

When the war was approaching and the Reorganization Act had made certain changes in his office, he tried again. He had hoped that the Office of Emergency Management would furnish a framework for the necessary expansion. But again its usefulness, except as a legal container, was nominal, and for the same reason—that those who had important responsibilities would not willingly tolerate an intermediary between themselves and ultimate authority. And the President was not sufficiently firm in rejecting this claim to establish firmly the custom of delegation. The most successful of the various attempts was the Office of War Mobilization, later converted into the Office of War Mobilization and Reconversion.[4]

The OWM was consented to by the President only when criticism for neglect of ordinary presidential tasks he could not perform became embarrassing. There were so many confusions and conflicts, so many snarls and delays, many of them traceable to lack of contact with himself, that something had to be done. What was urged by Administration opponents—and by some friends as well—was an Assistant President. Even the Truman committee (Senate Committee to Investigate the National Defense Program), which was so different from the aggressive and interfering committee during the Civil War, was insistent that changes were needed. It was in an effort to quiet a rising clamor that the OWM was set up and James A. Byrnes appointed to be its head. Byrnes had long seniority as a politician; also, he was a southerner and a conservative. It was thought that this would serve to make the position more prestigious than it would be with an occupant who was chosen for administrative capability. This proved to be true in the circumstances. The President actually did not allow his mobilizer to be by-passed. He seemed to have learned the lesson of earlier failures. Then too, he was so deeply engaged with strategy and military direction that he was willing to forgo other interests, however important. The OWM became the OWMR when the end of the war seemed imminent and a chaos of disestablishment could be anticipated if it was uncontrolled. Byrnes continued in the post. The office was liquidated in 1947.

That the easing up on the President represented by this succession of offices was not continued into the post-war era indicates at the least that such an extension of the Presidency was considered unsuitable in normal circumstances. It may have been considered that the duties of its occupant were those of the President himself and that no appointee ought to be entrusted with them. But the emergency of the war was hardly less demanding than that of recovery had been; and after Roosevelt was gone and Truman had succeeded him, there were other emergencies. Byrnes was there still to assist with the early ones, and he was soon succeeded by Fred M. Vinson, an equally respected politician;

[4] The OWM itself followed an earlier experiment—the Office of Economic Stabilization of 1942. Cf. Papers, 1942 vol., Item 97 and note. The OWM was set up in 1943. Cf. Papers, 1943 vol., Item 56 and note; and the OWMR followed in 1944. Cf. Papers, 1944–45 vol., Item 81 and note.

but after the OWMR was liquidated, the presidential office was again left with only the organization provided in the 1939 scheme. There was one individual now, with an amplitude of assistants, but still the ultimate and only decision-maker.

51

CREDIT TO ROOSEVELT AS AN ENLARGER OF THE PRESIDENCY RESTS partly on his experimentation with devices for better administration but more on his extraordinary achievements as a leader. There were very few occasions when he resorted to the Rule of Necessity in the drastic fashion of Lincoln. A number of times he seemed on the verge of it; but he usually preferred, even when his vast responsibilities weighed heaviest, to use his talents as a politician and wait for the slow operations of persuasion to legitimize what he felt must be done. His exasperation with those who opposed various phases of the recovery and reform program led to extra-legal recourses only in a few instances, and those not clearly out of limits. He was nearest to some such action when he was opposed in his efforts to prepare the nation for "defense." It is beyond doubt that he exceeded his authority when he made the so-called destroyer-bases deal with the British in September 1940, and his delegated powers did not really legitimize many of the wartime agencies created by his Executive Orders. As to the delegations themselves, they went far beyond anything known in previous crises. The Congress might dislike Presidents and might have come to detest this one, but there were few members who would risk unpatriotic votes.[1]

The destroyer-bases deal, which did stretch presidential powers, has to be related to its setting if it is to be understood why he dared undertake it without congressional authorization and why his competence was not challenged.

In the first place, the year was 1940; and in September of that year his third-term presidential campaign was at its height. But, in the second place, Britain and the Allies were in a desperate situation. The President obviously felt a compelling urge to give assistance and give it quickly, but he was also wary of the vociferous isolationists who might well be speaking—although opinion was changing—for a majority in the coun-

[1] As, it will be recalled, Lincoln, the Whig Congressman, would not risk one in Polk's Mexican War.

try. Churchill, from beleaguered Britain, was warning the President that Hitler's invasion plans might succeed and that if they did the British navy might be found on the other side of the struggle.

At the same time the Selective Service Act was before the Congress (it was passed on September 16). This the President had presented as a measure for "defense," but the modern meaning of the word, he had insisted, involved more than enlargement of the army and navy; it required the use of every possible means to ensure the nation's security. And it was in this orientation that the destroyer-bases deal also seemed to him allowable as well as necessary. He was handicapped by a precedent, however, which he found difficult to circumvent. The obstacle was surmounted only by a rather forced ruling of Attorney General Jackson; but, as in so many other instances, the legality of the transaction was less important than the public opinion that was crystallizing. The realization that the British navy was a bulwark for the United States had been hard for isolationists to accept, but it was suddenly apparent that Americans generally fully realized the fact. His quick sense of public feeling told the President he might act.

Nevertheless, an objecting opinion might have been a real obstacle. This was the more true because only recently Jackson had held that an old statute (of 1917) embodying the then rule of international law stood in the way of exporting warships built to be delivered to a belligerent. The opinion turned on the question of intent. The small ships formerly meant for Britain had been in process of being built, and the agreement to transfer them was in anticipation of their completion. But the destroyers Churchill was asking for later in 1940 were old ones possible to describe as obsolete; therefore, they could not have been built for the purpose of transfer. This, said the Attorney General, exempted them from the law of 1917. Such a classification did not, however, meet the broad requirement of international law that no neutral nation might furnish a belligerent with warships. This the President could not simply ignore.

But there was more involved in helping Britain than the transfer of naval vessels if her struggle was to be aided substantially. In 1938 the President had directed the army to turn back to private contractors many older weapons so that they might be replaced by newer ones. The contractors had then disposed of them to Britain and France. But the really massive use of this assumed Executive privilege did not occur until the fall of France in 1940 and the looming prospect that Britain might also succumb. At that time many rifles and heavy guns, together with ammunition, were transferred to the British. It was closely following this that the destroyer-bases deal was consummated. Even this was not the end. Lend-Lease was to follow. But fifty destroyers, even over-age ones, made a sizable gift; and the President was understandably reluctant to make it without some other justification than Britain's need. He found it in the suggestion to Churchill that in return Britain should grant (for ninety-nine years) leases to territory where strategic bases necessary to American defense might be built.

But there were complications, and they were of a sort that would rate as comic in any other environment. Churchill wanted the United States to be generous and offer the destroyers as a gift; presented as a trade, it would make him appear to be a poor bargainer. He afterward put it this way:

> The President, having always to consider Congress and also the Navy authorities in the United States, was of course increasingly drawn to present the transaction to his fellow-countrymen as a highly advantageous bargain whereby immense securities were gained in these dangerous times by the United States in return for a few flotillas of obsolete destroyers. This was indeed true; but not exactly a convenient statement for me. Deep feelings were aroused in Parliament and the Government at the idea of leasing any part of these historic territories, and if the issue were presented to the British as a naked trading away of British possessions for the sake of fifty destroyers it would certainly encounter violent opposition. I sought, therefore, to place the transaction on the highest level, where indeed it had a right to stand, because it expressed and conserved the enduring common interests of the English-speaking world.[2]

The compromise reached by these practiced politicians in the contest for advantage was embodied in the President's message to the Congress informing them of the action he had taken. It was sent on September 3, 1940; but he had prepared public opinion to an extent during August by announcing that bases were being bargained for. Along with the message, he transmitted Attorney General Jackson's opinion as well as the formal exchange of letters executing the deal. It will be noted that his message was only to *inform* the Congress of what he had done:

> I transmit herewith for the information of the Congress notes exchanged between the British Ambassador and the Secretary of State . . . under which this government has acquired the right to lease naval and air bases in Newfoundland, and in the islands of Bermuda, the Bahamas, Jamaica, St. Lucia, Trinidad, and Antigua, and in British Guiana; also a copy of an opinion of the Attorney General . . . regarding my authority to consummate this arrangement.

[2] *The Second World War: Their Finest Hour* (Boston, 1949), 408.

The right to bases in Newfoundland and Bermuda are gifts—generously given and gladly received. The other bases mentioned have been acquired in exchange for 50 of our over-age destroyers.

This is not inconsistent in any sense with our status of peace. Still less is it a threat against any nation. It is an epochal and far-reaching act of preparation for continental defense in the face of grave danger . . .[3]

It is difficult to take very seriously the bargaining for position between the two statesmen; and no one can really have believed at the time that giving the British fifty destroyers was not "a threat against any nation." It was, on the contrary, a decisive taking of sides. From neutrality the United States was advanced by it to nearly full collective security. In the press conference announcing the message that was being sent to the Congress, Roosevelt was at once bold and circumspect. When someone asked whether Senate ratification would be required, he said shortly, "It is all over; it is all done." But he felt the need for some explanation. He must have public acceptance.

Wendell Willkie, Roosevelt's antagonist in the current presidential campaign, had been consulted in advance and had agreed not to make an issue of the trade; but he had not been told that it was to be done by the President alone, and he felt that he had been deceived. He proceeded to denounce it as "the most dictatorial action ever taken by any President." But there was no severe reaction, and this in spite of a curious mistake made by Roosevelt in his press conference as he attempted a justification—one of the few historical errors chargeable to him. He told the reporters that his action was comparable to that of Jefferson in the acquisition of Louisiana. In that case, too, he said, "there was never any treaty, there was never any two-thirds vote in the Senate."[4]

The public reaction was favorable, and the neglected Senate was not unduly indignant; but a few voices were raised in protest. Professor Corwin wrote to the New York *Times* and subsequently said in his *President: Office and Powers* that "the transaction was directly violative of at least two statutes and represented an exercise by the President of

---

[3] *Papers*, 1940 vol., 391.

[4] What he recalled, evidently, was that Jefferson had pondered, as he himself had done, what his course ought to be. Jefferson had really felt that a constitutional amendment was needed to authorize the acquisition of territory; and it was this conviction that he had put aside in favor of response to the Rule of Necessity; but there had been an almost unanimous ratification of the treaty he had submitted embodying the terms of the purchase.

a power which by the Constitution is specifically assigned to Congress."[5]
But the power represented by the destroyer-bases trade was a good
deal less than that soon granted by the Congress under the Lend-
Lease Act.[6] That Act, incidentally, could be said to represent a ratification of the exchange; so, also, could the appropriation Acts which provided money for construction on the bases to be acquired.

But the deal, if it aided Britain in the exigent circumstances of 1940,
by no means solved all her problems. There were many other materials
she needed quite as badly and which could not be acquired in the
United States because of two legal difficulties—the Neutrality Act of
1939 and the older Johnson Act of 1934. Because of the first she was
required to pay cash for all the munitions she might buy—and her cash
had all been spent; and because of the second she was barred from
borrowing in the American market. The Lend-Lease Act was the President's solution. It was an amazing demand on the Congress for him to
have made, but it was an even more amazing one for the Congress to
have granted. It is a conspicuous illustration of the impulse to yield
authority generously in crises. The same had been done for both Lincoln
and Wilson. It would be taken back, and perhaps more would be taken
than had been given—that was also an irresistible impulse—but for the
time being the Executive's powers would be so great as to cause shudders among those who did not fully understand the institutions of the
Republic. This included not a few vociferous persons, some of considerable importance, in 1940; but opinion by then was swinging so
rapidly toward support for the Allies that even they were soon silenced.
The powers were given for two years (and twice renewed), and they
were broad enough to allow the President all the scope he needed not
only for aid to be sent abroad but for preparing at home to meet the
crisis of intervention.

Under the Lend-Lease authorization the President, whenever he
deemed it necessary for the national defense, could direct the manufacture in government arsenals or could otherwise procure "defense articles,"
and he could "sell, transfer title to, exchange, lease, lend, or otherwise
dispose of" any of them to the government "of any country whose defense" he deemed vital to the defense of the United States. He could do
this on any terms that he "deemed satisfactory."

In other Acts[7] the President was authorized to go farther and

[5] Op. cit., 289.

[6] U. S. Code (1940), Supp. IV tit., 22. Cf. Professor Corwin's *Total
War and the Constitution* (New York, 1949).

[7] Such as the Selective Service Act of that same September, by the
Priorities Statute of May 1941, etc.

practically to bring under government supervision all industry necessary to defense. And this, it must be recalled, was all before war had
been declared. Once this had been done, of course, the authorization
was enlarged. By the Second War Powers Act (of March 1942)
penalties were provided for failure to comply with presidential directives. Then there followed the Emergency Price Control Act in January
of 1942. The Office of Price Administration set up under this Act, together with the War Production Board, wielded powers hitherto quite
unknown in the United States, even during World War I.

The sense in which these wartime powers enlarged the Presidency
must be apparent. They were neither unconstitutional nor extra-legal—
that is to say, they had been delegated by the lawmaking body. It is not
of primary importance to inquire what the Court made of them; as in
most such instances, the need was past, or nearly past, by the time any
decisions affecting them were reached. But for what it is worth, the
Court was uniformly favorable—that is to say, a majority was. In one
case testing the penalties for violating the orders of the OPA, the Court
said that "the directions that the prices shall be fair and equitable . . .
confers no greater reach for administrative determination than the
power to fix just and reasonable rates" often held to be allowable. Justice
Roberts felt this to be mistaken and said so in an indignant dissent.
But this is the way it went; it was a President's war, and he fairly well
had his way.[8]

But neither the destroyer-bases deal nor the broad delegations furnish
the most interesting instance during the Roosevelt Administration of a
reach for powers to meet unprecedented responsibilities. More striking
was his admonishing of the Congress for not rising to its duty. The
illustration is somewhat like that cited in the case of Theodore Roosevelt
and the anthracite strike of 1902—that is to say, the threat sufficed
and the powers were not actually used. But they stand in the record
as having been asserted and not having been challenged.

It was in September of 1942 that the President demanded, in the most
peremptory way, that the Congress repeal forthwith a certain provision
of the Emergency Price Control Act and, in effect, told the legislators
that if what he required was not done, and by a certain date, he would
nevertheless act as though it had been done. To be sure, his demand was
accompanied by a justification so complete as to have convinced any
reasonable lawmaker that the stabilization he sought was vital to the
war effort, but still the notice in such terms was unprecedented. What
brought him to so drastic a warning was that food prices had been

[8] The case cited here was *Yakus* vs. *the United States,* 321 U.S. 414
(1944).

rising at a frightening rate, and this naturally led to requests for higher wages. An unbalance of this kind spreads like a disease throughout the economy, and it was this that the President felt must be stopped. He spoke, as he knew, to an especially lobby-ridden Congress, one to whose members he would again and again address protests and rebukes for their abasement before the representatives of special interests. This time it was the farm lobby. It had succeeded in adding to the Emergency Price Control Act provisions preventing any control of the price of farm products until a certain level was reached, a level which turned out to be so high as to be ridiculous. The indignant Executive finally warned the legislators that if they were unable to find their own independence he would act without their authorization:

> What is needed is an over-all stabilization of prices, salaries, wages, and profits. That is necessary to the continued production of planes and tanks and ships and guns at the present constantly increasing rate.
>
> Therefore I ask the Congress to pass legislation under which the President would be specifically authorized to stabilize the cost of living, including the prices of all farm commodities . . .
>
> I ask the Congress to take this action by the first of October. Inaction on your part by that date will leave me with an inescapable responsibility to the people of this country to see to it that the war effort is no longer imperilled by the threat of economic chaos.
>
> In the event that the Congress shall fail to act, and act adequately, I shall accept the responsibility, and I will act.

There followed the justification. It rested, it will be seen, squarely on the Rule of Responsibility:

> The President has the powers, under the Constitution and under Congressional Acts, to take measures necessary to avert a disaster which would interfere with the winning of the war . . . If we were invaded, the people of this country would expect the President to use any and all means to repel the invader . . . I cannot tell what powers may have to be exercised in order to win this war. The American people can be sure that I will use my powers with a full sense of my responsibility to the Constitution and to my country. The American people can also be sure that I shall not hesitate to use every power vested in me to accomplish the defeat of our enemies in any part of the world where our own safety demands such defeat. When the war is won, the powers under which I act automatically revert to the people—to whom they belong.[9]

[9] *Papers*, 1942 vol., 364–65.

This incident has seemed to some students of the Presidency to be an outrageous usurpation by the President of the powers belonging to another Branch. One was Professor Corwin, again, who felt that when Roosevelt said to the Congress that unless it repealed a statutory provision forthwith he would nevertheless treat it as repealed, and thus claimed for the President a power and right to disregard statutes, he went even beyond the position taken by Johnson in 1867 that he was not obligated by laws trenching on presidential prerogative. It was more presumptuous than the first Roosevelt's "stewardship theory," which had claimed for the President the right to do anything in the public interest that seemed imperative but had added the significant exception: provided he was "not prohibited by the Constitution or an Act of the Congress from doing it." The message, said Professor Corwin, could be interpreted only as a claim of power to suspend the Constitution in a situation deemed by him to make such a step necessary. In doing this, Roosevelt was "proposing to set aside, not a particular clause of the Constitution, as Lincoln had once done, but its most fundamental characteristic, its division of power between Congress and the President, and thereby gather into his own hands the combined power of both."[10]

To a later student, aware that nothing of a revolutionary nature did actually occur as a result of the Roosevelt assertion, and aware, also, that the threat had been effective and that within a month the Congress had passed the very important Stabilization Act (56 Stat. 765), it would seem that Professor Corwin—and others—had been unduly excited. He would be inclined to take more seriously a passage in the message not dwelt on by those who felt that Roosevelt had gone too far. This passage followed his assertion that the President may do what is necessary to avert disaster. In it he said that he had given "the most thoughtful consideration" to meeting the issue without further reference to the Congress but had determined on consultation:

> There may be those who will say that, if the situation is as grave as I have stated it to be, I should use my powers and act now. I can only say that I have approached this problem from every angle, and that I have decided that the course of conduct which I am following is consistent with my sense of responsibility as President in time of war, and with my deep and unalterable devotion to the processes of democracy.[11]

Professor Corwin would seem to be arguing the wrong issue. The question was not whether the President had the right to tell the Con-

[10] Op. cit., 303 ff.

[11] *Papers*, op. cit., 364.

gress what laws to pass or whether he had the right to disregard laws already passed. The issue was whether the President's war powers had been invaded by the Congress. If they had, then the question was whether the President should disregard the aggression and act on his own or whether he should warn the Congress to retreat—which is what he did. The opposite argument would rest on the presumption that the Congress can make *any* law and that the President must always respect it. But the Legislative Branch, disregarding the Rule of Restraint, may also exceed its prescription, as we have seen; and when it does, the President, being independent, may oppose the invasion and may behave as his interpretation of the incident requires him to do. The Roosevelt position, then, would not seem very different from that of Johnson after all. If the Congress had legislated in a field where the President's responsibility was prior and paramount, not he but the Congress was in error. And under the Constitution he had a right equal with theirs to say whether this was so. The Rule of Restraint must apply to the Congress as well as to the other Branches, and when it is disregarded it must be expected that there will be conflict.

Roosevelt's message was a statement, in a particular situation, of the applicability of the Rule of Responsibility. It will undoubtedly be followed by any future President who finds himself committed to a duty he must stretch his powers to meet.

52

WHEN PRESIDENT-ELECT EISENHOWER CONTEMPLATED THE VICTORY he had won in 1952 over an opponent more suited to the office, he ought to have been appalled by what lay before him; but there is no reason for thinking that he was. He seemed confident enough. But it was only too apparent that he had no clear idea of a President's responsibilities. He was not a politician but a soldier who had recently himself said that military men ought to eschew politics and had given good reasons for saying so. He had shown little interest in public affairs beyond the military range—and what he had shown had been embarrassingly naïve. The campaign he had just conducted was that of a puppet speaking for principals who had not fully explained to him what they had in mind. But he evidently did mean to be a father to the country, or perhaps a grandfather; at least he soon showed a distaste for the more arduous duties of office and retreated to the high ground of detachment from which he refused to be dislodged. This instinct for safe position served his purpose. The party chieftains had wanted a symbolic figure and they were willing to guard him from a naughty world; and he, in turn, was content to be that symbolic figure and nothing more.[1]

Those who were versed in presidential history could see that Generals Taylor and Grant were reproduced with some verisimilitude in this later professional soldier. There could be no greater contrast, however, than that offered by Eisenhower and his two immediate predecessors. Roosevelt and Truman, practicing politicians and men of the active and complex world, had been used to the give-and-take of party struggle and sensitive to the needs of the electorate to whom they owed preferment. Eisenhower seemed to feel that the voters had set him on a pedestal and that he ought to occupy it passively. True, he expressed himself stoutly as being against irreligion, inflation, and war; but that

[1] For a contemporary analysis of the Eisenhower method, cf. Richard Rovere's *The Eisenhower Years* (New York, 1956).

was about the nearest he would—or ever did—come to any definition of purpose. In one sense this agenda was suitable enough for a President. It focused attention on general objectives and formed a frame for the work of more active party stalwarts. It will be noticed that the presidential program did not include progress. This was left conspicuously to the captains of the economy. It was outside the realm of government —except as government might facilitate their operations. What this came to in the Eisenhower conception, Americans who voted him into office had eight years to learn—eight years of holding back, holding down, holding tight.

Eisenhower had written for him, and stumblingly read year after year, more pious words than any President of record. But his impress on the office was a limited one. In an exploration of enlargements not much attention to him is justified. There is, however, one contribution to be noted: the instruction of subordinates in the arts of briefing to which his army training had accustomed him. No President had ever known so well how to use a staff; but he needed a very large one for the method he followed, and the personnel of his office burgeoned amazingly in spite of the negative policy he consistently pursued. It had to. There was an immense bureaucracy at work, and someone had to sign its papers. Decisions of moment to the economy might be made in corporate offices—in Detroit, Chicago, or New York—but they must be translated into some sort of action. Also, most of the time he had a Democratic Congress to deal with, and this required elaborate arrangements for communication. But his most active interests of a positive sort had to do with defense and foreign aid, matters his prestige as a General helped immensely to forward and on which there were not many party differences.

The Republican domestic policy was the same as ever—decentralize, economize, and minimize—these were the themes, and they required repeated holding actions. Before it was over the President would have given a wonderful exhibition of versatility in using the veto, being able to collect strength when it was needed from the southern conservative Democrats. And this also would stand as an achievement of sorts.[2]

[2] The veto during the Eisenhower Administration was one of its more interesting facets. Its use enabled him to perform as the apotheosis of the Republican President. For six of his eight years there was a Democratic Congress, but he used the veto with consistent success (120 vetoes in the first seven years, not one of which was overridden). This was because he appealed to conservatives among the Democrats as much as to members of his own party. In this way he prevented, cut down, or reshaped welfare legislation of all kinds; expenditures, for instance, for schools, housing, old-age assistance, benefits for government workers, labor legislation—a long list. Perhaps the most interesting development was his indirect

If the generous expansion of his own office and the multiplication of perquisites seemed inconsistent with the theory of the minimal Presidency, this was a superficial view. What the government did, even negatively, ought to be done in a proper and businesslike way. Only by rigorous control could the expenditures of various agencies be held down and taxes kept at a minimum. It was one of the marvelous ironies of the Eisenhower years that the President could berate the Congress, repeatedly and with righteous emphasis, for "spending," and yet at the same time preside over what his predecessors would have regarded as an unimaginably extravagant expansion of his own office.

Of course it was not a happy situation that had been inherited from Truman. The office had been degraded by indignities, relieved only by a kind of cocky detachment on Truman's part; and there were still more important difficulties. Truman had allowed the Supreme Court (in the steel case) to tell him how he must define the Rule of Necessity and to insist that the Court would always pass on the alleged danger that invoked its use; he had allowed a cold war to begin that would torment the nation for an indefinite time to come and had conducted that war —*vide* Acheson and Dulles—with behavior, and especially with language, more suited to an alley fight than to international negotiation. Back of that, also, he had decided to use the atomic bomb to destroy two Japanese cities when the Japanese had been trying to surrender for six months past, thus convincing Asia that American racial bias was a fixed policy. Altogether, because of these and a number of other lesser mistakes and blunderings, the Presidency was at a lower point—although for different reasons—than it had been even in the Harding Administration.[3]

---

approach to the item veto so long the object of presidential hopes. He simply notified the Congress that parts of bills he did not like would not be administered. This was done selectively, and sometimes the refusal was not notified to the legislators but merely put into effect. But if the precedent stood and was further developed it might be very important. Cf., for background in this matter, C. J. Zinn, *The Veto Power of the President*, a report for the Committee on the Judiciary of the House of Representatives, 1951.

[3] Some responsibility, at least, for the Twenty-second Amendment, started on its ratifying journey by congressional action during his Administration, must be charged to Truman. It was a Republican measure, passed by a hostile Congress; but if he made any effort to halt its progress, it was notably ineffective. It would not bother Eisenhower, who had no need for compulsive influence in his last years; nor, for that matter, would he be bothered by the precedent of the steel case, but these would be serious for future Presidents of more active habit.

Eisenhower at least brought back a more becoming atmosphere of respectability. And there was one inheritance he owed to Truman—which characteristically he never acknowledged; neither was graceful in this way; both, indeed, were strangely petty—a beautifully reconstructed White House. It had once again fallen into hopeless disrepair during the Roosevelt tenure and had had to be demolished before it could be rebuilt. This was not the boon to Eisenhower that it would have been to another President, since he was much away in pursuit of change, exercise, and innocent pleasure. But still it was now a much more adequate place for the activities centering there. Visitors who had known it in other days remarked that the Victorian gloominess into which it had fallen had been remarkably relieved.[4]

For social purposes the change for the better was considerable. Entertainment could now be much more efficiently conducted, and visitors could be accommodated without crowding. The President's own study on the second floor and his adjoining quarters were still happily open to the south; also, there was no more need for their use as offices, so that the possibility of withdrawal and contemplation was heightened. With the adjoining offices in the West Wing and in the State, War and Navy building (about to be supplemented by an office building) the Presidency was for the first time well equipped for its routine work without the inconveniences borne by all Presidents in the past.

But now the organization showed some tendency to expand beyond reason, so that it might become something of a problem for the President to control just his immediate staff. The purpose of these assistants—to help him in the management of the immense bureaucracy—was in danger of being forgotten. There was a concern with public relations and with magnification of the Eisenhower personality that exceeded any former interest of that sort, and the President seemed to become more and more remote from the operations of the Departments and agencies. There was some recognition of this in the continuing multiplication of independent administrative groups outside the presidential establishment. Since the Humphrey decision these were responsible, if to any authority, to the courts. The President appointed their members, but he could not remove them, and consequently, even if he had wanted to, he could not control their policies. The result was periodic

---

[4] Early in May 1959 the Eisenhowers entertained, at the initiative of the Women's Press Association, all the living descendants of the Presidents. This was the first time such a group had ever been assembled, and they were able to make some interesting comparisons. Several had either been born in the House or had lived there as children, and all were struck with the cheerfulness and convenience of the rebuilt Mansion. Cf. the Washington *Post* and the Washington *Star*, May 4, 1959.

scandal and almost continuous suspicion that they favored the interests they were supposed to regulate. This was heightened by the kinds of appointments made by Truman and Eisenhower—mostly from among those who were somehow involved with the interest supposed to be controlled. This was on the theory that regulators ought to be expert and that only experience produced expertness. But one result was to continue old, and create new, intimacies, not in the public interest. There was an outright scandal in the Federal Communications Commission in 1958 and many more were rumored to be latent; but they led to no reform of the system. And there was no visible comprehension that what was lacking was responsibility to the President. By now the subtraction from the President's duty to the public in the matters dealt with by these agencies was very nearly complete.

Neither Truman nor Eisenhower had the remotest chance of being listed in the future as among the more competent Presidents; so much could be said even without the advantage of perspective. Neither made any contribution of note to domestic policy; but there was a striking contrast in their attempts at leadership. Both had to deal with hostile Congresses, or at least ones with a majority belonging to the other party —the hostility was not actually considerable. Truman attempted to push his Republican Congress; Eisenhower attempted to hold back his Democratic one. Truman was sometimes eloquent about civil rights and welfare proposals. But his lack of success in persuading the Congress to enact legislation was striking; almost nothing he suggested ever got done. Eisenhower being apathetic about all liberal causes, his influence was used to whittle them down or to smother them.

Eisenhower, having this negative purpose, had much more success with his method. He had the veto at his command, and when he could not prevent legislation to which he seriously objected, his threats, vigorously voiced, would often so reduce the costs and the scope of the bills he objected to that he could approve them. Not enough was left, usually, to endanger the annual budget, about which he took so literal a view. Enough conservative Democrats agreed with him to prevent the mustering of a two-thirds overriding majority. He became very skilled at preventing the threatening Democrats, pushed by their liberal members, from accomplishing their purposes. No President had ever prevented so much.

These comments apply strictly to domestic matters. It was, of course, a time when foreign affairs were dominant; and the best efforts of both statesmen had to be given to the devising and implementing of policies to meet the entirely new challenges of a changing world. Colonialism was dying, and this was agonizing for old allies France, Britain, and the Low Countries. New nations were creating themselves overnight without the competence or the resources necessary for independence.

And the competition with Russia which blundering diplomacy had allowed to develop after Roosevelt's death was a constant threat. Besides, the vast colossus of China was taking ominous shape in the East and was reacting, with almost constant fulminations against the United States, to a moralistic policy of non-recognition.

There were repeated crises, sometimes rising to intervention and potential world conflict. They occurred in Germany and in the Near and the Far East. There was nowhere in the world the peace of older days. Truman's best efforts, the Marshall Plan and then the device popularly known as Point Four (for technical assistance to underdeveloped areas), were imaginative attacks on the general problem of envy and its consequent hostility. But the development of the North Atlantic Treaty Organization, with subsequent Southeast Asia and Near East organizations of a similar sort, were linked to containment and had the effect of exacerbating relations with Russia. The patent weakness of these measures, compared with the enemy potential, prevented them from gaining the advantage they had been invented to produce. The nation was never able to deal with the now consolidated communist world from strength. And so accommodation was difficult: the bargaining had been calculated to take place in an atmosphere of fear, and the communists were far from being fearful.

Both Truman and Eisenhower gave their most imaginative efforts to these foreign problems; both made—or allowed to be made—mistakes, but both showed strength in the crises which followed from erroneous policies—Truman in Korea and in Berlin, and Eisenhower in Lebanon, for instance, and in other places where opposition evaporated temporarily before a show of determination. But although crises were handled for the most part with laudable courage, there remained the fact that they ought not to have developed at all, that if different policies had been pursued there might have been a reasonable peace in the world rather than continuous anxiety. This was more important because it was in the post-war years that the development of nuclear weapons took place and made resort to war finally absurd because certainly suicidal. The President's responsibility to his nation, for its present and future security, depended now on sheltering it from war, not in preparations for engaging in a successful one. But neither, during the Dulles regime—for John Foster Dulles influenced the Truman policies and dominated those of Truman and Eisenhower during the critical years—met this responsibility. They were fatally lacking in this respect.[5]

[5] For an account of the years 1945–55, the critical years in the development of nuclear weapons and of the Dulles policy with respect to them, the reader is referred to the author's *A Chronicle of Jeopardy* (Chicago, 1956).

It was not novel now for the President to take the lead in foreign affairs, even to the point of committing the nation to steps involving possible war; nor was it novel for weak Presidents to devolve upon strong Secretaries of State the direction of policy. Washington had realized that only the Executive was equipped to take the initiative in dealing with other nations, and Presidents since had followed the precedent. Grant had deferred to Fish, and even Cleveland had allowed Olney to take him far on the road to war. But never, in determining policy, had there been the deference shown to an individual not President that was shown to Dulles. Several times his attempts at containment of Russia and, after China had become a monolithic communist camp, his affronts to the government that, in spite of him, existed, led almost to attacks on the nations he so abhorred. It was a curious exhibition of Christian righteousness—Dulles was a prominent Presbyterian layman—which would have seen violence used without hesitation. Eisenhower is supposed to have intervened at the last moment on these occasions and refused to allow the use of armed force. But he went on allowing his Secretary to create incidents leading to the verge of these disasters. The Secretary was popularly given credit for mastering the dangerous art of "brinkmanship."

Yet although there was criticism rising to ridicule and, as nuclear weapons and missilery were perfected, a gradually spreading fear that some incident would become irretrievably acute, Dulles retained the initiative until he died during the closing years of the Eisenhower Administration. The Congress was futile. This was partly because the Democrats, out of power, were conscious that the Dulles policies had begun when they had had responsibility. At least as many of them took the line that more risks ought to be incurred as shrank from possible consequences. There never was a better demonstration that the making of foreign policy belonged inescapably to the President, even when delegated by him to another. It seemed improbable that the Congress, even if it should try, could ever recapture it.

What could be done by the President as Commander in Chief hardly needed the demonstrations provided by several Truman-Eisenhower incidents, but they at least served to confirm emphatically the President's unchallengeable ability to use the armed forces in pursuit of policy in any way he chose. But again, as in other instances we have seen, there was no doubt that approval for intervention would be forthcoming. Truman's Korean adventure was most doubtful; it was undertaken in the name of the United Nations without actual consent until after the commitment; but ratification prevented any serious challenge. And the use of the armed forces in other incidents, such as Lebanon, was at the request of threatened governments. These occasions merely served to confirm the freedom of the Commander in Chief to direct the military as he chose, and he would naturally choose to back up the policy he was pursuing.

The whole of the Truman and Eisenhower Administrations were passed in a state of emergency. There were repeated real or imagined threats from the communist states; and these were backed, or were thought to be backed, by weapons so terrible that minds shrank from consideration of their possible effect. The reaction to the constant peril was such an expenditure on weaponry as had never been conceived before in the wildest imaginings of the military; and there was a feeling in the Congress, and often expressed, that even the General in the White House was skimping on arms in the budgets he submitted. There went with this the usual hysteria of a period of anxiety. Senator Joseph McCarthy for a time played on this fear with enormous success, making himself famous by the simple method of accusing practically everyone else of treason.[6] The nation existed in a state of tension and mutual suspicion which can have been equaled only by the dissensions that tore the country apart as it got ready for the Civil War.

The significance of these characteristics of two decades, for our purpose, is that they tended to make permanent more and more delegations to the President. Especially the expansion of the military budget to two thirds and more of the total national expenditures immensely increased the importance of the President's role as Commander in Chief. With a General in the White House, and with the military services dominating the nation's interest and holding, as most people believed, the responsibility for their safety in a perilous age, it was an ideal time, it might have been supposed, for the development of something like a dictatorship. It did enlarge the Presidency, but Eisenhower went rather in the other direction. It would be difficult to explain this to an observer not well versed in the traditions of democracy. As has been noted, it was Eisenhower rather than the Congress who held down the more extravagant demands of the military Chiefs of Staff; not infrequently his requests were overridden and expanded by the Congress. It was he who calmly contained the aggressive McCarthy and damped down the hysteria about security. It was he who feared inflation with a crusader's righteousness. It was he who held back from using force when Dulles would have resorted to it in international disputes.

Taylor and Grant had not been notably militaristic Presidents either; neither had been aggressive. They, also, seemed to hold their important contemporaries in a kind of awe. But the awe that overwhelmed Eisenhower was reserved for the big businessmen who were his higher audience. What they thought good for the country, he thought good

[6] Cf. Richard Rovere's brilliant study, *Senator Joe McCarthy* (New York, 1959).

for it too; and he took pains to find out what they thought. They were his familiars at the White House and on his recreational sojourns. It was made plain by his behavior that military glory was less glamorous than achieving places of power in the industrial hierarchy.

He was one President who occupied the office with obvious relish. He enjoyed the deference that came to him from the mighty figures of the nation's elite; he responded to the adulation of the many people who needed the assurance of a father and found it in him; he enjoyed the perquisites of his powerful position—the houses and clubs at his disposal, the planes fitted out especially for his convenience, the many aides who protected and served him. Life was smooth and luxurious. His special ability to deploy and use assistants kept him from the arduous labors of his predecessors. He was a President in the modern manner. What had had its first considerable development in F. D. Roosevelt's regime had its apogee in Eisenhower's.

But with all his assistants, and with all the easing of life carried out so elaborately for him as President, Eisenhower was a failure in the first responsibility of his office. He had only negative aims and negative methods. He was a caretaker President. This lack of adequacy, in its way, as Truman's impulsiveness had in another way, illustrated again the structural weakness of the institution he represented. If one man was too impulsive and another too preoccupied with defense against wicked attacks on the budget, other Presidents, without exception, had been similarly lacking or preoccupied in other ways. Since men are Presidents, and since no man is perfect, no President will be perfect. The possibility sometimes occurred, rather vagrantly perhaps, to students of government that they might borrow the first principle of democracy for reform of the office. If many judgments are better than one and many men more likely to produce reasonable judgments, perhaps several Presidents might be better than one.

It was not unusual, in recent times, for thoughtful men to approach such a suggestion. President Hancher of the State University of Iowa was an example. In an address in 1955[7] he had this to say:

> The mere enumeration [of the President's functions], without regard to other demands on his time and talents, should be enough to show that the office is too comprehensive, too varied, too exacting and too isolated to be filled by any one man. The monarchs of Great Britain reign, but they do not govern. The Prime Minister governs, but he does not reign. Moreover, the Prime Minister is *primus inter pares,* and the authority which his office shares is a cabinet responsibility . . . But the President's authority and re-

---

[7] On the Shepared Foundation at the Ohio State University.

sponsibility are personal and ultimate. He may delegate, but he may
not share. He, and he alone, must bear both the authority and the
responsibility . . .

We need, he went on to say, a re-evaluation of those aspects of the
Constitution which assume a competency that men cannot be expected
to possess.

This was surely the kind of warning that Americans could not afford
to ignore. They were more frequent as time passed.

53

THE PRESIDENCY IS REGARDED PRIDEFULLY; PRESIDENTS EASILY ES-
tablish a rapport with the electorate, but there is nearly always some
criticism of their conduct and very often serious questioning as to the
worth of the institution itself. The President is said to have exceeded his
powers or to have used them in doubtful ways; to have played favorites;
to have condoned corruption; to have been guided by political considerations; to have tended toward regal behavior or, on the contrary,
toward a disgusting demagoguery—and sometimes the critics have
combined these last, as in the case of Jackson, who was called "King
Andrew." The doubts about the Presidency as an institution have gone
deeper and have been expressed in every generation. It was too strong
or too weak; it usurped the prerogatives of the Congress; its independence made policy-making and legislation slow and awkward; it attracted mediocrities or, on the contrary, ambitious men who were
greedy for power; it might turn toward dictatorship and, if it did, its
control of the armed forces would guarantee that it would succeed.

The proposals for change have been as frequent, almost, as the criticisms. Some have been reasonable and ably argued; others have been
carping and fanatic. And some, of course, have been purely partisan.
When, as has occasionally happened, a former critic has succeeded to
the office himself, he has found himself as little disposed to change
as the predecessors he criticized. So Jackson, who was a bitter critic
of J. Q. Adams, found many of the Adams policies ones he must adopt;
and Franklin D. Roosevelt continued many Hoover policies and
adopted much of his organization. The scope and opportunities of the
office, in spite of the inevitable accumulation of traditions, are its most
notable features.

The Presidency is indeed a volume to be written, not a script to be
read. And most Presidents have found their critics to be quite few in
number, however loud their outcries. Actually Americans have continued to be fascinated by the occupants of the White House as by no
one else in the Republic, and this, of course, is the reason that they can

be, as Wilson said, as big as they are capable of being. Or, it must be added, they can be the failures that their natures have determined. They can find, as Hoover did, that the respect and affection of the public can vanish as if by magic if they fail in their responsibilities.

We have seen serious questioning of the Executive as an independent Branch coming from students who have thought it necessary to change the structure of the government; and this has seemed more worthy of attention than the demands originating in political debate or in controversy among the Branches. The scholarly argument that the tripartite form was being adopted at the very time that the British were abandoning it has the weight of historic fact. Students have contended, moreover, that it has prevented the development of initiative, has led to inaction because of bickering over power, and more particularly has diffused responsibility as should never be allowed in a dynamic society. And the applicability of this caveat to the American case has sometimes seemed undeniable. We have paid attention to this kind of dissent, taking Woodrow Wilson as its most persuasive exponent. This was not only because he was the most eminent political theorist of a long generation but also because he subsequently became a two-term President himself, after which, he was still—it seemed—of the opinion that the British alternative was more desirable than the one chosen by the convention of 1787. If he, with all his learning and experience, felt the independent President unsuited to American circumstances, his judgment was entitled to respect.

He was by no means the only student who held this opinion. It could almost be said to have been orthodox among political scientists during Wilson's lifetime. There were variations, but Wilson was inclined to emphasize the Cabinet as the agency of British superiority—he spoke of "Cabinet," rather than "Parliamentary," government. In the *International Review*, some years before he published his first book, he offered a reason for thinking that the British solution was better:

> The merits of the two systems—Committee Government and Government by a responsible Cabinet—hinge upon . . . full and free discussion of all subjects of legislation; upon the principle stated by Mr. Bagehot that free government is self government—a government of the people, by the people . . .[1]

For it was his contention that the center of power in the United States had located itself in the irresponsible, almost anonymous, standing committees of the Congress, where there was no airing of issues, no free debate. They were inaccessible to democratic influences of any kind, and they could not be reached by the President. But if these committees

[1] August 1879.

were deprived of power and the Executive was made an arm of the Congress, there would be a transformation; policy would be made in open discussion, and it would be carried into execution under proper auspices and without insensate opposition.

There was not only academic support for this view; there were proposals for actually achieving its ends. One such was introduced as a bill by Senator Pendleton as early as April 1879. This provided that members of the Cabinet should occupy seats on the floor of the Senate and the House, with the right to participate in debates concerning their responsibilities, and that they should be required to attend the opening of Senate sessions on Tuesday and Friday of each week to answer questions. There was no action on the proposal, but there was widespread discussion. Among others who came to its support was a member of the New York Bar, Henry C. Lockwood, author of a book called *The Abolition of the Presidency*,[2] in which the Pendleton bill was said to be "one of the wisest propositions ever made in the history of our government." This was because it attacked "the almost unlimited power of the President," which shows well enough Lockwood's reason— and that of others—for hoping such a change might occur. His was a more drastic solution than most others; he wanted to go all the way back to the principle of the Continental Congress anterior to the Constitution and have the Executive made up of simple committees of the Congress:

> Our conclusion is that the Presidency should be abolished, and the following amendments to the Constitution be adopted: the supreme power of legislating and executing all laws of the United States shall be vested in the Congress (consisting of one body), which body shall be the final judge of its own powers, subject, nevertheless, to the right of the Executive Council, hereinafter provided for, at any time they shall elect, to dissolve Congress . . . and appeal to the people . . .

So it can be seen that he was nothing if not thorough. His revised Constitution would have allowed the Congress to appoint the Cabinet, and this body would have become the Executive Council he mentioned. Its chairman would have been the Secretary of State, and it would have had seats in the legislature and have been responsible to it for Executive behavior.

This curious throwback to earlier ideas was supported, as its author believed, by Spencer's *Political Institutions*. This influential nineteenth-century authority was quoted:

[2] (New York, 1884.) It was almost concurrent with Wilson's *Congressional Government*.

On the one hand it is needful that the men who have to carry out the will of the majority, as expressed through the legislature, should be removable at pleasure, so that there may be maintained the needful subordination of their policy to public opinion. On the other hand, it is needful that displacement of them should leave intact all that part of the Executive organization required for current administrative purposes . . .

There was behind this the implied belief that only the Congress—like the British Parliament—was truly representative, denying Jackson's claim, and that of other Presidents, that they are closely identified with popular sovereignty because elected by a national rather than a local constituency.

Although these proposals of the seventies and eighties brought about no actual changes, other movements, concurrent with them and also originating in dissatisfactions with government, did have some result. There was, for instance, a renewed concern about the civil service. And it was Senator Pendleton, too, who introduced the first bill for the establishment of a merit system; most of those, it seemed, who were interested in the one change were also in favor of the other.[3]

Others, more moderate, still thought constitutional revision necessary. Freeman's *Historical Essay on Presidential Government* (at p. 391) said:

The President cannot dissolve Congress, and he is in no way called on to resign his own office. Thus it is quite possible that the Executive and Legislative branches may be in discord for years. On the other hand, a President of whom Congress thoroughly approves may come to the end of his term of office when nothing calls for any change of men or measures, and though he may be re-elected, yet his continuance in office is at least jeopardized, and the country is obliged to go through the turmoil of a Presidential election . . . In truth the evil is one inherent in the form of government; it may, by judicious provisions, be made less baneful, but it cannot be got rid of altogether. It is the weak point of Presidential government—a weak point to be fairly balanced against its strong points, and against the weak points of other systems . . . If the President were elected by Congress, or by some body chosen by or out of Congress—if his Ministers were allowed to be members of Congress, or to appear or speak in Congress, the evils of

[3] Including, for instance, William Beach Lawrence, authority on public law and promoter of business ventures, who felt, he said, that the President was more a king than the British King. *North American Review*, November 1880.

the system would be greatly diminished, while the essential principle of Presidential government would remain untouched.

If this seems a strange way of not touching the "essential principle" of
presidential government, perhaps the very illogic shows what strained
efforts were being made to locate the source of dissatisfaction and to
propose a remedy.

This unsatisfactory something has seemed to a later generation to be
more a succession of incompetent Presidents—from Grant to Arthur—
than their independence. They wondered whether a structural change,
not in the general government but in the Presidency, might not be
indicated. But certainly Cleveland's vigor in contrast with the passivity
and circumspection of Hayes, the weak complaisance of Grant, and
the ineptness of Johnson, tended to demonstrate that the government
would work much better than had been supposed if men of wisdom
and initiative manned it. After Cleveland, it is true, there was not the
continued improvement that might have been hoped for. McKinley
was another Hayes, dignified but empty. Roosevelt was abnormally
effective but was immediately succeeded by Taft. Then after the
brilliant Wilson there came Harding, Coolidge, and Hoover. And, again
after another Roosevelt, the electorate opted for Eisenhower rather
than Stevenson, with every indication plain as to the kind of President
he would be. All these Republicans, with the exception of Hoover,
who was dogged by ill luck, were incapable of offering leadership and
dominating their eras; and if they had been competent, the evidence
seems to suggest that they would not have been chosen. There were, of
course, Wilson and the second Roosevelt. But it was necessary to acknowledge that since the Civil War, not counting Johnson, whose difficulties were special, there had been ten "weak" Presidents, two only
less weak, and no more than four "strong" ones.

There was something very wrong, if this counting was accepted, with
the process of selection. But it was not the weakness of the President
himself that those who wanted to reform the office centered on; most of
them were satisfied with the kind of Presidents the nation was getting, but they did want better administration. There was little more talk
of change to the British system after Cleveland. The new agitation
was for "efficiency and economy" to be reached by reform of officialdom.
To it generally can be attributed the modern Civil Service, the budget,
and the successive reorganizations of the Executive establishment during
and after the Roosevelt regime.[4]

Then there was the continuing Republican attitude that the Presi-

[4] The idea of Cabinet representation in the Congress has persistently
recurred since it was first suggested by Justice Story (according to Professor Corwin: *President, Office and Powers*, op. cit., 514) in Jackson's

dency was a potentially dangerous institution, a threat to laissez faire and pas trop gouverneur, a source, if encouraged and strengthened and especially if allowed to be occupied by a vigorous and ambitious

---

time. Story felt that the influence exerted by Cabinet members was "secret and silent" and, from that very cause, "might become overwhelming." When he said this he was talking about the activities of Jackson's second Cabinet, largely chosen from the earlier Kitchen Cabinet. He went on to say that the appearance of departmental heads would "compel the Executive to make appointments . . . not from personal or party favorites, but from statesmen of high public character, talents, experience, and elevated services . . ."

Garfield, many years later, advocated the appearance of Cabinet members on the floor of the Congress "but, of course, without a vote" (Works, II, 483). He shifted ground somewhat, however; what he hoped for, he said, was more open and direct relations between the legislature and the Executive. And this began a series of variations on this theme. There was evident a desire for an end to the bickering caused by mutual hostility. Wishing for good will was natural in Garfield's case, since he had lived as a Congressman through the sordid events of the Johnson impeachment trial and had seen the Senate's arrogant behavior toward Grant and Hayes.

After Wilson's excursions into this field, the argument was again taken up by Estes Kefauver, then a Representative, in the 1940s. His argument was summarized in The American Political Science Review, April 1944, 317–25. And Thomas K. Finletter again shifted the argument slightly in 1945 (in his Can Representative Government Do the Job? [New York, 1945]). He would have a joint Executive-Legislative Cabinet. But this idea, or a variety of it, was already in the air, having been suggested as a possibility by G. B. Galloway in 1940 and taken up by Senator La Follette in 1943, after first Wisconsin (in 1931) and then nine other states had created Legislative Councils having somewhat the same purpose and structure.

Thus there has been a persistent attempt on the part of theorists and practitioners to "bridge the gap," as they often put it, or "relieve the tension" between the Branches. Wilson, as we have seen, was the most thorough in his analysis, but interested not so much in good will as in securing practical progress and efficient leadership.

Many Presidents have adopted makeshift devices for liaison without giving away any powers; but a contemporary summary would have to record no progress either in the attempts to modify the constitutional situation, as Wilson would have done, or to induce the two Branches to regard each other with the friendliness that Garfield hoped for. And the tendency of modern theorists, after studying all this history, is to conclude that the tension so often deplored is necessary in a government of separated powers, and that any modification of it really goes to the heart of the tripartite system. They are very reluctant to agree that any change could stop short of abandoning its central principle.

individual, of demagogic proposals likely to burden business with regulations and increase the budget for welfare. Inevitably, however, in spite of delaying tactics and in spite, too, of Republican captures of the office with fair regularity, it expanded in every direction. It was impossible to prevent interferences in many fields where business practices were resented by the public. And labor, as it became organized, acquired enough influence to assert its claims; and these included governmental protections of many sorts from the exploitation of employers. Collective bargaining was legitimized, too, and became a responsibility of government to enforce. So it went. And responsibilities could seldom be disestablished once they had been accepted. Republican Presidents, no less than Democratic ones, administered a governmental organization of a size and scope undreamed of in Coolidge's day. Even when there was no emergency its employees remained many times those needed before assumption of new responsibilities during the New Deal.

It was in a kind of despair, because they could not get rid of the duties Roosevelt had assumed, that those who deplored the expansion joined in the efforts to make them more efficient. Thus the elaborate investigations of the Hoover Commissions, conducted by myriad experts, were authorized; and sometimes the recommendations were accepted. The enormous volume of *Reports* issuing from these endeavors baffled all but the most interested observers.

Apart, however, from the need for assessing the value of better operations with the criterion of efficiency in mind, there is always the matter of general objectives. And there was discernible in the Hoover attack on "inefficiency" a bias. It was the old Federalist-Whig-Republican one. There was an attempt to say what the government should and should not do. And much of the "reorganization" was simply an attempt to reduce governmental functions. The Hoover investigations being followed by another spell of Republican ascendancy there was another fairly formidable drive of this sort. Eisenhower was eager about this as about few other presidential activities. If he could not stop the "creeping socialism" that seemed to him so reprehensible, he would pass it on to the states. He proposed this to the Governors. They listened and thought him the amateur he undoubtedly was, as were also, in their opinion, the big businessmen from whom he got such directions. This drive on government, conducted from the very heart of government itself, was a failure. His became, perhaps while he was looking the other way, by far the largest and perhaps the best staff in presidential history, and it had more duties than any Presidency in time of peace. Nothing went to the states.[5]

[5] The message of decentralization was carried to state and local officials by spokesmen for the Administration on every suitable occasion. There

How could this really formidable campaign, headed by a popular President and conducted with all the elaborate apparatus of propaganda available to big business and to the now-enlarged Presidency, and conducted through eight years, be so colossal a failure? The inner citadel of government was controlled by those intending to contract its activities and to return the Presidency to its status during the McKinley or the Coolidge regimes; why could they not succeed? The explanation is, of course, to be found in the national demand for collective services. People still responded to revivalist exhortations—Eisenhower called his campaign a "crusade"—and evinced horror at the thought of unbalanced budgets, inflation, dishonest dollars, burdensome taxes, interfering bureaucrats, and restrictive regulations. But when the attack on the "spenders" and "do-gooders" was over and the crusade

---

was, for instance, a newspaper account of the policy as detailed to the City Managers Association by Robert E. Merriam, Assistant to the Director of the Budget, on October 25, 1957. The headline for the story read: "Ike's States Rights Policy Told to City Managers." But the city managers were not receptive to such a suggestion (the Washington *Post,* October 25, 1957).

A summary of the Eisenhower effort was made by Washington correspondent Roscoe Drummond in 1959; he said of the "noble experiment" launched at the Williamsburg Governors' Conference in 1957, intended to give back to the states some of the functions pre-empted by the Federal government and "to reverse the flow of power from the state capitals to Washington:

What has happened? Nothing has happened. There have been no accomplishments . . . no Governor has arranged for his state to recover a single function which the Eisenhower Administration has offered to give back. . . .

Mr. Drummond thought the reasons were obvious. He listed them:

1. The Governors of the more prosperous states have so much on their hands that they feel no Federal encroachment . . .

2. There are other Governors who theoretically would like to see certain functions recovered by the states but who cannot bring themselves to levy the state taxes to finance these functions even when the Federal Government abandons these same taxes.

3. There are also Governors who would rather have the states' rights issue to talk about than solve it. They know they can't recover a state right without recovering a state responsibility and when they complain about the Federal Government performing a service which belongs to the states, they really don't want the service performed at all, either by the states or Federal Government.

He went on also to say that "underlying all of these resistances by the states . . . is a weakness of every state government, which, until it is corrected, will prevent any important redress of the balance. That weakness is the distorted representation of rural districts in the legislatures." (the Washington *Post,* August 5, 1959).

had run its course, the government was bigger, stronger, more responsible than ever. So was the Presidency. It fell to Eisenhower, who seemed completely unaware of any inconsistency, to request the building of an entire new structure—the old State, War and Navy building having been by 1956 filled to overflowing—on Jackson Square to house the presidential staff, now numbering thousands.

It was quite clear that the Presidency was not going to be abolished, as had been suggested a few times; that it was not going to become an arm of the Congress, as had been proposed so often by serious students and statesmen; and that it was not going to decline in importance. It was, on the contrary, clearly destined to grow even larger and to acquire enhanced responsibilities. If this was true, then the problem was not to contract and limit it but make it more responsive to the demands certain to fall upon it.

★ 54 ★

THE LONG REPUBLICAN DOMINANCE GAINED FROM THE CIVIL WAR
and lasting into the twentieth century, interrupted only temporarily
by the Cleveland and Wilson Administrations, was a time of fantastic
economic expansion—but also of social change and disturbance. It was
natural that Republicans should claim credit for the expansion, dwell-
ing on the virtues of free enterprise, and that they should blame fate for
the accompanying ills—recurrent hard times, a rising cost of living, long
hours, low pay, and miserable living conditions. This was a politically
successful strategy until free enterprise produced a depression too
cataclysmic to be explained in the usual terms or to be treated with
the usual remedy—"allowing nature to take its course." The energetic
performance of Roosevelt from 1933 on produced the first real majority
the Democratic party had commanded since the Civil War. Neither of
the Democratic Presidents who had broken the long Republican reign
from 1860 to 1932 had had a clear and safe majority, and neither had
been able to pass on his office to a Democratic successor. The recourse
of the electorate to Eisenhower, even in later Democratic times, and the
perpetuation of the Republican-style executive, make it appropriate to
recall for contemporaries the views of the party able to hold the office
so persistently.

These were, and are, of course, the same views as those of the Whigs
who were the Republicans' ancestors, so there was nothing really new
about them, and they were doubtless ones that would always be held
by financiers, businessmen, creditors—the more prosperous citizens
generally: government ought not to interfere in private affairs, it had no
responsibility for welfare, and its operations ought to be kept at a minimum unless they were of assistance to business. It would not do to say
that repeated electoral victories were solely attributable to this appeal;
but it was in fact generally used in an era of success. The vote of the
veterans certainly helped in winning several close contests after the
Civil War, and the attribution of disloyalty to the Democrats was effective for a lengthy period; but this issue gradually lost its attractive-

ness, and the Whig economic and political doctrines reassumed their importance as political themes. Also, their sponsors continued to win, whether or not because of them.

But laissez faire states' rights and Federal weakness were negative theories, and it can be guessed that they might not have been so persistently associated with success if they had not been supplemented by the issue of radicalism just as patriotic slogans were losing their appeal. Talk about communism did not begin when the Russian Revolution first frightened men of influence in America; it was then that the persecution of radicals became open and official; but the representatives of big business and big finance—and conservative politicians —had been making loud outcries about radicalism ever since labor troubles had begun to appear. A certain number of repressed workers sought solace in socialist alternatives to the capitalism that seemed to bear so heavily upon them, but most of them remained as devoted to free enterprise as any capitalist. Nevertheless, they were accused of full apostasy if they dared question the beneficence of their employers. Working up a scare about revolutionary intentions among labor leaders was a favorite political device, and somehow they were always attached to the Democrats. The Republicans, once the party of Union and loyalty, easily became the party of Americanism and prosperity. The Democrats naturally did not accept classification as radicals any more happily than they had accepted the stigma of disloyalty, and they were even more reluctant to concede the Republican claim to prosperity. But they did have a tendency to espouse panaceas which repelled more solid citizens. They stopped short of suggesting any serious reorganization of the economic system; but a considerable number had a weakness for cheap money, they seemed more sympathetic to welfare schemes, and their concern for budget balancing easily gave way to appeals for spending. This frightened all those who had savings, insurance, or pensions, and all who were creditors. There seemed to be more of these—or more who voted—than there were of debtors. At least Bryan's challenges were turned back, and the Republicans continued to win.

The Democrats were so intimidated at one stage after their long immolation as traitors, radicals, and do-gooders that they sought respectability with desperate concentration. Even this did not succeed. If the electorate wanted Republicans, real ones were available; they would not accept a Parker or a Davis. It was only when there was a serious Republican split— between those who would have committed the party to a policy of progressivism and those who wanted no change from the old ways—that a Democrat could win. Wilson was a minority President; and after his two terms the return to Republicanism was immediate. Generally speaking— with an exception for the brief interlude of the New Deal in the wake of the depression—the period from 1912 on would be one of uncertain balance. Neither party could lay claim, successfully, to any special responsibility for national security or for domestic tranquillity. The Democrats had a national majority, it seemed, but the Republicans were able to regain and hold the White House.

What difference there was in social beliefs—and the Democrats strove mightily to erase that, strange as it may seem, since a party must have some claim to an attitude—continued the old contrast between conservatism and liberal-progressivism. But the Democrats claimed to be even more solicitous of business interests, even more devoted to free enterprise, even more capable of keeping open opportunities than the Republicans. To be sure, they were against *big* business, but not very clearly or emphatically, except in oratory, because it was not apparent what a big business, as opposed to a small one, was. But these issues tended to be played down rather than emphasized in campaigns;[1] and after Roosevelt's signal success with the Social Security issue after the long depression of the thirties, the Republicans claimed it as their own, much as the Tories in Britain had done with the welfare state, and the Democrats were so anxious to escape the radical label that they allowed this potential asset to evaporate. They lost the right to claim that theirs was the party of progress as presently they were to lose, under Truman, the claim to being the party of peace. They still longed to be known as respectable, economical, and patriotic.[2]

The tendency toward indistinguishability of the two great parties had an immense influence on the institution of the Presidency. In spite of Jackson's example, the Democrats tended to acquiesce, as in so much else, in the Republican conception of the office; it seemed to be part of their attempt to appear conservative. The Chief Executive was to be subordi-

[1] It ought to be noted, in this connection, how badly split the party was between progressives and conservatives. But a broad spectrum of opinion characterized both great parties and caused both to seek compromises during campaigns which brought them so close that their views became practically indistinguishable, except that each claimed to be more enthusiastically virtuous than the other.

[2] This tendency of parties to become almost indistinguishable forced electoral campaigns to concentrate on emotion rather than reason, something politics was likely to lead to anyway. The historian James Harvey Robinson once remarked of presidential campaigns that they were "designedly made into emotional orgies which endeavor to distract attention from the real issues involved, and they actually paralyse what slight powers of cerebration man can normally muster." He was looking at some thirty presidential contests, and perhaps those of the twentieth century were no worse than some earlier ones. W. H. Harrison's election was the most notorious political flim-flam of record.

nate to the legislature; he was to be kept in a restricted state. In spite of the agreement of both parties on this view, the Presidency actually developed in precisely the opposite direction. It did this because it was necessary for the nation that it should; it may have been an unwanted transformation, but the fact was indisputable. It developed more rapidly in Democratic times; but some Republicans—Theodore Roosevelt, for instance—were among the more notable expanders.

Crises enhanced the Presidency; when there was need for decisive action the Executive must supply it. But legislators only reluctantly reconciled themselves to exclusion from execution; they still interfered whenever they could, and they periodically claimed the right to give minute directions. But their impermanence in office, their ties to local interests, their need for support in campaigning, their dispersal of authority through committees—and perhaps the nature of those who offered themselves for office—made their claims to managerial functions absurd. There was no doubt that the Legislative Branch, under the pressures of a high-energy economy, was gradually being reduced to argumentation, to investigation, and to acquiescence in presidential planning. The Executive was more and more relied on by the electorate to divine its wishes, to formulate its policies, and to see that the measures necessary for national security and prosperity were taken and carried out. More and more it was assumed that the President must, if necessary, coerce or persuade the Congress. In this sense he was indeed the Chief Legislator as well as the Chief Executive.

It is strange, in view of this, that the presidential office hardly changed at all in the physical sense until the Administration of Theodore Roosevelt, and even then not radically. He is usually spoken of as the first "modern" President, but it was actually under Democratic auspices that the office was modernized; and this was not because the Democrats meant to enhance it, but because they had a series of crises to overcome and had to find the means for overcoming them. Two wars and a great depression fell to them to see through; and emergencies, as we know, call for strong Presidents with broad powers and administrative competence.

There had been a gradual growth of the Civil Service; but the Cabinet, enlarged to include Departments of Labor, of Commerce, and of Agriculture, was not much altered in status. And there had been an Interior Department since 1849. But the President's own staff was incredibly meager. In Grant's time the whole appropriation for his office had amounted to $13,800. For this he was supposed to employ a private secretary, a clerk or two, a stenographer, and a steward. He resorted, as Lincoln had done, to borrowing. Generals Babcock, Comstock, and Porter became his right-hand men; and he had, as aides, Generals Badeau and Dent. White remarked of this situation that "the personal assistance authorized for the President by Congress amply demonstrated that the

President was not expected to play a creative role in the administrative system." All through the Republican dominance, the Congress expected to —and for the most part did—designate the official to be in charge of any activities it authorized; it also expected that this official would accept "advice" about appointments outside the Civil Service and that each year he would return to the appropriate committees to report and ask for further appropriations: these were gone into in detail and were one of the most important devices for keeping the administrative personnel subordinated and submissive.

That his office was starved was only one, but an important one, of the evidences that the President was not expected to be Chief Executive. And the office did not grow as the nation expanded; it fell farther and farther behind, so that when Wilson had to organize for war there had almost to be an administrative revolution. White spoke of this lag:

> The President's office made an apparent gain during the McKinley administration, but the increase of staff was only partly the kind the President needed. By the appropriation act of 1901 Congress authorized a secretary and two assistant secretaries, two executive clerks, and four clerks, two of whom were telegraphers, as well as numerous doorkeepers and messengers. McKinley thus had authority to hire a personal civilian staff about equivalent to that which Grant had secured by detail from the army.[3]

It does not need to be said that Hayes, Garfield, Arthur, Cleveland, and Harrison had fared no better. Especially the private secretary, who could be extremely useful if he were a person of some caliber, was insufficiently paid—or paid attention to—to be of much account. Hayes had difficulty in persuading anyone to work with him and finally fell back on an old friend who was quite hapless and incompetent. When Garfield tried to persuade John Hay to become his secretary, Hay responded that "contact with the greed and selfishness of office seekers and bulldozing Congressmen" would be unspeakably repulsive. Cleveland had no better luck and finally spoke of paying for a competent person out of his own pocket.

Meanwhile it must be noted how difficult certain of the conditions fixed by the Constitution, or by immediately succeeding agreements, made the President's situation. If we think of him, for the moment, not only as a putative Chief Executive but as Chief of State, Social Mentor, National Planner, and Guardian of Security and Welfare, we shall understand better the dilemma in which he found himself—with so much to do and so little to do it with. And by now even Republican Presidents, however unhappily and however much against the general expectation, occupied an almost Jacksonian position. They often deplored it and often tried to

[3] *The Republican Era,* op. cit., 102.

slough off responsibilities, but their escape was impossible. Differences became ones of degree, no matter what the party.

The increasing difficulty Presidents found in getting through their work had part of its origin in the fairly unargued decision of the framers to have a single rather than a plural Executive. This was in the tradition of the Governorships, taken, it would seem, without realizing how different the situation of the future President would be from that of the existing state executives, as well as without imagining how the nation must expand. The first of these differences was one of simple scale, together with the enormous burden of powers and duties certain to accumulate gradually. But the second was the concentration upon one person of the hopes and fears of a vast continental country with the intensified glare of publicity resulting from spectacularly improved organs of publicity.

If this concentration had from the beginning been dispersed to a Council of Presidents there would have been no official mansion occupied by one conspicuous family; the President would not have become the sole Chief of State; he would not have been the leader of his party, or at least not the single leader; and he would not have borne alone the responsibility of planning for national security and internal welfare. Also, he would not have been, as he would eventually be forced to become, in spite of opposition views and of congressional obstruction, the sole director of the immense administrative machine. All these duties and responsibilities would have been shared with others.

Since he would not have been alone in the White House in semi-royal state, with relatives and associates of consuming interest to all his fellow citizens, it would not have been a matter of such consequence whether or not he had an invalid wife and irresponsible children, whether his secretaries and his physician were incorruptible and competent, or whether he possessed social graces as well as wisdom and political talent. He would not, in other words, have been the focus of interest and the symbol of Union for the whole American people, watched with avid curiosity and criticized inevitably by those with standards of conduct differing from his own.[4]

[4] Eisenhower's successors would be indebted to him for some changes in the demanding White House social routine. The closeness of nations as air travel and telecommunications improved made many former customs and procedures obsolete and offered new problems for solution. Diplomacy was vitally affected. Ponderous negotiation through ministries and ambassadorial establishments, so fondly clung to by the professionals, became more and more absurd. And even Eisenhower, whose disposition was to resist contacts among chiefs of state, had finally to give way as Wilson, Roosevelt, and Truman had done.

But if as Chief of State the President must also accept the duty of

We have already seen that this whole range of presidential experience is apart from, yet by custom involved with, the more serious duties of office. It can contribute to or can detract from success in leadership to an amazing degree. It is strange, for this reason, that the framers seem not to have realized the significance of the decision for a single Executive. Nevertheless, it can be imagined why it happened. Essentially it was because the nationalists or centralizers of 1787, who believed in a strong government and an effective Executive as part of the strong government, prevailed. Apparently no one asked himself whether a plural Executive, properly constituted, could be effective too. It was simply assumed that pluralism would mean division and dispersal of power, and so a less secure Union.

The New Jersey Plan, to be recalled as the counter, in the Constitutional Convention, to the Virginia Plan, contemplated a plural Executive, and that proposal was intended as the riposte of the small states to the large ones and of those who thought the Convention ought to "revise" the Articles of Confederation rather than adopt a new structure—"revised, corrected and enlarged" was the phrase used in the Paterson draft offered on June 15, 1787. Article 4, concerning the Executive, provided:

---

negotiating, another burden was added to his already impossibly heavy responsibility. Slowly the readjustments forced by this acceptance were registered. One that other Presidents would have been grateful for was that the "social schedule" of the White House was finally abandoned in 1959.

There had been eleven regularly scheduled social functions—six dinners and five receptions—even as late as 1953–54. The dinners had been for the Vice-President, the Chief Justice, the Speaker, the Cabinet, and the Ambassadors of foreign countries (two). The receptions had honored the diplomatic corps, the judiciary, the military, the Congress, and government Departments. As other Presidents had usually managed to do, using one or another excuse, Eisenhower reduced these obligations until in 1959 he abandoned them completely. The excuse given was that many foreign heads of state were continually being entertained and that most of those formerly invited to the old fixed functions were included among the guests on these occasions. (For an account of the Eisenhower accommodations to social pressure, see the Washington *Star*, August 12, 1959.)

But the fact was that choices were having to be made among presidential duties and that gradually more and more were being eliminated as more and more were also being delegated. The ceremonial functions would necessarily be sacrificed to those having to do with vital national interests. If this tended to shut the President away from casual and social contacts and made available to him only prepared, routinized, and formal opinions and digests, that was a penalty of asking one individual to do more than one individual *could* do.

That the United States in Congress be authorized to elect a federal executive to consist of——persons, to continue in office for the term of——years; to receive punctually, at stated times, a fixed compensation for services by them rendered, in which no increase or diminution shall be made, so as to affect the persons composing the executive at the time of such increase or diminution. . . .[5]

This matter was briefly referred to in the opening chapters of this book. And there was a good deal more in this draft making it plain that the Executive was not only to be plural but was to be an organ of the legislature, thus following the precedent of the Continental Congress. It was apparently concluded incidentally during this discussion that any plural Executive would be a weak and subservient one, not a necessary implication, but quite natural in the circumstances.

This apprehension would have repelled the nationalists and generally would have identified pluralism with weakness. At any rate, the advocates of a strong Union wanted the Executive to be independently chosen and *not* to be responsible to the legislature. And since the only models for this required a single individual, the plural form was not even considered. When this faction prevailed in the Convention, there was left only the question of the accepted President's powers and of his relations with the other Branches. But the choice of the Convention did not still the dissent. And Hamilton, during the next year in *The Federalist,* brought to bear on the continuing argument all the resources of his debating skill. In his exposition, too, we can see that the single Executive was considered to be necessary if "energy and responsibility," his two paramount criteria, were to be attained. This was because there must be "unity." As he put it, "Decision, activity, secrecy, and despatch will generally characterize the proceedings of any greater number; and in proportion as the number is increased, these qualities will be diminished." But the worst fault of the proposal for plurality, he felt, was that it "would tend to conceal faults and destroy responsibility."[6]

The discussion was ended with ratification. Once Washington was in office, offering his version of the Presidency, it seemed unthinkable that there could be an alternative; and soon the President seemed an expression of the very genius of American democracy. There never has been any serious renewal of the argument, so accepted has the office become—necessary to politics in operation as well as to government in process.

It is, however, possible to conceive that many of the deficiencies that

[5] *Journal of the Constitutional Convention of 1787* (1819 ed.), 123–27.

[6] The exposition of Executive duties and the argument for a single head ran through eleven numbers of *The Federalist*–from No. 67 to 77 inc.

grew upon government even by Republican tests, and many of the handicaps of the Presidency, even when the President was supposed to have a
restricted role, were traceable to the adoption of singleness rather than
plurality as a principle; also that the latent argument for plurality, never
raised seriously in recent times, might well rest on the greater efficiency
and effectiveness to be found in the plural as contrasted with the single
form. The impossible situation of the President pressing for powers and
organization consonant with the responsibilities to which he is inexorably
committed, and burdened with political and ceremonial duties he cannot
escape, makes some change imperative. And this is true even if Presidents
of the highest competence could always be expected to be chosen.

★ 55 ★

FROM TIME TO TIME—ALWAYS IN THE REGIMES OF THE STRONG PRESI-
dents or immediately afterward—expressions of fear about dictatorship
have had a certain prominence. These have never had any depth in popular feeling, but they have sometimes come from quite responsible persons.
The President, they have said, might determine that only he could deal
with aggressor nations or that only he could protect the people from
domestic predators. In some crisis, when the Rule of Necessity had been
invoked and most of the government's powers had been gathered into his
control, he might simply refuse to give them up. And, being Commander in
Chief, he could stand off any challenging authority. Alarmists at such times
have recalled Patrick Henry's exclamation when the President was suggested at the Convention, to the effect that he almost was, and might easily
become, a king. This has been the gross fear. A less exigent but equally
real one has been that, under the guise of Necessity again, but not necessarily in a dangerous crisis, the presidential powers might expand and
expand until freedom of enterprise and individual liberties might be lost.
The President would become a kind of Orwellian Big Brother. There
would be order and security, maintained by a vast officialdom, but there
would be no liberty, perhaps not even much privacy.

What actually has happened, as we have seen, is that as a result of
growing governmental responsibilities and consequent presidential ones—
because leadership and decision-making must center somewhere—the
Presidency has been enormously enlarged. But also we have seen that,
even though the enlargement has been enormous, it may possibly not
have been enough. And it has not been at the expense of the other
Branches.

Presidential aggression is quite incorrectly deduced from the contracted
scope of the Legislative Branch, which, because of its obvious unsuitability
for certain duties, has tended to increase its delegations and to restrict its
ventures into Executive territory. Aside from minor harassments, it has
tended to fall back on general definition, the marking out of limits, and
the setting of standards. This has involved a considerable growth of ad-

ministrative legislation in the process of extrapolating congressional directives. But much of the delegation has been to independent agencies whose inroads on the Executive have been far more serious than any made by the Congress directly. And the Comptroller General, acting as the deputy of the Congress, has increased his interferences with Executive action.

The Congress has, then, made delegations not only to the Executive but to two kinds of new creations in the attempt to escape its own inherent incapabilities—the independent agencies and the Comptroller General. And still it has not gone far enough to gain the time it ought to have for the better performance of its more suitable duties. These have too often been left to small unsupervised segments of itself and have been done irresponsibly—for instance, investigation and oversight, very important matters, have been seriously discredited by the conduct of committees and subcommittees in recent years.[1]

What the Executive has gained, aside from its repeated expansions in national emergencies, has come to it because of social and economic change. Most of it has been into new, not old, areas. There is an infinity of adjustments incident to the growth of population, improvements in tech-

---

[1] There was an attempt to cut down and reorganize these proliferating committees in the La Follette-Monroney Act of 1946. What started out to be a thoroughgoing reform of congressional procedures was much weakened in passage. It followed a period of extremely bad relationships between President and Congress during which a number of suggestive studies appeared. The most important of these was G. B. Galloway's *Congress at the Crossroads*. Mr. Galloway, in fact, was not only director of the La Follette-Monroney Joint Committee but also chairman of a committee of the Political Science Association on congressional reorganization. We have already spoken of the Galloway recommendation in another connection. He would have established a Legislative Council "to be composed of the Vice President, the Speaker of the House, the majority leaders in both chambers, and the chairmen of the reorganized standing committees" (sitting separately in each House). It would have been "the duty of the Legislative Council to plan and coordinate the legislative program of Congress and to promote more effective liaison and cooperation with the Executive." This suggestion was widely supported by political scientists (cf., for instance, "The Relation of the President to Congress" by W. E. Binkley, *Parliamentary Affairs*, III, 1 [London, 1949]). It was, however, ignored. Perhaps the Congress knew itself better than the political scientists knew it. But the committee system was streamlined, a reform which did not last; there were soon numerous special committees pursuing probes and investigations, their chairmen assiduously hunting headlines or just as assiduously covering up for favored interests, without any discoverable relationship to the legislative function, and without any effective oversight by the Congress as a whole.

nology, and the demands of a people learning to enjoy a high level of living, and many involve the government; but the Congress can do very little about them except to direct that the Executive or an independent agency assume responsibility. It must forgo even the specification of operations.

The intent of legislative Acts when delegations of this sort are made can be forwarded or defeated in administration. So far as it is the President who is charged with new duties, it has to be recognized that his person is not indefinitely expansible. He must delegate too; and these delegations are of more and more significant matters. He can make only a few of the decisions, the appointments, the communications with subordinates required in every working day; and one of the duties of his staff is to decide what the President shall decide. But what this means is that the Presidency becomes an institution, and to a certain extent an autonomous one. So far as the new duties go to independent agencies, it has to be recognized that such of them as are Executive ought not to go to them at all. That they have is partly because of the inefficiency and known overburdening of the Presidency. If it were more capable there would be a check to this particular tendency.

President Eisenhower went farther than any of his predecessors in not doing what legislation directed to be done, sometimes quite openly; but this reluctance to accept congressional judgment above his own was only an extension of the tendency shown by most of the modern Executives.[2] By no means were all such decisions actually made by the President himself; not infrequently he discovered such departures after the fact and had to assume responsibility for them. It must be noted that this is one of the inevitable characteristics of Executives of the Eisenhower sort. If the President does not himself attend to matters, those who do attend to them will modify their instructions to conform with their preferences—which may not accord with those of the Congress or even of the President. The extraordinary complexity and the immense volume of governmental duties made these modifications more likely as time passed. But there seemed no alternative to the increase of delegations.[3]

There has been an enlargement of staff which, if that alone could cure presidential incompetence and overwhelming responsibility, would have

[2] In Eisenhower's case it was usually a refusal to undertake as much —to spend as much—as the Congress had appropriated. Economy was the fetish of this particular Administration and inflation its most dreaded calamity.

[3] In 1950 the McCormack Act (64 Stat. 419) authorized the President to delegate many minor functions required to be performed by him under former statutes. The immediate result was dozens of Executive Orders assigning these duties to others.

sufficed. We have only to recall that so recent a President as Hoover had a staff numbering forty-two, and then to compare with this Eisenhower's twelve hundred. The growth to Hoover's forty-two had been a gradual and reluctant one through some hundred and forty years; Eisenhower's twelve hundred had accumulated in little more than twenty years. This would seem to indicate a belief that this expansion would create a satisfactory Presidency.[4] Yet the dissatisfaction has not been eliminated. In one or another respect the Roosevelt, Truman, and Eisenhower Administrations all were criticized for not getting through presidential work; and it became obvious that proliferation of staff was not a sufficient remedy. During the war Roosevelt neglected domestic concerns to concentrate on being Commander in Chief; and this neglect, however unavoidable, was notorious and costly. Truman, in spite of his large staff, made snap decisions of fatal significance—such as that to use the atomic bomb when Japan was already trying to surrender (which he may not have known) and, in another field, to seize the steel plants when he was not certain he could make the decision effective.[5] And Eisenhower, although he was more skilled in using staff and more willing to delegate than any of his predecessors, was still much criticized for inattention to many of his duties.

[4] Figures cited here are not to be taken as strictly accurate. There are many reasons why the presidential staff cannot actually be counted. In the first place, there are many borrowings. Presidents have frequently had numerous assistants who were on other payrolls. In the second place, individuals or groups in the agencies or Departments are put to work on White House assignments of various sorts. Also, sheer outsiders are asked to take assignments from the President and seldom refuse. These—and other—subterfuges have become less necessary with the growing recognition that the Presidency is an institution, not an individual. If a date can be assigned to the change of attitude in this matter, it is probably 1937. This was when the lucid *Report* of the Committee on Administrative Management was published. But it is always a mistake to assign too definite an origin to general developments of this sort.

[5] An incident referred to before. Unfortunately it cannot be discussed here at the length it deserves. It resulted in a new and curious judicial doctrine, called by Professor Tanenhaus "the relativity of Presidential power." Whatever else it did, this decision asserted the right of the Court to say when the Rule of Necessity should operate and perhaps to say what the President may do when it does operate. In only two former instances had the Court ventured to limit the Presidency. These occurred during the New Deal, and Roosevelt fought back with the Court reorganization plan of 1937. There is a short but helpful discussion of these issues in "The Supreme Court and Presidential Power" by Professor Tanenhaus in *The Annals* of the Academy of Political and Social Science, September 1956, 106–13.

It was often said, during his first six years, that he delegated so much as hardly to be President at all. But perhaps the most seriously sustained criticism was that the procedure had become clumsy and awkward, slow and confused. When so many minds with conflicting prejudices converge on one decision, the struggle for primacy among them may result in unhappy compromises and confused advice.

President Eisenhower was surrounded by the agencies surviving from the Truman and Roosevelt incumbencies together with some new ones.[6] What this formidable institution, rivaling now in numbers and in many other ways the legislative institution—although that too was expanding its staff in almost as spectacular a way at the other end of Pennsylvania Avenue—ought to become as it further developed had not been considered. There had been such concentration on administrative capability— the advances in budgeting, personnel management, and so on, were preceded by elaborate and lengthy campaigns to promote their adoption —that no substantial change in the Presidency itself seemed ever to be thought of. It was very generally assumed that the deficiencies of Wilson, Coolidge, Harding, Hoover, Roosevelt, Truman, and Eisenhower could be remedied by better organization and more assistants. It was apparently in this belief that Eisenhower bequeathed to his successor new proposals for a reorganized staff.

Yet such questions were hinted at. Professor Koenig, for instance, thoughtfully recalled:

Of the thirty-three men who have occupied the Presidency, at least several rank among the world's great statesmen, and six or more deserve ranking as "strong" Presidents. None . . . has represented

[6] Among them the enhanced Bureau of the Budget, in development since 1921 (for a short modern appraisal, cf. Robert E. Merriam, sometime assistant to the Director, later an assistant to the President, *The Annals*, op. cit., 15–23); the Council of Economic Advisers (established under the Employment Act of 1946 and in some measure a successor to the National Resources Planning Board, etc., of the New Deal); the National Security Council; and the Office of Defense Mobilization. It also ought to be noted that there were now a staff secretary and a Cabinet secretariat; the one presumably captained the President's personal assistants; the other, after so many years, regularized the life of the Cabinet, perhaps erecting it into the Council avoided by so many Presidents in the past. Besides these, the chairman of the Civil Service Commission now served as the President's Adviser on Personnel Management, this in avoidance of the recommendations of the reorganizing commissions that a personnel office be substituted for the Civil Service Commission, which had long outlasted its usefulness. (There was irony in this congressional reluctance to disestablish an agency it had seen created with such anguished reluctance and had for so many years regarded with hostility.)

the more extreme forms of political vileness. No dictator or despot, no scoundrel or profligate has appeared. Yet, as we well know, we have had men who have pursued folly, were naïve, indolent, or blind to reality while the storm clouds of tragedy gathered . . .

Not only have there been Presidents whose weaknesses have endangered the Union or the national security, but the present-day situation rather invites a return to mediocrity:

Television puts a new premium on affability. The winsome grin and mellifluous tonality do wonders for a Presidential candidate. The uncertainties of our nuclear age bring new mass stirrings of the father complex which makes anxious people overvalue the President as he appears and uncritical of him as he really is . . .

But to remedy all this, Professor Koenig suggests nothing beyond improvement of the "institutional side of the Presidency." Review of the recent expansions encourages him to say at least that

the inaction of a Buchanan or a Coolidge would nowadays be challenged by a variety of staff sources . . . the President would be expected to come forward with policy on a considerable number of more or less stated occasions . . . therefore, it would be far more difficult for a present-day Coolidge to count apples and serenely wear out his rocking chair while the country raced into economic doom.[7]

Pretty obviously there is much more to be said about the substitution of competence in the staff for competence in the President himself—that symbolic figure so often referred to in recent literature. But one thing at least may be said. A mediocre President with political charm is unlikely to become a dictator. His talents are of another sort; he longs for approbation and is apt to shrink from the responsibility for operating machinery he does not understand and for making decisions he knows are vital but which involve grave risks. But then democracy does not evolve in the direction of dictatorship anyway. It is more likely to create a diffused and witless authority—and staff may go toward remedying this. Dictatorship may be imposed by a determined minority on an underdeveloped society with a low-energy economy (Russia, for example); it may even be imposed on a high-energy economy whose people (like the Germans of the thirties) have a grievance they feel can be redressed by a conquest of neighbors who have pressed in on them or have deprived them of room to expand; but in the United States of the present, whose people have no large grievance, who have plenty of room and so have no

---

[7] The quotations here are from "The Man and the Institution," *Annals,* op. cit., 10 ff.

incentive to accept the disciplines necessary to conquest, and who have always been more likely to break up in dissension than to harden into totalitarian unity, a dictator is inconceivable except in time of peril. It is even difficult for some Americans to exploit others in the way elites have exploited submerged masses from history's beginning. Resentment among free people stirs easily and finds a champion who soon commands the power to compel redress. The United States is not a classless nation with no inequalities, but disadvantages for individuals are usually temporary. Envy and ambition have a ready scope, and there is a characteristic fluidity about status that baffles analysis. It is hard to keep anyone down who has abilities that ought to make him rise, and it is hard to keep anyone up who lacks the abilities that ought to keep him there. It is, in other words, an uncommonly persistent democracy; and it has, as John Dewey remarked, the self-repairing ability, got from its universal education, to keep it that way, an awkward and slow but reliable built-in safeguard.

The Executive of a nation thus incorrigibly committed to the processes of democracy is bound to operate as democrats will approve. He is not likely to move toward the gathering of more power, which he fears because he knows he cannot stretch his judgment to all its issues and because he always has a wary eye on his eager detractors. When wholesale delegation to the President occurs in war or in domestic emergency, he responds then to the demand for an unnatural unity, bringing focused powers to bear on the enemy or the problem; but once the emergency is past, or even when its end can be seen in the distance, the discipline vanishes like smoke in the wind.[8] And suddenly the wielder of emergency powers finds that he no longer possesses them. His administrative machine, even his military machine, controls a reluctant people. Any impulse he may have to hang onto his expanded prominence is soon discouraged.

But to say this is to say something Americans know and consider trite. And Presidents are always aware of it, even those who have been conditioned to military life and might be expected to have soldiers' views of discipline. There never has been a President—except perhaps the second Roosevelt in a curious modified way and in a most exigent crisis—who ever thought of dictatorship as possible or desirable; and if Roosevelt really thought of it at all, he thought of it in connection with the need to make exploiters, profiteers, and disrupters consider the public interest while the nation fought for its life. And the soldier-Presidents—Washing-

[8] As it began to weaken in 1944 and again after the Korean war, forcing the premature disbanding of military forces and the abandonment of control measures, in spite of all the President could do or say. Confusion and disastrous price inflation resulted, but they were evidently preferred to the disciplines that would have prevented them.

ton, Taylor, Grant, Eisenhower—have on the whole been more respectful of institutions they did not understand very well, not being politicians, than those Presidents who were professionals. But the argument need not be labored. There have been students—very respectable ones too—who at one or another juncture have voiced fears that dictatorship was about to be imposed. It must be said, however, that there has always been a certain unreality about their anguish. It could usually be suspected that an unreasonable animus activated their charges. They did not *really* believe what they were saying.

If dictatorship is out of character for the United States, although it seems not to have been for dozens of other nations; and if the President cannot, by using the cleverest administrative devices and by devoting to his duties the utmost industry, stretch his personal direction over the enormous machine he commands; and if he often cannot find the time, to say nothing of the capability, to make all the vital decisions he is supposed to make—then we do have to ask ourselves in what other way the institution can be enlarged to meet the looming responsibilities of an even more demanding future. It would be foolish to assume, too, that the percentage of great men chosen for the Presidency will rise. The record is not reassuring: six "strong" Presidents, six more acknowledged to have been competent; but this is only about one third of the total. And if we assess the increased literacy and thoughtfulness of the electorate against its tendency to allow itself the luxury of emotional attachments, the result is not too reassuring.[9]

Will there have to be an enlargement of the Presidency itself, not merely of its appurtenances, its staff, and its organizational spread, but of the person, the decision-maker, the national symbol? It would be possible, of course, to go back to the discussion of 1787 and see whether it would not now be resolved so that the President should in some way be plural rather than single. If one individual cannot by the utmost ingenuity ever be made to achieve more competency than the natural limit of man's energy and intelligence, and if this is not sufficient, this would seem to be the only solution.

Other nations have found it so. Except for the dictator-governed nations, the United States is very nearly alone in having a singular Executive.[10] Most of the greater powers have plural executives of one

[9] And it might be added that the most recent choices have not been such as to give assurance of improving judgment.

[10] Some republics, especially in Latin America, which seem to have separated and independent Branches, are actually dictatorships, the Legislative and Judicial Branches being subordinate. This is true, also, of the Fifth French Republic.

sort or another.[11] They may be Cabinets with a Premier responsible to the legislature—as in Britain and Scandinavia, Councils on the Swiss model, or committees chosen in conclaves of the elite—as in the Soviet Union and the Chinese Republic. But the vast responsibilities of the Executive who is also Chief of State and of party are nowhere expected to be assumed by a single individual except in the United States. This peculiarity of holding to a presidential form adopted in simpler circumstances than now prevail may be less a mark of virtue than of inertia, pride, or conservatism.

[11] The West German Constitution was, of course, largely American-made; it is therefore less interesting as an exception.

* 56 *

DISCUSSION OF THIS FURTHER PROBLEM NEEDS AT LEAST THE SPACE OF another book. It must be enough here to have stated the issue. We have seen the institution of the Presidency reach what would appear to be very nearly its maximum expansion without some sort of radical break-through. To achieve anything further, we may be forced to go back and start again at the point Madison found himself as the discussions were beginning that resulted in the Constitution of 1787. He had been thinking hard, but he had to confess that he had

> made up no final opinion whether the first magistrate should be chosen by the legislature or the people at large or whether the power should be vested in one man assisted by a Council of which the President shall be only *primus inter pares* . . .[1]

So drastic a proposal as a plural Presidency would no doubt be thought at first to be extreme by most Americans; but if the probable developments of the next few decades are seriously considered, it is clear that some sort of novel enlargement, something beyond the mere increase of staff or the addition of devices, will have to take place. What will probably happen at once, as indeed Eisenhower recommended, is further efforts at re-arrangement and additions to capacity. This will go on until all possi-bilities are exhausted. But the facts available forecast failure—that is, in-sufficiency. The President's many helpers, it is true, have enormously increased his capacity to meet issues as they arise. His decisions now are largely prepared for him before the necessity for action actually arises. He is no longer likely to be confronted with emergencies no one has anticipated. The system of allocating planning and preparatory work pre-cludes the possibility that anything important will be overlooked. The alternatives will come to him well argued and carefully refined so that a choice can be made with a minimum effort and a reduced probability of

[1] This was in a letter to Caleb Wallace, August 23, 1785. *Writings*, Hunt, ed., II, 169–70.

error. But there must always be the certainty in such a system that decisions will become progressively less those of the President and more
those of the assistants.

There is a physical fact that is overlooked surprisingly often. For the
same reason that a President cannot deal with a hundred agencies by
direct contact, he cannot deal with a hundred assistants either. He has no
power to stretch time or space. It is because of this that the Presidency has
already become a kind of plural institution. But because it is not recognized as such it escapes the requirements certain to be prescribed for
it if it were. The other Presidents are not responsible; they are hidden
behind the fiction that one individual does all, decides all, is all.

It is true that nowadays presidential work is infinitely better done than
it ever was before. Alternatives are, however, inevitably worked out and
presented in such ways that one presents itself as preferable to others. It
may be the best; it probably is. But wisdom is relative to objectives, and
such a way of determining objectives and ways of reaching them is
anomalous in a democracy. To confer such power and to allow its pos-
sessors to remain anonymous—how shall we explain this to ourselves? It is,
of course, only something—a further growth of something—inherent in
the organizational development of large-scale management; and it is
something, moreover, that students of the Presidency have hoped and
worked for. To give the office the best and largest possible organization
was to do the best for it that could be thought of. Yet lately many of them
have had second thoughts. To have policies governing the national behavior made in such an official dusk by persons not elected but appointed
is a serious matter.

Communications between the Chief Executive and his assistants have
to be privileged, and investigations may not penetrate the Executive enclave. That is a condition of separated powers. But it is interesting that no
issue between the President and the Congress during the Eisenhower
Administration was so sore as this one. The Congress was always prying
and probing, and the President was always reminding it that the Branches
are separate and that the Executive was exclusively his.[2]

---

[2] Two of many such incidents may be cited to illustrate the President's
vigilance in this matter. In 1959 the Congress passed a bill allowing
the Tennessee Valley Authority to finance itself by bond issues but provided for reporting to the General Accounting Office, not to the President.
Eisenhower refused approval until congressional leaders agreed, if he
would sign, to sponsor amendments removing the offensive requirement.

An even more striking case was provided by the presidential statement
made on signing the authorization for Mutual Security. Three amendments
had stipulated that information, documents, and materials relating to the
foreign-aid program should be furnished to the General Accounting Office
or to committees of the Congress. The President said:

Even Cleveland, who was as bluff and forthright as Eisenhower was conciliatory, was not more alert in defense of Executive privilege. And this had to be so, because Eisenhower had brought the office to a very high state of physical development, and it would cease to function at all if the lines of communication from his assistants to himself were open to exploration by another Branch. But that so many rejections of attempted inquiry had to be made may have been more a sign of uneasiness than of hostility.

It may indeed be necessary in the coming years to consider how policy for the nation can be more democratically made, how the President can actually be multiplied, how we may decrease the risk of anonymous bias as well as of presidential incompetence. It made less difference in 1861 that the bureaucracy was infiltrated with disloyal officials than it would today. Lincoln reached his own decisions without the help of a mountain of position papers and the digests of selected assistants. No President is likely ever to be so independent as this in the future. He is *primus inter pares*—but we may insist that those others—the *pares*—are legitimate objects of concern. They must be brought out into the open.

I have signed this bill on the express premise that the three amendments relating to disclosure are not intended to alter and cannot alter the recognized constitutional duty and power of the Executive with respect to the disclosure of information, documents and other materials.

This again has relevance to the development of the item veto and even suggests its extension to policy matters.

INDEX

DATE DUE
